When Truth Was Treason

When **Truth**

Compiled, Translated, and Edited by

Blair R. Holmes and Alan F. Keele

Foreword by Klaus J. Hansen

Was Treason

German Youth against Hitler

The Story of the Helmuth Hübener Group
Based on the Narrative of Karl-Heinz Schnibbe
With Documents and Notes

University of Illinois Press   Urbana and Chicago

This book is printed on acid-free paper.

Library of Congress Cataloging-in-Publication Data

When truth was treason : German youth against Hitler : the story of
the Helmuth Hübener Group / based on the narrative of Karl-Heinz
Schnibbe with documents and notes : compiled, translated and edited
by Blair R. Holmes and Alan F. Keele : foreword by Klaus J. Hansen.
   p.   cm.
Includes index.
ISBN 0-252-02201-7 (alk. paper)
   1. Schnibbe, Karl-Heinz. 2. Helmuth Hübener Gruppe (Resistance
group). 3. Anti-Nazi movement—Germany. 4. Mormons—Germany—
Biography. 5. Germany—Politics and government—1933–1945.
I. Holmes, Blair R. II. Keele, Alan Frank. III. Schnibbe, Karl-
Heinz. Jugendliche gegen Hitler. English. IV. Title: German
youth against Hitler.
DD256.5.W464   1995
943.086—dc20   95-3567
                                                               CIP

Contents

Illustrations follow page 142

Documents

Foreword: History and Memory

Klaus J. Hansen

My interest in the story of the Helmuth Hübener group is both personal and professional. I was born in the city of Kiel, about sixty miles
northeast of Hamburg, shortly before Hitler came to power in 1933.
Because my parents were Mormons, my early childhood memories
include being part of a vibrant Mormon community in Kiel—of Sunday school and church outings, of visits with children of church members, and of American missionaries having Sunday dinner at our
home. I also remember the ever-present symbols of the Nazi party
and the Nazi state—the parades, the flags, the uniforms, the music,
the salutes. I even remember seeing Hitler, who came to Kiel in 1938
for the launching of the heavy cruiser *Prinz Eugen*—a small figure in
a brown uniform, arms outstretched in salute, standing in an open
car.

To a six-year-old, both Mormonism and National Socialism were
part of the "given world," with the latter more ubiquitous and more
colorful and more exciting. If my father no doubt knew why Hitler
came to Kiel to christen a warship, I was thought too young to understand. However, two years later when the bombs of the RAF
rained down on us, I certainly knew why—though at the time I did
not draw the logical and moral conclusions of a sixteen-year-old fellow Mormon in the neighboring district of Hamburg. In fact, I did
not learn of the Hübener story until after the war, for in the spring
of 1941 my brother and I (together with many other children) were
evacuated to the south of Germany to escape the relentless hammer-
ing of our city by the RAF.

varia seemed safe enough from British bombers, but to a
ld from a large city this was an alien world dominated by
ic religion—no Mormons and hardly a Nazi. It was here,
4, that I heard the shocking news of the attempt to assassi-
r, which involved a relative of a prominent local family, the
ergs. Though branded a traitor at the time, Claus Schenk von
Stauffenberg was to become one of the celebrated heroes of the resistance to the Nazi regime. It was not until 1946, after German Latter-
day Saints were able to resume contact with each other in a war-rav-
aged country, that I learned that Mormons, too, could claim a hero of
the resistance as one of their own (though not many were eager to do
so). But it was not until much later, in the 1960s, after I became a professional historian, that I realized that to appreciate the full significance
of what Hübener and his comrades had done, it was necessary to have
an understanding both of the broader history of the German resistance
and of the history of Mormonism under Hitler. It seemed a daunting
task, and the only thing I published at the time was an oblique reference to Hübener in a review essay.[1]

Of the Germans during the Third Reich it cannot be said—unlike Hamlet—that it was conscience that made cowards of them all.
Quite to the contrary, it was conscience that made a few courageous
Germans overcome their cowardice. That is what united Hübener
and Stauffenberg, though they were separated by a veritable gulf of
class, rank, education, and religion—and by different motives. Ultimately, each was unique in his resistance to a regime he perceived as
evil. Most of Stauffenberg's fellow aristocrats made their peace with
National Socialism, and so did most of Hübener's fellow Mormons.
What made these two, and a few thousand others, say no to injustice
and inhumanity eludes disciplines such as social psychology and group
dynamics.

At the same time their example spurred others to resist as well—
in the case of Stauffenberg, hundreds involved in the plot to assassinate Hitler; in the case of Hübener, only three loyal comrades who
survived to tell a story that lacked the glamour of the 20 July plot
but none of the heroism. Both Stauffenberg and Hübener failed in
their attempts to rid the world of the Hitler regime, and both paid
with their lives. Yet to measure their actions by ordinary standards
of success is to misunderstand the true significance of what they did—
to bear witness not only in word but in deed to the dictates of human conscience, regardless of the outcome. To paraphrase the historian Hans Mommsen, the inner conviction was sufficient unto itself,
and requires no justification by "results."[2]

Yet since historians, ultimately, do not have an "explanation" for the workings of the human conscience, or for its absence, they feel compelled to place such actions within a historical context. Although the literature on the German resistance is voluminous, it isn't all that easy to locate the Hübener/Schnibbe story within that genre, because these young men acted alone, and what they did seems only vaguely rooted in the blue-collar social/cultural milieu of their families.

Much the same can of course be said of many who resisted National Socialism. As a class, the aristocracy did not oppose Hitler, and many joined the party. And while there was a core of resistance in the army, the military on the whole supported Hitler with enthusiasm. And yet, even if the individual conscience was the ultimate motivator, Stauffenberg's position gave him access to a few like-minded, high-ranking members of the military and the government, to the possibility of establishing a network, and to some hope of success.

The same was true of the Kreisau circle around Helmut James von Moltke and the Solf circle, and even more so of the resistance groups organized by the Social Democrats and the Communists—especially the Rote Kapelle (though these latter, because of their organizational structure, were the most easily penetrated by the Gestapo, and most of them were executed).[3] Perhaps a closer parallel is the case of Dietrich Bonhoeffer, who acted as an individual and from deep religious conviction.[4]

The Hübener group was unique also because these young men were among the youngest to resist the Nazi regime. Certainly, until 1941/42, those involved in the resistance were primarily older men (and some women). Even the Geschwister Scholl, who organized the White Rose group in Munich and were executed in 1943, were as university students some years older than Hübener.[5]

As the war dragged on, however, resistance among the young took on ominous dimensions for the regime. In the Rhineland, gangs of working-class youth organized as Edelweiß Pirates refused to attend Hitler Youth meetings, distributed anti-Nazi leaflets, and were involved in the murder of the Gestapo chief of Cologne. Twelve young men were publicly hanged in 1944.[6]

In the north, middle-class high school students calling themselves Swing Youth played North American swing music and jazz, and generally identified with an Anglo-American lifestyle—anathema to Nazi leaders, who arrested the ring-leaders and threatened to place the participants in concentration camps.[7] Undoubtedly, much of this resistance was social, and is at least partially explained by the phenomenon of gang culture, prevalent also in western democracies. There are those who have also accused the Hübener group of such motivations. While Hübener might have gotten some of his ideas and methods from groups such as the Edelweiß Pirates, a comparison with their activities highlights even more the ethical and moral imperatives motivating Hübener and his comrades.

For Mormons, it is no doubt tempting to derive such motivations from the religious faith of these young men. Yet such an assumption is problematic. Before the war there was widespread support for Hitler among German Mormons, who were encouraged by Church leaders to be obedient to the powers that be, in keeping with the Twelfth Article of Faith.[8] Not that many members joined the party (although some did). More common, at least in the early years of the regime, was an eagerness to identify supposed similarities between Mormonism and National Socialism—such as sacrifice of selfish, individual desires for the greater good of the whole. Hitler, it was said, had copied several of his social programs from the Mormons. Hitler didn't smoke or drink, and frowned on those who did. And so on.[9]

Yet such rationalizations were perhaps secondary to more fundamental reasons why Mormons on the whole acquiesced in the Nazi regime. Because of a turbulent history of persecution and migration, Mormons sought order and stability. Such values resonated strongly among German Mormons, who by and large came from economically disadvantaged strata of society, and who faced the disapproval of the "respectable" bourgeoisie and the established churches.

National Socialism appeared more sympathetic to certain outsiders. In spite of antichurch rhetoric, the Nazis in fact worked out a modus vivendi with most religions, Jews excepted of course.[10] The principled opposition of the Jehovah's Witnesses (many of whom died in concentration camps) to the regime could be seen as a special case because of their resolute refusal to accept the legitimacy of the secular state in any guise, even its liberal/democratic variant. It is significant that during the trial of the Hübener group, their church membership was not held against them. In fact, in the trial records the Mormons were reported as having a positive attitude toward the "new Germany"—though a report from the Hitler Youth leadership (opposed to clemency for Hübener) raised a question about the religious affiliation of the accused.[11]

German Mormons, ironically, may well have perceived the early Nazi years as a kind of golden age for their religion. Emigration to Utah declined, not only because it was now officially discouraged by both the Church and the Nazi state[12] but also because of increased economic stability among German Mormons. Centers such as Hamburg, Königsberg, Chemnitz, Stuttgart, and Nuremberg—among others—developed vigorous, active Mormon communities. Religious persecution, which had been common under the Empire and which had declined significantly during the decade and a half of the Weimar Republic, virtually ceased. An efficient network of railways and modern highways facilitated socialization among the Saints, aided also by one of the most modern postal and telephone systems in the world. Several larger urban branches were able to construct their own meetinghouses.

If Hitler was not exactly regarded as a patron saint of German Mormons, they preferred to see the hand of God working in mysterious ways. For example, the Nazis strongly encouraged genealogical research to prove Aryan ancestry.[13] Of course, this was beneficial to Mormons, who now had access to archives previously denied them. My father took great advantage of such opportunities. After the outbreak of war, when he was drafted into the German army and sent to Poland, he continued his genealogical research for our ancestors in the east, and saw this as providential. It was a frame of mind typical among German Saints, who shared quietistic millenarian convictions. God provided opportunities for building the Kingdom to those who could see them, even in the kingdoms of this world. In the last days, all of these would be destroyed, but it wasn't for the Saints to raise a hand against them. In fact, in a backhanded way, such activity would be counterproductive by delaying the building of the Kingdom. "Judge not, lest ye be judged" was a maxim much quoted by German Mormons. It was not a climate of opinion conducive to the activities of Hübener and his associates.

Opposition to the regime was unlikely for other reasons as well. German Mormons were too few in number, too exposed, and too scattered throughout the Reich to engage in effective actions of group resistance—unless they were prepared, like the Jehovah's Witnesses (and the early Christians) for certain martyrdom. Few indeed, even among those actively involved in the resistance, were prepared to go that far. Not even Bonhoeffer actively *sought* martyrdom. Though resistance might manifest itself in individual acts of courage, most was carried out within a context of tacit cultural support—a support not readily available to Mormons.

I learned something of this important difference after my evacuation to Bavaria. To me, the passive acceptance of the Nazis by the Kiel Mormons contrasted sharply with the passive resistance to the Nazis in my new home—since immortalized in a famous study by Martin Broszat and Elke Froehlich.[14] Rooted in a traditional Catholic, rural culture, this opposition did not lead to spectacular acts of open resistance but to a permanent war of attrition against representatives of party and state, aided and abetted by the head of the county government, who escaped being sent to a concentration camp only because he enjoyed the support of passive opponents of the regime in the higher echelons of the state government.

Under the circumstances, then, it should not be surprising that the story of the Helmuth Hübener group had an ambiguous response in the Mormon community. From time to time I was tempted to take a hand in the telling of the story, only to give up because I encountered extreme sensitivity among those who had been close to it, Hamburg Mormon leader Otto Berndt being very much the exception in the openness, frankness, and honesty with which he approached the subject. I somehow sensed that it was not for me, a north German Mormon, to interview church members who knew my family and who, for the most part, wanted to relegate the Hübener story to a past that was best forgotten.[15]

Though my father was not one of these, he was in many ways typical of those Saints who walked a fine line between collaboration and resistance. He served as a Mormon missionary in central Germany in the late 1920s, and after his release became somewhat intrigued by Hitler. He attended a number of party meetings, but decided rather quickly that Nazism was incompatible with Mormonism. Before the Nazis turned elections into a farce he had voted Social Democratic. As a missionary he had worked with many American companions and dreamed of emigrating to the United States. Keeping out of politics as much as possible, he devoted his energies to the Church, serving in the Schleswig-Holstein district in several capacities. In April 1940 he was drafted and (according to his request) assigned to the medical corps, in which he served throughout the war, never being required to fire a shot—in answer to his fervent prayer.

In recounting his military experience in later years, he always said that he did what he had to do, not so much because of the Twelfth Article of Faith but because of his family. Had he been required to fire a gun, what would he have done? He said he honestly didn't know. Would he have endangered his family for the sake of principle? It was a test he didn't have to face, and he was glad for that. But at the same time he admired Helmuth Hübener for his courage and for his principled opposition to a regime that was corrupt. And he was greatly saddened by his execution. But he also had great empathy for his friend Otto Berndt (Hamburg district president) and his predicament of having to distance the Church from the actions of the Hübener group, believing that it was his responsibility to save the many from the consequences of the actions—however admirable—of the few.[16] That these were not the imaginary fears of a man cowed by Gestapo threats is borne out by the fate that awaited the families of the conspirators of the 20 July 1944 plot.

Within a day or two of Stauffenberg's failed attempt on Hitler, the Gauleiter of our region, Fritz Wächtler, organized a demonstration at the foot of the castle of the branch of the Stauffenbergs who lived in our vicinity, and which I was ordered to attend in uniform as a member of the Jungvolk (a pre–Hitler Youth group). Unable to vent his hatred at Stauffenberg, who had been summarily shot in Berlin, Wächtler, with raised fists, led those assembled in a chorus of epithets against the "nest of traitors on the hill"—whose resident patriarch was an uncle of Claus. The ensuing mass arrests included all members of the extended family, even small children, in a vendetta of guilt by association—*Sippenhaft*, as Himmler called it.[17]

Young as I was, and intimidated by so much hatred, I recoiled at the monstrous injustice of such a spirit of revenge—though the climate of fear was such that it made me toe the line. I recall men in dark suits sitting in a back row of our church in Nuremberg—"Gestapo" our branch president whispered, and well remember my cautious and apprehensive turning of the radio dial lest I accidentally tune in a foreign station. I enjoyed being a member of the Jungvolk, but as I grew older, my father took pains to point out to me the incompatibilities between Nazism and Mormonism.

Sometime in 1944, while home on furlough, my father gathered us together, closed the door, and launched into a frank discussion of the fate of Germany. The war was lost, he said, or in any case, better be. For the time being, Hitler had bigger fish to fry, but should Germany win the war, we as Mormons would have to face persecution. Germany's defeat would be our salvation.[18] For a twelve-year-old member of the Jungvolk, even though a Mormon, these were hard truths to swallow.

At the time I did not think the summary execution of Stauffenberg unjust, though I was repelled by the spectacle of the show trials of the other conspirators and their slow, gruesome deaths by hanging, filmed on Hitler's orders. In the hanging of the Edelweiß Pirates in Cologne I can also see a modicum of justice—after all, they had committed murder, even if their victim was a chief of the Gestapo. By comparison the beheading of seventeen-year-old Helmuth Hübener seemed truly monstrous. On further reflection, however, I have come to see Hübener's execution in a different light—as an example of the conundrum of the relationship between legality and morality that exists in all societies but is particularly applicable to the Nazi state, as an illustration of what Hannah Arendt has called the "banality of evil."[19] There was no doubt that Hübener was guilty of having violated the "Decree about Extraordinary Radio Measures of 1 September 1939."[20] It was an extraordinary law for extraordinary times, but quite in keeping with laws against the dissemination of enemy propaganda passed even by the western democracies, and with harsh penalties—for example, against Lord Haw-Haw, Tokyo Rose, and Ezra Pound. Propaganda, after all, was a weapon perhaps more deadly than a regiment or a division of soldiers—as the case may be. Hübener's justification for what he did, then, was a moral one. It was a citizen's duty to oppose an immoral regime, particularly in wartime, when that war, in fact, had been unleashed by the machinations of a power-hungry madman and his lackeys. Such considerations, of course, did not affect the illegality of what Hübener had done, and the wheels of "justice" ground to their inexorable conclusion. This is also the reason why Hübener was to be disappointed in his prophecy, flung at the court that condemned him, that their time would come. It never did. The Nazi judiciary escaped judgment because what they had done may have been immoral, but it was most certainly "legal."[21] It is little wonder that after the war few members of the Gestapo expressed pangs of conscience; having performed only their legally mandated duties, they left the morality question to their accusers.[22]

There are, however, others (perhaps Stauffenberg) who might legitimately have raised questions about the morality of Hübener's actions, because they were intended to weaken the morale of a nation engaged in a life-and-death struggle—a struggle involving not only the Nazis and their ilk but the entire German nation. Stauffenberg himself had done his best to defend his country and had been badly wounded. His attempt on Hitler was not intended to weaken military resistance, but to stop incompetence and to effect an honorable peace, by honorable Germans. Had he known of Hübener and his group it is likely that he would have let justice—yes, even Nazi justice—take its course.

If Hübener's morality prevailed over Stauffenberg's, it was not so much because the young Mormon's motives were "more pure," or because Stauffenberg's bomb failed to kill Hitler, but because Hübener's acts were more consistent with the Allied policy of unconditional surrender (though not yet proclaimed when Hübener was executed). Even had Hitler been killed, it might not have changed the course of the war very much, because the Allies had shown no inclination to deal with the July conspirators.[23] In the end it was to be unconditional surrender, though the debate over which course might have been preferable is far from over. Where the two differed is that

Stauffenberg, as a German patriot, sought to salvage as much of his "holy Germany"[24] as he thought feasible, while Hübener, with less sentimental attachment, saw more clearly the need for a new beginning. What is indisputable is that the new Germany—at least in the west—is heavily indebted to the moral capital of both the Stauffenbergs and the Hübeners.[25]

Yet the survivors' cant that their deaths ennobled them (and us?) is cheap. More convincing is the view that by executing Hübener, the Nazis acknowledged the danger he represented to the existence of their order (more obvious of course in the case of Stauffenberg). Seen in this light, Hübener's actions were ineffectual only because the state, recognizing their seriousness, nipped them in the bud. Who knows what encouragement clemency might have been to others. As it was, the starting point for a new Germany had to be preceded by the terrible destruction wrought by the superior force of the Allied military machine.

Thus, if the "Year Null" was the aftermath of a climactic *Götterdämmerung*, it also marked a new beginning, both for Germany and for German Mormons. Shortly after his release from a French prisoner-of-war camp, my father went on another mission for the Church, helping to rebuild the scattered and battered branches in south and central Germany. Thousands of converts flocked to the Church, not a few seeing in it a refuge from the legacy of Nazism. For many, German reconstruction involved forgetting a past too embarrassing or too painful. Because the Resistance could be no fig leaf for personal honor, its memory had to be suppressed as well. The new West German state, however, in need of all the symbols it could garner to bolster its international standing, clearly understood the important role the Resistance would play in the legitimation of the Federal Republic. The East, on the other hand, proclaiming an unbroken "antifascist" tradition, was able to write off the Nazi past as a product of imperialist monopoly capitalism that was resisted heroically by antifascist workers, whose struggle had become reality in the workers' and peasants' state of the German Democratic Republic. The plotters of 20 July 1944—decadent and reactionary aristocrats and militarists all—were dismissed as class enemies, while the Hübener group, perceived as working class and with communist connections, could be incorporated as part of the antifascist resistance into the mythology of the German Democratic Republic. In any case, if the Nazi past was a problem, it was properly confined to the "anti-progressive" West German state.[26]

Ironically, German Mormons managed to evade the Nazi past in a manner not unlike that of the East Germans. For the Church on the whole there was, of course, no Nazi past, only historically embarrassing conduct by some mission presidents[27] and some compromising advice and perhaps some miscalculations by Church leaders such as Heber J. Grant and J. Reuben Clark, Jr.[28] The Hübener affair, likewise, could be seen as an embarrassment and with the rest of the Nazi past swept under the rug. For German Mormons, matters were of course a bit more complicated. For those who had joined the party and actively supported the regime there was guilt and shame. But this was no doubt also true of the majority of Mormons who had gone along only passively or even those who had resisted to some degree.

The immediate postwar emphasis by the Allies on "collective guilt"—the idea that all Germans, with the exception of those very few whose resistance had led to death or the concentration camp, were culpable—had the paradoxical effect of a backlash of denial. Even as the East Germans had their "antifascist" escape hatch, the German Mormons had "Zion," with headquarters in Salt Lake City, Utah, in the United States. In the early years after the war, German Saints looked to Mormon Utah as their spiritual and, in many cases, literal homeland, allowing them to escape not only the physical but also the psychological ravages of the German catastrophe. For most German Mormons, whether they immigrated to the United States or remained at home, the past was either buried or left behind—and with it the Hübener story.[29]

Yet before we can pass judgment on the German Mormons a better understanding of Mormonism under Hitler's Germany is required. While some pioneering work to that end has been done, the full story still needs to be told—without accusation and without excuses. Karl Schnibbe's account is a vital part of that story, and its telling overdue.

Introduction

Blair R. Holmes and Alan F. Keele

When the German scholar Hans Rothfels visited the University of Chicago in 1947 to deliver a lecture in commemoration of the 20 July 1944 assassination attempt on Adolf Hitler, he faced a greater challenge than is now recognized a half-century after the ill-fated effort to rid Germany of its dictator. At the conclusion of World War II, and for a substantial time thereafter, the western perception of the resistance to Hitler and the Nazi regime was that it was largely the efforts of a small group of dissatisfied "aristocrats" and high-ranking military officers. It was nearly inconceivable to outsiders that any, let alone a significant number of, Germans were or could have been openly opposed to and revolted against the system under which they lived.[1]

Representative of such a viewpoint was Gordon W. Prange, who edited a book of Hitler's speeches and writings for the American public and declared that "a whole generation of Germans has been reared in the fanatical spirit of National Socialism. This poses a grave problem for the future, for it is this Nazified generation with which the Allies must deal in the post-war world. To suppose that there will be many anti-Nazis among them, anxious to throw off Hitler's yoke, and to embrace a democratic order, is pure illusion. The *Fuehrer's* regimentation has been too intensive and too thorough for that."[2] The prevailing notion in the West during and immediately following the war was that there was little resistance to Hitler worth mentioning and that the German nation, as a whole, "voluntarily associated themselves with or submitted out of cowardice to the tyrannical rule of criminals, either through innate wickedness or from an acquired habit of blind obedience, or under the influence of some specifically baneful philosophy."[3]

The English-speaking public regarded the German people as "collectively guilty" for the rise and actions of the Third Reich, although there has been "no extensive or systematic examination of the evidence" to support such a notion. Nevertheless, two terms have been applied to the adult German population between 1933 and 1945: "collective guilt" and "collective responsibility." The former term implies moral blame, whereas the latter is more widespread and indicates that the adult German population contributed to the course of their country's history, even though some could not or did not foresee the results of the path they chose. Because, it was concluded, not all adult Germans could be considered morally culpable for the terrors of the Nazi era, they could be expected to share the consequences of the Hitlerian rule, hence the term "responsibility" became more commonly used than "guilt."[4]

With the passing of time and the cooling of passions, it has become easier to examine the German populace disinterestedly, and examination has established beyond doubt that resistance to the Nazis began before Hitler seized power and continued until the end of the war. This German resistance was largely unsuccessful and unknown, but it succeeded in demonstrating its existence and desire to rid Germany of an "immoral regime and put an end to crimes of incomprehensible cruelty and magnitude."[5] It is unfortunate that in the immediate postwar period the extent and nature of the resistance was not of significant concern to politicians or historians. As a result, many valuable opportunities to study the subject were neglected and have disappeared.

It is now known that, considering the totalitarian and terroristic nature of the Nazi state, German opponents to Hitler were much more numerous and ranged more greatly in age and occupation than was previously imagined. Given the brutal nature of life in Germany under the Nazis, the German penchant for submissiveness, the defenselessness of the population, and the fact that the citizenry had no legal recourse, it is astonishing that there were so many who did resist.[6] Because of the need for secrecy, the destruction or absence of records, and the number of persons involved, it will never be possible to determine precisely how many Germans perished as a result of their resistance. However, "official data show that between 1933 and 1945 about three million Germans were held at some stage in a concentration camp or prison for political reasons, some only for a few weeks, but some for the whole twelve years; of these approximately *800,000* were held for active resistance."[7] Even at the conclusion of the war, however, when the "bestiality" of the Nazi regime was revealed, little mention was made of those Germans "who had continually tried since 1933 to

arouse an indolent and skeptical public and speak for men ʾ
who suffered unspeakable tortures."[8]

The efforts of such a group to weaken, divert, or overtl.
Nazi system were clearly and almost totally without success. Tʾ
government was never seriously threatened by their efforts and
ified its policies in only a few, minor matters.[9] If so many Gerʾ
were opposed to the regime but still failed to affect it, the natʾ
question arises as to why they were so unsuccessful.

One of the numerous reasons for the failure of the resistance movement was that "so many Germans approved of Hitler and had little
sympathy for those who did not."[10] Hindsight might make one wonder how "so many Germans" could be blind to the criminality of the
Nazi regime, until we recall that the vast majority of Germans and
even many non-Germans could not see, or chose not to see, the dark
side of the picture.[11] Though most Germans were aware of arrests,
the existence of concentration camps, the disappearance of Jews, and
the destruction connected with the Night of Broken Glass, they were
unaware of the extent of the Nazi crimes. Even those who opposed
the regime were largely unaware of the mass exterminations of Jews
and other so-called subhumans.

The successes of the Nazi government also made it appear to most
Germans to be worthy of toleration, if not support. It is well known
that prior to the war, American and western European visitors and
observers of Germany often believed and remarked that Hitler was
working wonders and that National Socialism was overcoming many
modern problems. It was not until the German army suffered serious reverses in the war that the temper of the German people shift-
ed. Even at that, the struggle for survival was paramount, and the
loyalty of the population to the political and military leadership did
not suffer substantially.[12] The modern rise of a neo-Nazi movement
indicates that Hitler still has his supporters, persons who believe that
he was basically good and that the evil attributed to him is contrived.

The widespread belief in the existence and value of a *Rechtsstaat*
(state of law) made many Germans disinclined to oppose a government that came to power legally. The reputed loyalty of Germans to
laws and regulations, and their moral compunctions against violating the law surely played a role in their obedience to their government. Those in the military and civil service were also hampered by
their oaths of loyalty to the regime and the Führer.

Popular opposition to the Nazi regime suffered also from being
"scattered, isolated and easily controlled by security forces." The fear
installed in the populace by the harsh measures of the police state
greatly reduced opportunities to form conspiracies. As a result, it was

virtually impossible for large groups to coalesce and carry out acts that would threaten seriously the government. Most of the underground opposition, particularly the Communists, were destroyed soon after the Nazi takeover.[13]

One further reason for the failure of the resistance efforts was the ubiquity of surveillance. Although the Gestapo consisted only of approximately forty thousand operatives, there were almost countless other informants, such as the Sicherheitsdienst (SD), the police, party officials and members at all levels (the most notorious being the block leaders), Hitler Youth members, opportunists, criminals, teachers, vindictive neighbors or fellow employees, and children who were convinced that loyalty to the regime was greater than fidelity to one's family.

In light of the resounding failure of nearly all efforts to oppose the Nazi regime, we must ask why there was resistance, why Germans of nearly all ages and occupations risked their lives for a hopeless cause. It must first be recognized that few, if any, of the resisters engaged in their opposition knowing or thinking they would fail, although they recognized that possibility. Except for those possible few who sought personal gain, the resisters were concerned primarily with a higher good.

Those who have received the most attention were the soldiers and bureaucrats who sought to overthrow the Nazi government and themselves take power, "but by far the greater number of those involved were people who had neither political ambitions nor any hope of changing the course of history through the use of tangible power. They sought only . . . to preserve the integrity of the human spirit, believing that if this abided, the grace of God might find willing human servants when the time for rebirth was ripe. They served the church, the intellect, labor or tradition; and upon occasion they were merely young people who could not stomach what they saw round about them."[14] Their resistance to the Nazi government stemmed from its criminality, arbitrary injustice, dictatorial and police excesses, persecution of racial and political minorities and opponents, and the launching of a world war.

Many who opposed Hitler did so because they were convinced he was ruining Germany and had to be stopped before total destruction occurred. Others perceived that they were ruled by criminals who had no regard for human life. In all cases, they wanted to show that there was "another Germany," that not all of their countrymen were hateful, arrogant, and uncultured, and that Germany, once known as the land of "thinkers and poets," still possessed many good, honorable, and virtuous citizens.

Of course this took enormous courage, but heroism and courage were not lacking in Germany during the Nazi era and were present in three forms. One type of courage was "conventional" courage, the kind needed to fight in the trenches at the front or pilot a fighter plane. Another form of heroism was the "courage of routine," when in battle, in a concentration camp, or struggling for survival at home, "extraordinary responses became a standard." A third form of courage was that of "resistance," which did not require superhuman qualities but the proper use of human qualities and "above all the courage to follow [one's] conscience in isolation, even in the face of death, while at the same time maintaining a sense of relationship between ends and means."[15]

Those who engaged in resistance were basically alone, did not receive encouragement from fellow citizens or foreign governments, and faced enormous odds in their undertakings. Their individual acts of heroism were necessarily unknown or covert, because of the threat to families and friends that any oppositional stance posed. They expected no remuneration or notoriety and, for the most part, have vanished without our being aware of their names and deeds.[16] Because most of their acts of "resistance" were done secretly and anonymously, the question of what constituted "resistance" in the Third Reich necessitates a broad interpretation.

The praise and fame accorded to those who attempted to assassinate Hitler or who committed acts of sabotage were justified, but no less praiseworthy were the deeds of those persons who refused to salute the Nazi flag; who joined the army "to be safe from Nazi importunities or persecution"; who refused promotions at their places of employment, thus avoiding being required to join the Nazi party; who listened to foreign radio broadcasts; or who painted anti-Nazi slogans on the walls of buildings. In a pluralistic society, such deeds would hardly be considered politically dangerous or seditious, but in Nazi Germany they were deliberate acts of sedition for which one could pay with one's life.

Such "dissent" or "disobedience" in a totalitarian society "can legitimately be designated 'resistance' because that was how despotic Nazi leaders perceived it." German society under the Nazis was so highly politicized and the rules of everyday life so constrained that acts which would be accepted or unnoticed and sentiments which could be expressed without fear of retribution elsewhere were viewed as dangerous to the well-being of the prevailing system. Each act of dissidence, regardless of how apparently innocuous it seems to our society, was considered "dangerous," because the rulers of the German state had imported political claims into areas which had previously been considered private.[17] Thus, disagreement, dissent, or even lack of total compliance was threatening to those who dominated political power: "Where a regime has a monopoly on expressions of public opinion, it can portray its own interests as being congruent with those of the nation at large and any undermining of these as treason. The leaders of the Third Reich propagated this connection relentlessly. This is why even small acts of disobedience were truly resistance, because they threatened the totalitarian claims of the Nazi leadership."[18]

Because of such conditions, "there was always resistance, open and covert, in all social and occupational strata," with the result that unknown thousands gave their lives. This "resistance" caused the government increasing concern, as proven by the SD internal security reports. Especially during the war, the Nazi regime became worried about popular disaffection and increased its harsh measures against its own people.[19]

Those Germans who resisted faced an additional, largely unrecognized problem which did not exist for opponents of National Socialism elsewhere. Resistance outside of Germany was considered "legal," that is, resisters were fighting an oppressive occupying foreign power to reclaim their sovereign rights and regain their national liberty. Those within Germany who resisted the Nazi regime were committing treason by waging a war against their own country. Even though they might have been patriots in their own eyes and certainly were risking their lives, they were seeking the defeat of their own country, which increased their isolation from their fellow citizens.[20]

For the foregoing reasons, and because of the appeal of Nazism to the youth, the majority of those who resisted Nazism were adults, especially prior to World War II. Also, much of the active resistance, which involved sabotage or education, involved groups rather than isolated individuals. However, there were significant numbers of honorable and conscience-ridden youths who were opposed to National Socialism and took active steps to resist. Most famous were the White Rose movement in Munich, groups such as the Edelweiß Pirates, and the youth groups of the Communist Party.[21] It was to such groups that Helmut Guddat aka Kunkel, later Hübener, who resided in Hamburg, was drawn and from which he apparently developed his conspiratorial ideas. When we consider that the Gestapo infiltrated conspiratorial groups and doggedly pursued those who showed any form of resistance, it is noteworthy that Hübener, at the age of sixteen, began a conspiracy, succeeded for approximately six months in distributing virulently anti-Nazi literature, and was captured only due to his own carelessness.

One scholar of the German Resistance claims that many of the works on the resistance movement in Germany have "an inadequate basis of source material for an account of the concrete attempts to overthrow the Nazi regime," that "many who wrote of their own experiences knew and saw only a small section of the whole," and that many of the witnesses and participants "had either forgotten or preferred to forget the details."[22] Although the following account of four teenage boys in Hamburg who attempted to arouse opposition to the Nazi regime is modest in comparison to the descriptions of many of the more famous schemes and attempts to remove Hitler and bring an end to the terror of National Socialistic rule, it does provide a detailed and relatively comprehensive picture of the means by which the participants in the group which developed around Helmuth Hübener were brought to engage in resistance and the methods they used, because it is based on the personal accounts of those intimately involved in resistance.

In the following, the reader is provided, to an uncommon degree, with a detailed portrayal of the activities of the Hübener group. Because Karl-Heinz Schnibbe, Rudolf Wobbe, and Gerhard Düwer, the known co-conspirators with Hübener, survived their imprisonment and recorded many of their experiences, it is possible to present a relatively comprehensive description of their motivations, actions, and emotions associated with resisting the Nazi regime, as well as the results of their illegal behavior. One of the astonishing aspects of their actions was that they were not associated with or directed by adults, an independence which was virtually unheard of in resistance circles and which the Gestapo found hard to believe. Although Hübener likely drew ideas from other resistance groups, especially the Communists, the activities of the Hübener group were apparently developed and perpetrated by a small circle of teenagers.

The narrative portion of the following work is based almost entirely on the recollections of Karl-Heinz Schnibbe. Because the memoirs of Rudi Wobbe were published in a separate work in 1992,[23] shortly after his death, the editors have only selected those portions of Wobbe's words which elucidate Schnibbe's account, and prefer to let the individual stories remain distinct rather than mingling the accounts, which differ only in a few minor details. It is regrettable that Gerhard Düwer has not yet fully recounted his experiences, because the complete story of the only non-Mormon in the Hübener group would provide a valuable insight into how Hübener recruited and involved someone outside the LDS religious community. Nevertheless, Düwer's diary, a detailed chronology of the difficult trek westward from Graudenz in January 1945, has been included as Document 63 and provides important details and corroboration about that gripping episode of the story.

Besides providing an account of the activities and punishments of the conspirators, Schnibbe's narrative records many aspects of the daily life of a member of the blue-collar class in prewar Hamburg. It is obvious that the nature of his domestic life, religious affiliation, and social origins played a determining role in moving him to resist Nazism.

Because of the idealism and youthful exuberance of the Hübener group, they were not entirely aware of where their activities would lead them, or of the forces and consequences they were facing. Schnibbe indicated their innocence in a preface to his narrative:

> There are ominous, even fatal, moments when apparently harmless deeds decide between life and death. As the friend of my youth, Helmuth Hübener, sometime in the summer of 1941, invited me cordially to come to his apartment on a beautiful Sunday evening, I had no idea where that step would lead me. I could not imagine that I would soon participate in a full-fledged resistance against Hitler; be arrested, interrogated and condemned by the People's Court; and that I, as a result, would nearly be worked to death in various camps in Germany, Poland, and Russia.
>
> Even Helmuth, who certainly knew much more on that portentous summer evening than I, could scarcely have sensed that he had blazed a trail that would lead him on 27 October 1942 to the guillotine of the Nazi regime and that he at the age of seventeen would be the youngest resistance fighter to lose his life in Plötzensee, the infamous Nazi center of death.
>
> As I now reflect, however, I can see that it had to end thus, that this harmless invitation was a watershed preceded by definite antecedents and followed by a chain of decisive consequences.

The original basis for the following account was a series of interviews conducted with Karl-Heinz Schnibbe in 1990. The original documents in the case, presented here nearly in their entirety, are intended to enhance the description of the experiences of the Hübener group. Many, including the diary of Gerhard Düwer, are presented here for the first time.

Because nearly all of the materials were in German, the editors accept responsibility for any errors their translation might contain. We regret especially that it was impossible to translate adequately and include many of the expressions Schnibbe acquired during his imprisonment. The idioms and phrases of *Knastologie* (literally, "slammer-ology," prison jargon) he adopted provide an interesting and insightful commentary on the situation of those who were incarcerated by the Nazis or were prisoners of war, a commentary which will soon fade as the generation of those who experienced captivity passes away.

After consulting previous scholarship on the subject and conceiving the project, the editors assembled documents through correspondence with or searches in the following depositories: the Dokumentationsarchiv des Österreichischen Widerstandes, Vienna; the Berlin Document Center; the German National Archive, Koblenz; the National Archives of the United States of America, Washington, D.C.; the LDS Church Historical Department; and the Institut für Marxismus-Leninismus, Berlin, whose assistance was invaluable.

The editors are grateful to the Department of History and the Department of Germanic and Slavic Languages as well as the College of Humanities and the College of Family, Home and Social Sciences at Brigham Young University for providing some of the resources necessary to bring the story of the Hübener group to light. The editors are also highly appreciative of the assistance of Douglas F. Tobler, who was diligent in obtaining documentary materials. Above all, we wish to express our gratitude to Karl-Heinz Schnibbe for his willing cooperation and desire to preserve the story of his friend, Helmuth Hübener, to whose memory the following pages are dedicated.

When Truth Was Treason

I

Childhood in the
Shadow of the Swastika

Many years before I was born, before my father met my mother, something happened to him which was one of the first links in the chain which led, ultimately, to my resistance to the Nazis: he joined the Church of Jesus Christ of Latter-day Saints, commonly known as the Mormons.[1] My father, Johann Schnibbe, was raised on a farm in Hetthorn, near Wesermünde, which is in a beautiful area in the north German moor country west of Hamburg.[2] Late one winter night his father left a tavern on a bicycle and fell into a ditch of icy water. He lay there in a stupor for several hours before getting up and going home. As a result, he developed a fatal case of pneumonia and died soon thereafter.

The farm could not support the three sons—my father Johann (called Hans), Martin, and Georg. In fact, it could not support one brother adequately, so the younger boys left it to Martin. My father became a machinist's apprentice and worked for a short while on the railroad repairing locomotives. In 1911 he went to Bremerhaven, where he joined the merchant marines. During World War I he sailed to Africa, but was not involved in any hostile action. When the war ended, he worked for the Woermann Lines as a stevedore, as an overhead crane operator, and on a tugboat in the port of Hamburg until 1941, when he became subject to military service.

Instead of serving in the military, he was transferred to the Krümmel forest near Geesthacht, where he worked in a factory producing explosives, such as dynamite and gunpowder and other highly explosive products, though not the actual finished munitions. Some workers ended up being blown sky-high. For security reasons, no one was allowed to live nearby. The workers there were obliged to travel an hour on the train to work and an hour to return home.

While working in the port of Hamburg, Dad met a man named Theodor Verhaaren, who asked my father if he was aware that he had lived before coming to earth. My father said, "You're crazy," but he was interested immediately in what Verhaaren had to say. He followed Verhaaren to a dingy meeting place in an old school, where he spoke with five or six other Mormons. From that moment on, he felt there was something special about that church. He studied, read books, asked questions, and, in 1921, was baptized a member. Thereafter, he was an enthusiastic and totally converted Mormon, proclaiming the message to any or all who would listen to him, and to some who would not. Much to the chagrin of my mother, he often stood outside our house under the street lamp until late at night discussing religious questions with other members of the church or an occasional curious neighbor or fellow worker who had followed him home.

When my mother met him, she thought he was crazy, but he persisted and converted her eventually.[3] Like my father, she was from a modest background. Her father, Fritz Lütkemüller, was a fine cabinetmaker from Lüdelsen near Salzwedel in the Altmark, an area southeast of Hamburg.[4] He, too, came to Hamburg as a young man. He lived with us after his wife died. Like my grandfather Schnibbe, he drank a lot. When we went to church on Sunday, he went to what he called his "beer Sunday school." He belonged to a German men's glee club where singing was always harmonized with tippling. The Mormon church was the agent which pulled my parents and, through them, me and my siblings, away from certain national and familial traditions and pointed us in a new direction, a direction that had a profound influence on my life.

During World War I my mother had an experience which may have helped prepare her for Dad's discussions about life before birth, life after death, and the immortality of the soul. One night she had trouble sleeping, so she got out of bed and looked out the window. Suddenly, she saw her brother, Berthold, coming along the street in his uniform. She was excited to see him and said, "Come in, come in." He replied, "I can't." "What do you mean, you can't?" she said, and then he disappeared. The next day the infamous brown letter arrived informing the family that their son had died "for the kaiser and the fatherland."[5] My grandmother Lütkemüller died soon thereafter of a broken heart. She had lost other children when they were very young, and this was the final blow.

When my parents were married in 1921, they found an apartment next door to where my mother was born, on the second floor of a house in the Rossausweg, No. 32, in the suburb of Hohenfelde, an area not far from Hamburg's beautiful Alster Lake. At first they attended the branch of the LDS church in Hamm, which, after growing, became the St. Georg branch. In the early, difficult days of the Weimar Republic, there were usually only ten or twelve members present.[6]

Times were difficult for my parents. Inflation ran wild and a book of matches cost millions of marks.[7] People were paid their salaries every day and spent the money immediately, because the next day it would be worth even less. Food was scarce and it was difficult to buy enough coal to keep the apartments heated to drive out the damp north German cold. During this period, many people died of malnutrition, pneumonia, tuberculosis, and other related diseases.[8] Sometimes my father had a shortened workweek, but during the inflation of the early twenties and the Depression he managed to work rather steadily.[9]

Later, the Nazis blamed these difficult times on the Weimar Republic, but my parents did not. They, like Grandpa Lütkemüller and most of the other families in our working-class neighborhood, were supporters of the republic and the labor unions. I remember going to the Christmas parties in the enormous union hall, "das Gewerkschaftshaus," on the same street where our church branch met: the Besenbinderhof at the corner of the Große Allee. We received cake and marzipan there, all those good things we did not have often at home.

Like most union members, my grandfather was a Social Democrat and had a black, red, and gold flag that he hung out the window on holidays. He also had for his lapel a little insignia with three arrows and the word "Freedom" on it.[10] It was clear to all that he was a supporter of the republic. My father was not a member of the Social Democratic party, but he was sympathetic to their goals.[11] Even though he looked back at the Empire as a time of stability, my father referred to the kaiser as a "pompous ass." My parents and grandparents were certainly not Communists. Very few persons in our Hohenfelde neighborhood were. There were more Communists living further down into the city, in Barmbek, Altona, or Rothenburgsort, but our neighborhood was distinctly working class and we were always conscious and proud of it.[12]

Then Hitler and his SA[13] people appeared. The Nazis marched and the Communists marched. I remember well the brawls and the battles of the storm troopers and the Communists.[14] The Communists had a shawm[15] orchestra with only shawms, clarinets, and oboes. When they approached, the Nazis would come out of their haunts with chains and clubs and waylay them. They ambushed the Communists during the day, too, not only at night, but the Social Democrats, by and large, had fewer conflicts with the Nazis.[16] When I wanted to go somewhere any time after about 1930, my parents would often say, "No, today you stay home. They're planning a big confrontation today."[17]

Unemployment contributed to the situation.[18] The people in the SA prowled around in the habitual haunts of the unemployed, cooked up a few things here and there, gave them a little booze here and a little there, and anyone who wanted could be an auxiliary policeman for pay, even though most were thugs.[19] Many had criminal records and had been in prison before they joined the SA.[20] Horst Wessel,[21] for example, had previously been described as "an asocial element."[22]

The police did nothing; they were powerless. At first they tried putting the Nazis in jail, but gave up on it.[23] Then they were on the side of the Nazis, no longer neutral.[24] Thereafter, they marched with the Nazis.[25] The Communists, also, did terrible things, such as thrashing people. For the most part, though, it seemed to me there was not much shooting.

On our street lived a man named Domin, who was a totally fanatical Nazi. He was also heavily involved in the violence. I saw him often with a bandage on his head. He had a harelip and lisped when he spoke. We goofy kids made fun of him. We imitated his speech: "Heil Hitler! I am from the party and am here to haul away the deceased man. Please wrap him in two packages, because I am on my bicycle." Old Domin was a real sharpie, a 500 percent Brown Shirt.[26]

On 20 June 1922 my brother, Berthold, was born. He was named after my mother's brother, who had been killed in World War I. I came along on 5 January 1924, and was named after a character in the operetta *The Student Prince*. My sister, Karla Elizabeth, was born on 13 February 1925. Perhaps our family would have been larger if times had been better. My mother told me once that my father would have had twelve children if he could. Ours was a normal-sized family for the neighborhood and for the era. Of course, there were families with many more children, but they usually suffered a great deal in the hard economic times.[27]

A further limitation was our apartment. Everyone in our neighborhood lived in an apartment. We had two bedrooms, a living room, a kitchen, and a toilet, with no bath.[28] Like most people, we went to the municipal baths or had a bath in a large tin washtub in the kitchen. We stood in the tub in the evening and Mom scrubbed us before she wrapped us in a towel, dried us, and carried us off to bed on her back.

My father was quite strict, and my siblings and I were punished physically when we did something wrong. Dad either spanked us with his hand or, if it was more serious, got out his switch. That was a normal thing in Germany at the time. Fathers were authoritarian and no one saw any harm in it.[29]

Because my parents were strict, I worked relatively hard at school, that is, I did my homework, although I was not a serious student. I knew that I could never attend the university. Most people from our class could not afford it.[30] From my circle of friends, only one, Heinz Buske, went on to take college preparatory courses in the *Realgymnasium*.[31] As far as my parents were concerned, education was vocational training. As soon as I was old enough, I was to begin learning a trade. At first, I talked about becoming a sailor, but my father, who had been a seaman and worked at the port and knew about the bad morals of the seamen, said that first I should get a vocational skill.

In 1930, when I was six, I entered the elementary school at Wallstraße 22. Our curriculum always consisted of arithmetic, geography, singing, painting or drawing (my best subject), gymnastics, and history, although the curriculum was gradually changed.[32] At that time we had religious instruction, also, but that was gradually eliminated.[33] Foreign languages were not normally a part of the curriculum of the German primary schools of that era.

In school I was a rambunctious little fellow and was spanked by the teacher nearly every day. Perhaps that is why I entertained no further educational ambitions. I enrolled in an English course, and was kicked out when I did not memorize my vocabulary.

We were not taught civics or government, subjects in which we were sorely lacking when it came time to vote for or against the Nazis. Many of our teachers were Social Democrats, but no attempt was made at school to teach us about politics.[34] It was said we lived in a republic without republicans and a democracy without democrats. When the Nazis came into power, everyone was indoctrinated in their version of civics. We always had to start class with "Heil Hitler." There was no more "Good morning, children."[35]

Around 1936, probably in the sixth grade, one of my enthusiastic Nazi teachers was Herr Rolf, who was an active party member and a volunteer anti-aircraft gunner. I knew from what he said and from his party badge that he was a Nazi.[36] He did not have a gold badge, because a person needed to have been a party member before 1922 to have one of those.[37] He was a complete fanatic. Once, when I disagreed with him about some political issue, he said to me: "Schnibbe, you will land in jail yet." Some of the children laughed, yet he was right, because I was not one to be suppressed. I was always a free spirit and could not stand it that he had favorites, his pets. I started a fight with every one of them and beat them up. Then afterward I was beaten by the teacher, which is when he told me that I would land in prison.

Rolf was the head teacher. We had him in English and German.[38] He was the officer type. Later, he actually became an officer in World War II in the anti-aircraft artillery in the air force. From the beginning he must have been an enthusiastic Nazi, or he would not have advanced so quickly in his career.[39]

The school principal, Herr Platte, was a Nazi, also. I heard that he came back specially from the German colony Blumenau in Brazil.[40] He had been there a long time, but he did not want to miss the rise of the Great German Reich. He would send us into the auditorium, the entire school, when an orator from the party was there. At that time, though, things were not as well organized as they were later.

When the Führer spoke on the radio, we were all herded into the auditorium together and required to listen. While he was speaking we whispered and snickered a little, but for us it was a break from classes, so we welcomed such things. However, we had to sit still and listen, because it was demanded by the party.

The announcer on the radio would whisper quietly as if he did not want to disturb anyone. In that tone he would say: "The people are all gathered here and are waiting for the Führer." One could hear in the background some "Sieg Heil!"[41] when the Führer was coming, and then the music began, the "Badenweiler March," which was Hitler's favorite.[42] When the "Badenweiler March" was over, it was announced: "The Führer is coming!" Then we heard the roar: "Sieg Heil" and "The Führer is coming." It was a very dramatic event. During his speech and three times at the end "Sieg Heil" would be repeated and then the *Deutschlandlied* (see p. 281) and the Horst Wessel Song ("Raise High the Flag")[43] (see p. 282) would be played.[44]

As a child, one understood absolutely nothing of the speeches. Very seldom afterward was there a commentary by a teacher or one of the personnel. Once in a while it would be discussed a bit. There were practically no voices of opposition in the school.[45] We had Social Democrats, but never a teacher who made public that he was anti-Nazi.[46]

As I said, some teachers were already Nazis, and now they could be open about it. Their arrogance knew no bounds. The Nazis were generous and gave the teachers who were Social Democrats a choice. Those who did not want to go along were retired without a pension.[47] This did not occur immediately in 1933, but proceeded gradually. First they had to consolidate their power.[48]

In the beginning, until 1934–35, the Social Democrats were tolerated so long as they kept their mouths shut, but they were all forced to retire without a pension or join the Nazi party.[49] They were released without notice and had practically no chance to caution us. Their younger replacements were often Nazis.[50]

I was the only Latter-day Saint in my school, but I was not antagonized. My classmates and I never noticed differences, and we never worried about my church being different from theirs.

At school we typically had a mid-morning break and then ate our lunch from home. We could buy a bottle of milk or cocoa inexpensively at school, so we washed down our sandwiches with that. At one o'clock we were dismissed for the day, but before we opened our book bags, we tossed them in the corner and played for a while. In our area there was a park with a sandbox and other play equipment. We played soccer often and swam whenever it was warm enough. We joined a swimming team, also.

As children we had a good time with no worries. One of our favorite games was called *kippel-kappel*. Each player had a stick about two or three feet in length (the *kippel*), which was used to flip a smaller stick of about eight inches (the *kappel*) into the air. The *kappel* was placed over a small hole in the ground and then flipped into the air as hard and as far as possible. If another player caught the *kappel*, he could advance toward the hole and flip his *kappel*. Points were awarded by counting how many times a player could hit the ground with the *kippel* while the *kappel* was in the air.

During the winter we went skating on the frozen Alster lake or sledding on some nearby hills. In the summer we swam at the Schwanewiek swimming pool, which was part of the Alster lake. We went to school the entire year, except for a few vacations, including a longer one in August. Because our school was not air-conditioned, whenever the mercury went up to 29° Celsius (approximately 84° Fahrenheit), school was dismissed—it was called *Hitzefrei* (literally: "heat-free")—and we headed for the swimming pool. We always kept our swimming trunks handy in case of a hot day. When we got hungry after swimming for several hours, we went to a bakery and for five cents bought a bag full of trimmings which the baker cut from cakes.

One day, when dad was working on the tugboat, he arranged to meet us and we went on board and spent all day with him at the port. We climbed up the Jacob's ladder to a big freighter and the cook fixed us a special meal. Those were extraordinary times which I loved and will never forget.

On the day the Nazis took power, 30 January 1933, I was nine years of age. We were all herded into the auditorium at school and listened to Hitler's acceptance speech on the radio. All night, people paraded through the streets with torches, singing the Horst Wessel Song and others: "The old rotten bones of the world are quaking about the great war. We have broken the bonds of servitude; for us it was a great victory. We shall march on and on, even if all is destroyed; for today Germany shall hear us, and tomorrow the entire world"[51] (see p. 283). There were enormous celebrations and processions and other events that monopolized the evening. One could hear it all on the radio.[52] The sky was illuminated by the torches from the parade.

At the time, the majority of the population was swept along. By and large, we children were excited by the Nazis. They were excellent propagandists. They came with their flashy parades and we followed them like the Pied Piper to wherever their band concert was to be. People were swept away by the march music. As youngsters, we often went to the City Hall Square, which was changed to Adolf Hitler Square. Every weekend there was a concert there by a military or a police band. It was exciting. They played very patriotic marches.[53]

We saw the exciting party congresses on the newsreels and we listened to other Nazi orators like Joseph Goebbels on the radio. "The nation is getting back on its feet," we heard them say. There was new hope after years of political and economic decline. A kind of intoxication came over the entire population, especially the young.[54]

My mother was very musical. She told me that when she was young, she often went into music stores and put a coin into the nickelodeon and requested operatic arias, not popular tunes. I began attending concerts with her, mostly operas and symphonies, when I was very young. By the time I was seven years of age, I had joined the singing school in the Bühlaustraße, an organization that took talented youngsters who could not afford private lessons. Once a year our group presented a concert in the music hall. We sang classical numbers, some church music with Latin texts and many schmaltzy patriotic songs which I still remember well: "The German mountain woods stand green, the pine trees rustle softly. The German eagle, with eyesight keen, circles the heaven's corridors. The German rivers, clear they flow, in cracks in cliffs do blossoms grow. Oh, German woods, oh, rivers, oh, oh, eagle guard our borders" (see p. 283).

One of our neighbors, Karl Voscherau, was an actor at the Thalia-theater.[55] He arranged engagements for me and my sister on the stage as child actors. They were all minor parts, of course, but I became very interested in the theater. Later in my life, after I emigrated to the United States, I played in a German-language repertory company for many years.

My family acquired early a simple, silver-quartz crystal radio set which had a battery and was difficult to tune and was full of static, but with which we could listen to music at home. It crackled terribly. At least once a month we had to go to the Güntherstraße, where there was an automobile garage that recharged the batteries for a modest fee. After a day or two we could retrieve the recharged radio and would be able to listen again for a week or two.

Dramas such as "Verdun" from World War I and "The Heroic Struggle of the Germans" were presented. One could hear the grenades whistling and the machine guns shooting. It was all a radio play, but everything over the radio was fascinating. Nobody dared utter a word. At that time patriotism was loudly proclaimed just like in every other country. The Nazis, of course, promoted it a lot.[56]

Later, there was also a utility radio called the people's receiver (*Volksempfänger*)[57] which let us hear only that which the government wanted us to hear. We could not listen to anything else. Later, during the war, shortwave radios were forbidden.[58] (See Document 2.) A person was not permitted to have one. For the upper crust it might have been allowed, but not for us.[59] The propaganda disseminators were possibly afraid that people would start thinking, that we would discuss the war and much more among ourselves, that comparisons would be made, and doubts arise,[60] doubts about our infallible, greatest military commander of all times,[61] and doubts about our ultimate victory. (See Document 1.)

Once a month or so, we went to the movies. It cost thirty cents, which was often more than we could afford. Riding the streetcars cost ten cents for children and fifteen for adults, which was beyond our reach, so we walked almost everywhere. My father went to work on a bicycle every day, up Heidenkampsweg and through the city, about six or eight miles each way.

Like most German women, my mother went shopping every day. She did not have a refrigerator, merely a little pantry with a small open window covered by a grate to keep things cool. She went to the milk store with her little covered metal container and asked for a liter of milk. They ladled two scoops out of the large vat in the shop into our container. Then she went to the grocery store, the butcher shop, and to the fruit and vegetable shop. Once a week there was a fish market and a farmers' market. We always liked to go there, because they distributed free samples to nibble.

We had a large garden, a *Parzelle* or "parcel" of ground. It was called a *Schrebergarten*, after the physician Dr. Schreber[62] who recommended that the government allot small pieces of ground in such places as the odd-shaped lots between railroad tracks and highways to city dwellers so they could enjoy the sunshine, the clean air, and the vitamins in fresh, homegrown produce. Our garden was about an hour's walk from home, in the Dunckersweg, in Horn, near a well-known horse-racing track. We built a little hut there, a garden shed, which was expanded later. In 1945, when I was released from prison and inducted into the army, and again, when I returned from the prison camp in Russia, I found my parents living at the garden, because our apartment house in the Rossausweg had been destroyed in the bombing raids in August 1943.[63]

We had occasional church parties there in the evening, with paper lanterns in the bushes and along the paths. It was a wonderful oasis in the urban desert. On our way to the garden, we pulled a small, wooden-wheeled wagon, called a block wagon, which could be taken apart and stored in the cellar when not being used. We took, also, a little shovel and broom. All along the way we stopped to load horse manure for the garden. In those days, horses were used widely for such things as delivering beer or groceries or furniture, and the horses did not say "excuse me," they just dropped fertilizer everywhere and our garden benefited from it.

After picking the fruits and vegetables, we loaded them onto the wagon and took them back to our apartment, where mother bottled them. She turned a chair upside down on the table, tied a piece of cheese cloth to the four legs, placed a big pot under the seat, and poured in cooked rhubarb, black currants, red currants, gooseberries, all of which we had in our garden, and strained the juice for bottling or for jams and jellies and for rote Grütze.[64]

She had a device which made French-cut or slivered beans. You put the beans into a slot and turned the crank, and they came out perfectly slivered for canning. Mom filled a big container with beans and salt brine, which she covered with a linen cloth and weighed down with a large rock to keep them from floating until they were pickled.

In the basement we had a wooden cage approximately four by twelve feet, where we stored things like our block wagon and our briquettes of coal for cooking and heating. Some apartments had a "laundry kitchen" in the cellar, but we were required to wash in our own kitchen. Mom put a large pot on the stove and boiled the laundry and stirred it with a big stick. Later, she acquired the latest invention: a pot with a system of return tubes on the side which was not supposed to boil over. Doing laundry was a big job. The bed sheets needed to be stretched and pressed with heavy irons heated on the stove. Once a week the rugs were carried into the courtyard and hung over a rod and beaten with an instrument resembling a tennis racket to knock out the dust. Then they were rolled up again and carried back upstairs into the house. It was all hard work.

When I was growing up, we had gas lighting, instead of electricity. There was a coin-operated gas meter in the apartment. Mom put in a *Groschen* (a ten-cent piece) and it ticked away, supplying us with gas for forty-five minutes or so. When the lights dimmed, we dropped in more money. At the end of the month, the meter reader returned the extra money we had inserted. The gas meter was sort of a savings bank for poor people.

With so much housework, it is no wonder my mother did not have a job outside our home. Besides, it was not customary for women to have outside employment. My mother was expected to stay home and cook meals everyday, big pots of soup, for example, except on wash days, when she made rice pudding with sugar, cinnamon, and milk, which we especially loved. One or two days a week we had fish. Because we lived near the port, fish was relatively inexpensive and there was a good assortment. We had everything from green herring to red snapper, and all sorts in between, including shellfish and flounder. On Sunday we often had meat, but it was very expensive. Sauerbraten, roulade, a roast of some kind was the usual Sunday fare. During the week we sometimes had cold cuts for supper, but Mom always fixed our open-face sandwiches for us, and that was all there was to eat. We never went to bed hungry, but we probably could have eaten more.

The American missionaries came often for meals. Every day they went to some other church member's home for dinner. It was taken for granted that the members would care for them. By the end of their missionary service,[65] they usually had enough saved to travel through Europe, but we did not care. We loved the missionaries and looked up to them. We young people were especially fascinated by them, by their Americanness, by their broken German, and their wealth, or what seemed wealth to us. Even though these missionaries were probably from very poor homes themselves (this was the time of the Great Depression), they always talked like they were wealthy. They all had a car and a house, and to us that was wealthy. As a consequence, it never entered my mind that I could serve as a missionary. I was not an American and we were not wealthy. I believe most other young German Mormons felt the same.[66]

From the missionaries we learned that America was Zion, the Promised Land, the land of unlimited possibilities. However, there was no talk of emigrating, at least in my family, except once when I broke a neighbor's window with a soccer ball. I ran home and said to my mother, "Couldn't we emigrate to America before Herr Schmidt finds out?" I do not recall anyone from our branch emigrating, either, although this was a time when a lot of emigration occurred from certain areas.[67] After the war, of course, many left Germany for the promised land and our family followed them.

Before the war we were very patriotic. We loved our beautiful north German city with the large ocean liners (we called them "musical steamships") of the Hamburg-America line departing for exotic ports of call, and our large merchant-marine fleet, all these beautiful ships sailing into the world. Even we working-class Social Democrats responded to the surge of national pride out of which Hitler was making great political capital.

Perhaps the Latter-day Saints in a port city like Hamburg felt like they had already been gathered to Zion out of the worldly community. We were all very strong, almost fanatical, for example, about the Word of Wisdom, a church rule prohibiting the use of alcohol and tobacco, even though (or perhaps because) there were bars on every street corner.[68] Though all the children knew where the houses of ill repute were located, and when I was apprenticed as a decorative painter our shop was in the red-light district and I knew every girl by name, that was all. We were in the world, but not of the world.

My father was caught up in the Word of Wisdom and preached temperance to my grandfather Lütkemüller, but he finally gave up. He insisted, however, that we say a blessing on the food, and my grandfather was willing to join us in that. Even in church my father was always the preacher. When he gave an address they invariably needed to tug on his coattail to tell him his time was expired. He studied a great deal in the Holy Scriptures and in the limited church books available to us. As a result, he acquired a lot of knowledge and had a great deal to say about church doctrine. He became a traveling Elder[69] in the district, the one who took the sacrament[70] to the shut-ins and others who could not come to church. He taught them and saw to their well-being. The church was his life, and it became my mother's, too. The best friends of my parents, the Knapps, the Bergmanns, and the Berndts, were all Latter-day Saints.

We children, however, were less committed. On a warm Sunday we often wanted to go swimming but were told, "Nothing doing. Your place is in church." When it came to fasting,[71] Dad was a bit more lenient: "Well, you don't need to fast if you don't want to," he would say, "but since we're not cooking anything, there will be nothing to eat today. But you don't have to fast if you don't want to."

It was not that we did not like attending church services. We did enjoy it, and all our experiences in the branch were positive. We were a close-knit group and had fun together. Even social class differences were largely ignored. The Brey family, for example, who were quite well off (he bought and sold ships, I believe), were our friends in the branch, also. There were Christmas parties with Santa Claus and New Year's parties and picnics at our garden and sack races and remodeling parties at the branch house, where president Arthur Zander arranged for refreshments.

The church, of course, always kept us very busy. On Monday there was the priesthood meeting for males and the women's Relief Society; on Wednesday the Mutual Improvement Association for the youth; on Thursday there was choir practice; and Sunday we had Sunday school in the morning and sacrament meeting in the evening.

What I always found horrible was being assigned to go home teaching.[72] We had to go once a month to some members who lived three-quarters of an hour away from us. We did not have a telephone, so we always took our chances. When we were lucky, we met them; when not, we returned another day. My father was very exact about it.

We visited one particular family, which was an awful experience for me. The wife was always the same. When it came to the end and my father said, "We need to go. Would you like to have a prayer?" she always replied, "Yes, gladly. Would the young man do it please?" I dreaded going to that woman's house, because I knew for sure that I would be called on to pray again.

It was in the branch, also, that I became Helmuth Hübener's friend and he mine, and we became friends with Rudi Wobbe.[73] Little did we know at the time that these friendships would become matters of life and death and later would be tested in the fire.

I first saw the differences and noticed the gradual transition to Nazism in our branch. Still, no one spoke about this or about any other political matter in the branch until later. Most members were cautious and adopted a wait-and-see attitude.

Our branch president at that time belonged to the party and was enthused about it, which one could not hold against him. He saw good in it. At first everything was terrific, everything that the Nazis accomplished. No more unemployment, the autobahn was constructed, and every one had work under Adolf. Naturally, there were many people who were enthused about it. In our branch we had some who came in their SA uniforms to the meetings. Brother Paul Haase and his boys joined the SA, the Brown Shirts, and began wearing their uniforms to church.[74] I do not think they were the brutal, street-fighter types. As I recall, they were musicians and belonged to a military band. The SA gave them something with which to identify. That was part of daily life in the Third Reich.

In the Hamburg branch there was a man who belonged to the SS,[75] the Deathhead SS.[76] He was said to have taken part in the assassination of a Communist. The SS took the Communist out and shot him. That was an open secret. Whether he had fired the shot or not, I do not know. Six or eight men were involved.[77]

At first it was difficult to be negative toward the Nazis, even if one did not like them intuitively, because they improved the economy and gave Germany a new sense of purpose and destiny. Our family benefited, somewhat, because my father had fewer short workweeks after the Nazis came to power. For those who had suffered more deprivation, who had been unemployed for a long time, the improved economic climate was all the more welcome.[78] Within a few years after the Nazi takeover, the unemployment rate dropped from more than 30 percent to 0.[79]

I do not want to overemphasize the economic progress under the Nazis. They really helped mostly other Nazis, and overall, progress was slow. The lowly worker remained lowly, even under the National Socialist Workers' party, but when people are out of work they grasp at any straw, even if the pay is low and the job has been created by a rapid military buildup.[80]

At home we often talked about Hitler and his cronies. As I have said, my family members were all Social Democrats. My father was never a Nazi; he was a Socialist like my grandfather.[81] He had no sympathies for the Brown Shirts.

I can still see the flags that my grandfather hung out the window, black, red, and gold. That was the flag of the Socialists. Our next-door neighbor, Otto Schulz, a Nazi, hung the swastika flag out the window. Because of the different flags, there were numerous colorful streets in Hamburg. That was from 1930 to 1933, before the Nazi takeover of power. Afterward, it was dangerous to hang other flags outside. Some tried it, but they did not last long. The flags were soon hauled inside. My father saw and experienced many things, above all in the harbor where many Communists were employed. They were gradually arrested and incarcerated by the Gestapo.[82] My father would then come home and say, "Schultz went down the tubes." Many Schultzes went down the tubes.[83]

The Rote Hilfe[84] (Red Relief) took up collections at the harbor. This organization was for the Social Democratic wives whose husbands were in a concentration camp or in prison.[85] The collection was made for the family left behind. The Rote Hilfe was collecting for Schultz, because someone squealed on him and he had gone "down the tubes."

My father donated some, too. Then the receipt books were confiscated by the Gestapo, so now those brethren[86] knew who gave what to whom. Because of that, many were arrested and sent to Kolafu, the concentration camp Fuhlsbüttel.[87] My father suffered many sleepless nights about this, because he knew that his name was in the receipt book, but he was lucky. Perhaps his name was written illegibly.

From his buddies my father learned early about the concentration camps or KZ's.[88] The first ones were Hilfs-KZ's (provisional or wild concentration camps). The SA locked people in the cellar of the city hall and tortured them. The first Hilfs-KZ's were extremely brutal, unstructured concentration camps. They had been established by the SA. In the police prison, in the cellar, they did whatever they wanted. They were completely outside the law. The Nazis had the law on their side and were left untouched when they did such things. These poor devils were systematically beaten to a pulp and then, of course, were always forced to write that they had been treated well. At that time these things occurred not in such great numbers as later, but even so my father was aware of it happening.

Although my father had nothing in common with the Nazis, they won over many, because they cared well for the children and did other things that were viewed as being positive. For example, during school vacations, we children often went to Köhlbrand or Moorwerder, which were hostels along the Elbe river belonging to the school administration. We met at the subway station every morning at 6:30. Then our chaperon, a National Socialist teacher, would come and we would board the subway. A special train took us to the river, to the mooring place of the steamships, where we boarded a paddle-wheel steamer for the trip to the hostel. The ferry boats were named "Fortuna"—"Fortuna 1," "Fortuna 2," or "Hugo Basedow" after the owner of the boats, Hugo Basedow. They were large and beautiful white ships and traveled fast. A horde of children traveled on the boats.

What always fascinated us was the pumps in the engine room, the large pistons. During the trip to Moorwerder we needed to sit together and sing songs. We sang songs such as "Wildgänse rauschen durch die Nacht" (Wild Geese Whir through the Night) (see p. 284) and popular songs from other organizations.[89] Of course, we sang Nazi songs: "Ein junges Volk steht auf" (A Young Folk Arises) (see p. 285), "Unsere Fahne flattert uns voran" (Our Flag Flutters before Us)(see p. 285) and similar things, including "Das Engeland Lied" (see p. 286).[90]

Moorwerder was a large complex, perhaps 100 to 125 acres. There was a large playground, a sports area for soccer and handball, and a beautiful beach where we could swim. We played games or went swimming when the tide was in. It had private beaches that were fenced so no one could swim out too far. The children could build sand castles and play handball, volleyball, soccer and *Schlagball* (or *Völkerball* as it was called then), which was a kind of baseball. On the beach we had wagers to see who could build the most beautiful castles. And we made up our own games. It was great fun. We did it when the tide was out; and when the tide came in everything was washed away.

We had one game where a person threw small objects into the air. We called it *Produktsteine* (similar to the game of jacks). Or we had small sticks with numbers on them, which we let fall with a twist. Then you needed to be extremely careful in lifting one, because when you moved a different one, someone else had a turn (similar to the game of pick-up-sticks).

When we arrived in Moorwerder, breakfast was already prepared. There were three or four barracks, open on the sides. Benches ran along both sides, like picnic benches. The enamel kettles of hot chocolate stood in a row. Everyone received a hefty slice of raisin bread, perhaps two inches thick, and a mug of hot chocolate. At noon we got a big meal, which usually consisted of some kind of stout soup dish: peas, beans, or lentils.

In the afternoon we played more, or laid out lazily in the sun. There was also a first aid station. The nurse was a nice woman. When we were sunburned, she put salve on us. As children we enjoyed it. When one had a *Groschen* or even five cents, one could enter the canteen and buy a bit of candy, licorice, or some bonbons, a lollipop, or something else.

Before we left for home in the evening, we had a light, cold supper at 6:00. Each child received a couple of slices of bread, perhaps four slices with lunch meat, or something similar, and something to drink. Then the steamships came and took the approximately three hundred to four hundred children home. The next day we went back, and this lasted for our entire vacation. By the end of vacation we were tanned brown. The only thing we wore the entire summer was a bathing suit.

This was all very inexpensive for my parents, because it was sponsored by the government. That must have cost an enormous amount of money for so many children, but not all of the children in Hamburg participated. Many traveled with their parents on vacation. The excursion was only for those, such as my family, who could not afford otherwise to go on vacation. My mother was required to pay only a mark or two. The rest was contributed by the party. The parents were free of the children for the entire day; the children were well cared for, and there was no nonsense.

In those days children played a lot with lead soldiers, which started at the end of World War I. We had lead soldiers, Frenchmen with blue coats, German soldiers, and cannons, everything made of lead. They were genuine lead figures, flexible ones with swords. There were also small cannons with peppercorns for shot.[91] A friend of mine, whose family was better off, constructed an entire battlefield. We played war in the sandbox. We made scenes from World War I, from the Thirty Years' War, of mercenaries, and of Frederick II.[92] Old Fritz, the Battle of Leuthen,[93] and such were the idols of the Nazis.[94] They made a lot of films about Fritz.[95] It was their number-one propaganda effort.[96] It was easy to see that children were being educated in war.[97]

In 1934 or 1935 my mother had a shocking experience. She went shopping in the Lübeckerstraße, and returned home completely agitated and broken up and crying. She related how she wanted to cross a street. A bicyclist, a civilian, went traveling past. Then along came an SA man. The two knew each other and the storm trooper simply shot him down before the eyes of my mother. Of course, my mother did not know the reason why.[98] She did not report it; she did not need to. It was a major street and many people were there.

As we grew older, we were required to join the Jungvolk (Young Folk).[99] In 1936, at the age of twelve, I joined the Jungvolk. Two groups were available and we were obligated to join one of them.[100] Recruiters came through each neighborhood and were careful to register each boy. Scouting had been banned in 1934, so I never had a chance to become a scout. I had looked forward to it and was a bit disappointed. Still, all the children joined the Jungvolk, and at first it was very exciting. Young people were interested in the Jungvolk and the Hitler Youth because they employed clever tactics. By 1936 there were already six million children involved.[101] The children were well organized, which was exactly according to the plans of the Ratcatcher of Braunau.[102]

In the Jungvolk we were twelve-year-old Cubs (*Pimpfe*), still small children. What fascinated us about the Jungvolk were the field exercises, excursions, night hikes, sleeping in tents, sleeping in youth hostels, and various other kinds of training. We fought mock battles between our groups and marched to the beat of the long parade-corps drums. We had campfires and large bonfires on open places in the city to celebrate special pagan German holidays like the solstice festivals, and we sang all the sentimental, patriotic songs.[103] We were also allowed to shoot air rifles.[104] We had targets with circles and shot at them. We also had darts with feathers. One could shoot them and see exactly where they landed; plus, they could be used again. There were few accidents, because everything was supervised closely.[105]

They attempted in every way to convert the youth to their view, and they very often succeeded. It was a form of military training, but they were not yet referred to as battles. Things began with a little "attention," "left face," with a little drilling; everything was jovial, then came the tents, the shooting, the field exercises. Everything was directed toward slowly but surely educating the youth politically.[106]

For children who were a little older, there were also premilitary training camps, a bit more like the military, more inspections, guard duty, and such. They had to know map reading and a little bit about radios.[107] They also shot small caliber rifles with regular bullets.[108] Everyone also had a dagger. "Blood and Honor" was engraved on it. As Cubs, we did not have that. We had only the parade corps drums (*Landsknechttrommel*) for the fanfares. We also had military caps, waist belts, and shoulder straps. We liked it; it was fun for us young guys, the night duty, the field exercises, and the uniform. We received a black field jacket, a brown shirt, and then the leather lanyard. That was sharp! We had to swear an oath.[109] I can still give it.

In the Jungvolk the children were mostly well behaved. They wanted to be involved. No one needed to call them to order, only a little, such as "be quiet" or "shut up." It was all fascinating to us. We could hardly wait from one home evening to another.[110] We had the Nazi home evenings in a large warehouse near the Kuhmühlenteich, a pond near the Alster lake. There our leaders related the entire ideology of the Führer, the takeover of power, the struggle that was ahead, and the battle they waged in the march on the Feldherrnhalle[111] in Munich. All of that was crammed in. It always began with a song such as "Es zittern die morschen Knochen" (The Rotten Bones Tremble). It was part of the test of the German Jungvolk, that we needed to memorize the Hitler songs. Then Hitler's sayings were repeated and we were told when Hitler was born and such, his ideals and this and that.

We often remained overnight at our activities. We traveled Friday night, not far from Hamburg, put up a tent or slept at a youth hostel. We stayed there until Sunday and then returned home. Once I was also in the youth recreation camp with the Jungvolk, in Georgenthal in Thuringia, in the neighborhood of the Wartburg.[112] We performed field exercises there. Sometimes there was also a little shooting. Our food was prepared in a field kitchen. For us youngsters it was really something.[113]

Afterwards, of course, when I was fourteen, I was transferred to the Hitler Youth. It was a lot like the Jungvolk, except that we were permitted to wear a dagger with the words "Blood and Honor" stamped on the blade. By this time, I was beginning to become disillusioned by the Nazis.[114] I did not like it any more. The pressure and coercion did not appeal to me.[115] By then a person is more mature. At first, perhaps it was not so, but then the shouting and ordering no longer appealed to me.[116] I was, somehow, a free spirit and that did not suit me. I was simply not in favor of it, that someone would force me to throw myself into the muck.[117]

My parents, especially my father, must receive a great deal of credit for this, because they always made subtle, negative comments about the party. When I needed a Hitler Youth uniform, for example, the brown shirt with a shoulder belt and a neckerchief, my father said, "If they want you to have one, then they should provide the uniform."[118] And that is what the leadership of the Hitler Youth did, but I never put the uniform on. When I had to go on duty, I went in civvies. "Where is your uniform?" "It's in the laundry." It was always being washed. I never put it on.

After I came home from a meeting, my father often said, "Well, what kind of baloney did they teach you tonight?" This had a great deal to do with my developing skepticism, although I may not have been aware of it at the time. My father could see that Nazism, which relied on force instead of freedom, which enticed people to place their absolute faith in a man and in a political system created by men, was the opposite of the gospel of Jesus Christ. To him it was a competing religious system.[119]

I began to skip my Hitler Youth meetings as often as I could. Sometimes, when I did not appear for duty, the leader of the Hitler Youth came to see my father and asked, "Where is Karl-Heinz? Why does he not come to duty?"[120] Then my father always replied in mock anger, "Well, that is terrible! I will have some words with him! That's out of the question! He must go to duty! I'll give him the thrashing of his life when he gets home! Thanks for telling me." I stood behind the door and nearly laughed myself to death. When the leader was gone, my father laughed, too. He said, "You can always go, but it is your affair."[121]

Once more I went jauntily in my civvies to duty at our Hitler Youth home in the Reismühle.[122] Everyone came in uniform and with brightly polished boots. Somehow it did not please our group leader that once again my uniform was being washed, and so he had it in for me and wanted to disgrace me again. He bellowed at me and wanted to drill me terribly with push-ups, crawling, and all of that nonsense.[123] My tormentor was not any older than I was, so when I had had enough, I went over to him and told him to lay off and asked him if he was completely normal.[124] I said, "Leave me alone! Don't brag so much!" One word followed another, and then I gave him a shove. He yelled at me and I told him to shut up. He then yelled even louder, so I punched him in the face. By the finish I had trounced him in front of all the others. I was a little bigger than he and I really had gotten hot under the collar and I finally told him that he could kiss my ass, and then I went home.

When I arrived home I told Dad about it and he merely grinned. "Now I don't know what will happen," I fretted. "Well, what can happen?" he replied with a shrug, "Nothing." A few weeks later I received a letter from the area leader and was summoned to attend an honor hearing.[125] That did not last long. They no longer valued my membership. I was called in and then they read me a statement. On the grounds that I failed to obey an order, I was expelled from the Hitler Youth.[126] Did I have anything to say? I answered, "No, I have nothing to say." Then the matter was finished. Of course, they chewed me out, saying that it was a shame for a German to act that way, and so on, but that did not bother me any further. The process left me cold.[127]

I was completely happy and pleased that this uproar was over. Thereafter, when they had duty and drilled, I always went past nattily dressed in civvies. All my friends saw me and I stopped and smirked at them. My father grinned, also, when he heard that. My father was always on my side. He merely did not want any complications. He did not want to go to the hearing. I certainly had no notion that the Gestapo would remember the episode and hold it against me. In August 1942 all of this was dredged up again.[128]

But in this environment, where many were positively in favor of the Nazis, there was a current of opposition. My father was part of it, and he said so loudly, though he never participated openly in any opposition. He said, "They should leave me alone." I often heard my father debate with our neighbor, the SA man Otto Schulz. He was a harmless SA man. He loved a little hell-raising and rows and barroom battles and brawls ("dancing by seizing"), but I doubt he ever really harmed anyone or had anyone arrested, because he was not an evil man at heart, but he was enthused about brawling and was a genuine bruiser and felt that the party gave meaning to his life.

One of our neighbors said to my father once that he should keep his mouth shut. That was in approximately 1939 or 1940. My father had shouted, "That swine, that bloody cur!" Then the neighbor said, "Mr. Schnibbe, be quiet. I heard what you said down on the street. If they hear that, you will be sent down the river and never return."

The opponents of Hitler who were still left knew they could not succeed.[129] My father always said, "Man, this cannot go on like this; it will lead to war." Some spoke like that, but few did anything about it.

2

From Pogroms to War, from Radio to Resistance

Despite my bad experiences in the Hitler Youth and my father's fine anti-Nazi example, I doubt that I would have become an active member of a resistance movement if I had not known Helmuth Hübener. I would not have despised the Nazis less, but I may not have hit upon a particular plan of action like the one Helmuth had in mind. On the other hand, it might have been partially due to my intense dislike of the Nazis that Helmuth was moved further toward anti-Nazism.[1] I do not know. I think we influenced each other.[2] (See Documents 71 and 72.) I know that I told Helmuth about an experience I had in 1938 which left me totally shocked and horrified.

The ninth of November 1938 was the Kristallnacht (Crystal Night),[3] which struck suddenly throughout all of Germany. In the morning as I went to work, I could not believe what I saw. It looked like a war had started. Through the entire street, it was the Steindamm with many Jewish businesses, all of the windows were shattered.[4] Broken glass was scattered on the street and expensive furs and clothing and other goods were in the gutter. No one seemed to have any idea what had happened. Many people inquired, "Good heavens, what is wrong here?" I was greatly alarmed by it and could not understand why everything had been smashed.

Before then there had already been a lot of hazing of the Jews,[5] but the Nazis had not gone to such violent extremes. The SA had stood in front of Jewish businesses with placards reading: "Germans protect yourselves, do not buy from Jews!" We thought it would pass, but now it had gotten much worse.

I was an apprentice painter by that time and I worked at painting and decorating homes in the rich sections of Hamburg, where many

Jewish people lived, in the Isesstraße and on the Rothenbaumchaussee,[6] as well as in the business district on the Jungfernstieg at Neuen Wall and on the Großen Bleichen where there were many elegant Jewish businesses. Everything was wrecked, everything dumped out in the filth. Those who did such things were genuine thugs. I thought, "Man, oh man, what is going on here?"

All my Jewish acquaintances were very kind to me, and I occasionally got into political discussions with them. I remember very well one Jewish lady, Frau Doctor Frank. She was a nice woman and the owner of several apartment houses where we worked a lot. She told me she thought the Jews were in no real danger, because they were German citizens and were very important people with friends in high places.[7]

My boss often gave me travel money, fifteen or twenty cents, for the streetcar, but I saved the money and went on foot, because I was young and walking was not difficult. Only an hour or an hour and a half and I was home. That was in 1939, after the beginning of the war. Once, as I was going home from work, I went along the Grindelallee and came upon a spot where they had herded a group of Jewish people together. The Jews were being spat upon and laughed at on the street by the SS and SA men, who then forced the poor people to climb into their trucks amidst jeering and derision.[8] As I stood and watched, I became terribly upset. Afterward I went home and talked with my mother, and she said, "Son, it is best you forget what you saw. That is the way our lives will be now."[9]

Dr. Caro, the physician who brought me into the world, was a Jew and a good and fine man. When someone needed help, he came with his little satchel and made a house call. He came to our house often. He was truly a conscientious physician. Now, of course, we continued to go to our good old Jewish physician. At that time, however, people started to look at us askance and make slighting remarks, but he was our doctor and we visited him. However, when you wanted to visit a physician, you had to obtain a permission slip in the Allgemeine Orts Krankenkasse, the general city insurance office, where you were asked who the doctor was. If it was a Jew, as in this case, you often received an admonition, or an "I beg your pardon, who?" or a long, chastising look and were dismissed with "Heil Hitler."[10]

One day I needed to visit our physician again at his practice in the Ifflandstraße. As I entered, the door was locked and a sign said "Closed."[11] What the truth was, we did not know. We had no idea if he was sick or on vacation.[12] Later, of course, we knew well where he was, poor Dr. Caro. That was approximately at the end of 1939.[13] Although he had been a decorated officer and staff physician in World

War I, that no longer made any difference.[14] Frau Doctor Frank also disappeared shortly thereafter. I think she may have been able to get out of Germany in time and emigrate to the United States. If so, she would have been among the last to escape.[15] We were always told, "The Jews are the cause of our misfortune."[16]

Some of those who remained did not believe they were in danger. We often said to them, "You need to flee from Germany." They said, "They cannot do anything to us. We are German citizens. We were born here. This is our home. They cannot do such things." Oh yes, the Nazis could do it! They simply drove the poor Jewish citizens out of their apartments. They had to leave everything they owned. They were only permitted to take thirty to fifty pounds of baggage, no cash. The money was confiscated as "German property," as the Nazis called it.[17] Then important Nazis wasted no time settling down in the elegant apartments of rich Jews. How nice, these thugs must have thought, to sleep in a bed already made up![18]

Everything that the Nazis seized from the Jews was called "Aryanized."[19] Large signs were plastered on the display windows of the Jewish businesses which were "Aryanized." Thereafter the party moochers went in, the presumptive bastards![20]

At age fourteen, near the end of March 1938, a few weeks before leaving school, I went down to the government career advising bureau Am Raboisen, near the central train station. "What do you want to be?" the man asked me. "Well, I wanted to be a sailor, but my dad thinks that's an immoral life and he wants me to learn a trade, but I still like the sea and ships, so I'd like to be a ship's plumber or a marine steamfitter or something like that." The counselor said, "Hmmm, I don't think we have any openings in those areas right now. What else can you do? What's your favorite subject in school?" I told him it was art, so he sent me home to get some pictures that I had drawn with colored pencils. When he saw them he said, "You don't want to be a plumber, you want to be an interior decorator, a painter."

The minute he said that I was excited. I was immediately taken by the idea. He gave me the name of a firm: F. Georg Suhse, Painting Contractors, where I could apply to become an apprentice under the master painter, Johannes Ehlers. Because it was evening by then, I went to see Mr. Ehlers at his home. His wife let me in after I explained what I wanted. Mr. Ehlers entered and was very brusk with me. That was the way masters treated their apprentices in those days, I learned. They even boxed their ears occasionally.[21] He barked at me for a while and then he looked at my drawings. When he saw them, he said, "April first, 7:30 A.M. at the shop." "Don't you want to see my school grades?" I asked, holding them out to him. "Not interested. That's fine. You be there." I had the job; I was an apprentice decorator.

Once a week, on Tuesdays, I went to the vocational school in the House of Youth in the Museumstraße in Altona,[22] where I learned theoretical things, such as how to make and calculate bids, and how to figure perspective for lettering, and how paint is manufactured. On Thursdays I went to the Nagelsweg, where the painting and decorating guild had a six-floor apartment house that was empty for us to use for practice. The instructor, Herr Bähre, whom I never saw without a big black cigar, would come in with a large chisel and pound on a door with it and make big gouges and scratches, and say, "I want this door perfect, beautiful."

Of course, I did not start working on doors immediately. Being an apprentice in Germany in those days meant that one learned a trade literally from the ground up. For the first four or five months my job was to clean out the shop, sweeping and mopping the floors, and to go on errands delivering things to the eight or more journeymen who were working on jobs all over the city. After quitting time, I chopped firewood for the wife of the boss and ran errands, such as grocery shopping, for her, too. As an apprentice I worked fifty to fifty-five hours per week. During the first year I was paid 4 marks 80 a week. I gave my Mom 4.20 for groceries and my white painter's clothes, and kept 60 cents for pocket money. The second year my pay increased to 7.20 a week, and the third year it was 9.60. The journeymen, by comparison, made slightly more than one mark per hour, approximately 50 marks for a forty-eight-hour week.[23] I was an apprentice for three years, after which I took the difficult practical and theoretical journeyman's examination.

During the period of my apprenticeship, I continued my close association with my friends. Because the LDS church kept us involved, almost all of my friends, with a few exceptions, such as Heinz Buske at school and Peter Pflug, were in the LDS branch. Otto Berndt, Jr.; Erwin Frank; Gerhardt, Harald, and Karla Fricke; Helga Krüger; Nani Kreutner; and Marie, Hedwig, Arthur, and Werner Sommerfeld were some of my friends from the branch. My closest friends, though, were Helmuth Hübener and Rudi Wobbe. They were the ones who came often to my house and the ones with whom I went swimming or to the movies.[24]

Helmuth was the natural leader of the group. He was, simply stated, the smartest kid in the bunch. He had tremendous talent. He could take a pencil and whip out caricatures of Churchill and Hitler that were brilliant. Everyone liked him, I believe, because he got along well with people.

He lived with his grandparents, the Sudrows,[25] who were good Latter-day Saints, and he was their favorite, I believe. They were too poor to spoil him, but they doted on him a lot. Helmuth had two half brothers, Hans and Gerhard Kunkel, who were seven and five years older than he. He lived with the Sudrows because his mother worked a lot and, later, because she was remarried to a zealous Nazi named Hugo Hübener, whom none of the boys could stand.[26] Before Hugo adopted him legally, Helmuth's name was variously Gudat (also spelled Guddat), his mother's maiden name, or Kunkel, her first husband's name.[27]

Because Helmuth was a year younger than I and went to the *Oberbau*, or upper track at school, he began his vocational training about two years later than I did. The *Oberbau* was for those who were not in the expensive and elite university track, but were going into some other kind of challenging profession. Helmuth went into the upper administrative track of the Hamburg city social welfare department. He was a white-collar apprentice. Had he been from a family with status and wealth, he certainly would have gone to the university, because he had the intellectual capacity.

He was very widely read and loved to discuss things with me and Rudi and adult members of the church, as well as with people at his place of employment. A few adult members of the branch thought him a bit arrogant, but that was probably because they resented (as any adult German at that time would have done) a young person asking them difficult questions and pointing out flaws in their logic. Helmuth especially enjoyed engaging adults in political discussions, because they were often a bit naive, and he enjoyed picking them apart if they were wrong. He enjoyed displaying his intellectual and debating abilities. His intention, however, was not to embarrass people but to make them more careful about what they said, to make them support their opinions more rigorously with logic and evidence. In our church classes Helmuth was the one who knew the answers. He had studied the doctrines and knew them very well for a person of his age.[28]

Rudi was younger than Helmuth and I. His mother was a war widow.[29] Theirs was a good Mormon family, and I spent a lot of time at their home on Sundays between meetings. He lived quite a distance away, in Rothenburgsort. Helmuth's house in the Louisenweg was closer. Rudi became an apprentice mechanic. He, too, was not particularly fond of the Hitler Youth.[30] He was riding his bicycle one day when a Hitler Youth patrol tried to stop him, because he did not salute their flag.[31] He just rammed into one of them and knocked him over and pedaled away. Because they did not know who he was, they never caught him.

The patrols contained brawlers who went through the parks at night searching for juveniles, and those persons the Hitler Youth patrols captured were beaten up.[32] One time we, too, were chased by a Hitler Youth patrol. They tried to ambush us, but where we were we knew every bush, so we disappeared. We threw rocks at them and then ran away.[33] Having a skirmish with the Hitler Youth was not as serious as our later resistance activities, because then we were risking our lives.[34]

I hated those stupid flag patrols, too. Whenever they came along everyone had to stand at attention and raise their arms in salute.[35] I always turned a corner or stood in an alley or an apartment entrance if I could, and a lot of other people did too, because Hamburg never did go completely over to the Nazis.[36] There were too many Communists and Social Democrats there.[37] The place was very cosmopolitan and independent, because it was an ancient Hanseatic free city[38] with close ties to England. The Nazis knew this and they made Karl Kaufmann[39] the Gauleiter (regional party leader) in Hamburg because some felt he was sophisticated, and thus less like some of the other typical Nazi thugs who were the other Gauleiter around the Reich.[40]

We boys talked about the Nazi party, Communism, and the revolution. We noticed the great emphasis on military things. Helmuth said, "Where can all this militarism be taking us, this Army Day, Navy Day, Air Force Day business? It can mean only one thing: war is inevitable. And these Hitler Youth uniforms look just like the military ones. Obviously, they are preparing us to be soldiers, too."[41]

Our increasingly sour attitude toward the Nazis and Helmuth's outspoken political discussions with church members converged when Arthur Zander became president of the St. Georg branch. He and one of his counselors, Franz Jacobi, were Nazis. Jacobi was a very serious "super Nazi." He and Zander suggested that we start our meeting with the Hitler salute and bring a radio so that the branch members could listen together to Hitler's occasional Sunday radio broadcasts. The doors would be locked so that no one could leave during the speech.[42] All these things were opposed by people like my father and Otto Berndt, who was the other counselor in the branch presidency at the time and became, eventually, the district president.[43] "Don't you do that," Berndt told them. "This is a church of God, not a political meeting." Zander and Jacobi relented on most items, but some time before the war Zander put a sign on the branch house which read, "Jews are not allowed to enter."

The case perhaps best illuminating the political climate in the branch was that of Salomon Schwarz, a member of the Mormon faith in Hamburg, who looked "Jewish" and was generally held to be a Jew, even though he did not descend from known Jewish ancestors and had been raised a Protestant.[44] It was partially to discourage Schwarz's visits to the St. Georg branch that Zander hung out the sign forbidding Jews.[45] Salomon, however, was welcomed at the Barmbek branch.[46] When he attempted, in 1941, to get a certificate proving he was not Jewish, he was arrested by the Gestapo for not wearing the yellow Star of David with the word "Jude" written on it. He was placed in the ghetto in the Grindel area of Hamburg, and then he disappeared eventually.[47] (See Document 71.) He died in the concentration camp at Auschwitz.[48]

Of course, we knew the meetings were being monitored, so we felt that some displays of patriotism were good insurance. We posted on the bulletin board the letters of LDS soldiers serving in the military. Once, I saw at the branch house some Hitler Youth boys whom I recognized from my days with the Hitler Youth, and I said to them, "Hey! What are you guys doing here? You're not interested in our church."[49] They had come to make a disturbance, but left quietly a short time afterward.[50] Perhaps they lost their courage or saw one of our leaders in his uniform.

Even after the war started in 1939, and as late as 1941, many members of our branch supported the regime, albeit nervously. "Well, we are fighting against Communism," they would say, "and we need to support the powers that be. Besides, our boys are out there on the battlefield." At the end of 1941, though, when the United States entered the war after Pearl Harbor, many of the German Saints predicted the defeat of Germany, because of the Book of Mormon[51] prophecies concerning the fate of those "gentile nations" which fight against "Zion." After Stalingrad[52] the pessimistic attitude became more prevalent.

I do not wish to leave the impression that any of the Saints, including Arthur Zander and Franz Jacobi, were evil persons. They were not. Zander was a dedicated branch president, a natural leader of young and old, who took charge of things in the branch and made things happen. Under his leadership we enlarged the branch house and installed a baptismal font.[53] He made certain there was always cake and hot chocolate for the volunteer workers. He was an executive in a laundry detergent factory and supervised employees there, so knew how to organize people and get things done. We called him the Chief.

In spite of the growing militarism and Helmuth's premonitions of war, it was a shock when the news came over the radio on 1 September 1939, that the march into Poland had begun at 4:45 A.M. Now the watchword was: "Strike them with a vengeance." And then all hell broke loose in a breath-taking tempo that was called *Blitzkrieg* (lightning war).

When England and France declared war on Germany on 3 September, most people were shaken that it had actually come to this. Many persons were very opposed, including my father and mother. They could not understand it. Another war?! What a pile of crap!

Of course, many were enthused. All of the Nazis were in favor of "the only way to solve the Polish problem." It appeared as if our Führer and supreme commander could do nothing wrong. It was one big uninterrupted victorious triumph.

On our street lived a young man who was in the army and fought in Poland and was one of the first to fall. Then came more obituaries in the newspapers. Of course, everything was written large with the Iron Cross and "With Proud Grief" and "For the Führer and the Fatherland" and all of that baloney. It was all a lot of rubbish. Where was there such a thing as "With Proud Grief"? the people asked. Had anyone ever known a wife who did not miss her husband above all, or small children their father? And for what reason? people said. What did the Poles do to us? No one has the right to inflict so much harm on others. No good can come of it.

All of a sudden the war in Poland ended and the troops were back already.[54] There was jubilation and milling crowds. Many said, "I hope the war comes quickly to an end and they come to their senses." But that lasted only a short while, because on 3 October, German troops were transferred from Poland to the West.

On the western front nothing was happening. The French played soccer and the Germans watched, but a man such as Hitler could not sit still, and one day he attacked there, too. The gods were with Adolf and he was acclaimed again as the greatest military commander of all time. Our victorious troops returned home again and marched with beating drums through the Brandenburg gate in Berlin.[55] It was an immense victory parade and swept everyone along with it. Nevertheless, the populace yearned and hoped for peace at last and mourned the many victims on both sides.

Many saw nothing wrong with all of the campaigns and defended the whole rot. It was said, "The losses are small potatoes! We can endure that. What are a few dead, wounded, and missing? If you want to make an omelette you have to break eggs! As for the victims from the other side, they are of no interest to us. They did not need to start something." That was the talk in the party circles and among the worshippers of our beloved Führer. Sieg Heil and lots of loot and a big mouth.

I often discussed with my friends Helmuth and Rudi what we thought about such things. We saw each other once, twice, or three times a week and talked. Helmuth always told us things that caused us to say, "My goodness, how does he know that?" Could one really believe these brethren? Joseph Goebbels was a completely callous and hard-boiled minister of propaganda who could lie without blushing. When we heard the military reports, there were nothing but victories and everything on the ground was destroyed. Because Goebbels had a club foot, we called it "Doctor Clubfoot's Fairy-Tale Hour."

We did not know what was right and what not, because there was no news from abroad. We had only small utility radios, so that we could hear Hamburg, Berlin, and Munich.[56] Sometimes we received only one station and were supposed to believe what they told us. There was a lot of whispering: "Did you hear?"

Helmuth always said to us, "I need to make you a little more politically educated." He presented comparisons and forced us to think. I was always astonished at his knowledge and intelligence. I called him "the Professor," because he knew everything, or thought he knew everything.

At his job as an apprentice in the social office in the Hamburg government, he had access to the storerooms in the basement of the city hall, where forbidden books were stored, where we could not go. At that time Helmuth read books about all the European countries, of which we had no notion. He was always hungry for knowledge. I am convinced that Helmuth read many books which ordinary mortals never encountered in Germany at that time.[57] He read books about foreign policy, domestic policy, and the economic situation. We did not know anything, because we were not supposed to know.[58] Thus, Helmuth related a lot to us at that time and explained some things to us about which we had to keep our mouths shut. We asked, "Man, how do you know that?"

Helmuth was naturally convinced that the whole enterprise could not succeed. "Just think about it," he said. "England, France—it is strategically impossible! It just can't be. Germany is cut off, has no raw materials, everything will collapse." He had put two and two together and figured out what many had not. "Listen, an army needs so much gasoline every day, and this and that. It goes okay for a while, but then comes to a halt when nothing more is available."

When Hitler began the attack on the USSR in June 1941, most Hamburgers were stunned. On the day the war started, I was at the swimming pool at Ohlsdorf and had been swimming and was lying in the sun. There I heard the special announcement that German troops had crossed the border at 4:00 A.M. and that war with the Soviet Union was underway. I then heard discussions by the others who were lying on blankets in the sun. They said, "Good heavens, he certainly got himself into a mess!" They were skeptical and said, "Oh, boy, it'd be a miracle if they can pull this one off." I had already heard some say, "Oh, heavens, that won't work! That is a gigantic country."[59]

Helmuth also said to us, "It cannot succeed!" He had thought about it a lot and was firmly convinced of it. Thus it came about that he invited me to visit him in the apartment where he lived with his grandparents. His mother had been drafted and was a nurse who worked nights. Then she remarried. His grandparents were elderly people and always went to bed early.[60] So we were always alone to hear the news at ten in the evening.

I went there alone. At the time I did not know that our friend, Rudi Wobbe, was also part of it. Helmuth had merely said to me, "Come visit me sometime, I want to show you something." I was supposed to come a little late, not too early. I thought, "Oh yeah, his grandparents need to be in bed first," or something similar. I had no idea what he wanted to show me and so I arrived later.

When I entered Helmuth's apartment on that fateful evening, he showed me a radio. Helmuth's brother had brought the radio, a Rola brand, home from occupied France where he had served in the National Labor Service.[61] I didn't have any idea what this radio could do, this attractive, neat, little thing. Helmuth said to me, "It has shortwave." I replied, "Oh, *short*wave. What can you hear on it? France?" "Oh yes, and England, too," he answered. I said, "Man, are you crazy?" "No, not yet," he responded. "I want to show you something."

Then he showed me a flyer he had written based on the British newscasts. I read it. "Man, where did you get this? It can't be possible. It is completely the opposite of our military broadcasts."[62] "That it is," he said. "Do you have time?" "Sure," I answered. "Then let's hear it."

He turned out the light in the room and turned on the radio. The feeble light illuminated the numbers of the shortwave dial. He turned the radio up gently and at exactly 10:00 P.M. we heard the first four notes of Beethoven's Fifth Symphony. That signal (three shorts and a long, Morse code for "V," standing for victory) was given at the beginning of every broadcast of the British newscast in the German language. Then coming out of the ether in clear German I heard, "The BBC London presents the news in German." The Nazis often tried to jam such broadcasts, but on that night it was crystal clear. My heart was beating like mad, because I knew well that listening to enemy newscasts was strictly forbidden and severely punished.[63]

The first newscast that I heard dealt with the Russian campaign, code-named Barbarossa.[64] The official German military press releases printed in the newspapers and broadcast on German radio stations boasted of great successes in Russia. The number of enemy soldiers killed and captured was phenomenal, but little or no mention was made of German losses. "That can't be," Helmuth whispered to me, "somebody's lying."

Then I remembered other recent discussions with Helmuth at the church. He said on several occasions that the military press releases were lies. "Do you believe them?" he asked us. "Why not?" we said. "Why shouldn't we believe them?" "Because they are lying, that's why," Helmuth replied. I heard, also, that his friends at work called him "the man with connections." (See Document 10.) Now I recognized what his source of information was. He must have been listening to the BBC for several weeks.[65]

"Look," he continued, "it just doesn't make sense. We march into Russia and kill so many of their soldiers, but they have guns. They are shooting back. Put two and two together and you'll see that we're going to have some casualties on our side, too. And these British reports have a lot more details than ours, and they give their own casualties, not just the enemy's. Our news reports sound like a lot of boasting, a lot of propaganda, and theirs sound more realistic.[66] I'm convinced they are telling the truth and we are lying."[67]

That was something that enlightened me immediately. I could scarcely believe what I heard. The German military reports and the German news service had told us one thing and the BBC London told us something completely different. They were completely contradictory. The German news service said that the German military had had light casualties.[68] The British told us that the German army had already lost hundreds of thousands. Whom could one believe?

The English said that the German propaganda lied, and they gave precise numbers of sinkings to prove it. For example, the Germans claimed to have sunk the *Royal Oak*[69] approximately three times and it was still afloat. (See Document 46.) The Germans had also conjured up enemy casualty losses which were so high as to be impossible. From Africa the German news service had informed us that Rommel won over and over again. The British reported to the contrary that Rommel had received many setbacks, but admitted that Rommel had also won some important battles. (See Documents 35 and 41.) There was something about the English broadcasts that was, somehow, more realistic and credible. In contrast to them, the German transmissions were more vague and wanted to color everything and represent it gloriously. Naturally, it was clear that the Germans had lied.[70]

Listening was fascinating. It was impossible to leave it alone, because you just wanted to know more. A lot more became clear to me. Curiosity and a wish developed in me to know precisely what was occurring. I began then to doubt seriously the German military reports.[71] Even so, I had previously never really believed the whole circus. When I heard, "great advances, light casualties, small casualties," I thought, "Oh come on, how is that possible? That is a lot of baloney!"[72] I became convinced that the BBC told us the truth without a lot of clamorous trappings and bluster.[73] Even if it had been possible to believe half of it, it was shocking. The gentlemen in Berlin were deceiving us. The German people were being duped. Anyone who was not yet totally castrated intellectually and blind, shuffling along through this glorious period, must have noticed it. "Comrades, we are conquering ourselves to death."[74]

The newscast ended at 10:30 and I had to see to it that I got home. My parents were not enthused when I came home late. There could be air-raid alarms, because the English came now and then to visit us in Hamburg. My mother, of course, was worried about us when we were not there, and it was impossible to know where bombs would fall. As I said good-bye, I asked Helmuth if I could listen again, the next time he did. "Of course," he said. "Only you know, Kuddl, keep quiet." Man, to whom was he saying that? It was as clear to me as the nose on my face.

That's how my involvement began. I listened often with Helmuth to the English newscasts. The anxious feeling that we were doing something perverse or committing a crime abated gradually. Nevertheless, it was a certain thrill.

We began to concern ourselves with it more intensely. We obtained maps and followed the advances precisely. It was one *Blitzkrieg* after another. It is no wonder that the majority of Germans believed that Adolf had been sent from God and that he must be victorious. He had proved it. He smashed Poland in three weeks, France in four, and occupied all of Europe. That was obvious. Why should he not be victorious in Russia?[75]

At first we heard from soldiers who participated that the German soldiers in the Ukraine were received as liberators, because the natives were not really Communists; they hated the regime. The Germans made a good start; they distributed collective land immediately to the peasants. The farmers received their land and livestock, but they had no idea of what was coming.[76] It was all bait. Those first soldiers were the combat troops, but then came the SS and the little Hitlers, the commissars of agriculture and the special commissions.[77] Then began the looting. Thereafter the Ukrainians received nothing more to eat. One blow followed another, encirclement followed encirclement, and we always heard that 500,000 were captured, 300,000 were captured. We always asked ourselves, "How will they feed so many? They must have something to eat." We had no idea that those in the prison camps were starving, that many received absolutely nothing.[78]

But Adolf practically won himself to death in Russia. The distances became too great. Besides, each general wanted to get ahead of the others, because it rained decorations like never before.[79] It also rained deaths like never before. At first the newspapers were full of "proud grief for the Führer and the Fatherland," but afterward that gradually diminished. It was also no longer stressed so much by the party, because there were too many obituaries in the newspapers.

I could not go listen to the radio every time, every day. Because of my parents, I had to be cautious that I did not come home too late. Although I was seventeen years old, my parents were still very strict. When I left, I was always given a curfew when I had to be at home, due to the air raids.[80] It was not possible for me every night to dawdle going home. Thus, I requested of Helmuth that he write down the interesting things for me, because I knew that he had mastered stenography. "I'll do it," he said to me. I really didn't think he would.

Helmuth always listened enthusiastically. He did not neglect anything. He did, in fact, take shorthand notes and gave me excerpts so I would not miss anything. When we had the chance, we listened together, but it was always the two of us, still without Rudi.

At that time you heard a lot about political murders and how the Russian prisoners of war, who were called subhumans, were treated. Helmuth was very incensed over it. I believe this motivated him to produce his first leaflets.[81]

In the beginning they were rather small, perhaps four by six inches. There were only a few words on them, such as "Down with Hitler!" (See Document 28.) Another one stated "Hitler the murderer!"[82] One was "Hitler the seducer (*Verführer*) of the people." He made only ten copies[83] of these small leaflets and left them himself in telephone boxes with the notice: "This is a chain letter, so pass it on." Many people probably did pass them on, because not many of them were turned over to the Gestapo. (See Documents 3, 4, 5.)[84] At the beginning of August 1941 the flyers became larger, filling entire letter-size pages and were detailed, accurate accounts of major military and geopolitical issues.

Once, when I went to visit Helmuth again, he let the cat out of the bag. He asked me, "Kuddl, will you take part, too?" I didn't understand what he had in mind. "What should I do?" I asked. "I always listen diligently to the broadcasts, if the interference is not too bad." "Not that," he said. Then he showed me a little stack of type-written red leaflets. "We've got to get these into people's hands," he said, and gave me one to read.

A strange feeling began to rise in me and I started to get very sick, because I had a terrible foreboding. I asked Helmuth to explain to me exactly what the things were for, what their purpose was. My fears were justified. He said they were intended for telephone booths and mail boxes in apartment houses. Man, oh man, that was an ambitious undertaking! Those little handbills burned my hands like hot iron. I said to Helmuth, "If they catch us, we'll be in deep, deep trouble." You could read in the newspapers nearly every day about death sentences or imprisonment because of conspiracy to commit high treason.

I tried to speak with Helmuth about it to see if there was some other way, but he was completely convinced and would not be moved by any arguments. He declared to me again the abomination of the Third Reich and made it clear to me that it was the moral duty of every truth-loving person to combat the regime. I told him that I would think about it, because "to speak the truth these days is a fatal luxury." Helmuth was of the opinion that if we handled it carefully, it would work. I still had misgivings and a little fear. I could not get it through my head that this quiet, intelligent, clever young man was so cool and resolute. He said to me, "Think about it again and tell me for certain on Sunday. Take a few of these things with you when you go home and get rid of them! Don't forget, telephone booths and mail boxes, and always watch out. So long." And so I tore out of there and headed home as fast as I could go.

I was really uneasy and had a stomachache. I told myself that everything would go okay and that I would soon be rid of the seven annoying handbills. It was good thing that Hamburg was totally blacked out, because the darkness worked to my advantage. I kept a sharp eye out, because I really had no desire to end up in the clink.

I went home the fastest way, via Oben-Borgfelde to Klaus-Groth-straße, Alfredstraße, then Lübeckerstraße. On the way I put some in telephone booths. At Oben-Borgfelde I wanted to put some in mail boxes, but the house doors were locked. In the Klaus-Grothstraße and in the Lübeckerstraße I finally got rid of the flyers. That was a load off my mind; my heart thumped awfully. Man, was I happy to be free of them!

I was all worked up, especially when I met two policemen as I turned from the Lübeckerstraße onto Rossausweg, where we lived. I greeted the two with a Heil Hitler and wished them a good evening, which they cheerfully reciprocated. "Where could you be going so late?" one asked me. "Going home," I replied. "I live in Rossausweg 32. I was visiting a friend in the Reismühle." A friend of mine actually lived there, but I did not want to tell them where I had really been.

"Well, good night then young man, and hopefully there will be no air raids." I said good night, also, and left. I was just two heels and a cloud of dust. It was a good thing my parents were already in bed, because I was a nervous wreck. My stomachache worsened and I got diarrhea. If Helmuth had asked me then to deliver the handbills, I would have turned him down flat.

The following morning I saw things differently, and I told myself that if I were careful and only helped Helmuth now and then, everything would be all right. Nothing could go wrong. My mother asked me accusingly where I had been last night, why I had come home so late. I said that Helmuth and I had been chatting heartily and the time passes dreadfully fast when you're having fun. "Son, don't wear out your welcome by staying too long at Helmuth's grandparents'." If she had known what we really did, ouch, I dare not think about it.

On Sunday I met Helmuth at church again, as we had planned. "Well, how is it going?" he asked, laughing, and meant "You didn't go down the tubes." He continued and said, "If I know you, you got rid of everything all right." "And a lot more," I answered him. "How come, what else? What do you mean?" Then I had to laugh. I told Helmut that the blasted leaflets had given me the trots. I felt like I had been through a meat grinder.

Both of us laughed so heartily and loudly that Rudi Wobbe came up and asked what was so terribly funny. I said to Rudi, who was two years younger, that it was nothing for the ears of children. I still had no idea that Rudi was already involved as the third member of the conspiracy. "Come and visit me again some time," Helmuth said. "We need to chat some more, Kuddl." "Okay. When is it best for you, Helmuth?" "How about Saturday night?" "Okay. The same time?" "Yes, but don't come too late, Kuddl."

Fridays and Saturdays were the best days for me, because on the weekends I could stay out longer. During the week I had to go to the church with my parents in the evenings. I told myself that when I was eighteen, I would not go to church so much, that my father could no longer twist my arm, that I would be old enough to decide for myself. How gladly I would have gone to church with my parents when I was eighteen!

As I got ready Saturday afternoon to visit Helmuth, my mother asked me where I was going. "I think Helmuth and I will go to a movie," I told her. "Don't come home too late and be careful if there is an air raid. By all means, get into the air-raid shelter." My mother knew too well that we often stayed outside to watch when the search lights spotted a plane and kept the light shining on it. It looked like a little moth. Then the flak cut loose. That was really exciting, but was, of course, very dangerous, because after a couple of minutes the shrapnel fragments came falling down. They clattered all around us and some were damned sharp and had jagged points. Getting hit on the head with one of those could ruin your whole evening.[85]

At seven o'clock I sauntered over to Helmuth's apartment. He opened the door and said he had prepared a surprise for me. "How come, what kind of a surprise?" "Relax, Kuddl, you'll see." He grinned on all four cheeks. His grandparents were sitting in the living room. I greeted both of them. "Good evening, Karl-Heinz." We went into the kitchen, and lo and behold, the surprise was none other than Rudi. I was totally astonished to see him there with Helmuth. "Man," I asked, what are you doing here?" He answered, "What are you doing here? You, too?" Helmuth had recruited him in part because he lived in Rothenburgsort, a Communist neighborhood known for its anti-Nazi sentiment, where Helmuth wanted lots of leaflets distributed.[86]

"Since when, Helmuth?" "Since the beginning. The three musketeers," Helmuth said, and grinned. "Did you know about me, Rudi?" "Nah." "Why this secrecy, Helmuth, couldn't you trust us?" "Of course, but better safe than sorry. I wanted to see how things worked out for a while and if you had the stomach for this, because I must tell you frankly, Kuddl, that it was an uneasy feeling for me at the beginning, too. Let's go outside and get some fresh air."

It was a beautiful, mild, clear September evening. Hamburg was pitch dark. Would the Tommies come tonight? Perhaps they would leave us in peace. "Hamburgers, stay in your digs, we're going to Berlin to bomb the pigs."[87] We did not want to talk too loudly, because we always had the feeling that somebody would be disturbed or awakened. At night the city looked dead.

"Let's go on upstairs. It's about time; it will soon be 10:00 and a person can get melancholy out here in the dark," Helmuth said to us. "We can thank our Führer for that!" I said. "Shut your trap! Not so loud, Kuddl." "Yeah, I guess you're right," I muttered. "There will be a time when a wonder occurs, and then a thousand fairy tales will come true," Rudi trilled suddenly, imitating a popular song.[88] "Man, now listen to that screwball; you have missed your calling, sweetie." "Kiss my ass, my dear Karl-Heinz." "Uh uh, how refined. You want to accustom me to taking a bite, what?"

That's how we kidded around, and it looked like we were in the best of spirits. In reality, we were all nervous and knew precisely that what we intended was a criminal offense. The only one who was calm and cool as a dog's nose was Helmuth. His composure and calmness gradually carried over to us.

When we entered the apartment, his grandparents were already in bed. We went quietly into the kitchen and sat at the table, where the radio was located. We had about two minutes before the broadcast and Helmuth attempted to tune in London. That evening things bleeped and cracked and buzzed so much out of the ether that it was impossible to understand a word. We waited a few more minutes and tried it again. Very cautiously he turned the dial, but there was nothing doing. The jamming was too strong. To tell the truth, I was very happy that we couldn't hear anything that night.

We met together again and listened to the newscasts three or four times, and were gradually captivated, fascinated. It was hard to bide one's time before hearing the next English newscast. We knew precisely that it was dangerous, because we had read in the newspaper that illegal listeners were given a ten-year jail sentence, or life. We heard this over and over. "But," we said, "who can catch us when we listen to it with the radio turned down so low that late in the evening? First someone would need to come through the door. They would need to have a key to catch us." We did not worry ourselves about it. I always said, "Listening is not a crime; the crime is getting caught."[89]

Helmuth explained his plan to us that first night. He had decided not to distribute a few handbills now and then, but to carry on a full-fledged informational resistance, and asked us if we wanted to help him. I was alarmed and said, "Man, are you nuts? Are you completely off your rocker? What are you thinking of? Surely you don't suppose that we three can overthrow the government?" No, he did not want to do that. He was not that naive, but he said, "We can inform people, and demonstrate that there are groups who are opposed; then many persons can start to talk and say, 'Have you heard about this? That is amazing!'" Then came a long pause. I could not make up my mind at first; I had to think about it. Rudi, also, was hesitant about distributing the flyers.[90]

Helmuth felt obligated to inform the people in Hamburg what was occurring; he said he wanted many people to hear the truth.[91] He said, "We have learned from childhood to tell the truth." He was convinced that other people must hear the truth, and not everyone had a short-wave receiver. Not everyone could hear English broadcasts, or if they could, many had not done it because they were afraid.

Finally Rudi and I said, "Okay, we will help you. What is your plan?" Helmuth went into the living room and returned again a few minutes later, holding a pile of handbills in his hand. "What is that?" asked Rudi, who apparently had never distributed any of these longer handbills.[92]

The strange feeling began to well up in me again, but I said nothing. A question was raised, "Man, you know what this means. If they catch us, what then?" Helmuth answered: "Assuming, only assuming, that one of us should be stupid enough to get nabbed, which, as I see it, if we are cautious, cannot happen, I think he should agree not to squeal on the others."

We decided then and there, whoever might be caught should take all of the blame; he should not incriminate the other guys. "Okay, give no names." And if they say, "Yeah, you were surely with a friend," you just say: "Oh, yeah, he did not know anything, he knew nothing about it." The person who gets caught must take the entire blame. "What do you think of that idea?" "Agreed," said Rudi. "And you, Kuddl?" "The thought of going up the river does not appeal to me, but, because we must protect each other, it's all right." "Don't talk to anybody," Helmuth said. "It's too dangerous. Not to your parents, nobody! At church we will just shake hands and say 'How is it going? Everything OK?' 'Fine' and that is all."

We relied upon our promise not to tell anyone, but I wished later Helmuth had been able to follow his own plan better. Of course, we had no idea that when he was arrested they would torture him for two days until he finally caved in and mentioned my name and Rudi's, though he still didn't really implicate us. (See Document 10.)

"Good," said Helmuth, and stuck out his hand. "Shake on it." For a minute we held our hands firmly together. "Now I want to show you something else. I'll be back in just a minute." He went into the living room again and returned with a writing tablet. "Here," he said, "what do you think about this?" One page was covered from top to bottom with stenography. "What is it?" "German newscasts. As I listened, I took shorthand; and these," he said, showing us another bundle of notes, "are English newscasts."

"It's fantastic," Rudi said. I, too, was flabbergasted at his thoroughness. "This way, when you can't listen, I always have the latest news reserved for you." I was excited about the idea, because it was not always possible to visit Helmuth every night or every other night. "That's just the ticket, Helmuth." "So, and now on your way home get rid of a few flyers again," Helmuth said. "I'll do it," Rudi answered. "Give me some. Goodbye, Kuddl." We stuck out our hands and Rudi took off with twenty flyers. I wished him good luck. He distributed the handbills from Louisenweg through Rothenburgsort.

Helmuth kept about ten copies for himself. I received seven or eight and the stomach pains began again, but I said nothing this time. "I will get rid of these quickly and easily," I thought to myself. "So long, Helmuth, see you later and stay cool." "Thanks, Kuddl. My regards to your family, and be careful. Don't fall among thieves." "Cheer up, there's worse to come," I said and departed.

When possible, Helmuth used a duplicating machine now and then, but the thing did not work right. The copies were always a little dim and blurry, but he distributed them anyway. First it was necessary to type the masters, and then turn the handle, there was a cylinder, and so forth. It didn't work well; it was primitive. Helmuth preferred to make seven or eight carbon copies on the Remington typewriter, which were reasonably good. Sometimes he typed it twice so we would have more copies.

Because of his stenographic and typing skills, Helmuth was a clerk to President Zander, who needed someone to type letters to the soldiers in the field and do other secretarial work. Zander gave Helmuth a key to the branch house in the Besenbinderhof and permission to take a typewriter—Zander's own personal portable, first, and, later, the branch Remington—and work at home. (See Document 26.)

He also obtained from the church some of the paper he used. He often said, "Our only real crime is taking this paper from the branch." We had no idea where he got the rest of the paper. The Gestapo documents state that the early handbills were identified as paper from the social administration where Helmuth worked. We did not have big bundles of paper like those Hans and Sophie Scholl[93] used, who later practically let thousands of copies rain down from the rooftops. Afterward, the Nazis wanted to know the names of those who bought a lot of paper, especially carbon paper, but when we made our flyers, things were not yet so tightly controlled. Since Helmuth was writing letters to the troops and others from the branch, and since he did not need more than thirty or forty sheets a week, that amount was not difficult to obtain.

At church on Sundays, Helmuth would sometimes say, "Hey, we haven't seen each other for a long time. Why don't you come over and visit me? Let's do something together." That was our signal. Then I knew that Helmuth had cooked up a new set of leaflets and wanted me to help distribute them. At first, he had something for me about every two weeks. Then, as we became increasingly caught up in the project, as Helmuth became more obsessed with the idea of disseminating the truth, he made a new leaflet every week, and then twice a week.

In the entrance halls to German apartment houses there was always a bulletin board with a swastika, where the official proclamations were posted, for example, "Tomorrow Home Evening with Party Comrade So and So, Topic: Air-Raid Wardens." There was always something like that on the hallway board. The National Socialist party never left a family in peace. They wanted to keep the entire family busy day and night. We stuck our handbills on the bulletin boards with a thumb tack. For the Nazis that must have been very shocking. Helmuth even procured a stamp with an eagle and a swastika, so the flyers looked like official communications. When I think about it today, I still get goose bumps.[94]

That night I still had some handbills when the sirens began to howl, announcing an air-raid alarm. I had had a feeling the entire night that there would be an alarm, because the night was so clear and bright. I needed to get home quickly, so I ran the rest of the way and was not stopped. My mother was happy, of course, that we were all at home, except my brother who had been drafted into making explosives in a factory a good distance from Hamburg. He was on the night shift. "I hope there are no Brandenburgers there tonight and everything goes well," my father uttered. Brandenburgers were what the workers called it when something blew up or a fire broke out in the dynamite.[95]

Later that evening I sat next to our neighbor, Otto Schulz, in the living room and chatted. It was quiet outside and the flak was not shooting. "When they start to shoot, we need to go into the air-raid shelter," he said. Then I stupidly showed Schulz a handbill. "Read this. What do you think?" I told him that I had found it. He read it and turned pale. He became enraged and said, "Man, you idiot, where did you get that? Throw it away, burn the thing, don't pull such crap again. You stupid jerk, are you nuts? Do you want to send us all to the gallows, you monkey's ass? Do you know what you are doing?" "I didn't think I was doing anything wrong, and found it really interesting," I said to him. "Burn that crap immediately and don't ever bring such a thing into my apartment! Shut your trap and do what I tell you. I don't want to hear anything about it. If they catch you, they'll hang you."

It was fortunate that my parents and Otto's wife and his mother-in-law were standing downstairs outside the door and did not hear any portion of our "friendly exchange" and of my reprimand. I took a match and burned the flyer in the ash tray. "Do you have any idea what they would do to you if they caught you? Distribution of inflammatory pamphlets? That is conspiracy to commit high treason. They will smash you like a bug; they don't tolerate any horseplay." "But Otto, I didn't distribute anything." "Oh, yeah? You showed it to me. It makes no difference to them whether we are friends, neighbors, or brothers. It was distribution. My dear Kuddl, you don't know these brethren. You don't know what they are capable of. I know it, believe me."

Of course he knew it! He was an SA man. I then had to promise him and say, "I'll never do anything like this again." After that I never again brought one home and showed him. After the war, he told me that when I was arrested, he wanted to go to the Gestapo and say, "Look, the boy did not do anything, really. He showed me a leaflet once, and I really chewed him out." It was a good thing he did not, because they would have locked him up the same day. That was a very dangerous idea.

The sirens howled with an unchanging sound to signal the all clear. Everyone came upstairs and went quickly to bed. It was 1:30 in the morning. "Sleep well, Otto." "Thanks, and you, too. And you are aware, aren't you, who your friends are?" I did not need any help in understanding that.

If the confounded air-raid alarm had not come, I would have been rid of that flyer, but as we say in German, "If the dog had not stopped to take a crap, he would have caught the rabbit." One thing I certainly resolved to do, and always remained faithful to: I never brought flyers home with me that I could not distribute. When I could not get rid of some, because I thought I had been seen by someone, I either burned them or cut them into pieces that were thrown into the wind, so that I did not incriminate my parents. This habit may have saved my family from more problems, because when I was arrested the Gestapo searched our apartment very carefully.

As youngsters we always had a small gathering place, a cafe at the Landwirt train station. It was not a beer hall, but a restaurant, where I often went on Saturday night. Occasionally we had a little ersatz cake[96] that we'd scrounged up here and there, and met as a group of three or four other youths my age, including my girlfriend. She was doing her mandatory year as a domestic servant for some rich people at Alsterufer.[97] They were high party functionaries, because who else could afford a household servant? I read a flyer to the members of our group and they were, of course, dumbfounded, "Oh, my gosh!" and "Ah" and "Oh," but they all refrained from asking more about it. No one wanted to touch it with a ten-foot pole. Today I am glad, because if that had gone beyond that group, things might have been even worse than they were.

I never again tried to do such a thing and none of the boys or girls reported me. They likely forgot it and said, "He is nuts." No one was enthused. To my friend, Heinz Buske, I never said a word about it, for example, because I simply did not know his stand on such things. His brother-in-law was a captain in the German army at that time and his brother was a lieutenant. That was always a dangerous situation, so I kept my trap shut.

My fear when distributing the flyers gradually abated. At first I had terrific anxiety. I always thought that someone would come out of the next house and seize me, but that fear decreased.[98] You became accustomed to such things and became more daring. I even took the opportunity to stick a few flyers into coat pockets in a cloakroom. It was possible to recognize the coats of high party functionaries, because they had a thing hanging from them we called the golden pheasant.[99] After a while we weren't afraid anymore, though we were really playing Russian roulette.

On the morning following the air-raid alarm, we could lie in the sack a little longer. As I arose, my mother was already bustling about in the kitchen. "Well son, did you get enough sleep?" "Nah, I quit early. That stupid air-raid alarm." "Yes, it is difficult. I wonder who got the blessings poured out on them from above last night. Well, anyway, Hamburg was left in peace, thank heavens."

Everything made me sick. During the blackout a person felt like a prostitute working at night. The nerve-racking air-raid warnings and crouching in the cellar at night irritated us and always brought the fear that a bomb would fall on the roof.[100] Altogether the war was totally wretched. They lied to us and deceived us from all directions. We needed to be cautious about what we said and to whom we said it. It was almost impossible to trust anyone.

Many common items were no longer available, and other things were not for sale or were being rationed, we were told.[101] Yes, dear national comrades, we were informed, first we must bring to a victorious conclusion the war which was so insidiously forced down our throats. Forced down our throats? By whom? I wondered. We were the ones who had started the whole crap. The evil wizard was portrayed as God, but now he cannot conquer enough territory. The Russians, Poles, French, British, are our enemies, our leaders always said.

In my opinion, if the bigwigs would leave the people alone, they would get along with each other. I did not feel that a Pole or Frenchman or Russian ever did anything to harm me. I had no enemies, especially not the so-called enemies of the state, the Jews, who were to blame for everything.[102] One cannot kill people because they are Jews. Thank heavens there were some good persons who helped the persecuted and put their lives on the line.

Now we boys were also part of this effort. We never believed that we were in the position to overthrow the Nazi regime, by no means, but Helmuth always said to us: "What we can do is to warn the people. We can wake them up, we can bring them to the point of asking questions and saying: 'Wait a minute, something is not right. I want to hear that myself.' And when enough people hear the truth or are interested in the truth, then who knows?" We wanted to show people that it was not a benevolent regime with a few problems, but that the entire structure was thoroughly rotten.

One sign of the times was the many executions and the harsh sentences and detentions. Everywhere you could read "Forbidden," "Prohibited," "Not Permitted," and "Forbidden on pain of death." What kind of a country is that? I asked myself. How good can a government be if it is so afraid some little man might listen one time to an English station that it would execute him for it?

What a shitty time we are living in! Lies and political murders are the order of the day for the security of the state, of course. The poor Jews now have to wear a glaring yellow star with the inscription "Jew." It is high time the war came to an end!

These were my thoughts on that Sunday morning. Somehow, I was provoked. I had not had enough sleep. The stern reproach of the previous evening by Otto Schulz and my stupidity in showing him the flyer were upsetting to me. My father turned the radio on. "Let's hear whether our enemies are finally fed up and have begged our Führer's pardon." That was how my father slandered and amused himself immensely while my mother looked anxiously to see if all of the windows were closed. "You shouldn't talk like that. Someone might hear and report you!" Father hugged Mother and said, "Now don't you worry, old gal, everything will be okay!"

Snappy march music resounded from the loudspeaker, and then some radio commentator blathered something about the marvelous providence and that an infallible Führer was sent to us and it is better to be dead than a slave. It sounded as good as Christmas: "Unto us, a son is given. Heil-aluja! Heil-aluja!" Now we were presented with this drivel on a Sunday morning when the bells should have been pealing. Good grief, I mused, how deeply we have sunk! The German troops continuously conquered on all fronts with few casualties. We were always victorious, of course, and the other guy was always completely destroyed.

I had to laugh at the newscast. "Why are you grinning so stupidly?" my father asked me. "Don't you believe, you ruffian, what they are telling us there?" I said that I considered this the fairy-tale hour of the billy goat from Babbelsberg, which is another term we had for Goebbels. Our Joseph was lying to us again in good form. My father laughed. "You are too vulgar for me," he said, and went into his bedroom to change clothes to go to church.

Through Helmuth I knew the truth behind this constant victory stuff. I was also beyond believing these brethren anymore. "Are you ready, Karl-Heinz?" Mother asked me. "We need to hurry." "Okay, let's march off to church," I said. "Don't blaspheme, perhaps the time will come when you will be glad to go." We set off like a faithful family to receive spiritual nourishment, to learn from the word of the Holy Scriptures, to learn that man should love his neighbor and his enemy. With that commandment I had absolutely no difficulty, because I had no enemies, but the time came when it became difficult to love my enemies.

I locked arms with my mother and started chatting with her. "Mom, shouldn't we love our enemies?" "What is this, son?" she asked suspiciously. I then recited a little doggerel for her:

> Alcohol, as we all understand,
> Is the enemy of mankind throughout the land.
> Yet the Good Books agree,
> You should love your enemy.
> Now may love never end,
> And may your elbow always bend.

"What do you say to that?" She had to laugh. "You are such a character. Where did you get such a thing? You are full of nonsense. Do you want to start boozing?" She nudged me in the side. "Nah, not me. Alcohol doesn't interest me." "I should hope not. Think about your grandfather, how he fared because of boozing. It looks to me like you are in the right frame of mind for church service, and now behave yourself," my mother suggested.

We had reached the Besenbinderhof, where our meetinghouse stood. As I observed my mother from the side, everything was good about her; she was a beautiful woman. I loved my mother above everything.

Suddenly I asked, "What is going on here?" I could scarcely believe what my eyes saw. On the entrance door a sign had been hung, which said in large, plain letters: "Jews are forbidden to enter." My mother looked at me. I could see that she was grieved, and I remember the words she uttered to me then. "Son, try to forget it. This is a part of our daily life in Germany now." She shook her head and said faintly, "Must this be?"

Inside, we were, as always, greeted heartily and no one said a word about the sign. Nevertheless, I saw many dejected faces. I saw Helmuth. He signaled to me and I went over to him. He was very agitated. "What do you say about that? The Nazis ruin and poison all the good in mankind. There is really no more love any more among men.[103] Hatred is also trickling now into the houses of God. I will try to find out if this was done under pressure from the Gestapo."

We all knew that our church branch leader and spiritual advisor Zander was a party member. He never failed to wear his party badge proudly. Nevertheless, he was a good shepherd and was honestly concerned about the welfare of his sheep, in his own way, of course. In the Third Reich there were men who could serve two masters.[104] There were men who had the marvelous talent of being able to reconcile politics and the word of God, love and hate, and to help and comfort those who were persecuted as well as to slam the door in their faces.

"Now I need to tell you something. Hang on tight, because it will stagger you," Helmuth cautioned. "What is it, Helmuth?" "The Gestapo has arrested old Brother Worbs." "What? Heinrich Worbs? But why? He would not harm a fly." "I know that, but he allegedly made antifascist comments, and like always there was an informer who had him sent down the river."[105]

It came out that at the unveiling of a statue Brother Worbs once said, "My goodness, now we have one more butcher that we must salute," which somebody overheard.[106] He served time in a concentration camp and eventually came home again a broken man. When he returned, Helmuth wanted to know exactly what had happened. "I will ask Zander what Worbs did wrong. Drop in some time, Kuddl. I will know more then." Helmuth was the unpaid secretary for Zander and often conducted church and private business for him. If anyone could learn details, it was Helmuth.

At first Heinrich Worbs did not want to talk, because he had been required to sign a statement that he would tell nothing about it.[107] Afterwards, however, he did tell about his experiences. The guards had locked him in the stocks and let ice cold, freezing water trickle over his hands. When ice accumulated on his hands, his tormentors struck him across the hands with a rubber truncheon to knock the ice from his hands and to "keep them warm."[108] Shortly after his release from the concentration camp he died.[109]

The story about Brother Worbs so staggered me that I needed to sit down. I recognized more profoundly the danger in which we had placed ourselves. It could as well have been the three of us who were caught. I was convinced that the state police were hunting the person or persons who were distributing flyers and inflammatory handbills in Hamburg.

After such news I was absolutely no longer in the mood for religion, and I was happy when we sauntered home. My parents were very upset and shaken over the arrest of Heinrich Worbs. "What evil could the old man have done that he would be locked up and possibly hauled before the judge? My goodness, is no one certain of his life today?" asked my mother. "They have nothing better to do than to chase and badger old people. Why don't those bullies volunteer for the front? They are all overstuffed with food and don't have the strength to go. But the more they arrest, the more indispensable they become. I'll bet they receive ration cards for 'heaviest laborers,' because they work the night shift. They always come between three and five o'clock in the morning to arrest such a poor, unfortunate man."[110]

That is how my father talked to himself in a rage as we walked. "Be careful with your blabbering and don't talk so loud. You will cause trouble for us," my mother said. "If someone is standing behind the door in the staircase, he can hear everything. Just think what has happened to Heinrich Worbs. The same thing can happen to you. So please, keep quiet. You can think what you want, but don't think out loud." "Ja, you are right, Paula, but it is still true," my father grumbled.

Mother bustled around again in the kitchen, so we were soon able to eat lunch. She was a very good cook and what she cooked always tasted good. Because of the air-raid alarm the previous night we had all gotten too little sleep, and I became terribly drowsy after the meal. "I need to lie down for a long while," I told my mother. "I can hardly keep my eyes open." "Do that. If you're asleep you can't sin, and sweet dreams of sour pickles!"

3

Guests of the Gestapo

Helmuth was arrested on Thursday, 5 February 1942. He had wanted to extend his activities to include the French prisoners of war working in Hamburg.[1] Needing to have the leaflets translated into French, on 20 January he and his colleague Gerhard Düwer approached Werner Kranz, a fellow apprentice at the social administration. Kranz refused to cooperate and would not accept the paper Helmuth tried to give him. (See Document 8.) Their conversation was observed by Heinrich Mohns,[2] the overseer of loyalty and patriotism in the office. When Hübener and Düwer were out of the room, Mohns questioned Kranz about them. The following day Gerhard Düwer was summoned and the bubble burst. Mohns wanted Düwer to get copies of the materials from Helmuth. Düwer stalled for a while until Mohns put pressure on him by threatening him and telling him what would happen if he did not cooperate.[3] Finally, on 4 February, Düwer handed over copies of some flyers to Mohns. (See Document 7.)

Mohns had the Gestapo called and Helmuth was arrested along with Düwer the following day. Afterward, their homes were searched.[4] Düwer, of course, had been forewarned by his previous encounters with Mohns, but he had not warned Helmuth, possibly under instructions from Mohns,[5] so at Düwer's home the Gestapo agents found nothing, but at Helmuth's they discovered the radio, a pile of assorted leaflets, some notebooks with manuscripts of handbills along with some shorthand notes, and the Remington typewriter with seven unfinished carbon copies of a leaflet entitled "Who is inciting whom?" still in place in the roller. (See Documents 6 and 40.)

On the day they were arrested, three more flyers were turned in to a party block leader.[6] All of the flyers were found within one block of Helmuth's house. It was amazing to me that relatively few leaflets had found their way into Gestapo hands before this time.[7] (See Documents 3, 4, 5.)

I had absolutely no idea about Gerhard Düwer. Helmuth had never mentioned Düwer, because Helmuth was very cautious.[8] (See Document 9.) He also never told me anything about a group of Communists that certain people associated with them later claimed he had gotten to know at the Bismarckbad.[9] (See Document 68.) He only said to me once that he had gotten to know some interesting persons the previous week, whom I needed to hear sometime, but he left it at that. I knew nothing about them. I thought they were somehow from the social administration in Hamburg.

Helmuth had surely invited other people, also. (See Documents 13 and 14.) Some of them were probably from our congregation. I know he invited some of the Sommerfeld children to listen to the radio, but I do not believe they ever came, or, if they did, they were not interested. (See Document 72.) They did not want anything to do with it.[10] He asked some of them cautiously once, "Tell me, if you had the chance to listen to English broadcasts, would you listen?" He did not say that he did it. They said, "No, under no conditions. That is much too dangerous." Then he knew exactly where they stood.

He restricted the activity to our group, therefore, but he may have tried to extend the operation. If he did, we knew nothing about it. He was very clever in that way, for if we had known about it and something had gone wrong, we all would have been forced to walk the plank.

Life was cheap in the Nazi period. "Heads must roll for victory," was the common saying.[11] "If you say that, you'll lose your head," was daily talk. There was the death penalty for nearly everything, for enemies of the state, when someone stole something from a package for a soldier in the field—inevitably: the death penalty.[12] In our post offices there were placards notifying the populace that someone had stolen five cigarettes from a package being sent to a soldier. The thief was beheaded. He was a postal official and the state made a public example of him.[13] When a traveler was surprised by an air-raid alarm and, leaving his suitcase sitting on the train station platform, ran into the nearest air-raid shelter, even if he emerged hours later after the all clear, his suitcase was still there. Nobody had the temerity to steal it. If they had caught you, off with your head.[14]

Assaulting women during a blackout, such as in a park, was a crime against the blackout.[15] If the woman was also married to a soldier stationed in the field: the death penalty! "You are an asocial element, an enemy of the state, away with you!"[16]

We also knew about the killing of the mentally ill and retarded. They called it "mercy killing."[17] They even took us children from the schools on a field trip, where we were required to visit the mental asylums. When you are a twelve-, thirteen-, or fourteen-year-old youth and you see people in cages and everything, that is unsettling. They said, "Take a look, these people are not capable of having a life." I can understand why many said, "Yes, it is better that these people be released from their misery." I can still see in my mind's eye after all these years people, lying in cribs, who were over forty years of age with a large head and a body like a small baby. Today, of course, I see we do not have the right to take anyone's life.

I had no idea that Helmuth had been arrested. I saw him only a couple of times during the Christmas holidays. Over Christmas and New Year's I traveled to Lüdelsen for a week in order to bring a little food home with me from my aunt's farm.[18] I did not return to Hamburg until a few days after the New Year, which may have helped save my life. If I had been caught distributing leaflets after my eighteenth birthday on 5 January, it would have been curtains for me, so it was a very good thing I did not see Helmuth much after I turned eighteen. (See Document 52.)

When I returned and saw him in the church meeting, he said again, "Come visit me sometime." When I did, he had new flyers again. They were very vehement things with the titles "The Voice of Conscience" (see Document 36) and "The Year '42 Will Decide" (see Document 44). I distributed these, as well, but fortunately, the Gestapo could not prove that I had done it.

This was in the middle of January, and then I did not see Helmuth for a while. The last time I saw him was approximately fourteen days before his arrest on 5 February. Three days afterward, on a Sunday, we were asked by the branch president to remain a little while after the meeting. He had a very regrettable announcement to make, he said, and he told us to be there. There was nothing unusual about that and I was not concerned. I thought somebody must have been excommunicated or something.[19] Then the bomb dropped. Zander said, "A member of our branch, Helmuth Hübener, has been arrested by the Gestapo. I cannot give you any details, because my information is very sketchy, but I know that it is political. That is all."

My heart fell into the seat of my pants and I wanted to die at that moment. I have never been so scared, and I was literally sick. I looked over at Rudi and he looked at me. He was pale, but we could not speak. "What?" some other members of the branch around me were saying. "Helmuth? That is impossible!" I did not wait for Rudi to leave; I just wanted to go home. What little acting ability I had developed as a child actor I now needed, because I did not want my parents to think anything was wrong. I could not tell them anything. All they said was, "I wonder what he did."

I expected to be arrested myself, but I hoped fervently that Helmuth would remember our pact, that whoever got caught would take all the blame. The crucial question tormented us: did he tell, or will he tell?[20] I figured that I would also be arrested on Monday, but nothing happened. Then my hopes began to rise and I thought perhaps he'd kept quiet and they knew nothing about me.

Tuesday morning, 10 February, I went to work as usual. I was working with a colleague in an empty apartment, when right at noon someone rapped on the door. Sensing impending calamity, I went to the door myself. Two men with slouch hats and long, leather coats were standing there. They showed their badges: Secret State Police, and I immediately knew the game was up. "Gestapo. Are you Karl-Heinz Schnibbe?" "Yes." "Come with us."

They stuck me in an official car, a black Mercedes, and drove to my home. The driver sat in front, and one of the agents, Wangemann, sat in the back on my left. I sat in the middle, and the other agent, Müssener, sat on my right. I was still in my painting clothes.

Then, of course, came the question, "We know that you were part of it. How much do you know?" If they had said to me directly: "Listen, you don't need to tell us any fibs, your friend sang like a nightingale," then I really would not have known what to do, but they only asked, "Do you know someone named Rudi Wobbe?" I knew then that Rudi had also gone down the tubes, or would be going soon. They let him sweat for a week.[21] I said, "Yes, I know him. I know him from the branch." That was all. I did not say anything about him.[22]

When we arrived at the apartment, it was fortunate that no one was there. My father was at work and my mother was at the dentist. I let us in with my key. "Just stay put," they said. Then the two searched everything, the books, my bed, everything. Of course, they found nothing, because I never brought anything home with me.[23] The search lasted about an hour. Then we got back into the car.

The suspense was terrible. What should I say, what should I not say? They told me if I lied, they would beat me to a pulp. It was a terrible thing.

Then the question arose, how much do they know about me? I was, of course, terribly frightened. I am still amazed that I did not shit my pants right there in their Mercedes. I had no idea what would happen to me. I hoped that I would be interrogated and then I would go home. I had no other experiences like this and had no clue that they would keep me there.

They took me to the city hall, the headquarters of the Gestapo. We entered through the rear by a special door and then went into a type of elevator that did not stop. (This "paternoster," as it was called, was a slow-moving elevator without doors, which you just stepped onto, but you felt inclined to say the Lord's Prayer, hence the name "Our Father.") The elevator went only to the cellar to the Gestapo headquarters; the exits to the other floors were boarded up so no one could get out. As I discovered later, SS guards were posted on the floor by the elevator exits and on the stairs.

The first day was taken up with all of the personal matters such as my name, address, occupation, birthdate, and so on. I was arrested about noon and when we arrived in the city hall it was 3:00 or 3:30. These gentlemen had all the time in the world; they did not need to hurry. They interrogated me for half an hour.

They did not want to keep me overnight in the city hall. My name was called and I was handcuffed to another prisoner, and then away we went in the Green Minna, the green-painted paddy wagon, to Fuhlsbüttel—Kolafu: concentration camp Fuhlsbüttel. The Green Minna was completely full. I was astonished how many men were there, at least twenty to thirty prisoners.

Before the transport departed the city hall for Kolafu, I saw for the first time what was referred to in prison jargon or "jailbirdese" as "the hall of mirrors." It was long and painted a brilliant, glossy white and was brightly illuminated. I soon became very familiar with this room. But I had still not seen Helmuth.

That was also the first day I became acquainted with Tall Paul. I got to know him the first time when he herded us into the Green Minna. He was about two meters tall, like a giant animal. He was almost half a head taller than I.[24] He had huge feet. The next larger size was a child's coffin, we used to say. Man, could he stomp! And hands like a toilet lid. But at first I did not know his name for certain; I learned it later from another prisoner.

He was the director of transport and the chief torturer and was a brutal monster. He had the handcuff keys on a long metal rod and he used it to direct traffic. He had a very subtle trick: somehow, by pressing this rod against your neck, he could shut off the flow of blood to your brain. Then you would faint, because your artery was shut off. He was totally callous. After the war I learned that he was severely punished with a long prison sentence. It was rumored that some vengeful prisoners killed him in prison.[25]

Wangemann and Müssener did not go with us. At 4:30 they probably went home to their wives and children. What I could never understand was that these people could torture and hit other people all day long and in the evening go home and leave all of it behind them.[26]

When we arrived in Kolafu the first time, I did not know the house rules of the Gestapo. I had no idea that you always needed to run. They hauled me out and shoved me through the passageway. The antagonizer there was an SS man smartly dressed in gray and well groomed, a handsome fellow with polished boots and elegant riding pants, a completely sadistic, charming young man. I received terrific kicks in the rump and blows to the neck.[27]

I also did not know that you had to stand facing the wall in front of any door until the door was opened. They had already drilled me in the hallway with push-ups and knee bends. In the first position the hands were to be kept in front and the knees bent just slightly, and then you had to go down just a little, with a bit more knee bend, then the third position slightly more, and in position four you were nearly bent as far as possible. Then he let me sit there for five minutes or so in that position, and then jump up again. Oh, man; it was just pure torment!

At last I was put into a cell, and I found a Dutchman lying there. He had been arrested because he'd refused to work for the Germans.[28] He looked like he had been through a meat grinder, the poor guy. He had been there for ten days or so, and they had really beaten him badly. His face was black and blue and battered, cracked open, pounded bloody. When the door was opened, he jumped up, dashed to the wall and reported: He called out his name and number, Prisoner so-and-so, cell so-and-so, arrested for this and that reason. Then he said "in protective custody!"[29] (I always wondered: protection from what?!)[30] We did not have our individual prisoner's numbers yet, only the cell number.

I had absolutely no idea that I also had to make a dash to the wall. I stood still and gawked at what he was doing, and then I suddenly flew to the wall from a swift kick in the ass. I had never experienced such a thing. Then I had to shout out, "Schutzhaftgefangener Schnibbe, arrested for listening to enemy radio transmissions and for distribution of foreign news."[31] The first time I said "*alleged* listening" and then there was hell to pay. They really kicked my butt because I said "alleged."[32] In the "brown days" under Hitler one was condemned without having stood before a judge. There was always an absolute presumption of guilt.[33]

Then night came. We thought there would be peace. The darkness was good for my eyes, but sleep was unthinkable. My nerves were frayed. Although I was dead tired, I could not sleep. My eyes burned like never before, but sleep would not come. Yet the darkness was soothing somewhat to my frayed nerves, and I began to think about home, about my parents. Mom and Dad must be terribly worried about me by now, I thought. (See Document 67.) Well, maybe they will let me go soon. Then a full awareness of the hopelessness of my situation hit me and I cried quietly into my pillow for a long, long time, until I cried myself to sleep. Then I was awake again, because all of a sudden the light went on and the door flew open. We had to jump out of bed and dash to the wall like before, and make our report.

They did that about every twenty minutes, every half-hour, but not for the entire night. And then, I don't know what time it was, the door flew open and that animal was there again. That was, at the latest, perhaps one or two in the morning. "I only wanted to see if you were all sleeping well! Look out that something doesn't happen to you!"

He lifted the toilet lid with the paddle attached to his huge key ring and looked inside to see "if we are keeping things clean or behaving like swine." He examined everything with his gloves. There were no filthy cells! You could eat off the floor. Then he left. The light went out again and we could return to bed, but there was no hope of going back to sleep. That is how the first days went. In the evenings, when the guards were partying, it was quiet. In time I became more hardened, but it was clear that they wanted to get me psychically weakened, so that they could get a confession the following day.[34]

The harassment from a sadistic individual was all part of the program of the Gestapo. That's what they intended. They wanted to let us feel like we were asocial elements[35] and that we were crap, that they could do with us whatever they wanted. Those people had experience, they were hardened, but we also became hardened. Though we always feared for our lives, whenever they started harassing us, we thought: "Oh, this asshole, doesn't he have anything else to do?" As time passed, therefore, I became calloused against torment. That was a natural development. If that did not happen, you went to pieces. You could not endure it.[36]

In the morning at 5:00 the light went on again and there was a big racket. The bell sounded and everybody got up. The bell was a large, loud one, like in school. Then all of the lights went on in the cells and you had to get up. You had to wash and get ready and make your bed. That was one of their hobbyhorses. The bed had to be like a board. There could not be any wrinkles in the blanket. I did not know that beforehand. I was happy that the Dutchman helped me a little, otherwise I would have received a thrashing until I learned.[37]

The next thing we did was our early morning exercises. We had to go out into the hallway, where they shoved us along, into the courtyard in back of the prison, in the cold, in February, and they made us jump in place, which was just more harassment. All of the prisoners were required to go out.[38]

We were compelled to run three, four, five, or six laps around the courtyard before breakfast. We were then given ersatz coffee, which was called *Muckefuck*."[39] We prisoners called it *Arschbackenbrühe*, or "buttocks brew." It was thin coffee, "the terror of the lodgers." We also received a crust of dry bread, often just a heel, and that was all. We ate out of an enameled bowl with a flat bottom called a *Bütt* that reminded me of a chamber pot.

There was a water faucet in the cell that stuck out of the wall. Underneath we had a bucket, where the water was caught, and we could wash ourselves. We had no soap, until my mother brought some later. We washed and dressed, and then the cell was opened and we had to report again after making our dash to the wall.

After that we got ready to leave, when we would be summoned again: "Get ready for transport!" We had to stand at the back of the cell, the cell doors were opened, our names were called out, and we had to go out into the hallway and stand with our faces to the wall. We were always manacled together in pairs with handcuffs. If the Dutchman and I were both summoned, then we were manacled together. Or when the Dutchman did not go to interrogation, then another man and I were handcuffed together. We had to run down the hallway to the Green Minna.

We got into the Green Minna and were taken into the city hall to the Gestapo offices. The Green Minna was a relatively large vehicle. In addition to some solitary cells, it had benches on the sides where we sat. Of course, we all were given the order: "Shut your traps, don't talk with each other." No one talked. It was terrible, like a battalion of the damned. It was unbelievable how they intimidated people, even the prisoners who were highly qualified specialists, educated scientists and physicians. Every stratum was represented; these prisoners were not only from the proletariat, the working class.[40]

At the Gestapo headquarters we had to go into the hall of mirrors. It was on the floor where the Gestapo offices were. There were large lights in the room. The first time it was terrifically hot and there was a terrible, dazzling light. We had to stand at attention again facing the wall, with our noses approximately one inch from the wall. You wanted to do it right, so that you did not attract attention, because of fear of the horrible kicks. You did not know when they would come, when suddenly you would be kicked and your face smashed

into the wall and made to bleed.[41] Then you had a real p\
cause you made a mess on the wall.

If you concentrated too hard, you could not hold out
because you became dizzy and fell down. You needed to lea
under these new conditions. You needed to concentrate on so
else, you needed to say to yourself: "Kiss my ass, you sadi
tards, I'm not going to give you the satisfaction of seeing me fall
down." As soon as someone did fall down, a sadistic SS type would
kick him until he got up again. When this happened to me, they said,
"So, you wanted to cause Germany to fall, and now you are the one
who is falling, right?"

The first days were terribly difficult, but after a week it did not
bother you as much anymore.[42] Then you said to yourself as you entered the hall of mirrors: "We bear our fate with patience, our teeth
we firmly grit, for we elected Hitler, we're to blame for all this shit."[43]
I always thought about something else, concentrated on something
different. I thought about my vacation with my aunt in the country.
I closed my eyes just a little so as not to see the dazzling wall, and
now and then I sent a fervent prayer to heaven. If you did these kinds
of things, you could, perhaps, endure it. But, of course, when you
had to stand five, six hours until you were summoned, then everyone fell down. No one could endure that. I could not turn my head,
lest an SS man throw one of their heavy glass ashtrays at me, which
was another of their methods of enforcing the rules.

You could not go take a piss, so you learned not to drink much
before interrogation. The first time you slurped down your morning
coffee, but thereafter you didn't touch it, because you were not permitted to urinate. When your bladder was empty you could make it
through the day. They told you with certainty in the morning: "You're
going in today." Then it was off to the city hall again. And if they
didn't say that, then you could guzzle your coffee.

If you did not go for interrogation at the Gestapo headquarters,
then you were subject to the harassment in the prison. They had you
either way. They never left us in peace. We were harassed, we were
drilled, we were goaded, we were browbeaten, we were bellowed at.

On my first visit to the hall of mirrors I did not see Helmuth. That
occurred a few days later, but the same week. I was arrested on Tuesday, and on Thursday or Friday I saw Helmuth. They had obviously
made a mistake. They had placed Helmuth in the hall of mirrors so
that I had to pass by him when I entered.[44] I arrived there in the
morning, as I had on the first morning, and the second, and so on.
After an hour or two I was summoned to be interrogated. When I
returned, Helmuth was standing there. Perhaps Helmuth had been

.mmediately before me at the interrogation. I did not know. In any case there he stood, and because the SS sat at a large table in the middle of the room, the only way I could get to my place was to go along the wall past him. They should have placed him where I could not have seen him.

Helmuth had seen me coming, and as I passed him, he grinned a little for a moment, winked his eyes a bit, and then I knew for certain that the lad had kept mum, that he had not said much, that he had kept his promise and had taken the blame upon himself. (See Document 10.) I was so sure of this, certain enough in any case, that there was now a ray of hope.[45]

Had I not known that he had promised to take the blame upon himself, perhaps I might have contradicted him in some way in my testimony. Then there would have been another thrashing, there would have been punches. Their interrogation system was based on the fact that the other person did not know what you had said, and you did not know what he had said.

Sometimes they bluffed and said, "Come on, your friend said this and that." You thought, "My goodness, did he say that?" Then you had to be made of iron, because they suddenly asked you something else. After half an hour they asked the same question as before, only formulated slightly differently. You had to be on your toes. When the answers differed a little, they said, "Ha, ha, ha! Come now, something stinks here." You could not leave yourself wide open. You needed to remember what you had said. They were callous, and in order to survive under their system you needed to become more callous.[46]

I stuck by my statement; it made no difference how they twisted and turned things, or how the questions came. I only admitted: "Yes, I knew that Helmuth listened to the news, and I knew, also, that he wrote something down now and then." "In fact," I said, "it was because I could not always go there and listen, so I said, 'Helmuth, when something is interesting, could you copy it down, so that I can read it in the evening?' 'Yes,' he said, 'I will do it.'" That much I admitted. Then I confessed, also, that we attempted to listen once, but could not hear due to the jamming.

I did not tell them that we listened night after night. I told them that we tried once. They knew that the Germans had attempted to jam broadcasts. It did not always work, however, because the BBC had terrific transmitters and we could still hear. Sometimes it crackled a little, but we could hear. "And then he showed me a flyer once, and nothing more, that was all." I stuck by that story come hell or high water. (See Document 11.)

They bluffed and said, "Oh, yeah, Helmuth Hübener said . . ."

Then the interrogator pretended to read. I responded: "That cannot be. That is not correct. That is not true. He is lying, then." The first time I said this I received a ferocious smack in the chops,[47] but I stuck with my story. "I am sorry, that's the way it was."

The interrogators were the same people who had arrested me, Müssener and Wangemann.[48] A blonde female stenographer was there; she was always taking notes. What a profession for a woman! She saw a lot of tears and sorrow. She must have been a totally hardened sow, because a normal person could not endure such a thing.[49]

When Helmuth winked, I knew I was on the right path. But then I saw his face, and it was completely swollen and bloodshot, black and blue. They had beaten Helmuth to a pulp. Afterward, on the way to Berlin in the train, when we could converse a little, Helmuth referred to these interrogations. Our police guard had said, "Do not talk about the case," but we could whisper a bit among ourselves. Then Helmuth said, "I am sorry. I could not do otherwise."

From the Gestapo documents which I gained access to after the war (see Document 10), it is clear that Helmuth was systematically tortured after his arrest before he broke down and confessed anything.[50] Even then he mentioned me and Rudi only in passing, describing us more as curious friends than as fellow conspirators. He admitted that we, as his friends, were there once when he tried to listen to the BBC, but he told them very little. (See Document 15.)

They could not imagine that a seventeen-year-old boy could mastermind such a conspiracy. They wanted to find the adults behind the scenes. They thought there must have been a large ring which they could now break up. But there were no adults instigating us.[51] (See Documents 71 and 74.)

I do not know when my parents learned about my arrest. In any case, they did not know at first where I was. I vanished without a trace. I did not come home. "Where is the boy?" "I don't know." They contacted my boss and said, "Listen, Mr. Ehlers, our son has not returned home. Didn't he show up for work?" "Oh yes, I wanted to tell you that he went up the river." "Up the river? Why?" "The Gestapo." Then they knew that I was not dead, but they didn't know where I was and what had happened. They only knew that I was in some terrible trouble. They must have seen some connection with Helmuth's disappearance, though Rudi was not arrested until later.[52]

My mother went to Police Precinct 24 on the Lübeckerstraße, and they said, "Leave the name here. We will inquire. Come again tomorrow and then we will tell you something definite." Mother told me later, she did not know for a few days where I was. When she found out that I was in Kolafu, she thought: "What is going on?"

My parents inquired of the Gestapo, and then they knew that I was involved with Helmuth.

We had no nightshirts, only the clothes that we had on. I had my underwear—my undershirt, my underpants. I had not been permitted to get anything from my apartment, absolutely nothing. I had to travel there in work clothes, just like I was. I also had no coat, only my painting smock. I could sleep in my underclothes.

They told my mother she could bring laundry to me each week, as well as a hand towel and soap, toothpaste with a toothbrush, and socks and so on. (See Document 24.) She had to deliver them to the front door in a package with the name "Schutzhaftgefangener Karl-Heinz Schnibbe." She delivered it there and picked up the dirty, sometimes slightly bloody, laundry.

She also wanted to smuggle in a little chocolate or marzipan by sticking it in the laundry, but it did not work. The package was opened in the cell by an SS man, and he emptied everything piece by piece. When the candy fell out, he said, "Ah, what do we have here? Chocolate? Do you really think we would allow you swine to eat chocolate?" Then he ate it before our eyes or stuck it in his pocket, perhaps for his girlfriend.

I was interrogated for three weeks before the matter of the bicycle tires came up. First they asked me: "Tell us, did you ever swipe bicycle tires?" I said, "No, I didn't." Though they could not prove anything, they did not give up on the bicycle tires. At last they asked, "Do you know a Willi Vorbeck?" "Yes," I said. "He is a colleague with whom I worked and with whom I apprenticed." Willi Vorbeck, another journeyman painter, was there when I was arrested. He must have thought: "Now is my chance to have him take the blame." He swiped some bicycle tires out of the attic of the house where we were working, that bum.

But I did not hold it against him. It was not possible to get such things at that time. Perhaps he saw them in the attic and said to himself, "Man, that's exactly what I need," and took them with him. But he still stole bicycle tires and charged it to my account, the cur. Willi was not so dumb. At any rate, I met him once in 1949 when I returned from Russia. I did not say anything about it. What purpose would it have served? I was happy to see him again. He said, "Man, Karl-Heinz, you survived everything? That was a circus! Yeh, that was exciting." What should I have said, "Hey, you bum, you swiped some tires!"? Then he would have said, "Tires? What sort of tires? You must be out of your mind."

At the beginning of March we were told: "Get ready to go." The proceedings with the Gestapo were closed and we were to be delivered over to the court for further interrogation. We appeared before the judge in the investigative prison on the Holstenglacis.[53] Its abbreviation was UG.[54] We went through the gate, down and into the cellar, into the reception area, and there they reinventoried the private property we had with us when we were arrested. Everything was put again into large envelopes with our names on them and put into the closet. Everything was then locked up.

We were given our laundry, underclothes, and the prison uniform, which included a small, round, dark blue hat. Everything in the UG was of dark blue felt material, a dark blue jacket without a collar, simple, no pockets, and the pants. That was the prison garb.

Then we took a bath; the new arrivals needed to go into the shower. And then we went to our cells. At first we were in a cell in the cellar until we were put in other cells upstairs the first night. There we were locked in. I was alone in a cell and had absolutely no idea where anyone else was. I was not afraid, because by then I was an experienced prisoner. I had long weeks of terror behind me and was already hardened. What shook me was the immense quiet. It was so quiet, like a grave, that you heard no sound. We received some soup so thin that it went right through to your bladder. We called it "radio soup," because on the radio they always said, "We'll be right back." Then came the lockup and the lights went out at perhaps six o'clock. Then you could go to bed. It was so peaceful I felt like I was on vacation. The rest did my nerves a lot of good.

I knew by then that I would no longer be beaten by the Gestapo. Even though I lived in Nazi Germany, at least I was in the hands of the "legal system." That was a relief and I slept heavenly that night.[55] In the morning we were transferred to cells on the third floor, where we had to wait for six months until our trial. My cell was so situated that I could look down into the courtyard where the doomed prisoners on death row were allowed to exercise.

They would never permit you to lie around. I had a solitary cell, therefore my bed had to be hung up on the wall. I had to lift it up and hang it on a chain. Then I sat at a little, scrawny table. There was a stool, but that was all. There was nothing to read! We received toilet paper afterward, newspaper actually, cut in small squares, which I tried to read. There was absolutely nothing to do. Now and then you heard a rustling at the door, and you knew that the guard was peeking through the spy hole to see what you were doing.

There were a few more interrogations, but they were civil. They asked everything again. When that was over we were told to pack our things, and we were moved into cells down on the first floor, which was exactly above the place of execution. I lay there in my cell every morning between 4:00 and 5:00 when they fetched prisoners for execution. In Hamburg, in this "investigatory prison" there was a guillotine, where they executed people. During my stay there they executed someone every few minutes during that hour. I heard it every morning. When you are in such a building, it echoes a lot. I would wake up and hear the rustling of keys and the door opening. Then I heard a murmuring, "Get ready, it is time!" Then I heard some scream, "No, I don't want to," or crying. And then you heard a few blows and such. I did not know exactly what was happening. Then you heard steps. Approximately an hour later, a half-hour later, you heard the rattling of the horse and wagon hauling away the zinc coffins of the executed, those who had been beheaded. They were taken to the university for dissection. And then they returned with the zinc coffins. They used the same zinc coffins over and over.[56]

After some weeks we were transferred upstairs again. From there I could look down from a window. I always looked carefully. In the morning I took the opportunity to take a quick peek down there. It lasted only a minute. Then I calculated how many men went to the exercise round, and again the next morning, then I thought I knew how many had been executed. But there were always new ones being added. In Hamburg in the UG sometimes they executed five to eight persons in a morning—every day. Life was cheap.

My mother visited me sometimes, but she was not allowed into the UG. That was unthinkable. The "investigatory prison" was connected by a tunnel with the justice building. We went downward through a long hall through what seemed like at least seventy-five doors, which is how a prison is. Open, close. And then we went through the tunnel into the justice building, where we could talk, mother and I, always in the presence of a prison official, of course.

The visiting time was once a month. Ten minutes were allowed for the visit, but that depended upon the permission of the senior government councillor. He could say: "Let them have half an hour" or: "March back!" Mom always came faithfully. We were told "Preliminary notice of impending visit!" Then the cell was opened and the guard said, "Schnibbe, preliminary notice!" and I needed to go out where there was an official. He fastened his hand to my hand with cuffs. Oh, they were cautious.

My mother talked once with the senior government councillor and said, "Oh God, oh God, my son looks so thin and so emaciated. Would you be opposed if next time I brought a small piece of cake with me?" He then gave permission: "Do that, Mrs. Schnibbe, we will manage that." When she visited again, she had a small package and said, "Can I give my son a small piece of cake?" The guard said,

"No, that is strictly forbidden!" The senior government councillor said to the guard, "This is my concern. Wait outside a while. I will call you when it is time." Then he had to leave, and my mother gave me the cake; I could eat a piece of cake there. The councillor was present and asked a few questions, also, about what we had done. He merely shook his head and said, "Well, would you believe it!"

During the entire time of the visit I looked out the window. It was an ordinary room with ordinary windows. There was a large window without bars. All the cell windows were higher, small prison windows. You had to shove the table against the wall quickly and then put the stool on top, otherwise you could not reach the window. But here was a large, beautiful window. I sat and looked at the trees. In the meantime it had turned to summer. Oh, that was so beautiful.

I was hungry for freedom, to look outside. My mother always held my hand and said, "This won't be so bad, will it?" That was a terrible time. I was so young and naive concerning life. In prison I had already become hardened. I knew that for certain.

Once they put someone in my cell with me. He was a repeat offender, a professional criminal. He had been imprisoned six or seven or eight times. He knew for certain that this time he would receive preventive detention. He knew that he would never get out again. I told him what we had done. Not exactly, not everything, but only little things. He told me, "They will cut off your friend's head. You can count on it. They will finish off your friend. And you, you will receive a long sentence." "Nah," I said. "What do you know?" But he was right.

It was strange that he, as a professional criminal, had still been running around, and Helmuth, who did something once, had been thrown into prison, never to return to life. That's how the Third Reich was. They seemed to have more fear of Helmuth than of all of the professional criminals.[57]

Later I had someone else share my cell. I have forgotten his name. He had a wooden leg and hobbled. He was very young, probably in his thirties. He was a businessman in Hamburg who had sold clothing ration cards on the black market. That crime was punished severely. He received a prison sentence of at least ten years.

After five or six months our indictment came. (See Document 27.) When the indictment arrived, they transferred my cellmate. They said to him, "Pack your things!" And then I was alone again.[58] I picked up the indictment, and as I looked at it I thought I was done for. The entire indictment was stamped "Secret."

The charges consisted of conspiracy to commit high treason and treasonous aiding and abetting of the enemy.[59] When I read that the trial would be on 11 August at the People's Court[60] in Berlin, I would not have given anything for my life anymore. I told myself: either the death penalty or a long imprisonment. I was shaken. The entire time I was in prison I had suffered from constipation, because of too little to eat and not enough exercise, but when I read the indictment, three minutes later I developed diarrhea because of the fear. This document destroyed my sense of security like nothing else that had happened to me so far.

I already knew about the People's Court. It was talked about. It was feared. It was a great surprise that I was to be shipped to Berlin. I had not counted on that. When we were first arrested and after some in the UG told us their opinions, we thought it would be a juvenile court, a court for delinquents that would try us. Then some officials said, "Oh yeah, you are going to a court of lay assessors," a jury court. And then they said, "This is a more serious matter, it will come before the special court in Hamburg." That court had the authority to pronounce the death penalty. It was a political court. But now came the news: the People's Court!

After the indictment arrived, at least five or six officials came to my cell to see the man who had to go to Berlin. A juvenile delinquent is going to the People's Court? "Schnibbe, you have to go before the People's Court? My goodness, what did you do?" That was like the seventh wonder of the world. The People's Court was infamous as being the worst there was. I had the feeling that the officials respected us. They said, "I'll be damned! Man, you guys are really something!"

Because I was in solitary confinement, I could brood over my indictment. Of course, I had to return it after two hours. I read it once and had my fill. I said, "This is terrible; I don't want to know anything about it." They retrieved it and sealed it in the envelope. The prison officials were not permitted to take it. A man in civilian clothes came especially from the Gestapo to deliver it and to fetch it again. The prison officials were curious, of course. Perhaps they thought we had been functioning as spies for England. They thought they had gotten a bunch of real hot dogs.

One morning we were told, "Tomorrow at 10:00 you will be transported to Berlin, Alt-Moabit." We knew nothing about the prison, Alt-Moabit. They came for us and we were put together in the Green Minna. I saw Helmuth and Rudi there, and I saw Düwer for the first time. We were driven around to the Altona train station where there was a compartment reserved for us on the express train to Berlin. The windows were covered with paper and printed on it in large letters was: "Police Transport." We were dangerous criminals.

When we were in the Green Minna, each prisoner had his own guard. We sat on one side on the bench and they sat on the bench on the other side. The people at the train station stared at our guards in their uniforms and at us starved-looking and slovenly prisoners. They probably thought, those are mass murderers! We were four innocent boys! I was eighteen, Helmuth and Düwer were seventeen, and Rudi was sixteen.

In the train the people gawked in the door of our compartment, "What is going on?" The police said, "Move along, move along, this is a police transport." When the train set out, they took the paper down from the windows so that we could look out. We were ordered not to talk about our case, because of the danger of collusion. That was a lot of nonsense! We were going to be damned. All the collusion in the world could not have helped us. And so we went to Berlin.

4

Judgment and Destruction

When we arrived in Berlin, everything was arranged in a first-class manner with a Green Minna waiting. The Hamburg police guards delivered us over to the Berliners in exchange for a receipt and then took their leave again. We were taken to the infamous Alt-Moabit prison, where a crowd of cops harassed us, barking out in their Berlin dialect: "Come on in boys, we will take good care of you!"

In Moabit there were scoundrels and criminals and tramps and traitors. I thought, "Oh, for heaven's sake, why don't they bump us off immediately? They could save a lot of money." Alt-Moabit was the oldest prison in Berlin.[1] It was a haven for bedbugs and was full of lice and filthy, a terrible clink. We were separated again and isolated in louse-ridden cells. It was such a filthy hole that we didn't even have a toilet. We had a bucket with a lid where we had to sit to defecate and urinate. There was an overpowering stench that was terrible! Every morning the bucket had to taken out, and you needed to empty it and spray it out with water. Oh, that was miserable.

Although we were all weak and rickety, in Moabit they came up with the brilliant idea that we should do calisthenics in the mornings. They said we must exercise to be physically fit, even though we were nearly starved. We had sat in solitary confinement for six months and done nothing. In the UG we had not been required to do exercises. Now we were required to go down to the courtyard and do calisthenics. It caused sore muscles, because our limbs were all completely stiff. I could not do the exercises, nor could I walk back up the stairs.[2]

We had to listen to all manner of profane language. They called us swine, curs, scoundrels, criminals, traitors to our country, and so on. It was obvious that we were already guilty.

The entire courtyard in the prison was planted with chard, which they put into the soup, our main food supply, every day. At least it supplied us with some vitamins.[3]

We needed to work, too. We were required to fill little paper bags with mothballs. We were given a large sack of naphthalene balls and had to place three small mothballs into each of the paper bags. At night the small bags were placed outside the door. The stench was so powerful that it gave us headaches!

In Berlin I was visited for the first time by an attorney. I was informed: "Schnibbe, visitor!" "Who?" "I don't know, have no idea." Then I was led into a room, and there stood a man with a briefcase. He introduced himself and said, "Defense counselor Kunz. How is it going?" "Hmm," I said, "how should it be going? Wonderful as you can see. If things were any better, I could not stand it." "Oh yes," he said, "I understand. Don't worry, it won't be too bad. I will make the point that you are juveniles." I responded, "That is nice, thank you."

Right from the outset I sensed that he was too friendly, too chipper, too fatherly in comparison to all of the other beasts. Then he said, "Tell me, what did you guys do?" All of a sudden his question rang a bell in my mind. A voice said to me, "Careful! Don't say too much. Careful! This is a pile of fresh, steaming shit. Don't step in it!" I told him exactly what I had told the Gestapo and not a bit more. I did not trust him in the least!

If he had said at first, "Man, you have really made a mess of things, but we will see what we can do, . . ." perhaps I would have trusted him more. He probably would have reported it if I had said something. Perhaps they said to him, "Question the boy thoroughly and you, as a party member, Herr Doctor Kunz, you know exactly what to do."

He was with me for, perhaps, a half an hour. He said, "We will meet again on the court date." He only visited me once and did not take any notes.[4] Perhaps it was not worthwhile to write anything down. What could such a person do? What should he have done? If he were not a Nazi and if he had defended us too vigorously, they would have hanged him, too. They would have said, "You scoundrel, you are one of them." The system was completely corrupt, a system of cogs, one turning the other.[5]

Back in Hamburg they had put a criminal named Rubinke in the cell with Rudi. He is probably still sitting in prison today, if he has not died, because he had received a life sentence. He was not much older than I, perhaps three or four years. The Gestapo was using him as a stool pigeon and had told him something like: "Listen, sniff Rudi out a bit and tell us everything that he says, then we will make it a bit easier on you." They called it reduction of punishment.[6] Rudi was naive and considered himself a hero and sang like a nightingale.[7] (See Documents 50 and 51.)

Of course they did not let Rubinke free. The prosecution intended to call him to testify at the trial, but because he was a habitual criminal of very limited intelligence, they decided he would not make a credible witness.[8] They had their hooks into him, but he was not much good to them.

Knowing that this kind of thing happened, I did not say anything, especially to the other prisoners they put into my cell. When they said, "What did you do?" I replied, "Smoked in the movie theater" or "I pushed my grandmother down the stairs." I never said what I had done. In the beginning at Kolafu someone told me: "Trust no one! Trust no man! Pay attention, my boy, you are alone here, completely alone. Keep your mouth shut and trust nobody. They are all bums; they are all stool pigeons. They all want to earn brownie points and to have their sentences reduced."

I was in Alt-Moabit for about a week before the the trial, which was at ten o'clock on 11 August. The preceding night I was very nervous. On the one hand it was the most terrible night, but on the other I was happy that things were moving ahead and that I would soon know at last where I stood. The uncertainty was so terrible that I did not sleep much. I was alone in the cell. At eight o'clock the following morning things started moving. We had to get dressed and were handcuffed again. We got into the Green Minna and were driven to the Bellevuestraße to be tried before the People's Court.

We were given our civilian clothes for the trial, because we needed to appear respectable. Our clothes came with us from Hamburg to Berlin and went back to Hamburg after the trial. Everything was wonderfully in order with neckties and collars and such. When I had put my suit on, someone said to me, "That can't be your suit." It hung so loosely on me that I looked like a scarecrow. Oh, was that ever hilarious!

We were locked in a cell in the justice building to await the trial before the People's Court. When it was time for the trial to start, we were taken into a side entrance and up to the courtroom. We suffered more verbal abuse from the functionaries running around the building, who were all Nazis. None were the black-suited SS. They were just good party members in their brown uniforms. It was an exciting thing for them, having traitors like us. That apparently did not happen every day. We were not such a wonder for the Hamburg cops as we certainly were for the Berliners. They would not have gone out of their way to abuse ordinary, small, wise guys. In their eyes we were important criminals. We were important symbols, resistance fighters. I particularly recall one of them, a short, fat fellow. He really gave us a hard time. He said, "Now we'll see what kind of mess you've gotten yourselves into! Now you're gonna pay the piper, my friends!" As it was, I already had the willies about the whole procedure, but when he said that I knew what our fate would probably be. After that I did not cherish illusions any longer, because I was the oldest and probably the most cynical of the four.

Franz Ahrens wrote later about us: "We who were in the Resistance knew what resistance was. What these youths did was unbelievable, incomprehensible."[9] We, of course, did not know that it was unbelievable. We did not know we were heroes. We simply did it without much fuss. The interesting thing about the whole affair was that everyone took it for the seventh wonder of the world, which was why the people were still snarling at us, even at the trial.

We waited in the cell for approximately twenty minutes before our attorneys arrived and we were led upstairs into the courtroom. We sat on an elevated stand with the lawyers in front of us. In front of them was an empty area, and across the room the judges sat in an even more elevated position. It was a large courtroom, a typical German courtroom.

The judges were Vice President of the People's Court Karl Engert; Higher Regional Court Councillor Fikeis; National Socialist Motor Corps Brigade Leader Heinsius; Senior District Leader Bodinus; Senior District Judicial President Hartmann, who represented the public prosecutor; First State Attorney Dr. Drullmann; and Secretary of Justice Wöhlke. Next to Fikeis sat a high military officer, a high SS officer, and the court recorder. Fikeis presided over the trial, but Engert conducted some of the routine business. Fikeis and others had on their red robes, each with the swastika and the golden eagle, which the prisoners called the "vulture of rack and ruin."[10]

Before we entered, spectators were already sitting in the courtroom.[11] They stared incredulously when four young delinquents entered. My father had come from Hamburg and was there. (See Document 49.) He was the only person from any of our families who attended the trial. He had come alone from Hamburg and was staying with friends who were members of our church. When the mighty men entered, everyone had to stand up. About ten o'clock the opening statements and the formalities began, names were read, and so forth. Each person had to stand when his name was read, acknowledge whether it was correct, state his birthdate, residence, profession, and so forth. Then they went down the row of attorneys and asked if they had anything to reply. They all responded, "No."

They gave us what appeared to be a small intelligence test. They asked a few general knowledge questions and some crap like that before getting on to the interrogation about our crimes.[12] Helmuth was sharp as usual. He answered with flying colors. The rest of us were completely speechless, the result, in the first place, of lack of sleep, and then of our nervousness and state of agitation. In spite of that Helmuth answered immediately. He did not seem to be bothered by all this in the slightest.[13]

When Helmuth was done, Rudi's turn came, and Rudi had less to say. He was totally played out. Yes, he admitted wrongdoing. "But I didn't intend to break the law," Rudi stuttered. Then it was my turn. Because I was over eighteen, and thus technically an adult, with me they used the formal pronoun of address *Sie* ("you"), and the familiar pronoun *du* ("thou") with the others, who were still legally minors. They read back to me a portion of my statement and inquired if it was correct. I stood by what I had always said. They wanted to ask some trick questions, but I did not fall for them. Düwer did not say much.

When we had finished answering their questions, the witnesses were called. All of them were outside. Werner Kranz, Helmuth's colleague at work, was there, and the judges reprimanded him for not reporting Helmuth. There was a young soldier there named Horst Zumsande, who was summoned from his station in Thorn, because Düwer had once shown a flyer to him and his brother, Kurt.[14] (See Documents 9 and 11.) Then came Heinrich Mohns and Gestapo agent Müssener. Officer Wangemann was not there.

The main witness in the trial was Mohns, the political overseer of Helmuth's office. This superpatriot declared to the court that he was responsible to watch for anti-Nazi statements and to keep his office free from impure political thinking. In 1949 Mohns was convicted as a war criminal, but for some mysterious reason he was not required to serve out his sentence.[15]

After the witnesses had testified, there was a recess. The judges had a lunch break and we had to go into the cellar and did not receive anything to eat. After the recess, the judges had the spectators removed from the courtroom for state security reasons, as they said, because the leaflets were to be read aloud. The trial lasted until 5:00 in the afternoon, because they read and discussed every flyer.

The leaflets enraged the judges. In some of them Helmuth attacked Hitler and his speeches. "The Führer's Speech" (see Document 45), for example, was sarcastic and very ironic. There was one other about Reichsmarshal Göring, the Fat (see Document 37). The judges actually laughed at that flyer. I was speechless. They sat there and snickered, but, of course, the matter was deadly serious.

I was astonished how cool, clear, and clever Helmuth was. The court went over every detail in the leaflets and he recalled everything. He knew precisely when, how, and where he had conceived an idea and what he meant by it. It was obvious that the entire matter was not a mischievous, boyish escapade, but a serious undertaking to which he had completely dedicated himself.

Throughout the entire trial Helmuth stood like an oak and answered the questions. "Why did you do this?" "Because I wanted the people to know the truth." "Does that mean that the British atrocity stories are correct?" "Exactly!" Sometimes Helmuth was sarcastic toward Fikeis. When Fikeis asked, "Would you have us believe that the British are telling us the truth? Do you really believe that?" Helmuth responded: "Yes, surely, don't you?" The judges asked Helmuth: "You don't doubt Germany's ultimate victory, do you?" Thereupon Helmuth said to the judges: "Do you actually believe that Germany *can* win the war?"

At that point, of course, all hell broke loose. His attorney, Dr. Hans Georg Knie, turned around and scowled, as if to say, "Are you out of your mind?" It was completely clear to me that deep in his heart Helmuth knew prior to appearing before the People's Court that he would be sentenced to death. I believe he had made up his mind to conduct himself with courage and dignity.[16]

When the evidence had been heard, the judges withdrew to decide the verdict.[17] The door was opened and all of the spectators came in again and filled the hall. The judges returned and we all had to stand up again.

Fikeis berated us terrifically. He called us Bolsheviks, Communists, traitors to the fatherland, scum, asocial elements, vermin. "Vermin like you must be exterminated." My knees were knocking. I had no hope. I thought we would all receive the death penalty. My worst fears were partly confirmed when Helmuth received the death penalty and loss of his civil rights for life.[18] When this sentence was pronounced, the room grew deathly silent. I noticed that the people were shocked.[19] Then I heard people whisper: "The death penalty for the lad? Oh, no!"[20]

I received five years imprisonment. Rudi had a ten-year sentence imposed, presumably because he sang too much, particularly to Rubinke in the cell.[21] Gerhard Düwer received four years, because it could not be proved that he ever listened to the radio.[22] (See Document 52.)

Finally, they asked if we had anything to say. They began with Gerhard Düwer, who said, "No, I have nothing to say." "Schnibbe, do you have anything to say?" "No." "Wobbe?" "No." "Hübener?"

"Yes." Helmuth stood up and said fearlessly to the judges: "Now I must die even though I have committed no crime. So now it's my turn, but your turn will come."[23] His attorney again gave him that strange scowl, but Helmuth had said what he wanted to say.

As they took us back down into the cellar, people were standing on the left and right sides of the stairs forming a lane. As we passed, they all removed their hats and stood silently while we were led through the cordon down the stairs. For me it was clear: this act was in solidarity with us. They could not say anything or they would have been in deep trouble themselves.[24]

They shackled all of us again and put us in a large room, perhaps eight by twenty meters.[25] The iron bars on the windows and the sliding door made the room into a cell. We received a piece of bread and thin coffee, buttocks brew. Until then we had received nothing to eat. The handcuffs were removed from three of us, but Helmuth's hands remained cuffed behind his back. We ate our bread and I helped Helmuth to eat something. I broke it up and put pieces in his mouth. I was still shaking like an aspen tree.

Rudi and I talked with Helmuth. "Helmuth," I said, "I do not believe that they will do it. They will reduce or cancel the verdict. They only want to use you as an example, so that others do not start anything. They will not kill you. You are too young; that will be how it is."[26] "No, they will kill me," he said quietly. "Look at the walls."

The walls and the iron gate were completely covered with writing. There were small names and verses: "I must die," and "I do not want to die," "Farewell, beloved," "Goodbye Mother," and such. Every square inch was covered with references to people's death sentences. There were things written in foreign languages, also, in French, Polish, Czech . . .

I had seen my father in the courtroom. I waved to him and he waved back as though to say, "Chin up, boy, it's not as bad as all that," but after he heard how the proceedings were going, he sat despondently hunched over the whole time. He asked my attorney, Dr. Kunz, to obtain permission for him to talk with me. Immediately after the trial, my attorney went quickly to the judges before they left and said that the father of Schnibbe was there from Hamburg, and could he have permission to speak with his son. They deliberated a long time and gave my father five minutes.

A quarter of an hour after we were placed in the cell they called my name. I thought, "What now?" I was taken into a room behind the courtroom. A man was sitting there who said to me in his Berlin dialect, "Man, it is 1942, you will not be in jail long before they put you into the army. Be happy that you are safely in prison."

My father came to comfort me, but I had to comfort my father. When he entered the room, Father completely collapsed. I said, "Now, now, it is not so bad. Do not be concerned. I am alive." I spent the time comforting my own father. He had to leave and I went back to the cellar again.

Three-quarters of an hour later the guards returned. They said, "Wobbe, Schnibbe, Düwer, get ready to go!" We embraced Helmuth. "Farewell!" Helmuth had large eyes and now they were full of tears. "Good-bye, my friend!" We went back to Moabit and Helmuth went to Plötzensee to await his death.[27]

His last months on death row must have been miserable. It was commonly known that these places had the heating pipes torn out so that no one could hang himself. The prison clothes were only a smock, so that no one could strangle himself. Every ten minutes someone peeked through the spy hole. Inmates had only a small stool, a little table, and a bed made of planks, with no mattress. They had no blankets. In August, during the summer after the trial, that was probably all right, but it is hard for me to imagine what it was like on death row in the winter. No wonder Helmuth wrote in his farewell letter that he was glad for his life to end.[28]

No date was fixed for his execution. A part of his punishment consisted of his not knowing. He was first informed at 1:05 P.M. on 27 October that he would be executed that night after 8:00 o'clock. (See Document 60.) In the following seven hours he was permitted to write three letters that we know of, one to his mother, one to his grandparents Sudrow, and one to Sister Marie Sommerfeld, a member of our branch, whose children he often visited, who loved him almost like a second mother. The first two letters did not survive the air attacks on Hamburg, but the one to Sister Sommerfeld did.[29] (See Document 61.) That letter reveals that they must have given him wine to drink to calm him somewhat before his execution.

The documents reveal the cold-blooded bureaucratic efficiency with which his execution was carried out. They describe exactly the manner and time (8:13 P.M.) he was taken from his cell in Plötzensee, handed over to the executioner, Herr Röttger (ten seconds), placed on the guillotine by Röttger and his henchmen (eight seconds), and decapitated. (See Document 62.) His body was given to the Anatomical Institute of the University of Berlin. (See Document 59.) His grave is unknown.[30]

We remained two or three days in Alt-Moabit, because we had to wait until a larger group was assembled for transportation to Hamburg.[31] We were in a large, decrepit room where the bedbugs bit us continually. Everything was bug-ridden, and again we had to endure a lot of insults: "swine," "criminals," and "You got off too easily," and such.

On the first Sunday after the trial I was lying in my cell, waiting to be transported. The cell was approximately thirty meters away from the prison chapel. Suddenly I heard the organ playing.[32] I began to cry, sobbing without stopping for hours. I was racked with guilt: "Helmuth must die and we get to live." I wrote a letter to my parents in which I asked their forgiveness for having brought so much grief and sorrow to them. Many years later, organ music again caused a flood of tears and helped me to wash away all the pain and guilt of my ordeal.

They took us back to Hamburg in the prison transporter, a motor vehicle with a narrow hall and cells left and right. I was alone in a cell which was not larger than one meter square. There was only a bench in it where I could sit. There was a window, but it was made of milk glass. You could see only a small, bright square. When you had to go to the john, you had to rap on the door, and when it pleased the gentlemen, they let you go to the restroom. In the john the window was locked and obscured, also.

I sat alone in that small cell for six hours. Gerhard and Rudi were in the same vehicle in different cells. So it was back to Hamburg, back to the UG. From the UG I went to the police station in the Hüttenstraße (a building dedicated in 1985 as the Helmuth-Hübener House in Hamburg). I was placed in the basement where the cell was so terribly revolting that we were grateful we spent only one night there.

The next morning they took us in the Green Minna from the Hüttenstraße to Glasmoor, a work camp[33] in the peat area north of Hamburg, where we had to work digging peat.[34] I had no concept of what the work entailed. At that time Glasmoor was still outside of Hamburg, though today the city has spread beyond it.[35]

At Glasmoor we were eagerly awaited. Our fame had preceded us. The first question was always: "Where are the Berliners?" We became known at Glasmoor as "the Berliners," infamous criminals like Dillinger or Capone, but we did not look quite that malicious!

The director of the institution was an older official, who was there before the Nazi period. He was a good person and treated us well. He called us into his office and asked what we had done. We could tell that he was horrified at how we had been treated. He was enraged that we had received such severe sentences for minor offenses, but the others in the prison only knew that we came from the People's Court so they avoided us like the plague.

We were given cells in the upper story of the prison. I was put in a cell with a fellow who had killed his mother with a cleaver. There I was, a youth from a religious family in a cell with a psychopathic murderer!

Another prisoner there, named Rudi Wulf, was a hijacker of vehicles. He stopped cars by felling trees across isolated roads and then he robbed the passengers. The police were on his trail so he joined the Foreign Legion, but they caught him anyway. Somehow, I had a fear of that man. He always stared into the distance and had very creepy, fixed eyes. One day he was in the shoemaking shop and vanished again. The shoemakers had wax for waxing thread. While he was cleaning the room for one of the guards, he made himself a wax impression of the key. Then he reportedly made a copy with a file, opened the door, and disappeared.

The first thing he did was to go to the parents of his fellow prisoners and say they had sent him. "Why were you sent?" "Oh, I have been released and they told me that you would help me." They gave him money and provisions. He procured a pistol again and started robbing. The police set a trap and there was a shootout and he drew the short straw. They caught him and he was condemned to death and executed.

When the elderly director of the institution was pensioned, Dr. Krüger became the new director. He immediately took a liking to us Berliners.[36] Krüger arranged work for us in the tailor shop,[37] where I was permitted also to clean the room, polish the boots, and make the bed of Staff Sergeant Eggers, who directed the tailor shop. There was always a slice of bread for me on the table in his room.

It was while we were working there that we learned from a newspaper article that Helmuth had been executed.[38] We were horribly upset, but there was nothing we could do.

In some respects, life at Glasmoor was not so bad. It was just a large farm with pigs, cows, and everything like that.[39] After a couple of weeks we had to cut peat.[40] We were required to go into the bog in water above our knees. The bricks of peat were stacked up like loaves of bread.

After a couple of months of digging peat, I was made a painter.[41] There was a lot to paint at Glasmoor. There was a paint shop as well as a cabinet shop and a locksmith shop. Above all these shops was a stairway and a glass booth from which the guards could observe the work stations. Rudi was in the tailor shop the entire time. Düwer worked in the prison office and had a good life.[42]

One time Dr. Krüger had me summoned and said Privy Councillor So-and-So would like to have his kitchen painted. Krüger asked if I could be trusted to go there and return. "Of course!" I replied.

The path led an hour and a half through the woods. I painted his kitchen for him and went back. Running away was unthinkable, because the Nazis practiced *Sippenhaft*, the arrest of one's relatives.[43] I had injured my family enough already.

My parents were permitted to visit me every six weeks. It was a long way, because they had to go on foot from the main train station in Ochsenzoll, which was a two-hour walk.

We lived along from day to day, with an occasional air-raid alarm. During air raids I was required to go to the house of Dr. Krüger to carry luggage, valuables, and so forth down into the shelter. Then we were ordered to sit by the fire engine. The others were permitted to remain in bed during an air raid while Düwer and I remained up in case something caught on fire.

We were in Glasmoor during the great air raid of July 1943. We did not get hurt by it, but we could see Hamburg. The whole area of the city was one big, red glow. On the following morning the sun shone radiantly, but over Hamburg one could see only a huge dark cloud. Then the cloud spread out and covered Glasmoor as well, and for three days we could not see the sun. Approximately three centimeters of black soot fell from the sky and covered everything like black snow. When it began to drizzle, the rain was black as well. We could not understand how there could be so much smoke and soot.[44]

Two days later we were told the east wing of our barracks needed to be cleared. All of the prisoners went over to the west wing, so instead of eight there were sixteen or twenty to a cell when the refugees arrived, who were to be put in the east wing. Düwer and I and other trustees were required to help with the unloading. Some of the refugees were severely injured and others had received a nervous shock. Some had been buried and dug out of the rubble.[45]

I inquired if there were any from Hohenfelde, where I lived, and there were some. They were from the Reismühle neighborhood, from the Elisenstraße. I said, "I have heard nothing from my parents. How are things in Hohenfelde?" They said, "Everything is gone! There is absolutely nothing left there. Hohenfelde is totally destroyed!" I was greatly concerned and asked Staff Sergeant Eggers, who also lived in Hohenfelde, how things looked. He said, "Schnibbe, don't kid yourself, everything is gone." "Oh, good heavens! Where are my parents?" I was in the camp for nearly three months without news about my parents.[46]

Luckily, they were still alive. They could not come to visit me, because they had left Hamburg. At first they had gone into the air-raid shelter in the cellar. When the great fire storm began, they left the shelter and ran to the lake. Their apartment was gone anyway, so they fled. What saved my parents was that they lived close to the water, on the Alster lake, at the Kuhmühlenteich, the "cow mill pond," perhaps two minutes by foot away from our apartment. The only place safe from the fire when the fire storm began to consume the buildings was in the water.

Of course it was not completely safe, for out in the middle of the lake were three or four ship hulls chained together and on top of them were flak batteries which fired anti-aircraft shells. The shots whistled over their heads and shrapnel fell all around them.

After the air raid they were all gathered together on a large field and were told, "Get out of Hamburg, go away someplace!" They were asked if they had any relatives. On my mother's side of the family we had an aunt in Salzwedel, and that is where my parents had gone, but I did not know that. After three months or so they came back to Hamburg, and then my mother and father visited me. I was sincerely happy.

Father had a bandage on his head. I asked, "What happened?" He said, "From the fire storm." The wind had sucked up everything and a thick beam flew through the air and hit him on the head.

When they returned from Salzwedel, they applied for a Ley cabin.[47] It was all prefabricated, the four walls, the roof, everything, but at least it was a roof overhead. On our garden plot was only a small weekend hut that was not big enough to live in. It was torn down and the Ley cabin put there. There was plenty of rubble in the vicinity, so my father excavated bricks and somehow obtained sand and cement, and gradually constructed a foundation, completing the house with bricks. My parents lived there until the end of the war.[48]

We were in Glasmoor a little longer than a year, from August 1942 until the end of 1943, shortly before Christmas.[49] Then we were told: "Get ready to move out!" We were afraid we might be sent to Dachau or Auschwitz. There was a possibility that they would simply execute us. At first, we did not know where we would go, but it turned out that we were to work in an aircraft factory in Poland, in Graudenz on the Vistula, southeast of Danzig, where workers were needed.[50]

The day was set and the Green Minnas came in a group and shipped us to the main train station in Hamburg. When we got out, a cordon of police stood on the side where the theater was. One policeman stood next to the other, and we had to run through the middle to the train station. Of course, we could see that everything was destroyed. The people stared and likely thought that murderers and other such criminals were coming out. The train was ready, but had only three cars, because it was exclusively for us. It went via Hassen and Stettin through Pomerania to Graudenz.

5

Poland and the Long Road Home

We left Hamburg early in the morning and arrived in Graudenz late in the afternoon, then we marched from the train station to the aircraft plant. The camp where we were to stay was surrounded with barbed wire on a road quite a distance from the factory. When we entered we could tell that the camp had not been occupied for a long time, because it was in terrible condition; everything was filthy and neglected.[1] We were so tired the first night that we just hit the ground and slept.

The next day things started moving gradually when the administrative office was opened and the guards came. Some life stirred slowly in the clothing room, the commissary, the kitchen, and everywhere else, and things all got organized.

Many of the guards were Beutedeutsche, which is what we called those from Upper Silesia.[2] The name *Beutedeutsche* means something like "Opportunist Germans," which they were called because they had joined Germany when Hitler's Reich expanded. Some of these were pro-German Poles, who were also called "East Germans." Though they were German citizens, they spoke only broken German, since they had lived their entire lives in Poland. Every second word they spoke was *pironia*, which means dog.

The barrack where I bunked with Rudi and Gerhard was the administrative barrack, where the clothing room and the kitchen staff were. Dr. Krüger went with us to reopen this camp. In addition to Dr. Krüger there were Staff Sergeant Eggers, Staff Sergeant Jäger, and Police Sergeant Barts, all people we had known a long time at Glasmoor.

Barts loved to torment us and drill us after ten hours of work. He hounded us until we collapsed from fatigue.[3]

I became the barrack's leader, and Gerhard Düwer from the office remained with us, but Rudi was moved to the aircraft plant, where he was assigned to some technical tasks. He was a mechanic, so was transferred to some barracks where he could live together with those people.[4]

Our barrack was nearly always open, being closed only at night. When the columns came in from work and after the evening muster, the other barracks were closed, but ours remained open, because I fetched bread for the other barracks and needed to distribute the food.

Near Graudenz the air force had constructed an aircraft plant, a subterranean one where the damaged ME-109 Messerschmitt fighters were taken apart, the parts cleaned, and put together as new machines.[5] Out of two or three wrecks they made a new airplane.[6] One of our jobs was to wash the parts of the airplanes with a chemical solvent. Working with all of those chemicals was a difficult and dangerous job, and we had to work long hours every day, at least twelve hours.[7]

Blood and hair were still on some of the parts. We could see that Germany was on its last legs. The shot-up fighters came in on the train and some were really shot to pieces with not much left, but they used every part that could still be used, either from the landing gear, the hydraulic system, or whatever. Every month, two or three fighters were flown out of Graudenz, ready to fight.[8]

Of course, when the test pilots arrived we could watch them fly away. They climbed high and flew two or three times past the runway; then they waggled their wings. They went up and made a few tests and then the planes went to the front again.

Once we needed to paint a place where they performed static tests on the Messerschmitts, where they synchronized the machine guns and the motors, for example, so they could shoot through the propellers. It was there I became acquainted with Joseph Ratzkowsky, who was also a painter and was to be my superior. In the mornings he came to the door and waited, leaning on his bicycle while I was called to the door, and they came to let me out. That arrangement was by special order of the camp director. The camp guards did not care for us and would gladly have bumped us off, but they could not do anything. We marched across the road and over to the airplane plant where we had to go through the gate again, and then work began. For the entire day I saw no one else from our group.

Later I was ordered to camouflage the airplane hangers and the workrooms with special paint. It was a waterproof vinyl paint that I mixed in green and brown and applied to the roof and all of the surfaces, even the road, so that we could not be recognized from the air. I mixed a lot of camouflage paint, and after a while the entire area was camouflaged. I had to spray the airplanes a bright blue underneath and camouflage on top. I also lettered the doors of the adminstration buildings, the supply management, and the staff sergeant's area so that people knew what office to go to.

When I was first together with Ratzkowsky and the other Poles, they sounded me out a little and listened to my story. Naturally, they did not know at first if I was "genuine" and I did not know if they were "genuine." We needed to sniff each other a few times, but it did not take long until I knew exactly what Ratzkowsky and the other Poles were made out of and they knew what kind of guy I was. We developed an unconditional trust and got along wonderfully. Ratzkowsky was a first-rate fellow. He was missing a few teeth in the front, and when he laughed the gaps showed. He spoke broken German. Joseph gave me food and tobacco, because I had started to smoke, which reduced the hunger pangs.[9]

When he asked me if he could do something else for me, the first thing I asked was if he could smuggle a letter to my parents for me, which he did. (See Document 64.) If they had caught him, they would have hanged him. Oh, the Nazis were consistent about that. But my parents received mail from me and I asked them if they could send me a few little pastries or such, which my mother did. Each package was sent to Ratzkowsky and he gave it to me. I wanted to share the cake with him, but he said, "No, that is for you. You need it more than I."

I had a small workshop in the airplane plant and one in the administration building, where I did the lettering work. It was the workplace for several men, and I had a key to it. Once I went alone into the airplane plant and looked around and noticed that a guard was following me. He probably wondered, "What does this guy think he's doing wandering around by himself?" When I noticed him, I went faster; then he went faster, too. It was a Saxon, a police sergeant, who was a malicious customer.[10] I thought, "Just you wait, my friend, I'll fix you," and I went directly to the administration building. As I entered the administration building, he went to it, too. I ran quickly up the two flights of stairs to my workshop in the attic. I heard him open the door. As he came up the stairs, I unlocked my workshop, opened it, entered, and locked it. Then I heard him rattle each door, because he did not know where I was. I waited half an hour before going outside again. Being unable to find me must have aggravated him.

After I became really well befriended by the Poles, they offered to help me escape. Naturally, the temptation was always present. When the Poles told us that Germany was losing the war, I said, "We have known that for a long time. How do you know?" It turned out that they were all resistance fighters. We figured it was only a question of time, one year, a year and a half, and it would be over. They said, "So, when we hide you, we will hide you in Congress Poland."[11]

The temptation was great, but I knew precisely the moment I ran away my parents would be arrested because of *Sippenhaft* and would be forced to go to a concentration camp,[12] which I could not do to them. I explained this to the Poles. "Well, think about it some more." I said, "Thanks, but no thanks."

Afterwards I spoke with Gerhard Düwer about it. Gerhard and I had become firm friends. Although he had been partially responsible for our arrest,[13] that was all forgotten and forgiven. Now he was with us, because he belonged to the Hübener group. Because he worked in the administrative office, he helped me a lot by informing me about what was happening.

After the assassination attempt on Hitler of 20 July 1944, an order came for all political prisoners to be put into an extermination camp.[14] The Gestapo wanted to ship all of us to Neuengamme.[15] The order arrived and Gerhard knew that it had come. Krüger spoke with him about it, and they decided they would not follow it. Krüger immediately wrote a telegram to Berlin, to Gestapo headquarters in the Prinz Albrechtstraße and said, "The lads are to stay here. They are doing strategic military work. We cannot dispense with them. They are skilled workers on the Messerschmitt fighters, and must remain here."[16] That saved our lives, because nothing more ever came of it. If it had come to the point that we had been forced to go, I would have accepted the offer of the Poles. Gerhard said, "I will go with you." We would have done it.

The Poles once had a special surprise for me of which I had no inkling. I was going with Joseph Ratzkowsky and he was grinning from one ear to the other. He said, "Today we have something for you." I said, "What?" "Ah," he said, "I have a girl." They had a little doll for me, a Pole. I was supposed to have a little fun with her, with cute little Maria. When they all left me alone with her, we were supposed to disappear into the forest.

She was as bashful as I, very young, and did not know what to say or do. I was so ashamed that I turned as red as a tomato. I said, "No, no, no, I don't do that kind of thing. I can't do that." They were very disappointed, because she was a pretty girl. "What? You are nuts. . . . Man! Your only chance in life. No prisoner gets such an opportunity." I said, "No, I cannot do it. I have been raised otherwise. I don't do that kind of thing; that is out of the question for me." They could not understand it, but I had the feeling that the little Polish girl respected me greatly for that. The whole business was naturally embarrassing for her, because she must have felt like a whore. They had said to her, "Come on, you keep still now. We have a good political prisoner and you need to give him some pleasure. So, you will keep your trap shut, won't you?"

Joseph Ratzkowsky once took me with him into the city, into Graudenz, because we needed to go to the main workshop. He needed something and said, "Why don't you come with me? Come on." He pushed his bicycle alongside him. As the devil would have it, storeroom manager Krüger and Herr Kröger, the secondary school teacher, were coming toward us, also on foot. There were some young boys along, too. I assumed a completely military stance and greeted them; hands on the trouser seams, head to the left, and then we went further. We behaved as if it were completely normal, but I was fearful. They probably thought, "Oh yes, that is normal. The Pole Ratzkowsky signed for him and it is okay." To be sure, in the evening they watched to see if I was there. I was present there at the proper time, and nothing ever came of it.

We political prisoners in Graudenz were marked with a yellow triangle. We all had a large triangle on our backs and a smaller one on our trouser legs. In the other large camps the triangles of the politicals were red and the triangles of the criminals were green.[17]

Among our Polish friends there was a little Pole who was my girlfriend, whose father was an actor. She worked at the camp also and somehow had taken a liking to me. She always held her purse over the yellow triangle on my back when we went walking so that no one could notice. Otherwise, everyone could see it a half-mile away.

Although there was very close supervision, because the camp was filled with technical workers, Nazis, and guards, there was a lot of stealing and smuggling. That was extremely dangerous, but at the time we naturally smuggled a great deal. I obtained things from the clothing room, because the clothing big shot was stationed in our barrack. He gave me socks, which I smuggled to the Poles for cigarettes or something else. If we had been caught there would have been hell to pay.

We swiped everything, even the gasoline for the fire truck, for the motor, for the pumps. When I think about it, if someone had needed it and there had been no gas in it, I would have been in deep trouble.

Once they caught Rudi smuggling. In our camp a stockade had just been constructed, and Rudi was the first guest. He received three days of solitary confinement on bread and water, but we did not want to let him starve, so we slipped him something to eat.

At that time in Graudenz, between my Polish girlfriend and swiping food, I did not need to complain about having enough to eat. The cuisine was not lovely, but when I wanted to fill my stomach with potatoes, I could get enough.

There was a kind of soup with little fish in it that stared at you with their eyes. We called it the soup with ten thousand eyes. Rudi got stomach troubles from it. When he was living in my barrack he stunk up the entire room! We said to him, "Man, Rudi! Go to the toilet and take a crap!"

A more serious problem in Graudenz was that we had to suffer from the cold. It was very difficult to withstand the winter, because we had left our warmer clothing in Glasmoor. At the time we received new clothes, but it was all just flimsy camp material.[18] In the airplane plant and the work halls it was warm, but it was colder in the barracks. Of course, we had our round iron stove in the middle of the room and received a little fuel, and because we had connections, we could obtain more coal and briquettes. As a result, we had a relatively warm room. The other fellows did not sleep as warmly.

Adjacent to our camp were barracks with Russian women civilians who worked in the plant. The poor girls froze, because they did not get any fuel. We were on good terms with the single guard who went up and down the fence. We had given him a nickname, the Stork, because he walked funny. It looked like he was walking on stilts through the vegetation. For this reason he was not drafted into the army but was used as a guard. We told him to take a hike and he went away for a while. We gave the Russian and Polish girls to understand that they should all come closer to the fence, because the fence was high. When they approached, we tossed briquettes over the fence and then they had a warm room for once. They were very happy about it.

In the summer and the fall when the onions and the other vegetables were ripe, I told this guard, the Stork, to watch out for me when I climbed over the fence, because in the field of the airplane plant there was a vegetable garden for the factory canteen. The guard stood watch for me and I went up and over and harvested a little. When I did this at 3:30 in the morning, everything was quiet; otherwise, we could not have risked it. He opened the outer gate and I went over the inner fence and made my harvest. At a quarter after four I was back.

That was a dangerous thing, because there was barbed wire and other guards who were patrolling. There were dogs, also, but they were not out at night. When I returned, I gave the Stork his share. Of course, that was graft, but the guards didn't have any more than we did. Everyone needed to fend for himself as far as "grocery technology" (*verpflegungstechnisch*) was concerned, and we needed some fresh vitamins.

The Stork would come to the barracks, also, knock on the door and come to the window and ask for tobacco. When he said he wanted something to smoke, we gave it to him, because we could not afford to lose the guy's favor. We needed to be cordial to him, because we needed him to open the gate so we could get out to "organize" some food.

I had already learned the *verpflegungstechnisch* tricks in Glasmoor, but in Glasmoor it was not so easy to arrange, because we did not get out. We could do a little in the truck garden, but there was not much to get there. We found that sugar beet slices for the cattle, which they received for feed, tasted good; or we could scavenge a few potatoes used to feed pigs, but otherwise there was not much to be had.

In Poland I saw some of the persecution of the Jews. You heard rumblings of it, the Poles talked about it, and the neighbors knew. Only the Germans "did not know about it." The Poles knew about Auschwitz, Treblinka, Buchenwald, and all the rest, but did not tell much about it. They only hinted, because they were a bit fearful. They had to be careful and not say too much, but they knew everything. The Poles only said things like: "There are places where they make people walk the plank, where they do them all in."

Some even said, "Oh, the Jews, they stink, they are filthy, they don't work, they take our money." These types did not care much for the Jews, but most of the Poles were opposed to the persecution of the Jews. "What they are doing is not good." Those being persecuted were not only German Jews, they were also Poles and Polish Jews, and political prisoners, and Russian prisoners of war. We had talked about the existence of these camps, but we had no idea of their extent. Of course we knew that there were political prisoners in the concentration camps. We were political prisoners and were not treated with kid gloves, but even we were unaware of the full scope of the Holocaust.

Of course, I believed it, because I knew the Nazis. We had already heard in Graudenz about the shootings of Jews. We heard that the Gestapo, the special detachments, simply shot people in the forest. We also saw military police and the Security Service everywhere. They were all around in the camp and in the large airplane plant where there were many Russian and English prisoners of war and Polish civilians.

The English prisoners of war did not work with the machinery.

They only built roads and did grading work, manual labor. When it got cold the poor fellows were left to starve.[19] I stuck a loaf of bread under my arm once and took it to one Englishman. The bread was sliced up in three pieces to make it easier to hide. I looked to see if the coast was clear and gave a signal to the Englishman. He looked, and I said something, but he did not know what I wanted, so I went past and laid the bread down and pushed it over a bit. Then he saw it and took it.

The next day I went past again and wanted to know if everything was okay, and he gave a signal. I went closer and he laid a wool sweater on the ground for me, but I did not want anything in exchange for the bread. I left the sweater and went away, because the poor guy needed the sweater himself; they had nothing. There were fewer Englishmen, more Russians, but we did not make any contact like that with the male Russian prisoners of war.

We also saw some combat, even though the front was far away in Russia, because British and Russian planes occasionally came that far. They wanted to destroy the airplane plant, of course, but they could not find it. They could not make a concentrated attack, because it was too far from their bases and they were harrassed the whole way by German fighters shooting at them.

The Russians did not make any real bombing attacks. They flew around and we heard the motors roar, and there was an air-raid alarm. They dropped flares but not many bombs, at least nothing exploded. We saw a great many air attacks, but there was no damage. Often, when there was an air-raid alarm, just like in Glasmoor, I was required to go immediately to the administration building, where the dependents of the camp leadership lived, and help Senior Administrative Director Krüger and his wife carry luggage into the shelter.

We heard from the Poles that the front was drawing closer and closer. They told us precisely where the German lines were, so we always knew where the front stood. We heard that the German troops had suffered massive defeats such as in Stalingrad,[20] and that the German troops in Russia were faring very poorly and retreating along the whole front. On the airfield there was a regular squadron of fighter airplanes, and we noticed from their numerous sorties that the front was coming closer.

At that time we could not get a clear picture whether they would ship us back or whether the Russians would liberate us. Of course, we were all in favor of being shipped back, because we were afraid of the Russians. As the front came increasingly closer, things became more hectic and the atmosphere was terribly tense. We noticed anxiety among the German civilians, the technical personnel from the Reich.

Each Sunday we had to go out and spend the entire day outside of Graudenz with the civilians digging tank traps. The entire city came out, which naturally resulted in a mass of confusion. We had to dig very deep trenches, long holes in the middle of the forest, that tanks would drive into and could not get out of. They were gigantic holes with steep sides, but we had thousands of men with spades to dig them. We also had to build fortifications in the forests above Graudenz.

It was sandy soil and was hard work, but not for me. I was still very strong, but most of the others were rather weak. Of course, we received extra food out there. We got more bread and other nourishment. We had our own group and were kept separate from the others. Only prisoners were there, and next to us were the civilians. The digging gave us reason to think, "Ah ha! Look, it will soon be over." If the Russians were already defeated in Russia as the official German propaganda line had it, why do we need to build tank traps? They knew very well that the Russians were coming.

The winter of 1944 was very hard. The guards, the kitchen boss, and all of the administrative personnel celebrated the new year vigorously with a nice, big party. In January, two days later, our retreat started.[21] We were told: "No more work. Pack your things." "Why pack?" "We are going back to Germany." "Oh, in the train?" "On foot."

Our entire camp had to move on foot that January. It was so cold that the Vistula was frozen over. The bridge over the Vistula was too dangerous to cross, because it was covered with ice and blocked by the military, so we crossed on the frozen river.[22]

We had our rags and still some other things to wear, and they gave us what they had, such as any coats and footwear from the supply room, but it was not warm enough. They were low leather shoes, not boots. We had wool socks and stuck our pants in the tops of the socks so the wind and snow would not get in, then we trotted off. (See Document 63.)

Because we were assigned to the kitchen as assistants, we were responsible for all of the provisions and had to pull a wagon with the cooking utensils for the kitchen on it. There were enough of us prisoners to pull this wagon without problems and we traded off. So there we were, free, fresh, and gleefully under way. After us came another wagon pulled by two horses and loaded with all of the baggage of the administrators. Dr. Krüger and his wife sat on the wagon, in the cold on the suitcases. How the wind whistles in East Prussia! The Krügers lay under a quilt and had some blankets around their feet and wrapped around them, but you can't keep warm by sitting the entire day. Walking is much better.

On the first day we did not get any farther than fifteen or twenty kilometers. Of course, we were always told where we should be accommodated when we stopped for the night. The first night[23] they put us in a women's prison, with all of the women still there. When we arrived there was shouting and turmoil, and they wanted to know what was happening. We said, "We are going back. Ivan is coming." We knew the Russians were on our heels, because we could hear a rumble in the distance.[24]

We still always had to procure what we could, because we could not prepare a regular meal. Sometimes we had no opportunity to cook, and there were mostly only cold provisions, such as a piece of bread, and that was all. You could not cook under such awful conditions. Where could you get a kettle to cook for the entire camp? We often cooked in the laundry rooms of places where we stayed. In fact, most of the time we did that, because most of the houses had large laundry rooms in the cellar. In the laundry rooms there were large kettles built on top of brick fireboxes to heat the water. They were large enough to cook potatoes or whole pigs, if we could steal one, which was very dangerous, of course.

At the most, we received a warm meal three or four times a week. I always took a large pot of food and visited the Krügers wherever they were quartered. Because he had been so kind to us, I took it upon myself to help the man and his wife. The first few days many prisoners did that, but after a while nobody bothered himself any more. I searched for the Krügers, and it often took a long time until I found them, but they got a meal. Even if I only brought him some bread or smoked fish, he got something to eat every day. I could see that he got worse everyday, because he was not accustomed to harsh conditions. He was a bureaucrat, a pencil pusher. Then I got something to eat for myself and looked around for a place to sleep.

I was always on the lookout for something to scavenge, to "liberate." The first thing I procured was a nice large sled, not one to sit on, with regular seats, but one with a flat bed for hauling. The next thing I procured, that is, swiped, was a horse. There was plenty of feed, because every farm was deserted. All of the farmers had fled, and there was still enough hay in the barns. We gave this nag the name Belami, good friend. The horse answered to Belami and pulled the sled. There were some lads with us who could not walk anymore.[25] The sled could carry two at the same time. Our Belami followed us, always trotting splendidly behind us.

Once we entered a town where the farmers had slaughtered all of the pigs. They had just finished slaughtering and had cut the pigs in half and laid them on a footbridge to cool, so they could be transported. I saw it as a unique opportunity. The half pigs were nicely frozen and would keep in good condition. "Man," I thought. "I must take a little stroll over that way sometime." I kept a lookout and, when no one was there, I took Belami with me, loaded half a pig on the horse's back, and beat a hasty retreat.

Because it was not possible for us to thaw the entire pig, we needed a saw to cut up the meat. We finally hacked off chunks and cooked them. They were very nice. The pig was a godsend to our little group; not everyone got part of it. We could not roast it, so we boiled it in a laundry tub. We skimmed the fat, which was like drippings, from the water and let it get cold, then ate it with a spoon. It was useful in warding off the cold. We had to be preoccupied with food: if you didn't eat well, if you got diarrhea, for example, you would crap yourself half to death. We once swiped half a sack of sugar and ate pig meat with sugar. Our bodies needed sugar, because it gave us stamina, but I took a little too much. "Man," I thought, "if I get the runs and need to crap every three minutes, I will freeze my ass!" but nothing like that happened.

While it lasted, we could always cook some pig meat. When that was gone, there was the cooking broth or bouillon with some salt, which was nothing special. On those occasions, I always held on to my bread to eat.[26]

Once I was looking around again, doing a little procuring in a village and went a little outside of the village where I had already requisitioned a couple of loaves of bread. On the way back I suddenly heard behind me: "Halt! Stand still!" I looked around and there was an SS patrol.[27] Oh, good heavens! "Come here. Where did you come from?" I said, "From back there." "Papers!" "I don't have any." "What? Where did you come from?" I said, "From Graudenz, the airplane plant." "Aha, ran away, eh?" "No, we are prisoners." "A prisoner? That is worse." The interrogation lasted approximately three minutes. It was a short trial and then they stood me up next to the nearest tree. I was scared out of my wits: "Man," I thought, "is this the end, after all I've been through, to die like this?"[28]

Suddenly I heard someone say: "Schnibbe, what are you doing here?" It was Sergeant Eggers, in his uniform. He came up to me and the SS lieutenant said, "Do you know this man?" "Oh, yes," Eggers said, "he is with us. We are all here from the prison, from the labor camp at Graudenz. We are on our way back to the Reich." "Now then, get going," the SS man said. "Five more minutes and he would not have existed any more."

"Man," said Eggers, "Schnibbe, you asshole, can't you be careful, you stupid dog? Do you want to die this way?" Naturally, I was happy and thanked my Father in Heaven, I can assure you. When I returned to the shelter, everyone was snoozing. I first took care of the Krügers again and then I hit the hay.

Once we slept in the auditorium of a school. A lot of refugees had already arrived and every square foot was covered with sleeping bodies, and we had to bunk up under the rafters in the attic. There was a guy lying there and next to him was a place to lie down. Rudi was already lying on the other side of the guy. I asked the man, "May I lie down here?" but he was sleeping. As I laid down I jostled him a little, because he took up so much room. I was very tired after walking in deep snow for thirty kilometers, so I fell asleep immediately. In the morning when I awoke, he was still lying there. I said, "Man, aren't you feeling well? What is the matter with you?" There was no answer, so I looked at him more closely. He had already been dead for approximately a week.[29] I assume he was frozen or had died from exhaustion. I had slept the entire night with a corpse, but that did not bother me. No one there concerned himself about it. "If you are the son of God, save yourself."

I always cared for Belami, also. He always received a place indoors, in a warm and dry stall. There was always enough hay and sometimes a few oats. I could not give him too many oats, otherwise I thought he might founder. When we finally concluded our trek, I had to leave him behind, because we had no choice. What was I to do? I left everything I had requisitioned. He walked away a few feet, then turned and looked at me one more time. I was sorry. He must have ended up in someone's cooking pot, or the Russians took him. Later there were firefights where he had been, because the Germans and the Russian were always right behind us. I suppose they probably made mincemeat out of our good friend Belami.

In the morning we always began at six or seven. It had often snowed during the night and there was deep snow for us to march through again. It was bitterly cold that January in 1945.[30]

We saw a woman along the way, pushing her bicycle through the deep snow, which was very difficult with such small tires. Up front on the crossbar was a little saddle where a daughter sat holding onto the handlebar. In the back on the luggage carrier was a suitcase, and on the rear saddle sat another small daughter. The children were, perhaps, three or four years old. The poor little things were so cold it made me sad, but everyone was left to his own resources. After a day or two we met the woman again, but she no longer had the small children. She was alone with the suitcase, so we asked her where her children, the little kiddies, were, whether she had put them on the train or such. Then she cried and said, "They froze to death." That was such misery.

Although the front was thirty kilometers away, behind us we heard the rumbling and the shooting, and we were lucky to be able to stay ahead of the fighting. The motorized army troops were moving faster than we were, because we were, after all, walking. As a result of a dirty trick of the Gauleiter of East Prussia, Koch, all the civilians from East Prussia were fleeing also.[31] He did not give the people the opportunity to evacuate in time, but did it when the Russians had broken through, and then it was too late to escape except on foot.

Now and then we encountered a few vehicles coming toward the front and were ordered to "Clear the road again, German tanks are coming." We would hear a rumbling in front of us and get off the road. The refugees pulled off the road with their large, heavily laden wagons into the snow-covered fields where the axles were buried in snow. Then three or four tanks roared past and that was all, because the German army was already on its last legs. Then the poor civilians were in a miserable condition, because they could not get out of the field. They had to throw away half of their baggage so they could get out of the deep snow and back onto the road.

Every evening I scouted around again and requisitioned whatever I could. One could call that stealing, but it was not really, because we needed to live.[32]

Every night the Russian NCOD, the "noncommissioned officer of the day" as we always said, flew over us and dropped flares; it was bright, but that was all. No bombs fell.

By this time we were with Staff Sergeant Jäger, the head of the kitchen. He admonished us by saying: "Listen fellows, let's stay together and then we will make it. As soon as you all go off on your own you will be lost." I said amen to that. He slept with us. He hung his cartridge belt and his service revolver close by, and we were surely glad that we had someone with us to protect us. We were only a handful: Gerhard Düwer, Rudi Wobbe, I, and a few others, at the most, ten or twelve men. The others from the camp had broken up into other small groups.

We were always together and shuffled along all day through the snow. We had to walk like storks, because the snow was so deep. That was tiring, but we talked together to take our minds off our misery.

One evening, when we arrived in the next small hick town, we slept in another school, in the gymnasium, which was filled with rags. Someone had been making a collection of rags for a war drive, and the place was a foot deep with rags. That was our evening accommodation and it was as warm as if it had been heated. When you come in from being in the cold all day, you fall down and go to sleep immediately, you are so tired.

The hall was warm and there was a musty smell, a stench in the place, but better a warm stench than cold fresh air![33] Our entire group assembled for the first time that evening to cook up what we had to eat when I noticed that Düwer was missing and asked Rudi where Gerhard was. He said, "I don't know either. I saw him not long ago." We searched high and low, but Gerhard was not to be found. I thought that he had trotted off somewhere to take a crap.

Eventually I marched back again, the way we had come, approximately three or four kilometers, until I finally saw him sitting along the road. I said, "What are you doing here?" He said, "Well, I am so tired, I am resting." I said, "Come on, don't talk nonsense, you will freeze here." He said, "I am warm. Go on ahead. I will come along soon." I would have none of that, because when someone says he is warm, that is a danger signal. I grabbed him and held onto him, one of his arms over my shoulder, and we both lumbered along. He said, "Don't make such a fuss, I will be there soon." "Quiet. You are coming with me."[34]

The next day he complained of pain in his feet, which turned red and then black from frostbite! He had frozen his toes and a part of the foot, but fortunately not so badly that anything needed to be amputated. His flesh simply began to rot as if it had been burned. At first there were large water blisters which burst. He could scarcely walk, but he had no choice except to walk on his frozen feet.

He could no longer get his shoes on easily, because everything was swollen. I said to him "Once you get them on, don't take your shoes off or you will never get them on again. Keep them on. It will hurt, but keep them on." He said later that he had no pain, that everything was numb.[35]

We finally arrived at Bütow, a place outside Stettin, where the trains were operating.[36] At first we had a compartment to ourselves.[37] I helped lift Gerhard into the baggage rack above the seats and placed a blanket under his head. He took off his shoes and socks and let his legs hang out. What a stench! I swabbed him a little with cotton wadding in an attempt to dry out his blisters. We had nothing else to use, no medicine, but eventually everything healed again.

The train stopped again on a siding, still outside Stettin, and there was a terrible bombing raid. "Man," I said, "we are helpless, like sitting ducks!" We thought, "Well, we have made it so far, now we will catch a bomb on the noggin," but we survived that, too.

The train traveled on slowly and arrived at the train station in Stettin, or what was left of it. The Red Cross had established aid stations for the refugees.[38] I took off my prison jacket, covered up with a coat and hung out the window, and Rudi and I called out, "Here, we're refugees!" They always offered and we always accepted the sandwiches and coffee and whatnot. Then we made a stockpile of sandwiches, and that was lucky. That helped us, because I could no longer go out on my requisition forays from the train.

We stopped now and then, in some cases for as long as a day.[39] When the train stopped once, I said to myself: "This will surely take three, four, five hours. We can't go further, because the track is bombed. It needs to be repaired first." So Rudi and I took off again on our procuring rounds. Approximately three or four kilometers away from the train there was a Russian prisoner-of-war camp, so we went in there. They were no guards, because they had all fled. The prisoners were there alone and were singing and were in a good mood, because they knew that it would only be a few days until their compatriots arrived. We asked them if they had anything for political prisoners. They said, "Yes, in the kitchen." They still had something to eat, nothing special, but they had a kind of milk soup, a thin soup like "Wheat Hearts." They gave us a large milk can, which Rudi and I carried back to the train.

We had a ladle and I started serving. Our group was served first, of course, and then the other refugees. The women and children were all looked after. When I wanted to have some more, everything was gone. I had given it all away, but that did not matter.

We rolled slowly onward and came in due time to Mecklenburg, where we needed to get out of the train. The sergeant who was with us from the camp announced that we had orders to go to the Bützow prison, five or six kilometers from the train. We had to remain there during the night. We were there for a few days and slept in the gymnasium and did not get anything to eat there, except a very little bit of turnip soup.

The straw was completely red with lice. We said to ourselves, "We're not sleeping on the floor with lice!" but we ourselves were as lousy as pigs. We were always catching lice and cracking them between our thumbnails. You cracked ten lice and missed thirty. You could run your hand under your collar and would have five or six lice in your hand. We were filthy and our hair was matted. When we asked if we could bathe there, we learned it was out of the question: "This is only a transit camp. We push you on again as fast as possible."

There were not many more of us left. On the way, many ran away, especially those who were from parts of West Prussia and Poland, who were close to home. I never saw Dr. Krüger again once we were out of Poland. I heard that he was very sick and that he later said that we prisoners had saved his life. (In 1985, when the City of Hamburg honored the Hübener survivors on the occasion of Helmuth's sixtieth birthday, Rudi and I were guests of the city at all the sites of our incarceration in Hamburg. The director of the prison in Fuhlsbüttel, formerly Kolafu, told us that his predecessor Dr. Krüger, who had become the director of this prison after the war, mentioned to him that the prisoners saved his life on the trek west from Graudenz in January 1945.)

The officials arrived from the administration of our camp, and got everything rolling. They made a few phone calls, and after a few days it was off to Hamburg again, to Glasmoor. We were picked up in Hamburg; more precisely, from the main freight depot outside of Hamburg we were picked up by trucks and taken to Glasmoor. Hamburg was even more destroyed than before and was almost totally gone.[40]

6

From Political Prisoner to POW

Back in Glasmoor again our first job was to lie in ecstasy in the bath-tub, in wonderful, hot water! We scrubbed ourselves for half an hour and they cut our hair very short. All our things were washed and we were given delousing agents. First they sprayed us, and then our clothing was deloused. It was the first time in weeks that we had slept on a normal plank bed. We also located our civilian clothes again. That is how the German bureaucracy worked: even in calamity, everything was accounted for. You got a receipt for everything and everything was returned. That was the only thing good about it.

But we could not remain in Glasmoor, because they had other plans. We were sent to Hanöfersand, a former youth prison on an island in the Elbe river. Sergeant Jäger took over the kitchen there immediately and retained us. Rudi was in the machine shop, because he always said, "I'm a mechanic, I'm a mechanic." "Okay, then," they said, "you be a mechanic." He trotted around in the cold machine shop while Gerhard and I peeled potatoes and scrubbed carrots in a warm kitchen.

Then we heard that familiar rumbling again, because the British were very near. One day an announcement was made that a commission would be coming the next day. "What kind of a commission?" "Well, they are recruiting soldiers; they need soldiers." "We're safe," we thought, "we are asocials, we are ineligible for military service. We don't need to worry about it."

"Famous last words!" Gerhard could not be inducted, because he was still having difficulties with his feet and limped worse than ever.[1] They did not take Rudi, because he had received ten years and still had far more than half of it to serve. Therefore, they came to me and looked me over. I was healthy and had served the majority of my five years, so they said, "You are going into the army." What could

I do? If I had refused to go they would have hanged me. On the following day they said, "Your papers will be prepared."

I was assigned to the Adolf Hitler caserne in Oldenburg. The next day at 8:00 A.M. I was evacuated and the ferry took me over to Schulauweder, where I took the commuter train to Hamburg. Because I had my civilian clothes on again and had my conscription papers in my pocket, I was permitted to visit my parents briefly on the way to the train station. In the evening at 8:00 I had to be in Oldenburg.

Oldenburg is three hours by train from Hamburg,[2] and at 5:00 I needed to leave. Before I arrived home, it was already 11:00 or 11:30. Naturally, I did not have a new outfit and my old suit was wrinkled and tattered, but nobody stared at it. The Hamburgers all ran around in a similar condition. No one had anything better.

Mother had written me, so I knew where to locate my family. I had not seen them for nearly three years and they had no idea that I was coming. Because I had to flee from Graudenz, they no longer knew where I was, but they did not worry about me, especially my mother: "We did not know where you were, but we knew somehow that you were safe."

What a joy it was! I went there and Mother was happy. Dad was at work in "the Kiel milk factory," in the explosives factory. I had only a couple of hours with Mother before I had to leave again. Mother said, "Should we hide you? The war will soon be over." I said, "Mom, who guarantees that the war will soon be over?" She said, "Surely you can see that. They are telling us where the British are. They already took Lüneburg, so it can't be long now. They have already been shooting across the Elbe."[3] "No," I said, "that'd be too dangerous for me." She said, "We have ruins all around. We can hide you."

We might have succeeded, but if they had caught me, they would have hanged Mother immediately. I could not take that risk. "No, Mom," I said, "even if the war is nearly at an end, I still must put in an appearance in Oldenburg. That's in the area where the English are heading, anyway. If I'm captured by them I'll be all right. Therefore, I do not need to worry about it." The war lasted four more weeks, and to hide and supply me with food for four weeks would not have been easy. The patrols in Hamburg looked around all over in the ruins, because they knew that many deserters were there.[4]

Finally Mother said, "Come, I will go with you to the train station." We had to go on foot, because no trams went to the main train station. I had only a little suitcase and did not need anything more. When we arrived the train was already there. As I went to say good-bye to Mom, the sirens began to howl: air-raid alarm. Then I said, "Well, Mother, let's go quickly, it's about time for things to start happening."

"No, take your time," she said, "Most of the bombs have already fallen when the sirens start. They wait until the last moment."[5]

We went up the stairs again and out of the main train station. Around the corner in the theater was an underground bunker, deep underground. We went in with the crowd of people gathered there, so I had a chance to be with my mother for another four or five hours. The air-raid alarm lasted a long time until the all clear sounded, and we sat and were able to chat nicely.

About nine or ten I finally departed and arrived late. The soldiers were waiting for me at the station, but they knew there had been an air-raid alarm in Hamburg and that I had not simply gone AWOL. In Oldenburg I was taken to the Adolf Hitler caserne, which was approximately two or three kilometers outside the city. I was given quarters and I had a quiet minute. I ate and waited. They said, "You will have work to do soon enough, for now take a rest."

There was no shortage of provisions. It was already late in the war, but the procurement process, as far as provisions were concerned, always seemed to go smoothly for the army. You would not get fat on what there was to eat, but nobody needed to be hungry either.[6] We had to help in the kitchen, unloading bread and such. Once in a while we made some bread disappear, because we were specialists in stealing food.

In front of the caserne in Oldenburg was a slit trench in a zigzag shape. When you were hiding in the trench and a bomb fell, you were protected by the zigzag, so that you were not hit by fragments. One day there was an air-raid alarm. We had already heard the sirens wailing in the city. In the caserne they had the hand apparatuses, alarms with hand cranks. When they sounded we were all required to get into the slit trench, from where we could see the city.

We saw the bombers coming, which looked like small silver fish in the air. I said, "How many *are* there?" The entire sky was full of these glittering silver fish and the foil chaff they had dropped to confuse the radar sets. "Oh," someone said, "they are leaving Oldenburg in peace; they are flying on to Berlin or someplace." Then we saw the lead plane, the guide, which released its smoke bombs. It marked exactly where the bombs should be dropped.

It sounded as though someone had laid both arms on the keyboard of a mighty organ in a church. There was a terrible howl from the falling bombs. It was only a few seconds before we saw the mushrooms shoot up. Then everything was smoky and we could not see the city.

When all of the smoke had dispersed, the city was no longer there. Oldenburg was gone. That shocked me, because I had watched it with my own eyes. In Hamburg there were ruins everywhere, but here I actually watched it happen. It stunned me to watch the destruction of an entire city. I wondered how many blameless people were blown to bits there.[7]

One day we were told we needed to go to Bremen to get a train to Czechoslovakia. I was to be in the Fifth Army under General Schörner.[8] I asked someone: "How are we going to get to Bremen, on the train?" He said, "On the train? Here we travel on foot, my friend. It is only thirty kilometers. That is not bad."

We walked in a column under the trees bordering the road. The air buzzed with the American fighter bombers. They completely controlled the sky, so no one could risk running around in the open. They even machine-gunned the cows in the fields and appeared to be doing it with a vengeance.

Someone was always a lookout and shouted: "Air-raid alarm!" and we jumped into the ditch. Then the American fighter plane buzzed close to the tops of the trees, but the pilot did not see us. There of all places I thought again about how right Helmuth was. Where was the invincible German air force now? The Allies had complete air supremacy. Although the situation was deadly serious, I had to laugh. How ironic was the utterance of Hitler of 1933: "Give me ten years and you will not recognize Germany!"[9]

While we marched along there came a truck loaded with baggage. Refugees were riding on it, women and children. We said, "Are you nuts!? Don't you know that they will shoot you?" "Oh," one of them said, "we have lookouts on the front fenders and lookouts in the rear, too. When they see a plane, we stop quickly and run for cover and leave our things in the truck."[10]

The highway went straight for a ways and at the end made a bend and went into the forest. We could still see them until they went around the curve and were gone. We thought, "Let's hope they make it." Then we heard the drone of a motor and saw a plane peel off and dive. Then we heard the aircraft cannon firing. We said, "Let's hope they all got off the truck in time."

When we arrived there, none of them were alive and everything was shot to pieces. The plane came so quickly from behind they absolutely could not get away; it was already firing at them when they saw it. The suitcases were torn open from the bullets and were lying tattered and shot to bits. There were approximately eight women and children. We thought to ourselves, "Man, there was no reason for them to have taken that risk; they could still be alive."

We went on and eventually arrived in Bremen.[11] The thirty kilometers had required the entire day. When we arrived, an air-raid alarm sounded. Our commander told us: "Don't worry about it, just keep going to the train station." The train station was outside of Bremen. We continued marching during the air-raid alarm, past the ruins and could see that Bremen was totally destroyed.[12]

When we got onto the train, the locomotive had steam up and it departed. It was already a little dark and you couldn't see much. We went through to Königgrätz in Czechoslovakia during the night.[13] Eventually the train halted between stations along the route. Everyone had to get out and march away with our little suitcases in three files, although we didn't actually march in step. We had to walk briskly for nearly an hour before we arrived at the caserne in the neighborhood of Königgrätz.

There were approximately 350 to 400 new recruits and a couple of old soldiers with us. We still had no uniforms or any other military equipment. In the following days we received an ill-fitting uniform and heard a long speech by the propaganda officer. In the meantime we played soccer with the Czech youths. Our company commander, a captain, a NSCO (National Socialist Commanding Officer), noticed in my papers that I had been a political prisoner. Somehow he did not like me and called me on the carpet, but he could not get to me; I was too calloused. I only said to him what I wanted to say; he could ask as much as he wanted. From that time on he began to nag me, always assigning me extra things like pulling night guard duty. They strapped an Italian rapid fire pistol on me, and I had to stand guard in the caserne, marching up and down for two hours. I did not like that a bit, because I knew how the Czechs felt about us. They would have liked to have cut all of our throats.

The following day we learned to salute and I did not salute smartly enough. The captain dismissed all the others and I still had to drill alone for hours. He sat on a tree stump and I had to march back and forth, ten steps from him, stop, stand at attention and such, and it was never correct. I became angry, but I had to keep my mouth shut. He wanted to let me have a little extra.

One day we were told, "Your weapons are coming and then things will start happening." But the weapons did not come, thank heavens. One night there was a terrible ruckus in the caserne. With the alarm, everyone got up and packed things, thinking it was starting. "To the west." "What do you mean west?" "The Russians have broken through; the front has collapsed." We were only thirty to forty kilometers away, so we set out marching in a westerly direction toward Tabor.

In the meantime the Czechs rebelled and openly displayed their resistance, so the Germans brought in Czech hostages as protection, all of which made for an exciting time. I thought it was bad in the camps, but this was even more terrible. The Czechs stood around and grinned and gloated, because they knew very well that the Germans were turning tail.

As we marched along, suddenly we heard: "Stop!" Three American tanks were parked on the bridge ahead of us. All of the officers went to the battalion commander. "Should we attempt to break through or should we capitulate?" They had weapons and we did not. Half were in favor of fighting, half were in favor of surrendering. We could not have succeeded by fighting, so the Germans lowered their flag.

We were taken captive and the Americans put us all in a compound. What few weapons there were, some old German assault carbines, were handed over, and the Czechs collected them. The Czechs then came out of their houses, all carrying German rifles. We thought it was over with us. It was by this time the seventh or eighth of May and we knew the war would be ending soon anyway.

The Americans gathered up a few technically qualified men and departed, leaving us alone in the compound, wondering what would happen next. Soon we heard the rumble of tanks again. This time it was the Russians, because the Americans had agreed to let the Russians take this part of Europe.[14]

Though we were not particularly happy to be prisoners of the Russians, rather than the Americans, everyone, including the old soldiers who already had five years of war behind them, were relieved that there had been no fighting. They would have shot us to pieces, bumped us off like flies.[15]

The Russians said, "Now you are going home, but first you are going to a large assembly camp. There you will be sorted out, and then you'll be going home." We believed it, too, naive as we were.[16] The Russian soldiers with whom we became acquainted were good fellows. They gave us cigarettes and wine and said, "Ah, comrade, Hitler kaput." They were all happy that the crappy war was at an end. Before we marched into the assembly camp, some of our officers shot themselves, because they did not want to be prisoners-of-war.

The month of May 1945 was an extraordinarily hot, dry, and dusty month. There were approximately 6,000 to 8,000 soldiers guarded by twenty or thirty Russian guard details for the long column. We were thirsty, but in each town the Czechs stood in front of their houses and threatened us with their fists and swore at us like troopers. Their hatred was terrible. Most of them had handguns, all German pistols, and some rifles. They were celebrating the victory and their liberation by the Red Army.

For myself I could understand very well the hatred of the Czechs toward the Germans, after such a long occupation by the SS and Gestapo and all of the atrocities in the concentration camps and the obliteration of Lidice.[17] I know the redeeming feeling of liberation, because I was also a victim of the Nazis.

The Russians did not trouble themselves much about this. They permitted the Czechs to do what they wanted with the Germans, which included not giving the German soldiers anything to drink. On the third day of our march to the assembly camp—we were still approximately twenty-five kilometers away from it—some of our comrades became very sick. A sergeant from the artillery collapsed, apparently with sunstroke. Some wanted to leave him there: "Lay him under a tree and he will come to again." "But the Czechs will cut his throat." Two men remained there with him.

I tried once more to obtain water, but did not get a drop and was told that "German criminals all deserve to die!" We were chased from a farmyard by kicks and by a large dog. Suddenly two Russian guards appeared. One was a second lieutenant and, to our great astonishment, spoke fluent German. He said, "What is going on here?" We explained to him that we had gone to the farmstead to get water for the man who had sunstroke and was delirious, but the Czechs wouldn't give our sick comrade any water.

Then the Russians and another soldier and I went back to the farm. All of the Czechs spoke Russian. The Russian officer conversed with the Czechs about giving us some water. "Not for the German swine." "We are getting water," the Russians said. "Not for the Germans." The farmer swore at the Russians, because they would simply not let the damned Germans die, and made a terrible scene. Slowly but surely, the Russian lost patience, then all of a sudden he hauled off and slugged the farmer two or three times as hard as he could in the face and nearly knocked his block off.

The farmer had a dog, a regular large German shepherd, that bared its teeth and wanted to attack the Russian, but the other Russian killed the dog and held the rest of the Czech family at bay with his submachine gun. The Russian said again, "We are getting water." Then the Czechs brought water.

The Russian went with us into a stable, took a horse and a harness and hooked it to a wagon. All of the sick and a few old soldiers were loaded on, and we went off to Tabor where the large assembly camp was.[18] The farmer had not only earned himself a broken nose and enormous headaches for the next few days from his smack in the chops, he had had his dog killed and was out a horse and wagon. Through their persistent action the two Russian soldiers certainly saved the lives of a few German soldiers that day. One man's loss is another man's gain.

In the meantime something unusual also happened to me. We had to get away from the street, because a Russian tank was passing. It was rushing toward Prague and the tank crew was roaring drunk. It was a miracle they didn't run over anyone. They shouted, "Hey, comrades, Hitler kaput!" and threw bottles of wine and cigarettes down to us. Suddenly the tank stopped so quickly I thought they would all fall off. An officer jumped down and beat up a fellow very close to me and then shot him to death with a submachine gun, shot him full of holes. Afterward we discovered that the victim was a Russian who had fought on the German side. How the Russian officer knew that, I do not know; presumably he recognized him.[19]

Once an SS column came down the road at top speed. They tried to break out, because they were afraid that the Russians and the Czechs would kill them if they were captured.[20] Therefore, they tore along as fast as they could drive, shooting like crazy in all directions. We heard them coming and threw ourselves into the ditch for cover. An awful gunfight broke out, which, of course, lasted only a couple of minutes. When it was over, the bodies of the SS men were lying all over the place and the Czechs were ransacking the pockets of the dead. I was really terrified.

At last we came to a large German motor pool where there were hundreds of German trucks of all types, Horch, Büssing and Mercedes, all covered with tarpaulins. Suddenly I felt a rifle barrel stuck in my back. "Come on, comrade." The Russian soldier, one with a hat tilted on his head, took me to a large army truck. I was afraid and thought, "Now it is my turn. What have I done? I have never even fired a rifle." The Russian just grinned. "It is fun for him," I thought. He continued to push me further, and then he said, "Stop."

It was a large van with a tarpaulin on top. "Get in." No one would ever find me inside. But a surprise awaited me! The entire truck was full of salami sausages. The large ones were white. He indicated I should take as many as I could carry, so I filled my arms with about twelve huge sausages.

I covered the sausages with a blanket so that no one could see, tied it up and carried it over my back. They thought it was my bed roll or such. That saved the lives of me and a few comrades, because in Tabor we did not get much of anything to eat. There were nearly 30,000 soldiers to feed there.[21]

We camped in an open field where there was nothing else on the site. If the weather had been foul, we all would have perished, but it was hot and dry.[22] The camp was not encircled with barbed wire. If someone wanted to walk away, theoretically he could, but the Russians had guards every ten meters who fired their guns horizontally over us as we lay on the ground. What a racket! You could not raise your head when the tracer bullets whistled over.

We asked, "Do we get any bread or such now?" The bakers had joined forces and refused to bake bread for us Germans. "Not for the Germans, not a piece." The Russians said, "We'll give you one more chance." Still the bakers said, "No! We don't bake for the German swine."

The Russians said, "Okay, karascho, bake no bread." Then they arrested all of the bakers in the city and stuck them in jail. The entire city did not get any bread. After two days they were baking.[23] The Czechs baked a round bread that weighed, perhaps, three pounds, but that was for forty men.[24] Everyone received a thin slice, but that was better than nothing. My sausage helped out.

We dug a latrine, but after a week or so all of the water in the area began to taste like shit, because it was all polluted.

The Russians divided us into work detachments and we had to remove munitions.[25] The Germans had left live ammunition such as 88 and 105mm artillery shells lying around everywhere, which was, of course, very dangerous for the population. We had to carry all of that to a large pit, where it was detonated.

Once I had to work with a detachment whose specialty was the stealing of sewing machines. One Russian loved sewing machines, particularly the German brands such as Pfaff. He took us from house to house and, when we found a good one, we "liberated" it and carried it out to his truck. Unworthy machines we had to throw out the window into the street.

One other Russian loved discipline. His detachments were told to march and sing German military songs. The Czechs hated that, but he quietly held out his pistol and laughed the entire time while we marched and sang. One time a Russian ordered some Germans to beat up a few Czech teenagers who always loitered around, because they had pelted us with stones. The Germans beat them up, while the Russians held their pistols on them. The war was over, so the Russians were euphoric and they fooled around.

At first, the Russians and Czechs appeared to celebrate the victory together, but after a few days the mood was very different. The Russians seemed to take everything that they wanted: women, animals, and food. The Czechs gradually recognized that they had driven out the devil with Beelzebub. They began to tell us how greatly they hated the Russians. One of our Czech guards came to work with a sad face, because four or five Russians had raped his wife. "I guard you and they rape my wife! As far as I'm concerned, you can all go home right now."

Every day the Russians said, "Tomorrow you are going home." Then a Russian delousing crew came and we all had to go through delousing and our clothing was put into large delousing ovens. We were told: "Now you are going home." We also went to the barber and he cut off all of our hair.[26] Some were concerned with their looks: "Going home? With a bald head?" Still, I doubted it. Why would they go to the trouble of delousing us, just to let us go?

Soon we were distributed onto railroad cars. In the railroad cars the doors were bolted shut and you could hardly peek out.[27] We had no idea where the train was going. We believed we were going home until after about a night's travel, or a little longer, when we peeked out and saw the skyline of a large city on the horizon. When we came closer we saw a sign reading "Vienna." "Ha, ha, going home? Like hell we're going home."[28]

From Vienna we went to Hungary, and from Hungary to Rumania.[29] Yes, going home, dream on! During the entire trip there was not much to eat, at most only dry bread and water and some salted fish.[30]

It was hot in the train cars because there were no windows and the doors were shut tightly. There were two boards nailed together in a V shape and fastened to the door as a kind of crude urinal, a pee trough, we called it, and you had to piss into that.[31] There were a lot of men in a railroad car, but there was room to lie down. We were all thirsty. After a day's travel we did not receive much water, only just enough so that we did not die of thirst. The Russians sold us water in exchange for rings and watches when the train stopped and two men from every car got out and fetched water.[32]

Many men complained about this treatment, but I had heard that the Germans had transported Russian prisoners in open railroad cars in the middle of the winter, so I was less worried about our situation. Although I was a prisoner again, which I really for all the world did not want, at least I was happy that I did not need to be beaten and mishandled by the SS and the Gestapo. My captivity under the Nazis had hardened me, and I could endure the bad conditions without eating better than most of the others, so I kept my mouth shut and let the others complain.[33]

We traveled for what seemed an eternity! We stopped often while troop trains rolled past. It was three or four weeks, with a two-day stop in Rumania, where we waited for another train.[34] I remember that everywhere in Rumania it smelled like garlic.

One day the train stopped and two men from each car were allowed to get water. I was sitting by the door and simply fell out of the car, and suddenly I was standing by an enormous, unbelievably large river. It was the Volga. The water there was dirty, but that did not matter to me. I was so thirsty that I simply fell into the river and began to drink. Of course, I held my head deep under the water, because on the top there was a film of oil. I tanked up like never before and made up for the whole trip. Then I felt my stomach begin to rumble and grumble. I thought, "Now I am going to get diarrhea!" Because we were so thirsty we simply had to drink it, but we were lucky that our stomachs accepted the dirty water.[35]

This was one very large country! We traveled slowly, too, and stopped repeatedly to be checked by troops. Then we came to the steppes, where the train halted again and everyone got out. We had arrived, half-dead, at our destination. There were green rolling hills and nothing except the steppes, carpeted in wormwood plants and absinthe as far as the eye could see. "Where is the camp?" "You will soon build it," we were told.

We marched off and after one or two kilometers we saw four watch towers with barbed wire strung between them. Otherwise there was nothing else except weeds a meter high and a pile of building material that had been sent there before our arrival. We were supposed to build the barracks, if we wanted to live warm and dry, so we started working.[36]

Suddenly, forty or fifty civilians appeared, nearly all women, all of whom spoke German, that is, they spoke Swabian.[37] We were astonished to see them and had absolutely no idea where they came from until we learned that they were Volga Germans.[38] They lived in the nearest village, Bochvisnievo.[39] They all had dugout houses covered with dirt, where one wall, the south wall, had a window and a door. A stove pipe extended out of the mound. You went down a few steps on a plank, from where you then went into the clean, comfortable rooms.[40]

Most of the men were gone, taken into the Red Army and killed or missing, so I began to understand why we were brought to Russia. Our work was supposed to be in place of the work of the dead. We, who had destroyed Mother Russia, were obliged to help rebuild it.

Our camp commander said we would get three days off if we had the camp completed in two weeks. We built like crazy and made the deadline, but did not get any holidays. We built the foundation out of concrete and then made blocks out of concrete and used them to build. In our group of approximately 3,000 men we had carpenters, masons, and plumbers who did the job right.

The barracks were of wood and were prefabricated Ley houses, the ones named after Robert Ley. Inside to the left and right were double bunks made of planks and in the middle there was a stove. In one end there was a small dayroom with a bench and a wooden table. There were windows of double pane glass only in the day room; in the bunk areas there were no windows. The roof was a type of glazed tile and was insulated, because the weather was so cold. In the barrack a naked light bulb hung. That was all. Approximately 120 men lived in one barrack.

There was another kind of barrack, one with what we called a thunder beam. Actually, there were two thunder beams and in the middle was a shit pit. On each side there were about twelve seats separated by boards.[41] There was a crap commando that hauled the stuff out with buckets.[42] I never did that. For this commando they used those who had run away or had stolen, or such. Outside the wire we built barracks for the camp commander and for the officers. We also had a kitchen. In front of the complex there were rough-hewn benches which we sat on in the summer. In the summer we almost never went inside because it was so hot.

We built the barracks in the allotted time, because they had terrified us by telling us that the winter comes at the end of September, and "if you are not done by then, you will freeze your ass off." A Russian, our translator, said "I will leave it up to you whether you want to freeze your balls off or sit under a roof," so we set to work with a will.

The camp commandant was very friendly at first and we thought, "Not a bad commandant." But that was merely at first, because later he really screwed us royally. The saying arose among the prisoners that "What a Russian promises, he keeps (for himself)."[43]

The barbed wire fence was approximately four meters high, but it was not electrified. Inside the large fence was a lower fence and in between was no man's land. A light bulb that burned day and night hung over the main gate. There was a loud speaker that summoned us to roll call.[44] It was, in a word, a typical labor camp.[45]

In the middle of the camp was the food storehouse, where the Russians kept the provisions and delivered them to the kitchen. Our cook, a small, fat fellow, had been a chef by profession, and he, of course, wanted to cook good meals, but that was not possible. Our baker baked us good bread once, which the Russians then stopped immediately. There was no firm bread; the dough was watery. From the normal dough the baker had to bake three times as much. Water was added and the bread became slimy or gooey. There was everything imaginable in the bread: weeds, black and green seeds, and all possible odds and ends.

During the first days the meals were not bad. We received a good soup and so on, but that all ended. Afterwards the food got progressively worse.[46] When the cook got down to only fifteen kilograms of peas for five hundred men, we said, "Here we have radio soup. We'll be right back." We hung small signs on the doors: "If you find any peas in the soup, they are to be turned in to the kitchen."[47]

Per day we each had five hundred grams of bread, but that was the gooey kind, so that was not much.[48] It was so slimy that we said you could throw it at the wall and it would stick. Of course, no one ever tried it. In the morning there was a kind of coffee, a buttocks brew. There was a little bit of kascha, which was millet cooked thick.[49] The Russians put sunflower oil on it. We would have liked to have more of it,[50] but, of course, we did not get much.[51]

The Russians simply left their potatoes outside and they froze hard and black and looked like briquettes. We carried them in with a shovel, put them into a large bucket of cold water and thawed them. It needed to be cold water to take out the frost. We did that a couple of times and then they went into the soup, if you could call it that. They were not peeled, because they could not be peeled. They were merely black objects in the soup. This was cooked for a while and then fish heads were added. What slop! Not even a pig would have eaten it, but we gobbled it down, because we were hungry.[52] Not knowing what it was, we said it was undefinable soup. Yet if we had had more, we would have been happy.[53]

Gradually, we all started to starve. Many starved to death, died from edema, for example, from water accumulation caused by hunger.[54] Every two months or so we were required to strip and run around naked before a commission of physicians. They looked at our buttocks.[55] If there was still flesh there, you were still ok. If you were too thin, you were incapable of work and would be, perhaps, permitted to go home. When I was released, I weighed about forty-nine kilograms,[56] although I am 1.87 meters tall.[57]

Fall started overnight at the end of September. We woke up one morning and everything was gray. Everything, the trees and such, were covered with hoarfrost. It rained a little for a few days and became windy and cold, the leaves fell from the trees, and almost overnight it became winter. It began in October and went until May. Never in my life have I seen so much snow. It was up to two meters deep with drifts everywhere from three to four meters high. In places they were much higher.

It was also bitterly cold. The trees froze and split right through with a loud crack. Forty-five degrees below zero was quite common. The Volga was frozen over until May. Every Sunday in the winter we had to shovel the snowdrifts away for the blue express, the Siberian express from Moscow.[58] It came once a week, but other trains, freight trains, came as well. The railroad needed to be passable. The snowdrifts out there were up to ten meters high, so we had to dig a tunnel so the trains could get through again. We always carried the snow out of the tunnel as we excavated. That was hard work. Some men needed to go up on top and cut away the tops of the drifts so that everything did not cave in.

As soon as we were finished building the barracks, we went out into nature and shoveled trenches for the oil pipeline. The "tool" that we received was unbelievable. When you really dug into the ground and had a shovelful of dirt, the shovel bent backwards. You could not work with it.

It was typically Russian that there was no rest and that we needed to fulfill a quota. In Russia you always had to fulfill your quota 100 percent, then you received a large piece of bread.[59] The rations of those who accomplished less went down from there.[60]

At first, we Germans were suckers. The Russians gave us a quota, which we accomplished easily. Then what did we Germans do, we idiots? We did twice as much. In that case they raised the quota. That was still no problem for us. Once again we did more; once again they raised the quota. In time it was raised so high that no one could accomplish the quota.[61] We Germans are a very strange race; sometimes we are efficient to a fault.

Bochvisnievo was in an oil- and gas-producing region. We needed to dig trenches for gas pipelines and build pumping facilities. There was so much petroleum in the area that it always stunk and everything smelled like raw eggs. Even the water tasted like oil until we became accustomed to it. Petroleum and natural gas simply oozed out of the ground everywhere.

Our plumbers drove pipes into the ground until they hit gas. The gas flowed through pipes into the barracks so that each barrack had gas. The gas hissing out the end of the pipe in the middle of the barrack was simply ignited and allowed to burn in the open air of the room.

In the winter, as long as we could, we also had to lay pipes. We picked and hacked, and when you filled a bucket with dirt in a day, you were lucky, because frozen loam is as hard as steel. The Germans with their ingenuity developed a system. We had a chisel made, a suitably strong one and hammered it into the ground at the end of a trench. When it had penetrated a little, we pried off large chunks of frozen dirt. Our hammers were so large that you could only strike three times with one, then you were tired and your calories were completely expended, but we kept hacking away at the ground and gradually the trench got a little deeper and a little longer. When we were working down in the trench the wind did not blow so cold.[62]

One time we were surprised by a terrific snowstorm. The snow came horizontally and we could not see. On the way home we discovered that we were going in a circle. One's entire system was completely confused from the raging snow and wind. We were approximately sixteen kilometers away from the camp and had to go on foot. In the mornings the trucks took us out there, but in the evening they did not pick us up. "The SA is on the march," the Russians said, mimicking a Nazi cliché.[63] Eventually we encountered a farmer from the village, who allowed his horse to find its way home through the blizzard. He rode on his sleigh in his furs and we followed behind. The horse was smarter than the humans.

We worked also with civilians. Every day we were together with the Volga German women, who were paid for their labor. They were mostly women and young girls.[64] The men were not yet home from the army or were missing. Men were missing from every village. Russia had a lot of war dead. All together, with civilians, it was twenty million.[65] That was noticeable.

There were also the *zachluichonnies*, Russian civilians, who, for whatever reason, because of some offense ended up in a labor camp.[66] That was part of the Gulag system. Many soldiers were there, too, because every soldier who had been a prisoner of war in Germany was first reeducated for one or two years in a labor camp. Stalin held it against them that they had been captured. In Germany they had become acquainted with German culture, so it was felt they needed reeducation.[67]

They hated us. Because they had to pass through our camp, they were not disposed to talk to us, and we never worked together with them. They worked by themselves and did exactly the same work as we. They had guard towers, too, exactly like we did.

Everything was guarded in Russia. A Russian said to me once, after I had asked him why there was a man with a rifle guarding every piece of lumber in the landscape: "If you steal in Russia, you do bad; if you do not steal, you do badly."[68] In Russia there was nothing except smuggling and stealing. I have never seen so much corruption anywhere as in Russia.[69] Of course, everything there was in confusion.[70] Hitler had not left one stone standing on another. Everything was blown to bits.[71] I was no stranger to the requisition system myself.

We still wore our uniforms the first winter, because there was no winter clothing. We had coats and jackets, but they were just thin summer uniforms, so we had a lot of frostbite. In January and Feb-

ruary it was unbelievably cold, but finally at the end of March a ship-
ment of winter clothing arrived, the cotton wadding jackets the Russians called *fafeika*, and cotton wadding pants filled with genuine cotton. We received also the *walenkis*, the felt boots, and the Russian
caps with flaps, *schappkas*, you could fold down over your ears, which
was nice and warm. We also received wool mittens and could survive in the cold.[72] Before we received that stuff, we looked like bums
and had small, wool gloves, which soon fell to pieces.

During the winter each man looked out for the other, "Your nose
is white here and there." Then we rubbed snow on it.[73] We hopped
around the whole day, skipping and jumping up and down. Once we
made a fire, but the guard stomped it out. He had a fire where his
sentry post stood. He had a long sheepskin on the ground and a fire
in front of him, but we were not permitted to have a fire, because
we were the Germans. We jumped around like poisoned monkeys just
to keep our blood in circulation.

Naturally there were many cases of frostbite, mostly of the fingers
and toes. The sad part was, when a man had frostbite, he might be
locked up, for the Russians said, "He did it intentionally. It is sabotage." That was the beastliness of the whole affair. They thought we
had gotten frostbite because we wanted to get out of work.[74]

The nights were always too short.[75] Because we ate so much soup,
we had to go outside four or five times during the night to piss.[76]
That deprived one of sleep, because you needed to go out into the
cold winter. Of course, no one went outside and ran to the latrine.
They merely went to the door and pissed on the ground right in front
of the barracks.[77] The next morning there were "fir trees," three- or
four-foot-high yellow fir trees. They had to be hacked down with a
pick and carried away and then everything was clean again. The next
night it occurred again. That was miserable.[78]

The first winter was so awful that many died from fatigue, mental
depression, and starvation. Yet I do not criticize the Russians whole-
sale; they had nothing themselves. I saw what they had to eat; they
received exactly the same food that we got.[79] When the food bucket
was brought out, the guard received his share. The Russians were
hungry, too. The only reason they were not as starved as we were
was that they did not need to work so hard.[80] They received also some
more cold cuts and bread, but the soup was the same. We all lost
weight rapidly there. When we arrived in May everyone was still nice
and fat, but we went downhill quickly.

There were absolutely no holidays in Russia. Some Sundays they
left us inside, but we had to work from Monday through Saturday.[81]
The Russians did not believe in Christmas, so we had no Christmas

holidays. We wanted to bring in a little Christmas tree once, but they took it out again and threw it away. The Russians tormented us mightily.

At this camp, the prisoners also worked at building an entire small oil city with a schoolhouse, an office building and apartments, and a pump station. Most of the workers did not live in the barracks, but in houses in the city, where later the oil workers and the civilians, the party functionaries, and so on were to live. There were also welders, who worked fabricating the oil tanks.

This city was built fifteen to twenty kilometers away from the camp. The Russians wanted the city to look nice. Because some of us were decorators, we worked making the most elegant decorative moldings and stuccowork on the ceilings, for example. The Russians encouraged us to do our best work: "Now, do a first-rate job." We made forms out of wood for all the decorative medallions and so forth, poured plaster in them, removed them when they had hardened, attached them to the ceilings, and painted them. We did a remarkable job.

There was also a very handsome school. I worked there as a hod carrier, bringing bricks and mortar to the bricklayers. In the winter we had to build a fire in a kind of metal stove within the sand pile, because the sand needed to make mortar was frozen solid. The masons laid this steaming hot mortar on a brick and let the brick plop onto the wall. They had to do it correctly, because the bricks froze in place immediately and could not be adjusted afterward.

At first the walls were only whitewashed with lime. They made paintbrushes out of bast, the fibers of tree bark, and then simply added water to the lime and it was applied with the brush. When you got some of this stuff on your fingers, it burned holes in your skin!

With regard to the cold, we were relatively well off. We had the fire and the hot sand. I talked with other prisoners who froze their rumps off. One of the other fringe benefits of having the fires for the sand was that we took the soot out of the stovepipes, mixed it with machine oil, and polished our boots with it, because it made our boots black and clean-looking.

When we bathed, we went to the sauna used by the civilians. There was a prisoner who thought he was quite a big shot, because he was in charge of issuing clean clothing in the sauna.[82] His name was Adolf Wegener, and he had a little game which we did not know about until later. He bored small holes in the wall between his issue room and the sauna so he could look directly in where the Russian women were bathing.

It was no small wonder that he was glad to work there the entire day, soaking up the heat and the scenery. Adolf spoke fluent Russian, because he was from East Prussia, somewhere near the Russian border. This horny toad got a Russian woman pregnant, and the Russians made him an honorary citizen. Whether or not he ever went home, I do not know, but when we left, he was sitting there with his wife and child. Everyone was happy about that. He had lived by the motto: "If it feels good, it must be right; every man for himself!"[83]

The bum always cheated us. This big shot said, "Everyone who still has gold rings, wedding rings, and so on, give them to me, so that the sentries do not take them away from you. I will keep a record of them." Road apples! He traded them all away and we never saw the bum again. He constantly got us into trouble with the Russians, with "Ivan."

One other big shot there, whom we called *natschalnik* (boss)—I no longer remember his name—also caused us grief. He was a slave driver who always made us work harder than necessary. He drove us for months and had the best brigade and always overfilled the quota 100 percent. Oh, he was wonderful!

He spoke fluent Russian, also. He said he was a German and at first the Russians gave him free hand to torment us, but they apparently were amazed that he spoke such a pure, fluent Russian. We later also thought he looked like an Ivan, with his broad face, but no one thought about it at the time. He should have kept his trap shut until we arrived back in Germany.

One day he was gone and there was no more shouting. No one, including the sentries, knew where he was. After three or four days everyone in the camp had to fall in. The commandant came, and an interpreter told us that the *natschalnik* had been shot that morning. He was a deserter, a Russian soldier, who had fled to the German army, fought on the side of the Germans, and been captured by his countrymen. He had a German paybook and had changed his name. If he had kept his mouth closed, everything would have been all right, but because of his zeal and his shouting and his excellent Russian, he had given himself away.

Only twelve men could fit in the civilian sauna, so an eternity passed before you were able to bathe. We were so lousy and bug-ridden and filthy[84] that we were revolting even to the Russians, so we were eventually allowed to build our own sauna in the camp complex. Everything was done voluntarily in the evenings. First we dug a hole, then lined it with plaster and stones and installed a hot water system. We heated water outside in a boiler and then we had as much hot water as we wanted! We also heated stones in the fire and then poured water on them to create steam. We also had round basins in the bathhouse, where the water lines formed a star, and you could wash yourself.[85] There was no longer any excuse for being filthy. The only problem was that when you came home from work in the evening it was pitch dark and you had no more energy left for bathing.

So we were lousy in spite of our new sauna and the lice infested our clothes. Our beds—straw sacks—were full of bedbugs.[86] We washed our shirts and hung them outside, and in ten minutes they were stiff from the cold. We let them hang outside the entire night, because of the lice. The next morning we fetched our shirts again and thawed them. As soon as they were thawed, the lice and the bedbugs were crawling again, too. The Russian lice and bedbugs are as tough as steel and survive anything.[87] It is no wonder that Adolf lost the war; even the Russian lice were invincible![88]

One day the camp commandant and Tanya, the Russian physician, came to me and said, "Tonight you must go to the train station, a German physician, *Nemjetski vratsch*, is coming here." I had to bring him to the camp. At midnight the train arrived at the officers' camp. It was a cold winter evening, but it was the most beautiful experience that I'd had. The stars looked as if one could pick them. The sky looked deep, the stars glittered heavenly, and the wolves howled in the forest. When you heard one, you thought they were in a certain direction, then you heard one howling from another direction.

We knew the train station well, because we always unloaded coal there from freight trains. We waited in a type of waiting room. Dr. Wille arrived alone. He could not go anywhere else; he had to get out. He reported with a snappy salute to the sentry, a sergeant, and greeted me also in his Schleswig-Holstein dialect. I replied: "Schleswig-Holstein, encircled by the sea . . ." (see p. 287). "Man," he said, "are you from Hamburg?" From that moment on we were friends.

When we were underway he asked how the camp was. I said, "Not very good, it is a filthy camp." "Now then," he said, "they are all filthy, the camps. Dear boy, I want to tell you something. All of the Russian camps are filthy, many men are sick and there's no medicine. We have good specialists, good surgeons, good orderlies, good physicians, but no medicine."[89]

He had been in the army and been captured. Because our camp needed a German physician to help the Russian physician, he was ordered there from an officers' camp. He had his quarters where his treatment room was. As an officer he received, also, somewhat better nourishment. He saw what miserable condition I was in. I often visited him in the evening and then he would give me something to eat. For the first time I got a little white bread. White bread, what is that? For us that was a foreign word. We did not have it anymore in our lexicon, but it still existed.[90]

We also played chess there. I played chess enthusiastically.[91] We also chatted about old times. He was older than I. I was about twenty-two; he was approximately in his late thirties. He was not married, but he was engaged and always talked about his fiancée. He also showed me a picture of her, a lovely woman. She had a lot of jewelry; she must have been rich. She wrote him regularly, also. He was a typical physician with the typical duelling scar on his cheek that was the badge of honor for German university students.[92] He was a fine fellow, Dr. Georg Wille.

I had boils on my butt, my back, and on my neck from the lousy provisions. If you only eat slop, your body breaks out in boils.[93] He needed to lance them, to make a crucial incision and drain the pus. He had nothing with which to numb the spot, so he said, "Young man, this will hurt, so bite your teeth together." After making a quick incision he squeezed it to take out the root or the core so it could heal. He put some petroleum jelly and a bandage over it and said, "If it heals, then it heals." My entire back is still scarred.[94]

Tanya worked together with Dr. Wille. She was a physician and a lieutenant. She was cute and tall with blond hair and blue eyes. She came from Siberia, and had lost all contact with her family during the war. She was fairly certain that her father and brother had been killed in action. In the camp I had not noticed her at all, I had my own worries. She stopped me once and said, "Comrade, *viegisida*, come here!" I said, "Yes, Lieutenant." I looked at her, "Man, a blond woman, what does she want?" She spoke a little German to me: "You travel with me to Kuybyshev, go for medicine." "Yes, when do we leave?" "In two hours. Do you need to pack anything?" I said, "I have nothing, I am ready." She said, "Get provisions." I got dry bread, *suchari*, a little cube sugar, and such. For three days we had only cold provisions.

The camp received allocated medicines, but we needed to go to the main storage depot, and that was approximately one thousand kilometers away. Two barrels full of two hundred liters of gasoline each were loaded onto the truck. There was a civilian as driver, she as an officer, and I as a prisoner. I sat in the back of the truck and we took off.

Before leaving the camp I needed to report to my German commandant. He said, "Take care, we will see you in about a week." When the truck was out of sight of the camp, the driver stopped and Tanya climbed in back. She said to me: "Now we speak an hour of German, you help me. We speak an hour of Russian, I help you."

She had been in Germany with the army, but did not speak much German, because no one could converse with her. The first question she put to me was: "Do you believe in God?" I thought, "Now, wait a minute, that is surely a trap, careful. What kind of a stupid question is that?" Everyone knows that a Russian officer does not believe in God. I said, "Yes, of course I believe in God." She said, "Me too." I nearly fell off the truck. I would have nearly called her a liar. I said, "I don't believe that! A Russian officer does not believe in God." No, she said, she believed in God. "Tell me about your God." I told her what I believe about my God, and she said, "Your God is exactly like my God."

So then I had to tell her about my home. She wanted to hear about my parents and if I had a girlfriend in Hamburg. I blushed and said, "No, I have no girlfriend." She did not want to believe that. We laughed about that. I told her a little about my political involvement, but she did not believe that completely, either; anyway I had that feeling. She said she had never met anyone who admitted being an active Nazi, all of them claimed to have resisted Hitler.[95] I noticed her skepticism and said, "No, we do not want to talk about it, because I have the feeling you doubt my story."

Then we spoke Russian and she helped me, told me what I needed to say. She immediately admonished me: "Do not use Russian profanity. Try to stay away from it. It is a detestable habit." It had become terrible in the camp. The Germans used profanity so often that the commandant threatened them with arrest.[96]

At night we slept outside. Tanya crawled under the truck, the driver slept in his cab, and I slept in the back of the truck. It was marvelous: the wolves howled, the sky was bright with stars, and the night air was warm. We fetched our medicine from the depot and went home again. We were gone approximately a week. We brought along a whole lot of medication, not all drugs, exactly; some Band-Aids and iodine and bandages and aspirin.[97] We even brought ether and surgical tools, such as scalpels. Dr. Wille was as happy as a child at Christmas.[98] "Man," he said, "marvelous." She asked him, "Are you satisfied with me?" He said, "I could hug you." The both of them worked together well, because she had class and he had class.

I went on such trips several times. Once we were traveling a different direction along a river and we went swimming. It was approximately five or six meters wide with clear, clean water. It was hot, and Tanya stopped and said, "Now, we swim." I said, "Yes, but with what? I have no bathing suit, only underpants." That was a thin, mesh pant. I said, "Well, then, I cannot go swimming." She said, "It does not matter." So I took off my uniform and we swam in our underwear.

When she came out of the water, you could see through her under-wear, but she thought nothing of it. I was embarrassed and always tried to look somewhere else.

While we swam, the Russian driver snored and slept with his feet hanging out the cab window. Because I needed to relieve myself, I thought I'd just swim across the river quickly, where there was a small stand of forest on the other side. I said I would be back soon. "Ok," she said. I swam across and walked in my underwear into the forest where I was attacked by mosquitoes that I swear were a centimeter long.[99] I thought they wanted to carry me away. I had to stop defecating and depart the area hastily. I ran to the river and jumped in. I said, "Ow, there are mosquitoes in there." "Yes, yes," she said, "that is dangerous."

Three or four days later I began to notice what she meant. I got a stiff neck and every part of me hurt; I had headaches and even my hair and finger joints were painful. "Yes," she said, "valine fever." I asked, "What can we do?" "Absolutely nothing. I will give you a few tablets, aspirin for the fever, but you must see it through." I asked, "Is it bad?" "No."

She did not want to tell me the truth, because in my starved con-dition it was not a good thing to have. I began to run a high fever. For days the woman came every day into the dispensary, the sick room. Every day she sat on the bed and saw that I received my bread. She even bought me milk out of her own money, brought it to me and said, "You must drink milk." This woman was sent to me from God.[100]

I was so weak I could scarcely stand on my legs. Tanya spoke with the commandant, and one morning a Russian came in a cart with a small, shaggy horse hitched in front. She said, "*Sievitze*, take a seat." She got in with me. "Where?" I asked. "*Kokoi.*" "Why, what is that?" "*Votschivo.*" After about four or five kilometers we came to a collec-tive farm, a kolkhoz, and I was allowed to sit in the sun the entire day. She brought me yogurt, sour milk, bread, and two or three cooked potatoes, then left again. In the evening she returned and picked me up again. She took me out there for three days. I gradual-ly gained strength. Then we traveled away again together to get med-ical supplies.

In the meantime we had a wonderful band in our camp. Kurt En-gels was there, a blond, curly haired, handsome man. I heard him sing for the first time. They announced: "We have Kurt Engels here, the hero of the Dresden opera." The master of ceremonies always ex-aggerated everything a little, but this time it was no exaggeration: "He comes from Yemen, and sings the flower aria from *Carmen*." We had a piano and a piano player, and Kurt Engels could sing. Tears came to my eyes as he sang the flower aria, and I will never forget it.

Up front the first three rows were reserved for the officers, for the camp commandant, and some guards. While I was there in the room, who should come in dressed in a totally elegant wine red evening dress and with her golden blond hair? Tanya. Everyone stared, and I did, too, because that was one beautiful woman. She went up front and looked around, and when she saw me she came back and sat down next to me. Oh, that was worse than running the gauntlet. There was a whistling and a hooting and a tumult that was not to be believed. They thought I was a big lover. I, of all persons, and a Russian physician. My face turned as red as her dress. She laughed and laughed. The Russian officers looked around, but that did not bother them. So we listened to the program together.

We also had a choir director who assembled a men's choir. I sang tenor with the men's choir, which was fun for me. We needed to audition, of course, and had to sing some Russian songs. We had sheet music and instruments. In the camp we worked voluntarily on Sunday to earn musical instruments. For an accordion the entire camp worked one Sunday. They even constructed a stage.

In a large camp there were all kinds of people. We had professional musicians, soloists, architects, every skill was represented, from the completely clever to the completely stupid. We had people who could not read and write and highly qualified men. In the choral society we sang a Schubert song, the *Schöne Müllerin*, that I found exquisite.[101]

We had such events once a month, perhaps. It was not very often, because, after all, practicing was strenuous. After each performance, if the kitchen had an extra portion of food left over, they would let us have some. An evening with music and singing, proper, good music gave one strength again, me, in any case. Inwardly I said, "Life is beautiful. I must persevere. I must go home again. I will not go to the dogs, giving up is out of the question."[102]

The Russians have a tradition of male choirs that always fascinated me. During the summer in Bochvisnievo, when we needed to go outside at night to piss, no matter how often we went out, we always heard singing. It was the Russians out there in the background, singing all the time, the entire night. I thought, "Don't they sleep at all, or what is going on here?" The Russians sang at every opportunity, whether they were harvesting or mowing hay. One started, and all of a sudden six, seven, eight, ten, twelve people began to sing parts.

We always sang vigorously when we marched out of the camp. We always sang our camp's national anthem, that went: "We bear our fate with patience, our teeth we firmly grit, for we elected Hitler, we're to blame for all this shit." Some of the sentries in the camp were adamant: "Sing!" The Russians loved it, just like in Czechoslovakia. During the salvage work we always had to march in step and sing.[103]

But everyone comes to a point where you just don't give a damn. You are at a low point and cannot continue. There is absolutely no hope.[104] We were lied to forwards and backwards. Every day we heard: "Soon you're going home." "Well, yes, next month." We were all starving and were too weak to cope.[105]

The music and the little trips with Tanya put me on my feet again. I was out of the crude milieu of the camp, but my relationship with Tanya was purely platonic, a clean, nice relationship. Tanya was a fine person and noble person.

One day a newspaper came from Berlin, I think in March 1946, and I read it and could not believe my eyes. There was an account of our case, of the Hübener group. I showed it to Tanya, and she said "Ahah!" I think she finally began to believe me. I went to our political officer with it, but that was like talking to a wooden wall. He said to me coldly, "If you were such a good antifascist like you say, why didn't you throw yourself from the train when you were drafted into the army?" I thought to myself, "You are really completely stupid, my friend. I will never do you a favor and throw myself from the train. Whoever heard of such a thing?" I never said another word about it.

In the camp some read the newspaper article and attacked me, not literally but with words. "Because of you swine we lost the war." Those were the inveterate Nazis. The Russians proposed to me that I should report to the antifascist committee. I said to myself, "You jerks, you treat me like dirt," so I wouldn't even consider it.

The Russians sent members of the antifascist committee to Moscow for schooling and later released them in Germany as archcommunists.[106] I did not do that, even though for four weeks of school there would have been four weeks of good provisions. I had had it up to the gills. I was so crapped on by the Nazis, I thought, "Well, how will the Communists be any different?" That was exactly the same pile of manure, there were just different flies on it.

7

Ḥorror and Ḥumanity along the Volga

Eventually we were transferred. One morning approximately forty trucks arrived and everyone got on, thirty men on each in three columns of ten. We were only told: "Transport, leaving tomorrow, transport." We hoped we would be going home.[1]

However, we were transported to another camp, Yablonka. It was an eleven-hour trip to Yablonka, a larger camp immediately adjacent to the Volga. Of course, we had stopped a few times so that we could urinate, but when we arrived our legs were asleep. When I tried to stand up I keeled over.

Yablonka was located on an elevation above the Volga, which meant we always had to go up and down the hill. My bad luck was that my barrack was at the top and the kitchen was at the bottom, so to get food was a hardship for me. One man always went for three others, carrying four mess kits. Every fourth day I had a turn. That was bearable, because it wasn't every day.

Our camp was a factory site. The factory building was converted into a barrack, a rather large hall, not well insulated. It was cold, because there were large windows in it. There were also steel trestles where the cranes ran, but, of course, they had been removed. The first day we settled in, unpacked, and the next day went to work down at the Volga.

There, for the first time in my life, I saw the famous great rafts of logs. These were enormous rafts made up of many smaller rafts. The little rafts were four to five meters long and five meters wide, and a large raft was approximately thirty smaller rafts linked together, nearly a kilometer long.

The Volga boatmen had built houses on them, where they lived. There was even a large fireplace on the raft. The helmsman steered with an enormously large rudder. The rafts were not towed by boats, but drifted with the current of the Volga from the northern forests all the way to the mouth of the river. It was a three-month journey for them.

They anchored at our camp, and we disassembled the rafts where they were run ashore and moored. The Volga boatmen stayed for a few days and then left on the train with their wives and children to go back north and repeat the process with other rafts.

Our camp was the site of a great sawmill, and our job was to take logs out of the raft and haul them to the mill. We called ourselves the Volga commando. My work was with the winches and the engines that powered them. Above the river on the hill stood the Maibach engines, large, twelve-cylinder motors from the German military. We laid down tree trunks next to each other to form a corduroy road or slide, then we tied six or seven logs together with cables and whistled for the detachment above us to start the winches.

Up above, on the hill, the logs were stacked up in an unbelievable mountain of wood. From there the logs were hauled into the mill, where other detachments took over.

Once I witnessed a terrible accident when the cable snapped under a load and whipped viciously back toward us, cutting one of my fellow prisoners in half. In a split second he was lying near me in two pieces. As he died, he looked astonished, as if he could not understand what had happened to him. What a terrible thing that was to witness.

I remember another tragedy that happened in Yablonka. We were carrying mortar and bricks for a project there and we used the hods called *nossilka* that looked like a stretcher or a sedan chair.[2] They had two grips at the front and two at the rear. I worked with a young prisoner who was a music student. On one occasion he was in front and I was at the back, but because I could not see well where I was going, I stumbled over some bricks. I said, "Let's change; I am always falling over my own feet." After we changed places, we had not gone three meters when he fell down. I thought he had stumbled, and turned around to say something to him like: "See, it's not so easy back there, is it?" when I saw blood spurting out of his neck. A Mongol sentry had shot him for some reason, had used him for target practice or whatever. We had not heard the report of the gun. Perhaps it was an accident that the gun went off.

Someone summoned Dr. Wille, but the student was dead. The Mongol stood there, grinned and said, "Comrade kaput!" The other sentries took the rifle away from him and dragged him away immediately. I assume he was simply transferred, and that was all.[3] This was, naturally, a great shock to all of us. No one worked for the rest of the day. No sentry could have made us go back to work that day; we just talked all the rest of the time.

Dr. Wille had come with us from the other camp. He was there until all of us had gone home. He was still in the camp and said good-bye to us one at a time as we were sent home. Malaria was still stuck in my bones for a long time. It was not the type from the tropics, but the type we called "terzerna." I became very tired and at the end could absolutely go no further. Dr. Wille said, "You're coming into the infirmary."[4]

After I had been there approximately two days, my door opened and he came in and said, "What do you want?" I said, "Nothing." He said, "But you called me." I said, "No, I did not." He said, "You certainly did call me." I said, "I did not." But he checked my pulse, which was racing, and seeing my condition was serious, he immediately gave me an injection of camphor, which, I assume, saved my life.

Later he said to me, "Do you know, my friend, your heart was very weak. We came within a hair of losing you." He looked after hundreds of patients. If he had not believed I was calling out to him as he passed my door, I cannot believe he would have had the time to look in on me.

I didn't have another relapse for a long time, but I was, in fact, still sick when I was released.[5] I didn't make a complete recovery until I returned to Hamburg. Each time I had a relapse I was down for exactly three days with chills and fever. Then I felt better for about four weeks before another bout came. I always knew when it was coming, because I felt exactly like you do when you get up first thing in the morning and want to stretch. When I needed to stretch, invariably the next day the attack came, and I was sick again for three days. I could not stay warm with five blankets.

At that time I also worked burying bodies. We loaded them on a truck and drove out into the steppe where they were buried. I was always a little sentimental about the matter[6] and buried them so that they faced west, toward home. I also made a small cross out of sticks and picked a few flowers when there were some. Otherwise I placed a bouquet of green boughs on the graves.[7] I noted the names, that is, I attempted to remember the names. Three weeks later I had already forgotten all of the names, of course, because there were too many, more than ten.[8] Other burial details did the same. It was just one of the camp jobs.

Whenever someone died, Dr. Wille performed an autopsy on the corpse, cutting it open from the larynx down and then sewing it up with a cross-stitch, so when we loaded it on the truck, there was no longer any support inside the body. He had taken the organs out and laid them back inside again, so that everything was wobbly. As we loaded one of them onto the truck he belched. I said, "Are you still alive?" Then I thought, "Well, what is the matter with me?" Of course, we had to laugh. We knew full well that he was dead. We buried them stark naked.

Each time someone died, a commission came from the nearest city and investigated the death. The Russians did not want to be accused of operating death camps. I am convinced there were camps in Russia where people died and no one paid any attention, but where we were, they wanted to know exactly what was going on.[9]

All this maudlin stuff did not bother me, because I already had been through so much. What disturbed and disappointed me was the fact that although I had evidence from the Berlin newspaper that I had resisted Nazism, even with my name listed right there in black and white, it was of no avail. I went to the political officer, but it was no use, they didn't send me home. They needed me as a worker. I sometimes think I should send the Russians a bill for over four years of labor, because I had not done anything to them. But, as they say, "caught together, hanged together."

In the autumn we were required to harvest potatoes, and the prisoners lived on the farms with the civilians. Another prisoner and I lived with a family and helped them harvest their potatoes. Winter came so early there, that the growing season was very short, so there was little time after the potatoes became ripe before the ground froze. We needed to work furiously for one or two weeks. The soil was beautiful and the harvests were good, but the Russians often forgot to dig out all of the potatoes. They merely wanted to fill their quota. We prisoners received permission to gather the rest of the potatoes, so we harvested quite a large pile of potatoes. When the Russians saw that we had a small mountain of potatoes, they came and took them away.

It was unbelievable what they could make out of potatoes. Some of the dishes were quite tasty, but we were thoroughly full of potatoes, and when you eat only potatoes, you also get the runs. I had diarrhea and dysentery and it was painful. I had the feeling I needed to crap again, and nothing more came, only the nausea, cramps, and a little blood. When I thought it was getting better, ten minutes later I needed to run to the latrine again. I became increasingly worse and could almost not walk anymore.

A Russian woman got wind of where my quarters were and told an old babushka about my plight.[10] I was taken to the old woman's house. When I got there she climbed up to the attic and retrieved a sort of pepper, a kind of red paprika. She had a pot of squash soup bubbling on the stove, and she put the pepper into the soup, just waved it through the pot a few times. Then she fetched her Bible, the Tatar Bible, because she was a Tatar,[11] not a Russian, opened it in her lap, and began to mutter some kind of Tatar prayer, at the same time rocking forward and backward as part of her prayer ritual. It sounded like we were somewhere in central Asia.

When she was done praying, she put the soup on a plate and said, "Eat." I ate one spoonful and thought it was going to burn out my throat. Man, it was steaming hot and spicy hot! It was so hot I could not eat it, but she insisted, and I had to eat it all. I thought my innards were scorched, because I felt the heat all the way down. It was just amazing that the next day the diarrhea and the cramps were gone, and I felt better.

When we were out in the countryside harvesting potatoes we had no other medical assistance. If someone had a ruptured appendix, he would simply die before the physician could come, so it was a blessing to have an old shaman like this Tatar woman to help out with her folk medicine.

One time, for example, one of the men got a bad infection from riding in the truck out into the countryside. In the trucks there were always two gasoline barrels, one on the left and one on the right. One of them leaked a little, and the wooden floor of the truck had absorbed some gasoline, with lead in it. One of our comrades sat there and got a sore on his rear. It looked ugly and grew worse every day. The first day it was red; the second day he had blisters as large as chicken eggs. Then they broke open and stank. Everything festered and it was sickening. The poor fellow could not walk or sit, he could only lie on his stomach. We hoped that his blisters would dry out, but they only became worse.

Another babushka heard about it. She took me along with her into the fields searching for a particular kind of wooden fence post. It had to be just the right kind, well rotted. She scooped out the rotten wood with an old spoon, took it with her, dried it on the stove, and made a powder out of it.

When she took the powder into the sick man's room, he said, "Throw that old Russian out of here, she does not need to see my ass." We teased him about that a lot: "Your ass is not as beautiful as you think." She trickled the powder onto his blisters in a rather thick layer. After two days they started to scab over, and were soon completely healed. I assume that a type of penicillin had formed in the moldy wood and she knew that it would combat infection. I learned to appreciate folk medicine, even the use of garlic, from these experiences.

The Russians all smelled like garlic thirty miles away against the wind. You might not see a Russian, but you could smell him. They stank like garlic and yet were the most healthy people. They had dazzling white teeth, yet when we brushed our teeth, they watched dumbfounded. They laughed themselves half to death when we gargled.[12]

With all their problems finding enough food to eat, at least the Russians did not gorge themselves to death. They could purchase bread and other things in a bazaar, which was a bit like a black market. They were permitted to keep small numbers of cows or chickens, though the state took almost all the milk, eggs, and butter. They also had small gardens behind the houses where they cultivated vegetables and makhorka.

Makhorka was a very strong kind of tobacco.[13] Once I smoked a large makhorka cigarette wrapped in newspaper.[14] It nearly knocked me down, so I gave it to the next person. That single cigarette knocked out ten men. Thereafter I stayed with the papyrossas which Tanya obtained for me. They were made of a milder Crimean tobacco.

In the spring the Russians gathered wild onions, berries and any other edibles that grew in the forest and on the steppe. Nothing is more beautiful than the steppe in the spring. Overnight it became a purple carpet which stretched miles in every direction. The meadow flowers bloomed for only a couple of days, and then the onions took over. Wherever you went you could smell wild onions.

The bread they baked was made of rye and various seeds; it had everything imaginable in it. The flour was not cleaned, as we knew it in the west, but had black weed seeds in it. The bread was slimy and not good, but the Russians lived healthy lives.

In the evenings, while we were with the farmers, they all gathered together and we had to go out so they could look us over. They wanted to look at the German prisoners of war because most had never seen a German. This region was far behind the front during the war. They apparently thought the German soldiers had horns, were devils, but we were just young men, exactly like their own sons. Thus the ice was broken immediately.

The people were very warm and friendly; there was no hatred among them. An old woman cried. I said, "Why are you crying?" She said, "Oh, young man, I just have to think about your mother, how greatly she misses you." That was a sign to me that the Russians are good people.[15] Of course you can never know where you stand with a Russian. One may come up and embrace you and cry with you and five minutes later he smacks you one in the kisser; such is the mentality. It seemed to me that the Russians could be exuberant one moment and downcast the next.

From the new camp I was also sent to fetch medications from a large central provisions warehouse. Our trips always took us four weeks and were beautiful journeys, because we were in no hurry. We drove cross-country through the steppe, where there was a track just worn enough so you could faintly see the ruts. Our driver actually navigated by the sun and the stars. When you ask a Russian what time it is, he looks into the sky and tells you the time, very accurately. At night they can look into the sky and tell you exactly where north, south, east, and west are.

The interpreter in our camp, Tamara, was a pure soul. She was an innocent, clean girl, something hard to imagine in that environment. She was a young woman about twenty years of age. She had learned to speak German quite well in school and was sent to the prisoner of war camp as an interpreter. Her parents lived in Kuybyshev.

Once we needed to fetch office supplies and Tanya told Tamara: "Take Karl, you can rely on him." We fetched the things from a building in Kuybyshev. I was taken to a police precinct, where I was locked in overnight. I needed to get out once to go to the toilet and nearly laughed myself to death. The toilet was a hole in the floor where you just squatted down and crapped. The Russians took every opportunity to tell us that the Germans had no culture, and when I saw that I could only marvel.[16]

Tamara also introduced me to her parents. Though I was a prisoner of war, I was invited to eat. I was uncomfortable, because I knew they did not have much themselves. This, after all, was shortly after the end of the war, and the Russian civilians had suffered also. There was nothing much to be had. Hitler had destroyed everything upon his retreat, but the Russians were still a lovely people, a good people.[17]

Another person I got to know well in the camp was Sascha. We helped him haul office material and provisions. Sascha was the commissary lieutenant. He had been wounded and was very proud of his injury. He had been shot by a German machine gun, and he showed us the bullet holes which ran like stitching down his entire leg, one right next to the other, but he did not hate the Germans. He couldn't stand Hungarians for some reason, but he tolerated the Germans, although they had shot him full of holes. We liked that bum, even though he was a big drinker. He always took us with him to fetch provisions with the truck.

Sometimes we traveled with the train. We had an empty railroad car, because a camp that size required a mountain of provisions. At the depot, in the main provision office, everything had to be accounted for precisely, but Sascha, nevertheless, cheated the provision office. He had quick fingers. When he was counting out the items we were to take, he counted: "one, two" and very quickly "two" again, and then "three, four, five, five." The clerk there could not count as fast. Sascha then signed for the supplies and we loaded them.

He sold the extra provisions on the black market and bought vodka. Then he really went on a bender. While he was gone we needed to guard the truck. There was another German there with us. He was in the Africa Corps for a while, and when Africa was over, there was still time for him to be sent to Russia. He was from the Black Forest, a Swabian. The two of us stood guard over the truck and our Sascha went boozing. He took off his Russian pistol and shoved it under the provision sacks, because he knew when he was drunk, he was prone to start blazing away. We knew where the pistol was and had to keep our eye on it for him.

One time he returned drunk, as usual, and a hospital orderly, who was coincidentally in the city, saw him completely snoggered and us guarding the truck. He returned to camp before us and reported that Lieutenant Sascha was completely plastered and we were sitting on the provisions.

Sascha also offered us a drink. He said, "Come, we drink vodka!" Then he tipped up a whole water glass full of vodka and drank it in one gulp. The Russians always took a bite of an onion and then chased it with a slug of vodka. He was as drunk as a thousand Russians, as we used to say. He embraced us and said in his broken German: "Good, good comrade." I thought, "Man, leave us in peace." He wanted to give us some vodka, too. I said, "No, I do not drink." "But you must drink now." I could not get away from him, so I pretended to take a drink. Then he liked me; now I was a real man. We really did not drink it, but tossed it on the ground. He was so plastered that he didn't notice it.

When we returned to the camp, there at the camp gate stood the camp commandant, the political officer, and Tamara, the interpreter. The truck stopped and we all had to get down. The lieutenant, as was his right, had everything unloaded from the truck, everything weighed and the papers examined, and nothing was missing. Sascha had snookered the central depot. They wanted to know where he obtained the liquor. He said, "Bought it." "You did not have enough money." Then they interrogated us.

The commandant asked the questions in Russian and Tamara inquired of us in German. While she was asking, Sascha said in German, "Don't say anything, comrade, don't speak," whereupon the commandant said, "Damn it!" I understood Russian and spoke it fairly well, but the commandant did not know that. The commandant asked, "What did he say?" She said, "Nothing of importance." I said, "I don't know where he got the liquor, perhaps he got acquainted with a friend." "Did he steal provisions?" "No." When the matter was cleared up, Sascha said to us Germans, "Good, comrades, you go, you say: one bread." We received bread as a reward, because we did not squeal on him.

That was uncomfortable for little Tamara, who was mortified by the whole matter. She was a good girl and was too honest and naive. The prisoners of war were crude and told vulgar jokes, but she absolutely did not get the point of their obscene jokes. She was a completely clean, delicate, black-haired young lady. She looked a little like a Tatar and could have been from the Caucasus.

One time we were sitting on the train and a Russian officer, also drunk, came in with his wife and child. When Russians pushed their hats way back on their heads, clear down to the nape of their necks, that meant they were plastered. We had our hair shorn and I was burned brown from the sun and spoke Russian,[18] so I looked like a Russian. I had been brought up to offer my seat to a woman, so I stood up and said to her, "Please be seated." She sat down and her husband looked at us fiercely. He stared at us and asked something in Russian, which I answered. Then he said, "Are you a German?" I said yes. All of a sudden he flew into a rage: "You are no German. You are Russian. You fought under Vlasov, the deserter."[19] I said, "No, I am a German, not a Russian." He grew increasingly angry and got out his pistol and wanted to kill me, to bump me off on the spot.

Our sentries came to the rescue and Tamara was soon there. She said that I was a German. He said, "No, look at him, Russian!" So, though I was saved this time, thereafter I was cautious. I never spoke to the officers again in Russian. I kept my trap shut.

It was also while we were on the train that I saw a person attempting to jump onto the moving train, fall under the train, and be cut in half. The train was not traveling fast, so he came running up alongside. He was apparently also drunk. In Russia there were many drunkards. After the train stopped, what fascinated me was that there was no blood. Presumably the wheels crushed the tissues and sealed off the vessels. They did not make a big fuss about it. Everyone got out, they covered him up, and the train went on.

We spent the night in the train compartment. We had to lie on the wooden beds that folded down out of the wall. The stench in there from the garlic, the farts, the unwashed feet, and the smelly bodies of the men and women, and everything else turned my tongue green. The entire cloud rose up to where I was and I longed for cold, fresh air.[20]

In the mornings we got out when the train stopped, and first we washed ourselves and breathed deeply.[21] Our eyes were swollen from the stench. When we ate, the Russians shared with us chunks of bread and onions, but there was no butter. Some had sugar, but otherwise it was just dry bread. They just kind of mouthed it and gnawed on it until they could swallow it, then washed it down with cold tea.[22]

The adolescents were fanatics. I always called them the Russian Hitler Youth, because they were part of a youth movement. They came in the mornings to the train station and you needed to be on your guard against them. Among some of the sentries, too, there were some totally fanatic slime balls; they hated the Germans, and with good reason.

At one of the train stations where we were waiting we encountered a fabulous balalaika player. In Russia if it does not come today, it will come tomorrow; there's always plenty of time. What can you do? You must wait. Everyone was sitting around on the floor waiting for the train. It was like a bivouac. A blind man with long white hair was sitting there. They treated him like an old patriarch. They gave him gifts of money, a few kopecks, makhorka tobacco, paper to roll cigarettes, bread and such. Finally he rummaged around in his pack and brought out a scratched, filthy balalaika, and began to play. I had never heard such beautiful music. Tears came to my eyes. It was unbelievable how he could draw such sounds from such a battered instrument. In an instant the entire encampment fell quiet and no one talked any more.

When I experienced such things among the Russians, it always gave me a good feeling and restored my faith in humanity. On these occasions I saw the good in mankind, in the Russians too. When I heard that music and saw the old blind man and how they treated him, I said to myself, the Russian people are good, as individuals they're wonderful.

From Yablonka our camp went temporarily to Ufa and Saratov, because our labor was needed there. In Saratov there were coal trains which needed to be unloaded. Underneath the hopper cars there was a trip lever which we pulled, and the coal spilled out. We shoveled it onto hods like the mortar hods and dumped it onto a huge pile nearby. We worked around the clock there. I worked the night shift. Although we did everything by hand and were very tired, a couple of thousand men can unload a lot of coal.

Then we unloaded flour and heavy machinery from Germany. The Russians disassembled entire factories in East Germany and shipped them to the Soviet Union.[23] We unloaded train cars full of precision tools, lathes, dynamos, motors, and all kinds of machines, and piled all of these machines outside in the weather, because there was no storage room for them. It was not long before they were completely ruined by the rain and snow.

When I returned to Yablonka again, I was soon so undernourished and weak I could hardly walk. The staff physician, Georg Wille, spoke with the political officer, who agreed that because I was so starved I should be given work in the camp bakery.[24]

The first day the bakers played a joke on me. The dough was kneaded by hand in a kneading trough approximately two meters long that was full of flour and water. When I entered, the bakers said, "Come over here. Are you hungry? Have you already eaten? Well, then eat first." Bread, oh man! I thought I was in heaven.[25] When I had eaten, they said, "Ok, come help now, scrub your fingers and arms and then dig into the dough here; knead." I stuck my arms into the dough and could not get them out again. I was so weak I could not move. They nearly laughed themselves to death. They said they understood how weak I was, and just had me help clean up for a while. After a couple of weeks of more food, I could knead just like them. I worked in well and became strong.[26]

They had a wooden vat there half filled with water, into which they tossed bread to let it ferment. We then drank the liquid with a ladle. It tasted like alcohol and was pungent like carbonated mineral water and really gave you gas. When one of us came near, the other men ran away because of our flatulence. Before the flatulence subsided a bit, you could not even stand yourself. We used to say: "Now that was a Boom Brand: one fart and nobody can stand."[27]

While I was working in the bakery I became acquainted with a young man named Helmut who had been in the Waffen-SS,[28] in the division that was known as Adolf Hitler's honorary body guard.[29] He was just a kid who'd been recruited because he was a big, strong Aryan-looking boy. When the Russians took Berlin, he was captured. To capture an elite SS man was a big deal for the Russians, and they interrogated him over and over. The poor fellow would not have harmed a fly. He was harmless, but he was often in the detention bunker located in the middle of the camp.

He was being interrogated one time and was sitting in his cell when I had the night shift. In the morning, when the labor details were out working, I went back to my barrack to sleep. My route went past the clink where he was being held, so I called out: "Are you still in there?" "Yes." So then I would toss half a loaf of bread through his window.

Once, however, unbeknownst to me, a political officer was interrogating him in his cell. A half loaf of bread went flying through the window again and practically landed in the officer's lap! That was the end of my career as a baker. They said I did not have the right to take bread with me.[30] I was discharged and had to return to the Volga to drag logs.[31]

When I left the bakery I was strong, because I had been stuffing myself and had filled out and was well nourished. Of course, the poor, starving soldiers in my work detail made comments, "Come here, you pig, you have eaten for three, now work for four." They teased me from morning until night. I said, "Keep your mouth shut, leave me alone." But they did not keep their traps shut.[32] One was particularly venomous, so I told him a couple of times he should keep his mouth shut. I gave him a shove and then clobbered him with my fist and probably hit him a little too hard. I had lost my patience and I should not have done that, but we were all riled up, which was understandable considering that we were always crammed together with the same people day and night.[33]

He fell down unconscious and it took about fifteen minutes until he came to again. Because I thought I had beaten him to death, I died a thousand deaths myself. I was in shambles until he finally came to again. With tears in my eyes I excused myself. Because I was still in good condition, I could afford to give him some of my food. We became the best of friends afterwards. He played the guitar wonderfully.

It's amazing how quickly the body deteriorates when you don't have enough to eat. It was not four weeks before I was just as emaciated as the others and was very shaky on my legs. When I woke up in the morning, I felt perfectly well, but after three hours it was over. I was so weak I could hardly walk or put one foot in front of the other. My legs were like two sticks with a ball in the middle. Sometimes we prisoners looked at ourselves and broke out laughing. I would have preferred to crawl into a corner and die like an animal.[34]

Because of malnutrition I became night-blind. As soon as twilight came, I couldn't see a thing, just large, red rings. Dr. Wille said, "Well, yes, it is not good, but not so bad, either. If it does not last too long, there will be no permanent damage. It is just a vitamin shortage."[35] Dr. Wille still had a little cod liver oil left, and in order to prove his theory, he gave me half a teaspoon full of it. I could see again at night immediately. That lasted for a week.

I knew that we were not receiving proper vitamins, because our camp commandant had reportedly sold some of our camp provisions on the black market and in their place served us stinging nettle.[36] Because stinging nettle was said to contain vitamins, we called him the vitamin king.[37]

In March or April we were again told, "Now you are going home." We had already heard that so often that we no longer believed it. We had to appear again before the commission.[38] With my decrepit body I had absolutely no rear end any more. If you still had buttocks, then you were okay, but I had no more buttocks, everything was gone. A group of prisoners to be released was assembled and I was part of it, but we still did not believe it.[39]

We had to go through the "Louse Control" again, putting our arms up, so the Russians could look carefully again to see if you had your blood group tattooed under your arm, if you, in other words, had been in the SS or not, or if you had a scar, which might mean you had removed the tattoo. Even at this late date, they still found some who had kept it hidden.[40] Then we had to pack our bags, line up, and we were told: "Off you go." We were excited, we trembled, hoping that nothing would go wrong. We could not believe it.[41] Outside were fourteen or fifteen trucks and we all got on the trucks and sat there in rows. There were approximately three hundred who were released at that time.

Georg Wille came and wished me well. As we marched out of the camp, Tanya was standing by the gate to shake hands with me one more time and say good-bye. She said she was happy that I was going home. I asked her, "Am I really going home?"[42] "Yes," and she said to me, "Karl, we will not see each other any more in this world. We will meet again in heaven." She shook my hand, embraced me, and then I climbed onto the truck. I regret that I was so sick and so excited that I didn't say anything meaningful to her; I could only mutter a short good-bye and say "Thanks."[43]

8

home and healing

The main highway was in the middle of the Volga, right on the river. The Volga was frozen over, although it was already April. After we were loaded onto the trucks we traveled over the ice to the nearest railroad. The ice cracked and creaked and there was a layer of water on top, but somehow we managed to make the trip.

We traveled some 80 to 100 kilometers to a larger train station where we were first dispersed to work in the city. We shoveled snow and cleaned up streets and sidewalks. Of course, we thought they had just deceived us again, but in the afternoon we were loaded into the trucks and taken to the train. We would have preferred to keep working to sitting in the train cars, because in the city we had been able to duck into the entry areas of apartment houses to get warm. It was still cold, because it's still winter in Russia in April. In the train cars we were given very little fuel for the stoves. We shivered the entire night and the next day, but we could certainly endure that, if we thought we were going home.

Late in the evening the train started and headed westward. After traveling for a week we arrived in Brest-Litovsk.[1] We had to go through the louse control again, raise our arms, and there again some were sorted out. You were scared to death each time; hopefully they would not grab you for some reason again, hopefully our journey would continue. We were placed in different railroad cars. This time the doors were nailed shut, because we were to travel through Poland and the Poles did not want German prisoners there. We could not look out, could see absolutely nothing, but it only took two days to cross Poland.

As we traveled the weather changed. In Germany it was already spring. We opened the doors of the cars and let our legs hang out. We traveled through West Prussia in the direction of Frankfurt on the

Oder river. I was completely shaken by what I experienced after we crossed into Germany. It was 1949, over four years after the war, yet during the entire trip there were women standing at the stations holding placards: "Do you know Günther so-and-so? Do you know Hans so-and-so?" None of them knew where their husbands or sons were. Another thing shocked me: These women had to beg bread from us, from POWs, late returnees as we were called.[2] We thought, "Good heavens, what's going on in Germany? Are things that bad here?"[3]

In Frankfurt on the Oder we received fifty marks discharge money, but the money remained in the camp. We could purchase three bread rolls, a quarter pound of sugar, and a beer, or whatever you wanted, and that added up to fifty marks. They used the same money there over and over.

I met a man from Hamburg in the camp in Frankfurt on the Oder and asked him to visit my parents, because he was traveling directly to Hamburg. I thought: "OK, he says he will but later he'll forget it." But he actually looked them up, went to see them, and told them I was in Germany. Of course my parents were very happy that I was finally back in Germany, safe and sound, after seven years of being away from home. After seven years, as we say in German: "Shit on a stick is also a kind of flag."

One night we stayed in Erfurt, which earlier was the flower city of Germany. From the train we needed to go to our quarters, an auditorium, on foot. We also received something to eat. They tried to entertain us there by presenting a small variety program.

In the railroad cars, which were filthy coal cars or such, I must have gotten a sliver in my arm, because I developed an infection in my left arm. It was all filled with pus where it had festered. I reported to the physician in Erfurt and he examined it. He said to me, "Young man, I am going to give you some advice. Try to hold on. Tomorrow you will be on the other side. See it through. If you stay here, heaven only knows when you will get back over there to West Germany." Those POWs who had their homes in East Germany were separated from us here. They went one way and we went another, toward the west. The physician was concerned that I could get put into a hospital in East Germany and be kept there forever.

My condition became increasingly worse. I had a fever from the infection in my arm and I feared blood poisoning, because the infection was so close to my heart! The doctor said I should hold the arm up the whole time, but it still took two more days until we were across the border. We traveled from Frankfurt via Erfurt and crossed the border near Helmstedt, not far from Göttingen. We had to cross the border on foot.

Our Russian guards went with us to the border, then they stopped, and we went through the no-man's land, approximately two hundred meters wide. There the former prisoners of war did something which made me ashamed. When they were across the no-man's land, on the British side, all of them turned around, dropped their pants, took out their penises and pissed toward the Russians, and then took their Russian caps and threw them back into the no-man's land. The Russians turned away in disgust. I didn't participate in this insult, but I was ashamed.

Once across the border a few of our comrades attacked people who had functioned in Russia as informers and thrashed them terribly. They had worked for the Russians and the others knew it.[4] They had harbored that animosity and thought to themselves, "Well, as soon as we are free, we will get revenge. If you work for the Russians you are a squealer, a traitor, but the day will come sooner or later when they will not be there to protect you."[5] The British did not appear to concern themselves and did not intervene.

When we arrived in the West, we had to file through corrugated sheet metal huts filled with pictures of prisoners. We all had to look at them, in the hope we might know some of them. Surprisingly, there were some there whom we recognized. "Yes, man, that is so and so, I saw him a few weeks ago. Yes, he is still alive," and so forth.

When we emerged from these huts, the Salvation Army and the English Red Cross had a large table loaded with cake and hot chocolate, and we got something to eat for the first time in a long while. I can still remember clearly being loaded onto a large stub-nosed British truck and being driven into Göttingen. I got very dizzy and weak and only remember getting down from the truck, when I must have fainted. When I came to again, I was in bed in the Göttingen university hospital.

They operated on me the next day, in the evening. After they placed me on the gurney and rolled me into the operating area, I still had to wait my turn. I peeked around and saw they were operating on someone's back. Although he was anaesthetized with ether, when they cut and pushed and pulled on him he moaned and groaned. I thought, "Oh, good heavens, they say, 'You feel nothing.' Oh, my." "Man," I said, "What am I getting myself into?"

Later I met the other fellow again. I said, "When you were being operated on, that must have been painful." Then he said, "I felt absolutely nothing." I said, "You groaned and made a fuss." "I did?" he said, "I felt nothing. Hmm, apparently it's just nerves."

They got everything ready and placed the mask over my mouth and nose and sprinkled drops of ether on it and told me to count backwards from 100: "99, 98, 97 . . ." I think I reached 93, then I was gone. They cleaned everything out, scraped out the inflammation. When I awoke again, I was in the recovery room.

When I awoke in a wonderfully beautiful white room, with clean white bed linen, where there were beautiful white gardenias, I suddenly heard children's voices singing. I thought I was dead and now this was heaven. But it was a choir of children from the Mormon congregation in Göttingen. Somehow, they had learned that I was there and had come to greet me. It struck me as uncanny that they were singing a song from our children's songbook whose text was very familiar to me:

> Oh, I had such a pretty dream, mama,
> Such pleasant and beautiful things;
> Of a dear little nest in the meadows of rest,
> Where the birdie her lullaby sings.

> A dear little stream full of lilies
> Crept over the green mossy stones,
> And just where I lay, its thin sparkling spray
> Sang sweetly in delicate tones.

> And as it flowed on toward the ocean
> Through shadows and pretty sunbeams,
> Each note grew more deep, and I soon fell asleep,
> And was off to the Island of Dreams.

> I saw there a beautiful angel,
> With crown all bespangled with dew.
> She touched me and spoke, and I quickly awoke,
> And found there, dear Mama, 'twas you.

I felt as if I had finally come home.

We were x-rayed from top to bottom, everything. The German, Swedish, English Red Cross was there and examined all of us, and from our troop, when we arrived, 30 percent had tuberculosis! I did not have it, thank heavens. My lungs were clear, but many others' X rays were shadowy, white.[6] Nevertheless, I still had malaria.

I thought, now that I was free, I would really eat a lot, but the physicians warned me about that, because in my weakened condition overeating could be fatal. They related to me a case of a discharged prisoner who received a lot of provisions because his parents lived in the country and had sent him ham, butter, and so forth. He gobbled all of it and died.[7] I received oatmeal gruel, a boiled egg, and mashed potatoes. Now and then I received a lean piece of veal. Just from this fare alone my physician feared I might gain weight too quickly. Each morning I had to be examined: blood pressure and heart rhythm before and after exercise, and so on.

I remained in Göttingen for eight weeks. In the meantime I had written to my parents. They wanted to come and visit me in Göttingen, but I talked them out of it, because they still had no money. I said, "That would cost too much money. Wait a few weeks, I will still be here. You can wait that long."

At that time my brother, Berthold, was getting married. He wrote me, "It would be wonderful if you could come to the wedding. I would like to have you as my witness." I had a fever, but I went to the physician and said, "Doctor, I must go to Hamburg." He said, "Like hell you must! You must remain in bed." I told him about my brother. "Under no condition," he said. "We cannot assume the responsibility." I said, "What if I go anyway?" "It's true," he said, "we cannot stop you, but you must sign a note stating that if something happens to you, we are not responsible for it." Then he asked me, "When will you come back for more treatment?" I said, "I'll be gone a couple of days at the most, because the marriage ceremony will not last long, and then I will be back." We scheduled when I would come back again.

The hospital paid my trip to Hamburg, but getting back was my affair. In the morning about four or so, my express train left for Hamburg. When I got on the train, people could see immediately where I was coming from. From my wooden shoes and the Russian clothes, they surely knew that I was a late returnee.[8] Women came up to me constantly with questions: "Ah, excuse me, did you just come from Russia." I said, "Yes, as a matter of fact, I did." "Do you know my husband by any chance? I have not heard anything from him for a long time." Oh, that was so heart breaking! It was continuous. Each woman asked about her fiancé, about her brother, about her husband, or about her son. It was terrible how many were still missing. I simply could not endure it any more. Finally, I found a place directly by the compartment door and wrapped myself in the window curtain there so that no one could see my clothes anymore.[9]

Our train finally crossed the Elbe. When I knew that I was home, I cried like a little boy. I remember it as though it was yesterday. I was in Hamburg at 10:11 in the morning. I knew the route I needed to take to get home. From the central train station I had to catch the 31 or the 16 line, so I waited until the streetcar came. However, I had no money. I said to the conductor, "I need to go to Bauerberg." Whereupon he said, "That'll be thirty cents." I said, "I have no money." He said, "Well, then, you must get out at the next station." That nearly created a revolution in the streetcar.

The longshoremen from the third shift, from the night shift, were on their way home in the morning. They nearly threw the conductor out of the tram. "Can't you see, you stupid sap, where this man is coming from? Can't you see that he is a late returnee from Russia?"[10] Simultaneously ten or twelve people wanted to pay for me. Now, the poor conductor had only been doing his duty. If the inspector had come along he would have been in trouble, but I was touched by the people's generosity.

My father said to me later that at the very time I must have been walking up our street, Mama grew very restless. She had been somewhat restless the entire morning. She had sensed my approach when I came home years before on my way to being inducted, and now she had the same kinds of premonitions again. She had been looking out the window the whole time. Dad said, "Mama, what is the matter with you? Now, sit down, you are driving me crazy." "I know," she said, "I don't know what is wrong with me, I am just restless."

My father gave me his weekly ticket to the streetcars and said, "Take the tram down to where your brother is working so he'll know you're home." He had a job in the Labor Exchange for actors at the new Pferdemarkt, in the Moeggebergstraße. I got freshened up and went to see my brother at his work. I went in and inquired where Mr. Berthold Schnibbe was. At that moment he was talking to an actor. He saw me coming and left the actor sitting, stood up, came up to me, and embraced me. It was a great joy and we made quite a joyful noise together.

He said to his division boss, "Look, my brother has just arrived from Russia!" The boss said, "Well then, go home, take a holiday. Call it a day." "Well," he said, "I just left someone waiting in my office there . . ." The boss said, "We will take care of it." My brother knocked off for the day and we went casually strolling through the city, chatted a little at first, talked about this and that.

The following day my brother got married. It was a church wedding, and the service plus the wedding celebration afterward were quite exhausting for me. All the wedding guests were friends, acquaintances, and relatives, who were delighted to see me and made quite a fuss. It was very taxing, but I held out to the end. I was miserable because I did not feel well in the least. I had a fever and was shaky on my legs. I was really just half a man. The doctor was right.

At that time I became acquainted with Jean Wunderlich and Walther Stover. Wunderlich was president of the West German mission for the Mormon Church and Stover was president of the East German mission, which at that time included Hamburg. Stover and I were the wedding witnesses. These men needed to return to Frankfurt am Main the following day. Wunderlich said, "We are going to Frankfurt. Isn't Göttingen in that direction? We will take you with us." He had his large DeSoto, which he'd shipped over from the U.S. At that time huge American cars were the seventh wonder of the world in Germany.

My parents had no money, but they had a lot of provisions and clothing, because the American Mormons had sent an enormous amount of relief supplies to postwar Germany. It was divided, with a third going to the Catholics, a third to the Lutherans, and a third to the Mormons. Otto Berndt, that efficient man, was the president of the branch and had rented an old air-raid shelter as a warehouse, and it was full to bursting with supplies.

Because I would be traveling by car to Göttingen, a gigantic suitcase full of cans of peaches and pears was packed for me, to be shared with those in the hospital, because even the physicians and the nurses there did not have enough to eat.

I had thrown away my old Russian clothes immediately! They were burned. They were such terrible things! The linen underpants needed to be tied on with a kind of strap on the bottom. From the treasure in the warehouse I was permitted to take with me an entire wardrobe consisting of two pairs of slacks, a business suit, several shirts, many socks and pairs of underwear, and a pair of shoes. It was not used stuff, but all first-class, brand-new American clothing. Overnight a shabby "Ivan" became a very stylish "Ami."

Wunderlich and I and his chauffeur, Hans Dahl, and a couple of others traveled in Wunderlich's large DeSoto to Göttingen. When we pulled up into the driveway of the hospital, which occurred exactly at noon, when all the patients happened to be lying around outside having their mid-day rest, they were astonished to see me arrive in such luxury. I gave the provisions to the physicians and the nurses, because they received little or no salary. Those were still hard times in Germany in 1949.

I still needed to remain some weeks in Göttingen. I still had several attacks of malaria, with the urge to stretch and with fever and chills. We were well taken care of in Göttingen. Every day we late returnees received tickets to the operettas. They played Lehar and Strauß and everything, wonderful stuff. We also received movie tickets. What always struck me as strange was that there was always a group of women and girls standing out in front of the hospital. They all wanted to get acquainted with someone. Most of the men were inside the hospital. Otherwise, there were no men.[11] They knew that the men had movie tickets and everything for free. The men were not opposed to the idea. They had been celibate for years. They were all as horny as sailor shit, as we used to say. Naturally there was a lot going on.[12]

I wrote my mother and told her when I would finally be released and be a completely free man. She was at the main train station and picked me up, because my father was working. It was the third of July, that's how long I needed to stay in the hospital. She was overjoyed, my dear mother. My parents and my grandfather Lütkemüller, who had gone back to Lüdelesen during the war, still lived in the prefabricated Ley hut on our parcel of land. My mother had gone over into East Germany and had smuggled her father back over the "green border," that is, through the forest.

Provisions were obtainable only on ration cards, but because my father sometimes worked two eight-hour shifts as a crane operator, and because I had been a prisoner of war, we could both receive "Ration Cards for the Most Heavy Laborers." These, together with the provisions and clothing sent by the American Mormons, provided a semi-secure existence for us in that terrible time.

Psychologically, my adjustment was not so easy. Because of my restless nature and my coarse manner, I often hurt my mother's feelings. I was very rude, but she never said anything. Throughout my entire prison experience I had become calloused. That was a simple fact of survival.[13] If you were not furiously self-serving, others trampled you. You needed to be that way.[14] At the time it did not occur to me, but I stepped on the feet of many others.

My mother, for example, was very happy on one occasion when Aunt Anna had invited us to tea. We were all happy, and she had decorated the table so nicely, everything was beautiful. We sat down and I did not eat a piece of cake. I stood up and left, because I could not endure it. I do not know why; I was restless, fidgety. I did not know what I should do or where I wanted to go.[15]

That was in the afternoon about four. I roamed around and came home on the last tram in the morning about 1:30. Of course, Mother was still up and crying. "What is the matter?" I always became more nervous when I saw her crying. I said, "Ah, Mama, I don't know. I must deal with it myself. Just wait, I am sorry."

Every day it was like that. It was a prison psychosis.[16] I felt lost and always looked around to see if someone was behind me with a rifle, because I always felt under guard. I did not know what to do with my freedom, was very nervous and restless. I had always had fences and barbed wire around me, sometimes electric barbed wire, and now all of a sudden I could do what I wanted. I could not resolve it. This condition lasted for months.[17]

I always awoke during the night completely bathed in cold sweat, and experienced in dreams all the terrible days of the camps. During the day I was also lost.[18] I had become accustomed to the profanity and the beatings and the strict rules. I went into the penal institutions as a teenager and remained a teenager.[19] I never grew up; in that time I never developed as a person. I lived entirely for myself and was totally egoistic. I was lewd, crude, and rude.[20] I feared that my soul was crippled for life, that I actually would never be able to become fully human again.[21]

Then, in the late autumn, Mother said to me one Saturday, "Come with me today, into the city. There is an organ concert at noon in St. Peter's church in the Mönckebergstraße, and we wanted to go there sometime."[22] I said, "Okay." I always liked these old churches anyway, these large, Gothic churches. The nave of the church was very pretty, solemn, and peaceful. We went inside and sat down and listened to the organ music, and they played everything, Haydn, Bach, and such. I was deeply gripped by the music and became melancholy. I had a lump in my throat and began to cry. The people stared at me and said to my mother, "What is the matter." They wanted to help me. Mother said, "No, leave him alone, it's OK." They thought, "Well, what is wrong with the woman?"

I wailed for nearly two hours. Afterwards I felt better. It was as if something was cleansed inside me. Afterwards I was still not completely normal, but I felt much better. Somehow the depression was gone and my soul was free. Strange that it was precisely the organ music, such as that I had heard in Berlin immediately after the trial, when I learned that Helmuth would be executed, which summoned forth within me all the hurt of the last seven years.[23]

I also became acquainted with educated persons. I have strived my entire life to associate with better people and have always admired people who were intellectual. I got to know some fine persons and could converse again. I breathed and felt good, that I was a free man.[24] I still needed a lot of medical assistance, because I was a long way from being healed, but it was looking up. I was on the sick list for nearly a year after I returned home.[25]

People think, when they come home, everything will be well again, but nothing is well again. It is a terrible struggle.[26] When I was a child and was torn away from my home, the world was a completely different place, there was a dictator and a war. Now, when I came home, there was peace and a democratic society. In the meantime seven years had passed. People were different; times had changed. I could not fit into the pace of modern postwar life. Nevertheless, I had a zest for life; I could not get enough.[27]

I wanted to normalize my life; I wanted to get to work again immediately.²⁸ I went to visit Johannes Ehlers, my old boss at the F. Georg Suhse Company. His wife greeted me at the door and said he had died. She wanted me to start immediately with the company. "You'll begin in the morning," she said. "I can't," I said, "the doctors said I shouldn't start so soon; I'm supposed to wait six months." I was still always very run down. I had received some reparation monies, so although I lived with my parents and helped them with expenses, and really wanted to work, I also wanted to follow the counsel of the doctors, because I knew what terrible consequences could follow.

Therefore, I waited. Later I took a job with Adolf Reineke. He had lived a long time in America and had returned to Hamburg. He did not like it in America. Reineke was a master painter, and I got along well with him. We called him Grandpa, because he was older. He said, "Come here, young men, take a look at what I've brought you." He had a carton of cigarettes for the smokers. He always thought of his employees.

We were required to work on Saturday until noon. When I arrived home about 12:30 in the afternoon, Mother said, "Do you want to eat something?" I said, "No, no, I only want to bathe quickly, and get dressed up nicely." Then I went to see my good friend, Gerhard Düwer. We killed the entire afternoon, the evening, and the night. About eight or eight-thirty in the morning we returned to his home. His mother cooked breakfast for us, with lots of strong coffee. We stuffed ourselves and laid down for a couple of hours. Then we were on the move again, and danced all of Sunday and on through Sunday night.

On Monday morning I went to work tired from all this carousing. I left my work clothes at Gerd's. I changed my clothes, left my good clothes there and picked them up the next day. I went to work for the entire day and got home about 4:30.

By then I was worn out. I came home and could no longer keep my eyes open and was reeling. My mother said, "My goodness, where did you come from? You look a sight!" I was not hungry, I just wanted to hit the sack. About 5:00 I was in bed and the next day I went to work again. The next weekend it was the same routine. I craved life. I even went out quite often in the evening during the week, and I seldom got home before the last streetcar ran, which was about 1:00 A.M. At 7:30 I was back at work.²⁹

Above all, I enjoyed going dancing. There were approximately ten women or young girls to every man. You had your choice. For me this was just a lot of harmless fun. We went to restaurants where they had table telephones. You had a table, a telephone, and a lamp illuminating your phone number which was large enough to be read across the room. Oh, the calls we received from other tables! "Do you want to dance with me?" We had a lot of fun.

One time I went dancing again with Gerhard to a place called the Lüpscherbaum. I noticed while I was dancing, that I needed to stretch. That was a sign to me that I was about to have an attack of malaria. I said to Gerhard, "We had better go home." "How come?" I said I was getting malaria. He said, "Come with me. No problem, we will take care of that." We went into the bar and sat down. The bartender came up. Gerhard said, "Ten cognacs!" The bartender looked and said, "Where are the other eight guys?" "Just give us ten cognacs." Gerhard said, "I will drink one, the others are for you." I said, "You must be crazy." "You drink them all," he said.

"I don't like alcohol." He said, "Down the hatch. Believe me, it will help you." Boy did I get soused. After two hours I could not find my ass with both hands. I was as drunk as a thousand Russians and was miserable. Gerd said, "OK, now I'll take you home." He called a taxi and delivered me to my house. He said to me, "Remember, I know nothing about this." He told me later: "I just pushed you out of the cab and took off."

When I went in stinking drunk, I thought my mother would have a heart attack. With a lot of crying, Mother put me to bed. Thank heavens I did not break anything, but the next day I had headaches and a hangover to end all hangovers. My mother said, "Tell me, is this necessary? You have already shown us everything you are accomplishing in life, but this is the limit! Now the gentleman comes home drunk!" I tried to explain it to her. "Yes, yes," she said, but of course she did not believe me. But to our amazement, the malaria was gone. The germs must have all died of alcoholism; they were all drunk as skunks. Since that time I have never had another attack of malaria. Dr. Gerhard Düwer's magic elixir cured me for good.

I received reparations money from the state. When I returned from Russia and got out of the hospital, finally, I received an invitation from the Biberhaus, from the social administration where Helmuth had worked.[30] I went there and they introduced themselves and greeted me with great respect. They told me that all kinds of help was due to those persecuted by the Nazi regime. I was one of them and could prove it. First, they sent me to a department store, where I could select a suit, shoes, a complete wardrobe. It was all paid for by the government. I also received several thousand marks in cash. I received that amount of money three times.[31] The last time I paid my steamship trip to America with this cash.

The people from the VVN,[32] the Union of Those Persecuted by the Nazi Regime, looked me up and said they had written the Soviet government back in 1947 in the hope of obtaining the release of all German antifascists who had ended up in Russian captivity. In my case it was unsuccessful, but it pleased me that there were people who wanted to help me.

I began to go to church again. I was received in a very friendly manner, and my smoking did not appear to bother them very much. My friend Rudi, of course, was also in the congregation. He was freed in 1945 from Hanöfersand by British troops. He was given a pistol, the Nazi guards were put behind bars, and Rudi was told to guard them.[33] Rudi had then served as a missionary for the church and had returned before I was released. He had promised Heavenly Father if he survived he would go on a mission. Rudi was the only one in our congregation who was willing to talk about Helmuth and our experience. I wanted to tell everyone about it, but no one wanted to hear anything. (See Document 67.) They all wanted the past to remain in the past.[34]

I did a lot of visiting. I visited our old neighbor, the SA man, Otto Schulz. Tears came to his eyes when he saw me. In the denazification hearings conducted by the Allies, Otto lost his former position with the Post Office. He was demoted to letter carrier and lost his pension. I would have gladly helped him, but as Helmuth said early on: he was a party member and a party moocher, and that was the inevitable result.

About that time there was also an investigation of Dr. Krüger. He was entitled to receive his former position as a prison director, because he claimed, correctly, that he had not been a Nazi. I, Gerhard, and Rudi, among others, were invited as witnesses. We and the others testified that he was a good man, was not a Nazi, and that he had, in fact, saved our lives.[35] Many years later, after his death, his successor at the Investigatory Prison told me, when Rudi and I attended the memorial service of the sixtieth anniversary of Helmuth Hübener's birthday and were permitted to visit all of the old prisons in Hamburg, that Dr. Krüger spoke very often and very highly about the prisoners who, on the trek from Graudenz, had saved his life.

Toward the end of 1949 I had reached the point that I believed that I could think about getting married. I had gotten acquainted with a young woman who liked me and had a motherly instinct, and who always said, "Oh, you poor boy!" For my part, I suppose I wanted someone to whom I could cling. We had enough money, I had a job, what stood in our way?

My mother said to me, of course, "Son leave that girl alone. You are not ready yet. You are still a big child." I became angry. I thought to myself, "What do they know how I feel and what I think?" I was already twenty-five, going on twenty-six. I was old enough. Mother said, "Don't make that mistake, you will regret it."[36]

How right my mother was. I thought when we were married, that it would be heaven on earth. That did not last long, because inwardly I was still not mature enough. One must bear in mind that seven years of my life had stood still. I did not need to shave and nothing had developed within me. I was still an adolescent.[37] She naturally wanted a normal husband, but I was not normal, because all of my selfish survival strategies stood in the way.[38]

I felt trapped in marriage. I was not mature enough to have any consideration for anyone else and did not want to admit that I had made such a huge mistake. Divorce is a serious thing in our culture, and I did not want to discredit my family. So the years just went by with each of us essentially living alone under the same roof. I went every day to visit my mother, the only person who understood this aged adolescent.

In the spring of 1951 my brother Bert immigrated to the United States. My wife's mother already lived there, too, so in January 1952, we decided to emigrate. We had our tickets and enough money to return if we did not like it there. I said to myself: it is an adventure, a long trip from which I can always return as soon as I get tired of it. But I liked it. I found work in my trade, learned English, bought a large American automobile, and then a house.

Through the years I matured and eventually divorced, became, I believe, a nicer person, and married a lovely American woman, a teacher. I now travel regularly back to Germany, which I very much enjoy, but I feel at home in the U.S., and am always glad to return.

Rudi emigrated, also, and until his death of cancer in January 1992, lived in the same town, Salt Lake City. Both of Helmuth's half brothers, Hans and Gerhard Kunkel, live there, too, as well as many others from our Hamburg Mormon community. Until their deaths, Arthur Zander, Otto Berndt, and Marie Sommerfeld also lived there.

I very often think about Helmuth and our resistance work. The longer I live, the more I see in the world around me, the more I recognize how right Helmuth was to do what he did, and the more I admire him. Because I survived, I consider it my duty not to let Helmuth's life and death fall into oblivion. Now that I have told our story from my point of view, I invite my readers to verify the truth of what I have said by reliving through the following original documents the events as they unfolded.

The St. Georg Branch, about 1936. Front row: fourth from left, Rudi Wobbe; fifth from left, Karl-Heinz Schnibbe. Second row: seventh from right, Otto Berndt, Sr. Photo courtesy of Karl-Heinz Schnibbe.

Gestapo photos of Helmuth. Photo courtesy of Karl-Heinz Schnibbe.

From left, Rudi Wobbe, Helmuth Hübener, Karl-Heinz Schnibbe. Taken about 1941. Photo courtesy of Karl-Heinz Schnibbe.

Helmuth Hübener shortly before his arrest, age sixteen. Photo courtesy of Karl-Heinz
Schnibbe.

Helmuth in about 1940. Photo
courtesy of Karl-Heinz Schnibbe.

Schnibbe family about 1932.
Left to right: Berthold, Karla,
Karl-Heinz. Photo courtesy of
Karl-Heinz Schnibbe.

Karl-Heinz shortly before his
arrest, age seventeen. Photo courtesy of Karl-Heinz Schnibbe.

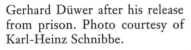
Gerhard Düwer after his release from prison. Photo courtesy of Karl-Heinz Schnibbe.

Karl-Heinz standing in a cell in the basement of the Hütten prison in 1984, forty-two years after he was incarcerated there. Photo courtesy of Karl-Heinz Schnibbe.

Karl-Heinz visiting the Gestapo prison at Fuhlsbüttel in 1984. This is now a memorial museum. Photo courtesy of Karl-Heinz Schnibbe.

Karl (left) and Rudi (right) standing before a picture of Helmuth in the Helmuth Hübener Haus in Hamburg in 1985. Photo courtesy of Karl-Heinz Schnibbe.

Caricature drawn by Helmuth in his notebook, on a page containing notes for a leaflet. Courtesy of the Berlin Document Center.

School in the Louisenweg 150–52, attended by Helmuth. Photo courtesy of the Stadtteilarchiv Hamm.

Ein Monat ist es her, seitdem Rundfunk und Presse in Deutschland
grossspurig das Ergebnis der Wollsammlung bekanntgab. Ueber   7o
Millionen Stück, verkündete Goebbels. Über 7o Millionen Stück !
Doch wo sind diese 7o Millionen Stück geblieben ? Die Soldaten
der Ostfront, die Soldaten im hohen Norden jedenfalls haben sie
nicht bekommen. Sie schreiben nichts davon, nur dass sie frieren
frieren und frieren und vergeblich auf warme Winterkleidung war-
ten.
Wo aber sind sie dann geblieben die 7o Millionen Stück - Pelze,
Pullover, Handschuhe, Unterwäsche und Jmier ?? Sollte es doch
etwa stimmen, was ein neutraler Journalist - sein Name müssen w
wir aus begreiflichen Gründen geheimhalten - in seiner Zeitung
schrieb ? Sollte er recht behalten,wenn er von der zunehmenden
Rohstoffknappheit in Deutschland sprach, wenn er erwähnte, dass
Wollsachen in nächster Zukunft nicht mehr auf die Reichskleider-
karte, sondern nur noch in dringlichsten Fällen auf Bezugschein
abgegeben würden ? Die Zeit wird es lehren, ob man nur deshalb
das deutsche Volk um Woll- und Peltssachen prellte, damit man
sie ihm dann grossindiger Weise später auf Bezugscheinen wieder-
geben kann. Die Zeit wird es lehren !

    Der "Josef" steht im Rundfunkhaus,
    der Arme, weiss nicht ein noch aus.
    ' Wie bring ich's nur den Leuten bei,
    Dass Hitlers Rechnung richtig sei ?
    Wie kommt er's auch sagen -ungeniert -
    er hätte alles mit einkalkuliert !'

    Was Josef spricht, klingt nur sehr schwach;
    Da ist ein Jammer; Weh und Ach:
    'S'ist Winter und 's ist bitter kalt."
    (Noch kälter, wenn man draussen knallt,
    weil man beim Schiessen furchtbar friert.
    Hat Hitler denn das nicht mit einkalkuliert ?)

    'Wir stehen im Ringen um Leben und Sein.
    Es währt nicht mehr lange, dann sind auch sie klein.
    Sie greifen schon lange - wie sagt Goebbels noch -
    Mit letzten Reserven auf dem letzten Loch !"
    (Das Stalin seit langem den Krieg siegreich führt,
    Das hat Euer Führer wohl auch einkalkuliert ?!)

    'Wir stehen im Kampfe, stehn an seiner Genue
    Drum gebt alle viel für die Wollsachenspende !"
    Je bettelte Lieboeis um glaubte auch nun,
    und würde es auch deinen Wünsche nach tun.
    Man würde still alles vergeben, und hätte dann selbst
    nichts zum Leben;

    Ergebnis sehr flau, das kann man schlecht sagen,
    To sagt man, sie spendeten Eisterwagen.
    Ob halbvoll, ob voll oder garnichts war drinn',
    Das Volk komm zu fragen erst garnicht in Sinn;
    Denn Rundfunk und Fritsche - sie reden geschmiert:
    'Der Führer hat alles mit einkalkuliert !"

    Ja. Hitler ist schuld, dass das Volk muss verappen
    Von seinem Vorrat, dem ohnehin schon knappen.
    Für Hitlers Irrtum zahlt das Volk nun die Kosten,
    was hilfts,Russland bleibt ein verlorener Posten.
    Dass Stalin sein Heer jetzt zum Siege hinführt,
    Das hatte der Führer n i c h t einkalkuliert !!

Im Namen
des deutschen Volkes

In der Strafsache gegen

1) den Verwaltungslehrling bei der Sozialverwaltung in Hamburg Helmuth Günther H u b n e r, geboren am 8. Januar 1925 in Hamburg, zuletzt dort wohnhaft gewesen,

2) den Schlosserlehrling Rudolf Gustav W o b b e, geboren am 11.Februar 1926 in Hamburg, zuletzt dort wohnhaft gewesen,

3) den Malergesellen Karl Heinz S c h n i b b e, geboren am 5. Januar 1924 in Hamburg, zuletzt dort wohnhaft gewesen,

4) den Verwaltungslehrling bei der Sozialverwaltung Hamburg, Gerhard Heinrich Jacob Jonni D ü w e r, geboren am 1.November 1924 in Altona, zuletzt in Hamburg-Altona wohnhaft gewesen,

sämtlich z.Zt. in dieser Sache in gerichtlicher Untersuchungshaft,

wegen Vorbereitung zum Hochverrat

hat der Volksgerichtshof, 2. Senat, auf Grund der Hauptverhandlung vom 11. August 1942, an welcher teilgenommen haben

als Richter:

Vizepräsident des Volksgerichtshofs Engert, Vorsitzer
Oberlandesgerichtsrat Fikeis,
NSKK Brigadeführer Heinsius,
Oberbereichsleiter Bodinus,
Oberführer Gaugerichtsvorsitzender Hartmann,

als Vertreter des Oberreichsanwalts:
Erster Staatsanwalt Dr. Drullmann,

als Urkundsbeamter der Geschäftsstelle:
Justizsekretär Mohlke,

für Recht erkannt:

Es werden verurteilt:

H ü b n e r wegen Abhörens eines Auslandssenders und Verbreitung der abgehörten Nachrichten in Verbindung mit Vorbereitung

- 2 -

zum Hochverrat und landesverräterischer Feindbegünstigung zum Tode und zum Verlust der bürgerlichen Ehrenrechte auf Lebenszeit,

W o b b e wegen Abhörens eines Auslandssenders und Verbreitung ausländischer Rundfunknachrichten in Verbindung mit Vorbereitung zum Hochverrat zu

10 - zehn - Jahren Gefängnis,

S c h n i b b e wegen Abhörens eines Auslandssenders und Verbreitung ausländischer Rundfunknachrichten zu

5 - fünf - Jahren Gefängnis

und D ü w e r wegen Verbreitung von ausländischen Rundfunknachrichten zu

4 - vier - Jahren Gefängnis.

Auf die erkannten Freiheitsstrafen werden den Angeklagten Wobbe, Schnibbe und Düwer je fünf Monate der erlittenen Haft angerechnet.

Das sichergestellte Rundfunkgerät Marke "Rola" und die Schreibmaschine Marke "Remington" werden eingezogen.

Die Angeklagten haben die Kosten des Verfahrens zu tragen.

Von Rechts wegen .

The official indictment. Courtesy of the Berlin Document Center.

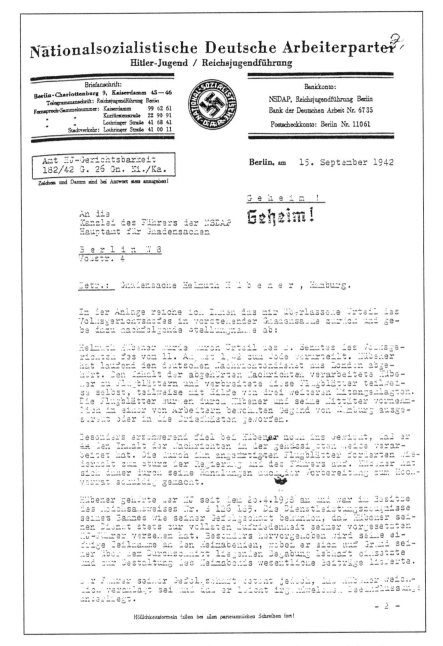

Nationalsozialistische Deutsche Arbeiterpartei

Hitler-Jugend / Reichsjugendführung

Briefanschrift:
Berlin-Charlottenburg 9, Kaiserdamm 45—46
Telegrammanschrift: Reichsjugendführung Berlin
Fernspruch-Sammelnummer: Kaiserdamm   99 62 61
  „   „   Kurfürstenstraße 22 90 91
  „   „   Lothringer Straße 41 68 41
  Stadtverkehr: Lothringer Straße 41 00 11

Bankkonto:
NSDAP, Reichsjugendführung Berlin
Bank der Deutschen Arbeit Nr. 67 35
Postscheckkonto: Berlin Nr. 11061

Amt HJ-Gerichtsbarkeit
182/42 G. 26 Gn. Hi./Ka.
Zeichen und Datum sind bei Antwort stets anzugeben!

Berlin, am   15. September 1942

G e h e i m !

Geheim!

An die
Kanzlei des Führers der NSDAP
Hauptamt für Gnadensachen

B e r l i n   W 8
Vo.str. 4

Betr.: Gnadensache Helmuth H ü b e n e r , Hamburg.

In der Anlage reiche ich Ihnen das mir überlassene Urteil des
Volksgerichtshofes in vorstehender Gnadensache zurück und ge-
be dazu nachfolgende Stellungnahme ab:

Helmuth Hübener wurde durch Urteil des 2. Senates des Volksgerichtshofes vom 11. August 1942 zum Tode verurteilt. Hübener
hat laufend den deutschen Nachrichtendienst aus London abge-
hört. Den Inhalt der abgehörten Nachrichten verarbeitete Hübener zu Flugblättern und verbreitete diese Flugblätter teilweise selbst, teilweise mit Hilfe von drei weiteren Mitangeklagten.
Die Flugblätter wurden durch Hübener und seine Mittäter vornehm-
lich in einer von Arbeitern bewohnten Gegend von Hamburg ausge-
streut oder in die Briefkästen geworfen.

Besonders erschwerend fiel bei Hübener noch ins Gewicht, daß er
in den Inhalt der Nachrichten in der gehässigsten Weise verar-
beitet hat. Die durch ihn angefertigten Flugblätter forderten wie-
derholt zum Sturz der Regierung und des Führers auf. Hübener hat
sich immer durch seine Handlungen auch der Vorbereitung zum Hochverrat schuldig gemacht.

Hübener gehörte der HJ seit dem 20.4.1938 an und war im Besitze
des Reichsausweises Nr. 3 126 185. Die Dienststellungszeugnisse
seines Bannes wie seiner Gefolgschaft bekunden, daß Hübener seinen Dienst stets zur vollsten Zufriedenheit seiner vorgesetzten
HJ-Führer versehen hat. Besonders hervorgehoben wird seine ei-
frige Teilnahme an den Heimabenden, wobei er sich auf Grund seiner über dem Durchschnitt liegenden Begabung lebhaft einsetzte
und zur Gestaltung des Heimabends wesentliche Beiträge lieferte.

Der Führer seiner Gefolgschaft betont jedoch, daß Hübener weich-
lich veranlagt sei und daß er leicht irgendwelchen Beeinflussunge
unterliegt.

- 2 -

Höflichkeitsformeln fallen bei allen parteiamtlichen Schreiben fort!

The Hitler Youth national leadership's rejection of an appeal for clemency.
Courtesy of the Berlin Document Center.

Berlin, den 27. Okt. 1942

Gegenwärtig:

Erster Staatsanwalt   R a n k e

als Vollstreckungsleiter,

~~Justizangestellter   K a r p e~~
Justizsekretär   R e n k

als Beamter der Geschäftsstelle.

Die unterzeichneten Beamten der Reichsanwaltschaft beim
Volksgerichtshof begaben sich heute zur Vollstreckung des
gegen   Helmuth H ü b e n e r
ergangenen rechtskräftigen Todesurteils in das Strafgefängnis
Plötzensee in Berlin.

Um ~~Uhr wurde der zur Vollstreckung des Urteils be-~~
~~stimmte Raum betreten.~~ Der Scharfrichter   Röttger
aus   Berlin   meldete, dem mit der Leitung der Vollstreckung Beauftragten, daß er mit seinen Gehilfen zur Durchführung
der Vollstreckung bereit stehe. In dem vorderen Teil des durch
elektrisches Licht hell erleuchteten Vollstreckungsraumes befand
sich ein schwarz verhangener Tisch, auf dem ein Kruzifix und
zwei brennende Kerzen standen. Der hintere Teil des Vollstreckungs-
raumen, in dem das Fallbeilgerät steht, war durch einen schwarzen
Vorhang abgetrennt.

Die Unterzeichneten nahmen hinter dem Tisch Aufstellung.
Der Scharfrichter stellte sich mit seinen drei Gehilfen vor dem
geschlossenen Vorhang auf.

Anwesend waren ferner:

Verwaltungsoberinspektor   R o h d e

Der Vollstreckungsleiter ordnete die Vorführung des Verurteilten an. Dieser wurde um 20 46 Uhr, die Hände auf dem Rücken ge-
fesselt, durch zwei Gefängniswachtmeister an der Richtstätte
vorgeführt. Die Tür des Vollstreckungsraumes wurde geschlossen.

Die Personengleichheit des Vorgeführten mit dem Verurteilwurde sodann durch den Vollstreckungsleiter festgestellt. Er
beauftragte darauf den Scharfrichter mit der Vollstreckung des
Urteils des Volksgerichtshofs vom 11. August 1942.
Sofort wurde der Vorhang zurückgezogen und die drei Gehilfen
des Scharfrichters traten an die Stelle der beiden Gefängniswachtmeister.

Der Verurteilte gab keine Äußerung von sich. Er war ruhig
und gefaßt. Er ließ sich ohne Widerstreben vor das Fallbeilgerät
führen und dort mit entblößtem Oberkörper niederlegen. Der Scharfrichter trennte sodann mittels Fallbeils den Kopf des Verurteilten vom Rumpfe und meldete, daß das Urteil vollstreckt sei.

Die Vollstreckung dauerte von dem Zeitpunkt der Vorführung
bis zur Übergabe an den Scharfrichter 16 Sekunden und von der
Übergabe an diesen bis zur Meldung des Scharfrichters, daß das
Urteil vollstreckt sei, 8 Sekunden.

Ranke

View of Plötzensee execution room with guillotine. Photo courtesy of In-
formationszentrum Berlin.

Bekanntmachung.

Der am 11. August 1942 vom Volksgerichtshof wegen Vorbereitun
zum Hochverrat und landesverräterischer Feindbegünstigung zum Tod
und zum dauernden Verlust der bürgerlichen Ehrenrechte verurteilt
17 Jahre alte

Helmuth Hübener
aus Hamburg

ist heute hingerichtet worden.

Berlin, den 27. Oktober 1942.

Der Oberreichsanwalt beim Volksgerichtshof

Red poster announcing Helmuth's execution. Courtesy of the Berlin Document Center.

Prisoners march single file through the vast Russian landscape. From *Stacheldraht-Hunger-Heimweh. Eine Erinnerung*, text by Johannes Kurt Klein, drawing by Georg Hieronymi (Düsseldorf: R. Bärenfeld Verlag, 1955).

No matter the weather, prisoners were always carefully counted. From *Stacheldraht-Hunger-Heimweh. Eine Erinnerung*, text by Johannes Kurt Klein, drawing by Georg Hieronymi (Düsseldorf: R. Bärenfeld Verlag, 1955).

Hacking at the frozen ground with iron crowbars. From *Stacheldraht-Hunger-Heimweh. Eine Erinnerung*, text by Johannes Kurt Klein, drawing by Georg Hieronymi (Düsseldorf: R. Bärenfeld Verlag, 1955).

One of the worst jobs was to carry away the contents of the latrines. From *Stacheldraht-Hunger-Heimweh. Eine Erinnerung*, text by Johannes Kurt Klein, drawing by Georg Hieronymi (Düsseldorf: R. Bärenfeld Verlag, 1955).

Prisoners always somehow found a way to make music. From *Stacheldraht-Hunger-Heimweh. Eine Erinnerung*, text by Johannes Kurt Klein, drawing by Georg Hieronymi (Düsseldorf: R. Bärenfeld Verlag, 1955).

Talking on the grapevine. From *Stacheldraht-Hunger-Heimweh. Eine Erinnerung*, text by Johannes Kurt Klein, drawing by Georg Hieronymi (Düsseldorf: R. Bärenfeld Verlag, 1955).

A welcome shower with little water and even less soap. From *Stacheldraht-Hunger-Heimweh. Eine Erinnerung*, text by Johannes Kurt Klein, drawing by Georg Hieronymi (Düsseldorf: R. Bärenfeld Verlag, 1955).

Is there enough body fat left to do some more work or should this prisoner be sent home? From *Stacheldraht-Hunger-Heimweh. Eine Erinnerung*, text by Johannes Kurt Klein, drawing by Georg Hieronymi (Düsseldorf: R. Bärenfeld Verlag, 1955).

Prisoners always tried to bury their comrades facing home. From *Stacheldraht-Hunger-Heimweh. Eine Erinnerung*, text by Johannes Kurt Klein, drawing by Georg Hieronymi (Düsseldorf: R. Bärenfeld Verlag, 1955).

Finally able to open the door and enjoy the sights and smells of home. From *Stacheldraht-Hunger-Heimweh. Eine Erinnerung*, text by Johannes Kurt Klein, drawing by Georg Hieronymi (Düsseldorf: R. Bärenfeld Verlag, 1955).

Documents

1

Decree about Extraordinary Radio Measures of 1 September 1939

In modern war the enemy fights not only with military weapons but also with means to influence the people mentally and spiritually and break down their resistance. One of these means is the radio. Every word that the enemy transmits into our homeland is obviously a lie and designed to inflict damage on the German people. The administration of the Reich knows that the German people are aware of this danger and it expects, therefore, that out of a sense of responsibility each German will elevate it to his proper duty absolutely to refrain from listening to foreign stations. The Council of the Ministry of Defense of the Reich has issued the following ordinance for those citizens who are lacking this sense of responsibility.

The Council of the Ministry of Defense of the Reich decrees with legal force for the area of the Greater German Reich:

§1
Intentional listening to foreign radio stations is forbidden. Violations will be punished by imprisonment. In lesser cases a prison sentence can be imposed. The receiving equipment employed will be confiscated.

§2
Whoever willfully distributes the broadcasts of foreign stations which are designed to endanger the strength of resistance of the German people, will, in particularly severe cases, be punished with death.

§3
The provisions of this ordinance are not applicable to acts undertaken in the course of official duty.

§4
For trials and decisions regarding violations against this ordinance, the special courts have jurisdiction.

§5
Criminal prosecution pursuant to §§1 and 2 shall occur only at the instigation of the state police offices.

§6
The Minister for Education and Propaganda of the Reich issues the requisite legal and administrative regulations for the enforcement of this ordinance, and inasmuch as they involve criminal regulations, this shall be by mutual agreement with the Minister of Justice of the Reich.

§7

The decree enters into force with its promulgation.

Berlin, 1 September 1939.

Source: Ministry of the Interior, Reichsgesetzblatt (Berlin: Reichsverlagsamt, 1939), 1: 1683.

2

Against Parasites of the People[1]

A radio decree of the National Ministry of Justice, signed by State Secretary Roland Freisler, concerning the conducting of criminal proceedings on the basis of the ordinance "Against Parasites of the People." 12 September 1938.

Germany stands in a battle for honor and right. The model for every German today more than ever is the German soldier. Whoever wrongs the people instead of living up to that example no longer has a place in our society.

For the ruthless struggle against these parasites of the people the Ministry for the Defense of the Nation has created the necessary legal basis.

I expect all judges and state attorneys to apply the ordinance with the same ruthless, rapid, harshly powerful determination and energy with which it was issued. Not to apply the most extreme severity in the face of such parasites would be treason to the fighting German soldiers!

Moreover, all participants must assist in making sure that the crime, the indictment, the trial, the judgment and the execution follow immediately upon each other with no delays.[2] All participating judges and state attorneys are to transmit this order immediately.

Ordinance of 12 September 1939. Source: Ministry of the Interior, Reichsgesetzblatt (Berlin: Reichsverlagsamt, 1939), 1: 1679.

3

Chief of Police, Hamburg
Police Station: 43rd Police Precinct
No. 92/42
Hamburg, 4 February 1942

Report

Mrs. Flögel delivers a flyer.

On 4 February 1942, about 9:00 o'clock, a married woman, Mrs. Bertha Flögel, née Baum, born 29 April 1904 in Altona, residing in Hamburg, Kreuzbrook 2 IV, appeared in the Precinct and delivered the enclosed flyer. Upon being questioned she made the following statement: "Today, about 9:00 o'clock, I was in the telephone booth in the Louisenweg-Süderstraße to make a call. In the telephone booth I found a flyer, which I herewith deliver. I do not know who left the flyer there."
The flyer delivered by Mrs. Flögel is attached to the report.

/s/ Gebhardt, Master of the Protective Police

Source: Berlin Document Center

4

Chief of Police, Hamburg
Police Station: 43rd Police Precinct
No. 92/42
Hamburg, 4 February 1942

Report

Weltien, office clerk, delivers the enclosed flyer.

On 4 February 1942, about 7:45 p.m., the office clerk Carl Friedrich Weltien, born on 5 July 1901 in Hamburg, residing in Süderstraße 205 II, appeared in the Precinct and delivered the enclosed flyer.
Upon being questioned, Weltien made the following statement: "The flyer was handed over to me today about 6:30 p.m. by the mechanic Frehse, resident at Süderstraße 205 I. Allegedly Frehse found the flyer in the mailbox attached to his stairwell. It is unknown who placed the flyer in the mailbox.
"Previously, on 3 February 1942 about 5:30 p.m. a flyer was given to me by my apartment neighbor Schwedlick, resident at Süderstraße No. 205 II. I delivered this flyer to my local branch of the National Socialist German Workers' Party for further action. I suspected foreign workers who are working on jobs in the basement of the building at Süderstraße 205."

/s/ Hein, Master of the Protective Police

Source: Berlin Document Center

5

National Socialist German Workers' Party
Regional Administration Hamburg
District Hamburg 5
Hamburg, 10 February 1942
Division: District Leader Bi/L

To the
Secret State Police
Hamburg
City Hall

Re: Enemy Propaganda

In the enclosed I am sending you a transmitted, duplicated writing from the local chapter Hammer Deich, that was turned in to the apartment of cell leader P. Weltien in the Süderstraße 205. The writing was found in an envelope and was tossed into the mailbox by an unknown culprit. Further similar writings, which are found in the possession of the police authorities, were found in the telephone booth Süderstraße/corner Louisenweg and in other mailboxes in Süderstraße 205.
Heil Hitler!

/s/ Brandt, District Leader

Source: Berlin Document Center

6

Secret State Police
State Police Agency
B. No. II P—126/42
Hamburg, 5 February 1942

Report

About 2:00 o'clock p.m. Municipal Bailiff Matthiessen reported from the Social Administration—Biberhaus—that an administrative apprentice employed there was suspected of listening to the prohibited news service of enemy broadcasters and of distributing the transmitted reports in the form of flyers. The undersigned and Criminal Secretary Müssener went to the office of the social administration. The investigations conducted at that location and office revealed that the administrative apprentice *Helmuth* Günther Hübener, born 8 January 1925 in Hamburg, residing in Hamburg, Sachsenstraße 42, with his parents, had given in the course of the last weeks to one other apprentice, to wit: *Gerhard* Heinrich Jacob Jonni Düwer, born 1 November 1924 in Altona, residing in Hamburg-Bahrenfeld, Bahrenfelder Kirchenweg 53, with his parents, several of the aforementioned flyers. In the meantime, this person was sent by Bailiff Matthiessen to his apartment with the commission to fetch the flyers. This concerns flyers with notes from an enemy news service, which bore the notation

"This is a chain letter . . .
So pass it on!"

Hübener admitted in the short oral interrogation to having prepared and distributed the flyers. He listened to the radio reports in the apartment of his grandparents, Louisenweg 137, second floor, with a receiver belonging to one of his inducted brothers, and wrote them down on paper.

To search the apartments of Düwer and Hübener a car was requested. At Hübener's place more flyers were found, which with the radio and the typewriter used to produce the flyers were confiscated to secure them for the moment. No incriminating material was found in the apartment of Düwer, nevertheless the radio apparatus of his parents was secured also, because there was a suspicion that Düwer had also listened to forbidden foreign broadcasts. Düwer and Hübener were arrested about 5:00 p.m. and taken to the police prison. Both are members of the Hitler Youth.

In the course of the day three of the questionable flyers found in mailboxes and telephone booths were sent from the 43rd Police Precinct.

/s/ Wangemann, Criminal Inspector

Note: During the search of the apartment of the grandparents of Hübener seven more flyers in the process of being produced were found in the typewriter used for this purpose, which was confiscated. Hübener was prevented by his arrest from completing these flyers, which bore the title "Who is inciting whom?"

/s/ Müssener, Criminal Secretary

Source: Berlin Document Center

7

Report

Re: Administrative Apprentice Helmut Hübener, born 8 January 1925

I. Address: Hamburg 1, Sachsenstraße 42
II.   ”   :   ”   Louisenweg 137 II, with grandparents

On the afternoon of 20 January 1942 the above-named administrative apprentice attempted in my workroom—305—to press a folded paper into the hand of his comrade, apprentice Kranz, in the presence of apprentice Düwer, which paper, nevertheless, was absolutely rejected by Kranz. Because all his coaxing was to no avail, Hübener, accompanied by Düwer, disappeared with the questionable paper.

The thought came to me immediately that it must have to do with a forbidden matter, and I subsequently spoke with the apprentice Kranz in the most gentle manner; I determined that Kranz found himself in a very complicated situation. After a short discussion Kranz opened his heart and told me literally: Because of this matter he had not slept the entire night, and he felt it necessary to inform me of his concern.

Kranz described to me briefly the facts of the case, that he had already put down in his account of the fifth of this month. Thereupon I ordered Kranz to tell Hübener that he'd changed his mind and arrange to obtain from him these short accounts which he wanted translated into the French language. Hübener did not offer the administrative apprentice Kranz the accounts in question, which is why Kranz cannot further state what the contents of the papers were.

On 21 January 1942, in other words one day later, I established contact with the administrative apprentice Düwer, because in the meantime I had determined that Düwer could succeed in obtaining something tangible from Hübener.

During the entire period I endeavored to obtain documents from Düwer or Kranz, which I finally succeeded in doing on the afternoon of 4 February 1942.

Administrative apprentice Düwer gave me two chain letters, which have since been put in the file, and upon being questioned informed me likewise that still more documents were to be found in his apartment, which he would place at my disposal on Friday, the 6th of this month.

In the meantime, Düwer received instructions to fetch the documents immediately.

Hamburg, 5 February 1942
/s/ Heinrich Mohns

Source: Berlin Document Center

8

Hamburg, 5 February 1942

Report

Re: Helmuth Hübener

On Saturday, 17 January 1942, H.[elmuth] H.[übener] asked me if I had learned French in school; you see, I had opened a notebook with French vocabulary words in the front. I confirmed having learned French. Thereupon H. H. asked if I could do him a favor. I said: If it is not too difficult and too long. What is it? It is only two small accounts. What do they contain? I cannot tell you that. Well then, in that case I cannot take it on. You will get something for it. It appeared to me immediately that something was not right. I asked again about the content of the accounts. Thereupon he informed me in confidence that he with others was slipping inflammatory letters to prisoners, mainly. Also, they write military postal letters to not entirely reliable German soldiers; he had lists of them. Thereupon I replied that it was not a possibility for me. On Tuesday, 20 January he tried, nevertheless, to give me the aforementioned accounts, but I did not accept them.

/s/ Werner Kranz, Hamburg-Rahlstedl, Loherstraße 38

Source: Berlin Document Center

9

State Police Agency Hamburg
Hamburg, 5 February 1942

About the Person:
Düwer, Gerhard Heinrich Jacob Jonni

From the age of seven to eleven I attended the primary school in Bahrenfeld. From 1935 to 1942 I attended the secondary school in Altona. At Easter 1941 I graduated from the school with average grades. After graduation I became an administrative apprentice at the social administration in Hamburg. On 4 September 1933 I joined the Hitler Youth, to which I still belong today with the rank of youth comrade.

About the Case:
On 1 December 1941 I began my apprenticeship with the social admin-

istration in Hamburg. I also became acquainted there with the apprentice Hübener, at first only by sight.

Through our mutual activity I came to know him better; we did not associate privately. At the beginning of January 1942 Hübener came to me once and asked if I wanted to join a secret club. What he meant with this secret club he did not tell me at first. I asked for some time to think it over, and then he said he would tell me what it was about. The next day I also had a conversation with him. I asked him what the deal was with his club. Then he explained to me that it involved a spy ring, which was working to overthrow the regime. He told me also that he listened to broadcasts on the radio, which he then wrote down. At first I concluded that his statements were absurd, and then he intimated to me, too, that everything was only nonsense. I must point out that in regard to listening to the broadcasts he spoke only of himself, but when he referred to the club he used "we" and "us."

I still want to mention here that Hübener, before he came to me, had approached the apprentice Kranz with a request to translate something into French for him. However, Kranz declined, and then he came to me and talked with me about it; he explained to me at the same time that he would talk to the office overseer Mohns about the matter. I did not converse further with Kranz about it.

One day, it could have been the middle of January, Hübener came to me and gave me a typed page and encouraged me to read it. I read the page and without expressing myself about it, tucked it away and took it home. From this writing I could see at once that it was an inflammatory flyer directed against Germany. I must mention here that Hübener did not tell me where he obtained the writing, and I did not think at first that it consisted of reports of monitored English broadcasts. I had, in taking the page home and locking it in a box, simply the goal of gathering materials of this nature in order, at the proper time, to denounce Hübener. On 30 January Hübener came to me again and gave me four sheets with similar contents, which I read likewise and took home. A third time, it was 4 February, I received four similar pages again.

Question: To whom did you show these flyers, and who read them?
Answer: The flyers that I took I showed to Horst and Kurt Zumsande, who live in the same house, and they read them, too.
Question: Did you talk about the contents of the flyers?
Answer: Yes, we did. We became convinced that it was nonsense and we laughed about it. No other persons saw these flyers, nor did I talk with others about them.
Question: Why did you keep these flyers at home and did not, as it would have been your duty, make a report about it to your superior authority?
Answer: The evidence that I had then did not appear to be adequate, and I had the intention to gather still more and then talk with my father about it. Nevertheless, I could never talk with my father, because no opportunity presented itself to me. My father is with the Security Service of the SS and comes home only every third day. I recognize that my behavior

was not correct and I am now suspected of having cooperated with Hübener. However, that is not correct, and I declare again, that I merely wanted to gather material against Hübener.

Question: Your parents possess a radio, so did you also listen occasionally to foreign news broadcasts?

Answer: No, I did not. I did not have any opportunity, because I was never alone at home. It might well have happened that an English transmitter got through and some was understandable, when one listened to a German station. Nevertheless, I never heard a continuous transmission and never made the attempt. I cannot make any further statements.

read personally and found to be correct
/s/ Gerhard Düwer

Certified with the note that Düwer was returned to police custody.
/s/ Müssener, Criminal Secretary

Hamburg, 6 February 1942

Upon being summoned, the administrative apprentice for the executive civil service Werner Kranz appears, born 3 April 1924 in Tondorf/Lohe, resident Hamburg-Rahlstedt, Lohestraße 38, and gives the following transcript concerning the Hübener-Düwer affair:

Hübener was transferred together with me as an administrative apprentice from the central administrative office on 1 April 1941 to the social administration for training. I became acquainted with Hübener in the administration school, where he attended the same class with me. I was together in the social administration with Hübener in the central tracing file from 1 June to 30 June 1941, and later, since 1 December 1941, employed in the cashier's office. We were not on friendly terms. Outside of work time we did happen to meet regularly on Thursday evenings for four weeks from 5:30 to 7:30 p.m. for dancing lessons with our dance teacher Schacht at the Holzdamm. We met neither before nor after the dancing lesson. I know nothing about Hübener's domestic and economic situation. I also do not know where he lives. On Saturday, 17 January 1942, as we had instruction in the administrative school, Hübener, who sat adjacent to me during the instruction, asked, while I took notes in a tablet for French vocabulary, if I had learned French. I answered his question affirmatively, whereupon he asked me further if I wanted to do him a favor. I answered him that it depended, I needed to know first what there was to translate and what its contents were, because I am not perfect in French. Hübener declared that he could not tell me any more about it. Sometime later, it could have been during a class break, Hübener shared with me quietly that "they" were producing inflammatory brochures, which they wanted to give to the prisoners, and that he had a card file of the military addresses of soldiers who were not entirely reliable and patriotic. I told him that such a thing was out of the question for me and urgently advised him to cease his activity. He repeated, however, that he wanted to bring "something" to me on Monday. With that the conversation ended. On Monday, 19 January 1942, we had not talked about the matter and Hübener had also not given me any papers. On the following day, the 20th of the month, he tried secretly to press some folded papers into my hand. I did not accept the writings and declared to him that I, under no condition, would accept or read them. The administrative apprentice Düwer, who had entered the room with Hübener, was present at this conversation. They left the room together again after I refused. The acting shop steward of the cashier's office, Mr. Mohns, observed this incident and, after the exit of the administrative apprentices Hübener and Düwer, made an observation, something to the effect: "don't let yourselves get caught." In the course of the afternoon, Mr. Mohns asked me what was going on, whereupon I disclosed the incident and informed him too, that I had already spoken briefly with my father on Saturday, the 17th of the month. I did not report it immediately, because the scope of the activities was unknown to me, and at first I did not take them seriously. I would never have believed Hübener capable of such an act. Hübener was always very talkative, and I had the impression that he read a lot and that he had obtained his knowledge, also in the political field, from reading. In occasional political discussions, he was very well informed. Because he is also artistically gifted, he often made caricatures of foreign statesmen. I did not know that Hübener, with the exception of the administrative apprentice Düwer, attempted to distribute the inflammatory writings to other administrative apprentices. I have also never seen Hübener talking in any way with other administrative apprentices about inflammatory writings and so on.

Düwer first informed me on Tuesday, the 20th of the previous month, I don't know whether it was before or after the incident with Hübener, that he already knew that Hübener had been distributing inflammatory writings. He was in agreement with me that it needed to be reported. I did not talk about it with any other administrative apprentices; also not with other persons, with the exception of my father and Mr. Mohns.

6 February 1942
read aloud, verified, and signed
/s/ Werner Kranz

Certified,
/s/ Matthiessen

The foregoing interrogation of the administrative apprentice Werner Kranz was conducted by Municipal Supervisor Matthiessen, of the Municipal Administration of the Hanseatic City Hamburg in his offices.

The original of the interrogation is found in the folder, page 15a of the documents.

/s/ Müssener, Criminal Secretary

Source: Berlin Document Center

10

State Police Agency Hamburg
Hamburg, 5 February 1942

About the Person:
Hübener, Helmuth Günther

In 1931 I entered the primary school in the Louisenweg, which I attended until 1938. From there I attended the upper track at Brackdamm school until April 1941. Thereupon I entered my apprenticeship as an administrative apprentice for the executive civil service.

About the Case:

Upon Interrogation:

I am ready to make a complete confession. I admit to having listened for a long time to German-language newscasts of an English broadcasting station, taken notes of what I heard, to having duplicated this with the typewriter and to having distributed it by means of flyers.

read and found to be correct

/s/ Helmuth Hübener

Certified with the note that the interrogation was interrupted because of the late hour and Hübener was remanded to police custody. Only after lengthy remonstrations and explicit admonitions[3] was Hübener moved to give a confession about the scope of his destructive activity.

Hamburg, 9 February 1942

Hübener, brought from police custody, states further:
How I came to this activity I cannot rightly say myself. I must mention at once that no persons stand behind me who have induced me in this matter. I alone am responsible for this. The only reason I could give is that [I wanted to] appear particularly well informed in conversations through my superior knowledge.
In March or April 1941 my brother brought a radio set with him from France when he was released from the National Labor Service. My brother was home only two days, because he was immediately drafted. The radio set was first of all taken to be repaired, and at the end of April I received it back. While experimenting with the radio I ran across the English newscast. During the subsequent period prior to my arrest I listened to this newscast about 4 or 5 times a week. I must mention here that I lived with my grandparents, because my parents are employed during the day. Because my grandparents go to bed very early, I had the time and opportunity in the

evening to hear these newscasts after 10:00. In my circle of apprentices at my office we often discussed current events, and I wanted, as I have already indicated, to know more than the others on those occasions. I do not know whether someone suspected that I was listening to the English broadcaster, but I assume it, because I was generally dubbed "the man with connections."

Question: How did you get the idea of distributing what you heard by means of flyers?

Answer: I have two schoolmates, one of whom is with the National Labor Service and the other is in the finance school in Thorn. I have remained in contact with both of them through correspondence. In these letters I have also made reports for them about what I heard from the English newscasts. I never told them, of course, where I obtain the news, but presented them as facts. Later I simply began to enclose these newscasts in the form of a flyer with the letter in order not to need to write the same thing twice. I must add here that I was often visited by an acquaintance, he is eighteen years of age, who belongs to the same religious community as I. This person, Karl Heinz Schnibbe, residing in Hamburg, Rossausweg 32, once read a letter that I wanted to send, and in which political news of this type was written. He displayed a great interest for these newscasts and asked me to convey these newscasts to him also. I must have talked with him about the origin of these newscasts, because he knew that I listened to the news broadcasts of British radio stations. Thereafter, in order to save work, I copied these newscasts with the typewriter—I had previously taken them down in shorthand—and then enclosed a flyer in each of the letters to the aforementioned schoolmates and also gave Schnibbe a carbon copy.

Question: Did your schoolmates show any interest in this news?

Answer: The one who is with the Labor Service, Horst van Treck, after a short while forbade any further sending of such letters. However, the other, in the finance school in Thorn, Franz Prumnitz, answered my letters, but did not show any interest at all for the other news.

Question: But considerably more than three flyers were produced; what happened to the others?

Answer: First of all, I, in fact, produced only three flyers for the aforementioned persons. It was only later, it might have been the beginning of January 1942, that I began to converse with the apprentice Düwer about these newscasts. Because I had with me two flyers, which originally were intended for Schnibbe, I showed him those. Düwer then retained these flyers and asked me if I had more of them. Because I did not have more, I also made one in the future for Düwer. Counting the original, which I kept, there were, in each case, five flyers.

Question: Did Düwer comment on what he wanted to do with the flyers?

Answer: No, he never said anything to me about that. He only told me once that he had shown one to another apprentice, I believe his name was Neuss, from the administrative school. One day before my arrest, he told me that he read the flyers at a private party, which took place at his home when his parents were absent, and also, that he had stuck some of them in mailboxes. Altogether Düwer received 15 flyers from me. Whether what he told me about the use of them corresponds with the facts, I do not know.

Question: How many flyers, in each case, were produced after each listening, and where are they?

Answer: After each listening I did not, as a general rule, produce flyers, but wrote down that which, in each case, appeared the most important to me, and when I had enough together, then I combined it into a flyer. I did that either weekly or every fourteen days, according to how much I had together. In the last while, then, I made six or seven of the flyers at one time. In the meantime, a large number of the flyers had collected which I did not dispose of. In order to dispose of them, I came up with the idea of putting them in mailboxes, hallways and, in one case, in a telephone booth. I also did this, namely, one evening and one morning before I went to work.

Question: How many flyers were distributed in this way?

Answer: A total of about 15 flyers were distributed in this manner.

Question: Were you unaware that listening to and distributing such newscasts is punishable with severe penalties?

Answer: Yes, I was aware of it. But I was firmly convinced that it would never come out.

Question: What was the mentality that led you to listen and distribute these things? What were you thinking?

Answer: First of all, it was my intent to furnish my school comrades with newscasts, which they can get neither at school nor in the National Labor Service. But that my impulse to listen and distribute could someday develop in this manner I never anticipated and it was also not my original intent. I had no particular reason to throw them in hallways and mailboxes. I merely wanted to get rid of the flyers which had, in the meantime, accumulated.

Question: Wasn't it simpler and safer just to burn them?

Answer: It would have been, but that idea never occurred to me.

Question: Düwer said in his statement that initially there was talk of a secret spy ring, in which the flyers were produced and distributed, is that correct?

Answer: It is correct that I expressed myself like that to him. But it was only a pretext to make myself important, and I assume also, that he interpreted my remarks in that manner. I must reaffirm, that I alone am completely responsible for my deed and did not receive orders from anyone.

Question: The witness Kranz asserts that the translation of such flyers into French was desired, with the intent of passing these flyers to prisoners of war and politically unreliable soldiers. Is that correct?

Answer: It is correct; I did turn to Kranz with this in mind, but did not say to him that it involved flyers. Kranz first wanted to see what was to be translated, and when I then brought two flyers with me, he declined, without having seen at all what it was about. Düwer was also present at this incident. Whether Kranz was informed by Düwer, I cannot say. It is also correct that I said the flyers were to be passed to prisoners and unreliable soldiers.

Question: Was this your intention?

Answer: I never had the intention of passing such flyers to prisoners of war, although I did consider including such flyers with the letters that I needed to write. It never came to a realization, because these letters were checked before their dispatch, and then the flyers would have been discovered. I must mention here, that I was obligated to write these letters under the direction of the president of the congregation of the religious community to which I belong, Mr. Zander. Before it was mailed, each individual letter which I wrote under his direction was examined by him personally. These letters were sent only to soldiers who belong to our church. The typewriter which I used to produce the flyers and was located in the apartment of my grandparents belonged to Mr. Zander.

Question: Did Düwer say also, how often he had such private parties, of which he spoke, and who took part?

Answer: He told me about it twice, and, in fact, it was once at his home and another time at a friend's. Who was present at these private parties I cannot say, because nothing was said to me about them.

Question: Did Düwer talk about what went on at these private parties?

Answer: No, he did not inform me of anything more precise. He only just told me that they played records and that it was really terrific.[4] Over the course of time I bought about 20 records (dance music) myself for Düwer. If he had records other than those, I cannot say.

Question: Did you only write letters under the direction of Mr. Zander, or did you also write your own letters to soldiers?

Answer: Except for the letters I wrote under the direction of Mr. Zander, I wrote only to my brother and to van Treck. Otherwise, I wrote no letters.

personally read and found correct
/s/ Helmuth Hübener

Certified with the note that Hübener was returned to police custody.

Düwer, brought forward from police custody, declares upon inquiry, that he received 9 flyers altogether from Hübener. A private party in the home of his parents was never held, also the reading of the flyers at this occasion never occurred. Other than the already-mentioned neighbor children Zumsande, he never showed the flyers to anyone. He allegedly never participated in a private party, although he knows that the neighbor children, in the absence of their parents, held such an event. He does not know who participated in it.

Düwer, who made his statements only hesitatingly, gives the impression of being stubborn. He was returned to police custody.

/s/ Müssener, Criminal Secretary

Hamburg, 17 February 1942

In August 1941 the attached inflammatory writings, which contain, on the one hand, *personal attacks upon the Führer* and, on the other, *newscasts of the London radio station,* were returned through the police precincts, to which they were delivered, and sent through the German Post Office. It emerges from the accounts under consideration that these inflammatory writings were thrown by the perpetrators in hallways, mailboxes of the German Post Office and on the open street in the Hammerbrook and Rothensburgsort parts of the city. The investigations conducted in due course did not lead to the identification of the perpetrators. Because paper used exclusively at the social administration was used in the production of the inflammatory writings, the suspicion grew stronger also that the perpetrator or perpetrators are to be found among the employees of the social administration. Nevertheless, the steps taken did not lead to any success.

Because the production and distribution of the inflammatory writings partially chronologically and spatially coincide with the flyers produced by Hübener and also various of these writings are identical or contain very similar texts, the suspicion is obvious that Hübener also produced and distributed these writings. Therefore, Hübener was brought again from police custody. Under remonstrations and the pressure of evidence, Hübener admitted also to have made and distributed these inflammatory writings. In addition, he states:

"I admit to having prepared and distributed the inflammatory writings in question. It could have been in August when I produced these inflammatory writings. Their contents deal likewise with the reproduction of newscasts of the London station. I produced these writings also in the apartment of my grandparents."

Question: How many of these inflammatory writings were produced and where were they kept?

Answer: It could have been approximately 60 copies, I cannot say more precisely. From these writings each time I gave a copy to the sales apprentice Horst van Treck, at that time at National Labor Service military postal number 39281, formerly resident with his parents at Louisenweg 139. What Treck did with these inflammatory writings I cannot say. The mechanic and machinist's apprentice Rudolf Wobbe, residing at Hardenstraße 15 III with his parents, received approximately 20 copies. I gave Wobbe the task of trying to dispose of the writings, which meant to distribute the writings. What he did with the writings, I do not know. For myself, I tossed my inflammatory writings, it could have been approximately 20, in the hallways, on the public street and in mailboxes in the Spaldingstraße, Eiffestraße and Grevenweg.

Question: What motivated you to produce and distribute such writings?

Answer: I was dissatisfied with the newscasts which the German radio reported and wanted to furnish other people with newscasts, which the English news reports presented, and which I held to be partially true, so that they could also learn something from these reports.

Question: Were you completely unaware of the criminality of your conduct?
Answer: Certainly, I was completely aware of it, but I never figured that it would ever become known.
Question: With what typewriter were these inflammatory writings produced?
Answer: The inflammatory writings in question here I produced with a portable typewriter, which is the property of Mr. Zander. He placed the typewriter at my disposal in order for me to write letters. Then later I was given the large typewriter, which was confiscated from me, and with which I wrote the large flyers. Otherwise, I wrote one flyer on an office typewriter in district office 4A, Frankenstraße 43.
Question: Were any further writings produced and distributed by you in this or a similar manner?
Answer: No, no other writings were produced or distributed by me.
Question: Was any oral propaganda carried out based on these newscasts from the London radio?
Answer: No oral propaganda was carried on by me. I used written material exclusively.

personally read and found correct
/s/ Helmuth Hübener

Hamburg, 20 February 1942

Hübener was summoned from police custody once again in order to be questioned about the reasons for his behavior.

Question: What motivated you to continue to listen?
Answer: As I already said in my first interrogation, curiosity motivated me to listen. Through reports in the daily newspapers about the English newscasts and through conversations with other persons I was first made aware of it. When my brother brought the radio set with him, I decided to inform myself about these newscasts. After I had listened to these broadcasts a few times, doubts arose in me about the correctness of our newscasts. To begin with, I kept these newscasts to myself or, at the most, mentioned something from them in conversation. But the longer I listened to the newscasts, the larger my doubts became. Finally, I could not do anything else, I had to listen to the London broadcasts.
Question: What reasons did you have to distribute these newscasts?
Answer: I felt the need to share with others that which I heard. Because I could not keep everything in my head, I made notes and then copied them on the typewriter. At first, I had only the intention of giving what I had written to my friends. After a while this did not satisfy me, and so I began to distribute the notes that I had written down during the newscasts in the way already described. It was my firm intent to point out to others the differences in the newscasts, because I myself had already become dissatisfied and believed much of the English broadcasts. It was not my intent to make the general public dissatisfied or to incite them at all, I never thought about that, I merely wanted to inform them of the difference in

the reporting. In order to achieve that in a broader circle without endangering myself, I turned to producing the flyers.

Question: On part of the flyers you wrote "chain letter"; were you aware what a chain letter is and what a broad range that kind of distribution can assume?

Answer: I read the expression "chain letter" in a book. I assumed from that, that such a letter went from hand to hand and thus passed through the largest possible number. Because it was my intent to provide the largest possible number with these newscasts, I wrote on the backside of the flyer "chain letter." I calculated that this expression is universally known and would be treated in that sense.

Question: How many persons, in your view, would read such a letter and pass it on before it would be destroyed?

Answer: I cannot say exactly. I marked 12 flyers with "chain letter" and figured that perhaps some would not be passed on. At least 8 or 10, in my view, were certainly passed on. Now if, as I figured, each time an entire family received such a flyer, reads it and then passes it on, and the next family does the same and then, perhaps, also distributes its content orally, this makes a rather large number, and that is what I wanted to accomplish.

Question: Did you never think, then, what risk you would run and that you would be severely punished, if you were discovered?

Answer: I was fully aware of that; I knew that such a thing would be severely punished, but I calculated that it would never be discovered.

read and found correct
/s/ Helmuth Hübener

Certified with the note that Hübener was returned to police custody.
/s/ Müssener, Criminal Secretary

Source: Berlin Document Center

11

State Police Agency
Hamburg, 10 February 1942

About the Person:
Schnibbe, Karl Heinz

From my 7th to 15th year I attended the primary school in Hamburg and graduated after 8 years. After my graduation I entered the painting trade with the firm F. G. Suhse, Bökmannstraße 36. I ended my apprenticeship on 1 April 1941. At this time, I am still employed by the same company as a journeyman painter.

About the Case:

Upon Interrogation:

I have known Hübener for many years; for approximately two years we have associated together as friends. It could have been approximately the middle of 1941 when Hübener mentioned to me that he was listening to the newscasts of the British Broadcasting Company on a radio set which his brother had brought from France. It is possible that he told me also when and how often he did it. But today I cannot recall any more about it. One day, I do not know anymore when it was, it could have been in the autumn of 1941, he declared to me he was writing down on the typewriter the newscasts which he heard. At that time he showed me a sheet of paper which was filled with typing on one side. I read this writing and knew immediately that it dealt with newscasts from an English station. Because I was interested in these reports myself, it was only curiosity, I told him that he should copy these reports for me. It is possible that I said also that he should give me a sheet each time. Of course, I cannot recall exactly. During the following period I received some such pages from him. There were, in my opinion, not more than three. He, of course, showed me more and I read them, too. The last time I received such a sheet from him was at the beginning of January 1942.

Question: What became of these flyers and who, besides you, read them?
Answer: The flyers were burned by me on the same day I received them. I did not show them to anyone else.
Question: Did you speak with anyone else about the contents of these flyers?
Answer: Yes, I did, and in fact with an acquaintance from the congregation. I shared with this acquaintance, it was Rudi Wobbe, his residence is unknown to me, some of the contents. I emphasize expressly that I did not show him the flyers.
Question: You were often in the apartment of Hübener, did you jointly listen with him on occasion to the newscasts of the English station?
Answer: I never listened with him. I admit that we attempted once to listen to the English station, but it was not possible, because there was too much jamming. I never tried it again.
Question: Did you know that, besides yourself, other persons received such flyers?
Answer: He told me once, that besides me one other colleague received flyers from him. Who it is, he did not tell me. I also did not know that he distributed flyers in other ways. I was first made aware of this on Sunday, 8 February 1942 by the leader of our religious community Mr. Zander. He told us at a meeting that one of our congregation had been arrested because he listened to and distributed English newscasts. He encouraged us to report anyone who did such things. I cannot make any further statements.

read personally and found correct
/s/ Karl Heinz Schnibbe

Certified with the note that after his interrogation Schnibbe was provisionally taken into custody and delivered to the police prison Fuhlsbüttel. He did not have any personal effects with him. His arrest card was used as a temporary identification card in the prison.
/s/ Müssener, Criminal Secretary

Hamburg, 11 February 1942

It can be determined from page 2 of the completed documents of Mohns's account that Düwer, as he also declared in his interrogation, asked for the flyers from Hübener in order to collect them as evidence. As a matter of fact, Mohns, as can be determined from his account, approached Düwer with a commission of that kind. In order to bring about a completely accurate clarification, the deputy shop steward

Kurt Heinrich Martin Mohns

born 14 January 1899 in Hamburg, resident in Hamburg, Bornstraße 4 III, was summoned to the interrogation at police headquarters. Mohns testified:
On 20 January 1942 the administrative apprentices Hübener and Düwer came into my office, in which the administrative apprentice Kranz also had his station. Hübener attempted to press a folded sheet of paper into the hand of the apprentice Kranz. He was supported in this by Düwer. Kranz declined to accept. I then became aware of the three and said to them "I hope you fellows are not involved in any forbidden business; watch out, that you don't end up in a concentration camp!" At that Hübener and Düwer left the room laughing. As soon as both of them had left the room, I requested an explanation from Kranz. Kranz explained to me that he was supposed to translate a document, an inflammatory pamphlet, into the French language for Hübener, who claimed to have connections with French prisoners. He, Kranz, of course, refused this request. On the following day then, I met both of the apprentices, Düwer and Kranz, in order to prevail upon them to obtain an inflammatory document from Hübener, in order to use it as evidence. Both agreed to it. On 4 February 1942 I received two such inflammatory documents from Düwer, after I, in the meantime, had approached him again.

Question: Did Düwer immediately say voluntarily that he still had more of these writings at home or was he asked about it by you?
Answer: I am of the opinion, I cannot say precisely anymore, that I asked him about it. In any case, he admitted having still more writings at home. He received from me the commission to bring the writings with him the following day. On the following day, it was on 5 February, Düwer nevertheless failed to bring the writings, because he allegedly had forgotten. After that I then reported it immediately to my superior, the director of the cashier's office, Mr. Graf, who took further action.
Question: You claim, that you, in the period from 21 January until 4 February repeatedly approached Düwer and asked him about the writings. What did Düwer say to you then?

Answer: Düwer always said to me, that he still had no writings.

read personally and found correct
/s/ Heinrich Mohns

Certified,
/s/ Müssener, Criminal Secretary

After being summoned, there appeared the two brothers,

salesman apprentice Horst (1) Zumsande, born 9 February 1924 Hamburg, and the student Kurt Zumsande, [born] 12 June 1925 in Kiel, both resident in Hamburg-Bahrenfelt, Adickesstraße 63 ground floor with their parents and explained under inquiry:

We are on friendly terms with Düwer. He comes often to our apartment. One day, it was about two weeks ago, I can no longer recall the exact day, Düwer visited us again at our apartment. Besides me and my brother, there was another acquaintance present named Karl Horst Pipo, resident in Hamburg, Grindelallee 6 c/o Karstens. It is possible that the three of us played cards. I no longer know what Düwer began a conversation with us about. In any case, he took the opportunity to show us a typewritten sheet of paper and encouraged us to read it. After we had read the beginning of the writing, we immediately handed the paper back to him. We did this first, because it was very difficult to read and, second, because it was clear to us that it dealt with things that must have originated from an enemy radio station. When we casually threatened to report him, he made a disparaging gesture and said "Pooh, you have no proof." Except for this occasion, he never showed us flyers again. I can still remember that it was two flyers that he handed us.

Question: Did Düwer, before he displayed the flyers, also talk occasionally about such things?

Answer: Yes, he did. I know that in this connection he once spoke about Dakar, English landing forces, and about General Rommel. At that time I could not form a clear image in my mind about his statements and wrote some key words on a scratch pad without his noticing. I made these notes because he had already told me once before about a secret club, I believe he called it "Spi." [Ed. note: the German word for espionage is *Spi*onage.] I wanted to use these notes at the proper time as evidence to denounce him. I must point out that Düwer first came with such things after the middle or end of January 1942, I never heard about such things from him before.

Question: Was there ever a private party given by Düwer?

Answer: I do not know, but I believe not. There was, of course, such a gathering once in our apartment. But Düwer did not participate.

read personally and found correct
/s/ Horst Zumsande

/s/ Kurt Zumsande

Certified with the note that the Zumsande brothers were released again after their interrogation.
/s/ Müssener, Criminal Secretary

Source: Berlin Document Center

12

State Police Agency
Hamburg, 18 February 1942

About the Person:
Wobbe, Rudolf Gustav

I attended primary school in Hamburg, Stresowstraße 16/18 from 1932 until April 1940 and graduated from the 8th grade.

About the Case:

Upon Interrogation:
I admit having distributed flyers with the text from newscasts of the London station.

Question: How did you get the flyers?
Answer: It could have been in August 1941, when I received flyers from the administrative apprentice Hübener. He gave them to me with the charge to read through and distribute them. It could have been 15 copies, I can no longer say exactly. They were small sheets in the form of handbills.
Question: Did you know where Hübener obtained the flyers?
Answer: Yes, I knew. When I asked him about their origin, he told me that he listened to the London radio station and then transcribed the newscasts with a typewriter.
Question: Did it not dawn on you that you are liable for prosecution, especially since you knew the content and know also where they originated?
Answer: No, I never thought about that. Only later, when I had distributed the flyers, did I recognize that I had committed a great blunder.
Question: Where and how were the flyers distributed by you?
Answer: I tossed the flyers in stairwells and mailboxes in Billhorn, in the Röhrendamm, Mühlenweg, Markmannstraße, Lindleystraße, and Canalstraße. In addition I attached them now and then to the bulletin boards found in stairwells.
Question: How often did you obtain flyers from Hübener?
Answer: I received flyers from Hübener twice, namely the small ones once,

which I distributed, and once it was four or five large ones. The large ones, which I received with the same charge, I burned after I read them.

Question: Do you know of other persons who received flyers from Hübener?

Answer: No, I know of no other persons.

Question: How often did you listen to the newscasts of the London radio station?

Answer: I've never listened to the London station. I admit, though, to have tried about three or four times to listen to this station. It was not possible for me, because it cannot be received on our old radio set.

Question: Did you listen to this station together with Hübener in the apartment of his grandparents?

Answer: It is true I was often in the apartment with Hübener, but we never listened to the station together. In the apartment I merely received the flyers from him.

Question: Why did you distribute the flyers, did you have a reason, were you dissatisfied with something?

Answer: I had no reason for this. I do not know myself how I came to do it.

read personally and found correct
/s/ Rudolf Wobbe

Certified with the note that Wobbe was returned to police custody.
/s/ Müssener, Criminal Secretary

Source: Berlin Document Center

13

Secret State Police
Hamburg, 11 May 1942
State Police Office Hamburg
B. No. II P—126/42

Upon being summoned, there appeared at the office the financial candidate

Franz Walter Prumnitz,

born 2 February 1925 in Hamburg, residing Osterbrook 58 IV, with his parents. Informed of the subject of the interrogation and admonished to tell the truth, he makes the following statements:

Hübener is known to me from school. We attended the upper-track school at Brackdamm together. Shortly before our discharge from school, I was with him in the apartment of his grandparents about two or three times, where we did our schoolwork together. After our graduation from school we only associated while on duty with the Hitler Youth. Graduation from school was in March 1941. In June of the same year I entered the finance school in Thorn, where I remained until 3 April 1942. During that time I had a vacation one time, namely from 18 December 1941 until 5 January 1942. Before my vacation I once received a letter from Hübener, in which he imparted only information of a personal nature. During my vacation I also visited Hübener once; it was between Christmas and New Year's. When I was getting ready to leave and was already standing at the wardrobe in order to put on my coat, he showed me a sheet of paper; it was a thin tissue paper that was written with the typewriter. He gave me the sheet with the words "Do you want to see what the foreigners say about us," or something similar. I can no longer say exactly. I just glanced at the paper very fleetingly and returned it with the words that it was of no further interest to me. Although I did not read everything exactly, I could still determine that it pretty much contained the opposite of what our newscasts contain.

Question: Did it become clear to you, that the content dealt with enemy propaganda?

Answer: Yes, that is what I thought immediately.

Question: Did you ask Hübener where he obtained the writing, or did Hübener give an explanation about it?

Answer: I did not ask him about the source, because it did not interest me, and he did not offer any explanation.

Question: During your vacation, did Hübener show you such writings often, or did he talk about such things with you?

Answer: No, he did not do that, because I did not see him again during my vacation.

Question: When you were back in school again, did Hübener still write to you? Did he write about such things in these letters?

Answer: When I was back in school again, I received one letter from him, which was written by hand. This letter contained information mainly concerned with Rudolf Hess, but what was otherwise contained in it I cannot say anymore. But I still recall that these messages were entitled "What the foreign press is reporting."

Question: Did you answer this letter, and were you, in particular, interested in this report?

Answer: I answered the letter, but I had no interest in the report of the foreign press.

Question: Did Hübener write even more letters containing similar reports?

Answer: I received mail from him two or three times; I can no longer say exactly. This mail did not involve handwritten letters, but consisted of envelopes that held nothing further except the typewritten sheets like he had shown me once.

Question: Did you read these writings, and what happened to them?

Answer: I read the first such writing that came in the mail. The others, upon opening the envelope and determining that it again concerned foreign reports, I destroyed unread. They were torn up by me and thrown into the trash can. No one besides me saw the writings.

Question: You knew exactly that it was concerned with reports of foreign radio stations, therefore with enemy propaganda. Why did you not make a report?

Answer: I did not think about it. I cannot give any other good reason. I was not interested in such things and considered the matter finished after I had destroyed them.

Question: Were you aware that the distribution of such newscasts is considered a crime or, at least, a punishable action that one must report?

Answer: I did not know that it involved a crime, but I was aware that Hübener would be punished if he were discovered. That it was my duty to make a report, I did not know. I had the intention to reproach him in a letter and warn him. But I later gave it up and did not concern myself about it any more.

Question: Did you ever think about what Hübener intended with the distribution of such newscasts, and that he could have sent such newscasts to yet other persons besides you?

Answer: I did not think about the purpose of his sending such newscasts, neither did I assume nor did it occur to me that he might have had other persons besides me in mind to receive such newscasts. On the basis of our acquaintance, I considered it as purely personal information. If I had been aware of the criminal nature of his conduct, I also certainly would have made a report. I can make no further statements about this matter and declare to have spoken the truth.

personally read and found to be correct
/s/ Franz Prumnitz

Certified with the note that Prumnitz after his interrogation was released again.
/s/ Müssener, Criminal Secretary

Source: Berlin Document Center

14

Secret State Police
Hamburg, 19 May 1942
State Police Agency Hamburg
B. No. II P—125/42

There appeared at the office the radio operator

Horst Willy van Treck,

born 9 December 1923 in Hamburg, at present with the 3rd Air Regiment 311, and made, when informed of the subject of the interrogation and admonished to tell the truth, the following statement:

Hübener is only known to me under the name of Kunkel. We have been acquainted since our school days and played together as children. After our school days we did not cultivate a particularly friendly association, at most we went together occasionally to the movies. His political outlook is unknown to me, because we never talked about politics. One exception was our conversations about current events. Hübener and I had quarreled temporarily and then about in March or April 1941, when we were reconciled, we got together again. In the following period I was in his apartment about five or six times, that is in the apartment of his grandparents, with whom he lived. We talked then about really mundane things or listened to music, partly phonograph, partly radio music. My visits to him lasted, at most, one to one and one-half hours, so that I was home again regularly about 9:30 or 10:00.

Question: During your visits, were, other than musical performances, newscasts heard on the radio?

Answer: No, newscasts were never heard in my presence.

Question: Did Hübener once give you a small leaflet written on the typewriter?

Answer: It could have been July or August 1941 when Hübener gave me about 10 or 15 small notes that were written with a typewriter.

Question: Did you read the notes and can you still recall what was written on these notes?

Answer: I read some of the notes. As far as I can remember, there was something about Russia, and about alleged losses that we were alleged to have had, with descriptions of the regiments. Also, the Führer was attacked in these handbills and designated as the one responsible for the war. Further, the Führer was called "a mass murderer, traitor and warmonger." It is possible that there was even more on the handbills, but I can no longer remember exactly.

Question: Did Hübener say to you where he obtained these handbills and how he came upon their contents?

Answer: I asked Hübener about the source of the handbills. He said to me that he had drawn them up himself and had taken the contents from the English newscasts.

Question: Did Hübener tell you how many such handbills he had produced, and who other than you had received handbills?

Answer: No, he did not tell me.

Question: Did Hübener tell you what you should do with these handbills?

Answer: Yes, he said I should pass them on.

Question: What did you do with these handbills?

Answer: After I had read them, I tore the handbills into pieces in his presence and stuck them in a storm-sewer grate in front of the house. Hübener did not want me to do this and tried to take the handbills away from me.

Question: Did you know that such handbills were also being distributed?

Answer: No, I heard nothing about it.

Question: Did Hübener approach you again with such handbills?

Answer: No, he did not. Since my induction into the National Labor Service on 29 August I have been together with him several times, but we never spoke again about this matter.

Question: When you were with the National Labor Service, Hübener nevertheless remained in contact with you by correspondence. Other than personal information, did these letters contain information of a political nature?

Answer: During my affiliation with the National Labor Service, I received about four or five letters from him. In the next to the last letter there was also information from the English newscasts. What it contained, I no longer recall. In the answer to this letter, I informed him that he should discontinue writing me such letters in the future. I then received mail once more from him. It was an envelope which contained nothing else except a flyer. I read the flyer and knew at once that it involved enemy propaganda. I destroyed this flyer immediately after reading it.

Question: Why did you neglect to report to your superiors, especially since you knew that Hübener was involved with the distribution of enemy propaganda that was aimed at the decay of the German will to resist and the overthrow of the national socialist German state leadership?

Answer: I did not think any more about the whole matter and let it drop. Today I see that I did not behave properly, and it would have been my duty to give a report about this. Concerning this matter I cannot make any further statements and declare to have stated the truth.

read personally and found to be correct
/s/ Horst van Treck

Certified with the note that van Treck following his interrogation was once again released to the appropriate field court martial.
/s/ Müssener, Criminal Secretary

Hamburg, 20 May 1942

In order to clarify a contradiction in regard to the whereabouts of the flyers, Hübener was questioned again today in the interrogation rooms of the investigatory prison. Concerning this matter he stated:

It is not correct when van Treck maintained that I gave him 10 or 15 of these small handbills at one time. I know positively that he received them in two installments. The first time he received approximately 5 or 6, and this was in or in front of the apartment of my grandparents, I can no longer recall precisely. Standing in front of the house door we looked over and discussed them. I must correct myself, I did not give him, as just stated, 5 or 6, but it was considerably more. From the bundle which I gave him, in front of the house door he searched for those that were written most clearly and that was 5 or 6 copies. These 5 or 6 copies were not all of the same leaflet, but they were copies of different ones. Approximately a week later I gave him handbills once again, how many there were and by which opportunity this occurred, I can no longer say with certainty. But I believe that it was at least 10 copies. When van Treck further maintains that he ripped the handbills in my presence and stuck them in a storm-sewer grate, that is not correct. I know further that we once had an argument about the handbills in front of the house where he lives. He reproached me about the matter, saying that what I was doing was not right, and said further that some day I could get in big trouble over it. If I remember correctly, he told me further on that occasion that in the future he would not accept any such handbills from me. I also did not offer him any again, and it was never discussed again. What van Treck did with these flyers, I do not know. I remember that during the argument he wanted to give back the handbills. But I did not take them back. We separated after that, rather agitated. I consider it possible that he destroyed the handbills following this argument, in any case, I do not believe that he distributed them. From the beginning he was opposed to the distribution.

read personally and found correct:
/s/ H. Hübener

Certified with the note, that the original of the interrogation is enclosed in an envelope.
/s/ Müssener, Criminal Secretary

Source: Berlin Document Center

15

Hamburg, 24 February 1942

Final Report

In August 1941 in the city districts of Hammerbrook and Rothenburgsort, inflammatory writings were distributed, which were found in hallways and mailboxes, as well as mailboxes of the German National Post Office and on the street. The contents were, in part, reports from the English radio which were designed to endanger the resistance strength of the German people, in part, horrible invectives against the Führer, like "Hitler the Murderer, People's Seducer, People's Corrupter, People's Traitor," and so on (B1.20 and envelope B1.21 of the documents).

The inflammatory writings were the work of an administrative apprentice for the executive track in the Hamburg social administration, *Helmuth* Günther Hübener, born 8 January 1925 in Hamburg, residence: Hamburg, Sachsenstraße 42 (B1.11 of the documents). Hübener, who earlier bore the name of his mother, Guddat, was adopted by his stepfather. His parents were both gainfully employed, so he lived with his grandparents, Louisenweg 137. In this residence, since March/April 1941, he also listened continually and unlawfully to the newscast service in the German language of enemy broadcasters, with a radio that his brother brought from France at that time, and indeed until his arrest he allegedly listened four to five times weekly, usually in the evening at 10:00 without the knowledge of his grandparents who were already sleeping at that time (B1.13 of the documents). The reports listened to are allegedly said to have made such a great impression and exerted such a great influence on him that he could not stop listening and he considered the reports to be completely correct. With the distribution of the flyers he allegedly intended for the general public to note the differences in reporting. It is psychologically interesting that Hübener completed a short time previously a final project in school, in which a completely positive attitude to the Führer is to be observed. The work is included as an attached exhibit.

From the formerly mentioned inflammatory writings he prepared until August of last year approximately 60 copies. He distributed approximately 20 copies himself in Hammerbrook, approximately 20 copies he gave to the mechanic's apprentice *Rudolf* Gustav Wobbe, born 11 February 1926 in Hamburg, Hardenstraße 15, with his mother (Personal Data B1.22 of the documents), which he distributed in the Rothenburgsort area. He knew that it involved intercepted inflammatory newscasts from a London station.

Together with Hübener he did not listen to the radio messages, but attempted nevertheless to listen alone to foreign stations with the radio apparatus belonging to his mother.

Hübener gave approximately the same number to another friend, the salesman apprentice Horst van Treck, who was later inducted into the National Labor Service (Military Post Office No. 39281) where he is currently. Whether van Treck also distributed these flyers, his interrogation must reveal.

In the meantime, no inflammatory writings of this type were found in Hamburg, nevertheless, at the beginning of February, flyers appeared in the Hammerbrook area containing detailed notes from the English radio propaganda service. With considerable skill, the most sophisticated broadcasts were selected, which were suited to have a demoralizing effect. On these inflammatory writings was a notice "This is a chain letter, so pass it on." Through the vigilance of the party overseer at the social administration office in Hamburg, we succeeded in identifying Hübener as the producer of these inflammatory writings. He was arrested on *5 February 1942*. In his interrogation he then also admitted to having prepared the first inflammatory writings cited. Of the last completed inflammatory writing (Envelope B1.4 and Envelope B1.15a of the documents) he himself threw approximately 15 copies in hallways and mailboxes in Hammerbrook. He included inflammatory writings several times in letters to a school friend Franz Prumnitz, address: Finance School in Thorn. Aggravating the case further is that he sent the sheets also to the aforementioned Horst van Treck, who was, in the meantime, inducted into the Labor Service.

In the middle of 1941 he informed further another friend, the painter journeyman Karl-Heinz Schnibbe, born 5 January 1924 in Hamburg, residence: Hamburg, Rossausweg 32 (Personal Data B1.16 of the documents), that he listened regularly to the newscast service of an English station, and in the fall of 1941 Hübener explained to him that he wrote down with the typewriter the newscasts which he heard. Hübener then also let Schnibbe read the notes and encouraged him to make regularly a copy of the inflammatory report for him. He received also various flyers from Hübener, but he did not want to distribute them, nevertheless, he shared the contents with the aforementioned Wobbe. Schnibbe attempted, further, to listen mutually with Hübener to foreign stations.

In addition, and finally, Hübener delivered to apprentice *Gerhard* Heinrich Jacob Jonni Düwer, born 1 November 1924 in Altona, residence: Hamburg, Bahrenfelder Kirchenweg 53, likewise employed at the social administration, approximately 12 of the last produced inflammatory writings. He gave some of the sheets to 2 friends to read and related to them oral extracts from the news sheets. Hübener, Wobbe and Schnibbe have belonged since 1938 to the Hitler Youth, the latter, because of failure to obey orders, was expelled at the end of 1939. Düwer has been a member of the Hitler Youth since 1933, he was mustered on 3 February 1942 into the tank corps or heavy artillery, but was deferred until further notice.

The parents, who had no idea of the activities of their sons, have never aroused suspicions in regard to political or criminal espionage.

/s/ Wangemann, Criminal Commissioner
/s/ Müssener, Criminal Secretary

Source: Berlin Document Center

16

District Court Hamburg
Division 120
Hamburg 36, 27 February 1942
File Number 120 Gs. 60/42
Criminal Case against Hübener et al.

Arrest Warrant

1. the administrative apprentice at the social administration in Hamburg
   Helmuth Günther Hübener,
   born on 8 January 1925 in Hamburg,
   residence: Hamburg 1, Sachsenstraße 42,
   member of the Church of Jesus Christ of Latter-day Saints,
2. the mechanic's apprentice
   Rudolf Gustav Wobbe,
   born on 11 February 1926 in Hamburg,
   residence: Hamburg, Hardenstraße 15 II. with his mother,
   member of the Church of Jesus Christ of Latter-day Saints,

3. the painter journeyman
   Karl Heinz Schnibbe,
   born on 5 January 1924 in Hamburg,
   residence: Hamburg, Rossausweg 32 I.,
   member of the Church of Jesus Christ of Latter-day Saints, (Mormons),
4. the administrative apprentice at the social administration in Hamburg
   Gerhard Heinrich Jacob Jonni Düwer,
   born on 1 November 1924 in Altona,
   residence: Hamburg-Altona, Kirchenweg 53 ground floor,

are to be brought to detention pending trial, because they are strongly suspected (see reverse side) of crimes punishable in accordance with §§83 sections 2 and 3, figure 2 and 3, Penal Code, 43, 47 Penal Code, §§1, 2, 5 of the decree concerning extraordinary radio measures of 1 September 1939, §§1, 3, 9 of the Juvenile Code.

Detention pending trial is being imposed, because the object of the investigation is a criminal act.

This warrant of arrest is subject to the right of appeal.

The defendants are accused as follows:

1. *Hübener:* of continually conspiring and, in part, acting jointly with others in Hamburg from April 1941 until February 1942
   a) to have prepared a treasonable undertaking, whereby the deed, in part, was directed at making the German National Defense Forces incapable of fulfilling their duty, to weaken the German Reich against attacks upon its external or internal stability, further to influence the masses through the production and distribution of writings and in consequence herewith
   b) intentionally listening to foreign broadcasts and further in coincidence with a) newscasts of foreign stations, which are intended to endanger the resistance strength of the German people, and to have distributed this willfully,
2. *Wobbe:*
   a) of having prepared a treasonable undertaking, whereby the deed was intended to influence the masses through the distribution of writings and in consequence herewith,
   b) to have attempted intentionally to listen to foreign stations and further
   c) in coincidence with a) newscasts of foreign stations, which are intended to endanger the resistance strength of the German people, and to have distributed this willfully,
3. *Schnibbe:*
   a) of having attempted to listen to foreign stations and through a further independent deed
   b) newscasts of foreign stations, which are intended to endanger the resistance strength of the German people, and to have distributed this willfully,

4. *Düwer:* of having distributed willfully newscasts of foreign stations, which are intended to endanger the resistance strength of the German people,

to wit: Hübener, Wobbe, and Düwer [are accused] as juveniles.

Source: Berlin Document Center

17

National Socialist German Workers' Party
Region Administration Hamburg
District Hamburg 5
Hamburg, 24 February 1942
Personnel Office Division/N.

To the
Secret State Police
here
Your telegraph inquiry of 20 February 1942
11 P 126/42

Re: Johannes Schnibbe, born 9 October 1891 in Hethorn near Wesermünde residence: Hamburg, Rossausweg 32 I.

The above-named makes a positive and correct impression. In political respects nothing unfavorable was known. Schnibbe is active as a preacher in the congregation of the Church of Jesus Christ of Latter-day Saints. This church congregation is legally recognized and stands on a firm footing with the present government. As we ascertained, his son is in detention, which causes the parents great sorrow.
   Heil Hitler!

/s/ [illegible], District Leader

Source: Berlin Document Center

18

National Socialist German Workers' Party
District Hamburg 7
Hamburg-Altona, 27 February 1942
Flottbeker Chaussee 73 (Donnerschloß)

To the
Secret State Police
State Police Office Hamburg
Report/Section II ¶ No. 126/42
Hamburg 36
Stadthausbrücke 8

Re: Adolf Hinrich Düwer, born 22 March 1893, and family
     Hamburg-Bahrenfeld, Bahrenfelder Kirchenweg 53 ground floor
     Your telephone inquiry of 20 February 1942

The above-mentioned Düwer belongs to the DAF [German Labor Front],
the NSV [National Socialist Volk Welfare], the RLB [Reich Teachers'
League] as well as the Technical Emergency Relief. Since June 1940 he has
been called to the Security Service of the SS. D[üwer] is married and has a
son, who belongs to the Hitler Youth. The Düwer family enjoys a good reputation in their respective local branch, and no negative information is known
there about the above-mentioned.
    Heil Hitler!

/s/ Piwitt

Source: Berlin Document Center

19

National Socialist German Workers' Party
Region Hamburg
District Hamburg 4
Personnel Office Division/Jo.
Hamburg, 10 March 1942

To the
Secret State Police
State Police Office Hamburg
-P2-
Hamburg 36
Stadthausbrücke 8

Re: Mrs. Wobbe, born 27 October 1901
     residence: Hardenstraße 15 II
     occupation: cleaning woman[5]
     your telephone inquiry of 20 February 1942

Aryan, widowed, 1 child (in the Hitler Youth).

Not a member of the National Socialist German Workers' Party and the NSV [National Socialist Volk Welfare]. Member of the DAF [German Labor Front] since 1939. Honorarily active as subdivision leader in the NSKOV [National Socialist War Martyrs' Welfare].

Behavior vis-à-vis political leaders and collectors unobjectionable, contributes to donations, WHW [Winter Relief Agency] and Eintopf [One-pot Meal].⁶ Meetings and events of the local branch are visited.

In respect to politics and character we have no reservations.

Heil Hitler!

/s/ [illegible], District Personnel Office Director

Source: Berlin Document Center

20

National Socialist German Workers' Party
Region Hamburg
District Hamburg 4
Section: Personnel Office/Jo.
Hamburg 1, 12 March 1942
An der Alster 12

To the
Secret State Police
State Police Office Hamburg
- 2 P -
Hamburg 36
Stadthausbrücke 8

Re: Hübener Family, Sachsenstraße 42
      Political Judgment
Re: your telephone request of 20 February 1942

Aryan, number of children: 5
Occupation of husband: Laborer
H[übener] has been a member of the Nazi party since 1 May 1937 and the DAF [German Labor Front] since 1934, wife a member of the NSV [National Socialist People's Welfare].

H[übener] was earlier in the Stahlhelm [Steel Helmet], since 18 February 1934 in the SA, currently corporal.

The swastika flag is displayed, good behavior vis-à-vis political leaders and collectors, participates in donations, WHW [Winter Relief Agency] and Eintopf [One-pot Meal]. Meetings and events are visited.

With regard to politics and character there are no objections.

Heil Hitler!

The District Leader
by commission [illegible]
District Personnel Office Leader

Source: Berlin Document Center

21

Letter from Emma Hübener

Hamburg, 8 March 1942
To the General Public Prosecutor
at the Hanseatic Higher Regional Court

My son Helmuth was born on 8 January 1925, in Hamburg. Helmuth
was a bright, intelligent boy. From the sixth year on he attended the Elementary School in the Louisenweg; he was a good student and after the third
grade was transferred to the upper-track at Brackdamm. Helmuth was gifted and ambitious as a student, his grades were good, his behavior, diligence
and attentiveness were very good! His attendance was regular except for a
few days of sickness. Because Helmuth was very diligent and gifted, my husband and I allowed him to take lessons in stenography and typing; he attended the courses and learned very well. His knowledge of English was
good, also, and he wanted to pursue a civil service career. Helmuth belonged
to the Young Folk and was automatically taken into the Hitler Youth in April
1939. His conduct at home was always very good, we seldom needed to scold
him, he obeyed immediately. We as parents were very pleased with the boy,
because he continued his studies so willingly and diligently. His graduation
certificate was good. His political essay was also very good and is on file.
Until the summer of 1941 Helmuth lived and spoke only for our Führer
Adolf Hitler. That is why it is inexplicable to me and my husband how this
matter could come about. We knew nothing about it. I also took a close look
at his work and could say that he sent letters with completely harmless contents to the front, the shorthand notes will surely still be available. Because
I am busy working as a nurse, Helmuth ate with my parents and came home
a few evenings during the week. His grandparents can also give Helmuth
nothing but a good recommendation; he was diligent and well behaved, he
did not smoke and was always at home at night and continued to practice
on the typewriter. Because my parents also knew nothing about him doing
such a foolish thing, they cannot conceive of it either. When Helmuth was
transferred during the summer back to the Biberhaus, I asked him how he
liked his present work. For an answer I received: very well, Mama, but they
are all oriented completely different, are not at all so much in favor of our

Führer Adolf Hitler. I replied afterwards: do me one favor and do not involve yourself with it. Then I never again conducted further conversations about politics and work. I cannot help thinking the cause of the incident must stem from the Biberhaus and I must assume that he was misled by someone.

Signed with the German Greeting,[7]
Mrs. Emma Hübener
Hamburg 1 Sachsenstraße 42, ground floor

Source: Berlin Document Center

22

Letter from Johann Schnibbe

Statement about my son Karl-Heinz

Karl-Heinz was born in Hamburg on 5 January 1924. At the age of six he entered the elementary school in the Wallstraße, where he went through all eight classes. He was an average student. He was also in the Hitler Youth. From 18 to 31 July 1939, he was in the summer recreation camp in Thuringia. Later he had to carry out camouflage work for the military, which was very strenuous for him. In his vocational work he also had long days because of the long distances, therefore he was often tired in the evening and did not attend the Hitler Youth, until he gradually fell away. As parents we could not complain about him. He was obedient at home and came home punctually at night. He was also not slovenly and debauched. In general he was still rather childish and interpreted everything on the lighter side. We often had the impression that he was easy to influence. We never had conflict with neighbors or strangers because of our children.

I would like to state still further that since 1921 we have belonged to the Church of Jesus Christ of Latter-day Saints and that until today we have spent most of our free time there. We have also taught and raised our children in that faith. We have never belonged to any kind of political party prior to the [Nazi] takeover of power; nor were we active in such. And it pains us endlessly that our son Karl-Heinz took part in this affair. For that reason we have had many sorrowful days and nights. We would really like to wish and ask that our son not be harshly judged for his offense.

Heil Hitler

J. Schnibbe
21 March 1942

Source: Berlin Document Center

23

Chief State Counsel
of the Hanseatic Higher Regional Court
Hamburg 36, 25 March 1942
File Number: Js. 11/42
Criminal Case!
Juveniles!

In re: Criminal case against HÜBENER et al. charged with conspiracy to commit high treason.

Without compensation

Enclosures: Investigatory Documents Js. 11/42

To the
Attorney General at the People's Court,
Berlin W 9
Bellevuestraße 15

In accordance with the circular directive of 18 December 1934-IIIa 25371 regarding processing of important criminal cases, Numeral III, I hereby transmit the Investigatory Documents Js. 11/42 against

1.) the administrative apprentice at the social administration in Hamburg, *Helmuth* Günther Hübener, born 8 January 1925 in Hamburg, resident at Hamburg 1, Sachsenstraße 42, member of the Church of Jesus Christ of Latter-day Saints,
2.) the mechanic's apprentice *Rudolf* Gustav Wobbe, born 11 February 1926 in Hamburg, resident at Hamburg, Hardenstraße 15, II., member of the Church of Jesus Christ of Latter-day Saints,
3.) the painter journeyman Karl Heinz Schnibbe, born 5 January 1924 in Hamburg, resident at Hamburg, Rossausweg 32, I., member of the Church of Jesus Christ of Latter-day Saints,
4.) the administrative apprentice at the social administration in Hamburg, *Gerhard* Heinrich Jacob Jonni Düwer, born 1 November 1924 in Altona, resident at Hamburg-Altona, Kirchenweg 53 ground floor,

and include the following accompanying report.

In August 1941, inflammatory writings were distributed in the Hamburg districts Hammerbrook and Rothenburgsort, which were found in hallways, house mailboxes, in mailboxes of the German Post Office and on the street. Some of the examples of these writings are contained in B1.21 and the other exhibits. For the most part, they contain extracts from the inflammatory broadcasts of the London radio station, in part they have the following wording:

"Down with Hitler
Seducer of the people
Corrupter of the people
Traitor of the people
Down with Hitler"

Further inflammatory writings were found in February 1942 in the city district Hammerbrook in house mailboxes and in a public telephone booth. These documents, contained in B1.4, are literal reproductions of English inflammatory broadcasts, of which one bore the notation:

"This is a chain letter
. . . so pass it on!"

The investigations conducted have revealed that the producer of the inflammatory writings is the accused Hübener. Hübener, who is an administrative apprentice for the executive track at the Hamburg Social Administration, has confessed to having listened continuously since the beginning of 1941 to the inflammatory broadcasts of the London station, to having partially copied the broadcasts and then to having reproduced them with a typewriter. In August 1941 he produced about 60 copies of such writings, of which he sent one copy to the sales apprentice Horst van Treck in the National Labor Service, military postal number 39281, handed approximately 20 copies to the co-accused Wobbe for distribution and himself placed the remaining writings in mailboxes and on the street in Hammerbrook and Rothenburgsort.

Also, Hübener produced and distributed the writings found in February. A search of his apartment uncovered further transcripts of the London station, which are contained in B1.15a and others. He admitted that he listened to the London station at first out of curiosity. He gradually came to the conviction that these inflammatory broadcasts, in contrast to the German newscasts, were in accordance with the truth, and that he felt the need to be self-important with his knowledge. For this reason he decided to undertake the distributing of the broadcasts. Hübener listened to the English broadcasts on a receiver belonging to his grandparents, who allegedly had no knowledge of the activity of the accused. The typewriter, on which the writings were produced, Hübener received from a certain Mr. Zander with the commission to write letters on the machine to the members of the Church of Jesus Christ of Latter-day Saints (Mormons) in the military. Zander, the director of this Mormon sect, is likewise allegedly said to have known nothing of the activity of Hübener.

The accused Wobbe has confessed to having received approximately 15 inflammatory writings from Hübener in August 1941 and to having distributed them in Rothenburgsort as ordered. In addition, Wobbe attempted himself approximately three or four times to listen to the London station. This allegedly was not successful, because the receiver was too obsolete.

The accused Schnibbe learned from Hübener in the autumn of 1941 that he was listening to the inflammatory broadcasts from London and partially copying them. After he had read such notes, he asked Hübener to copy the reports for him. He claims subsequently to have received approximately three times from Hübener a copy of the inflammatory broadcasts, nevertheless he claims to have burned them after reading. He admits only to having informed the accused Wobbe about the content of an inflammatory broadcast. Further, he confessed to having attempted with Hübener in his apartment to listen to the London station. He was unable to hear details because of strong jamming.

The accused Düwer received approximately 12 of the inflammatory writings produced in February 1942. Two of these pages he gave to friends to read, and he also shared with them orally extracts from the contents of the writings.

All of the accused were members of the Hitler Youth. Only Schnibbe, because of refusal to obey an order, had been expelled at the end of 1939 from the Hitler Youth.

The accused *Hübener, Wobbe,* and *Düwer* are still juveniles.

All of the accused in this matter have been, since 27 February 1942, held in investigatory custody in the investigatory prison of the City of Hamburg, on the following charges:

Hübener and *Wobbe* because of conspiracy to commit high treason, as well as listening to and distributing radio newscasts from foreign stations,

Schnibbe and *Düwer* because of listening to and/or distributing newscasts of foreign stations.

Against Horst van Treck, named by Hübener, presently with the National Labor Service, to date no charges have been filed.

Immediate judicial measures by the Investigating Judge of the People's Court are not deemed necessary.

In commission:
/s/ Stegemann

Source: Berlin Document Center

24

Letter from Rudolf Wobbe

Investigatory Division, Hamburg City
Investigatory Prison, Hamburg City
Hamburg 36, Holstenglacis 3

Sender: Wobbe, Rudolf
Addressee: Parents
Hamburg, 1 March 1942

My dear Mama!

I have thankfully received your dear letter and Alfred's note. Please write Alfred the necessary lines so that he is informed. I read your letter many times a day and am very unhappy that I must now sit in prison. I regret it so much, I can not cry any more. Dear Mama, I know that you grieve and cry very much, but I ask you, hold your head up too, I must bear it also. I hope and pray that I will receive a mild punishment and soon be home again. For the things that you brought to me, I thank you again heartily, it tasted magnificent. I still need 1 box of shoe polish (there are brushes, etc. here), my slippers, above all envelopes, but no stamps, only cash, 1 bootjack; everything else is listed on the front. In the trade school I lent a classmate my "machinist's book," it's a guy named Alfred, he sits in the first row. Perhaps you could look for it on a Wednesday, Augerstraße 7b, the class is called "Bsvo 15" with Mr. Meyer and Mr. Stiegen. The book is called "The Machinist's Manual." So far that is everything. This morning, when I got up, I kept thinking about home and you. Hopefully we will meet again in good health, do not work so much at home, etc. And do not forget your Rudi. Say hello to Jan, Kalli and Lisa, too, Grandma and Alfred, hope to be reunited with you soon at home. Many greetings and kisses from your Rudi, who is thinking about you.

My cell number is 5/54.

Source: Berlin Document Center

25

Letter from Helmuth Hübener

Excerpted Copy

Investigatory Prison
Js 11/42

Sender: Hübener, Helmuth
Recipient: Parents
Hamburg, 5 April 1942

. . .

After 1 April I have now been receiving a daily newspaper and I am very pleased with it. Now when I read daily of the bravery and endurance of our soldiers on the eastern front and think about Gerhard, who is one of them, when I catch sight daily of new reports of the heroic battles of our submarines and air force, I can't imagine how I once could have been so stupid and stubborn to read the newspaper with so much prejudice, and place more faith in the inflammatory and biased reports of those in London who cook up abominations, that is, those of the London radio. For this stupidity I now have to sit here behind bars, and I believe it is for the best. For who knows whether I really would have come to my senses by myself. So now I live here on hope—for believe me, it is not easy for me to sit day after day from morning until evening between these four walls.

Still, I understand that there must be a punishment, even if I really did not believe it would be so harsh. And the day will come when I will be free again and then I will also be present when you celebrate your birthdays or feast upon your Christmas cake with obvious relish.

. . .

Source: Berlin Document Center

26

Letter from Otto Berndt

Church of Jesus Christ of Latter-day Saints
West German Mission
District: Hamburg 6 April 1942

To the Secret State Police
in Hamburg. Stadthausbrücke

Approximately 9 weeks ago the juvenile Helmuth Hübener (Guddat) was arrested by you because of radio crimes. Helmuth Hübener, who lived with his grandparents in Louisenweg 137, appropriated in an illegal manner a typewriter that was located in a locked cabinet in our branch house in Besenbinderhof 13a. He told our branch custodian, Diedrich Meier, who lives at Besenbinderhof 13a, that he had received permission from Mr. Arthur Zander, the president of the St. Georg branch, who lives at Hübbesweg 34, to take the typewriter home with him. That did not correspond to the truth. Helmuth Hübener (Guddat) was occasionally called upon to perform minor tasks, among them to write letters with the typewriter. Because of this activity, he assumed the right to use the typewriter at home. When I learned about it, I requested that he immediately bring the typewriter back again. The next day H. Hübener (Guddat) was arrested and the typewriter confiscated. In the name of the above-mentioned church and as its legal representative in Hamburg, I would like now to assert the ownership of the church, and request the Secret State Police to return the typewriter. Because, so far as I am informed, the documents have already been submitted to the Hanseatic Special Court, I request the Secret State Police to relay this request to the proper public prosecutor's office. Because I have already troubled myself in this matter, I was encouraged to forward this request in this manner.

Heil Hitler!

/s/ Otto Berndt

Source: Berlin Document Center

27

The Superior Attorney General of the Reich
Berlin, 28 May 1942
at the People's Court
8J 127/42g
In Custody!

Re: 1, 2 and 4 juvenile!

Indictment

B1. 11/R   1) The administrative apprentice in the social administration in Hamburg *Helmuth* Günther Hübener from Hamburg 1, Sachsenstraße 42, born on 8 January 1925 in Hamburg, single,

B1. 1a   no prior record,
B1. 1/R,29,30/31   temporarily detained on 5 February 1942 and by virtue of the warrant of arrest of the District Court in Hamburg of 27 February 1942—120 Gs 60/42—since that day in investigative custody, at present in the investigatory prison Hamburg-City in Hamburg,

B1. 22/R   2) the mechanic's apprentice *Rudolf* Gustav Wobbe from Hamburg, Hardenstraße 15 II, born on 11 February 1926 in Hamburg, single,

B1. 1a   no prior record,
B1. 21,29,30/R,34   temporarily detained on 18 February 1942 and by virtue of the warrant of arrest of the District Court in Hamburg of 27 February 1942—120 Gs 60/42—since that day in investigative custody, at present in the investigatory prison Hamburg-City in Hamburg,

B1. 16/R   3) the painter journeyman Karl Heinz Schnibbe from Hamburg, Rossausweg 32 I, born on 5 January 1924 in Hamburg, single,

B1. 1a   no prior record,
B1.15,18R,29/30R,32   temporarily detained on 10 February 1942 and by

virtue of the warrant of arrest of the District Court in Hamburg of 27 February 1942—120 Gs 60/42—since that day in investigative custody, at present in the investigatory prison Hamburg-City in Hamburg,

BI. 7/R 4) the administrative apprentice in the social administration in Hamburg *Gerhard* Heinrich Jacob Jonni Düwer from Hamburg-Altona, Kirchenweg 53, born on 1 November 1924 in Altona, single,

BI. 1a no prior record,
BI. 1/R,29/30R,33 temporarily detained on 5 February 1942 and by virtue of the warrant of arrest of the District Court in Hamburg of 27 February 1942—120 Gs 60/42—since that day in investigative custody, at present in the investigatory prison Hamburg-City in Hamburg,
all without defenders as yet,

I accuse the defendants of having in the period from spring 1941 until the beginning of February 1942 continuously in Hamburg and in part jointly in the same manner

I. *all of the accused*
  1) deliberately listened to or attempted to listen to foreign radio stations,
  2) to have willfully distributed newscasts of foreign radio stations which are designed to endanger the resistance strength of the German people,

further in coincidence with the punishable deeds designated under I

  1) to have undertaken domestically, during a war against the Reich, to lend support to the enemy power and to have inflicted a detriment on the military strength of the Reich,
  2) to have conspired to change the constitution by highly treasonous activity, with force or through the threat of force, whereby the deed was directed toward influencing the masses through the production and distribution of publications,

These are crimes according to §§1 and 2 of the decree on extraordinary radio broadcasting regulations of 1 September 1939, §80 Section 2, §83 Section 2 and 3 No. 3, §§91b, 47, 73 Penal Code, §3 Juvenile Code, §1 of the Decree for Protection against Juvenile Felons of 4 October 1939.

Since the spring of 1941 Hübener listened continually to the English radio and since the summer of 1941 compiled flyers of the contents of the broadcasts, which were determined to promote the demoralization of the German will to resist and the goals of enemy propaganda to overthrow the leadership of the German state. Hübener distributed these flyers in Hamburg and in addition sent them by mail to acquaintances who were located outside of Hamburg.

Wobbe, Schnibbe and Düwer also listened to foreign stations or attempted to listen, and, further, distributed in inflammatory leaflets the contents of the English radio reports written down by Hübener by handing them on or by orally reporting them.

Essential Results of the Investigations

I. *The Subversive and Demoralizing Goals of the Enemy War Propaganda*
England and its allies, when they started the war in September against the Reich, operated on the assumption that they would succeed with the assistance of their war propaganda, just as they did in World War I, in shattering the resistance of the German people and inducing the elimination of the leadership of the state. Therefore, immediately after the start of the war our enemies engaged all of the propaganda means at their disposal for these purposes. The foreign radio particularly placed itself in the service of these endeavors by arranging for transmissions in the German language.

II. *The Criminal Offense of the Accused Hübener*
a) *Listening to the English radio and the oral transmission of what was heard.*
The accused Hübener, who has been, since 1938, a member of the Hitler Youth and, furthermore, is a member of the Church of Jesus Christ of Latter-day Saints, listened regularly, as he admitted, in the apartment of his grandparents from about the end of April 1941 to the radio apparatus of his brother, which was seized after his arrest, to wit: four or five times weekly to the newscasts of the London station. He always received this station at 10:00 in the evening after his grandparents had gone to bed. He shared the contents of these English reports in conversations about current events, which he conducted frequently with the apprentices in his office and other acquaintances, recapitulating these to the participating persons.

b) *The production and distribution of small flyers.* Approximately in the summer of 1941 the accused Hübener proceeded to write down the contents of the English newscasts heard and to develop flyers. First of all, he completed a number of small flyers written on one side, of the type contained in envelope B1.21a of the documents, in which vile insults and libels of the Führer, calls for his overthrow as well as inciting statements about the status of the war were repeated, through which the belief in the final German victory was to be shaken and the resistance strength of the people broken. For a description of the contents of the individual flyers, of which nine different kinds have been confiscated, you are referred to Section IV of the indictment. For the production of these flyers Hübener used a portable typewriter which the president of his religious congregation, Arthur Zander, had provided to him for the purpose of writing letters to the inducted military personnel from their religious community. As Hübener stated, he produced altogether approximately 60 of these flyers. He gave approximately 20 of these sheets to the co-accused Wobbe with the commission to distribute them. Further, he entrusted one copy of each issue, that is 15 flyers, to the business apprentice Horst van Treck, while he distributed the remainder in August 1941 in the districts of Hammerbrook in Hamburg by scattering them on the street or in hallways, as well as through tossing them in mailboxes.

c) *The production and distribution of full-page incendiary leaflets.* A while after the distribution of the smaller flyers, the accused Hübener began to assemble into detailed leaflets each week or every two weeks, the notes he had made about the contents of the English newscasts he had heard. Altogether the drafts or copies of 20 different inflammatory leaflets of this nature were confiscated. These leaflets, whose contents are given briefly in detail in Section IV of the indictment, contain, in addition to the English reports about the status of the war, which is intended to undermine the trust of the German people in its leadership and to shatter its strength of resistance, base insults and accusations about the Führer and his colleagues, inflammatory attacks on the actions and designs of the national socialist leadership of the state, as well as the summons to bring the end of the war through the overthrow of the Führer.

For the production of the inscriptions and the duplicates of the leaflets Hübener usually used the Remington typewriter seized at his arrest, which the already-mentioned Zander placed at his disposal in place of the portable typewriter lent earlier, in one case he also used a typewriter at his office. From the individual issues of these leaflets Hübener claims to have produced each time at least three to five and, later, six to seven copies. The last prepared flyer, in an edition of seven copies, "Who is inciting whom?" was, at Hübener's arrest, still in the confiscated typewriter. From the editions of each leaflet Hübener claims to have sent a copy each to the already-mentioned business apprentice van Treck, who was at that time in labor service, as well as his school friend Prumnitz, who was attending the finance school in Thorn. Further, he handed his co-accused Schnibbe since about the autumn of 1941, and since the beginning of January 1942 the co-accused Düwer, copies of his inflammatory leaflets. Düwer, to whom he claimed to have given altogether approximately 15 flyers, told him later that he had shown them also to other persons. Further, as the co-accused Wobbe stated, Hübener also gave him four or five such flyers with the direction to distribute them. About 15 further leaflets, including those copies found in envelope B1.4a of the documents, Hübener tossed in hallways or mailboxes or placed them in telephone booths in the Hammerbrook district in Hamburg. The majority of these inflammatory flyers he inscribed with the direction "This is a chain letter, so pass it on!" in order to have the individual flyers made available to the greatest possible circle of persons.

In the second half of January 1942, as the administrative apprentice Werner Kranz testified, Hübener met him with the intention of having him translate two of his completed inflammatory leaflets into French. Hübener explained to Kranz that he wanted to send the leaflets to politically unreliable German soldiers and he also wanted to give them, after they were translated, to prisoners of war. Hübener admitted to these statements, but declared that he merely "toyed with the thought" of sending them also to the inducted members of his religious community whose addresses Zander had placed at his disposal; nevertheless, he claims he did not get around to carrying out this intention. However, Hübener claimed that he did not intend to make the inflammatory leaflets accessible to prisoners of war. Nevertheless, in view of the translation commission given to Kranz, this defense is unbelievable.

d) *Statement about the interior aspect of the crime.* Concerning his motives, the accused Hübener admitted in a summary at his interrogation on 20 February 1942 that he at first decided to listen to the foreign radio merely out of curiosity. After listening several times to the London station he claims to have doubted the accuracy of the German news and came so strongly under the influence of the enemy war propaganda that he claims to have felt the need to inform his friends also about the content of the English news. But because this "in the course of time no longer satisfied" him, he claims to have turned finally to making the general public acquainted also with the intercepted news. He allegedly chose the route of producing the flyers because he did not want to endanger himself with the distribution of the enemy news. He knew that listening to and distributing such news carries with it the threat of severe punishment.

That Hübener, in spite of his youth, already possessed a sufficient capacity of political discernment is revealed in the composition "The War of the Plutocrats" attached to the documents, which he completed in about the spring of 1941 as his concluding thesis in school.

III. *The Criminal Offense of the Accused Wobbe, Schnibbe and Düwer*

1) *Wobbe.* The accused Wobbe, who has been a member of the Hitler Youth since 1938 and, further, is a member of the Church of Jesus Christ of Latter-day Saints, received from Hübener in August 1941 15 to 20 copies of the small flyers mentioned in section IIb of the indictment. Hübener explained to him that he gathered the content of these inflammatory writings from the intercepted reports of the London station, and encouraged him to read them through and distribute them. Wobbe carried out this commission as directed. He tossed the flyers in hallways and mailboxes in the district of Rothenburgsort in Hamburg and, in addition, attached some sheets to residential bulletin boards.

Later Hübener gave the accused Wobbe four or five more copies of a full-page inflammatory flyer, which is mentioned in section IIc of the indictment, with the charge to distribute these also. Wobbe claims, nevertheless, to have burned these flyers after he had read through them.

The accused Wobbe attempted three or four times himself to listen to the London station on the radio of his mother. He allegedly was not successful in receiving the broadcasts of that station.

Concerning his motives, Wobbe claimed that he himself did not know how he came to the criminal offense. Only after the distribution of the flyers did it dawn on him "that he had committed a great blunder."

2) *Schnibbe.* The accused Schnibbe, who also is a member of the Church of Jesus Christ of Latter-day Saints, and further, until the end of 1939 belonged to the Hitler Youth, nevertheless was expelled from this party organization because of refusal to obey an order, learned from Hübener in about the summer of 1941 that he listened regularly to the broadcasts of the London radio station. Around the fall of 1941 Hübener also showed him for the

first time two of the inflammatory writings that he had constructed from listening to enemy newscasts. Schnibbe, who claims to have interested himself in these reports out of curiosity, thereupon requested Hübener to let him have a copy of his flyers in the future. As Schnibbe explained, Hübener then handed him in the following time until January 1942 several such inflammatory writings, and, in fact, according to his assertion, a total of three copies and entrusted him in addition a number of further flyers to read in passing. Schnibbe claims to have burned the inflammatory writings given to him without having made them available to other persons. On the other hand, he explained, as he admitted, "some of the contents" of the flyers to the co-accused Wobbe.

The accused Schnibbe was also present once when Hübener tuned the radio of his brother to the London station in order to listen to the English news. Nevertheless, as Schnibbe claims, the reception was not possible at that time because of strong jamming activity.

3) *Düwer.* The accused Düwer, who has been a member of the Hitler Youth since 1933, learned from Hübener at the beginning of January 1942 that he listened to news from the London station and prepared inflammatory writings. Hübener mentioned in that connection that the production of the flyers ensued on instruction from a "spy ring" and urged Düwer to join this "ring." With these representations, which did not correspond to the truth, Hübener claims only to have pursued the goal of "making himself important." Hübener, as he admitted, gave the accused Düwer already during the first conversation about the making of the flyers, two of his inflammatory writings and in the following period gave him further flyers, in fact about 15 copies in all. The accused Düwer, in contrast to the portrayal by Hübener, maintains that he only gave him nine flyers. The first of these writings he claims to have received in the middle of January 1942, four more on 30 January and the remainder on 4 February. Düwer claims to have accepted these flyers merely because he planned "at the proper time" to report Hübener.

At the end of January 1942 Düwer gave the flyers received from Hübener to two young men his age, Horst and Kurt Zumsande, to read over. According to the statements of Horst Zumsande, on this occasion his acquaintance, Karl Horst Pipo, was also present. Moreover, Düwer once informed the brothers Horst and Kurt Zumsande, as Horst Zumsande testified, on a previous occasion about operations in the African theater of war, which he obviously took from the reports of the English radio reproduced in the inflammatory writings of Hübener.

Further as the deputy overseer Heinrich Mohns and the administrative apprentice Kranz testified, Düwer accompanied the accused Hübener on 20 January 1942 when he wanted to give Kranz the two flyers intended for translation into French, the acceptance of which Kranz nevertheless declined. After this incident Mohns instructed the co-accused Düwer, likewise Kranz, to obtain for him some of the flyers prepared by Hübener as evidence. Düwer declared himself ready to do this, however he handed him two such flyers only later, on 4 February 1942, after he previously had put him off with the explanation "that he still did not have any writings."

The accused Düwer maintained that he himself never listened to English stations and also never attempted to tune in such stations. Nevertheless, he admitted that he occasionally heard an English station on the radio of his parents on the frequency of the German stations and could understand some of it.

IV. The Contents of the Confiscated Leaflets

1) *The small flyers.* Of the small flyers produced by Hübener in the summer of 1941 nine different versions were confiscated, which have the following contents:

Flyers No. 1 and 9: The flyer with the headings "Hitler's Guilt" and "Hitler Is the Sole Guilty One" contain the allegation that the unrestricted air war against the civilian population was not begun by the British air force but by the Führer.

Flyer No. 2: In the flyer "Hitler, the Murderer!" the Führer is accused of having brought about the death of the military commander in Serbia General von Schröder.

Flyer No. 3: This flyer bears besides the subversive summons "Down with Hitler . . . the People's Seducer, People's Corrupter, People's Traitor," the V-symbol recommended by the enemy propaganda at that time as an advertising medium for the victory of the enemy powers.

Flyer No. 4: In the flyer "Who is lying?" it is argued that the reports of the Germany High Command of the military are unbelievable.

Flyer No. 5: In the flyer "One and one-half million" it is asserted that thus far one and one-half million have been killed in Russia, in addition listening to the London radio station is encouraged, whose times of transmission are given.

Flyers 6 and 7: The flyers "They are not telling you everything" and "137th Inf. Div." contain assertions about alleged heavy losses of individual German units in Russia.

Flyer No. 8: The flyer "Where is Rudolf Hess?" contains inflammatory statements about the flight to England of the former deputy of the Führer.

2) *The full-page leaflets.* In the full-page leaflets produced by Hübener, of which 20 different types have been seized, the following is argued:

Leaflet a (=k): In the leaflet "On page 199 in Hitler's 'Mein Kampf' it says" there is an attempt to demonstrate that the German news about the state of the war is incorrect, and listening to the London radio is encouraged, whose transmission times are stated.

Leaflet b (=o): In the inflammatory writing "3 October—3 February" it is claimed that the predictions of the Führer about the course of the Russian campaign did not come true, that the German troops on the eastern front have been "whipped".

Leaflet c (=g): The pamphlet "Monthly Military Overview December/January" contains statements about alleged German reverses and losses on the eastern front and in Africa.

Leaflet d (=n): The leaflet "The Voice of Conscience," which deals with an alleged "Christmas message" from Rudolf Hess over an English station, contains the worst insults and libel of the Führer and his colleagues, statements about the enormity of the German war losses, in which the German reports are represented as incorrect, as well as the encouragement to abolish the German leadership.

Leaflet e: In the pamphlet "Battle against the bolshevistic subhumanity" on the basis of a comparison between the alleged resources of the Axis powers and of the enemy states the supply situation of Germany and its allies are designated as "critical," while the resources of the enemy powers are represented as "inexhaustible."

Leaflet f: The inflammatory writing "The Nazi Reichsmarshall" contains terrible insults and libel of the Reichsmarshall as well as statements about the alleged inferiority of the German air force.

Leaflet g: In the pamphlet "The Riddle of Hess," horror stories about the alleged reasons for the flight to England of the former deputy of the Führer are repeated.

Leaflet h: The inflammatory writing "Hitler Youth" contains libel of the Hitler Youth leadership, crude insults of the Führer as well as a summons to disobedience against the Hitler Youth superiors.

Leaflet i: In the pamphlet "Weekend Incarceration" the introduction of juvenile detention in the Reich is commented upon in an inflammatory style.

Leaflet l: The leaflet "Who is inciting whom?" contains inflammatory statements about the entry of Japan into the war.

Leaflet m: In the pamphlet "Comrades in the South, North, East and West!" the English drive into Cyrenica at the end of November 1941, the situation on the eastern front, the sinking of the aircraft carrier "Ark Royal," as well as the establishment of "Iron Savings" are made the subject of subversive statements.

Leaflet p: In the leaflet "I've calculated for everything" the wool collection program becomes the occasion for commenting in an inflammatory fashion upon the status of the war, and an English-American offensive on the European continent is announced.

Leaflet r: In the inflammatory writing "In the East Asian theater there are still numerous attack bases" the German people are called upon to bring about the end of the war by the overthrow of the Führer. The leaflet contains further accounts intending to horrify which concern the death of General Field Marshal von Reichenau, of Colonel General Udet and of Colonel Mölders, as well as inflammatory views about the status of the war on the eastern front and in North Africa.

Leaflet s: The pamphlet "Perfidious Rome" contains inflammatory and subversive statements about the battle in North Africa, as well as about Italian colonial policy.

Leaflet t: In the leaflet "As is now known" the characteristics of the Italian people and the fighting strength of its military are made the subject of inflammatory views.

Leaflet v: In the inflammatory writing "A Wave of Oil" it is maintained that the alleged shortage of oil of Germany and its allies guarantee the victory of the enemy powers.

Leaflet w: In the pamphlet "Voice of the Homeland" there is an attempt to make church controversies serve the subversive endeavors of the enemy.

Leaflet x: In the leaflet "Victorious advance into the shining battles of annihilation" the Japanese successes are labeled as meaningless and the outlook for Japan's victory is placed in doubt.

Leaflet y: In the inflammatory writing "1942—the Year of Decision" the defeat of the Axis powers is predicted and the German people encouraged to overthrow their governmental leadership.

Leaflet z: In the pamphlet "The Führer's Speech" there is an attempt to represent the statements of the Führer about the status of the war as unbelievable.

V.

The head office of the state police in Hamburg filed the complaint against the accused Hübener, Wobbe, Schnibbe and Düwer pursuant to the crimes with which they are charged according to §§1 and 2 of the ordinance concerning the extraordinary radio measures.

Evidence
I. *The joinders of the accused:*
   1. Hübener: B1.11/15,20/R,24R/25,29,
   2. Wobbe: B1.22/24,29,
   3. Schnibbe: B1.16/18,29R,
   4. Düwer: B1.7/9R,15,29R;
II. *The witnesses:*
   1. Deputy Overseer Heinrich Mohns, Hamburg, Bornstraße 4 III: B1. 5,18R/19,
   2. Administrative apprentice Werner Kranz, Hamburg-Rahlstedt, Loherstraße 38: B1. 6,9R/10R,10b/R,
   3. Business apprentice Horst Zumsande, Hamburg, Bahrenfeld, Adickesstraße 63: B1. 19/R,
   4. Criminal secretary Müssener: B1. 1R,9R,12R,15,18R,19,19R,21,24,25, 26R;
III. *The documents and miscellaneous exhibits:*
   1. The criminal record extracts about the accused: B1. 1a,
   2. The confiscated leaflets: B1. 4a,15a,21a,
   3. The composition prepared by Hübener "The War of the Plutocrats": B1. 25R,44,
   4. The confiscated radio, "Rola" brand: B1. 1/R,13,27,
   5. The confiscated typewriter "Remington" brand, No. LD 67 792: B1. 1/R,14R,20R,27.

I adjure that the accused Helmuth Hübener, Rudolf Wobbe, Karl Heinz Schnibbe and Gerhard Düwer be tried before the Second Panel of the People's Court, that the continuation of the investigatory imprisonment be terminated, and that they be given defense attorneys.

Source: Berlin Document Center

28

Down with Hitler———

People's Seducer[8]
    People's Corrupter
        People's Traitor

Down with Hitler———

Source: Berlin Document Center

29

Who Is Lying?????????????

The official Report of the German
High Command of the Armed Forces

Quite a while ago they claimed
the roads to Moscow, Kiev
and Leningrad were open.

And today—six weeks after
Germany's invasion of the USSR,
severe battles are still occurring
far from
these places.

This is how they are lying to us!

Source: Berlin Document Center

30

137th Infantry Division
5th Infantry Division
8th and 10th Tank Divisions
111th Motorized Division
Flak Battalion of the 16th Tank Division
The Great Germany Regiment
135th, 311th, 372nd, 485th, 178th, 179th
and 253rd Infantry Divisions
in the struggle against Soviet Russia
sustained the heaviest casualties.
Altogether 1½ million
German and Austrian soldiers
lost their lives.
For that you can thank Hitler!!!!

Source: Berlin Document Center

31

Where Is Rudolf Hess:

Goebbels is silent, because he must be silent. But we speak, because we can speak.

Rudolf Hess, formerly the first confidant of your Führer, sits today in a London military prison and is in good health.

He fled, because he could no longer look upon the irresponsible murders of his Führer.

He fled, because he did not want to accept any responsibility for the victims of the invasion of the East, which was already decided even then.

He fled, because he has a heart.[9]

Source: Berlin Document Center

32

Hitler Is the Sole Guilty One!

By means of the unlimited war in the air, several hundred thousand defenseless civilians have been killed.

But the R.A.F.[10] is not to blame for these killings. Their flights are only in reprisal for the raids of the Luftwaffe over Warsaw and Rotterdam, where unarmed women and children, cripples and old men were killed.

Source: Berlin Document Center

33

On page 199 in Hitler's *Mein Kampf* it states: ". . . and so the English soldier could never feel that he had been misinformed by his own countrymen, as unhappily was so much the case with the German soldier that in the end he rejected everything coming from this source as 'swindles' and 'bunk.'"[11] That was in the World War! Shall this revealing sentence perhaps also find its application in this war?!

Upon closer examination of the reports (of the TRUTH???) coming out of the High Command of the Armed Services and the abominable Goebbels propaganda machine, it appears very clearly to have found its application. These people lie, lie, lie and are now entangled in lies to such a degree they hardly notice that with one blow any facts can place the stamp of LIE on their constant swindles. But does that bother the Lords of Berlin's Wilhelmsplatz, does that bother Goebbels, does that bother Fritsche and Dietrich or all the important and petty politicians and armchair politicians?

Even if actual successes are lacking, such are being officially fabricated so that the German people do not notice that not everything that glitters is gold.

If the reports of the High Command of the Armed Services and the official Italian communique actually coincided with the truth, where then would the proud Royal Navy be, where then would the R.A.F.[12] be, or where then would London, Liverpool or Birmingham be?!

Yes, if these reports actually rested upon truths, then they would exist no more, neither His Majesty's navy, nor the incomparable air force, nor the great cites of his motherland. Yes, if the report of the High Command of the Armed Services were actually a "Report of the Truth," like the Führer himself recently expressed so "beautifully" in one of his speeches, then the Battle of the Atlantic would already be decided, and 44 battleships, 20 aircraft carriers and many dozens of cruisers, destroyers, torpedo boats and submarines would be resting on the bottom of the sea. Yes, if . . .

However, the facts look otherwise. Of course, the methods by which the German Propaganda Ministry compiles such numbers of losses are clever, but are never so good that they cannot be refuted by facts, and these facts are:

fourteen battle ships
eight aircraft carriers

in other words, about a third of the losses reported by the High Command of the Armed Services.

No matter how Goebbels postures, or Fritsche screams bloody murder in the ironic manner peculiar to him, these numbers stand and remain standing until a new list of casualties—not that of the High Command of the Armed Services—but of the British Admiralty, gives further information. Are you a friend of the truth?

The broadcasts of the English radio, which can be received all day, will also satisfy your requirements.

The London radio sends daily broadcasts at

2:00 a.m.: Broadcast for the German military
6:00 a.m.: Broadcast for workers on the early shift
6:30 a.m.:   ”   ”   ”   ” ”   ”   ”
6:40 a.m.:   ”   ”   ”   ” ”   ”   ”
10:00 a.m.: Broadcast for the German military
7:45 p.m.: Broadcast for German sailors
8:00 p.m.: Evening broadcast for workers or farmers
10:00 p.m.: Evening news broadcast

Source: Berlin Document Center

34

3 October–3 February! Four months have passed, 120 days, since the Führer proclaimed in his latest arrogant speech: . . . the campaign in the East is already decided! . . . He was far off the mark, for although he still claimed to be able to see "extremely large" bolshevistic casualties in the withering crossfire, nevertheless he miscalculated. The campaign in the East is no more decided today that it was perhaps in July, August, September or on 3 October.

It is already a difficult piece of work for Goebbels and his Nazi propagandists to cover this fact and to put down Hitler's remark as never uttered. They attempt this in all possible ways, they employ every trick, artifice and piece of sophistry, speak about the terrific cold, the Russian winter, which determines the nature and manner of the operations—like the High Command of the Armed Services report already said at that time. But for all that, they have completely forgotten that this "General Winter" was also derided, ridiculed and pilloried by Hitler more than once, when he said on 30 January of the past year, for example: "They look forward to the winter, but I say to you: the German people are absolutely prepared for winter!" (Tumultuous Applause).

The German people are absolutely prepared for winter: hence they were recently permitted to donate their woolen and fur clothing to the soldiers, who are apparently not so well prepared for winter.[13] Although the "Black Corps" wrote (arrogantly and optimistically) as early as September of last year that winter would facilitate the operations, because then instead of the muddy, bottomless roads, at least hard frozen roadways would be available to the irresistible advancing tank units and infantry columns.

But they miscalculated. It is true that snow and ice now lie everywhere, but the German advance, or better said, the "last definitive battle of annihilation" has still made no further progress. On the contrary! Wherever the German soldiers achieved local gains in the autumn by the loss of men and materiel, the victory banners of the Russians already wave again today. The German soldiers are beaten! But not the German Propaganda Ministry, not by a long shot. Ok, so it's winter, no problem, they just put a new piece of paper in the typewriter and begin a new game.

They are starting rumors about how well things are going. The worker in the tram, the salesman in the office, the housewife while shopping, yes, even Little Heinz during his school class—all talk about it, and one whispers it to another, that everything is well planned! Hitler is the greatest strategic genius. He has lured the last (in other words the "last" ones once again) bolshevistic reserves from Siberia, thus making it easy for the Japanese to attack Russia in the flank. He acts as if there were nothing but blockheads in Moscow who could not count to three and did not have the faintest clue about strategy, isn't that so, Herr Goebbels? To what degree this farfetched rumor will fall on fertile soil among the people cannot be said, but how little this absurd nonsense corresponds to the facts will be known in all clarity when Spring places a different stamp on the operations.

Source: Berlin Document Center

35

Monthly Military Review, December–January

Eastern Front: In the north, in the middle, as well as in the southern combat sectors and in the Crimea, the winter offensive at the beginning of November took a favorable course. While the defenders of Leningrad have already penetrated the encircling German positions in several places, the "iron ring" around the city is no longer what one would expect of iron, namely that it can withstand small or even large tests of its breaking strength. Everywhere Russian combat patrols have pushed wedges forward, and it may not be a question of whether, but of how long the envelopment will endure, for the news is already arriving that gigantic contingents of troops have been set in march, aiming at a pincer movement on the grandest scale. Tichvin, the strategic railroad junction on the northern front, has found itself now firmly in Russian hands for several weeks, likewise Cholm, which plays an important role for further movements of Russian troops.

Middle Front: Also in the Moscow combat sector, hardly a day passes in which new stories are not reported of the successes of General Sukov in resisting and attacking, and the Russian winter, about which Hitler and the German propaganda promised us the sun and the moon when they believed it would facilitate the German moves forward, is now just the opposite: an ally of the Russians, and Kalinin, Kaluga, Klin and Starissa are now, after having been successfully recaptured, cornerstones of the Russian advance, while in Malo Jaroslavecz tens of thousands of German soldiers had to bleed to death, and in Modshaisk numerous German infantry and tank units were encircled and completely destroyed in heavy battles lasting for days. Testimony thereof is borne out by the numbers of German losses disclosed by official Russian sources, which losses in January alone amounted to over 50 thousand men taken into Russian captivity, while as yet incalculable masses of dead and wounded covered the battlefield. And that in one single month.

Donets Front: Even in the south, where the Russian winter does not occur in such severity, bolshevistic armed forces under the command of General Timoshenko, who was already declared dead by Goebbels's propaganda, are extraordinarily active. Nevertheless, strategic reasons forbid more detailed information about these operations.

Mediterranean Front: For the fourth time Bengasi has changed its occupier, for the fourth time German and Italian armed forces march west with the goal of capturing Alexandria. But also for the fourth time the little and large "Fritsches" in the Berlin headquarters are deploying a vigorous propaganda campaign; but despite conferring of decorations and promotions, this will not succeed for a fourth time. The forces of General Auchinlek are retreating in order to escape encirclement and to avoid larger losses. But Rommel does not consider this. He always throws his exhausted soldiers and also a few fresh reserves into the battle anew, and always the rear guards of the British Empire's troops inflict heavy losses on men and materiel. Over 36,500 captives and about 20,000 dead, those are only some figures on the debit side of the terrible ledger of the German Africa Corps. Come what may, Rommel is defending, despite temporary counterthrusts and counteroperations, a lost cause, and every day the inevitable fate draws closer, from which the big-mouthed Italians cannot be saved either.

Hitler gives the rallying cry for the tenth year: Certainty about Final Victory! Current military events speak a different language, and the irresponsible optimism of the Führer can scarcely change anything about that.

Source: Berlin Document Center

36

The Voice of Conscience! As the Führer's deputy in May of last year departed from Augsburg and Germany for all time in the middle of the night and under cover of fog in a Messerschmitt, the shaken Goebbels propaganda apparatus could think of nothing else to say, except: "Comrade Hess has been suffering a long time now from hallucinations!" Then they were silent, in order to silence this chapter of history forever. But Hess talked and is delivering this year, as he does every Christmas, a message, but much about it has changed. Hess no longer spoke over German radio waves, but exclusively over some shortwave stations of the "hereditary enemy"—over the English shortwave station G.S.A. with antennae aimed at the United States. Hess spoke no more about peace, no more about the great German struggle for freedom, nor did he appeal to the resistance strength of the German people. His message amounted to one big accusation against the arsonist who started this war, the originator of incalculable sorrow and unspeakable misery—Adolf Hitler! Hess, a comrade in arms during the planning period and a faithful counselor in the "years of building," the same Hess now raised the curtain and exposed the reckless mass murderer Hitler.

Here are some revealing extracts from the message: "As I made my momentous decision and left the Reich in an airplane in May of last year, I acted only out of the most pressing motives, only with heavy heart and sorrowfully. For I knew that not a few of my countrymen would see therein treason toward my fatherland. Nevertheless, it is not so!! I left Germany to save my life. The unscrupulous assassination methods of the Gestapo, which are denounced in foreign states, were only too well known by me, methods which began with a courier flight, a state visit etc., and then a little later end with telegrams of condolence about the unfortunate airplane accident, obituaries and state funerals." Isn't this short paragraph terribly revealing? Doesn't it cast a completely revealing light on the peace-loving (!) Führer, who embellishes every sentence of his speeches with references to God, Providence and higher powers? Doesn't it function like a ray of light in the darkness? Now we gradually begin to see why recently in one week three of the highest German aces fell victim to a "tragic accident" in the midst of a "peaceful" journey. But it gets better. Let's read:

"Indeed the nefarious plan of the Führer to attack the Soviet Union, contrary to all agreements and in spite of the friendship and nonaggression pacts, in the midst of peace, caused deep resentment. We had, in fact, obtained personally the assurance from Foreign Minister Molotov that concentrations of troops on the Russian-German border were never directed against Germany and only were of somewhat extraordinary size because they were intended to decrease the concentration of troops on the eastern borders, and thereby calm Japan's rising nervousness regarding Manchukuo. I was against Hitler's plan from the beginning, and numerous generals with me; for it was clear to us that after the drastic bloodletting in France, which in truth—I am now free to tell it—cost us several hundred thousand men, and after the extraordinarily costly campaign in the Balkans, now the truth can be told, which even today is not completely ended, we could not endure a new bloodletting which doubtless would cost millions more, that such a bloodletting undoubtedly would have a calamitous end. But Hitler was of a different opinion, he raged as he noticed our disapproving attitude, and threatened to take over the supreme command of the army himself. It was these dissensions in the highest leadership that caused the attack on the U.S.S.R., which was originally planned to begin on Hitler's birthday, the 20th of April 1941, to get underway only approximately two months later. But I, who had been the strongest supporter of the "peace party," was played out. After Hitler had first conferred several hours with Himmler and Göring, I was summoned and assigned a mission to have conversations in Paris with Admiral Darlan, who even before the beginning of the French campaign of 1940—supported by lovely German money—was a true friend of Hitler, and shared with Hitler the blame that the French soldiers could only resist the onslaught of German infantrymen and of the German tanks for a short time, because their morale was secretly undermined and their strength of resistance was neutralized even before the outbreak of the campaign, despite the Maginot Line which was said to be impregnable. Me, go to Paris?! Yes, accompanied in an airplane by several higher SS and Gestapo officers. I smelled a rat: in my mind's eye I saw the fate of Colonel General von Fritsch, who disappeared on a flight over the Polish front. I now knew that my time had come! That is why I fled—not with a courier plane to Paris, but with one of the newest Heinkel bombers to England. . . ."

This paragraph is so informative that one must read it not once, but ten, twenty, thirty times, to be able to grasp it completely. We can again see the confirmation of the fact that although Goebbels and with him all of the small and large "Fritsches" of the Berlin Wilhelmsplatz Hate Center are really fantastic liars, only one small ray of light suffices to prove their deceitfulness, to prove that though Nazi propaganda is often crafted right down to the last detail, it seldom coincides even in one point with the facts.

In conclusion, the former Deputy Führer addressed himself in moving words to the German people and said: "If some of my German brothers in their ignorance put me down angrily as a traitor, if they want to stone me because of my—in their eyes, vile—conduct, I can only reply to them: I am a German and will always remain one. I was a party member as long as it was worth it to engage its power for a peaceful work of construction. Nevertheless, I am not willing to bathe my hands in the blood of hundreds of thousands of German soldiers. In this I am man enough and responsible enough to put an end to the matter. And it would be nothing but desirable, if the German people would join with me in showing the same responsibility and make an end to the matter!! But as long as things are quietly endured or tolerated, the man, the father or the son given up for a cause which can never benefit the community of the people, the general public, but only special groups, Hitler will continue to believe in the 'inexhaustible' reserve strength of his people and in the unconditional determination of each individual to sacrifice himself. And as long as these things are quietly tolerated, he will not rest in turning his plans for imperialistic world conquest into actions. . . ."

Do you want to tolerate having the happiness of your life taken from you, and your children cheated out of the most beautiful years of their lives? Do you want to tolerate this??

Source: Berlin Document Center

37

The Nazi Reichsmarshall

Yes, good old fat Hermann: Reichsmarshall. Who would have thought it? His comrades from the first war, whose debtor he still is today? Or did he ever think about it himself? Oh yes, he has something on the ball, this little rogue with the saucer eyes. A dazzling career, a pretty actress and a very ample salary that is not to be sneezed at, but no brains. No, really not, as big as his head is. Nevertheless he always talks freely without inhibitions about things, so that the business is becoming uncomfortable even to Hitler.

When the R.A.F gets around to bombing Berlin, you can call me Meier,[14] he said at the beginning of the war. Today the streets of Berlin show clear evidence of the British air offensive, yet Göring is still Göring, and he is glad that he is. And then there is that ever so popular slogan: 1000 for one! Also a glaring hoax; because today the German air force is happy if it can simply fly over the islands once in a while without suffering heavy losses and bloody heads from the air defenses. The Air Marshal of the Nazis can certainly still draw an enormous dividend—he is a shrewd war profiteer and businessman—from his war factories,[15] nevertheless the dream of an unlimited air superiority of his flying armada, one that gets more unlimited all the time, is getting closer and closer to its end. There will be a rude awakening.

For Winston S. Churchill said: If it must be, our brave bomber crews will bring death and destruction over Nazi Germany!! We do not wish it, have never wanted it, but the deaths of many thousands of murdered persons in Rotterdam, Belgrade and not least in France, Norway and Poland, the blood of many freedom-loving brothers in the Europe suppressed by Gestapo terror, must not remain unatoned.

Retribution will come one way or another, Herr Göring.

Source: Berlin Document Center

38

Hitler Youth

German youths, are you actually aware of what the Hitler Youth is and what goals it pursues? You cannot know it. Your high-handed leaders and subleaders always preach about comradeship, while they exclude themselves from the circle of comradeship. They feel just fine in their element when they can tyrannize the intimidated youths, when they can tyrannize *you*. Or do you perhaps want to dispute that they want to make you submissive with all the means available. They threaten you with disciplinary punishments, police measures and have your freedoms taken away from you, from you Germans, and stick you in so-called weekend detention.

Do you know such buildings? No? Well, at the next opportunity you will get to hear about them.

So this is the Hitler Youth, praised far and wide. A compulsory organization of the first order for the recruiting of Nazi-enslaved national comrades. Hitler and his accomplices know that they must deprive you of your free will at the beginning, in order to make submissive, spineless creatures out of you. For Hitler knows that his contemporaries are beginning gradually to see through him, the suppressor of free nations, the murderer of millions.

Therefore we are calling out to you: Do not let your free will, the most valuable thing you possess, be taken away. Do not let yourselves be suppressed and tyrannized by your leaders—high-handed kings in miniature—but rather turn your back on the Hitler Youth, the tool of the Hitler regime for your destruction.

We are with you and you can always count on our help!

"Endure to the end, Germany awake!"

Source: Berlin Document Center

39

Weekend Incarceration[16]

German boys! Do you know the country without freedom, the country of terror and tyranny?

Yes, you know it well, but are afraid to talk about it. They have intimidated you to such an extent that you don't dare talk for fear of reprisals. Yes, you are right; it is Germany—Hitler-Germany!

Through their unscrupulous terror tactics against young and old, men and women, they have succeeded in making you spineless puppets to do their bidding.

But it's you, German boys, who must also suffer under the Gestapo terror. You are especially mistreated in the Hitler Youth.

"You are the future of Germany," they tell you, but then you are tyrannized and punished for any little offense.

The "Weekend Jail" is an affront that tops everything. For the smallest infraction during Hitler Youth duty, you will be sentenced to several days of incarceration. You will need to spend your nights in a small room with the temperature reaching the boiling point, suffering the indignities of a condemned criminal.

Yes, this is the future of Germany!

Source: Berlin Document Center

40

Who is inciting whom?

"Roosevelt has his war!"—that laconic comment was all the German radio broadcaster and commentator could think to make on the day of the Japanese surprise attack. "Roosevelt has his war!" Did it not sound a little ironical, that which the Goebbels propaganda machine trumpeted forth on that momentous Monday morning?!

Indeed: All accusations against the American federal government—no matter how many transmitters and wave lengths they are broadcast over, or in how many languages—are devoid of any basis in fact. They are false, malicious and are still symptoms of the deepest hatred, even when the ones who tell them somehow manage to keep a straight face, though it is the straight face of a corpse.

Who started it? It was not Roosevelt, not Knox and not Stimpson, but purely and simply the Tokyo war cabal, at whose bidding the first blood flowed in the giant east Asian arena, right in the middle of perfect peace they treacherously slaughtered the first civilians. No inflated pretext, no matter how often repeated, can gloss over the reprehensibleness of this "genuine Japanese" heroic deed. It is documentarily established, that all of the guilt falls on Japan, on Japan alone.

Already in 1919, scarcely a few months after Japan was rewarded for its betrayal of imperial Germany—which it actually should have thanked for its rise to military greatness—by being given some of the most choice German bases in east Asia, a whole quantity of new claims were being argued in a "Plan of National Reorganization" from Ikki Kita—a book which is more treasured by the Japanese militarists than the Bible.

Under the "promising" slogan: "The state is justified . . ." one after the other, the various Japanese-imperialistic lusts for power find here their expression. "The state is justified in conducting war. . . . The state is justified in waging war on any nation whose possession of territory is unnaturally large(!) . . . Example: Australia must be wrested from England, East Siberia wrested from Russia. The state is justified in starting a war in order to free oppressed peoples. Example: India must be freed from the foreign yoke, and China freed from its foreign oppressors(?)."

But because India "heartily" tells Japan thanks but no thanks, and free China under Marshal Chiang Kai-shek is not in the least bit in need of "help" from Tokyo, because it does not fear in the least "foreign oppressors," who apparently exist only in the empty heads of the Demei agents, these human-itarian, kind promises of help from Mr. Kita mean nothing other than:[17]

Source: Berlin Document Center

41

Comrades in the South, North, East or West! Again we send a report to you about the military and political situation. And it was necessary to do this be-cause the profusion of events in the last days are being almost completely si-lenced or rewritten in empty phrases by the official German positions.

The British advance in North Africa: Several times we have already spo-ken about the successful battles of the Royal Air Force and the Royal Navy against the supply line of General Rommel, but again and again the broad-casts in German, English, French, Italian or who knows what language, over long- and shortwave, declare it was really not so bad, and that over in En-gland they're just exaggerating a little once again. Now, we begin to see just how phony this "mouth offensive" of Fritsche's was as the events in Mar-marika show. On the morning of 18 November, the strike forces of the Brit-ish Empire crossed the Egyptian-Libyan border on a broad front and ad-vanced with great verve against Rommel's indestructible desert warriors. And by the following day the headquarters in Cairo was able to report that Rom-mel's position between the coast and Sidi Omar had been crossed on a front that was 150 kilometers wide, and that the British flag was already waving over numerous forts. Meanwhile, one German victory report followed the other, while the High Command of the German Armed Services was being driven—"victoriously"—to its own ruination. Fort Capucco fell, Gambut was taken, fast-moving troops were advancing from Girabub and threatened Rommel's supply line 200 kilometers south of Tripoli; the number of pris-oners rose, but the High Command of the Armed Services still remained victorious, the air force was on the high road to victory, and lo and behold: the German navy was becoming active off the African coast. To hear them talk, if things continue like this, the Führer and his Highness, the Reichs-marshall "Omnipol" will be celebrating Christmas in Cairo and make a vic-torious New Year's Day speech to their beloved fellow denizens of the en-tire planet. Now, the essential thing is that none of this calculated optimism from the official reports of the High Command of the Armed Services corresponds to the facts. Capucco fell, Bardia fell, the encirclement around Tobruk was broken, and on 27 November contact with the advancing troops of the worldwide British Empire was made, and even if the battle in North Africa is still not over, there can be no more doubt about its outcome after just two weeks of fighting.

Now news from throughout the world: East Africa: The last bastion of the Italian resistance in Abyssinia was finally conquered with the capture of Gondar. With this, thousands of Italian and native elite troops became British prisoners of war and now tens of thousands of Allied troops were thus freed for action in North Africa. Eastern Front: While the capture of Rostov was reported already on 22 November, with much fanfare, after a seven-day battle, German forces were unsuccessful in staving off the threat to Rostov by Russian units led by Marshal Timoshenko, who had allegedly been "cut off," and on 27 November he succeeded in penetrating into some outer districts of the city. Even the High Command of the Armed Services cannot conceal this unpleasant fact and must admit the loss of Rostov's industrial quarter (see the report of 29 November 1941). Nevertheless, when the report attempts to gloss over the facts with shabby assertions and empty phrases, it can no longer change reality, no matter how much is said. The halo of invincibility has been broken once again. Nazi-Germany: Does anyone still have in their possession a newspaper from the first of January 1941? Probably not, but in some heads a small recollection still lingers about what stood in giant headlines on the first page of the newspaper that day. And what did it say? It was the New Year's message of the Führer, who concluded with the words: The year 1941 will bring the most glorious completion of our victory. This victory has now gone sour. At most, good old Hitler can comfort us by promising that next year things will happen, but next year the decisive victory will also no doubt be postponed, etc., etc. The war is already decided. Hitler missed the bus, the bus with which his faithful deputy [Hess] now beats a hasty retreat to England.

Source: Berlin Document Center

42

I've Calculated for Everything

It's been a month now since the radio and the press in Germany grandly announced the results of the wool collection program. Over 70 million articles, Goebbels proclaimed, over 70 million! But where are these 70 million articles? The soldiers on the eastern front, the soldiers in the far north, in any case, haven't received them. They do not write about them, only that they are freezing, freezing and freezing some more, and vainly waiting for warm winter clothing.[18]

Where then are the 70 million articles—furs, sweaters, gloves, underwear and skis? Maybe what an unnamed neutral journalist wrote in his paper was right? Is he correct in writing about increasing shortages of raw materials in Germany, when he mentions that woolen articles are to be issued only in the most pressing cases and only on ration cards? Time will tell whether or not the government cheated the people out of their woolens and furs only graciously to allow them to buy them back later on ration cards. Time will tell!!

Poor "Joseph" stands at the microphone,
Entirely unable to bring forth a tone.
"How am I going to convince the *Volk*
that Hitler's figures aren't just a joke?
How could he have said—so embarrassing—
That he's calculated for everything?"

What Joseph says sounds pretty slack;
Oh woe is us, alas, alack:
"It's winter now and bitter cold."
(Even chillier when you sit in a hole
'cause shooters always seem to freeze.)
Didn't Hitler calculate for these?

"We're engaged in a struggle with hands and feet,
It won't last much longer 'til the enemy's beat.
They've been running along on their last breath
—So Goebbels says—soon comes their death.
(For the fact that Stalin has won of late
I suppose the Führer could also calculate!?)

"We're engaged in a battle, at the turning place
So everyone step up the wool-collection pace!"
That's what Goebbels begged for, and he also believed
That you'd follow his orders and be deceived.
That everything you own you would quietly give,
and keep nothing at all on which to live.

The results were poor, oh how that forebodes!
So we'll say that they donated many trainloads.
Whether half-full, full or completely hollow,
The *Volk* is too dumb to really follow.
'Cause the radio and Fritsche, they speak with clout:
"The Führer has calculated everything out!"

Yes, Hitler's the reason the people must share
From their meager belongings whatever they'll bear!
For Hitler's mistakes the *Volk* must now pay,
What good now is Russia, it's lost anyway.
And that Stalin now marches the victor in the war,
The Führer neglected to calculate for.

But in '41 the big break will come,
That's how the Führer's speech last year did run.
The soldiers now know of his tendency to err,
While Hitler keeps promising, "*This* is the year."
When the Allies all get moving there *will* be a rout
But then Mr. Hitler will be "calculated out."

Soldiers on the home front! Soldiers on all fronts! The Führer has promised you that 1942 will be decisive and this time he will stop at nothing to keep his promise. He will send you by the thousands into the fires in order to finish the crime he started. By the thousands your wives and children will become widows and orphans. And for nothing! The European Front stands fast and the Rütli-oath[19] is unanimous, unanimous the promise—the promise of all Allied peoples:

We want to be united now as brothers,
Not separate in danger or in need!
We wish to live in freedom like our fathers
Preferring death to living servitude!
We place our highest trust in God Almighty
And fear no kind of human power.[20]

The European Awakening has begun: in reply to the laughably audacious contention of the Axis propagandists that in a month or so the U.S. has already been badly damaged by the Japanese attack and that "Roosevelt's dream of having a say on the continent of Europe is nothing more than a dream," American air, land and sea forces have now taken up positions in the north of Ireland. Berlin, Rome and Tokyo may try to veil the dimensions of this landing and may gloss over it with sneering gestures, but time will tell who spoke the truth. And then, when the Allied and American forces set foot on the Continent, when American and British squadrons bring death and destruction over the Reich, when the Allied and U.S. fleet enters the battle of the Atlantic with fresh reserves; then deeds will speak a more eloquent language; then with Hamlet, our only reply to the illusionary soap-bubble blowers in the Wilhelmstraße will be:

"Words, words, words!"

Source: Berlin Document Center

43

The Voice of the Homeland

"The Bible not God's word. Merely a scheme of the Jewish world to en-
slave mankind. The product of an overactive fantasy."
This is the red thread which is found in each of the "freespiritual" or
"neo-heathenistic" filth-pamphlets. "The Bible, Not God's Word." That is
the title of one of the filthiest and most intemperate brochures of the great
Anti-Christ, General Ludendorff.
Why all this campaign against the Bible, holy writ? The answer to this
question should not be too difficult if one knows the contents of the Bible,
especially the many prophecies which pertain mostly to the latter days, to
the days when heathenism and idolatry will take the upper hand, when the
great Anti-Christ will arise in the midst of a peaceful period and will conquer with power or with cunning one country, one kingdom after another.
This time has come now; the Anti-Christ has established his "Reich."
Ludendorff knows this just as Hitler does, and they are attempting to take
the Bible away from the German people, so that they will not be able to see
through the insidious plans of Hitler and his followers in advance.
Christians, arise, open the Bible, read what it says in the Book of the
Prophet Daniel, 11:20:

> And in his place shall
> Stand up a vile person, to
> Whom they did not intend to
> Give the honor of the kingdom,
> But he shall come in the midst of peace,
> And obtain the kingdom by flatteries.

To whom does this apply better than to the Führer: by means of bold
phrasemongering and grandiose promises he and his comrades succeeded in
winning the majority in the Reichstag.

Source: Berlin Document Center

44

Comrades in the North, South, East, West. Friends at home!
A new year has begun, a year upon which Hitler has set all of his last
hopes in this struggle, which is in fact already hopelessly lost. 1942, the Year
of Decision, will decide decisively, we are told, it will show that until now
deeds still triumphed over words, even when these words, one is tempted to

say: these dictionaries full of words, spring from the mouth of a certain Herr Dr. Josef Goebbels.

Nazi propaganda is good, it is very good, but it is still not good enough to make gleaming, never-before-seen-in-history kinds of victories out of miserable defeats and costly retreats, out of lost battles and hopeless confusion without anyone noticing that something is rotten. Hitler's New Year's proclamation reveals this in all clarity. What a pathetic deal that was! He is by no means likely to alleviate the dissonance and dejection among the German people.—Whose ears are not still ringing with the cries of despair from "handsome Joseph" who has delivered us from Bolshevism? But I say unto you, they will perish by their own works!—What a transformation!! Hitler, the same Hitler who the previous year could not say enough about how well everything was going, now feels himself delivered from Bolshevism, although from June to December 1941, to listen to him tell it, he strode mightily from one "final destruction" of Bolshevism to another, and although he smashed or captured the last Russian reserves not ten or twenty, but believe it or not, no fewer than twenty-six times. This same poor old Hitler must now be plagued by incurable paranoia, in addition to his craze for taking over the world and his megalomania. But Hitler feels threatened by a phenomenon, namely bolshevism, which according to his own report, the report of the VERY reliable High Command of the Armed Services, must already be long decaying on the wide steppes of the East!—if the report of the High Command of the Armed Services corresponded to the facts. Nevertheless, day after day, the news reports that bolshevist concentrations are being destroyed in "his honor," completely wiped out by spirited counterthrusts resulting in severe losses for the enemy, and anywhere the enemy breaks through, he is immediately repulsed with heavy casualties, blah, blah, blah. It no longer remains a secret that the Russian winter offensive is daily gaining ground westwardly, and that day after day the strongest German key positions fall victim to them. Rostov, Kaluga, Klin, Tichvin—place names, which, before the onset of winter, were reported as conquered in one of the best propaganda blitzes ever staged, places about whose strategic and economic importance Superior Counselor Fritsche and his colleague, Rolf Bathe, as High Command of the Armed Services commentator, could not talk enough, are again today serving as starting points for further Russian winter campaigns. Malo Jaroslavecz, Mouzhaisk, places a few weeks ago where Hitler once again claimed to have struck a final battle of annihilation, are today the mass graves of countless numbers of German and its allied infantry and tank divisions, which the bolshevistic attacks repulsed successfully in courageous counterthrusts.

Just as tendentious and illusionary is the German propaganda campaign about the North African theater of operations. Rommel wins and sweeps and strikes in one battle of annihilation after the other, reports glory, earns the oak leaves with swords and other lovely medals and decorations, but all this notwithstanding apparently does not notice that he must soon die of thirst in the dry and extremely arid deserts of Tripoli if he does not soon choose to surrender in this hopeless struggle.

Hitler and his "comrades in arms" in the Palazzo Venetia in Rome know this only too well, only too well, and, therefore, are purposely trying to divert our attention to East Asia. But even the most stupid schoolboy in every village knows that the European showdown cannot be won in East Asia. And even if Japan momentarily exploits its surprise attack, which is contrary to international law, and still achieves many a victory, that still does not detract from the hard reality that Germany is doomed.

In the East Asian theater there are still numerous offensive bases against Japan itself. And General-Minister President Tojo and his imperialistic camarilla can rely on that; when they consider the timing appropriate, England, the U.S.A., China and the Dutch Indies will use these bases. The struggle for survival in East Asia will not be won in such exotic villages as Ipoh or Kuala Lumpur. The decisive battles will be fought at the gates of Tokyo, and the allied fleet will strike when they believe the time has arrived, and not when the Japanese fleet would like to have them in their gunsights.

Tokyo may well still scoff and joke, one illusionary soap bubble after another may rise up from and burst in the Wilhelmsplatz Propaganda Ministry in Berlin, the Italian Agenzia di Propaganda may well continually bestow premature laurel crowns over and over on a defeated army—the year 1942 will be decisive, Hitler says. Where, in the East, in Africa or in Asia, perhaps?? Hitler himself does not believe that. The decisive turning point will occur in another place. It will occur when it dawns on the German people, long held in darkness, when they are tired of the unspeakable burden of war and would gladly like to throw off the burden.—The year 1942 will decide. And this decision is reserved for the German people to make, it is reserved for each individual German to make, even if he now participates in the bloodbath provoked by Hitler and his comrades, even if he is reluctantly dressed in field gray in snow and ice or in the glowing heat of Africa. This decision is reserved for each and every German, including widows and orphans, the victims of the Hitleristic blood vultures, to avenge themselves on the man who is responsible for all of the untold grief, who is responsible for countless German soldiers losing their health in the indescribable cold, manning hopeless positions with inadequate winter equipment: he is to blame that hundreds of thousands wait in vain for their husbands, sons, and fathers to return.

Germans, arise, make your decision, a determined deed can still rescue you and your country from the abyss to which Hitler has led you with his sweet talk. Make your decision before it is too late!

Headline: The European Awakening. *Dateline:* Berlin: After the beginning of the month Hitler assumed the solitary supreme command of the army; to all appearances a reorganization of the military leadership corps is in process, such as has not been seen since his seizure of power. General Field Marshal von Bock was removed from the command of the middle army group, von Reichenau, who was not willing to dance to the tune of his Führer, suffered an accident after the pattern of Fritsch or Halder and ended a little later with a state funeral. And still five other leading generals find themselves in Berlin hospitals and it's not difficult to surmise their fate in advance. *Dateline:* Hamburg-Billstedt: In Hamburg-Billstedt in recent weeks numerous arrests were carried out by the Gestapo, because people were meeting evening after evening to listen to the broadcasts of the London radio in the German language. *Dateline:* Bern: from Switzerland it is reported that recently numerous illicit sales of gold from Germany were uncovered, deals in which some of the leading German military personnel also took part. *Dateline:* Ankara: From Turkey comes the news that in the course of 22 and 23 January agents of the Axis powers and employees of the German news agency were arrested because of espionage. *Dateline:* Switzerland: On the occasion of the federal holiday, leading representatives of the government delivered a declaration to the effect that any hostile infringement on the neutrality of the Confederation would be answered with armed force.

Source: Berlin Document Center

45

The Führer's Speech!

The Führer spoke and he really spoke a great speech. Believe it or not, this mixture of phrases and vacuous idioms lasted longer than 2 hours. 2 full hours—yet Hitler was unable to give any answers to the question which at this moment concerns everyone. Hitler spoke and spoke, but he avoided expressing himself. Why the German and allied troops on the east front are now being driven day by day from the best positions, with extremely heavy casualties; why does Rommel try, in spite of the prevailing setbacks and defeats, in spite of two failed offensives, to set in motion a third equally hopeless offensive; why has the allegedly superior air force for many months now no longer shown itself in massive attacks upon England; why do the sinking figures of the reports issued by the German High Command of the Armed Forces on the "Battle of the Atlantic" decline from day to day, although Hitler already believes this battle to have been won? Why? About this the "false prophet" Hitler wraps himself in silence, but nevertheless—in spite of everything—he had enormously much to say.

For nearly 2 hours the Führer continued this vacuous beating of his gums, for nearly 2 hours he blew one soap bubble after another. But still, despite this, and despite the numbers of small and large "Fritsches," the numbers of propagandists, politicians or armchair politicians and scribblers, who are also willing to trim to size this or that sentence, to garnish Hitler with glimmers of hope and calculated optimism, in order to make it palatable to the man on the street, Hitler has lost his halo. After the extraordinary prophecies of the past year, after dozens of futile promises of ultimate victory, scarcely anyone still believes in him and in his prophetic words.

This stenographic transcription of an English news broadcast was translated from shorthand.
Hamburg, 5 February 1942
/s/ Fleuker

Certified
/s/ Pollman 21 May 1942

Source: Berlin Document Center

46

Comrades in the East, South, North or West! In the intervening time so many new things have occurred in the military and political areas that we make an extra report. The largest submarine in the world has been sunk. Those were the words of the broadcaster of Radio London on 13 November at 10:00 in the evening, as he announced the report of the sinking of the aircraft carrier Ark Royal. And it is a fact; for this victorious ship was already reported as severely damaged six times by the braggarts in the German and Italian propaganda ministries. But also at the beginning of the war, on 26 September 1939, the ostentatious victory fanfares and the "Victory over England" song resounded over short and long waves to all the world, the Iron Cross, I and II class, were already bestowed with great tara tara, the Ark Royal has already been sunk once before! On page 120 of the book *Our Battle in Poland* it says literally: "In the North Sea, German airplanes attacked an English fleet and sank a large aircraft carrier (Ark Royal) with a 300 kilogram bomb. . . ." Now, if this is really true, is there anyone left who still could be amazed by the enormous German figures or reported sinkings in the Battle of the Atlantic? Yes, on 15 November the propaganda minister Dr. Josef Goebbels raised the veil for us and cleared everything up. We thank him most politely.

If one must really launch such lies into the world, but which can at any moment be documentarily refuted, in order to maintain the morale of the homeland and the fighting spirit of you soldiers, how bad off must things be already, how wobbly the "impenetrable front" of the ministerial counselor Fritsche must already appear. In fact things look like this: to finance the war, money is needed, and because this money is accumulating so slowly, new funds must be procured. So they seize upon the slogan "Saving for Iron." Every German who is gainfully employed will be voluntarily forced by threats to take part in this savings campaign. 13 or 26 Marks, those are the installments, which every month the German worker must pinch from his already scanty wage, so that more cannons, tanks and airplanes can be produced for the further subjugation of Europe and the world, although the outlook for repaying this disguised war loan is placed very, very much in question. Of course, it is said that the repayment of the balance of your savings will take place exactly one year after the conclusion of the war. However, what happens before that, what can yet happen, this they apparently forgot to point out to the German worker. Now, gone is gone and lost is lost; whoever neglects to invest his money in time, will sooner or later lose it yet; that is the view of numerous foreign financial experts, and it looks like they will be right in the long term.

And now a short overview about the important military events of the last few days. In Russia the cases of frostbite and freezing increase, particularly among the units newly arrived from the west, which without adequate training were immediately put into action at the battles for Leningrad and Tula. In other ways, German operations are moving forward only very slowly with great privations and hardships. The capture of Rostov cost many thousand German soldiers, among them numerous men of the Organization Todt and National Labor Service who had been trained in these organizations for military service. Since 18 November, British forces stationed on the Egyptian-Libyan border are in combat contact with German and Italian tank units. Despite all of the attempts of the High Command of the Armed Services to gloss over them, the operations of the Allies have taken a satisfactory course, and in several places have already been able to cross the Libyan border. The encirclers of Tobruk are immediately threatened. In East Africa the surrounded divisions are facing total annihilation if they do not choose capitulation. Even the German and Italian magazines and newspapers no longer make any secret about it and are writing articles expressing their sympathy to those who have suffered losses. Near Gibraltar a submarine was sunk and in the English Channel two PT boats were sunk. Further reports and the recently announced special report will follow shortly.

Source: Berlin Document Center

47

Johannes Schnibbe
Hamburg 24, 7 May 1942
Rossausweg 32 I

To the
Attorney General at the People's Court
Berlin—W9
Bellevuestraße 15

Re: The Case of Hübener et al. (juvenile), document number IS 11/42

In the above-mentioned criminal case my son *Karl-Heinz Schnibbe*, born 5 January 1924, residing with me, was taken into custody.

Because of this matter a great sorrow has come over me and my family, under which we understandably suffer extraordinarily. This all the more so as our son received an upbringing in our home, which makes it incomprehensible how my son could be drawn into such an affair. It can never be my intention to influence the court's decision, although it naturally is the most ardent wish of my wife and me that my son emerge from this highly unpleasant affair with some leniency, for in spite of the alleged offenses of my son, our parental love is great, and strong enough to forgive him even for this.

According to the inquiries made by me, the preliminary investigation is essentially closed, and it is, therefore, our fondest wish that the main trial will be soon begun, in order that we be freed from this disquieting uncertainty of what will become of our boy. The purpose of my present letter is, therefore, politely to request the Attorney General to plead as much as possible that the proceedings be expedited. I am aware that the present shortage of personnel already necessitates a delay of the matter.

I request of the Attorney General once more, our great love and concern for our youngster, despite his actions, fills us most profoundly, and I hope that you, Herr Attorney General, have the most complete understanding for this. Should it, therefore, become possible to accelerate the process, a great concern and sorrow would be taken from us.

I would, therefore, be thankful to you, if I could await from you a favorable reply in this matter. I thank you in advance, Herr Attorney General, for your gracious efforts, and close with

Heil Hitler!

/s/ Joh. Schnibbe

Source: Berlin Document Center

48

Letter from Marie Wobbe

Hamburg, 17 June 1942

Subject: The Criminal Case of Hübener et al.
87. 127/42 Juvenile

I hereby request an acceleration of the above-mentioned case, because my son, who is 16 years old, is suffering greatly emotionally in confinement. It is also for me, as a widow, very hard to be required to watch my only child go to pieces emotionally from the results of confinement. I am a war widow employed as a custodian. My husband died from a severe wound which he incurred in the former war. That was such a severe blow to me that I had to be hospitalized with acute meningitis. My life hung by a thread. Physicians warned me against allowing myself to get upset anytime in the future. My nerves are all frayed because of my son's grief. I request, therefore, once again an acceleration of the case of Hübener et al.

Heil Hitler,

Mrs. Marie Wobbe
Hamburg 27
Hardenstraße 15 III.

Source: Berlin Document Center

49

Joh. Schnibbe
Hamburg, 30 June 1942
Rossausweg 32 I.

To the
Attorney General
at the People's Court
Berlin—W9
Bellevuestraße 15

Re: In the Case of Hübener et al. (juveniles),
      Document Number JS: 11/42

Because I have learned that now in the near future the trial is to take place in the above-mentioned criminal case, in which my son Karl-Heinz, born 5 January 1924, and taken into custody on 10 February of this year, and that my son Karl-Heinz also will receive a defense attorney, I would like to re-quest the Attorney General politely, to be so kind as to send me the address of the defense attorney, so that I can establish timely contact with him.

I also would like to request that I be permitted to attend the trial.

About my son Karl-Heinz himself, I would still like to note, that he, as well as we his parents, suffer emotionally extraordinarily through this great concern for our son. I would like really to take the liberty to say that he accepted the copies without having thought the least about it. He really had no evil intentions. We as his parents have bestowed on our children an up-bringing which makes it incomprehensible to us that our son Karl-Heinz could have been drawn into this horrible affair. We would like to ask the Attorney General not to judge his offense too harshly.

I would be thoroughly thankful to you, Herr Attorney General, if I could anticipate receiving a quick reply.

I thank you in advance very much, Herr Attorney General for your gracious efforts and close with

Heil Hitler!

/s/ Joh. Schnibbe

Source: Berlin Document Center

50

Certified Copy[21]

On the subject of Rudolf Wobbe, Hamburg Investigatory Prison 5, Cell 54.

I was stationed with Wobbe since February 1942 in a sell where he tol me the following:

At my frend Hübener's with his grandparents and him I lissened to the English broadcasting station, there the following was announced. The German troops in Russia is always retreating more. Whoever volunteers for the SS is committing sooicide. Adolf Hitler is the greatest murder of men of . . . tol me further that there is an agent behind Hübener . . . whoever always Hübener a lot of money for his listening and . . . copied but Wobbe never got none of it.

He tol me further that they had a Dutchman at home[22] and that he tol bad things how it was going in Holland. He tol me that in Holland hunger revolts was always breaking out and that it looked very dark for the German soldiers in Holland. Wobbe tried further to gain ground with me by agitating against the Führer and the armed services. He said that what the Germans in Holland, Denmark and Norway done was not war but murder and plunder. I warned Wobbe numerous times but he always said that what he said was correct. Further, he cursed about the SS in Fuhlsbüttel that people is mishandled and tyrannized there, that no real man would join there.[23]

He tol me further. He had, in addition, committed a burglary and that he had bought provisions from a comrade although he knew that they was stolen.

/s/ Bernhard Rubinke
4 July 1942

Source: Berlin Document Center

51

Secret State Police
Hamburg, 10 July 1942
State Police Office Hamburg
B. No. II P—126/42

Upon being brought forward from investigatory custody, there appeared the mechanic's apprentice

Rudolf Gustav Wobbe

born 11 February 1926 in Hamburg, and made the following statements regarding the denunciation of the interrogated prisoner Bernhard Rubinke:

Upon interrogation:

It is correct that I shared a cell with Rubinke. We conversed about my case, and on this occasion I also told him what was written on the flyers which I distributed. On this occasion we also came to discuss the expressions with which the Führer was described. I admit the possibility of having used the expression mass murderer or something similar with reference to the Führer, but this was not my personal view, instead, I used these words because they were written on the flyers, and we were talking about them. It is also correct that I told Rubinke something about the newscasts of the English station, which I listened to once with Hübener. If I can remember correctly, I said to him that the German troops were always retreating and the Russians were always advancing. I also told him about the conditions in Holland, and that there were repeated hunger revolts. Whether I told him more about Holland, and where I obtained this news, I no longer know, but it is possible that I heard this by listening to the English station, but it can also be that Hübener told it to me. That I supposedly said what the Germans did in Holland, Denmark and Norway was not war but murder and plunder is not correct, at least not in this manner. It is possible that I represented the war as murder and plunder. I cannot recall details of everything I said on that day. I also did not think about it as I spoke with him about these things.

It is correct that I spoke with Rubinke about food ration cards. Our conversation in this regard concerned a matter that lies further back. While still attending vocational school, I once bought 2,000 grams of meat stamps from a school comrade. I used these meat stamps for myself without saying anything to my mother about them. On this matter I was interrogated in May of this year as a witness during the proceedings before the court.[24] It is possible that I, as I spoke with Rubinke about these stamps, mentioned that they could have originated from a burglary. In any case, I did not commit a burglary, and in that Rubinke must have understood me wrong.

personally read and found to be correct
/s/ Rudolf Wobbe

Certified with the note that Wobbe was returned again to investigatory custody. The alleged agent behind Hübener is merely a conjecture of Wobbe and it was in that manner he claims to have expressed himself also to Rubinke.
/s/ Müssener, Criminal Secretary

Source: Berlin Document Center

52

Verdict of the People's Court

In the name
of the German people
in the criminal case against

1.) the administrative apprentice at the social administration in Hamburg *Helmuth* Günther Hübener, born 8 January 1925 in Hamburg, most recently residing there,
2.) the machinist apprentice *Rudolf* Gustav Wobbe, born 11 February 1926 in Hamburg, most recently residing there,
3.) the journeyman painter Karl Heinz Schnibbe, born 5 January 1924 in Hamburg, most recently residing there,
4.) the administrative apprentice at the social administration in Hamburg *Gerhard* Heinrich Jacob Jonni Düwer, born 1 November 1924 in Altona, most recently residing in Hamburg-Altona, all of whom are currently in legal detention in this matter,

because of conspiracy to commit high treason

the People's Court, Panel 2, renders its judgment on the basis of the main trial on 11 August 1942, in which the following took part

as judges:
Vice President of the People's Court Engert, Presiding
Chief Justice Fikeis,
Motorized SA Brigade Leader Heinsius,
Senior District Leader Bodinus,
Senior District Judicial President Hartmann,

as representatives of the Prosecuting Attorney:
First District Attorney Dr. Drullmann,

as Clerk of the Court:
Judicial Minister Wöhlke

The court orders:

The following to be sentenced:

Hübener, for listening to a foreign radio station and distributing the news heard in connection with conspiracy to commit high treason and treasonable support of the enemy:

to death

and the loss of his civil rights during his lifetime,

Wobbe, for listening to a foreign radio station and distributing foreign radio news in connection with conspiracy to commit high treason:

to 10 (ten) years imprisonment

Schnibbe, for listening to a foreign radio station and distributing foreign radio news:

to 5 (five) years imprisonment

and Düwer, for distribution of foreign radio news:

to 4 (four) years imprisonment.

The defendants Wobbe, Schnibbe and Düwer will each have five months of the imprisonment already served credited to their terms of imprisonment.

The impounded radio set, "Rola" brand, and the typewriter, "Remington" brand, are to remain impounded.

The defendants are to bear the costs of the proceedings.

IN ACCORDANCE WITH THE LAW

Findings

In the main trial, the following was established on the basis of the deposition of the witness, criminal official Müssener, as well as the witnesses Heinrich Mohns, Werner Kranz, Horst Zumsande, in connection with the admission of the defendants, and from the content of the leaflets and flyers which were the object of the trial:

I.

The defendant Hübener is now 17 years old, his father is engaged currently in the Security Service, the mother is at home. He attended the primary school and entered the upper track at school in 1938. His overall school record, that he received upon graduation in the year 1941, was extremely good. Since April 1941 he has been an apprentice for the upper administrative service.

Hübener joined the German Young People in the year 1938, was then placed in the Hitler Youth and belonged to it until his arrest. In the Hitler Youth he was, as the panel made certain, adequately adjusted and schooled.

Since his childhood he has belonged to the religious community "Church of Jesus Christ of Latter-day Saints."

Wobbe is currently 16 years old. His father is dead. He attended primary school, is a mechanic's apprentice and is in his second year of training. After earlier being in the German Young People, he also has belonged since 1938 to the Hitler Youth and is a member of the same religious community as Hübener.

Schnibbe, who is now 18 years old, also attended only primary school, learned the painting vocation and is now a journeyman painter. He is also a member of the "Church of Jesus Christ of Latter-day Saints." In the year 1939 he was expelled from the Hitler Youth because of failure to obey orders.

Düwer is now 17 years old. After primary school he attended middle school in the years 1935 to 1941, and has been since December 1941 an administrative apprentice with the social administration in Hamburg. He has been a member of the Hitler Youth since 1939.

All of the defendants were, as the panel made certain, adequately tested in the Hitler Youth.

None of the defendants has a prior criminal record.

II.

1.) In March 1941, the brother of the defendant Hübener brought a radio with him from France and left it with his grandparents. Two days later he was inducted into the military. The defendant Hübener had the radio repaired, brought it back to the apartment of his grandparents, where he too lived, because his parents were both employed, and as he played it he discovered the German news broadcast from London. He listened to the transmission, he enjoyed it and was so captured by its influence that from then on he listened to it about 4 or 5 times a week, while his grandparents slept. He relayed the contents in conversations about current events to other apprentices of his office and acquaintances.

Beginning in the summer of 1941, Hübener converted the contents of the intercepted English newscasts into flyers and leaflets. At first, he produced 15 different small leaflets, written on one side, and over time, from 3 to 5 copies of each were made. Nine such leaflets were seized. They contained insidious insults and slanders against the Führer, encouraging his overthrow as well as inflammatory statements on the conduct of the war.

Two leaflets carried the heading "Hitler's Guilt" and "Hitler bears the sole Guilt." They contained the assertion that because of the unlimited air war against the civilian population, hundreds of thousands of defenseless civilians were killed, that this air war was begun not by the English air force but by the Führer and represented only the retaliation for Warsaw and Rotterdam on the part of England.

A third leaflet, "Hitler the Murderer!" accuses the Führer of having caused the death of the military commander in Serbia, General von Schröder. Concerning this, Hübener admitted in the main trial that it was not known to him in which manner Schröder lost his life. He believed the English newscasts.

A further flyer carries in addition to the subversive appeal: "Down with Hitler," the words: "People's Seducer, People's Corrupter, People's Traitor," as well as the "V" for Victory sign, then recommended by enemy propaganda as an advertising slogan promoting the victory of the enemy powers.

In a fifth leaflet "Who is lying?" the reports of the High Command of the Armed Forces are represented as lies.

In a further leaflet "One and one-half millions" it is claimed that up to that time one and a half million men had fallen in battle in Russia. In addition, listening to the London radio is encouraged and its broadcast times quoted.

Two further leaflets "They are not telling you" and "137th Infantry Division" talk about the heavy losses of individual German units in Russia and lay the blame on the Führer for the fate of the widows and orphans.

The last leaflet seized, "Where is Rudolf Hess?" argues that Hess fled because he could not stand by and watch the irresponsible murders by the Führer and did not want to shoulder the responsibility for the attack in the east.

For the production of these flyers, Hübener used a portable typewriter belonging to his religious community. On it, in accordance with instructions from Arthur Zander, president of the community, he was supposed to write military letters to the inducted members. Altogether he produced about 60 leaflets. Approximately 20 he handed over in August and September 1941 to the codefendant Wobbe with the charge to distribute them. One copy of each issue he entrusted to the sales apprentice Horst van Treck. The rest he distributed in the city district of Hammerbrook in Hamburg, which is predominantly inhabited by blue-collar workers, by scattering them on the street or in hallways or throwing them in mailboxes.

Wobbe learned from Hübener, when he gave him leaflets for the first time, that they concerned newscasts which the London station had sent. Nonetheless, in each case he read through the sheets, and afterward received the commission to distribute them. He deposited them in the city district of Rothenburgsort, of which the preponderant part is also inhabited by blue-collar workers, in hallways and mailboxes and tacked some also on building bulletin boards.

2.) Some time after the beginning of the publication of the small leaflets, about the beginning of autumn, Hübener began to compile the notes, which he made for himself on the contents of the intercepted English reports, every eight to fourteen days into detailed flyers. Altogether the drafts or duplications of 20 different slanderous pamphlets of this kind were composed. The flyers contain, in addition to the English reports about the state of the war, vile insults and insinuations about the Führer and his co-workers, inflammatory attacks against the measures and designs of the National Socialist state leadership, as well as the challenge to bring about the end of the war through the overthrow of the Führer.

In the flyer that begins with the words: "On page 199 in Hitler's 'Mein Kampf' it says," there is an attempt to demonstrate that the German news broadcasts about the war situation are incorrect, and encouragement is given to listen to the London radio, whose call signs were given.

In the inflammatory writing "3 October—3 February" it is argued that the predictions of the Führer about the course of the Russian campaign did not come to pass, and claimed that the German troops on the east front were "defeated."

The leaflet "Monthly Military Review December–January" contains statements about alleged German reverses and losses on the eastern front and in Africa.

The flyer "The Voice of Conscience," which concerns an alleged announced "Christmas message" from Rudolf Hess over an English station, contains the most outrageous insults and slanders of the Führer and his co-workers, comments about the extent of the German war losses, in which the German reports are represented as incorrect, as well as a call to abolish the German national leadership.

In the leaflet with the title: "Battle against the bolshevist subhumans," on the basis of a contrast between the alleged resources of the Axis powers and of the enemy states, the situation of Germany and its allies with regard to supplies is characterized as "critical," while the resources of the enemy powers are presented as "inexhaustible."

The inflammatory writing "The Nazi Reichsmarshall" contains grievous insults and slanders of the Reichsmarshall Göring, as well as statements about the alleged inferiority of the German air force.

In the leaflet "The Riddle of Hess," horror stories about the alleged reasons for the flight to England of the former deputy of the Führer are repeated.

The inflammatory writing "Hitler Youth" contains slanders of the Hitler Youth leadership, crude insults of the Führer as well as an appeal for disobedience toward the Hitler Youth authorities.

In the leaflet "Weekend Incarceration," the opinion is given in an inflammatory manner on the establishment of juvenile detention in the Reich.

The leaflet "Who is inciting whom?" contains inflammatory statements about the entry of Japan into the war, which in a venomous manner is given the blame for the outbreak of the war with America.

In the leaflet "Comrades in the South, North, East and West!" the English advance into Cyrenica at the end of November 1941, the situation on the eastern front, the sinking of the aircraft carrier "Ark Royal," as well as the establishment of the "Saving for Iron" program are made the topic of demoralizing statements.

In the leaflet "I've Calculated for Everything!" the wool collection program becomes the impetus for a commentary in an inflammatory manner on the status of the war, and announces an English-American offensive on the European mainland.

In the inflammatory writing "There are in the East Asian theater still numerous attack bases," the German people are summoned to bring about the end of the war through the overthrow of the Führer. Further, the flyer contains horror stories which are concerned with the death of Field Marshal von Reichenau, of Colonel General Udet and of Colonel Mölders; [as well as] commenting upon the status of the war on the eastern front and in north Africa in a manner detrimental to the Reich.

The leaflet "Perfidious Rome" contains inflammatory and demoralizing statements about the battle in North Africa, as well as about Italian colonial policy.

In the flyer: "As Now Will Be Known," the characteristics of the Italian people and the battle strength of their armed forces are made the topic of inflammatory statements.

In the inflammatory writing "A Wave of Oil," it is claimed that the alleged oil shortage of Germany and its allies assures the victory of the enemy powers.

In the leaflet "Voice of the Homeland," an attempt is made to enlist religious controversies in enemy efforts at demoralization.

In the flyer "Victorious advance on brilliant battles of annihilation" the Japanese successes are presented as meaningless and the prospect of Japanese victory cast in doubt.

In the inflammatory writing "1942-the year of decision," the downfall of the Axis powers is predicted for 1942 and the German people are urged to overthrow their national leadership.

In the leaflet "The Führer's speech," the explanations of the Führer about the state of the war are represented as being unbelievable and "vacuous phrasemongering."

For the preparation of the final typed copies and the duplicate copies Hübener, as a rule, used a Remington typewriter, which the aforementioned Zander put at his disposal in place of the portable typewriter, in one case also a typewriter in his office. From each individual leaflet, Hübener produced at first two copies and, since Schnibbe requested a flyer from him, three to five and later six or seven copies. The last flyer, being prepared with seven copies, "Who is inciting whom?" was still in the typewriter at the time of Hübener's arrest. Of the individual leaflets he sent one copy each to the aforementioned apprentice van Treck, who was with the Labor Service at that time, as well as to his school friend Prumnitz, who attended the finance school in Thorn. Four or five leaflets he entrusted to Wobbe with the instruction to distribute them. Wobbe read them, but did not follow the instruction, but burned them. Once again, Hübener threw approximately 15 flyers in the city district of Hammerbrook in hallways or mailboxes or placed them in telephone booths. The majority of the inflammatory writings he adorned with the statement: "This is a chain letter . . . so pass it on!"

Already in the summer of 1941, Hübener told the defendant Schnibbe that he regularly listened to the broadcasts of the London radio station. In the fall of 1941 he showed him two inflammatory writings and informed him that he had compiled them from the content of the newscasts heard. Schnibbe liked the contents and requested that Hübener in the future entrust him with a copy of each leaflet. In the following period until January 1942, Hübener passed to him several inflammatory writings and, moreover, temporarily lent him further flyers for perusal. Schnibbe burned the inflammatory writings given to him after he had read them, without making them accessible to other persons. However, he told Wobbe some of the content, in particular the news about the battles in Africa and the retreat of Rommel.

At the beginning of 1942, Hübener told the defendant Düwer that he was listening to the news from London and was fashioning it into inflammatory writings. He mentioned falsely in this connection, in order to make a particular impression, that he produced the flyers on the orders of a "spy ring" and remarked that Düwer, if he wanted, could also join this ring. Düwer declined. At the same time, Hübener handed him inflammatory writings and entrusted to him other flyers in the following period until 4 February 1942.

In the presence of Karl Horst Pipo, at the end of January 1942 Düwer presented two leaflets to his contemporaries Horst and Kurt Zumsande to read through. As they, after they had read the first sentences, returned the leaflets because of the subversive content, he nevertheless read the leaflets to them. Before then he had already once reported to the brothers Zumsande about the proceedings in the African theater, which he had taken from the radio reports reproduced in the inflammatory writings of Hübener.

On Saturday, 17 January 1942, Hübener approached the administrative apprentice Werner Kranz with the request to translate flyers for him into French, which he would give him in the future. For the moment he could not say anything about the contents. Because the matter appeared suspicious to Kranz, he refused. Hübener explained to him that he sent flyers to politically unreliable German soldiers and wanted to slip the translations to prisoners of war. Three days later, accompanied by Düwer, he came into Kranz's office and wanted to slip him two flyers. When Kranz resisted, he left the room with Düwer. The occurrence was noticed by the deputy party overseer Mohns, who was present. The same day he took Kranz aside and on the following day Düwer, and learned from them about the activity of Hübener. Mohns ordered Düwer to procure supporting evidence for him. But the latter responded to the order only after numerous remonstrations, during which he always maintained, contrary to the truth, not to have any evidence in hand. Finally, on 4 February 1942 he handed him two flyers. The previous day he had been summoned and apprised of the consequences of conduct harmful to the state.

During his imprisonment, Wobbe found himself for a while in a cell with a prisoner named Rubinke. As they mutually related why they were arrested, Rubinke questioned him about the content of the radio reports. Wobbe related that he had heard, among other things, that the German troops in Russia were constantly retreating, that anyone who voluntarily enlisted in the SS was committing suicide and that Adolf Hitler was the greatest mass murderer.

3.) Wobbe attempted three or four times himself to listen on the radio set belonging to his mother to the news of the London station. However, he did not succeed in receiving the transmission.

Schnibbe wanted also to hear the transmission from London one time with Hübener. Though Hübener tuned in the set, because of strong jamming, reception was impossible.

It has not been proved that Düwer also listened to foreign radio newscasts. According to his admission, which was not contested, only once, as he was listening to the German station, did some words of an English station break through.

The established facts in this section are admitted by all of the defendants.

III.

1.) The bill of indictment charges all of the defendants with a continuous felony according to §§1 and 2 of the ordinance about extraordinary radio martial law of 1 September 1939, moreover, it charges the defendant Hübener with treasonable support of the enemy (§91b Penal Code) and conspiracy to commit high treason (§§80 Sections 2 and 3 No. 3 Penal Code).

2.) All of the defendants have admitted to having known about the ban on listening to foreign stations and the distribution of foreign radio newscasts detrimental to the Reich. In addition, they admitted the following:

Hübener: The English news had in contrast to the German reports, which he heard also, represented the events in a favorable light for England and in a detrimental light for the Reich. But because they had treated everything much more thoroughly than the German reports, he held them to be correct on most points and felt himself obligated to inform other people so that they too could experience the truth and be better instructed. Nevertheless, he never intended to influence others or to make public enemies. He only wanted, in a manner of speaking, to pass on the news "as a mouthpiece." The thought of furnishing the flyers to French prisoners and inducted members of his religious community came to him suddenly. He dropped the idea again. The title "Comrades in the South, North, East and West" he only chose in order to impress his own colleagues.

Wobbe: The subversive content and "what it was about" first came to his awareness when he received the four large flyers from Hübener. For that reason he no longer distributed, but burned, them. With the distribution of the flyers he did not have anything particular in mind, and especially did not intend to injure the Reich or otherwise incite against the government. With his attempt to tune in the English station, he wanted to hear the news himself once.

Schnibbe: He read the news only out of curiosity. When Hübener tuned in the English station, he was only visiting coincidentally.

Düwer: He only read both flyers to the Zumsande brothers because he was on friendly terms with them and assumed they would say nothing further. He only accepted the flyers in order to denounce Hübener when the opportunity arose. He also informed Kranz of this, but the latter replied that he had already spoken with the witness Mohns.

IV.

1.) That the defendant Hübener made himself guilty of a continuous felony by the unlawful intentional listening to English radio news requires no further substantiation according to the sense of §1 of the radio ordinance.

The defendants Wobbe and Schnibbe also committed this felony, by tuning in the English station in order to listen to the news, [even though they] got no reception. However, this does not change anything legally, for he [sic] intentionally acted contrary to the pronounced prohibition in §1 of the radio ordinance.

Schnibbe maintains that he visited Hübener coincidentally when he tuned in the radio. The time of the evening, however, indicates that this occurred intentionally. Otherwise, it is inconsequential, whether he came with this intent. The decisive thing is that when Hübener had tuned in the transmission, he intentionally listened. That they could not understand anything as a result of the jamming is immaterial for the constituent facts of the case. An intentional violation against the pronounced prohibition is present in any case.

Such a violation is also evident, if the prohibition against listening is appropriately considered, in the fact that Schnibbe instructed Hübener to furnish him regularly with a flyer about the English newscasts and then actually read the flyers provided to him. Then he consciously and intentionally sought to obtain the content of the newscasts for himself on a regular basis, and in this process merely inserted Hübener as an intermediary between himself and the radio receiver. It cannot therefore be argued that he thus did not hear the words of the English announcer. The fundamental intent inherent in the prohibition spelled out in §1 of the radio ordinance is to prevent the influence of enemy propaganda via radio. Schnibbe violated this intent just as clearly as if he had listened directly. It goes without saying that the good, healthy common sense of all politically right-thinking persons dictates that this deed deserves to be punished.

In Düwer's case, it has not been proven that he listened to foreign transmissions or intended to do so. An acquittal was not applicable, because a guilty verdict for such crimes is commensurate with the felony he committed according to §2 of the radio ordinance.

2.) All of the four defendants are guilty of a crime according to §2 of the radio ordinance. There needs to be no further substantiation of the question whether the news from London effectively endangered the resistance strength of the German people, given the content of the leaflets and flyers. The effectiveness is obvious and was also obvious to the defendants. The evidence about the deliberate distribution by Hübener and Wobbe needs no further substantiation. It is obvious also with Schnibbe, who communicated only some of the material to Wobbe, and with Düwer, who furnished the news to three friends. Neither of the two defendants maintained they urged the others to remain silent. Just as they passed the news along, it was obvious to them that the others could also do the same. In fact, Düwer thought about this very thing. His friendship did not justify him in assuming that the others would say nothing. The danger that the materials would be further distributed did not restrain any of the defendants from giving them to their friends.

Düwer's rejoinder, that he only accepted the flyers in order to report

Hübener at the proper opportunity, is false. In any case, it would not free him from his accountability of having made himself guilty of repeated distribution. His rejoinder is contradicted by the fact that he only handed over the flyers to Mohns after several reminders and after having been admonished by Mohns when Mohns took him to task, which frightened him, but before that time he falsely stated that he did not possess any leaflets. The required complaint has been filed by the state police for the prosecution of the defendants, who are charged with the radio felonies cited (§5 of the radio ordinance).

3.) The German-language news broadcasts from London intend to wear down the home front in the Reich and thus to tip the advantage in the war to the enemy powers. Given the totality of the war, their broadcasts are to be considered acts of war and are much more likely to serve their purposes than other methods of propaganda, because they can be received simultaneously in the entire Reich by all who possess a suitable radio set. Whoever, as has occurred in the present case, passes on newscasts originating as enemy propaganda, and thereby exposes others to their demoralizing consequences, is participating in the enemy's acts of war and aids and abets the enemy in injuring the Reich. By aiding and abetting the enemy, therefore, he brings about in actual fact an objective realization of treason in the spirit of §91b of the Penal Code.

Hübener felt the demoralizing consequences of this on his own attitude. Nonetheless, he recorded the contents of the messages, worked them up in a venomous manner and distributed the leaflets and flyers in part by himself, in part through Wobbe, in a manner which, despite the limited means at his disposal, promised the greatest possible success. Therein lies conclusive proof that he consciously and willfully aimed at distributing the demoralizing consequences of these communications. By so doing, he also satisfied the fundamental stipulation of §91b of the Penal Code.

The leaflets and flyers repeatedly encourage the overthrow of the Führer and the government. Consequently, they aim at a forceful and, therefore, treasonable (§80 Section 2 Penal Code) alteration of the constitution. The arguments, which in Hübener's case prove that he satisfies the stipulation of having aided and comforted the enemy, impel the court to the view that he adopted this goal under the influence of enemy propaganda, and for this purpose wanted to influence the masses by producing and distributing leaflets and flyers. He is therefore guilty of conspiracy to commit high treason in the spirit of §83 Sections 2 and 3 No. 3, 47 of the Penal Code.

The court also adjudged the defendant Wobbe guilty of the same crime. He read the flyers. That their contents constituted high treason was always obvious to him. Nevertheless, he went forth to distribute the leaflets in a blue-collar district, thus indicating that he had adopted the contents and intentions, at least as far as these were focused on the overthrow of the Führer and the government, and that he intended, jointly with Hübener, to influence the masses in preparation for this overthrow. Because the court lacked evidence about his innermost intentions, it did not deem it necessary to arraign him for the crime of aiding and abetting the enemy. The idea of a violent overthrow of the constitution suggested itself to him at his age more than that of aiding and abetting the enemy.

4.) Inasmuch as each of the defendants committed several crimes, they stand in coincidence with one another (§73 Penal Code).

It is not proven that Schnibbe made himself liable for prosecution after 5 January 1942, on which day he attained the age of 18. He was thus at the time of the deed a juvenile like the other defendants. There is no indication, either from the personal behavior of or from the impression made by the defendants, of any circumstances which suggest that any of them was incapable, based on his mental or moral development, of understanding the illegality of the deed or of behaving in accordance with that understanding. All of the defendants possessed, particularly on the basis of the instruction which they received in the Hitler Youth, adequate political maturity.

V.

1.) The public prosecutor submitted the petition to prosecute Hübener according to §1 of the ordinance against juvenile felons. Two of the conditions of that ordinance are clearly fulfilled. Hübener, at the time of the deed, was over 16 years old. Protecting the German people requires that a juvenile guilty of such serious crimes be punished as an adult. The court reached the conviction that the third condition also exists, namely, that Hübener can be considered equal to a person over 18 years of age because of his mental and moral development at the time of the crime. Since the crime was committed just 6 months before, namely in February of 1942, the court was well able to make this judgment directly, without having to call an expert witness on the matter.

Hübener, who was characterized by the witness Mohns as an excellent and reliable co-worker, demonstrated in the main trial an intelligence which stands far above the average for youths of his age and was far superior to the 18 year-old defendant Düwer, who is physically much larger, and by no means below average, and who also attended 6 years of high school. His assignment to the executive track indicates that he always showed above-average abilities. For his final examination in school he submitted a political essay "The War of the Plutocrats," which is admittedly largely a compilation, but which in its style would never lead one to suspect that he was then only in his 15th and 16th years. The work is, in its inner contents and maturity, the work of a person far above 18 years. The same impression is made by the contents of the flyers which Hübener composed under the influence of the newscasts. Also in this case, no one would guess, even if he knew that their contents were composed from transcripts, that they were written by a youth of only 16 or 17 years. Also, our examination of his general knowledge, his political knowledge and his ability to make judgments, as well as his appearance before the court and his behavior, show without exception the picture of a precocious young man, intellectually long since having outgrown his youth. Also, that his moral maturation might somehow have lagged behind the other, was not in evidence in any way. Even in the way the crime itself was carried out, there are no indications that this was the act of an immature youth.[25]

Consequently the defendant was to be sentenced as an adult.

Decisive for the sentence imposed on him in the spirit of §73 of the Penal Code was that his case involved a particularly egregious distribution of foreign radio transmissions. This is demonstrated by the noticeably venomous content of the flyers and especially by the fact that Hübener distributed them in a working-class district of a city in which, as a result of the destructive air raids that the city has been exposed to, the danger of a seditious effect is particularly great, the more so, according to the statements of the criminal investigator Müssener, that one cannot yet say that Marxism has been completely eradicated in Hamburg. The defendant was aware of the danger of his propaganda and of the reasons for it. Therefore the death penalty, which is compellingly prescribed, must be imposed on him. It would have been pronounced even if this were not a particularly severe case in the spirit of §2 of the radio ordinance. Inasmuch as the extended threat of punishment from §91b Section 2 of the Penal Code is excluded, because severe consequences of the deed cannot be ruled out, the punishment would have been drawn from Section 1 of the Penal Code. In the event of a choice between death and life imprisonment, the decision could only have been rendered for the death penalty, because the gravity and danger of the deed and the need to protect the people require it, despite the fact that the defendant is a juvenile. The defendant himself revealed during the examination of his intellectual maturity that the interests of the community take precedence over the fate of an individual, and that he who opposes the people and the Führer must be eradicated, particularly in the current difficult times.

In consequence of the perfidy of the deed, the defendant was deprived of his civil rights for life (§32 Penal Code). §9, Section 5 of the Juvenile Court Law is not applicable in the present case in pursuance of §1 of the regulation against juvenile felons.

2.) For the same reasons as in the case of Hübener, the panel substantiated, both by the manner of the distribution of foreign radio newscasts and by the contents, that Wobbe's case was also particularly severe. In the place of the death penalty which is justified by §73 of the Penal Code, the panel has returned a verdict of ten years imprisonment, the maximum penalty permissible under §9 of the Juvenile Court Law. Given the difficulties of the times in which the Reich is struggling for its existence, in which it is a matter of to be or not to be, the full force of the law cannot be stayed, even for juveniles, when someone, as the defendant has done, takes a stand in a dangerous and insulting manner against his people and the Führer.

3.) Both of the other defendants are to be punished in accordance with §2 of the radio ordinance in consideration of §9 of the Juvenile Court Law. Because in the case of Schnibbe, who obtained knowledge from the contents of the radio transmissions from London over a longer time period, there is no amelioration under §1 of the radio ordinance, and the punishment for him is the same as under §2 of the radio ordinance, since the spirit of this paragraph does not specify a punishment in particularly egregious cases. The guilt of Schnibbe and Düwer, in the case of the latter of whom likewise a particularly egregious crime cannot be assumed, stands far behind that of both other defendants. The extent of the deed is smaller, also. For all that, given the interest they took in the newscasts, and given the nature of the deed, they must also be dealt with severely. Because Düwer only violated §2 of the radio ordinance, the punishment for him was set a bit lower than for Schnibbe, and he received a four-year, Schnibbe a five-year prison sentence. To impose an additional penalty, as the prosecutor proposed, was disallowed for Schnibbe because of the magnitude of his punishment. Moreover, it can be said of none of the defendants that they had been deprived of the necessary training in the spirit of the Hitler Youth.

4.) Inasmuch as the defendants have been sentenced to prison, in accordance with §60 of the Penal Code, five months of the incarceration already incurred was credited to them. A deprivation of their civil rights in accordance with §9 Section 5 of the Juvenile Court Law is not indicated. Educational measures called for by the Juvenile Court Law are not required in their case.

5.) The confiscation of the radio set that was used for listening, is based on §1 of the radio ordinance, the confiscation of the typewriter on §93a of the Penal Code.

6.) As a consequence of their conviction, the defendants are to bear the costs of the proceedings according to §465 of the Code of Criminal Procedure.

/s/ Engert
/s/ Fikeis

Source: Berlin Document Center

53

Letter from Emma Hübener

Hamburg, 8.14.42
Attorney General at the People's Court
Berlin W.9, Bellevuestraße 15

File Reference 8J 127/42g

I request for me and my mother permission to speak with my son Helmuth Hübener. Having initiated a petition for clemency with my attorney Dr. W. Grotenfend, I entreat the Attorney General at the People's Court for clemency for my son. He is surely still too young and wants to make amends for everything, everything, therefore, please heed the pleas of a sorely tested mother. Helmuth was really my sunshine and was such a good boy, there is not a better youngster, but it is so sad that he has made a mistake. Please hear my entreaty and just give him the opportunity to make up for it. I request a speedy reply to whether I can speak with my son Helmuth.

With the German greeting,

/s/ Mrs. Emma Hübener
Hamburg 1
Sachsenstraße 42, ground floor

Source: Berlin Document Center

54

Notary Judicial Counsel W. Grotefend
Notary Judicial Counsel Dr. G. Kohlsaat
Notary Werner Grotefend
Attorneys at the Hanseatic
Higher Regional Court, Regional Court Hamburg
and District Court
Hamburg-Altona, 15 August 1942

To the
Attorney General
at the People's Court
Berlin W.9
Bellevuestraße 15
8.J.127/42g

In the criminal case against Helmuth Hübener I am sending the enclosed power of attorney of the stepfather of the condemned.

Acting for him and his wife, the mother of the condemned, I request the death penalty imposed on their son be commuted to a prison term by an act of clemency.

The sentence was handed down, according to the notification by the public defender, because enemy radio broadcasts were listened to and newscasts of the same were distributed, which constituted conspiracy for high treason in the spirit of §3, Section 3, Numbers 1–3 of the Penal Code of the Reich and aiding and abetting of the enemy power according to §91b of the Penal Code of the Reich.

The condemned was born on 8 January 1925. Thus, at the time of the commission of the deed not yet 17 years old.

During his life to date he conducted himself in a completely impeccable manner. He attended primary school until he entered the upper track, and always received good grades. As the testimonials in the attached documents reveal, his conduct was always very good, as was his diligence. His accomplishments were adjudged satisfactory. Likewise, the condemned has always brought joy to his parents and his grandparents, with whom he lived. Also in his apprenticeship at the Hamburg social administration, he proved a success. He was ambitious and assiduous and applied himself by attending evening classes in order to make good progress in his training and in his occupation.

When his brother, who is at present a Private First Class at the eastern front, was inducted, he gave his brother his large radio set. For fun, he attempted to receive as many stations as possible and discovered that he could hear enemy transmissions. Out of youthful levity and from a certain need to stand out among his friends and acquaintances by virtue of possessing particular information, he continued his listening and brought what he heard into conversations. As a result of his youth, he was not aware of the severity of his criminal offense. He did not understand the consequences which might result from his actions. Neither criminal predisposition or inclination were the causes of his crime, but rather youthful light-mindedness and thoughtlessness.

As is shown by the enclosed letter of the condemned written from prison to his family members, it first became clear to him during his imprisonment what he had actually committed. These letters prove that he regrets his criminal offense most deeply, and that he is most desirous, after completing a sentence, to make good the wrong committed through his personal efforts. The letters reflect his love for his family, his readiness for penance and above all, his sincere desire to make good. His past life gives the guarantee that the condemned will subsequently conduct himself impeccably.

His stepfather, who is currently a member of the Security Service, his mother, who performs her nursing duty in a nursing home in Hamburg, his brother, who is stationed on the eastern front, appeal for the requested pardon to be granted.

The return of the enclosures after use is requested.

/s/ Grotefend

Source: Berlin Document Center

55

Dr. Knie
Attorney and Notary
Berlin W.8
Friedrichstr. 82 II
Berlin, 17 August 1942

To the
Attorney General
at the People's Court
Berlin W.9
Bellevuestr. 15

Petition for Clemency
for the administrative apprentice Helmuth Hübener
presently at Berlin-Plötzensee,

8J 127/42g

The condemned administrative apprentice Helmuth Hübener, born on 8 January 1925, who was sentenced to death by the 2nd Panel of the People's Court on 11 August 1942, pleads herewith

for mercy.

The appellate body, when considering the constituent facts, may well wish to take into consideration that the condemned was not yet 16¼ years old at the time when he began to commit the offenses with which he has been charged. According to his statements, he merely acted at first out of curiosity and then came under the influence of this seditious enemy propaganda. While the condemned certainly at first did want to distinguish himself in the eyes of his comrades with his knowledge, and wanted to impress them, doubts came to him then through the newscasts of the enemy broadcaster. As a result of his youth, still not inwardly mature and firm, he succumbed to this enemy propaganda and committed the deeds with which he has been charged. Therefore, he was not yet 16¼ years old when he came under the influence of the propaganda of the enemy. Its poison established itself in his young mind, and then in the course of time he could no longer free himself from it, and was drawn more and more into this entanglement.

It should further be noted, that the condemned was earlier in every respect positively oriented, as was particularly demonstrated by his final school project, which he chose himself. Only by listening to the enemy transmissions did he come to this simply incomprehensible conduct, which was totally contradictory to his former nature and behavior.

One cannot, therefore, see in the condemned a precocious criminal, who operated out of some strongly developed moral depravity, but a person who, as a result of his youth, of his immature character, yielded to temptation.

Further, the irregular family relations in which the condemned grew up may also be taken into consideration. The condemned was born an illegitimate child. His sire has only just now admitted the paternity, and only recently the current husband of his mother gave him his name. Neither did the condemned have, therefore, the firm hand of a father to lead him.

In consideration of all of these conditions, a reprieve may appear to be justified, so that this young man is once more given the opportunity to prove through his later life that this was a matter of a single error, which he deeply and bitterly regrets.

/s/ Knie, Attorney at Law

Source: Berlin Document Center

56

National Socialist Workers' Party
Hitler Youth, District Hamburg-East (282)
Main Office I.
Hamburg 26, 17 August 1942

Service Certificate

The juvenile Hellmuth [*sic*] Guddat, born on 8 December 1925, residing at Louisenweg 137 c/o Sudrow, has been a member of the Hitler Youth since 20 April 1938, and discharged his duty in Cadre 14 of the District Hamburg-East (292) until 1 December 1941.

He discharged his duty to the complete satisfaction of his superiors and always distinguished himself through his eager participation in the home evenings. Unfortunately, he occasionally permitted himself to be influenced for the worse by other comrades. His behavior toward his comrades was always friendly.

Director of the District Hamburg-East
/s/ Asmus, Senior District Director

Source: Berlin Document Center

57

Secret State Police
Secret State Police Office
IV A 1 c—8185/42
Berlin SW 11, 28 August 1942
Prinz-Albrecht-Straße 8

Express Letter

To the
Attorney General
at the People's Court
in Berlin W 9
Bellevuestraße 15.

Subject: Plea for clemency in the criminal case against the administrative apprentice Helmuth Hübener, born on 8 January 1925 in Hamburg.

With regard to: Your letter of 14 August 1942—*8J 127/42*
8 Gns. 106/42

Enclosed: 3 three-part photographs of Hübener

Hübener, to be sure, was the heart and soul of the activities of this group, but his open confession at the first police interrogation bears testimony that he, despite his severe criminal offense, was still morally uncorrupted. Even if he, according to his own admission, was thoroughly aware of the criminal nature of his behavior, he may not have been at his youthful age of 16 mentally mature enough to recognize the consequences of his deed down to the last detail. Obviously the destructive reports of the enemy propaganda influenced the young man so strongly that he could no longer summon the strength to free himself from them.

The motive for his deed is, above all, certainly to be sought in a certain egotism vis-à-vis comrades of the same age and older. His title of "The Man with Connections" given him by his friends, undoubtedly contributed to strengthening his megalomania and led him again and again to distribute the newscasts he heard, in order to justify his reputation to his friends and acquaintances.

That Hübener until shortly before his crime showed a positive attitude toward the state and the Führer emanates from his completed final project in school.

I recommend clemency.

By Commission:
/s/ [illegible]

Source: Berlin Document Center

58

National Socialist German Workers' Party
Hitler Youth / Youth Leadership of the Reich
Office of the Hitler Youth Jurisdiction
182/42 G. 26 Gn. Ni./Ka.
Berlin, 15 September 1942

To the
Chancellery of the Führer of the NSDAP
Central Office for Clemency Cases
Berlin W 8
Voßstraße 4

Re: Clemency Case Helmuth Hübener, Hamburg

In the enclosure I return to you the sentence entrusted to me of the People's Court in the aforesaid clemency case and deliver, in addition, the following decision:

Helmuth Hübener was sentenced to death by judgment of the 2nd Panel of the People's Court on 11 August 1942. Hübener continually listened to the German news service from London. Hübener made the content of the intercepted newscasts into flyers and distributed these flyers partially himself, partially with the help of the three others accused. The flyers were largely scattered or thrown by Hübener and his accomplices into mailboxes in an area of Hamburg inhabited by workers.

Particularly aggravating in the case of Hübener is that he had worked up the contents of the newscasts in the most hateful manner. The flyers prepared by him repeatedly encouraged the overthrow of the government and the Führer. Therefore, Hübener, through his actions, made himself also guilty of conspiracy to commit high treason.

Hübener belonged to the Hitler Youth since 20 April 1938 and was in possession of national identification card No. 8 126 185. The service record of his district, as well as his cadre, indicate that Hübener always discharged his duty to the complete satisfaction of his superior Hitler Youth leaders. Particularly emphasized was his enthusiastic participation in the home evenings, in which he was able to engage so vigorously because of his above-average ability, and that he made substantial contributions to the content of the home evening.

However, the leader of his cadre emphasizes that Hübener is inclined to be a weakling, and that he is easily influenced. His behavior in the association of the Hitler Youth was disciplined and friendly.

The domestic relations of Hübener were described as thoroughly in order. His mother is employed as a nurse in a state institution, while his stepfather is a member of the Security Service. Hübener's parents enjoy a good reputation.

In agreement with the evaluation by the Hitler Youth, the opinion held of Hübener by those in his office in the social administration of the city of Hamburg also emphasizes his mental agility, rapid perceptiveness and orderly behavior.

Hübener held neither an office nor a rank in the Hitler Youth. He was also not in possession of any decorations of honor or achievement. Hübener was expelled from the Hitler Youth effective 10 September 1942.

The gravity of Hübener's crime and the danger that the strength of resistance of the people in the war could be adversely affected by his crime, make the execution of the death sentence against Hübener necessary. In addition, it is clear, given his above-average mental abilities, that Hübener, despite his youthfulness, must have been thoroughly aware of the gravity and consequences of his crimes. Even the good conduct of Hübener in the Hitler Youth cannot be allowed to make Hübener's crime appear in a more favorable light.

It is regrettable that in the judgment of the People's Court against Hübener the question remained open, whether and to what extent the religious sect to which Hübener belonged is to be ascribed as the intellectual originator of Hübener's crimes.

Heil Hitler!

On instruction of the Chief of the Office of the Hitler Youth Jurisdiction.
/s/ Nille, Senior District Leader and Hitler Youth Judge

Source: Berlin Document Center

59

The National Minister of Justice
Berlin, 19 October 1942
IVg 10A 916/42g

SECRET
Urgent!

To the
Attorney General
at the People's Court
in Berlin
Personally
or his official representative.

On 8J 127/42g from 21 September 1942

Enclosures: 1 volume,

1 green booklet,
1 envelope with 1 arraignment document, the
    Decree of 15 October, clean retyped copy
1 accompanying copy of the decree,
1 press notice

In the criminal case against

Helmut Hübener

sentenced to death by a judgment of the People's Court of 11 August 1942
I forward to you a clean retyped and certified copy of the decree of 15 October 1942, with the request that you arrange with the greatest haste for all necessary subsequent actions. The undertaking of the execution is to be entrusted to the executioner Röttger. When the cadaver is given to an institute according to No. 39 of the Reichs Ordinance of 19 February 1939, the Anatomical Institute of the University in Berlin is to be considered.

By Commission
/s/ Dr. Crohne

Source: Berlin Document Center

60

The Attorney General
of the People's Court
Berlin, 27 October 1942
SJ 127/42

Present:
    First State Attorney Ranke
    as Executory Leader,
    Secretary of Justice Renk
    as Officer of the Secretariat

The undersigned officials of the Attorney General at the People's Court proceeded today to the Plötzensee prison in Berlin. Here about 1:05 p.m. in the company of the representative of the director of the prison

    Senior Administrative Inspector Rohde and
    the Institutional Physician, Government Medical Counselor Dr. Schmitt

they sought out in his cell the individual condemned to death, Helmuth Hübener.
    The Executory Leader declared to the condemned, who was guarded by

two prison officers, after he had ascertained his identity, that he was appearing by instruction from the Attorney General of the People's Court. He then read slowly and clearly to the condemned the determinative portion of the judgment of the 2nd Panel of the People's Court of 11 August 1942, and thereafter the decree of the National Minister of Justice of 15 October 1942, according to which the Minister resolved, on the basis of the authority granted him by the Führer, not to make use of his right of clemency, but to let justice run its course. He revealed to the condemned further, that the execution of the judgment would occur on 27 October 1942 after 8:00 p.m., recommended that he prepare himself for his final hour and pointed out that he could direct his final requests, if any, to the prison officials.

Hereupon the undersigned departed the cell of the condemned.

During the notification the condemned remained completely quiet and calm.

/s/ Ranke
/s/ Renk

Source: Institut für Marxismus-Leninismus

61

Letter from Helmuth Hübener

Dear Sister Sommerfeld and Family,

When you receive this letter I will be dead. But before my execution I have been granted one wish, to write three letters to my loved ones.

I want to thank you for the letter you sent to me, dear Sister Sommerfeld, which they withheld from me. I also want to thank you for the many happy hours I was able to spend in the circle of your family. Please remember me kindly. I am very thankful to my Heavenly Father that this agonizing life is coming to an end this evening. I could not stand it any longer anyway! My Father in Heaven knows that I have done nothing wrong. I am only sorry that in my last hour I have to break the Word of Wisdom. I know that God lives and He will be the proper judge of this matter.

Until our happy reunion in that better world I remain,
Your friend and brother in the Gospel,

Helmuth

Source: Marie Sommerfeld

62

The Attorney General
Berlin, 27 October 1942
of the People's Court
8J 127/42

Present:
First Public Prosecutor Ranke
as Director of Execution
Clerk of the Justice Department Renk
as Executive of the Secretariat

The undersigned officials of the Reich's Attorney General's Office of the People's Court, today visited the penal institution Plötzensee in Berlin for the purpose of executing the condemned prisoner

Helmuth Hübener

who was legally sentenced to death on 11 August 1942.
The executioner from Berlin, Röttger, reported to the officers that he and his assistants were ready to commence with the execution. In the foreground stood a table covered with a black tablecloth, upon which were placed a crucifix and two burning candles. The back of the room was separated from the rest by a black curtain, which hid the guillotine from view.
The undersigned officers took their place behind the table and the executioner took his place with his three assistants in front of the closed curtain. Also present was First Inspector of Administration, Rohde.
The Director of Executions then ordered the condemned prisoner to be escorted into the room. At 8:13 p.m. the condemned man appeared with his hands shackled behind his back. Two prison guards escorted him into the room, locking the door behind them.
The Director of Executions then identified the condemned man as the one sentenced to death by the People's Court on 11 August 1942 and told the executioner to proceed. Immediately, the curtain was withdrawn and the three executioner's assistants took hold of the condemned man, who was calm. The prisoner showed no resistance when he was placed before the guillotine. With his shirt removed, he was placed upon the apparatus and the executioner removed the head from the body of the condemned man with the guillotine. He then reported the sentence carried out. The procedure took ten seconds from the time the condemned entered the room until he was turned over to the executioner, and eight seconds from when he was turned over to the executioner until the executioner reported that the sentence had been carried out.

/s/ Ranke
/s/ Renk

Source: Institut für Marxismus-Leninismus.

63

The Diary of Gerhard Düwer

My Period of Imprisonment

5 Feb. 1942	Arrest in the Biberhaus with subsequent house search.
6–27 Feb.	Police Prison Hamburg-Fuhlsbüttel (SS custody)
28 Feb.–27 July	Investigatory Prison City of Hamburg
29 July–1 Sept.	Investigatory Prison Berlin-Moabit
11 Aug.	Main Trial before the *People's Court* in Berlin (2nd Panel)
2–9 Sept.	Investigatory Prison City of Hamburg, A-Bldg.
9 Sept. 1942– 28 April 1944	Criminal Prison Glasmoor

a) 9 Sept.–11 Nov. 1942	Tailor Shop
b) 12 Nov. 1942–28 April 1944	Office

29 April 1944– 21 Jan. 1945	Prison Camp Graudenz (Office)
21 Jan.–15 Feb.	Flight from Graudenz
15 Mar.–8 April	Youth Prison Hanöfersand
8 April	Release

Flight from Graudenz to Hamburg

21 Jan. 1945	March from Graudenz, quarters in village inn.
22 Jan.	March to Neuenburg, District Court.
23 Jan.	March to a large estate, barn.
24 Jan.	March to Groß. Wollenthal, barn, 6 of us doing cooking duty on farms.
25 Jan.	March to Pr[ussian] Stargard, District Court.
26 Jan.	Rest in Pr[ussian] Stargard.
27 Jan.	March to an estate, barn, Russian camp kitchen.
28 Jan.	March to Neukrug, barn, inn, slaughter house.
29 Jan.	March to Berent, District Court.
30 Jan.	Rest in Berent.
31 Jan.	March to a small village, marched all night.
1 Feb.	March to Bütow, District Court, evening entrained.

from 1–11 Feb.	By train from Bütow via Schlawe, Köslin, Kolberg, Greifenberg, Naugard, Gollnow, Stettin, Berlin, Wittenberg to Bützow.
from 11–14 Feb.	Penitentiary Bützow.
from 14–15 Feb.	By train from Bützow via Lübeck to Glasmoor.

Flight from Graudenz to Hamburg

"Get up!" From a deep sleep I started up, astonished faces all around; but then everyone in the room was suddenly wide awake: "Alarm!" Were the Russians finally advancing, had they broken through? A frightening question. We recalled the conversation of the previous evening; we had vigorously disputed whether the Russian troops would succeed or not. We knocked on the wall of B-room; no one there had heard anything. Had we all been dreaming? Some crawled immediately back into bed, my friend Kuddl [Karl-Heinz Schnibbe] and I likewise, others dressed, the hour was a little before three, quiet returned again. After five minutes rapid steps, First Sergeant Eggers and Staff Sergeant Jäger stormed in: "Everyone out of bed!" The kitchen crew had to pack up the mess immediately, prepare travel rations, load the supplies, distribute the surplus. Hardly had our six comrades gone to the kitchen, when we other six zipped over to the administration barrack. Pitch-black night and besides that in the morning the fog rolled in too, so that one could not see five meters. In the administrative offices wild disarray prevailed. Superior Administrative Counselor Krüger, First Lieutenant Kröger, and First Lieutenant Eichwald were already excitedly running back and forth through the rooms and hallways. But F. Pape and I. Fenner were peace and quiet personified; the latter surprised us with the news that about one hundred men were to be released immediately. We had also nearly completed packing our personal things. Our buddies would look after everything else. Our four comrades helped pack the administrative materials. While everything seethed and boiled around us, everyone ran around excitedly and was furiously packing, Heinz and I sat at our typewriters from 3:30 a.m. until about 1:00 in the afternoon and processed the hundred comrades who were to be released, namely those who had shorter sentences, up to one year. Each of us had to process fifty men. There was one break of ten minutes, that was all. In the meantime the entire camp was ready for the departure. Meanwhile, all the office supplies had been packed and then properly stowed on the wagon and sled by our other four comrades under the leadership of Kuddl. Hastily we choked down some bites of lunch, then we sprinted to our rooms, to the kitchen, grabbed the very last items, packed them and then Kuddl-Heinz and I joined the kitchen crew, which with us was seven men strong with its own wagon and sled. As a vanguard of about two hundred men we left the camp at 2:00 in the afternoon in the direction of the city of Graudenz, escorted by about forty guards. Our column slowly wound its way through the streets of Graudenz, viewed by the inhabitants with curiosity and, partially, with concern. We also heard from them that in the morning the last trains in the direction of Germany had departed, and some of our comrades had caught them. The difficult part lay before us. The bridge over the Vistula was already blocked, so we went down the steep slopes of the banks of the Vistula and crossed the Vistula above the bridge. Because the ford over the Vistula was somewhat sandy and there was only pack ice all around, the sleds moved forward with difficulty, whereas we with our wagon and both large baggage carts moved along well and had been on the other bank for a long time already before the main detachment arrived. That day, as most days on the trek, we were mostly without guards, because we seven represented the elite of the camp, and were now the foremost trustees of the officials. Our column was already strung out over a long distance, but after two hours the difficult ford was finally accomplished, and we could pull our wagon and sled together on a tolerable road on the other side of the embankment. But already on these remote roads we ran into the wild confusion of the retreat, and it was here, also, where we became acquainted with the worst evil of the following weeks: waiting! All of the roads, even the smallest, were overloaded with all types of vehicles, and we could only advance slowly. After darkness fell, by taking back roads, we finally arrived at our day's destination. The traffic slacked off markedly in the evening hours, we could go at a snappy march pace and arrived at our destination about midnight, a small village near the Vistula. That we were able to reach it was due to the fact that there was bright moonlight and clear, frosty weather. A village inn was to be our quarters. Quickly the most necessary things like quilts and eating utensils were unloaded and then brought into the large hall, the floor of which was covered with straw. After a hearty supper, everyone went quickly to sleep. Of course we seven from the kitchen crew had quite a meal with butter, bread, and bacon, as well as some bottles of ice-cold beer. A good cigarette concluded our first day of flight.

A radiant morning dawned, houses, fields, and woods were covered with hoarfrost, and it glittered over the broad landscape. We ate quickly, packed everything well, and we were ready for departure. During the night some of our comrades, natives of the vicinity, withdrew from further participation in the trek by running away; of course nothing could be done about it, and so we went forward again. The highway was frozen hard and smooth, good for the sleds as well as the wagons, and we could set a good march tempo. Our kitchen wagon moved like the fire department, and we took over the lead like on the previous day. With a quick pace, always following the Vistula, we covered a good piece, especially since the road was free of all traffic, which was explained by its being parallel to the front. After a short rest, already by afternoon we saw the little city of Neuenburg positioned on the heights above the Vistula. The mastering of the heights cost us a lot of precious drops of sweat, but we still surmounted them. It was also there where we met a small column, which, for the most part, consisted of bombed-out people from Hamburg who had found a new home in West Prussia. Because there were some from Hamburg among us, there was a friendly shaking of hands and telling of stories all around, for the strict camp rules had yielded to a certain freedom. After a short journey through the little city, we were received cordially at the courthouse. The quilts and provisions were taken down from the wagon, and then we kitchen personnel moved into a good cell in the cellar. Food, above all good food, was our motto, and we stuck to it today, too. The rest of the afternoon passed with smoking and chatting and soon everyone, in spite of the close quarters, lay in deep sleep. The second day of flight was successfully completed. We had beautiful, clear weather and good roads, even though it did not get any warmer than 5 degrees above zero [Fahrenheit], but the most important thing was, that so far we had done well.

The next morning we almost were able to get caught up on our sleep, but then the day began with surprises. The order was: civilian or institutional clothing. We chose civilian clothes, just to be on the safe side. The second point was the reorganization of the entire column. Some of the defective sleds were abandoned, the others were assigned more men in order to achieve a faster march pace. Anything that was somehow dispensable was left behind. We kitchen personnel still took approximately thirty blankets and our boxes of butter and bread. Now things really looked like a bunch of refugees had been there: there were discarded items everywhere, deserted boxes and chests. Both of our large wagons were unloaded, too. Apparently alarming news about the rapid advance of the Russians had arrived. Finally, about 10:00 a.m. we departed from Neuenburg. We had barely left the city when we heard: turn back! and we had just barely been looking forward to the open, good road. It was the wrong road, so we crisscrossed through the city until we finally reached the right road to Pr[ussian] Stargard. Though we had always stayed on the side roads during the first few days, now, as a result of the Russian troops approaching increasingly close, we needed to use the main roads of the retreat, where we then immediately ran into a mess of numerous little refugee columns and truck columns of the armed forces. But the traffic still rolled along without friction, especially since the weather was lovely. Our kitchen wagon held the lead again today, and the snappy tempo of both of the last days could be maintained, if not, as a matter of fact, increased. Every day, naturally, we took small breaks, in order to prevent anyone from getting worn out, but our meals were taken mostly on the march. The feeding of the entire body of men during the retreat went well, and if things did not work out once in a while, then we "liberated" things to eat as we went along. We had already loaded our cook wagon in Graudenz anticipating approximately ten days of travel, so that we had enough, especially since bread was also distributed at certain points locally as we went along. Late in the afternoon we reached our quarters for today, a large estate, quite a distance from the road. We were directed to an enormous barn as our night's lodging, where we immediately made ourselves at home, but it was too bad that there were gaping cracks in the walls of twenty and thirty centimeters through which the wind blew like crazy. Four of us men still needed to cook the meal that was distributed every evening. Our comrades came back late, all armed with a bucket full of food. The main group was already asleep, we were the only ones awake, and we had our dinner by the gleam of some flashlights. We didn't get to sleep for a long time yet. As in the first night, now also some tried to slip away; some escapes succeeded, but some of our comrades had to be tied up and left in the barn until the morning. But at last the crowd settled down and each man crawled as well as possible under covers and straw, because in the meantime it had become extremely cold, and an open barn at 13 degrees below zero [Fahrenheit] is really nice! Kuddl and I crept close together and slept, as we did the other nights as well, side by side. Loud snoring soon announced that we had successfully survived the third day of the trek.

We were awakened in the dark, we packed and ate quickly and then took off. Some comrades had heard thundering in the distance during the night. The Russians were therefore really pushing hard behind us. We were caught in a large bulge in the front line, as our superior administrative counselor explained, hence the early departure, and as soon as we could see anything at all, we withdrew with all haste. It was foggy and bitter cold, but the roads were smooth and that was the main thing for us. Our column showed good teamwork. Now we stayed in the middle of the column! As it got light, we also reached the large, main road, which was the retreat route that went at an angle through West Prussia toward Pomerania. Groups of refugees, columns of military trucks, marching infantry, French and Russian prisoner of war camps, even English POWs were among them, everybody in a mad rush. We conversed with the English and were given all kinds of things by them, because they received lots of things from home, which to us was truly amazing. Our snappy pace was now a thing of the past; we had to fall into line in the endless columns, but on this fourth day we still went forward enthusiastically. We met still other prisoners from the camps, prisons, and penitentiaries of West Prussia; it was a colorful mixture of peoples, and in between always the large groups of refugees, the population of East and West Prussia, who had to desert house and home, in many cases voluntarily, but also frequently upon the orders of the party. Large trucks were loaded with the last of what they still called their own, and still they would not have anything to do with us, because we looked poorer than they. The weather cleared up in the course of the morning, and the rumbling drew closer and closer; it was sometimes so close that we thought the Russian tanks might appear behind us the next moment, but it disappeared again in the distance. In the evening we reached our day's destination after a strenuous march, Großes Wollenthal. Our billeting officers, Staff Sergeant Jäger and F. Pape, were waiting for us at the entrance of this relatively large village. We seven from the kitchen went immediately to our quarters at a farmer's place, who had a big kettle in his laundry room in which we were supposed to cook. The rest of the column was accommodated in a large barn in the middle of the village. We hustled around, killed a pig at the butcher's, obtained potatoes from a neighboring farmer, we had ingredients ready to make soup and we had lard, that made for a hearty meal for the men. In the evening Kuddl and I went for a little walk in the village; there were a few nice girls in the town, we posed as refugees, and we ended the day with a nice evening spent with them and their families. It was nice to be a civilian again and to pass a few hours

in pleasant company. When we returned, our superior administrative counselor was right in the middle of a visit to our quarters, in order to give
each of us a cigarette, also Staff Sergeant Jäger was generous with us; the
other comrades had also obtained some straw, and so we snoozed around
the warm kettle. The fourth day had ended and again we had made good
progress.

In the morning at seven sergeants Eggers and Barth approached our kitch-
en with the cry, "Isn't the coffee ready?" But we were a real kitchen crew,
and had already cleaned out the kettle and filled it with water the evening
before, which was nearly hot. We built up the fire quickly and put in the
coffee, and before the two first sergeants reached our quarters, we announced: "Coffee's ready." They looked astonished, but we had pulled it off
once again. The weather today was hazy, the air felt like it was going to snow,
and in view of that we fortified ourselves properly, above all with lots of fat
pork. Then we were off, our destination Prussian Stargard, which we must
reach today by all means if we wanted to get out of the bulge in the front.
The rumbling of the front, if one could even speak of a front, had become
stronger overnight. That drove us to greater haste, and on this day we covered a lot of ground. Underway we met many straggling troops, who roamed
around behind the front without leadership. Apparently complete chaos dominated the entire eastern sector. They had all suffered terribly. We soon saw
Prussian Stargard lying before us, but suddenly a traffic snarl occurred, and
simultaneously an icy, sharp wind seized us, mixed with stinging driven snow
particles. We arrived in the city at dusk, where everything was topsy-turvy.
Tank traps blocked the way, wrecked vehicles and dead horses hindered progress.
We reached the courthouse late, where we were to find accommodations for
this night. We drove the wagons and sleds into a corner, quickly unloaded
them, and then we got nice, warm cells in the cellar of the building. Because Heinz and I still had something to do in the administration building,
on the way back we were able to bring a sack full of bread, which we had
seen earlier. We were lucky to get back into our cell through the huge crowd
that was milling around in the hallways. Among our comrades, of course, a
great joy prevailed over the unexpected reinforcement of our supplies. Now
the kitchen had things twice as good. We had enough lard, there was just a
shortage of bread sometimes. A few pipes were smoked, we had more than
enough tobacco. It was the same with sugar, each of us always filled his pockets in the morning, which we ate while marching. In spite of the rumbling,
to which we had already become accustomed, we fell asleep rapidly, not sus-
pecting what the next days would bring us. At the end of the fifth day we
were still as fresh and adventurous as on the first.

On the following day we could properly sleep our fill for once. We did
not need to cook, no one disturbed our sleep, no alarm, no scurrying and
racing, only the thundering of the artillery drew nearer. But we slept until
broad daylight, ate, smoked and could otherwise do what we wanted. We
sang and played music; we were in a great mood. In fact, Kuddl and I took
a bath, very hot, in a beautiful bathtub, yes, the two of us succeeded in making the impossible possible. Afterward we felt born again. How badly we

needed this day of rest we could see when we looked at ourselves. We still did not know what the following days would bring, only that the thunder of the front drew dangerously near in the course of the day. In the afternoon it began to snow, too, and in the evening an amazing snowstorm swept over the city. The shelling had come closer; we would soon be directly on the front. Once again we ate heartily, then we made sandwiches for the next two days, and everyone laid down early to rest, conscious that any moment an alarm could come. The sixth day was over.

In the early morning it really happened:—Alarm! We ate with all haste, packed and then took off. The terrible snowstorm had raged throughout the night and continued with undiminished force. Wild confusion reigned in the yard of the courthouse. Various groups had found lodging there and each wanted to get away as quickly as possible. After a lot of difficulty we were the first on the street with our wagon. Gradually the columns assembled. Now we also became conscious of how loud the shelling was. Suddenly there was the roaring of airplanes overhead, then a wailing and some heavy detonations very close by. We had to admire the daring of the Russian pilots, who flew their missions in such weather. But after this bombing raid we took off. During the night the occupants of the town had also received orders to evacuate, and everyone hurried as quickly as he could to get out of the city. Out on the highway we were greeted by a terrible storm. While we still had some protection in the city, out there it was gone. Although the roads were blown clear of snow by the wind, nevertheless the storm raged so strongly that we had to struggle forward step by step. We could no longer keep our pipes lit, besides the pushing and pulling of the wagon, we had our hands full trying to save our faces and ears from freezing. Although we had muffled ourselves up like old women, it was difficult to protect our faces and ears from the frost, and we continually rubbed them with snow, because the snowstorm got worse and worse. Gradually the snow began to settle on the road, because the wind could no longer blow such great amounts of snow away, so that we could make progress only with great difficulty. But we kept struggling further with all of the doggedness of our young years. Then a large forest appeared before us; although we had some shelter there from the icy wind, the snow was three times as deep there as on the open highway. Our column stretched miles apart, and everybody tried to get through this snowy wasteland as quickly as possible. Both of our other large wagons with the horses and the sleds with their large team of men got along well, but we with our heavy-laden wagon fell further and further behind, but again and again we pulled ourselves together and we, too, finally got through the forest. However, it was then suddenly dark again and the storm settled in again with renewed force. No sooner had we gotten out of the forest when we encountered the rest of our column coming toward us, who, though they still wanted to reach the day's destination, had turned around in the face of the storm's renewed fury, and we all took up quarters with many refugees in a large estate quite a distance off the road. The refugees found shelter in the stables, whilst we crawled into a barn. Even though there was enough straw on hand, it was of no use in warding off the icy wind, because the barn was really leaky, and snow came quietly sifting in. After we had eaten, it was still necessary to cook, and a detail of five men went out to accomplish this task. But the rest of us rolled ourselves in all of the blankets we had available and tried to sleep. When Kuddl and Werner returned after a while, we were covered with snow. They were billeted in the kitchen of an adjacent Russian POW camp and did their cooking there. Because there was still room for one more man in the kitchen, I went along, and after we had stuffed ourselves with bread and fat, hot pork, we flopped down dead tired around the cauldron to sleep. The seventh day of the trek was over, till then the most difficult day, and the first day on which we did not reach our daily destination.

When we woke up the next morning, the snow was even deeper. It wasn't snowing very hard, but any further travel with our lovely cook wagon was now unthinkable. No sooner had we ascertained this, when the hectic running around began: we made coffee, looked for a sled, packed everything, etc. But when it was finally time for departure, we had found a small, light wagon with two little horses in front and a nice sled; the kitchen team was ready to go. Envied by the entire column, we took the lead; nothing could bother us now. Kuddl Heinz and I were on the sled, the other five comrades on the wagon, and our trip continued. Unfortunately, we had to leave our "liberated" pigs behind, we could only stow one pig weighing approximately three hundred pounds, but because of this the Russian prisoners of war, to whom we gave the rest of the pigs, had a holiday meal too. Things went well until midday, but then a terrible wind came up again, combined with a hard, sticking snow, which caused us a lot of trouble. As bad luck would have it, once again we needed to traverse a giant forest. Once again the column got strung out and soon each man attempted to go forward by his own devices. Even where ten or twelve men were pulling and pushing each individual sled, several were abandoned and our comrades attempted to get to our destination by hitching rides on military trucks, wagons pulled by tractors or on foot. Both of our little horses endured the ordeal bravely, and in the afternoon we had achieved our destination: an inn in Neukrug. Before this blizzard, we had lost approximately 60 of our 200 men who had escaped or frozen to death, but the worst was yet to come. But now we had no idea how great the losses of the last two days were. We posted a sentry on the road in order to intercept some stragglers, and in fact by evening approximately twenty to thirty men still arrived. In the meantime, we had set up a slaughterhouse behind the inn; we put half a pig in the cauldron, and then we cooked a soup, which had so much fat in it that you couldn't find the soup, but we had earned it; we were frozen to the bone, we could not get warm at all. When the meal was distributed, and we had also had something to eat, Kuddl and I went to a military guard room, which we had noticed previously. There was a large stove going there, before which we squatted until 2:00 a.m. in order to finally get warm. We drank the wonderful coffee by the liter, half sugar, half coffee, which the soldiers gave us. We turned down their offer of alcohol, because we needed to be on the march again in three hours, though we did have two little shots to get our blood flowing, and then we just kept eating the fatty meat we had brought along. About two o'clock we went back over to our quarters, grabbed a couple of hours of sleep; we had been underway now for eight days.

The next morning the weather was clear, the terrible snowstorm had ceased. Even though we had slept little, we took courage again after a proper breakfast. First we took inventory of our supplies. Approximately twenty-five men had to stay behind in Neukrug with severe frostbite, so that we only had about one hundred men fall in for the continuation of the march. During the night the wind had scoured the loose snow from the road, so that a tolerable pace could be maintained. We had not been able to move swiftly along for days now. All the roads were overcrowded, there were traffic jams again and again, hours of waiting in icy winds, but our slogan was "forward!" The rumbling of the front became fainter again, apparently the Russians also had not made much progress in the last few days, but nevertheless we kept on hurrying; we were certainly not out of the danger zone. Not long after noon we already could see our destination: Berent, lying in the valley, but then everything halted suddenly, we could go no further. The entrance to the city was clogged with military columns and masses of refugees. We waited for hours, then those of us who were on foot got underway first, then a few of the smaller sleds which we still possessed, and finally the rest of us succeeded in reaching Berent by going across the open fields with unspeakable difficulties. We raced through the city to the courthouse, where everybody was waiting with great anxiety for the kitchen. This time we occupied quarters in the attic of the building, where it was damned cold. Three comrades were needed to cook, the other four of us fixed things up for ourselves as well as possible. Later we were served a first-rate meal by our comrades, and we had some hot milk with sugar as a bonus just for us, and then we crawled under the quilts and slept and slept, we had a lot to catch up on. The ninth day of our trek had come to an end.

The next day we were able to sleep delightfully late, and then we had a good breakfast. Now I also noticed that I had frozen my foot. I only told Kuddl about it, because all of the sick were being left behind. My ears and face were frostbitten too. On that day I could not do much about it, because there was no medicine available, and besides, twenty men had to be released, so there was work to do all day. "Proper food and keep warm," was Kuddl's advice, and I followed it, too, and moreover I went to bed early. Above all, we had the opportunity in Berent to replenish our supplies again; we succeeded in "liberating" a box of margarine and some cans of meat; for the next four days we did not need to have any worries. Our comrades who were released went to Germany on the last trains that were still running, we still had to march for two or three days and then board a train in Bütow in Pomerania. We had been underway already for nine [sic] days.

The next morning we did not need to get up very early; the immediate danger appeared to be over. I had bound my foot tightly and got my shoe on fine, so that I had some hope of making it all right the last days. Our departure was delayed for hours, because many of our comrades were still in the city. There was hardly any more order; everyone had the opportunity to desert, but most wanted to return home and therefore remained together. When everyone was finally all together, it had turned 2:00 p.m. and we started out. Our column was noticeably shrunken. We only had the two large wagons, our cook wagon on runners, and three or four smaller sleds, everything else had been left behind; we hardly numbered one hundred men. Thus we had a large number of men on foot, which benefited us a good deal the next night. The roads had become rather firm again, and we made good progress, but soon delays occurred. Sergeant Morentz, Kuddl, and I went ahead to explore the situation. We saw the endless columns of refugees, traveling two and three abreast, and the columns of the military, which had reserved for them two small lanes free for traffic going to the rear and to the front, because, as a matter of fact, troops were actually still going to the front once in a while. Next to the road there was a forest. There was forest as far as the eye could see; the entire road was blocked for the next ten kilometers. We were told over and over again that many of the columns had been stuck there for over two days. Morentz wanted to turn around, but that made no sense, because we were several kilometers ahead of the others, and besides it was getting dark. No village, no house, only the quiet, dark forest. Campfires blazed up, a romantic picture! Finally there came some movement into the endless columns, and after several more hours sergeants Engel and Steiner arrived with the smaller wagon and several comrades. Morentz got on, we tossed his bicycle up on the back and held on ourselves to the back, because we had learned that the wagon was also loaded with bacon, butter, sausage, and sugar. Kuddl and Werner wanted to explore the vicinity, but unfortunately there was nothing doing. Shortly thereafter came a sign: Bütow 17 km. A moment later both disappeared, as I learned later, they wanted go to Bütow on their own, which they succeeded in doing. In their opinion, I could not keep pace on such a long march. Because I was also unsuccessful in finagling myself something from the wagon, I let it travel on and likewise set out to Bütow. In the meantime it was pitch-black night and the roads appeared to be completely blocked. Except for a few military trucks the traffic was completely motionless. I hitched rides back and forth on these trucks in order to find our cook wagon. By some miracle I found it about midnight; Heinz and two other comrades were still there, likewise sergeants Struve and Patzold. They had loaded some bread and bacon. First, I "liberated" myself a sausage and some bread and properly fortified myself. We could, indeed, still get ahead in short spurts, but then finally we could go no further. And it was just our luck to come to a stop right on a hill and right where the forest ended. We passed long hours here in the icy cold. Our comrades marched past, their few belongings on their back; the few sleds we still had had been left behind. The large wagon was still a long way behind, they said. Finally we brought Struve and Patzold to the point that they were willing to take off with us, the question was: how? We found a way out. Through large snowdrifts and deep ditches we succeeded in reaching an open field and now we went forward through snow more than knee deep. Our good horses also did not leave us in the lurch this time; they made it.

Once, in the dark, we all tumbled down a steep incline with everyone riding on the wagon and sled, but the incline was like a ski jump, so that we suddenly flew several meters through the air. We could still leap off in time, before the wagon and sled both crashed together. It was fortunate that no great damage resulted; we were able to continue the journey. Now we could use the large road again, and here, after a short distance, we met the smaller wagon with Engel and Steiner, so that all of the provisions were now back together again. There were four officers and four of us. We saw none of our comrades again until the next evening. The way was now free on the main road, on the adjacent bumpy roads or cross-country. We had come to within ten kilometers from Bütow and hoped to be there at midday. Suddenly the order came down that the road needed to be completely cleared. It was said that a tank division was on its way to the front. We took the next byway, and as it became light we reached a small village. We placed our wagons in a courtyard and lit an immense campfire, made coffee, and dried out our wet and tattered clothes. While the four officers slept around the fire, we guarded the wagon. First Heinz and I, then the other two comrades. This way each could sleep half an hour. Looking ahead as always, Heinz and I stowed twenty loaves of bread and about thirty pounds of margarine, bacon, and sugar on our wagon for any eventuality. When it got quite light, we left the courtyard. The main highway was still blocked, and we tried to reach the connection with other roads in the direction of Bütow over fields and through forests. In the course of the afternoon the weather became nice again. The eleventh day of our trek had dawned. The sun smiled on us and it was also no longer so bitter cold. After a few hours we again finally reached the road which led to Bütow; but it was now twenty kilometers away, we had, in other words, gone far astray. Certainly our comrades were waiting for us, above all for our provision wagon. After a short rest, about midday we crossed the Pomeranian border. Until here the rumbling of the front had followed us, now by this time we heard it only occasionally and then very faintly. In the afternoon we traveled for hours through large, extensive forests. When we again had a clear view, Bütow was lying unexpectedly before us. We had finally made it. We quickly inquired about the location of the courthouse, and as we arrived there, we were received jubilantly by our comrades, who had already given us up for lost. Quickly we served some meals from the kettles, pea soup, gruel, and dessert; because we hadn't had any for so long, it tasted twice as good. About seven o'clock our train was supposed to depart. We quickly took our sacks of provisions from the wagon, packed everything well and then went to the train station. Kuddl still "liberated" everything that was not riveted and nailed down, and brought up the rear with it. In the train he requisitioned places for us, everything was quickly loaded and then the train slowly started to move. Our trek on the highway was at an end; we required eleven days to reach Bütow. Overtired as we were, we fell asleep with the peaceful feeling that we were finally out of the greater part of the mess. Sleeping, to be certain, was somewhat uncomfortable, but we were accustomed to everything. Six men slept on the two benches, one between our legs and one in one of the overhead luggage racks, while our things were stowed in the other. We didn't wake up until the next day from deathlike sleep. The train had been stopped, as some comrades told me, already since midnight. Now I finally found time to examine my foot somewhat more closely, which also pained me considerably. Terribly swollen, it was impossible to take my shoe off. So we got a bread knife and cut it off and the sock with it. The entire front part of my foot was just a bloody, pussy mass; now what? We had neither bandages nor cleaning materials, the only person who might have such things was the medic, so I limped over there. I was successful, got the whole mess cleaned up, put some salve and wrapped some paper bandages around it, then put my stocking on again, slipped it into my shoe, and at least I could limp around with it now and then. I now took the place in the luggage rack in order to rest. Now the train at last got underway and rolled further on into Pomerania. In every train station, even the smallest, a ration distribution station of the Red Cross had been erected, which was to attend to the refugee trains. When we had delays at the stations, which happened rather often, we went procuring; at first I could still go along, afterward this became impossible, because I could not walk any more. Once we were sitting in the restaurant in a small train station, when the train suddenly pulled out; what now? Kuddl and Rudi could have made it, but they did not want to leave me in the lurch, so they made a chair for me with their arms, I got on, and then we ran full tilt around the corner and actually caught the last car of the train. I pulled myself up into a window, my comrades swung up onto the steps, we were lucky once more: who knows what would have happened if we'd been stranded there. Because they were so overcrowded, catching another train was unthinkable, and who would pick up prisoners anyway? In any case, we were greatly relieved when we were finally sitting, or lying, as the case may be, again in our places. The first few days we occasionally received warm meals that were cooked underway. In this manner, after many adventures, we finally arrived at Schlawe. Here we received the "happy" news that the Russians were already deep in Pomerania and the train lines appeared closed; the only open stretch was along the coast via Köslin, Kolberg, and then in an arch toward Stettin, which was great, if we had already been in Stettin! Perhaps the Russians were already there before us. Even if we had nothing to fear, it still meant an unpleasant delay; who knows how long we would then be stranded? The Russians would certainly not take time to examine our claims that we were persecuted by the Nazis; they had more important things to do at first, rather, they would take us prisoner first and ask questions later. In the afternoon the muffled rumbling of the shelling, that we had already escaped for days, reached over to us again. Apparently, our train was redirected during the night, because the next day we arrived in Köslin. From Köslin we went to Kolberg. Here we still had the unusual luck that the mail was being sent out, and so we wrote like mad and this mail actually arrived in Hamburg, in fact sooner than our last mail from Graudenz. Then our train inched its way further along via Greifenberg, Naugard, Gollnow, to Stettin. We spent endless days on the journey; again and again we had to endure hour-long, even day-long waits, frequently on an open stretch of track. Once we had a 36-hour delay. Even though we had supplied ourselves well with provisions, nevertheless they were totally used up during these long days, even though we were always able to replenish our inventory again. One night Kuddl and I had the good fortune to receive a box full of sandwiches from two nuns. When all was said and done, Kuddl had a rare talent for liberating things. He also already had found himself a little girlfriend, and her cousin was entrusted to me, a little, sweet girl, dark, wonderful hair, and dark eyes like mine. Although we were now being more closely guarded again, we still spent pleasant hours together. At night, when the train rushed through the peaceful countryside, the countryside that was still peaceful, at any rate, yes it did occasionally rush along as well, we sat by the open window when Kuddl sang nostalgic songs of home in his wonderful voice. Often tears came not only to the girls' eyes but to our eyes as well. We really hoped to be home soon; we still had our parents, but the girls had both lost their homes, and little Inge had lost her parents in addition. I believe that all four of us will never forget these priceless hours. In Naugard, where there was still a large prison camp, the sick and those not capable of marching were detrained. In spite of the fact that everyone, including the officers, knew that I could not walk, Kuddl succeeded in hiding me, and so I made it through all right; I did not want to be left behind in some hospital, I wanted to go home. Finally Stettin, long yearned for, appeared before us. Everyone can imagine our happiness as we arrived at the main train station in Stettin on the evening of 8 February. We should originally have changed trains here, but now we were told that the train would travel on to Berlin, because the route was still not immediately threatened by the Russians, and so we dared to hope that we had now made it. Unfortunately this was also the hour of parting from Inge and Lore, who wanted to go further with Lore's parents into Mecklenburg. Of course we promised to write soon, but as of today I have never heard anything from them again. After its short stop, our train then traveled further in the direction of Berlin. We had barely left the city when American bomber formations launched a large attack on Stettin. As we distanced ourselves more and more, it looked very nice, even as terrible as it was. But a short time later individual airplanes attacked trains traveling or stopped on this route. Now, of course, the trains traveled at top speed; our train also set a devilish pace in the direction of Berlin. As soon as we traveled slower, the whole bombing business started over, until finally the morning dawned and brought an end to the whole affair. In Berlin itself everything appeared to be clogged, for we required the entire day and the following night to go from Eberswalde into and through Berlin. Endlessly long trains were on the open tracks, freight trains full of refugees, who camped in the streaming rain on flatcars with all their personal belongings. A terrible sight. Of Berlin I have only the impression of a completely ruined city. During the night we still stopped for a while at the train station in Wedding; there were ruins all around, not a person to be seen, everything deserted. We were happy when we finally left Berlin. The only stretch where our train traveled at the regular speed was the stretch from Berlin to Wittenberg. In Wittenberg our car was coupled to the passenger train that traveled via Bad Kleinen to Bützow. Bützow was the gathering point for all of those coming from the eastern prisons, camps, and penitentiaries. On this stretch we also had delays lasting for hours, and so we first arrived in Bützow on a Sunday, 11 February, after we had had nothing to eat for days already. I had not left the luggage rack for the last days, first because of weakness and second because my foot had worsened terribly. A half-hour march, where Kuddl and Rudi dragged me along, and we reached a penitentiary that sat like a fortress on a height. Finally a destination. Now we were no longer worried about how our trek would end. Because the penitentiary was overcrowded, the chapel was cleared out and the piteous remnants of the institutions from the east were stuck in there. The entire room was spread with straw, and each man flopped down exactly where he stood. Completely exhausted and dog tired, the first thing we did was to get some sleep. The following day half the men reported to the medic. Most of them had third-degree frostbite. My foot was also thoroughly cleaned, smeared with salve, and wrapped up. Then we had the time and leisure to make ourselves a little human again. Otherwise we played cards until we passed out and slept. My comrades were so filthy and lousy that in some places the straw was red from lice. Those of us from Graudenz had maintained ourselves the best, and more of us had made it back than the others. Groups arrived there that had a complement of only ten men! How happy we were when on Wednesday evening the call resounded: "Graudenz get ready!" We threw on our tattered clothing quickly and went to the door. I limped along as fast as I could. Then suddenly we were told: only forty men are leaving. There was a wild jostling; naturally everybody wanted to go, especially when they said that we're going to Hamburg. Kuddl pulled me with him toward the front, and we were the last ones who made it. I had nothing, apart from what I was wearing, because the last things had been stolen from me in the penitentiary, for which Kuddl had beaten the perpetrator half to death, because stealing from a comrade is the worst there is in such situations. I never received anything back, everything was probably already sold under the table. And thus I did not need to carry anything, and because we had had a few days of rest, I could make it the half-hour to the train station. The other fellows were supposed to come the following day, and they actually arrived in Glasmoor two days after we did. As we approached the train station all we could see was an endlessly long freight train, an empty passenger car in between all the freight cars, where we boarded, forty men and five officers. In the evening, then, the train rattled away with us. Destination: Hamburg. In spite of the rattling, we slept soundly into the next day. When we awoke, we were already in Hamburg. The trip went via Lübeck, as we were informed. At five o'clock in the morning we traveled through the main train station in Hamburg, but then we were switched and switched, once we were at the harbor, once in Altona, but finally we reached the correct track and landed at midday in Ohlsdorf. Here they were to decide whether to take us to Fuhlsbüttel or to Glasmoor. Shortly thereafter First Sergeant Barth came back with the happy news: Glasmoor! That was a joy, because many did not have pleasant memories of Fuhlsbüttel. In the afternoon, then, the Glasmoor truck came and hauled us away. We had departed from here in fine style and now we returned to Glasmoor as a most bedraggled lot! Only a few old Glasmoorers were still there. When the large red tower appeared before us we felt that we had returned to our home after a long wandering. Our flight over thousands of kilometers, through ice and snow, through good and bad days, was at an end. We received a hearty reception by the director of the institution; we were in Hamburg-Glasmoor again, at home again. We had made it. The end of the war was at the door; nothing else could happen to us.

Source: Gerhard Düwer

64

Letter from Karl-Heinz Schnibbe

December 12, 1948
My dear parents and brother and sister,

How often will I yet have to communicate with you in writing? I would never have believed that I'd still have to be here, but over and over I've been mistaken. Now again I'm hoping that this will be the last time I'll have to write to you. Christmas will soon be here. How I'd love to be in the circle of my loved ones, whom I've missed and done without for so long; but fate is terribly hard; fate doesn't inquire about the wishes or the needs of human beings. It must be fated to be this way, or things would not be as they are. Yet I do not want to give up. I want to continue to endure, because someday Spring will come, and then there will be happiness without end. How are you all otherwise? I hope you're all still well. I'm also well. I send you all my most heartfelt greetings.
Always thinking of you,

your son and brother Karl-Heinz

Source: Karl-Heinz Schnibbe.

65

Statement of Otto Berndt

In the summer of 1941 an incident took place in the Hamburg District [of the LDS Church] that caused me more fear and anxiety than I have ever experienced in my life. Three young members of our church, Helmuth Guddat, Rudolf Wobbe and Karl Heinz Schnibbe, who were from 16 to 17 years old, had listened to a British radio program that was aimed to lower the resistance of the German people. They had not only listened but also written down and duplicated the news they had heard and then distributed this information in various places in Hamburg. They had left sheets in telephone booths, put them on walls and other places. Of course, this was a very dangerous undertaking and the Gestapo didn't waste any time in arresting them. The Gestapo did not think that these young boys were able to do anything like this without having someone to inspire their thinking. The stepfather of Helmuth Guddat, not a member of the church, accused Elder Otto Berndt of being the instigator and the leader of this conspiracy.

For three days I was thoroughly questioned by the Gestapo. The fact that the office equipment of the Hamburg District, of which I was the president, had been used in typing and duplicating this dangerous information caused much concern. When I went to the police headquarters I prayed like I had never prayed before. When I entered the rooms and the questioning started, I felt that my spirit left my body and another spirit entered and took over my thinking. I was asked hundreds of questions in rapid succession and I, or I should say the spirit or the higher power that had possession of my body, was able to answer them all without any hesitation. I was very sure of myself. After three days of questioning the officers felt that I or the church I represented had nothing to do with the crime committed by these three young men. In the course of the questioning I was able to show that our church was not an American church and that we had nothing to do with the U.S. government. All our records had been confiscated by the Gestapo. They were checked and later returned. Questioned about tithing, I was asked why our church forces its members to pay tithing. I told him that we didn't force our members and that only 28 to 30 percent of them did pay tithing. He thought it was an awful lot of money to pay and so I asked him if he didn't spend that much for his political party, considering all the time and money involved.[26] Then the question of genealogy was brought up. I had to prove that I was an Aryan. Since my ancestors had been living in Germany for many generations and since I had my lines traced back about eight generations, to the surprise of the investigating officer who was only required to have proof for the last three generations, I was able to pass this test with flying colors.

At the conclusion of the hearing I was asked, and I had to sign a statement to this effect, whether I had been treated with courtesy during the investigation. Since this was true, I signed this statement. The officer asked me if I had been afraid during these last three days. I answered the question in the affirmative. He asked: "Why?" I told him that I had heard rumors about the cruelties committed by the Gestapo. This ended the questioning and I was free to go home.

So far I had only heard rumors. A year later [sic] a member of the Hamburg District, Brother Heinrich Worbs, was arrested and returned six months later from a concentration camp. I then knew that the rumors were true. At this time a monument honoring one of the Nazi heroes had been erected in Hamburg. Brother Worbs made the remark to someone to the effect that they had built another monument for one of their butchers. This someone was an informer and he went to the next policeman and had Brother Worbs arrested. In the concentration camp he had to undergo awful cruelties. After his return he related to me that in the middle of December he was stripped naked and his hands were put into stocks. Then water would constantly flow down on his hands and freeze. Every three or four hours a guard would come and knock off the ice with a rubber hose and say: "This will keep your hands warm." When Brother Worbs returned from the camp he was a broken man and died soon after.[27]

The three young men who had been arrested were taken to Berlin to the High Tribunal or *Reichsgerichthof* [sic]. Brother Helmuth Guddat showed at this time remarkable courage. However, his fate was sealed and he was sentenced to die. His head was chopped off with an axe [sic].[28] Two hours before his execution he wrote a deeply moving letter to his parents containing this sentence: "I have only two hours left, then I have to appear before my God."

I felt that Brother Helmuth Guddat (Hübener) was a deeply religious boy and I was saddened by his death. On the Sunday following the execution the mother and the grandmother of the boy attended the sacrament meeting in one of the branches in Hamburg. I had cautioned the brethren not to mention the name of the boy in the meeting. However, one of the very zealous brethren said, referring to Brother Guddat: "If I had had a rifle I would have shot him!" This was in October 1942. He had previously been excommunicated by the mission authorities on 15 February 1942. Brothers Wobbe and Schnibbe were not. This was done to avoid further difficulties with the [Nazi] party and to show that the church had nothing to do with the treason these boys were accused of.[29]

When I was questioned by the Gestapo I was told to see that the accused Helmuth Guddat was cut off by the LDS Church. I flatly refused to do this and explained to them that he would pay for his crimes, but that the Church had no right to excommunicate him.

The excommunication certificate was signed by President Anthon Huck and by Branch President Arthur Zander. I protested against this action and I believe that my protest and that of other members prevented the excommunication of Brothers Schnibbe and Wobbe.

In conclusion, let it be said that the Saints who believed in the ideals of the New Germany did like Saul of Tarsus in persecuting the Christians; they did what they did because they believed it to be in the best interest of the

Church and the country. Repentance and forgiveness has been manifested by all concerned after the war.

Ca. 1961.
Source: Historical Department, Church of Jesus Christ of Latter-day Saints, Salt Lake City, Utah.

66

Statement of Rudolf Wobbe

It was in the spring of 1941. Helmuth Hübener's brother, Gerhard Kunkel, had brought back from France on a leave from the Wehrmacht, a shortwave radio. With this Helmuth started to listen to the BBC London broadcasts and later told me about it. We both continued to listen to these broadcasts frequently. Then Helmuth suggested we do what had been proposed by the speaker of the broadcast and print handbills so that the German population would be made aware of the truth, to which I consented. Helmuth took shorthand notes of the news, typed them and made at first carbon copies only. Later, we used a mimeograph to make more copies. The handbills were about postcard size. We made 60 each with the following titles:

"What happened to General Schröder, the Army Commander in Serbia?"
"Hitler the Murderer!"
"The Hitler Youth we were forced to join."

The handbills had been typed and mimeographed at Hübener's place of employment, the social administration of the City of Hamburg, Biberhaus, and also at the St. Georg Branch meeting hall. Brother Hübener was at this time the branch clerk of the St. Georg Branch.

We placed the bills in mailboxes, telephone booths, and even on the official Nazi party bulletin boards that had been placed in the entrance halls of the large apartment houses. I also put them in the mailbox of the local NSDAP (Nazi) party branch office.

Later, Helmuth Hübener used standard size paper and wrote essays entitled "I have considered everything!" Also, "The Reichs-Marshall (Hermann Göring)" and others.

The judgment against these three young people read in part: "These handbills contain, besides the British war news, profane slanders and suspicions of the Führer and his fellow workers; agitated attacks against measures and institutions of the National Socialist government, as well as a challenge to bring about the end of the war by overthrowing the Führer."

Helmuth Hübener, who inspired and led this conspiracy, was a highly intelligent, friendly and congenial young man, who disliked violence. He was a member of the St. Georg Branch of the West German Mission.

Our dislikes against the party increased steadily from our earliest youth. We had been waiting for several years to be Boy Scouts. When we were finally old enough we were told that this organization had just been disbanded and we were forced to join the Hitler Youth. We also witnessed how members of the Hitler Youth threw rocks and broke the glass of the windows in our meeting hall. At one time I overheard Arthur Zander, the branch president, say to Sister Emma Haase, who had brought a handbill to the meeting hall that had been dropped by British planes, that he would see to it that she would be arrested and put in a concentration camp if she repeated this again. I just couldn't understand such an attitude. All these things increased our dislike of the party and even some of the brethren in our church.

Mr. Mohns was the *Betriebsobmann* of the NSDAP social administration in Hamburg, and as such responsible to the party that nothing happened that was in any way against the government. He was the watchdog. Like many of his fellow party members he was conscious of his own comfort and was involved in some of the black market business. He had been watched by his overseers and was aware of it. One day he listened or had heard of a talk given by Helmuth Hübener to the apprentices that was very much against the government. He reported the activities of Helmuth Hübener and Gerhard Düwer, another one of the conspirators, not a member of the LDS Church, both employed at the social administration. On 5 February 1942 these two boys, 17 and 18 years old, were arrested by the Gestapo.

I had heard that they had been arrested, and on 10 February 1942 I heard from Karl Heinz Schnibbe's mother and sister that Karl Heinz Schnibbe had also been arrested. I expected to be arrested also and considered going away, but I didn't know where to go, and so I stayed. While I was sitting in a class of the vocational school at the Angerstraße 7 in Hamburg on 18 February 1942, I was called out of the class by two officers of the Gestapo and was told that I was under arrest. These officers, one of whom was a Mr. Müssener, took me to my mother, who had been visited by these same men in the morning and been informed of the charges against me. She couldn't believe it, for I had never told her anything of this activity. But now I had to admit to her that it was so and left her heart broken. I was now taken to the police headquarters and questioned and threatened for a whole week. The investigating officers tried to get me to admit that my mother was also mixed up in this affair. This I couldn't do, which made the officers angry to the point that they roughed me up but good.

During this time I was back and forth between the headquarters and the concentration camp Fuhlsbüttel. SS units guarded this camp. I saw the other conspirators, Hübener, Schnibbe and Düwer once a day during exercise time in the courtyard of the prison. However, we were not permitted to speak to each other and we never did. In March 1942 we were transferred to the Hamburg *Untersuchungsgefängnis*. There we received our trial notices. Trial was set for 11 August 1942. Meantime, we stayed at the *Untersuchungsgefängnis* together with the criminals. There was no violence and the food was fair. At this time I never saw any of my former acquaintances with the exception of my mother, who was permitted to visit me every other week.

In the first days of August I was taken with the three others from Hamburg to Berlin where the trial was to be held. Four policemen guarded us. Here we were able to talk together for the first time since we had been arrested. Our guards told us at this time that we had nothing to be afraid of, that they should have given us a good spanking and sent us home.

In Berlin we were taken to the *Untersuchungsgefängnis* Moabit and kept there until trial date. The trial took place before the *Volksgerichtshof*, Second Panel, at Berlin Bellevue and started at 9 a.m. on 11 August 1942. First we were given IQ tests and were questioned about schools attended, and so on. Reference was made to an essay written by Helmuth Hübener which was so well written that it could have been the work of a thirty-year-old assessor. Then we were tested in our knowledge of the party and its political aims. Helmuth Hübener was asked what he thought about the party according to his beliefs. He answered that he didn't like the party and held the Church of Jesus Christ of Latter-day Saints in high esteem. He was also asked why he had passed handbills among the working classes. He answered: "Hamburg will always stay in opposition against the party."

Some of the handbills were read by the prosecution to the amusement of the judges, who were dressed in blood-red robes that had been embroidered with a large emblem of the German Reich, and who were often referred to as the "blood tribunal."

In his concluding remarks the prosecutor asked for a death sentence for Helmuth Hübener, for me a term of seven years in a penitentiary, if not a death sentence, and for Karl Heinz Schnibbe and Gerhard Düwer five years in a penitentiary. The attorneys asked the court for leniency because of our youth. Then the court withdrew for deliberation and appeared again at which time the following sentences were pronounced:

Hübener: death penalty
Wobbe: ten years imprisonment
Schnibbe: five years imprisonment
Düwer: four years imprisonment

We were then asked if we had anything to say. Hübener was the only one who responded by saying: "Wait, your turn will come also." We were taken back to our cells and Helmuth Hübener and I shared a cell with a Swiss spy, who had also been sentenced previously to die, for about one hour. I said to Helmuth: "Gosh, how terrible." All he could say was: "They are all out of their minds." We were both in a state of shock and were not able to say much. At this time we could not fully comprehend the extent of this judgment. We had heard of fake trials and didn't really know what to expect and if we should take this sentence seriously. We recalled what the guards had told us on the train to Berlin and didn't know what to think. I am sure Helmuth Hübener did not expect to be executed at that time.

Then we returned to the *Moabit-Untersuchungsgefängnis*. Since my arrest in February to this time in August, I had lost fifty pounds due to the meager food supply, bad treatment and, mostly, worry. In thinking ahead I could not comprehend how I could be locked up like this. It was solitary confinement at that time for the next ten years. I felt very discouraged and my morale was very low. In this state of mind I wrote to my mother and told her that I wouldn't blame her if she would denounce me as her son and if she didn't want to see me anymore after what I had done to her. Then I asked her to write me an answer if she still loved me and wanted me to come back to her, after what I had done.

Death seemed sweet to me, a liberator from the awful treatment I received in this lonely cell at Moabit. I didn't write it this way to my mother, but she must have read it between the lines. Her letter had been written with all the love a mother felt for her wayward son. She still loved me and was willing to wait for me, no matter what. She told me not to ask for her forgiveness, but for the Lord's, and to ask Him for guidance and strength and for a strong testimony of the truthfulness of the Gospel, so that I would be able to endure all things. I wept reading that wonderful letter from my mother and received the strength I needed to overcome despair and dejection, and I felt a lot better afterward.

I asked the prison chaplain for a Bible, which was given to me, and in reading the Holy Scripture I began to understand the Gospel of Jesus Christ. I had gone to the Church of Jesus Christ of Latter-day Saints in Hamburg because of my mother's influence. I didn't have a testimony in those carefree days in Hamburg with my friends, who were now in the same prison with me, but now I prayed and I read the scriptures and understood, and felt a great joy in my heart. Was this the reason why the Lord had permitted that I'd be taken to this place of hopelessness?

On 9 September 1942, I was transferred with Karl Heinz Schnibbe and Gerhard Düwer to the Glasmoor prison. Helmuth Hübener stayed in Moabit from where he was later transferred to Berlin-Plötzensee, where he was beheaded with a battle-axe [sic] on 27 October 1942.[30] I read about this in a paper we were able to read in Glasmoor. I was shocked and felt terrible about it.

All three of us were placed in the prison tailor shop. Mr. Franken, a master tailor, was in charge of us and we started to learn the tailor trade. Later, Düwer was transferred to the offices and Schnibbe to the painters. I remained in the tailor shop until we were transferred to Graudenz, West Prussia. The treatment in Glasmoor was according to the guards we had. Those who were Nazis treated us generally pretty rough. Others treated us as human beings.

In Graudenz I worked for a transfer from the tailor shop to an airplane factory, where I could work in my profession, which was granted. A Dr. Krüger was in charge of the prison in Graudenz who was very understanding and helped us in any way he could. He was also a psychiatrist. Once I had a good talk with him and in conclusion he told me that if it hadn't been for my religious background, I would not have been able to live through these last years. He was also very interested in the Gospel and I was able to teach it to him. After the war I met him in Hamburg and in talking to me he was very grateful that I did not resent him. At this time he told me that several guards in the camp who hated us "politicals" more than the "criminals" tried to get us transferred to a concentration camp. However, Dr.

Krüger was able to use his influence and to save us from what would have been almost certain death for us. Subsequently, I testified in his behalf when he was tried as a war criminal, and he was able to be cleared from any crimes he was accused of, and able to occupy a leading position.

A carbuncle developed on my neck during my stay in Graudenz and I was hospitalized with a high fever. Before I was able to regain my health we were ordered to leave, because of the approaching Russian armies. This was in January 1945 and it was very cold. We had to build sleighs on which we placed the guards and our bundles and suitcases. Intermingled with the endless treks of refugees and soldiers, we pulled our crude sleighs westward in the bitter cold of winter. Many of us didn't make it and about thirty prisoners died before we were able to catch a train going west. I was still suffering from the effects of the fever and was very weak as we started this march. As I was dragging behind one day and hardly knew where I was going, a guard hit me in the neck, causing the carbuncle to open, spilling pus over my clothing and back. My wound had not been dressed in any way and was not taken care of until we arrived at the penitentiary of Bützow-Dreibergen. There, one of the inmates was able to secure some kind of a knife with which he opened the carbuncle, relieving me of an agony that had caused me much suffering. During the trek from Graudenz to Bützow-Dreibergen we were told by the guards to limit our baggage to 25 pounds. This elimination process was handled by the guards. While we were standing outside, the guards went through our meager belongings, took what they wanted and put it in their suitcases. We had to put their suitcases on the sleighs, pulling the same load after it had "changed hands."

I would also like to say that from the time of my imprisonment until my release the population of lice and similar pets increased steadily. There was little I could do about it. We were able to take a bath every two weeks, at which time there was one shower and one piece of soap available for a few minutes for about twenty men, and if I was lucky enough to grab the soap long enough there were some doubts if I would be able to rinse it off. The little clothing we had was usually worn all the time and not washed too often.

After five days in Bützow-Dreibergen we were taken to the Elbe island Hanöfersand, a former youth penal institution. This place had been bombed and we were assigned to cleanup details. My fellow inmates from Hamburg were at this time released and assigned to a battalion (*Strafbatallion*) that was made up of prisoners. They were both sent to fight the Russians in the last days of the war. Karl Heinz Schnibbe, unfortunately, was captured by the Russians and kept in a prison-of-war camp three years [*sic*] after the war.

In Hanöfersand I was assigned as a machinist and stayed there until April 1945, at which time the British army was approaching the camp rapidly. In these last frantic days of the war an order had been issued that all political and foreign prisoners should be transferred to the concentration camp Neuengamme, near Hamburg. I heard about this from one of the friendlier guards, a Mr. Pape. Knowing what to expect there, I told him that I would try to escape. He assured me his support and promised to give me any new information. Later, he told me that Neuengamme had been filled to capacity and that we were to be transferred to Glasmoor prison, a place I had already been acquainted with, where we were brought to subsequently.

Some of the French prisoners had been able to escape from Glasmoor and reach the British lines. There they met a group of French officers who had been liberated shortly before. They and a group of British soldiers were able to come to the Glasmoor prison.

A week later a commission arrived from Hamburg who reviewed all the cases. I was released as one of the first ones. The criminals were not released and had to stay. I returned to Hamburg where my mother was overjoyed to see me. As soon as I could I attended the meetings of the church where I was greeted with open arms by my brothers and sisters in the Gospel. Soon after I was given a job. Since then I have filled many responsible positions in the church, including a mission.

In conclusion, I would like to say that I have learned that the "Lord is mindful of His own and remembers His children." We ask for strength and He gives us trials. I am grateful for the testimony I received and for the support and strength the Lord gave me to endure these hardships.

Rudolf Wobbe
Salt Lake City, Utah
17 April 1961

Source: Historical Department, Church of Jesus Christ of Latter-day Saints, Salt Lake City, Utah.

67

"I Knew Helmuth since 1928"

Irmgard Becker, born 1916, recalls:

At that time I lived in the Angerstraße 38 by the military train station. I knew Helmuth, Karl-Heinz Schnibbe and Rudolf Wobbe, because they, like me, were members of the Mormon congregation. The congregation numbered approximately 2,000 members and was located in the Besenbinderhof 13a. It was a factory building. I knew Helmuth since 1928. At that time he was three years old. I actually only knew him by the name Kunkel. When he was fourteen or fifteen, he said, when anyone addressed him as Kunkel: "My name is Guddat." I was astonished when I heard the name Hübener for the first time. When people started calling him Hübener I do not know. At first I said I do not know him. His mother never came to the congregation with a husband. She sang in the choir; she had a very deep voice. But she was not regularly in attendance. I knew the grandparents also. But I assume that the grandfather was the second husband of the grandmother, because they were named Sudroff. As long as I knew them that was what they were called. The three children, Hans, Gerhard and Helmuth lived there with them. The family made a good impression.

I knew Helmuth as a quiet boy. But he was an independent thinker. You could tell that when you looked at him. He always had a remarkable look on his face, very thoughtful and very profound. This is a very tragic story.

In the congregation of the church we were all together a lot and talked a lot. I never spoke with Helmuth about private matters. He would more likely tell such things to the youths of his own age.

I was never shown a leaflet by Helmuth. That would have required a lot of courage. You must remember what kind of a time that was: everyone watched everyone else. I know of one young man who lived in the Wendenstraße, the Frank family; there were eight children. This young man once brought home a flyer that Helmuth had written. The mother saw it. She immediately threw it in the kitchen stove and said: "Don't ever bring such a thing home again!" Only after the arrest of Helmuth, Karl-Heinz and Rudolf did I hear from Karl's mother Paula Schnibbe, that the leaflet came from Helmuth.

Helmuth and Karl-Heinz were in the Boy Scouts. In the communion rites of the sacrament, the youths also carried out sacred rites. They also presented—as befitting their age—little addresses and discourses which they had prepared themselves. Helmuth had brains. It is really a shame that he lost his life. It was already mentioned that he wrote letters to those in the military.

In our congregation the whole incident was passed over in silence. It was really terrible. It really was something awful. The parents of Schnibbe were downright sick after the arrest.

The execution was also not discussed in the congregation, as with political matters in general. I met with Paula Schnibbe and we talked about it. But as little as possible. You had to be so careful that you did not say one word too many. But word of the execution was spread around.

I never spoke with the Sudroffs after the arrest. It is possible that they went to the branch in Barmbek until their deaths. We had to give up our meeting place in the Besenbinderhof in 1941; the rooms were used as a munitions depot. After that the branch was divided, one part going to Barmbek, one part to Altona. I went to Altona. Most of the Mormons emigrated after the war.

It is incomprehensible what happened then.

It is a shame, really a shame, about Helmuth.

Source: *Begleitheft zur Austellung um das kurze Leben und Wirken des Helmuth Hübener*, Catalogue of the exhibit in the Hamburg Municipal District Archive [Stadtteilarchiv] of Hamm, 26 October–10 December, 1992.

68

"Afterwards I just couldn't get over the fact that the Nazis had the gall to cut off the head of a seventeen-year-old."

Jupp Wieczorek: My son once visited me alone before he was inducted. That gave me the chance, while working outdoors, to talk with my son personally without being watched. My son told me that he had worked with Hübener; and that he had also worked with their comrades as well.

Ida Wieczorek: There were four boys: there was Paul Liedel, Hans Beier, and our Jobi, together with Hübener. There were certainly still more of the youth that I do not know personally. And they were always sitting around together in our apartment.

Franz Ahrens: Just a moment, was that also here in the Stangelstraße in this apartment?

Ida Wieczorek: Stangelstraße 8.

Franz Ahrens: Across the street, then.

Ida Wieczorek: Yes. And it was like this: in back there was a courtyard and a stairway to the cellar. When things got hot, they had to get away. But I had the good fortune to have the key to Dr. Horn's property in Barmbek [possibly Bahrenfeld; see also Sander, "Helmuth-Hübener Gruppe," in Hochmuth and Meyer, *Streiflichter*]. I had the key, because I worked for Horn. And they knew what was going on with father and all of us and helped us quite a bit. And so the lads could meet there instead of in our apartment.

Jupp Wieczorek: Dr. Horn was an attorney.

Ida Wieczorek: Yes, Dr. Horn was an attorney. But these boys, I would like to mention this, they also met often with several young friends, also opponents of Hitler, in the Bismarck swimming pool, where they went swimming. Although our Jobi actually could not swim, they always took him with them. And they got acquainted there with Hübener and then brought Hübener to the point that he recognized, even though he was a Christian, that what Hitler was doing was not Christian either.

Franz Ahrens: He knew that you [were] Communists . . . ?

Ida Wieczorek: Yes, yes, . . . and he did not always approve of that but he gradually involved himself in the activities of our boys and helped with what they did. And if they were not in the Bismarck pool, they were in the country in Dr. Horn's cabin. . . .

Franz Ahrens: Did the boys listen to foreign radio stations in Dr. Horn's cottage?

Ida Wieczorek: I cannot say if Mrs. Horn, who did everything for the lads, also gave them a radio set, but in our apartment they lay there in the dark many nights . . . listening to foreign stations. I would just like to mention that Hübener was an upright, clean, fine lad that I immediately took

to my heart. Afterwards I just couldn't get over the fact that the Nazis
had the gall to cut off the head of a seventeen-year-old.

Source: Begleitheft zur Austellung um das kurze Leben und Wirken des Helmuth Hübener,
    Catalogue of the exhibit in the Hamburg Municipal District Archive [Stadtteilarchiv]
    of Hamm, 26 October–10 December, 1992.

69

"He Was Always a Straight-A Student"

Rolf Attin, born 1924, and Hans-Theo Roß, born 1925, relate:

From April 1937 until April 1941, we attended with Helmut the same
grade in the upper track at the Brackdamm school. That was the middle
school in Hamburg, which had the advantage at that time that you could
also graduate with your university preparatory degree from the upper track.
That was, we think, only the case in Hamburg. It was entirely a school for
boys. It was torn down just a few years ago; it stood there for a long time. I
often went past it and thought of my school days.

We were students who came from Rothenburgsort, from Hamm and from
Hammerbrook. We were joined together from the various primary schools.
I [Rolf Attin] was at first in the elementary school in the Louisenweg, then
in the elementary school in the Ausschläger Weg and then in the upper track
at Brackdamm. I cannot remember Helmuth from the first two schools. [Hel-
muth also attended these schools in the same sequence.]

At that time you had to pay tuition. And for normal mortals, like all of
us from these areas were, who were not blessed with riches, it was always a
sacrifice for the parents. You could receive subsidies also, but even then I
do not believe it was free.

Our teacher was August Meins. He was already old, to our way of thinking, and lived in the Hasselbrookstraße.

For a while Helmuth sat diagonally behind me on the other side of the
aisle. In the course of the four years that we were in school with Helmuth,
we noticed that he could sometimes be a really witty fellow. He was jovial;
he liked to laugh. He was fond of life and open-minded. He was not a home-
body or a loner. In any case, he did not make such a serious impression during his school days as he does in his photographs. In those he is a complete
stranger to us. Perhaps when he was still in school he had not thought so
much about everything. Sometimes we played jokes together. I cannot recall exactly if that was still the case in the last year.

Helmuth was above average in intelligence. He was always a straight-A
student. August Meins had a soft spot for German literature. We picked to
pieces the dramas of Schiller and Goethe. We then wrote essays about them.

I [R. Attin] think I remember that Helmuth was above all really superb in German and German composition. Mr. Meins once had him read aloud his essay as a glowing example of how you should introduce and construct essays. That was not the case with mathematics, I believe. The relationship of Helmuth to our teacher Meins must have been quite a good one.

I [Attin] talked a lot with Helmuth about books. And he read books that were over my head. I thought: what the heck is he reading? For me the maximum was an adventure story or a Wild West romance, but he already was reading substantial books.

He was a close friend of Franz Prumnitz. We always saw them together during recess. As I [Attin] recall, Helmuth was not particularly athletic. He and Prumnitz really fell behind in that area. That was not their forte. During our school days Helmuth was substantially smaller than I; he was a little chubbier. Only at the end of our school days was he larger than I and had become thinner and more muscular. During his spare time he went his own way; I do not know if he had contact outside school with Prumnitz. In the school we did not know he was a Mormon. Helmuth said nothing about his private matters. He also said nothing about political matters; apparently he was on his guard about that. In general, we did not talk about political matters or the Nazi regime. That was not a topic of discussion at all. And not from the teachers' side either. I only know that there was a certain pressure for you to join the Young Folk and later the Hitler Youth. But we did talk about the war. Also about air-raid alarms and bombing attacks on Hamburg. From the remarks that our teacher made to us about it, we could never have inferred that he was an outspoken Nazi (he did wear the party badge). On the contrary, when the war broke out, he still said we should not take everything too lightly, because the English were also someone of significance. At the start of the war we were all euphoric. National Socialism was drummed into us. We were not permitted to listen to foreign stations, and you actually took everything that was told us as the "gospel truth."

We never went on a class outing, but we had a school hostel in the country in Langenhorn. We were out there once and had to hurry, because Adolf Hitler was delivering an address. We sat there in a kind of stretched out barrack, a larger recreation room. An old radio was playing there. We had to listen to the speech. Today I can't recall anything about the content. That was the only time that we went for a trip together. Strange to say, we were also never photographed, there was not a class picture, as I recall. Never. In my [Attin's] opinion, Helmuth was predestined to take the entrance exam for the university, but he did not. That was also certainly a matter of the expense.

After our school days Helmuth once crossed my [Attin's] path here in Hamm; he looked considerably older. More mature somehow. I noticed that immediately. I thought to myself: his must be a difficult life. It was hard at that time. It must have been in the fall of 1941. We talked only shortly: how's it going, how's the job, and he said: "I am an administrative apprentice." He did not tell me anything more.

In the school we only addressed each other by surname, and he was called

"Kunkel." At an administrative review or such I first learned that he was officially named Helmuth Hübener, and only called Kunkel. I thought, why is that? Hübener is much nicer than Kunkel. I did not know him by the name Hübener.

I first learned about his death 25 years later, in 1967, by means of a story in the newspaper, where it said: "Helmuth Hübener died 25 years ago." I could not believe my eyes. I thought it could not be true. I would never had dreamed of such a thing. What he did was not that serious.

Today it is still incomprehensible, to kill him because of such a thing! A child!

Source: *Begleitheft zur Austellung um das kurze Leben und Wirken des Helmuth Hübener,* Catalogue of the exhibit in the Hamburg Municipal District Archive [Stadtteilarchiv] of Hamm, 26 October–10 December, 1992.

70

"Helmuth Was Different from the Other Students"

August Meins, Helmuth's teacher, recalls:

From 1937 until 1941 I was a teacher in the upper track of the Brackdamm school which Helmuth Hübener attended. At that time he was still called Kunkel. I learned about his later fate at the time he was executed. I was at that time on a class excursion in Hungary with my new class. I was very upset over his tragic death; it was a horribly filthy thing for them to do. I remember Helmuth very well as a person, but less about his academic accomplishments, because it has been too long ago. He had a good friend in the class. He was named Franz Prumnitz. The two boys were together often; whether their friendship lasted after their school days, I do not know.

Helmuth was different from the other students. He was independent and went his own way. But at the same time he did not isolate himself from the others. He was not a braggart. He was a likeable boy, who was very modest—though with a modesty that was nearly like a feeling of inferiority. He never would have admitted this complex himself. There were many reasons for it: his illegitimate birth, his poor circumstances and so forth. Certainly he was never utterly enthused about the Hitler Youth. He also entered the Young Folk late, 1939, perhaps as a cover.[31] Because of his nature he was teased a lot by the class, but he was never offended and could not be perturbed. The question always concerned me as a teacher: what brought him to this act of resistance? Was it not stupid? Not in its conception, but more in the structure. He must have known that resistance was pointless. But perhaps I was too old to be able to recognize his motive. In my opinion, it is certainly possible that there were many factors in his behavior that came from outside through other persons and ideas. What made him overnight into a resistance fighter, we will never know. But that should also not be our task. Whether he came to it by himself or was influenced by other persons, one thing is certain: what he always did was his own deed, he never permitted himself to be led or exploited by any groups.

His favorite subjects in school were geography and history, in contrast to mathematics, which he liked less. He worked a lot by himself and was very diligent. I never had to call him to order. I know nothing about the work mentioned in the declaratory part of the judgment; surely it was written under another teacher. He also participated in sports by always taking his place, but there were no outstanding achievements to report.

If I came close to describing his resistance as stupidity, I meant that with reference to his person. Resistance itself did actually fit his character, but resistance of this type? It was often noticeable: he was a resistance fighter through and through. He sat in the front row opposite me. I could always observe exactly his reaction, his eyes, when different things in the class were discussed by the class. I knew that in many cases he thought like me. He was a resister, but it was a cautious resistance. Everyone noticed that. Many disliked him for that reason. It was, at least at that time—hence his words before the People's Court astonish me—a completely different attitude than that of Hermann Peters, a Communist, whom I also had in the class in those years and who today is working as a teacher in the east zone.

I knew absolutely nothing about his Christian views. In the upper track there was no religious instruction and our conversation never came around to religion. I always thought he was a Communist. He was the only one in the class with his particular outlook. For that reason he was teased sometimes.

As I already said, he worked a lot by himself. He was tough, quiet and persistent. Although he often went his own way, you noticed that he could exercise a great influence on people.

We never talked about his—or our—thoughts. In front of the class you did not dare make the slightest allusion. You would be in danger immediately. But I sensed his thoughts.

Source: *Begleitheft zur Austellung um das kurze Leben und Wirken des Helmuth Hübener,* Catalogue of the exhibit in the Hamburg Municipal District Archive [Stadtteilarchiv] of Hamm, 26 October–10 December, 1992.

71

"I Was in a Group with Helmuth"

Friedrich Peters, born 1920, recalls:

Like Helmuth Hübener I am a Mormon. I became acquainted with Helmuth in our congregation. It was in the Besenbinderhof, that is, in St. Georg. Earlier I was in Altona, but then came to the Besenbinderhof in 1938, where I got acquainted with Helmuth in about February 1938.

I became a soldier in 1940 and was then in Hamburg only on leave. Helmuth was a Deacon in 1938. At that time I was already eighteen years old. The Mormon church is not political. But nevertheless in 1938 the first American missionaries were expelled from the country. Our youth organization, "Boy Scouts," was already forbidden in 1936; at the same time many members were arrested, interrogated, mishandled and put in coercive detention. From 1933 to 1945 our church was also listed in the Index of those to be persecuted. We had to delete our creed, section 134, "Explanations regarding governments and laws." But we did not do it. Our meetings were regarded as public and therefore we were ordered to fly the swastika flag. I had, under commission of the branch, to purchase the flag myself. But we never flew it. When we did it once, we discovered that it did not look pretty and we lost the spirit. Because our church had an American air about it, there were certainly people who did not want to escalate this political matter unnecessarily.

I was in a group with Helmuth. We did not talk about political matters, but certainly about religious matters. Then in about 1939–40 the North German Refinery approached our church, because they were very concerned about their Jewish employees. Under the aegis of our system for taking care of our members, we helped the Jews of the North German Refinery by—mostly at night when the streets were empty—loading their things on "Scottish carts" and then transporting them to the Hannover train station. Helmuth Hübener, Karl-Heinz Schnibbe and Rudi Wobbe were there. Each time they were underway for two and a half hours.

At that time I lived in Hamm, in the Wendenstraße. Outside of the church we had no contact; Helmuth was too young for that. Then when our congregation's Jewish members were no longer permitted to come to the meetings, we went after the Sunday evening meeting to visit Salomon Schwarz. Sometimes there were about 20–30 people who were crowded around him in his little flat. Helmuth was there, too. He was the littlest. We then discussed the gospel together. In sports Helmuth was absolutely nothing. We were often at the Hanseatic athletic fields in Rothenburgsort, and he was never there. Whether he went swimming, I don't know.

He was the intellectual type, who was interested only in intellectual things. I also saw his stepfather, Hugo Hübener, in 1940 at the beginning of the war. He was in uniform.[32]

It was a Sunday morning in the branch when I talked with Helmuth about his stepfather. We got around to talking about it. Helmuth's stepfather had been in France as a soldier. Helmuth told me all about the weird things he had done: he hauled all kinds of things home that he had requisitioned in France and sold them here.[33] I know that Helmuth was enraged at him for doing such things. He did not care for his stepfather at all. Helmuth had written him off, he'd cooked his goose in Helmuth's eyes. Helmuth complained vigorously about his stepfather. He had quite a sense of honor. He was kind of a little twerp, quite stocky and made a really intelligent impression; he was also very active in the church. Later I also thought his stepfather was not very likeable, and that might have been a reason for the flyers, for why he was so opposed to the Nazis. Helmuth was rather collegial, but he was a particular type. He was not for the Nazis. I believe I once heard a sermon by Helmuth. Everyone gave such sermons. He was very intelligent. In the classes and groups that we had, there was, of course, a lot of discussing and talking. He participated freely. I thought sometimes, he's a half-Nazi, somehow, but he was not that at all. He was just using that as a cover. You could not see clearly what was on his mind. Later, of course, you knew why he had done this. He wanted to maintain his cover as long as he could in order to accomplish his work. He was intelligent enough to figure that out. He was not with the Nazis. And when such a little person goes against the Nazis, then he is OK. And you liked him, too. Wobbe and Schnibbe, they were a bit larger and older,[34] but he was the driving force.

He also held the office of "Teacher" in the church, when he was still very small, 13 or 14. He gave you the impression that he understood the times better than the others. You could have a good friendship with him. But our five-year difference in age naturally made a big difference—when you are 20 and a 15-year-old comes along. . . . He was not particularly exuberant. He liked to discuss issues—Wobbe, Schnibbe and all the others could not come close to him. He was the intellectual leader.

I also became acquainted with Helmuth's mother once. We youths traveled to Barmbek together to a meeting that we were presenting for the parents. His mother was there, too. I know that he lived with his grandparents, but I have no recollection of them.

I know from accounts—when Helmuth was arrested in February 1942—that some of the people from the branch were arrested and interrogated, also. They thought the church was behind the matter. They didn't think such a young person could have done such things all alone. But they let them go after a day.

After he was executed, they excommunicated him from the church; I was very enraged about it, after I heard it. I was on leave in Hamburg and was very upset about the excommunication. In general not everyone in the branch was in favor of it. The Mormon church as such has a principle that you support the state which at the time has jurisdiction over you. We do not want to say by that that we support what is negative. But at that time we endured the Nazis; what else could we have done? But if I had been the bishop or Arthur Zander at that time, I would have forbidden Hübener to do it, because it says that we should obey the laws of the land. This was also the reason that we were not exactly happy about what Helmuth had done. If I had known about it, I would have spoken with him and made it clear to him: you know you can do everything, but to do that you are too small. That does not mean that that which he did—his heroism—was not very courageous; that is a completely different matter. The excommunication from the church must be considered in that light; he went against the rule: "Thou shalt obey the law of the land."

After 1945 he was completely reinstated. I am personally of the opinion that we did not need to do anything about the excommunication.

It was already bad enough that he was decapitated. That was a very difficult thing.

I first learned about the execution in 1942 by the red placards and the newspaper when I was on leave in Hamburg. In the branch no one knew anything about it.

Without being a bad Mormon, Helmuth did very many things that he actually should not have done, but which he took upon his own head.

Source: *Begleitheft zur Austellung um das kurze Leben und Wirken des Helmuth Hübener*, Catalogue of the exhibit in the Hamburg Municipal District Archive [Stadtteilarchiv] of Hamm, 26 October–10 December, 1992

72

"He Was Terribly Beaten Up"

I knew Helmuth for a long time. He was a friend of my son Arthur. They knew each other from the church. The youths in the church had formed a nice circle, who were always very happy together. I still recall today how Helmuth often said, "You will yet hear something really great about me. I will be known everywhere." At that time he was already involved in his resistance work, about which we, however, knew nothing. He did not say it because he was a braggart. It was more of a promise to those around him that he would someday really apply his intelligence, which he possessed, to something meaningful. But we did not know what to make of it. Nevertheless, before he talked that way he became a member of the Hitler Youth, about which he was very enthused at the beginning. Full of pride he told about "his" National Socialism, and I needed to warn my children about saying something in his presence which could have been dangerous for them. You need to know that we were opposed to the Nazis and spoke secretly about them.

Helmuth went around a lot with my son and with Wobbe and Schnibbe. Schnibbe was a regular go-getter and "daredevil," who always had everything possible on his mind. We would have thought him more likely than Helmuth to be involved in a resistance activity. It could be, also, that Helmuth was influenced by him, because Schnibbe had been tossed out of the Hitler Youth because of insubordination.

When Helmuth received the radio that his stepbrother Gerhard Kunkel brought from France, he was transformed. The BBC transmissions must have impressed him greatly. His grandparents, with whom he lived, had no idea of his activity. Helmuth was the secretary of the Hamburg branch president Zander and thus in the church leadership. He had a lot to do in that capacity, so his grandparents did not notice anything. He had to write letters and prepare the minutes. He was a good-natured and jovial person. He was very intelligent, for which reason the Nazis punished him as an adult. I still have a picture of him at home when he was acting in a play at the church. I remember one episode: we had a sister in the church, Annemarie Schwarz. She was half Jewish, and as the pressure on the church from the Nazis became greater, the leadership of the church had to ask Sister Schwarz not to come to church any more. Helmuth was very angry about this incident and said so very clearly. He thought very fairly. Still, as mentioned, we all knew nothing about his resistance.

I was well acquainted with his grandmother; every Friday we cleaned the church together. One day when I came to work, I noticed his grandmother. She was kneeling in front of the podium and had raised her hands and prayed and pleaded aloud to God. I walked up behind her and she did not notice me. Then I tried to calm her: "What is the matter?" "Something terrible has happened," the words gushed out of her. I asked if perhaps something had happened to Gerhard, who was stationed at the front; if he had been killed. "No, but I wish that Helmuth had been killed, that he were dead." "But why Helmuth? Nothing could have happened to him." Then she told me everything exactly. Helmuth had been arrested at his place of work by the Gestapo. After a few days the Gestapo brought him back to the apartment of his grandmother. He was terribly beaten up, and his grandmother cried out in terror when she saw him. She wanted to ask him something. Why were you arrested, what has happened? Helmuth wanted to speak to her, but the officers tore him away. They were not permitted to exchange a word. Helmuth had to show everything he owned. They confiscated his radio as well as his typewriter. They found paper and some flyers still in his possession. Then he was taken away again. His friends were arrested a few days later.

Then he went to Berlin. The boys were in investigatory custody a long time. At first I had a terrible fear that they would seize my son Arthur, too. He had always been with Helmuth, and perhaps he also belonged to the resistance group. Arthur had just been drafted into the Labor Service. At that time he was lying sick in a Berlin hospital. I traveled to him with my daughter. We told him everything, and he was able to calm us: he did not belong to it and he knew nothing about it.

Brother Schnibbe, the father of Karl-Heinz, traveled to Berlin to the trial. We did not believe that the boys would receive harsh punishments. They were so young; they were still children. We believed they would acquit Karl-Heinz and Rudolf and lock Helmuth in jail for a few years. Mr. Schnibbe related later about the trial: "If only I had not gone. It was terrible. Helmuth was brought before the court like a hardened criminal. He was bound with heavy chains. My son and Rudolf were not shackled. The judgment read: Schnibbe six [sic] years; Wobbe ten years; and Hübener death sentence. When Helmuth heard the sentence, he collapsed. His friends wanted to help him, but they were not permitted. Helmuth fell to the floor and Karl-Heinz and Rudolf were held back.

It was a terrible time for us. We all liked Helmuth so much. He was a good boy. He always called me Mother Sommerfeld. Although our President Zander always said that there was little point, that letters would not reach him, we wrote to him. We tried to help him and comfort him in his difficult imprisonment. He never received the letters. However, his relatives who visited him informed him that we had written. He was very thankful for that.

Five appeals for clemency for Helmuth were submitted. They hoped to change the punishment to lifelong imprisonment. One appeal came from his father, one from his fellow employees. But nothing did any good. One evening, some weeks after the judgement, I was sitting with my daughter. She was reading in the newspaper. Suddenly she read aloud: "The death sentence of Helmuth Hübener was carried out yesterday." I was very shaken and cried: "Now they've executed him after all." My daughter asked: "How come, do you know a Helmuth Hübener?" "But of course, that is Helmuth Guddat!" You must know that we knew Helmuth only by the name of Guddat. His stepfather, Hugo Hübener, gave him the name Hübener, in fact this happened during his detention. Hübener, the stepfather, apparently was on better terms with the Nazis and believed he could help him by the adoption that he carried out at that time.

Helmuth was a good boy. He visited us often. My daughter accompanied him on the piano and he sang. It was a wonderful time then, and it was now all over? It was terrible.

We lived in Hamm, in the neighborhood near Helmuth, who lived in the Louisenweg. He often asked Arthur to visit him in his apartment late in the evening. But I would not permit it. "What do you want to do?" I asked. "Helmuth's grandparents are already asleep and you will only disturb them." But Helmuth surely wanted to initiate Arthur into his secret.

After the death sentence I tried to comfort his grandparents. They were completely in despair. "And that he was also excommunicated from the church!" his grandmother said. Later she lost her life in a bombing attack on Hamm. Unfortunately she never experienced Helmuth's reinstatement.

When I heard about the death sentence, I wrote a consolatory letter. Unfortunately he never received it, but he knew about it.

One day after I had heard about the execution, I received a letter from Helmuth written a few hours before his death. Unfortunately I no longer have the letter. It was lost in the bombing attack. He wrote a total of four farewell letters. To his mother, to his brother Gerhard Kunkel, to his grandparents and to me. I no longer remember verbatim what he wrote. But the letter was very long. I still know some passages:

Dear Mother Sommerfeld!
When you receive this letter I will already be dead. I was permitted to wish for something before my death. I wished to be permitted to write some letters. I thank you for your consoling letter, which I unfortunately did not

receive. But I am happy that you have not completely forgotten me. Unfortunately I have broken the Word of Wisdom in the last hours of my life. Soon everything will be over. Keep me in good remembrance. I have not done anything wrong. I thank God that I will soon be released from this agony.

When I read the letter, I had to think about his words: You will yet hear something really great about me.

Source: *Begleitheft zur Austellung um das kurze Leben und Wirken des Helmuth Hübener*, Catalogue of the exhibit in the Hamburg Municipal District Archive [Stadtteilarchiv] of Hamm, 26 October–10 December, 1992

73

"We Would Not Have Given It Away and Treasured the Value of the Letter"

Hedi Radtke, née Sommerfeld, relates:

My brother Arthur Sommerfeld was very good friends with Helmuth through the contact they had in the church. My brother is two years older than Helmuth and was already in the National Labor Service when Helmuth, Rudi and Karl-Heinz began distributing the flyers. Helmuth knew English well, and one of his relatives in the army had brought a very good radio from France, which made it possible for him to receive English stations. Helmuth was a frequent visitor in our home; you could almost say that he spent nearly every evening with us. He liked to read and was a bookworm. We often played games when we were gathered around the table. As you know, the boys were often together. We never got well acquainted with his mother, but we knew his grandmother Sudroff very well through the church; she also brought him to church. Helmuth's mother was married for the second time. This second husband was, as we said, a "party man." I think he was a member of the SS.

I knew nothing myself about the activities, but my brother was informed about them; at the beginning of this matter he was still at home, but shortly thereafter he had to go into the Labor Service.

After the arrests we traveled to visit my brother to find out if he knew about it and had taken part. Helmuth listened to the English stations himself and printed flyers in the church office, my brother told us. My mother, Marie Sommerfeld, said at that time: "It is lucky that Arthur was not here, perhaps he would have been involved also."

On the last night of his life Helmuth wrote a letter to my mother in which he took leave of us. We could no longer find the letter after the death of my mother and assume that she had placed it at the disposal of a journalist and these people had kept it. Unfortunately we cannot prove anything, so this piece of history was lost. We would not have given it away and treasured the value of the letter.

Source: *Begleitheft zur Austellung um das kurze Leben und Wirken des Helmuth Hübener*, Catalogue of the exhibit in the Hamburg Municipal District Archive [Stadtteilarchiv] of Hamm, 26 October–10 December, 1992

74

"When I Went to Work on My Mother's Birthday, 28 October, Red Placards Jumped Out at Me from the Advertisement Pillars: 'Helmuth Hübener Executed'"

Helmuth was born in Hamburg on 8 January 1925. He had the maiden name of my mother for his surname, he was called Helmuth Guddat. My mother was divorced from Kunkel. From this marriage came two children, Gerhard and I [Hans]. Helmuth was our half brother. Later, during the war, my mother married the worker Hugo Hübener, who adopted Helmuth during his detention. We lived with my mother in Hamm. She raised her three children alone. She was employed by the state mint. Later she was a nurse. After that time we lived with our grandparents in the Louisenweg. We lived in humble circumstances.

In 1931 Helmuth was enrolled in the elementary school in Louisenweg. Since his earliest childhood Helmuth, like all of us, belonged to the Church of Jesus Christ of Latter-day Saints. This church had a scout troop. This group existed until 1934. Up to that point Helmuth belonged to the group. In 1937 on the basis of his excellent school accomplishments, Helmuth entered the upper track at the school in Brackdamm. Helmuth went through this school with great success; he passed his exams very well. He wrote a thesis about plutocracy. To this end he utilized many books with political and economic contents. If you are searching for particular effects and influences, I cannot tell you much.

Helmuth grew up in modest circumstances. He could never go on a trip. But by himself he did a lot for his education. Various sciences were his hobby. He read very much. Helmuth was a good orator and actor. In plays which the church produced we noticed that. In 1939 Helmuth joined the Young Folk; later he joined the Hitler Youth. He was very enthused about the National Socialist state. He held an office; I believe, at the end he was a file leader.

After he obtained the middle school certificate in 1941, Helmuth became an apprentice of the executive administrative track. He worked in the Biberhaus and the city hall. His resistance activity began in the beginning of 1941. At that time he received as a gift a larger radio from our brother Gerhard.[35] He listened to so-called enemy stations and at first made little flyers which he wrote on the typewriter with many carbon copies. He distributed these in Hamm, Hammerbrook, and Rothenburgsort. I knew of his activity myself.

How did he come to be a resister? Although he was enthusiastic about the Nazis (he did this until his arrest in order to cover himself), he soon began to think about everything in his environment. He read the newspaper and informed himself, as far as you could actually call that which was in the German press information. Later he compared the German press with the foreign radio reports. In the city hall he had the opportunity to read books in the municipal archive, which other libraries had not had for a long time. He read books about the USA, about the Soviet Union and other countries. He occupied himself with other forms of government. Consequently he got acquainted with the "enemy powers" and he had studied their strengths. And although the Nazis appeared to be doing well in the war, he proved that in the long run a victory against such an enormous enemy is not possible, just on economic grounds alone. Helmuth distributed the newscasts of the BBC to the people and commented on them from his political and religious viewpoint.

Helmuth wanted to become a young civil servant and he prepared himself for the necessary examination. He had to present a comprehensive project (unfortunately I cannot think of the title; it dealt with a civic subject). He was busy with the preparation of the first draft and had obtained a lot of material. So he improved his mind in every way. Helmuth, Rudolf Wobbe, and Karl-Heinz Schnibbe always raised their sights to higher and higher goals (in my opinion Schnibbe did not induce Helmuth to resistance, he only came to it later).

They soon duplicated the flyers. Then they sent them to the front, and that was subversion of the military forces! They distributed the leaflets in the worker districts, because from those who had suffered the most from war and National Socialism, the workers, they anticipated understanding and support. They also wanted to produce the flyers in French. Thereby they came into contact with too many people. That was dangerous; I warned Helmuth about it. But he had become somewhat careless because of his successes (people whispered about the leaflets).

At Christmas 1941 I warned Helmuth. We went dancing together, and on the way home we talked about everything. Nevertheless they raised their sights higher. On 7 January 1942, the entire group was arrested [sic]. The previous day was Helmuth's 17th birthday. I was there when Helmuth came with the Gestapo and undertook a search of the apartment. Afterward my brother Gerhard appeared before a court martial (because he had delivered the radio and had accepted subversive documents from his brother). The Gestapo could not imagine that a 16-year-old, alone, by himself, carried out this scheme and composed these clever flyers without adult help. They believed he was a member of a large adult resistance organization. They tortured Helmuth severely to get him to betray his "backers."

He was incarcerated in Fuhlsbüttel. Later he went to Berlin. Brother

Schnibbe, Sr., told us about the trial before the People's Court. Helmuth had courageously given an account of himself. You could tell from his face the agony of his detention. The "judges" wore red robes. Helmuth shouted: "Do you really believe that Germany can win this war?" The trial was not long. Then came the shameful sentence. I know about three appeals for clemency that were submitted: from the public authorities [in Hamburg], from the Hitler Youth unit, from his stepfather. By the way, the informer from the Biberhaus was later (after the war) sentenced to two years imprisonment. Unfortunately the appeals were not successful.

When I went to work on my mother's birthday, 28 October, red placards jumped out at me from the advertisement pillars: "Helmuth Hübener executed." My mother learned about it through the newspaper. We never received a letter that informed us where he was buried. My mother suffered a great shock at that time. She lost her life together with my grandparents in the bombing attacks in 1943. Helmuth wrote her a letter of farewell. The letter was heartrending.

Source: *Begleitheft zur Austellung um das kurze Leben und Wirken des Helmuth Hübener*, Catalogue of the exhibit in the Hamburg Municipal District Archive [Stadtteilarchiv] of Hamm, 26 October–10 December, 1992

Song Texts

The German National Anthem:
"Deutschland, Deutschland über alles"
(Germany, Germany, above All)

Deutschland, Deutschland über alles,
Über alles in der Welt,
Wenn es stets zum Schutz und Trutze
Brüderlich zusammenhält;
Von der Maas bis an die Memel,
Von der Etsch bis an den Belt;
Deutschland, Deutschland über alles,
Über alles in der Welt!

Deutsche Frauen, deutsche Treue,
Deutscher Wein und deutscher Sang
Sollen in der Welt behalten
Ihren alten, schönen Klang,
Uns zu edler Tat begeistern
Unser ganzes Leben lang;
Deutsche Frauen, deutsche Treue,
Deutscher Wein und deutscher Sang!

Einigkeit und Recht und Freiheit
Für das deutsche Vaterland!
Danach laßt uns alle streben
Brüderlich mit Herz und Hand!
Einigkeit und Recht und Freiheit
Sind des Glückes Unterpfand;
Blüh' im Glanze dieses Glückes,
Blühe, deutsches Vaterland!

(Germany, Germany above all,
Above all in the world,
As long as it holds together in brotherhood,
Protectively and defiantly;
From the Maas [river] to the Memel,
From the Etsch to the Belt;
Germany, Germany above all,
Above all in the world.

German women, German loyalty,
German wine, and German song,
Shall retain in the world
Their old, beautiful sound,
To enthuse us to noble deeds
Our life long.
German women, German loyalty,
German wine, and German song!

Unity and Justice and Freedom
For the German Fatherland!
For this let us all strive
Fraternally with heart and hand!
Unity and Justice and Freedom
Are the guarantors of happiness.
Bloom, in the glow of this happiness,
Bloom, O German Fatherland!)

The Horst Wessel Song:
"Die Fahne Hoch"
(Raise High the Flag)

Die Fahne hoch!
Die Reihen dicht geschlossen!
S.A. marschiert mit ruhig festem Schritt.
Kameraden, die Rotfront und Reaktion erschossen,
marschier'n im Geist in unsern Reihen mit.

(Raise high the flag!
Close up the ranks tightly!
The S.A. is marching with quiet, firm tread.
Comrades, shot dead by the Red Front and reactionaries,
Are marching in spirit with us in our ranks.)

"Es Zittern die Morschen Knochen"
(The Old Rotten Bones of the World Are Quaking)

Es zittern die morschen Knochen
Der Welt vor dem großen Krieg,
Wir haben den Schrecken gebrochen,
Für uns war's ein großer Sieg.
Wir werden weiter marschieren,
Wenn alles in Scherben fällt,
Denn heute hört uns Deutschland
Und morgen die ganze Welt.

(The old rotten bones of the world are quaking
About the great war.
We have broken the bonds of servitude;
For us it was a great victory.
We shall march on and on,
Even if all is destroyed;
For today Germany shall hear us,
And tomorrow the entire world.)

"Der deutsche Bergwald steht in grün"
(The German Mountain Woods Stand Green)

Der deutsche Bergwald steht in grün,
Die Tannen rauschen leise,
Der deutsche Aar schlägt stark und kühn
Im Blauen seine Kreise.
Die deutschen Ströme fließen klar,
Es blühen die Felsenspalten,
Du deutscher Wald, du Strom und Aar,
Ihr sollt die Grenzwacht halten.

(The German mountain woods stand green,
The pine trees rustle softly.
The German eagle, with eyesight keen,
Circles the heaven's corridors.
The German rivers, clear they flow,
In cracks in cliffs do blossoms grow.
Oh, German woods, oh, rivers, oh, oh, eagle
Guard our borders.)

"Wildgänse rauschen durch die Nacht"
(Wild Geese Whir through the Night)

Wildgänse rauschen durch die Nacht
Mit schrillem Schrei nach Norden—
Unstäte Fahrt! Habt acht, habt acht!
Die Welt ist voller Morden.

Fahrt durch die nachtdurchwogte Welt,
Graureisige Geschwader!
Fahlhelle zuckt, und Schlachtruf gellt,
Weit wallt und wogt der Hader.

Rausch' zu, fahr' zu, du graues Heer!
Rauscht zu, fahrt zu nach Norden!
Fahrt ihr nach Süden übers Meer—
Was ist aus uns geworden!

Wir sind wie ihr ein graues Heer
Und fahr'n in Kaisers Namen,
Und fahr'n wir ohne Wiederkehr,
Rauscht uns im Herbst ein Amen!

(Wild geese whir through the night
With a piercing cry on their way north—
A perilous journey! Take care, take care!
The world is full of murders.

Journey through the night-drenched world,
Gray traveling squadrons!
The tumult flashes in bright bolts, it ranges and rages wide,
The battle cry shrieks.

Whir on, travel on, O gray host!
Whir on, travel on north!
When you shall have returned to the south over the sea,
What shall have become of us!

We are, like you, a gray host
And march in the name of the kaiser,
And should we march without returning,
Whir us in autumn an Amen!)

"Ein Junges Volk Steht Auf"
(A Young Folk Arises Ready for Battle)

Ein junges Volk steht auf zum Sturm bereit,
Reißt die Fahnen höher, Kameraden,
Wir fühlen nahen unsere Zeit,
Die Zeit der jungen Soldaten.
Vor uns marschieren mit sturmzerfetzen Fahnen
Die toten Helden der jungen Nation,
Und über uns die Heldenahnen,
Deutschland, Vaterland, wir kommen schon.

(A young folk arises ready for battle,
Hold the flags higher, comrades,
We feel our time approaching,
The time of the young soldiers.
Before us the dead heroes of the young nation march,
With their battle-tattered banners,
And above us our heroic forefathers,
Germany, Fatherland, we're on our way.)

"Unsere Fahne flattert uns voran"
(Our Flag Flutters before Us)

Vorwärts, vorwärts, schmettern die hellen Fanfaren,
Vorwärts, vorwärts, Jugend kennt keine Gefahren.
Deutschland wird noch fortbesteh'n,
Werden wir auch untergeh'n.

Vorwärts, vorwärts, schmettern die hellen Fanfaren,
Vorwärts, vorwärts, Jugend kennt keine Gefahren.
Ist das Ziel auch noch so hoch,
Jugend zwingt es doch.

Unsre Fahne flattert uns voran,
In die Zukunft ziehn wir Man für Mann,
Wir marschieren für Hitler durch Nacht und Not,
Mit der Fahne der Jugend für Freiheit und Brot.

Unsre Fahne flattert uns voran,
Unsre Fahne ist die neue Zeit.
Und die Fahne führt uns in die Ewigkeit,
Ja, die Fahne ist mehr als der Tod.

(Forward, forward, the bright fanfares call,
Forward, forward, youth know no dangers.
Germany will continue to exist,
Even if we are destroyed.

Forward, forward, the bright fanfares call,
Forward, forward, youth know no dangers.
Even if our goal is that high,
The youth can accomplish it.

Our flag flutters before us,
We move ahead into the future, man for man.
We march for Hitler through night and hard times
With the flag of youth for freedom and bread.

Our flag flutters before us,
Our flag is the new era.
And our flag leads us into eternity,
Yes, our flag is greater than death.)

"Das Engeland Lied"
(Song of England)

Heute wollen wir ein Liedlein singen,
Trinken wollen wir den kühlen Wein.
Und die Gläser sollen dazu klingen,
Denn es muß, es muß geschieden sein.

Gib mir deine Hand, deine weiße Hand,
Leb' wohl mein Schatz, leb' wohl mein Schatz,
Leb' wohl, lebe wohl,
Denn wir fahren, denn wir fahren, denn wir fahren
Gegen Engeland, Engeland.

Und sie flattert und sie wehet auf dem Maste,
Sie verkündet unseres Reiches Macht,
Denn wir wollen es nicht länger leiden,
Daß der Englischmann darüber lacht.
Gib mir deine Hand, deine weiße Hand,
Leb' wohl mein Schatz . . .

(Today we want to sing a little song,
We want to drink the cool wine.
And the sound of our glasses clinking shall accompany us,
For it must, it must be decided.

Give me your hand, your white hand,
Good-bye, my darling, good-bye my darling,
Good-bye, good-bye,
For we are marching, for we are marching, for we are marching
against England, England.

And it flutters and it waves upon the mast,
It proclaims the power of our realm,

For we cannot longer suffer
That the Englishman mocks it.
Give me your hand, your white hand,
Good-bye my darling . . .)

"Schleswig-Holstein Meerumschlungen" (Schleswig-Holstein, Encircled by the Sea)

Schleswig-Holstein meerumschlungen,
deutscher Sitte hohe Wacht,
wahre treu, was schwererungen,
bis ein schönrer Morgen tagt!

Schleswig-Holstein stamm verwandt,
wanke nicht mein Vaterland!
Schleswig-Holstein stamm verwandt,
wanke nicht mein Vaterland!

(Schleswig-Holstein, encircled by the sea,
The lofty watchtower of German morals,
Oh, keep faithful that which has been so dearly earned,
Until a more beautiful morning dawns!

Schleswig-Holstein, kin-related,
Do not waver, oh my fatherland!
Schleswig-Holstein, kin-related,
Do not waver, oh my fatherland!)

Notes

Foreword

1. Klaus J. Hansen, "Are We Still Mormons?" *Dialogue: A Journal of Mormon Thought* 4 (Spring 1969): 101–6.
2. Hans Mommsen, "German Society and Resistance to Hitler," in *From Weimar to Auschwitz* (Oxford: Polity Press, 1991), pp. 208–24.
3. Standard accounts of the resistance are Peter Hoffmann, *Widerstand, Staatsstreich, Attentat. Der Kampf der Opposition gegen Hitler*, 4th ed. (Munich: Piper, 1985); Peter Hoffmann, *The History of the German Resistance, 1933–1945* (Cambridge, Mass.: MIT Press, 1977); and Michael Balfour, *Withstanding Hitler in Germany* (London: Routledge, 1988).
4. Eberhard Bethge, *Dietrich Bonhoeffer: Man of Vision, Man of Courage* (New York: Harper and Row, 1970).
5. Inge Scholl, *Students against Tyranny: The Resistance of the White Rose, Munich 1942–1943* (Middletown, Conn.: Wesleyan University Press, 1983).
6. Matthias von Hellfeld, *Edelweißpiraten in Köln* (Cologne: Pahl-Rugenstein, 1981); Detlev Peukert, "Youth in the Third Reich," in Richard Bessel, ed., *Life in the Third Reich* (New York: Oxford University Press, 1987), pp. 25–40.
7. Peukert, "Youth in the Third Reich"; Michael Kater, *Different Drummers: Jazz in the Culture of Nazi Germany* (New York: Oxford University Press, 1992).
8. "We believe in being subject to kings, presidents, rulers, and magistrates, in obeying, honoring, and sustaining the law." J. Reuben Clark, Jr., First Counselor in the First Presidency of the Church, who had visited Germany in 1937 and 1938 on behalf of the Foreign Bondholders' Protective Council, reported that he was "favorably impressed with living conditions there, and he took particular note that there was widespread support for Hitler among the German Saints" (D. Michael Quinn, *J. Reuben Clark: The Church Years* [Provo, Utah: Brigham Young University Press, 1983], p. 202).
9. Joseph M. Dixon, "Mormons in the Third Reich: 1933–1945," *Dia-*

logue: A Journal of Mormon Thought 7 (Spring 1962): 70–78; Alan F. Keele and Douglas F. Tobler, "The Führer's New Clothes: Helmuth Hübener and the Mormons in the Third Reich," *Sunstone* 5 (Nov.–Dec. 1980): 20–29; see also Gilbert Scharffs, *Mormonism in Germany* (Salt Lake City: Deseret, 1970), pp. 79–90. My own interpretation follows that of Keele and Tobler rather than that of Scharffs and Dixon, who are more defensive of Mormon relations with the Third Reich.

10. Ernst Christian Helmreich, *The German Churches under Hitler* (Detroit: Wayne State University Press, 1979); Klaus Scholder, *The Churches and the Third Reich* (Philadelphia: Fortress, 1988); in spite of its title, Victoria Barnett's *For the Soul of the People: Protestant Protest against Hitler* (New York: Oxford University Press, 1992) shows how much members of the "Confessing Church" compromised with the regime.

11. "It is regrettable that in the judgment of the People's Court against Hübener the question remained open, whether and to what extent the religious sect to which Hübener belonged, is to be ascribed as the intellectual originator of Hübener's crimes." See Document 58.

12. In the decade prior to Hitler's accession to power in 1933, nearly 2,700 German Mormons immigrated to the United States, between 1933 and 1939 only ninety-one. When President Heber J. Grant, during his visit to Germany in 1937, asked German Saints to refrain from emigrating to Utah, assuring them that things would be well for them in their fatherland, the address was largely symbolic, perhaps intended to reassure the German government regarding the intentions of the Church leadership, since emigration had already been reduced to a trickle (Douglas Alder, "German-Speaking Immigration to Utah, 1850–1950" [M.A. thesis, University of Utah, 1959], p. 76). By 1939 Church membership in the Greater Germany (including Austria) had reached nearly 15,000.

13. Otto Berndt was able to take advantage of this in his interrogation by the Gestapo: "I had to prove that I was an Aryan. Since my ancestors had been living in Germany for many generations and since I had my lines traced back about eight generations, to the surprise of the investigating officer who was only required to have proof for the last three generations, I was able to pass this test with flying colors." See Document 65, "Statement of Otto Berndt."

14. Martin Broszat and Elke Froehlich, *Alltag und Widerstand: Bayern im National-Sozialismus* (Munich: Piper, 1987); see also Ian Kershaw, *Popular Opinion and Political Dissent in the Third Reich: Bavaria 1933–1945* (New York: Oxford University Press, 1983).

15. In a telling incident a Mormon friend only slightly older than I confronted me in a veritable rage: We weren't like dogs, having to dig up the bones of the past.

16. Document 65, "Statement of Otto Berndt." It was the local branch president who removed Hübener's name from the records of the Church, over Berndt's objection.

17. In an address before the assembled Gauleiter on 3 August 1944, Himmler claimed that *Sippenhaft* was an old Germanic custom. They would say: "This man has committed treason, his blood is tainted, it is the blood

of a traitor, it must be exterminated. In a vendetta all members of a clan, to the last member, would be eliminated. The Family Count Stauffenberg will be extinguished to the last member" (Peter Hoffmann, *Widerstand, Staatsstreich, Attentat: Der Kampf der Opposition gegen Hitler,* 3d rev. ed. [Munich: Piper, 1979], p. 639). Although the SS had orders to shoot them all before the arrival of the Allied troops, because of chaotic conditions at the end of the war and a resolute army commander, the Stauffenbergs and most of the other families were saved from execution (ibid., pp. 640, 657–58).

18. Otto Berndt was told by a Gestapo officer, "Make no mistake about it, Berndt. When we have this war behind us, when we have the time to devote to it and after we have eliminated the Jews, you Mormons are next." "When church members hoped for victory in the war, Berndt would reply: 'You be grateful to God that we will not win it'" (quoted in Keele and Tobler, "Führer's New Clothes," pp. 24–25).

19. Hannah Arendt, *Eichmann in Jerusalem: A Report on the Banality of Evil* (New York: Viking, 1963).

20. See Document 1.

21. There are those who saw in the death of Dr. Roland Freisler, president of the *Volksgerichtshof,* in the air-raid shelter of the "People's Court," an element of divine retribution.

22. Schnibbe does precisely that. He does not understand how these men can commit torture "all day long and in the evening go home and leave all of it behind them" (p. 52). However, it is doubtful that the interrogating Gestapo officers, Wangemann and Müssener, personally tortured prisoners. The brutal treatment and the beatings in the early days of interrogation was carried out during transport and in jail by lower-ranking guards from whom the higher-ranking officers could distance and isolate themselves—"see no evil, hear no evil." An official directive in 1941 decreed that so-called *Verschärfte Vernehmung* (a euphemism for torture) was permitted only in the interrogation of Communist and Marxist functionaries, Jehovah's Witnesses, and saboteurs. Any exceptions required the personal permission of Reinhard Heydrich. A modified directive by Heinrich Müller, chief of the SD (Security Service), in 1942 specifies some of the methods: reduced rations of water and bread, hard bedding, darkness, prevention of sleep, tiring exercises, beatings with a stick (if more than twenty strokes were administered, the beating had to be attended by a physician). Under no circumstances should a paper trail be left (Hoffmann, *Widerstand,* pp. 641–42).

23. Patricia Meehan, *The Unnecessary War: Whitehall and the German Resistance to Hitler* (London: Sinclair-Stevenson, 1992); Klemens von Klemperer, *German Resistance against Hitler: The Search for Allies Abroad 1938–1945* (New York: Oxford University Press, 1992).

24. His last words, before he was shot in the courtyard of the high command of the German army in the Bendlerstraße in Berlin in the early hours of 21 July 1944, were, "Es lebe das heilige Deutschland!"

25. Ian Kershaw, "Resistance without the People?" in *The Nazi Dictatorship: Problems and Perspectives of Interpretation,* 3d ed. (London: E. Arnold, 1993), pp. 150–79.

26. Klaus Mammach, *KPD und die deutsche antifaschistische Widerstandsbewegung 1933–1939* (Frankfurt: Röderberg, 1974); Andreas Dorpalen, *German History in Marxist Perspective: The East German Approach* (Detroit: Wayne State University Press, 1985), pp. 418–28.

27. Editors' note: The most egregious example is an article by East German mission president Alfred C. Rees entitled "Im Lande der Mormonen" which appeared in a special issue of the Nazi party organ *Der völkische Beobachter*, dated 14 April 1939. Doubtless an attempt to curry favor with the government, the article makes Mormonism sound like the fulfillment of Nazi teachings. It concludes, "Mormons are people who put this healthy doctrine into action."

28. For complex reasons ranging from anti-Semitism to anti-British isolationism, there was, in fairly broad circles even in the United States, considerable initial enthusiasm for Hitler and for the New Germany. (For a more thorough discussion of this matter, see Keele and Tobler, "Führer's New Clothes," p. 27 and nn. 25–27.) As noted above (n. 12), President Grant assured German Saints in 1937 that things would be well for them in their fatherland. See also Quinn, who placed Clark "deep in the mainstream of isolationism" (*J. Reuben Clark*, p. 205), and saw his response to Nazi Germany as virtually identical to that of Charles Lindbergh, who (according to Wayne S. Cole), while he "disapproved of much that occurred in Nazi Germany, . . . admired the German efficiency, spirit, and scientific achievement and technological accomplishments. To a degree he began to 'understand' and sympathize with certain German attitudes and actions in the 1930s, even when he did not approve of them" (Cole, *Charles A. Lindbergh and the Battle against American Intervention in World War II* [New York: Harcourt, Brace, Jovanovich, 1974], p. 31; as quoted in Quinn, ibid., p. 202).

29. Unfortunately, Douglas Alder's M.A. thesis concludes before the wave of postwar Mormon emigration from Germany, which may well exceed the figures of the pre-Hitler period.

Introduction

1. For an excellent discussion of this phenomenon, consult Klemens von Klemperer, "Widerstand-Resistance: The Place of the German Resistance in the European Resistance against National Socialism," in Hedley Bull, ed., *The Challenge of the Third Reich: The Adam von Trott Memorial Lectures* (Oxford: Clarendon Press, 1986).

2. Gordon W. Prange, *Hitler's Words: Two Decades of National Socialism, 1923–1943* (Washington, D.C.: American Council on Public Affairs, 1944), p. 120.

3. Hans Rothfels, *The German Opposition to Hitler, an Appraisal* (Chicago: Regnery, 1962), p. 16.

4. Michael Balfour, *Withstanding Hitler in Germany 1933–45* (New York: Routledge, 1988), p. 262.

5. Peter Hoffmann, *German Resistance to Hitler* (Cambridge, Mass.: Harvard University Press, 1988), p. 127.

6. Karl-Dietrich Bracher, "Problems of German Resistance," in Bull, *Challenge of the Third Reich*, pp. 60–61.

7. Peter Hoffmann, *The History of the German Resistance, 1933–1945* (Cambridge, Mass.: MIT Press, 1977), p. 16. Emphasis added.

8. Rothfels, *German Opposition to Hitler*, pp. 18–19.

9. Those who opposed National Socialism also had little influence on the configuration of the postwar Germanies, though there were a few notable exceptions such as Willy Brandt, who opposed Nazism from exile in Norway and Sweden and later became chancellor of the Federal Republic of Germany, and Eugen Gerstenmaier, a member of the Kreisau circle arrested after the 20 July 1944 assassination attempt on Hitler, who later became a leading member of the federal assembly.

10. Balfour, *Withstanding Hitler*, p. 78.

11. It is interesting to note, however, that Hitler never received a majority of popular support in an election. The only free election in Germany following the Nazi seizure of power on 30 January 1933 was held on 5 March 1933 and resulted in the National Socialists receiving 43.9 percent of the vote. In light of the changes that had already occurred in Germany and the conditions under which political opponents functioned, this was a stunning rejection of the Nazis (Hoffmann, *German Resistance to Hitler*, p. 13).

12. Ibid., pp. 71–72.

13. Ibid., pp. 53, 60.

14. Helmut Gollwitzer et al., eds., *Dying We Live: The Final Message and Records of the Resistance* (New York: Pantheon, 1956), pp. xvii–xviii.

15. Johannes Steinhoff et al., eds., *Voices from the Third Reich: An Oral History* (Washington, D.C.: Regnery Gateway, 1989), pp. 529–30.

16. "Even now it is hard to identify with any certainty the regional, gender or class base of the Germans who resisted Fascism. Records were not kept; resistance groups worked separately and underground, with the minimum number of contacts, for safety's sake" (Christine King, "Pacifists, Neutrals or Resisters: Jehovah's Witnesses and the Experience of National Socialism," *Bulletin of the John Rylands University Library of Manchester* 70, no. 3 [1988]: 149).

17. Robert Ley, the director of the Nazi Labor Front, declared that "in National Socialist Germany such a thing as a private individual does not exist" (Rothfels, *German Opposition to Hitler*, p. 28; see Ronald Smelser, *Robert Ley: Hitler's Labor Front Leader* [New York: Berg, 1988], p. 201).

18. Jill Stephenson, "'Resistance' to 'No Surrender': Popular Disobedience in Württemberg in 1945," in Francis R. Nicosia and Lawrence D. Stokes, eds., *Germans against Nazism: Nonconformity, Opposition and Resistance in the Third Reich* (New York: St. Martin's Press, 1990), pp. 351–52.

19. Rothfels estimates that at least 12,000 Germans suffered the death penalty for political reasons, which might be a low figure (*German Opposition to Hitler*, p. 15; see also Hoffmann, *German Resistance to Hitler*, p. 57). Broszat estimates that, apart from the military courts and concentration camps, the civil courts pronounced at least 15,000 death sentences, in many cases "simply for public criticism of the regime" ("The Third Reich and the German People," in Bull, *Challenge of the Third Reich*, p. 93).

20. Klemperer, "Widerstand-Resistance," pp. 47–48.

21. "The young people in the Edelweiß groups or in the Packs were more deeply involved in the Resistance and in the sacrifices which it demanded than is generally known. It is reported, for instance, that in Krefeld at least 30 percent of the Hitler Youth were secret members of the Edelweiß. The concentration camp at Neuwied (Apr. 1944) was intended solely for boys under twenty. Giving evidence in court in 1939, a Gestapo agent stated that 'at least 2,000 boys & girls' were organized in the Pack in the whole of Germany" (Rothfels, *German Opposition to Hitler*, p. 15).

22. Hoffmann, *History of the German Resistance*, p. xi.

23. Rudi Wobbe and Jerry Borrowman, *Before the Blood Tribunal* (Salt Lake City: Covenant Communications, 1992).

Chapter 1: Childhood in the Shadow of the Swastika

1. The church is also often referred to as the LDS Church.

2. Hetthorn lies approximately ninety-five kilometers nearly due west of Hamburg and directly south of Bremerhaven. The town was not listed in the 1894 German gazetteer, but had a population of 121 in 1933 (Frederich Müller, *Müllers Grosses Deutsches Ortsbuch* [Wuppertal-Barmen: Post- u. Ortsbuchverlag, 1938], p. 420).

3. Pauline Schnibbe joined the LDS Church on 3 September 1922, less than ten months after her husband became a member on 28 November 1921 (Church of Jesus Christ of Latter-day Saints, Historical Department, Church Records of Members, Hamburg, Germany [1922–1948], microfilm roll no. 68794).

4. Lüdelsen is a small community located approximately 110 kilometers southeast of Hamburg. In 1933 its population was 449, an increase of fifteen persons since 1894 (Frederich Müller, *Müllers Grosses Deutsches Ortsbuch*, p. 635; Wilhelm Keil, *Neumanns Orts-Lexikon des Deutschen Reiches* [Leipzig: Bibliographisches Institut, 1894], p. 515).

5. This is not an unusual claim. In his autobiography, Hans Count von Lehndorff recounted that on the night of 14 January 1943, his brother, who was fighting in the Leningrad area, appeared to him in a dream. Hans knew from the dream that his brother was killed in combat, which was confirmed a few days later by a telephone call (*East Prussian Diary: A Journal of Faith, 1945–1947* [London: Oswald Wolff, 1963], p. 212).

6. In 1924, the year of Schnibbe's birth, the LDS membership in Hamburg was second only to that of Chemnitz in the German-speaking areas of Europe, with a total of 1,239 members ("Annual Mission Statistics," 1924, LDS Church Historian's Office, Salt Lake City, Utah, cited in Gilbert W. Scharffs, *Mormonism in Germany* [Salt Lake City: Deseret Book Company, 1970], p. 64).

7. By late November 1923 the value of the mark had declined until the exchange rate reached one trillion to one, a level of inflation that made the currency virtually worthless (Erich Eyck, *A History of the Weimar Republic*, 2 vols. [Cambridge, Mass.: Harvard University Press, 1962], 1:266).

8. Germany continued to experience higher death rates than the victorious powers, partly due to malnutrition. Tuberculosis was particularly noticeable and "civilian deaths shot up in October 1918 (when they were nearly 2½ times as high as they had been during September), remained extremely high in November, and returned to average wartime levels only in March 1919. . . . By 1919 and 1920, despite the continued shortages of food and fuel, it had returned to pre-war levels; from 1921 onwards it fell well below pre-war rates, continuing the long-term improvement which has characterized German mortality during the past century" (Bessel, *Life in the Third Reich*, p. 224).

9. In 1925 unemployment in Germany exceeded one million for the first time. By the end of January 1931, 4.9 million Germans were seeking employment (Eyck, *History of the Weimar Republic*, 2:50, 300). Because the burden of providing for the unemployed often fell on urban communities, they excluded as many as possible from claiming entitlements. By 1933 there were 1.2 million registered unemployed persons in Germany who were receiving no benefits (Wolfgang Ayass, "Vagrants and Beggars in Hitler's Reich," in Richard J. Evans, ed., *The German Underworld: Deviants and Outcasts in German History* [New York: Routledge, 1988], p. 210). In 1926 6.6 percent of the working population of Hamburg was unemployed. By 1933 the number had risen to 29.2 percent (Karl Ditt, *Sozialdemokraten im Widerstand. Hamburg in der Anfangsphase des Dritten Reiches* [Hamburg: VSA Verlag, 1984], p. 19).

10. On 26 April 1933, the Nazi regime forbade any further meetings or demonstrations by political opponents. A few weeks later it was also forbidden to display flags, lapel pins or any other non-Nazi political symbols (Ditt, *Sozialdemokraten im Widerstand*, pp. 60–61).

11. Since the mid-nineteenth century, Hamburg was a stronghold of the working-class movement and was an extraordinarily strong location for the trade unions and the Social Democratic party. Between 1918 and 1933 the Social Democratic vote in Hamburg exceeded the national average by 7 to 8 percent. By 1933 the SPD had approximately 57,000 members in Hamburg, making it the second largest Social Democratic district (Ditt, *Sozialdemokraten im Widerstand*, pp. 13–15, 22).

12. In 1923 less than 25 percent of Hohenfelde's inhabitants were members of the working class. All of the adjacent districts had from 25 percent to 65 percent working-class populations (Richard Comfort, *Revolutionary Hamburg: Labor Politics in the Early Weimar Republic* [Stanford: Stanford University Press, 1966], p. 155). Hohenfelde was also one of the strongest centers of Nazi voters in Hamburg (Ditt, *Sozialdemokraten im Widerstand*, pp. 19–20).

13. The letters SA stood for Sturmabteilung (Storm Detachment), whose members were the early private military force of the Nazi party.

14. Rudi Wobbe recalled when a demonstration of Communists was fired upon by Nazis from a building along the march route. While most of the demonstrators fled, one group "raced up the stairs after the Nazis and a battle ensued. Soon I saw the machine-gun and several bodies flying off the roof.

With the Nazis thus disposed of, the marchers regrouped and the demonstration continued" (Wobbe and Borrowman, *Before the Blood Tribunal*, p. 2).

15. An ancient wind instrument similar to the oboe, the shawm with its shrill, nasal sound was quite different from the brass and percussion instruments used by the traditional military bands. It was used in parades before and after World War I by the political Left as "a conscious gesture, a counterreaction to Prussian military music" (Willy Schumann, *Being Present: Growing Up in Hitler's Germany* [Kent, Ohio: Kent State University Press, 1991], p. 4).

16. Prior to the Nazi takeover of power in Germany, the Social Democratic and Communist parties were almost alone in opposing National Socialism (Ditt, *Sozialdemokraten im Widerstand*, p. 13).

17. The vicious attacks of political enemies often stemmed from the flaunting of party strength, thus taunting one's opponents. The so-called propaganda marches often led to brawls and, in some cases, open warfare. The most famous clash in Hamburg occurred in Altona on "Bloody Sunday," 17 July 1932. The police president granted permission for the Nazi paramilitary forces to march through the workers' quarter of Altona. Entire blocks of buildings were occupied by Communists, who fired upon the approximately seven thousand Nazi troopers. Eighteen persons, including two SA members, were killed, mostly from stray police bullets. One SA participant claimed that "we had 13 or 14 dead that day" (Otto Kumm, "One Could Try the Communists or Join the Nazis," in Steinhoff, *Voices from the Third Reich*, p. xxix). After the Nazi takeover of power in Germany, fifteen Communists in Hamburg were tried for murder; four persons were executed and the others received prison sentences. "Bloody Sunday" was the emotional term applied to Sundays when the largest and most violent political clashes occurred (Christian Zentner and Friedmann Bedürftig, eds., *The Encyclopedia of the Third Reich*, 2 vols. [New York: Macmillan, 1991], 1:21, 93).

18. Unemployment leads to increased radicalization. The blue-collar workers moved more toward the Communist party, while the white-collar workers became supporters of Nazism. More than half of the SA was drawn from unskilled or semiskilled workers, of whom 70 to 80 percent had been unemployed (Conan Fischer, *Stormtroopers: A Social, Economic and Ideological Analysis, 1929–35* [London: George Allen and Unwin, 1983], pp. 26, 46; Jürgen W. Falter, "Unemployment and the Radicalisation of the German Electorate 1928–1933: An Aggregate Data Analysis with Special Emphasis on the Rise of National Socialism," in Peter D. Stachura, ed., *Unemployment and the Great Depression in Weimar Germany* [London: Macmillan, 1986], pp. 207–11).

19. In July 1932 a meeting of three hundred "tramps" occurred in Hamburg in which complaints were voiced about abuses in and the high cost of rooming houses, inadequate pay in workers' centers, and the poor condition of municipal night shelters. The Nazis were active in this area and attempted to rescue "fellow Germans who had got into difficulties through no fault of their own." It is estimated that a "good many of the homeless must have found their way into the arms of the SA . . . attracted by the prom-

ise of food, shelter, uniforms and plenty of action" (Ayass, "Vagrants and Beggars," p. 211).

20. "In many cases of SA/SS members and leaders . . . their fathers had died . . . or lost their livelihood during the childhood or adolescence of the respondent. Nearly one-third grew up in poverty, and another one-sixth as half-orphans. Nearly two-thirds of them became unemployed or bankrupt in the republican years. The socially declining and highly mobile Storm-troopers, finally, had the highest unemployment rate in the 1930s" (Peter Merkl, *The Making of a Stormtrooper* [Princeton: University Press, 1980], p. 154). "In those turbulent months no one in the SA inquired about social origins. . . . Temporary delinquents and hardened criminals were taken to the bosom of the Movement. . . . Such persons were in fact more sought after than the ordinary solid citizen; for they had the virtue of possessing hard fists. And there were still a good many recalcitrants among their fellow coun-trymen who had to have the fact of their wonderful good fortune pounded into them" (Hans Gisevius, *To the Bitter End* [Boston: Houghton Mifflin, 1947], p. 65). Hermann Rauschning, the president of the Danzig senate in 1933–34, claimed that the cruelty of the SA and SS was increasingly refined and "dealt out" to political opponents as "part of a definite political plan" (*Hitler Speaks: A Series of Political Conversations with Hitler on His Real Aims* [London: Thornton Butterworth, 1939], p. 88).

21. Horst Wessel was the commander of SA Storm Unit 5 in Berlin when he was killed in 1930 at the age of twenty-two by members of the Red Front, a militant Communist organization. A poem he published in 1929 was set to music and became known as the "Horst Wessel Song" and was viewed much like a national anthem by the Nazis. Contrary to a common belief at the time, Wessel did not write the music. He wrote new words and "hotted up the tune," which stemmed from Viennese cabaret music at the turn of the century (Ernst Hanfstaengl, *Unheard Witness* [New York: J. B. Lippin-cott, 1957], p. 156).

22. Hans Gisevius, a Gestapo employee, alleges that Wessel was a pimp who was killed by Aly Hoehler, also a pimp, in a quarrel over a prostitute (*To the Bitter End*, pp. 59–60). Ernst Roehm, the leader of the SA, had a circle of homosexuals around him, although several members of this group, considered perverts by the Nazis, were killed when the SA was purged in 1934. The Nazis were willing to exclude those who were politically reli-able, regardless of their past, from the asocial category, but expanded the definition of asocial to include a wide range of others who were deemed genetically unhealthy, socially inefficient, and politically or ideologically unreliable, or any persons viewed as alien to the German community (*Ge-meinschaftsfremde*). Three basic groups were considered as being outside the realm of the German community: the ideological enemies, such as the Communists, whose beliefs were considered a threat to national morale; the "asocials," who were socially inefficient and offended the norms of German society; and the biological misfits deemed threatening because of their race or some genetic defect (Jeremy Noakes, "Social Outcasts in the Third Reich," in Bessel, *Life in the Third Reich*, pp. 83–84). The draft of a

law introduced as the "Community Alien Law" declared that "a person is alien to the community if he/she proves to be incapable of satisfying the minimum requirements of the national community through his/her own efforts, in particular through an unusual degree of deficiency of mind or character" (Hanfstaengl, *Unheard Witness*, p. 81).

23. After 1933 the regular police rarely took part in such activities, having "virtually abdicated while retaining their nominal positions, and the various private armies brawled and killed at will, while they stood by" (Edward Crankshaw, *Gestapo, Instrument of Tyranny* [New York: Viking Press, 1957], pp. 43–44).

24. On 5 March 1933, the Nazis became the strongest party in Hamburg. Minister of the Interior Frick transferred control of the police to Standartenführer (Colonel) Richter of the SA. As a result, the apolitical police became highly politicized and "claimed the right to determine the nature of social relationships. . . . which led to new conceptions of police power that laid the basis for the police state" (Gerhard Rempel, *Hitler's Children: The Hitler Youth and the SS* [Chapel Hill: University of North Carolina, 1989], p. 47; Ditt, *Sozialdemokraten im Widerstand*, p. 35; see Joseph Schorer, *Als Hamburg unter den Nazis lebte: 152 wiederentdeckte Fotos eines Zeitzeugen* [Hamburg: Rasch u. Rohring, 1986], p. 17).

25. After 1933 the regular police took little, if any, part in the brutal activities of the Nazis on the streets of Germany, because the Nazis used the police for their own terroristic ends by transferring police functions to members of the Nazi party and the SA, the SS, and the Stahlhelm. Hermann Göring issued a directive to the police making them accomplices of the SA and SS, and telling them it was their duty "to avoid anything suggestive of hostility to the SA, SS and Stahlhelm" and that it was the "business of the police to abet any form of national propaganda" (cited in Crankshaw, *Gestapo*, pp. 47–48). By 22 February 1933 Göring added 50,000 auxiliary police to the regular forces merely by issuing armbands and weapons to members of the SA and SS, thus giving them complete police powers. Within eight months this merging of Nazi organizations with the police resulted in approximately 600 deaths and over 26,000 persons being incarcerated as "police prisoners" (Hoffmann, *History of the German Resistance*, pp. 9, 15).

26. Because a brown shirt was part of the uniform of the SA and other party branches, beginning in 1926, the term was often used in reference to members of the Nazi party.

27. For a German couple married between 1915 and 1920 with a husband employed as a nonagricultural worker in a city with a population exceeding 100,000, the average number of children per household was 2.18 (John E. Knodel, *The Decline of Fertility in Germany, 1871–1939* [Princeton: Princeton University Press, 1974], p. 218).

28. Of the structures constructed for housing in Germany in 1929, small apartments (one to three rooms including a kitchen) accounted for 53.7 percent of the buildings. Many apartments had a living area of 32 to 45 square meters, which provided only minimal comfort (Colin G. Pooley, ed., *Housing Strategies in Europe, 1880–1930* ([New York: Leicester University Press,

1992], p. 246). In 1940 the average number of persons in a dwelling in Germany was 3.5 and the number of rooms per person was 1.2 (Graham Hallett, *Housing and Land Policies in West Germany and Britain* [London: Macmillan Press, 1977], p. 11). Housing problems increased with the construction of the wrong type of apartments. Between 1933 and 1940 an increasing number of apartments were constructed so large that workers could not afford to pay the rent, which resulted in extensive overcrowding in smaller apartments. By the beginning of the war in 1939, one-third of the dwellings in Germany were substandard (Hilde Oppenheimer-Blum, *The Standard of Living of German Labour under Nazi Rule* [New York: New School for Social Research, 1943], p. 49, cited in Richard Grunberger, *A Social History of the Third Reich* [London: Weidenfeld and Nicolson, 1971], p. 217).

29. German fathers were traditionally strict, aloof and often cruel to their children. In the late nineteenth and early twentieth centuries, authoritarianism, strict obedience, and corporal punishment were considered an essential part of the education of German youth. See Aurel Ende, "Battering and Neglect: Children in Germany, 1860–1978," *Journal of Psychohistory* 7, no. 3 (1979–80): 252–53, 258; Antoine Prost and Gerard Vincent, eds., *A History of Private Life: Riddles of Identity in Modern Times* (Cambridge, Mass.: Harvard University Press, 1991), p. 523; Eda Sagarra, *A Social History of Germany 1648–1914* (New York: Holmes and Meier, 1977), pp. 98–99; and Alfons Heck, *The Burden of Hitler's Legacy* (Frederick, Colo.: Renaissance House, 1988), p. 52.

30. University-level education in Germany was "based on the assumption that students would be well-to-do" (Balfour, *Withstanding Hitler,* p. 23). There was no provision for adequate scholarships. Schnibbe, Hübener and others of their social cohort could not afford the tuition of the secondary schools. It was Hübener's "greatest desire to attend the university, but he knew it was unlikely he ever would." He told Wobbe that "you have to have a rich father to attend the higher institutions of learning, so that leaves me out of the running" (Wobbe and Borrowman, *Before the Blood Tribunal,* p. 17). In 1931 approximately 5 percent of the students in higher institutions of learning came from the working class (Bernd Zymek, "Schulen, Hochschulen, Lehrer," in Dieter Langewiesche and Heinz-Elmar Tenorth, eds., *Handbuch der deutschen Bildungsgeschichte,* vol. 5 [Munich: Verlag C. H. Beck, 1987], pp. 178–79). The middle class was so concerned that their children receive a higher education that the level of competition nearly excluded potential students from the lower class. A university education, which set a person apart from other Germans, was the ticket to higher social status and potential affluence. On 25 April 1933, the Nazi regime issued the "Law against the Overcrowding of German Schools and High Schools," which limited to 15,000 the number of new students who could enroll each year in a high school (Hans-Georg Herrlitz et al., eds., *Deutsche Schulgeschichte von 1800 bis zur Gegenwart* [Königstein: Athenäum, 1981], pp. 145–48). In 1939 there were only 40,645 university students in Germany (Michael Steinberg, *Sabers and Brown Shirts: The German Students' Path to National Socialism, 1918–1935* [Chicago: University of Chicago Press, 1977], pp. 21–24).

31. The *Realgymnasium* was a secondary school requiring a mixture of a strong, traditional, classical education and a scientific/technical curriculum (excluding Greek and including Latin, calculus, physics, and chemistry) preparatory to entering the university. By 1936 it had become the predominant school of its type (Detlef K. Müller et al., *The Rise of the Modern Educational System: Structural Change and Social Reproduction 1870–1920* [New York: Cambridge University Press, 1987], pp. 45–51). The development and diversity of *Gymnasien*, however, did not change the fact that completion of the classical *Gymnasium* was still the most common route to enter the university (Steinberg, *Sabers and Brown Shirts*, p. 22).

32. On 9 May 1933, the curriculum was changed to incorporate four basic principles: (1) "the German school must form political man"; (2) historical instruction must emphasize events after 1914; (3) the students' "vision of racial differences must be sharpened"; (4) greater emphasis was to be placed on physical fitness (cited in Hans A. Schmitt, *Lucky Victim: An Ordinary Life in Extraordinary Times 1933–1946* [Baton Rouge: Louisiana State University Press, 1989], pp. 54–55).

33. Not all German schools prior to the Nazi era offered or required courses in religion (Inge Deutschkron, *Outcast: A Jewish Girl in Wartime Berlin* [New York: Fromm International, 1989], p. 2). In 1936, for schools which had religious instruction as an integral part of the curriculum, the time allotted to physical training increased from two to three periods per week and increased again in 1938 to five periods per week at the expense of religious instruction. After 1934 religion was no longer a subject required for graduation and attendance at school prayers became optional (Grunberger, *Social History of the Third Reich*, pp. 288–89). Religious denominational schools were abolished in 1936. Protestants and Catholics were permitted to have religious instruction by a clergyman of their own faith once a week. Church holidays which fell during the week were no longer celebrated and special prayers were banned. In 1938 all teachers were required to resign from any professional religious organizations to which they might belong (H. W. Koch, *The Hitler Youth: Origins and Development, 1922–45* [London: MacDonald and Jane's, 1975], pp. 172–73). Physical education preempted other subjects. At least four hours during each week and three weekends each month were dedicated to athletic activities, maneuvers, target shooting, and hiking (Rempel, *Hitler's Children*, p. 179). Excellent performances on the sports field could compensate for poor academic marks in major subjects (Marianne Mackinnon, *The Naked Years: Growing Up in Nazi Germany* [London: Chatto and Windus, 1987], p. 123). As a result of the increase of Nazi youth groups' activities, which were considered a valid substitute for scholastic activities, the curriculum was often upset or altered "and made us limp or skip through our studies. . . . Many dedicated teachers boldly confessed displeasure at having to sacrifice academic standards on the altar of the war" (Mackinnon, ibid., p. 63). Children of high-ranking Nazi party of military officials were permitted to graduate despite a "lackluster performance." (Deutschkron, ibid., p. 22; see also the Directive of the Minister of Science, Culture, and Education cited in Fricke-Finkelnburg, *Nazionalsozialismus und Schule*, pp. 241–42).

34. Gunter Otto concluded that the spectrum of political beliefs of his teachers ran from Prussian-Conservative to Social Democratic, but few of his instructors were tied to any political party or active therein. "I became acquainted with only a few of my teachers whose political positions were recognizable" ("Es war alles so normal—und doch ganz anders," cited in Wolfgang Klafki, ed., *Verführung, Distanzierung, Ernüchterung. Kindheit und Jugend im Nationalsozialismus. Autobiographisches aus erziehungs-wissenschaftlicher Sicht* [Weinheim: Beltz Verlag, 1988], p. 147).

35. When the Nazis came to power, few students or teachers gave the Hitler salute. On 22 July 1933, the Minister of Science, Culture, and Education decreed that the "German Greeting" (Hitler salute) was mandatory in all secular schools ("Nach dem 30. Januar 1933: . . . schon bald im braunen Hemd dabei," in Harald Focke, ed., *Alltag unterm Hakenkreuz. Wie die Nazis das Leben der Deutschen veränderten* [Hamburg: Rowholt, 1979], p. 15, cited in Renate Fricke-Finkelnburg, *Nationalsozialismus und Schule. Amtliche Erlasse un Richtlinien 1933–1945* [Opladen: Leske u. Budrich, 1989], p. 226). Students were to rise and stand at attention when their teacher entered the room and raise their arms in the Nazi salute until the "person of authority" returned the salute and gave them permission to be seated (Schmitt, *Lucky Victim*, p. 59). After 20 July 1944 all civil and military authorities or employees were required to use the Hitler salute during the course of their duties and whenever on the grounds of their place of employment, whereas prior to that time only the SS was obligated to give the Hitler salute.

36. Members of the Nazi party generally wore their party badges on their lapels. It was common for members of the Nazi Party who were teachers and for Hitler Youth to wear their uniforms to school (Andreas Meyer-Landruth, "A Pole Was Hanged in the Marketplace," in Steinhoff, *Voices from the Third Reich*, p. 103).

37. The Golden Party Badge, also known as the Party Golden Badge of Honor, was the highest Nazi party order after the Blood Order and was awarded personally by Hitler to fewer than 100,000 party comrades, "those who have particularly distinguished themselves in the National Socialist movement and the attainment of its goals" (Louis L. Snyder, *Encyclopedia of the Third Reich* [New York: McGraw-Hill, 1976], p. 124; Zentner and Bedürftig, *Encyclopedia of the Third Reich*, 1:352).

38. Klaus Granzow's teacher in German was a female member of the Nazi party, who required her students to study and memorize poetry dealing with military subjects, particularly wars and victories (*Tagebuch eines Hitlerjungen 1943–1945* [Bremen: Carl Schünemann Verlag, 1965], p. 18).

39. For thousands of lower-level civil servants, teachers, and others, a commission in the Wehrmacht was often a shortcut to greatly enhanced social status and advancement (Grunberger, *Social History of the Third Reich*, p. 36).

40. Blumenau was one of the most well known and successful German colonies in Brazil. Founded in southern Brazil in 1850, it retained its German character longer than most other German colonies in South America (Frederick C. Luebke, *Germans in Brazil: A Comparative History of Cultural*

Conflict during World War I [Baton Rouge: Louisiana State University Press, 1987], p. 22).

41. "Sieg Heil" means, literally, "Hail Victory." The term was used as a cheer at Nazi meetings.

42. The march commemorated the capture of the French town of Badonviller on 12 August 1914. According to a police ordinance of 17 May 1939, the march was to be played publicly only in Hitler's presence (*Amtliche Mitteilungen der Reichsmusikkammer*, 12 Jan. 1938, p. 79, cited in Joseph Wulf, *Musik im Dritten Reich. Eine Dokumentation* [Hamburg: Rowohlt, 1966], pp. 134–35). When a group of German prisoners of war were finally being released in the autumn of 1955 to return to Germany, they were asked to give the Russian band a request for some music. The prisoners selected the Badenweiler march, "and the Russians actually played it" (Heinz Pfennig, "A Half-Loaf of Bread—What More Could My Heart Desire?" in Steinhoff, *Voices from the Third Reich*, p. 158). See also Zentner and Bedürftig, *Encyclopedia of the Third Reich*, 1:62; Germany, Ministry of the Interior, *Reichsgesetzblatt* (22 May 1939), 1:234.

43. The Horst Wessel song was, in essence, a second national anthem (Jochen von Lang, *Adolf Hitler: Faces of a Dictator* [New York: Harcourt, Brace and World, 1968], p. xvi).

44. Because of the length of the songs, younger students often lacked the strength to maintain the Hitler salute, so that by the beginning of the Horst Wessel song, at the latest, their "less trained arms fell asleep and noticeably began to sag" (Hans Scheuerl, "Eindrücke und Erfahrungen aus bewegter Zeit," in Klafki, *Verführung, Distanzierung, Ernüchterung*, p. 67).

45. Denunciation by students was certainly possible. An inadvertent word or negative comments about a speech by a public figure or some writing in the Nazi press could be construed as political opposition. Because of their membership in Nazi organizations, students used their misperceived political superiority to control teachers. Erich Dressler recalled that "the teachers had no understanding of the Führer's slogans such as 'The education of the character is more important than the education of the intellect.' They drilled us with Latin and Greek, rather than teach us things that we could use later. We decided not to let ourselves be influenced by their outmoded views, and said that to their faces. If our Latin teacher gave us an endless section of Caesar, we simply did not translate it and excused ourselves on the grounds that we had had service in the Hitler Youth during the afternoon. Once one of the old fogies gathered his courage and protested about it. He was reported immediately to the Group Leader, who went directly to the principal and saw to it that this teacher was dismissed. From that day on the question of homework was clear. If we were not in the mood, then we had been 'in service' and no one dared to say anything against it" (Grunberger, *Social History of the Third Reich*, p. 286, cited in Focke, *Alltag unterm Hakenkreuz*, pp. 87–88).

46. Because the Nazi regime was unable to produce enough "political teachers," the political education was frequently left to the traditional teachers, most of whom were nationalistic, but rarely enthusiastic Nazis. What

political discussion there was was short and superficial before attention was turned to the topics in which the teachers were interested and in which they had been trained in the pre-Nazi era (H. W. Koch, *Hitler Youth*, p. 174). The majority of non-Nazi teachers went through the motions of giving the Hitler salute upon entering the classroom, as required by law, but it was often done in a mechanical way and, sometimes, in a derisive manner (Reinhold Pabel, *Enemies Are Human* [Philadelphia: John C. Winston, 1955], p. 16).

47. Social Democratic teachers were required to declare formally their departure from the Social Democratic party or relinquish their pensions (Ditt, *Sozialdemokraten im Widerstand*, p. 72). Teachers who had not displayed political sympathies previously were inclined to support the Nazi bid for power in the hope that their salaries would improve. Between 1 September 1930 and 31 March 1933 the average drop of teachers' salaries was 30 percent (Herrlitz, *Deutsche Schulgeschichte*, p. 133).

48. On 7 April 1933, the Nazi government issued the "Law for the Reorganization of the Civil Service" which removed opposition in administrative positions. Employment was terminated for those whose "political activities did not guarantee" that they would defend the National Socialist state (Deutschkron, *Outcast*, pp. 12, 23–24). Those of non-Aryan descent who had not served in World War I were to be dismissed and their children were not permitted to attend secular schools. Approximately 4 percent of the civil servants were dismissed immediately or pensioned, because of political reasons. Teachers and policemen comprised the largest groups to be removed (Ditt, *Sozialdemokraten im Widerstand*, p. 47). By 1935 15 percent of the female teachers in girls' secondary schools had been dismissed, as had all Jewish teachers in public schools (Grunberger, *Social History of the Third Reich*, p. 260).

49. By 1936 all primary and secondary school teachers had joined the Nazi party or the National Socialist Teachers' League, and were "persuaded to exert pressure on their pupils to join the *Jungvolk*" (H. W. Koch, *Hitler Youth*, p. 112). By 1937 63 percent of the civil servants were members of the Nazi party, whereas only 11 percent had been members in 1933 (Marlis G. Steinert, *Hitler's War and the Germans: Public Mood and Attitude during the Second World War* [Athens: Ohio University Press, 1977], pp. 29–30). Between 1933 and 1935, 637 teachers in Hamburg were dismissed (Focke, *Alltag unterm Hakenkreuz*, p. 84). Hitler had stated that "the youth who does nothing but study philosophy, who keeps his nose in a book . . . is no German youth" (*Völkischer Beobachter*, 16 Aug. 1922, cited in Prange, *Hitler's Words*, p. 121).

50. During the Nazi era it became a regular practice in considering teaching appointments to give credit for participation in Nazi party activities. In some cases this meant the waiving of professional examinations (H. W. Koch, *Hitler Youth*, p. 172). The shortage of teachers was increased due to the movement of teachers into other branches of education, the Nazi party, or the Wehrmacht. In 1938 the entrance requirements for training as elementary teachers were lowered (Grunberger, *Social History of the Third Reich*, pp. 293–94).

51. One of the most popular and widely recognized songs of the Hitler Youth, the song was written by a person who was a member of the Catholic Youth Movement. The final phrase was often sung enthusiastically, defiantly, and falsely, inserting the word *gehört* ('is ours, belongs to us') instead of *hört* ('hears'), as: "Denn heute gehört uns Deutschland; und morgen die ganze Welt" ("Today Germany is ours and tomorrow the entire world will be ours") (H. W. Koch, *Hitler Youth*, p. 88). It was "an example of unofficial indoctrination of children and teenagers with plans for global conquest" (Schumann, *Being Present*, p. 26).

52. Martin Koller remembered vividly when his father brought a radio home and "at once the world barged into our living room." On the "Day of Potsdam" (5 Mar. 1933), when the ceremonial opening of the Reichstag occurred, all of the ceremonies and speeches were broadcast to the German people, who were amazed and gratified that the new technology of radio permitted them to "take part in what was happening in the world," or so they thought (Martin Koller, "The Combat Soldier Was an Ideological Symbol for Us," in Steinhoff, *Voices from the Third Reich*, p. xxxvii; see also Zentner and Bedürftig, *Encyclopedia of the Third Reich*, 2:723–24).

53. The influence of martial music was a calculated part of the Nazi propaganda to enthuse and intoxicate the German people, especially the young, with its hypnotizing nature. See Schumann, *Being Present*, p. 25; Focke, *Alltag unterm Hakenkreuz*, p. 14.

54. Hans Zmarzlik recalled that "the 'disgraceful dictation of Versailles' was impressed upon us in the school. Now . . . things went forwards and we were the 'Guarantee of the Future.' That meant little, because family and school were still decisive, but the staggering self-confidence of adolescence came in handy to devaluate the resistance of our elders as blindness regarding the new age. Our loyalty to Hitler's state was thereby strengthened involuntarily" (cited in Focke, *Alltag unterm Hakenkreuz*, p. 15).

55. The Thaliatheater was one of Hamburg's three major centers of drama. Like the Schauspielhaus, it was more traditional and conservative, although producing modern works on occasion (Werner Jochmann, ed., *Hamburg. Geschichte der Stadt und ihrer Bewohner* [Hamburg: Hoffmann u. Campe, 1986], 2:233–34).

56. Of particular importance for the German youth, from the perspective of the Nazi party, were the Wednesday night home evening broadcasts which started at 8:00 and lasted an hour. All German youths were supposed to listen to special educational programs. Other broadcasts for the youth prepared by the Hitler Youth and sponsored by the propaganda service were presented throughout the week (H. W. Koch, *Hitler Youth*, pp. 127–28).

57. This radio was designed and built in 1933 on the request of the Propaganda Ministry, and received only medium wavelengths, so foreign broadcasts could scarcely be heard, usually only in border areas (Else R. Behrend-Rosenfeld, *Ich stand nicht allein. Erlebnisse einer Jüdin in Deutschland, 1933–1944* [Frankfurt am Main: Europäische Verlagsanstalt, 1963], p. 235). The low price of the radio (35 marks) made it accessible to most Germans, and permitted the Propaganda Ministry to influence the thinking of the German people by

providing carefully edited news reports (Zentner and Bedürftig, *Encyclopedia of the Third Reich*, 2:1004). "Millions of listeners could be constantly exposed to the incessant series of mass rallies, parades, harvest festivals, opening cere-monies, memorial day celebrations, state funerals and, above all, Hitler's speeches" (Schumann, *Being Present*, p. 42).

58. Jews were eventually forbidden to possess a radio or telephone or to go outside after 7:30 P.M. (Mathilde Wolff-Mönckeberg, *On the Other Side: To My Children: From Germany 1940–1945* [London: Peter Owen, 1979], p. 33). This restricted greatly their cultural relaxation and intellectual stimu-lation (Behrend-Rosenfeld, *Ich stand nicht allein*, p. 74).

59. On 15 January 1942 Hitler ordered that only Göring, Foreign Min-ister Ribbentrop, Field Marshal Keitel, Postal Minister Wilhelm Ohnesorge, Interior Minister Wilhelm Frick, head of the Reich Chancellery Hans Lam-mers, and Goebbels were permitted to listen to foreign broadcasts. All oth-er ministers required permission from the Führer, while those with permis-sion could extend the right to listen to a few persons in their own areas of responsibility. On 11 February Goebbels noted in his diary that it was "ter-rible how many prominent persons are now trying to prove to me that they cannot continue their work without permission to tune in foreign stations" (Louis P. Lochner, ed., *The Goebbels Diaries 1942–1943* [Westport, Conn.: Greenwood Press, 1970], p. 80, cited in Steinert, *Hitler's War*, p. 153; see also Dieter Borkowski, *Wer weiß, ob wir uns wiedersehen. Erinnerungen an eine Berliner Jugend* [Frankfurt am Main: Fischer, 1983], p. 116).

60. Goebbels justified issuing the "Extraordinary Radio Measures" by claiming that the home front needed to be protected from lies and propa-ganda to avoid the collapse at home and the alleged "stab in the back" Ger-many experienced during World War I (Robert Gellately, *The Gestapo and German Society: Enforcing Racial Policy, 1933–1945* [Oxford: Clarendon Press, 1990], pp. 140–41). Hitler feared greatly that informing the German popu-lace of defeats or permitting any kind of enemy propaganda to be heard would have devastating effects (Steinert, *Hitler's War*, p. 2).

61. Field Marshal Wilhelm Keitel, the head of the Oberkommando der Wehrmacht (Wehrmacht High Command), was part of the Führer's inner circle of military planners and the link between the military and the politi-cal leaders. He coined the descriptive phrase of the Führer as "the greatest commander in chief of all time," which was shortened to the acronymn *Gröfaz* (*Größter Feldherr aller Zeiten*). The acronym was a source of ridicule due to its resemblance to the slang word *Fatzke*, which meant "fop, dandy." *Gröfaz* gained in popularity, but could get a person who used it uncautious-ly into trouble (Schumann, *Being Present*, p. 71). Keitel's reward for devel-oping such a term was being referred to by his fellow officers with the mock-ing title *Lakaitel*, meaning "lackey" (*Lakai*) (Zentner and Bedürftig, *Encyclopedia of the Third Reich*, 1:493).

62. Daniel Gottlob Moritz Schreber (1808–61) was also an advocate of public health, gymnastics, and children's playgrounds (*Brockhaus Enzyklopädie* [Wiesbaden: F. A. Brockhaus, 1973], 17:10).

63. In 1919 Hamburg had a population of 900,000, which grew during

the 1920s to 1.2 million. In 1937 the "Greater Hamburg Law" allowed for the incorporation of several nearby cities into Hamburg, raising the population to 1.8 million. As a result of the extensive bombing in Hamburg during World War II, the population in 1943 decreased to one million (David Rodnick, *A Portrait of Two German Cities: Lübeck and Hamburg* [Lubbock, Tex.: Caprock Press, 1980], p. 207). Four of the five Mormon meeting houses were destroyed during the bombing raids, and thirty members of the church were killed in a single night (Scharffs, *Mormonism in Germany*, p. 105).

64. Rote Grütze is a jelly made of red currant or raspberry juice and thickened with corn starch, eaten in a bowl with milk.

65. In that era, missionary service usually lasted two and one-half years.

66. In 1930, 152 of a total of 290 Mormon missionaries in Germany were natives. Most of the native Germans, however, were not full-time missionaries but served on a part-time basis only (Scharffs, *Mormonism in Germany*, p. 84).

67. In the decade preceding the Nazi takeover, 2,683 German-speaking members of the LDS Church emigrated, mostly to Utah. During the period of Nazi rule prior to World War II, only ninety-one persons emigrated, partly due to the church's discouragement of further emigration. No records of emigration were maintained during the war. Following the war, there was a steady increase of German emigrants ranging from 9 in 1946 to 710 in 1958, with a total of 4,492 from 1946 to the end of 1958 (Douglas D. Alder, "German-Speaking Immigration to Utah, 1850–1950" [M.A. thesis, University of Utah, 1959], pp. 122–23).

68. Between 1929 and 1933, as the per capita consumption of beer consumed in Germany decreased by 43 percent, the social functions of some bars changed from neighborhood hangouts to Nazi "haunts." The SA approached failing or new bar owners in working-class districts with a guarantee of sales in exchange for using the premises as political stations. Such SA-occupied bars became targets of attacks by the local Communists and Social Democratic activists (Eva Rosenhaft, "The Unemployed in the Neighbourhood: Social Dislocation and Political Mobilisation in Germany 1929–33," in Richard J. Evans and Dick Geary, eds., *The German Unemployed: Experiences and Consequences of Mass Unemployment from the Weimar Republic to the Third Reich* [London: Croom Helm, 1987], pp. 208–9).

69. Because the LDS Church has a lay ministry, all males above the age of twelve have the possibility of holding a priesthood office. Males under the age of twenty-one held offices in the Aaronic or lower priesthood. The higher or Melchizedek priesthood offices were for adults, the first office being that of Elder.

70. In the LDS Church, "the sacrament" is the term used for the equivalent of communion or the eucharist.

71. LDS Church members were encouraged to abstain from eating for a 24-hour period once a month and donate the savings realized therefrom to the poor.

72. Male members of the LDS Church above the age of twelve were assigned to visit members of the congregation on a monthly basis to determine their welfare and needs.

73. Helmuth Kunkel, as he was known at the time, joined the LDS Church on 27 May 1933. Helmuth was known also by the surname Guddat, his mother's maiden name. He did not receive the surname Hübener until his mother married Hugo Hübener in 1941. Rudi Wobbe and his mother joined the LDS Church in June 1935, three months after the death of Rudi's father (Wobbe and Borrowman, *Before the Blood Tribunal*, p. 6).

74. By donning a uniform, the wearer shed his personal and civilian identity and was obligated to take orders, sometimes from his social inferiors, which distanced the individual from his social bearings. Wearing a uniform also made a person feel part of and be more aware of the vast power of the German Reich. Nazi functionaries with executive responsibilities were considered "bearers of sovereignty" (*Hoheitsträger*) (Grunberger, *Social History of the Third Reich*, p. 77).

75. The SS (Schutzstaffeln or guard echelons) were originally the black-shirted personal guards of Hitler and were later transformed into a mass army on which rested the ultimate exercise of Nazi power. The SS served as political police and were assigned the duty of administering the concentration and extermination camps (Snyder, *Encyclopedia of the Third Reich*, pp. 329–30). The SS were, essentially, a police organization dedicated to maintaining the principles of National Socialism and were described as "the elite formed of the most savage daredevils. . . . thugs . . . paid somewhat better for the effectiveness of their fists and the toughness of their consciences" (Gisevius, *To the Bitter End*, p. 66).

76. The early Deathhead SS units were recruited from the toughest SS formations and served as concentration camp guards. At the outbreak of war, some of the units were released from concentration camp service and provided the nucleus for the SS Panzer divisions. They became infamous for their fanaticism during combat and commission of horrible war crimes (Snyder, *Encyclopedia of the Third Reich*, p. 330; Zentner and Bedürftig, *Encyclopedia of the Third Reich*, 1:184).

77. One of the methods used to assure the allegiance of Nazi followers was to involve them in committing "punishable acts in order to keep them under complete control." Squeamish or unreliable members who participated in crime were thus bound more firmly to the party's organizations, especially the SA and SS (Rauschning, *Hitler Speaks*, p. 99).

78. From 1930 until the autumn of 1932, one-third of the German workers had become unemployed and the weekly earnings of those still employed had dropped 33 percent (Oppenheimer-Blum, *Standard of Living*, p. 15, cited in Grunberger, *Social History of the Third Reich*, p. 186).

79. The rate of unemployment in Hamburg was greater than in the Reich as a whole and comparable to the unemployment rates in other large cities. At the end of 1932 Hamburg had an unemployment rate of 28 percent. The age group from 20 to 59 made up 88.5 percent of the unemployed. By June 1933 Hamburg's unemployment was 30.02 percent. By the end of 1936, Germany had achieved *full* employment (Elizabeth Harvey, "Youth Unemployment and the State: Public Policies towards Unemployed Youth in Hamburg during the World Economic Crisis," in Evans and

Geary, *German Unemployed*, p. 143; Detlev Peukert, "The Lost Generation: Youth Unemployment at the End of the Weimar Republic," in Evans and Geary, ibid., p. 176; Anthony McElligott, "Mobilising the Unemployed: The KPD and the Unemployed Workers' Movement in Hamburg-Altona during the Weimar Republic," in Evans and Geary, ibid., p. 236; Wolfram Fischer, *Deutsche Wirtschaftspolitik, 1918–1945*, 3d ed. [Opladen: C.W. Leske, 1968], p. 108).

80. "Most modern studies . . . continue . . . to describe the liquidation of unemployment as . . . a marginal benefit of rearmament" (Avraham Barkai, *Nazi Economics: Ideology, Theory and Policy* [New Haven: Yale University Press, 1990], pp. 5, 196). One of the earliest successes of the Nazi regime was to create the perception that conditions were improving, when such might not have been the case. "The regime managed to generate an atmosphere in which propaganda and auto-suggestion transformed people's appraisal of their own concrete situation" (Grunberger, *Social History of the Third Reich*, pp. 203–4). The percentage of national income spent on wages between 1932 and 1936 dropped from 64 percent to 59 percent.

81. After 1930 until the Nazi takeover, the National Socialist vote in elections in Hamburg was usually 4 to 6 percent lower than the NSDAP votes elsewhere in Germany (Ditt, *Sozialdemokraten im Widerstand*, p. 19).

82. Gestapo is the shortened version of *Geheime Staatspolizei* (secret state police), an organization that became the "key link in the terror system and police state, and attained a reputation for ruthlessness and cruelty, so that the very mention of the name filled the hearts of contemporaries with dread and foreboding." The Gestapo is still recognized as representing the worst aspect of the Nazi regime for the German citizens due to its extralegal and arbitrary nature regarding arrest, detention, and torture (Gellately, *Gestapo and German Society*, p. 3).

83. Members of the Communist and Social Democratic parties immediately suffered the consequences of the Nazi takeover. The courts accepted the judgments of the Nazi jurists that political opponents of the Third Reich could not be shown mercy or granted privileges. Instead, they were to be considered "the most vicious of criminals." In July 1935, 150 Social Democrats in Hamburg were brought to trial simultaneously. A Communist conference in October 1935 calculated that in Germany 393 party members had been murdered, 21 sentenced to death, 21 given life imprisonment, and 860 given prison sentences totaling 3980 years (Ingo Müller, *Hitler's Justice: The Courts of the Third Reich* [Cambridge, Mass.: Harvard University Press, 1991], pp. 53–56). By 1936 nearly all of the 60,000 "real cadre of Germany's communists" were dead, in exile, or in concentration camps. The Nazis viewed the Communist party as a greater threat than the SPD, so concentrated first on ridding Germany of communists (William Allen, "Social Democratic Resistance against Hitler and the European Tradition of Underground Movements," in Francis R. Nicosia and Lawrence D. Stokes, eds., *Germans against Nazism: Noncomformity, Opposition and Resistance in the Third Reich* [New York: St. Martin's Press, 1990], p. 193).

84. The Rote Hilfe was closely aligned with the KPD (Communist Par-

ty of Germany), but not all who supported it were Communists (Hans-Günter Richardi, "Der gerade Weg. Der Dachauer Häftling Karl Wagner," in *Solidarität und Widerstand, Dachauer Hefte. Studien und Dokumente zur Geschichte der nationalsozialistischen Konzentrationslager* 7 [Nov. 1991]: 55). Rather, "a large portion of the leftist, pacifist citizenry" adopted the "benign political attitude" of the Rote Hilfe, whose primary purpose was to support political prisoners, not all of whom were members of the Communist party (Dieter Fricke et al., eds., *Lexikon zur Parteiengeschichte,* 4 vols. [Cologne: Pahl-Rugenstein, 1983], 1:752, 3:134).

85. Between 6 March and 30 July 1933, the Nazis conducted 850 raids in Hamburg and arrested 2,000 persons, mostly Communists and Social Democrats (Ditt, *Sozialdemokraten im Widerstand,* p. 46). By the end of the summer of 1933 it was estimated that 100,000 persons, mostly political opponents of the Nazis, had been deprived of their freedom and 500 to 600 had been killed. The SA was the organization most involved in the arrests and bloodshed, and established at least thirty "wild" concentration camps in Germany for the "enemies of the state" (Gellately, *Gestapo and German Society,* p. 40).

86. In the LDS Church, the term "brethren" refers to the authorities on the various levels and has a positive connotation. In reference to Nazi leaders, the term is negative and is equated with swine, bastards, and so on.

87. The acronym *Kolafu* stems from the German words *K*onzentrations *Lager Fu*hlsbüttel (Concentration Camp Fuhlsbüttel).

88. While many Germans knew little or nothing of camps such as Auschwitz, a great number of them knew there were concentration camps, which was a "particularly severe form of punishment [with] thrashings, poor food, hard labor and persecution." It was not uncommon to hear threats such as "You belong in a concencration camp" or "I'll send you to a concentration camp." The earlier form of the term "KL (*Konzentrations Lager*)" was changed by the German state to "KZ" because it had a harsher, thus better, sound (Jürgen Henningsen, "Vielleicht bin ich heute noch ein Nazi," in Klafki, *Verführung, Distanzierung, Ernüchterung,* p. 215).

89. When it came to singing, the Nazis and Hitler Youth were not above adopting popular songs from other organizations, including the Communists, which were "borrowed" because of their rousing nature and emotional appeal. Walter Flex's "Wildgänse rauschen durch die Nacht," for example, was a song stemming from the Great War. In some cases new lyrics were added to familiar tunes. Few of the songs sung originated with the Hitler Youth. Far more were taken from the pre-1914 youth movement, which in turn had derived its songs from traditional German folklore (H. W. Koch, *Hitler Youth,* pp. 40, 68, 134–35).

90. The "Engeland Lied" or "Song of England" was a patriotic drinking song from World War I which included the refrain "For we are sailing against England," Germany's great naval opponent (Schumann, *Being Present,* p. 53). A popular youth board game, the purpose of which was to see who could sink the most British warships, was entitled "We sail against England" (Focke, *Alltag unterm Hakenkreuz,* p. 47).

91. German boys who lived in port cities developed a mania for collecting ships made of lead, which were exact replicas of German merchant marine and naval vessels, as well as famous foreign ships. The prices were exorbitant, but the models were so highly desired that young men saved their money diligently to acquire more ships, or asked for them as gifts at Christmas and on birthdays. Young boys spent long hours reenacting famous naval battles with their accumulated fleets (Schumann, *Being Present*, p. 51; Granzow, *Tagebuch eines Hitlerjungen*, p. 11).

92. Frederick II, king of Prussia (1740–86), was referred to affectionately as "Old Fritz" because his military successes made Prussia into one of Europe's great powers (Schumann, *Being Present*, p. 10).

93. The Battle of Leuthen occurred on 5 December 1757 and resulted in Frederick inflicting a smashing defeat upon the Austrian forces.

94. Hermann Rauschning claimed that Frederick was the posthumous "forerunner" and "venerated hero and model" for Hitler, who, when he had completed successfully his political struggles, was going to rebuild Germany and fulfill his dream of emulating the Prussian king with his "work of the creative statesman and legislator, the pioneer artist and city builder, the prophet and founder of a religion" (*Hitler Speaks*, pp. 246, 258).

95. Films praising Frederick II and Bismarck and emphasizing militaristic virtues were common during the Weimar and Nazi periods (Julian Petley, *Capital and Culture: German Cinema 1933–45* [London: British Film Institute, 1979], pp. 7, 99, 106). Approximately 1,150 films were produced during the Nazi era, of which one-sixth could be classified as straight political propaganda. However, every film had an educational and political function. The goal of the films was, according to Goebbels, "to educate without revealing the purpose of the education, so that one fulfils an educational function without the object of that education being in any way aware that it is being educated, which is also indeed the real purpose of propaganda" (Erwin Leiser, *Nazi Cinema* [London: Secker and Warburg, 1974], pp. 12, 124). Because their intent was propagandistic, such films were certainly not always historically accurate (Borkowski, *Wer weiß, ob wir uns wiedersehen*, pp. 112–13). See also Horst Rumpf, "Geboren 1930, zwischen Formeln groß geworden. Einige Schritte zur Selbstverständigung," in Klafki, *Verführung, Distanzierung, Ernüchterung*, p. 249; and Hanfstaengl, *Unheard Witness*, p. 83.

96. The admiration for Frederick II had risen greatly since the Prussian unification of Germany and the creation of the German Empire. Prior to 1933 great numbers of books written for youth praised the possession and development of the Prussian traits of order, sacrifice, and obedience. The Nazis played upon these traits and attempted to tie them to the concept of the superior race. Hitler read voraciously about Frederick and Napoleon to draw parallels for his developing policies concerning Germany and a future war. Frederick was Hitler's hero and he quoted extensively from the king's successes in building Prussia in the face of great odds. Frederick, however, knew when to quit. Hitler, upon transferring his allegiance to Napoleon, imitated that military leader's policy of not knowing when to stop, a situa-

tion which had disastrous consequences for Germany (H. W. Koch, *Hitler Youth*, p. 146; Hanfstaengl, *Unheard Witness*, p. 41).

97. Klaus Granzow recalled one of his school teachers, who was a Nazi party member, requiring the students, as punishment for their misdeeds, to copy the biography of Frederick the Great ten times with an emphasis on the military campaigns (*Tagebuch eines Hitlerjungen*, p. 37). Perhaps the most popular reading material for young men, instead of comic books, were dime novels (*Groschenhefte*) of war experiences such as the exploits of Guderian, Rommel, or Günther Prien. Each week a new story appeared (Focke, *Alltag unterm Hakenkreuz*, p. 51).

98. Upon their seizure of power, the Nazis systematically destroyed the traditional German values of justice and order and replaced them with a system based on violence. The dominant trait of the Nazi leaders was violence and those persons soon rose to the top who were the most violent. Once the Nazis were established in power, members of the SA wanted to continue the "revolution" and did so by seeking out "enemies of the state." The definition of "enemy of the state" was broadened to include any person against whom a storm trooper held a grudge. "People who had never harmed anyone were horribly abused. Innocents who had been picked up by chance were beaten half to death" (Gisevius, *To the Bitter End*, pp. 100–104). By July 1933 the leader of the SA, Ernst Röhm, was alarmed enough by the level of violence that he condemned publicly "the settling of personal scores, unacceptable brutality, robbery, theft and looting" by storm troopers (cited in Fischer, *Deutsche Wirtschaftspolitik*, p. 197).

99. A division of the Hitler Youth for boys between the ages of ten and fourteen. At the age of fourteen, boys entered the Hitler Youth and remained until the age of eighteen. For girls between ten and fourteen, there was the Jungmädelbund (League of Young Girls) and from fourteen to eighteen the Bund deutscher Mädel (League of German Girls). In Wobbe's case, the Nazis set up a table in front of each class in his school and required each child in turn to pass in front of the table, where they were asked questions about their parents and involvement in the Nazi youth programs. When Wobbe said that he did not have the ten Pfennig to join, he was informed that it did not matter and that he was from then on a member of the Young Folk and was expected to report for service the next Sunday (Wobbe and Borrowman, *Before the Blood Tribunal*, p. 7).

100. As of 1 December 1936, all German youths were required to join the Hitler Youth or the League of German Girls.

101. At the end of 1932 the Hitler Youth claimed 107,956 members. With the Nazi takeover of power the ranks increased drastically. Besides the addition of youth organizations formerly associated with political parties, twenty youth leagues dissolved themselves and joined the Hitler Youth, increasing the membership to 3,577,565 at the end of 1933. The annexation of Austria and the Sudetenland saw the membership surge to 8.7 million, nearly half of whom were girls, by the end of 1938 (H. W. Koch, *Hitler Youth*, pp. 101, 113).

102. This was a common euphemism for Hitler, who was born in Brau-

nau, Upper Austria, on 20 April 1889. Hitler was also referred to as the Pied Piper of Braunau.

103. The initiation test of a Cub, after which he received his dagger, consisted of repeating synopses of Nazi dogma, the verses of the Horst Wessel song, map reading, and participation in the mock war games and collection drives for waste paper, scrap metal, glass, and so on. New Cubs were expected to be able to run 60 meters within twelve seconds, jump a distance of 2.75 meters, put the shot, and participate in a cross-country march lasting a day and a half. The method of teaching the songs left a permanent impression on the youngsters. "The leader recited the words of a song to a group of 30 Young Folk, who were then encouraged to repeat the words for hours until the song sunk in. . . . No poem learned in school made such an impression" (Rumpf in Klafki, *Verführung, Distanzierung, Ernüchterung*, p. 231). See also Werner Klose, *Generation im Gleichschritt. Ein Dokumentarbericht* (Oldenburg: Stalling, 1964), p. 100, cited in Grunberger, *Social History of the Third Reich*, p. 277.

104. Below the national level, the Hitler Youth was organized into five regional *Obergebiete*. In 1935 the *Obergebeitsführer* of the Hitler Youth, Helmut Stellrecht, remarked "that it is a remarkable attitude for a nation to spend, out of a number of years, hours in perfecting handwriting and spelling, when not a single hour is available for shooting." Thereafter, the Hitler Youth undertook to make the rifle an integral part of the education of its male members with the expectation that they would serve as soldiers at some future date. By 1937 a rifle school had been created and by 1938 1.5 million members of the Hitler Youth were trained in shooting, with the military playing an increasing role in supervising the field activities of the Hitler Youth (H. W. Koch, *Hitler Youth*, pp. 113–14).

105. In spite of the close supervision of the Nazi youth groups, there were fatal accidents. Between 1 April 1933 and 1 August 1939 there were 649 deaths from the following causes: drownings (139), traffic accidents (257), sport accidents (43), field exercises (14), freezing (35), and firearms (27) (Bundesarchiv Koblenz, NS 28/30, Bl.. 1, cited in Matthias von Hellfeld and Arno Klönne, *Die betrogene Generation. Jugend in Deutschland unter dem Faschismus. Quellen und Dokumente* [Cologne: Pahl-Rugenstein, 1985], p. 128).

106. Willy Schumann (born 1927) estimates that between the years he became old enough to join the Young Folk and his service in the military and subsequent imprisonment, he had spent thirty-six months in some sort of camp within less than eight years. Because of the discipline and control in the various "camps," he does not marvel that he still has an aversion to authority (*Being Present*, p. 35).

107. To take advantage of the traditional *Wanderlust* of German youth, Hitler Youth and military authorities went further than the Boy Scouts had done in teaching map reading, camouflage, orientation, and outdoor survival. "Groups of boys even learned how to reconnoiter by engaging in fairly realistic maneuvers, which were more like cowboy and Indian tussles than military exercises" (Rempel, *Hitler's Children*, p. 179).

108. Members of the Jungvolk and Hitler Youth became familiar with

lethal weapons on an unprecedented scale. In 1938 nearly one million youths participated in shooting competitions. Boys as young as ten were instructed in the use of dummy hand grenades. The Cubs became acquainted with a wide range of weapons, ranging from blowpipes and clubs to swords, pikes, and small-bore rifles. The training reached its zenith when "during military maneuvers, youngsters stand with yearning eyes behind blazing machine guns" (Grunberger, *Social History of the Third Reich*, p. 282). See also Rempel, *Hitler's Children*, p. 181; *Frankfurter Zeitung*, 13 December 1938; *Der Bund* (Bern), 22 April 1940; Thilo Scheller, "Wehrerziehung im Spiel," in *Erzeihung zum Wehrwillen* (Stuttgart: Rat, 1937), p. 321.

109. The oath of the Jungvolk was repeated every 20 April, the anniversary of Hitler's birth: "I promise to do my duty at all times, in love and faithfulness to help the Führer. So help me God" (H. W. Koch, *Hitler Youth*, pp. 112–13). The oath of the Hitler Youth was similar: "I promise always to do my duty in the Hitler Youth, in love and loyalty to the Führer" (Mackinnon, *Naked Years*, p. 53).

110. Schnibbe's initial enthusiasm was not shared universally. Prior to 1933 the "home evenings" played a minor role in Nazi youth activities, because so much time and effort was devoted to political campaigns. After January 1933, they were held frequently and were widely considered boring and shallow: "The *Heimabende*, for which we met in a dark and dirty cellar, were marked by a fatal lack of content. The time was spent on collecting fees, on checking uncountable lists and learning off by heart the words of songs whose poverty of content could not be missed even with the best of effort. Discussion of political texts, as for instance from *Mein Kampf*, quickly ended in general silence" (Melita Maschmann, *Fazit. Kein Rechtfertigungsversuch* [Stuttgart: Deutsche Verelagsanstalt, 1964], p. 25, cited in H. W. Koch, *Hitler Youth*, p. 126). Gunter Otto also considered the home evenings "boring and meaningless and, as a rule, poorly organized." The participants were worn out by word games, while charades were nearly the "high point." Singing was a significant part of the proceedings (Otto in Klafki, *Verführung, Distanzierung, Ernüchterung*, p. 122).

111. A great hall constructed in Munich by the Bavarian King Ludwig I between 1841 and 1844 to honor German military heroes. The *Putsch* on 9 November 1923 included a march to the hall, but collapsed when the Bavarian police fired on Hitler's Nazis near the Feldherrnhalle.

112. The Wartburg's significance was its role as a site of earlier German activities which pointed to the acclaimed definition and uniqueness of Germany and the fact that it was a place of refuge for Martin Luther in 1517. The Wartburg Festival was tied closely to the romantic notion of the origins of the German nation (Horst Bartel et al., eds., *Sachwörterbuch der Geschichte Deutschlands und der deutschen Arbeiterbewegung*, 2 vols. [Berlin: Dietz Verlag, 1969], 2:782; Hellmuth Rössler and Günther Franz, eds., *Sachwörterbuch zur deutschen Geschichte*, 2 vols. [Munich: R. Oldenbourg, 1958], 2:1361).

113. Upon entering the Jungvolk, prospective members were on probation for two to six months. Upon completing the probationary period, the

candidates underwent a test which combined sports, close combat, and ideological questions, mostly about the history of the Nazi party. The exam culminated with a test of courage such as jumping in full battle gear from the first floor window of an apartment house into a net. Upon passing the test successfully, the new members received the knife, shoulder strap, and insignia (H. W. Koch, *Hitler Youth*, pp. 112–13). Hitler declared to Rauschning that "weakness has to be knocked out of" the youth, that he wanted "a violently active, dominating, intrepid, brutal youth" that "must be indifferent to pain" and "learn to overcome the fear of death under the severest tests" (*Hitler Speaks*, p. 247).

114. By the time she was thirteen, Marianne Mackinnon had lost her original euphoria about being in the Nazi youth movement and "felt bored with a movement which not only did not tolerate individualists but expected its members to venerate a flag as if it were God Almighty, and which made me march or stand en bloc for hours, listen to tiresome or inflammatory speeches, sing songs not composed for happy hours or shout 'Führer, give your orders, we are following you!' or one of the many slogans which, somehow, went into one ear and out the other" (*Naked Youth*, p. 55). While underground in Freiburg in 1943, Else Behrend-Rosenfeld observed that the son of the family hiding her did not attend the Hitler Youth service. He responded to his mother's remonstrance that "most of those in my class go very seldom to service, no one bothers himself about it, because nearly all of the squad and group leaders are soldiers; and we have, at the most, only three enthusiastic Nazis in my class" (Behrend-Rosenfeld, *Ich stand nicht allein*, p. 237).

115. According to the "Law concerning the Hitler Youth" promulgated on 1 December 1936, all children aged ten and above were compelled, in conjunction with the school and the family, "to be educated physically, intellectually and ethically in the Hitler Youth in the spirit of National Socialism to serve the *Volk* and the national community" (*Reichsgesetzblatt*, I, No. 113 [1 Dec. 1936], p. 993).

116. The compulsory nature and enormous size of the Hitler Youth led to impersonal routine, which suffocated the enthusiasm and personal contact that characterized the early movement. Increasing numbers of youth engaged in nonpolitical rebellion against mandatory physical training and political indoctrination, and formed their own groups to pursue other interests, such as hiking, dancing, and listening to modern music, especially from England and the United States. Local authorities throughout Germany despised modern youth culture, because they felt it led to decadence and was corrupting the German youth (Klose, *Generation im Gleichschritt*, p. 152, cited in Grunberger, *Social History of the Third Reich*, p. 283).

117. Schnibbe's experience was not unique. The compulsory nature and institutionalization of the Hitler Youth resulted in frequent disillusion and unfortunate results. The aim of the Hitler Youth was to indoctrinate and control the German youth to the degree that they would have "no significant life . . . outside the Hitler Youth" (Rempel, *Hitler's Children*, p. 59; see also H. W. Koch, *Hitler Youth*, p. 113). Helmuth Hübener (Document 39)

derided the coercion and punishment attendent with the Hitler Youth. The Edelweiss Pirates in Düsseldorf, a group opposed to the Hitler Youth, had the motto: "Eternal war on the Hitler Youth," because, as one member explained, "every order I was given (in the Hitler Youth) contained a threat" (cited in Detlev Peukert, "Youth in the Third Reich," in Bessel, *Life in the Third Reich*, p. 31; see also the account of Karl-Heinz Janßen in Focke, *Alltag unterm Hakenkreuz*, pp. 45–46).

118. For some German families, the compulsory Hitler Youth membership created financial problems because of the need to purchase the obligatory uniform and pay the monthly subscriptions for periodicals and supplies (Grunberger, *Social History of the Third Reich*, p. 276).

119. Many German parents were uneasy about the Hitler Youth, which promoted a lifestyle and system of values different from their own, which were from the age of Wilhelmine Germany. Between 1933 and 1936 the Nazi government attempted to win the loyalty of the parents for the Hitler Youth movement, but once membership in the Hitler Youth became mandatory, such efforts were abandoned, because parents were obligated to accept the organization much like they were required to accept the Nazi party, the Labor Front and the military. Part of the reason for having duty on Sunday was to interfere with the church attendance of Hitler Youth members (H. W. Koch, *Hitler Youth*, pp. 130, 168, 220).

120. Members of the Hitler Youth knew also that if they did not appear for service, they would be fetched, which often led to punishment and recriminations (Rumpf in Klafki, *Verführung, Distanzierung, Ernüchterung*, p. 229).

121. Schnibbe's father was engaging in an act of self-preservation. Those who complained about young men serving in the Hitler Youth ran the risk of being arrested by the Gestapo, while anyone who willfully kept a child from performing his Hitler Youth duty could be punished by up to five years' imprisonment and a maximum fine of 10,000 marks (Heck, *Burden of Hitler's Legacy*, pp. 186–87; Rempel, *Hitler's Children*, p. 68).

122. Service usually occurred on Wednesday and Saturday afternoons into the early evening, from 3:00 to 6:00, but could take place on other days, especially Sunday morning. The activities included home evenings, exercises, close order drill, singing, sports, and marching in the districts of the city. The exercises were premilitary training and were largely calisthenics (Otto in Klafki, *Verführung, Distanzierung, Ernüchterung*, p. 120).

123. One of the attributes of the Nazi movement was that relatively young persons were given positions of enormous authority. In the Hitler Youth, their power status relative to their ages was an extremely unusual phenomenon in Germany. As a result, such young leaders developed an air of haughty superiority toward the older generation and were often inclined to view their own actions as matters of national significance and to abuse their perceived superiority over others. One of the common slogans of the youth movement was "Jugend muß von Jugend geführt werden" (youth must be guided by youth), which the Nazis used to exploit the "instinctual rebellion" of the younger generation against their elders, thus bringing them more

closely under the control of the Nazi state (Schumann, *Being Present*, p. 23; see also H. W. Koch, *Hitler Youth*, p. 131).

124. Because of the need for trained leaders to serve in the military, the older and professional Hitler Youth leaders were inducted, leaving boys of sixteen and seventeen leading groups of younger youths numbering 500 to 600. Smaller units of the Hitler Youth were led by still younger leaders (H. W. Koch, *Hitler Youth*, p. 233).

125. Wobbe had a similar experience, but did not respond to the summons. He had an altercation with a Hitler Youth leader who attempted to force him to attend a meeting. After being pushed around, Wobbe warned his antagonist to leave him alone, whereupon the Hitler Youth leader informed Rudi that he could not do anything about it, because the leader was in uniform. When the leader became more belligerent, Wobbe landed a blow which knocked out his antagonist, then fled. That was his last dealing with the Hitler Youth (Wobbe and Borrowman, *Before the Blood Tribunal*, pp. 12–13).

126. The expulsion occurred near the end of 1939. This information is contained in the introductory pages of Document 11, a routine form asking for biographical information. Because they are otherwise redundant, Document 11 is cited in this book without these biographical pages.

127. Schnibbe was fortunate, because the Hitler Youth had a wide array of "repressive weapons," ranging from "individual warnings, raids and temporary arrest (often followed by release with the public branding of a shaven head) to weekend detention [see Document 39], corrective education, referral to a labor camp, youth concentration camp or criminal trial" (Peukert, "Youth in the Third Reich," in Bessel, *Life in the Third Reich*, p. 34).

128. Any offense against discipline or order within the Hitler Youth made members subject to legal prosecution. Those expelled from the Hitler Youth could not join the Nazi party or any of its affiliates, and most vocations, especially the civil service, an academic career, or becoming a military officer required previous membership in the Hitler Youth. Parents of expelled Hitler Youth lost the support granted by the Ministry of Finance. There were "regional" and "superior" courts to deal with recalcitrant members, with penalties ranging from warnings to expulsion. A single judge heard the cases and applied the penalties. The hearings were confidential and no legal representation was permitted. Between July 1939 and August 1941, 2,701 youths (including ninety-nine boys accused of "bad attitude" or "violent acts") were expelled from the organization (Rempel, *Hitler's Children*, pp. 59, 69, 273).

129. Many persons were enthralled by the apparent economic gains and Germany's success in becoming a great power and revising the provisions of the Treaty of Versailles. However, those Germans who were skeptical and intelligent observers recognized that the foreign policies of the Hitlerian government would lead to war (Schumann, *Being Present*, p. 43).

Chapter 2: From Pogroms to War, from Radio to Resistance

1. The oppressive measures against their church contributed greatly to the mutual dislike of Hübener, Schnibbe, and Wobbe for the Nazi govern-

ment. Gerhard Düwer was drawn to their circle because he shared their disdain for the coercive methods of the Hitler Youth (Ulrich Sander, "Helmuth-Hübener Gruppe," in Ursel Hochmuth and Gertrud Meyer, eds., *Streiflichter aus dem Hamburger Widerstand 1933–1945* [Frankfurt: Röderberg Verlag, 1969], p. 327).

2. Friedrich Peters, a member of the Mormon congregation, claims that although Wobbe and Schnibbe were physically larger than Hübener, it was Helmuth who was the driving force ("Ich war mit Helmuth in einer Gruppe," in *Begleitheft zur Austellung um das kurze Leben und Wirken des Helmuth Hübener*, Catalogue of the exhibit in the Hamburg Municipal District Archive [Stadtteilarchiv] of Hamm, 26 October–10 December 1992, p. 17). Because some portions of this source have been included in the collection of documents, such references are listed hereafter by their respective document numbers. Otherwise, further references hereafter are referred to as *Begleitheft*. See Document 71.

3. Two days previously, a Jew, Herschel Grynszpan, assassinated Ernst vom Rath, the Third Secretary of the German Embassy in Paris, which provided Hitler with a justification for attacking the German Jews. Local Nazi party members, the SS and SA, and groups such as the Hitler Youth went on a rampage which resulted in extensive damage to Jewish religious and commercial buildings (Snyder, *Encyclopedia of the Third Reich*, p. 201; Zentner and Bedürftig, *Encyclopedia of the Third Reich*, 1:515). Between 171 and 177 synagogues were burned or demolished, while approximately 7,500 Jewish businesses were looted and destroyed. Numerous rapes of Jewish women occurred, as well as the murder of ninety-one Jews. The number of Jews incarcerated in concentration camps ranged from 20,000 to 30,000 (Anthony Read and David Fisher, *Kristallnacht: Unleashing the Holocaust* [London: Michael Joseph, 1989], pp. 73, 87). In Hamburg, Gauleiter Kaufmann strictly forbade the pogrom. The commando units (most likely the SS) from neighboring *Gaue* were involved in initiating the Kristallnacht activities in Hamburg (Hermann Graml, *Reichskristallnacht. Antisemitismus und Judenverfolgung im Dritten Reich* [Munich: Deutscher Taschenbuch Verlag, 1988], p. 25). There is little doubt that Joseph Goebbels was the force behind the events in an attempt to improve his political capital with Hitler (Uwe Adam, "How Spontaneous Was the Pogrom?" in Walter Pehle, ed., *November 1938 from "Kristallnacht" to Genocide* [New York: Berg, 1991], p. 93).

4. In June 1938, Jewish-owned businesses were required to make public their non-Aryan nature by painting the names of the owners on the fronts of the stores, emphasizing the names "Israel" or "Sarah," which all Jews had been obligated to add to their names (Deutschkron, *Outcast*, p. 30).

5. By February 1933, the Nazis threatened and pressured the approximately twenty thousand Jews in Hamburg, who were told that the day of reckoning was coming. Non-Jewish Germans were warned and advised not to patronize Jewish businesses (Schorer, *Als Hamburg unter den Nazis lebte*, p. 18).

6. The Jews were the largest minority group in Hamburg in the early twentieth century. It was estimated in 1933 that there were 19,000 Jews in

Hamburg, and a total of 24,000 in the greater Hamburg area. By 1940 the number of Jews had decreased to 7,000 (Rodnick, *Portrait of Two German Cities,* pp. 222–31).

7. After the 1936 Olympics, the Nazi government stepped up its efforts to force the Jews out of Germany. The "Aryanization" of the economy began in 1937 and by 1938 pressure on the Jews was "unbearable." In June 1938 a wave of arrests began, followed in October by the deportation of 17,000 Jews to Poland and in November by the Crystal Night. Because the Jews were not leaving the Reich fast enough (approximately 300,000 had emigrated by October 1941), emigration was halted and plans were developed for the "final solution" to the "Jewish problem." It is amazing that the 222,000 Jews remaining in Germany in 1939 and comprising only 0.32 percent of the population could be held responsible for so many of Germany's problems (Steinert, *Hitler's War,* p. 133).

8. The first groups of Jews to be arrested included those with criminal records and those viewed as vagrants or work-shy (Hoffmann, *German Resistance to Hitler,* p. 38).

9. "Good" German boys soon learned in school and the Nazi youth groups that Jews were not worthy of their association and, in a sense, were not really "German" (Heck, *Burden of Hitler's Legacy,* pp. 52–55).

10. In July 1938, Jewish physicians lost their licensing (Deutschkron, *Outcast,* p. 30).

11. The Wobbe family had a similar experience. Upon approaching the office of their Jewish physician, they discovered the doorway blocked by a storm trooper who told them that "no German citizen would willingly patronize a Jewish doctor." Mrs. Wobbe declared "we do" and pushed the trooper aside. That was the last time they saw their family physician. On their next visit they encountered a sign hanging on the door which read "Der Jude ist raus" (The Jew is gone) and discovered that an Aryan physician, who was a member of the SS, had taken over the office (Wobbe and Borrowman, *Before the Blood Tribunal,* p. 24).

12. Other German patients of Jewish physicians posed the same questions after their family doctors disappeared suddenly and mysteriously. The only information Ines Lyss gathered was that the Jews were put into "protective custody" camps so they would not be killed by those who hated Jews. An SS soldier informed her that the Jews "are receiving the best treatment and are eating well." Not knowing otherwise or what to believe, many Germans took such statements at face value (Ines Lyss, "You Open Your Mouth about Any of This, We'll Kill You and Your Family," in Steinhoff, *Voices from the Third Reich,* p. 317).

13. After the Crystal Night, Jewish men were seldom seen on the streets in many German cities, because they had been sent to concentration camps or were hiding. Else Behrend-Rosenfeld claimed to have been able to recognize Jewish women on the street, not because of their alleged "racial characteristics," which many did not possess, but "from the sheer stony, facial expression, that each bore as a mask; from the fixed, staring eyes, which no one detected, but which seemed to look through everyone" (*Ich stand nicht allein,* p. 65).

14. Jewish academics, civil servants, lawyers, and intellectuals were removed shortly after the Nazi seizure of power. The medical profession enjoyed a few years of grace until the Nazis removed 5,500 Jewish physicians, approximately 10 percent of the total. This decline, plus the decrease in specialists and the shortening by two years of the medical training required for a degree, reduced the general level of health care in Germany (Grunberger, *Social History of the Third Reich*, pp. 220, 456–57).

15. The last shipload of Jewish refugees to leave Germany sailed for Cuba on the liner *St. Louis* on 13 May 1939, with 930 passengers. Cuba, the South American states, and the United States refused to accept the refugees, so the liner undertook to return to Germany. During the return voyage, some persons took poison and others slit their wrists. At the last moment Belgium, Holland, Great Britain, and France agreed to accept the refugees (Pierre Joffroy, *A Spy for God: The Ordeal of Kurt Gerstein* [New York: Harcourt, Brace, Jovanovich, 1969], p. 182). Jews attempting to emigrate to the United States faced difficulties. They needed to prove that they had relatives in the USA who could provide for them, so they would not become public charges. In addition, the American government had a quota for Jews. During one month in Stuttgart 110,000 Jews applied for the monthy allotment of 850 visas. After the start of World War II, some Jews were successful in escaping from Germany, often by taking circuitous routes. Some went to Switzerland, while others went to the United States via Shanghai. Others paid enormous sums for visas to emigrate to Palestine. Not all who attempted to escape were successful (Deutschkron, *Outcast*, pp. 48–49, 68).

16. It was common in Germany to echo this phrase from the historian Heinrich von Treitschke ("Unsere Ansichten," *Preußische Jahrbücher* 44, no. 5 [1879]: 559–76; see also "Herr Grätz und sein Judenthum," ibid., no. 6: 660–70).

17. The regulation of 26 April 1938 required Jews to register their assets, foreign or domestic, in excess of 5,000 marks, which gave the Nazis an inventory of all substantial Jewish holdings and thus made it easier to dispossess wealthy Jews (Deutschkron, *Outcast*, p. 30).

18. The larger German cities, especially Hamburg and Berlin, were less anti-Jewish than smaller cities or rural areas, which did not have significant bourgeois and Marxist-influenced populations (Grunberger, *Social History of the Third Reich*, p. 458).

19. The Nazi term for the transfer of Jewish property into "Aryan" hands in order to "de-Jew the economy" (Zentner and Bedürftig, *Encyclopedia of the Third Reich*, 1:45). On 2 December 1937, the *Hamburger Tageblatt* reported that as a result of the efforts to "de-Jew" (*Entjuden*) the German economy, 1,200 Jewish businesses in the city had been closed and transferred into Aryan hands (Schorer, *Als Hamburg unter den Nazis lebte*, p. 19). By 1938 the German government decided to eliminate the German Jews from the national economy and reduce their numbers by having them emigrate. The internal revenue service and the local police were given lists of wealthy Jews, whose property was to be seized (Hoffmann, *German Resistance to Hitler*, p. 38).

20. "Party moocher" refers to the term *Parteigenießer*, a pun on the term

Parteigenosse (party member). Corruption was widespread among members of the Nazi party and higher officials were often more corrupt than those below them. Grunberger claims that "thanks to the 'Führer principle,' the Party's mechanism for internal control operated in such a way that the penalties for corruption varied in inverse proportion to its extent. Small-scale derelictions by petty officials committed within the sight of the man in the street frequently earned exemplary retribution, while crime at the top regional or national level largely went unpunished" (Grunberger, *Social History of the Third Reich*, p. 91).

21. Some employers believed erroneously that they could inflict corporal punishment on apprentices. In Wobbe's case, journeymen felt it was their place to assault apprentices when considered necessary (Wobbe and Borrowman, *Before the Blood Tribunal*, p. 10; see also *Frankfurter Zeitung*, 1 Sept. 1937, cited in Grunberger, *Social History of the Third Reich*, p. 269).

22. Altona is one of the communities incorporated by Hamburg when it became a metropolitan area.

23. In 1937 the average hourly wage for skilled male workers was 78.5 cents (37.68 marks per week). Women with comparable skills were paid a third less than their male counterparts. During the early years of the Third Reich, the purchasing power of workers dropped 15 percent, but improved later (Grunberger, *Social History of the Third Reich*, p. 189). The normal working hours of juveniles were 48 per week. By December 1939, because of the war, the ceiling was raised to 54 hours per week for boys younger than sixteen, and 56 for those sixteen and older. If their labor was considered essential to the country's needs, inspectors could increase the maximum number of working hours (C. W. Guillebaud, *The Social Policy of Nazi Germany* [New York: Fertig, 1971], p. 76).

24. Youths under the age of eighteen were forbidden to attend movies which contained dancing or kissing. To avoid the Hitler Youth patrols stationed in the theaters to check identification, the boys dressed as sharply as possible, wearing white silk scarves and Homburg hats to appear older than they were. One of the films the boys saw was *Jüd Süß* (The Sweet Jew), the most famous anti-Semitic film produced by the Nazis. It was first shown on 5 September 1940 and was acclaimed to be "especially valuable politically and artistically—worthwhile for young people" (Zentner and Bedürftig, *Encyclopedia of the Third Reich*, 1:477–78). Hübener was enraged by the portrayal of the Jews as a "lecherous, grimy and treacherous people" and believed the film portrayed the Germans as "a nation of hateful and arrogant people." The film roused such strong emotions in some viewers that attacks against Jews and Jewish businesses occurred after showings of the film (Wobbe and Borrowman, *Before the Blood Tribunal*, pp. 18–19).

25. The name is spelled in various ways, including Sudroff and Suderov. After Helmuth's maternal grandfather Gudat died, his grandmother married Johannes Sudrow.

26. After his mother married Hugo Hübener, Helmuth was invited to live with them, but his aversion to his step-father was so strong that he preferred to reside with his grandparents (Wobbe and Borrowman, *Before the Blood Tribunal*, p. 14).

27. Helmuth's mother moved from Tilsit with two children in March 1923. While she was estranged from her first husband, a teamster named Johann Kunkel, she had a liaison with a co-worker, a master engraver at the Hamburg mint by the name of Karl Oswald Vater, who she claimed was Helmuth's biological father. After her divorce from Kunkel, she married Hugo Hübener, who adopted Helmuth on 4 September 1941 ("Versuch einer Familiengeschichte" in *Begleitheft*, p. 3).

28. "Helmuth was not afraid to tackle the hard parts of the gospel and wasn't at all shy in challenging uninformed adults if they didn't know the doctrine well. He sometimes asked the American missionaries such deeply thought out questions that he embarrassed them. They, in turn, would get a little gruff and tell him to leave things alone, that he was too young to ask such questions. Some adults even thought he was impertinent, but mostly Helmuth was just curious. It's true that he enjoyed rattling people's chains just a little. He just wanted to wake them up and make sure they were seeing all sides of a question. If Helmuth really wanted to, though, he could have demonstrated a dazzling display of intellectual fireworks that would have outdistanced even the most educated of the brethren" (Wobbe and Borrowman, *Before the Blood Tribunal*, p. 18).

29. The father of Rudi Wobbe had a bullet graze his kidney during World War I. The resulting injury plagued him for the remainder of his life, such that he often complained of "feeling sluggish and tired." He died on 6 March 1935 (Wobbe and Borrowman, *Before the Blood Tribunal*, p. 5).

30. Wobbe's experience with the Nazi youth groups was almost entirely negative. His first home evening, where he initially found "a lot of camaraderie and group singing," deteriorated when the meeting turned to demeaning the Jews and accusing them of horrible crimes. When Wobbe asked for proof, "they started shouting at me as if I were crazy." Some time after attending his first home evening, which was also his last, he was invited to attend a summer camp. Besides being derided for his religious beliefs, he was the victim of harassment and hazing, which ended his association with the Hitler Youth. Upon returning home to Hamburg from the summer camp, "I hurried to the party office to return the uniform. . . . I didn't want anything more to do with those people" (Wobbe and Borrowman, *Before the Blood Tribunal*, pp. 7–8).

31. Groups of the Hitler Youth in uniform were renowned for causing mischief. In one case in Munich, a group broke the windows of an apartment of a Latin teacher for giving low marks. When the police arrived, they were frustrated, because they were not permitted to arrest members of the Hitler Youth who were in uniform (H. W. Koch, *Hitler Youth*, p. 168).

32. In 1934 the Patrol Service (Streifendienst) was introduced into the Hitler Youth to exercise functions comparable to the military police. The Patrol Service cooperated with the Gestapo and the SS, an association formalized in 1938. The duties of the Patrol Service were identical with those of the SS (H. W. Koch, *Hitler Youth*, pp. 111–12). "The slightest deviation among young people became [a] treasonable departure from the inflated 'moral code of the youth movement.' It was no longer a question of shared

values, as in the traditional German youth movement, which allowed for individual cultural, social and sexual expression, but rather a matter of uniform organization, official ideology and prescribed activity" (Albert Müller, *Die Betreuung der Jugend: Überblick über eine Aufgabe der Volksgemeinschaft* [Berlin: F. Eher Nachf., 1943], pp. 54–55, cited in Rempel, *Hitler's Children*, p. 47). "Smoking, drinking, improper saluting, tramping, curfew violations, singing of prohibited songs, disorderly conduct in billiard halls and dance halls, and similar aberrations from the puritanical Nazi code of conduct" were subjected to the intervention of the Hitler Youth Patrol Service, which was also intended to serve as a reservoir for future SS recruits. In larger towns and cities the patrols raided movie theaters, cabarets, billiard halls, and coffee shops looking for curfew violators and youngsters violating other rules. In many communities street patrols were conducted several times a week (Rempel, *Hitler's Children*, pp. 61–62, 104).

33. As German society became increasingly politicized and nazified, youth groups acting out of a hatred of Nazism engaged in activities opposing the Nazi state. Some bands of working-class youths, such as the Edelweiß groups, sought out Hitler Youth members and beat them up. The Hitler Youth retaliated and considered it their duty to attack illegal youth groups, which were viewed as enemies of the state (King, "Pacifists, Neutrals or Resisters," p. 149; Rempel, *Hitler's Children*, p. 58).

34. Being captured by a Hitler Youth patrol could also have serious consequences. The "Police Order for the Protection of Youth" (which had the power of law) issued in June 1940 by Himmler went beyond the earlier curfew regulations and included the prohibition of tobacco and alcohol consumption by persons under the age of sixteen. "Violators could be imprisoned for three weeks and fined 50 Marks, while adult accessories could be fined 150 Marks and incarcerated for six weeks" (Rempel, *Hitler's Children*, p. 70).

35. Whenever the Nazi flag passed by on the street, everyone was expected to come to attention and render the Nazi salute. Alongside the marching columns were storm troopers who kept an eye on the crowd. Whenever they spotted someone who was not saluting the flag properly, they swarmed through the onlookers and beat up the offender (Wobbe and Borrowman, *Before the Blood Tribunal*, p. 4; see also Heck, *Burden of Hitler's Legacy*, pp. 68, 84).

36. It was also necessary to salute the banners of passing SA or SS formations or run the risk of being beaten up. William Shirer noted that it was often necessary when walking to duck into stores to avoid saluting or the possibility of assault (*Berlin Diary: The Journal of a Foreign Correspondent, 1934–1941* [New York: Knopf, 1941], p. 15). In a court case filed by an onlooker who had failed to salute the flag, the public prosecutor stated that "although there is no law enjoining a compulsory salute, the custom of this greeting has nevertheless established itself and non-adherence to it is therefore an obvious act of provocation" (*Völkischer Beobachter*, 1 Feb. 1935, cited in Grunberger, *Social History of the Third Reich*, p. 76).

37. Rudi Wobbe recalls that when Helmuth was asked at their trial why

he had distributed the leaflets in the working districts of Hamburg, he replied: "Hamburg remains what it is, that is, revolutionary" (Rudolf Wobbe, "Um ein Haar wäre auch für mich die Todesstrafe ausgesprochen worden," in *Begleitheft*, p. 21).

38. Early in the fourteenth century, when it had a population of 7,000, Hamburg applied for membership in the Hanseatic League (Rodnick, *Portrait of Two German Cities*, p. 194).

39. Karl Kaufmann (1900–1969) helped found the Nazi party in the Ruhr area and was the Gauleiter for Rhineland-North from 1924 to 1929, when he was moved to Hamburg. In 1933 he became also the Reich Governor for Hamburg. In 1942 he became the Reich Commissioner for Overseas Navigation and was made an SS-Obergruppenführer, the equivalent of a general. In May 1945 he refused to defend Hamburg and handed the city over to the British forces (Zentner and Bedürftig, *Encyclopedia of the Third Reich*, 1:492; Ditt, *Sozialdemokraten im Widerstand*, p. 19).

40. Kaufmann's interest in the arts led to the misconception that he was cultured and covered the fact that he was a brutal man who participated in the interrogations of prisoners. He declared in 1933 that the prisoners in Wittmoor were not punished enough. When prisoners in Kolafu failed to give what he considered the respect due him by failing to rise when he entered the room, he ordered all political prisoners be put in one place, be watched more closely, and be more severely punished as a group. Any prisoners who peered out of windows should be shot at without warning. Kaufmann was known to strike prisoners being interrogated with a ring of keys and to urge torturers to apply their skills more rigorously (Gertrud Meyer, *Nacht über Hamburg. Berichte und Dokumente* [Frankfurt: Röderberg Verlag, 1971], pp. 19–23). Many of the more prominent Nazi leaders were less well educated and came from lower social classes than did more middling or ordinary members of the Nazi party. Of the thirty Gauleiter, twenty-seven came from small towns and twenty-three had only an elementary school education. Five of the Gauleiter had attended a university, but only three of them had completed degrees. Nearly half of the Nazi leadership came from the rural parts of southern Germany and had lower-middle-class backgrounds (Harold D. Lasswell et al., "The Nazi Elite," in *World Revolutionary Elites: Studies in Coercive Ideological Movements* [Cambridge, Mass.: MIT Press, 1965], pp. 197–98, 294, 313). In selecting his Gauleiter, Hitler "always looked for the bawling sergeant-major type, ready to use their fists if need be" (Hanfstaengl, *Unheard Witness*, p. 190).

41. Beginning in October 1939, the paramilitary training of the Hitler Youth increased, usually on weekends and conducted by former Hitler Youth members who had seen combat and been decorated. In 1941 instruction by frontline officers became an integral part of Jungvolk and Hitler Youth training. The paramilitary training of boys fifteen and older was enhanced by three weeks of basic infantry instruction in special defense preparation camps (*Wehrertüchtigungslager*). Young officers who were products of the Hitler Youth training had "an education behind them the essence of which was the elimination of the intellectual and moral content of literature and . . . are well

equipped for the task of deliberately destroying part of the globe in the name of the Aryan mission" (Klose, *Generation in Gleichschritt*, p. 251; see also H. W. Koch, *Hitler Youth*, p. 236; Schumann, *Being Present*, pp. 104–9).

42. Wobbe recalled that the branch president "conveniently provided a radio" for the Wednesday-night youth meeting so that they could listen to a speech by Hitler or Goebbels before proceeding with the planned social activities (Wobbe and Borrowman, *Before the Blood Tribunal*, p. 32).

43. A district president was a lay leader who supervised several branch presidents. A branch was a local congregation.

44. Schwarz, who joined the LDS Church on the same day as Rudi Wobbe and his mother, was descended from a Hungarian Jewish mother who had been abducted by Russian soldiers during World War I and raped, which resulted in her pregnancy with Salomon (Wobbe and Borrowman, *Before the Blood Tribunal*, p. 27).

45. In its Godesberg Declaration of 1939 the United National Church of German Christians demanded the purification of the church from Jewish influence and requested that the Jews attend separate services, because "one could not be expected to receive Communion next to a Jew." Other Protestant churches abandoned their Jewish coreligionists (Steinert, *Hitler's War*, pp. 138–39). Helmuth was incensed that the LDS branch he attended excluded Jews from attending church services (Sander, "Helmuth-Hübener Gruppe," in Hochmuth and Meyer, *Streiflichter*, p. 327). When confronted for having posted the sign forbidding Jews to attend LDS services at the St. Georg branch, Arthur Zander, a Nazi party member since 1933, declared, "I am just following party lines" (Wobbe and Borrowman, *Before the Blood Tribunal*, p. 28).

46. In 1943 the Barmbek branch also posted a sign on its door forbidding Jews to enter (Scharffs, *Mormonism in Germany*, pp. 100–101).

47. In 1941 Schwarz was incarcerated in a concentration camp for "educational purposes." When he returned, he was in poor health. A short time later he was ordered to move to the Jewish ghetto, from which he was sent to Auschwitz in 1943 (Wobbe and Borrowman, *Before the Blood Tribunal*, pp. 29–30).

48. For a detailed account of the case of Salomon Schwarz, see Wobbe and Borrowman, *Before the Blood Tribunal*, pp. 27–31.

49. With increasingly large numbers of Hitler Youth leaders serving on the front lines, churches attempted to reassert their influence over the German youth. To combat such efforts, the Sicherheitsdienst (SD) enrolled the Hitler Youth Patrol Service in "the clandestine surveillance of religious services." The Hitler Youth observers were to note "how the churches affected the population, what methods they used and the kind of political positions they took." Church meetings and members were observed by Hitler Youth patrols "to make sure their activities were purely religious and did not degenerate into political acts." There is evidence that the surveillance of churches by Hitler Youth patrols was widespread (Rempel, *Hitler's Children*, pp. 62, 75, 101).

50. The Hitler Youth was encouraged to play fanfares outside of churches

or use other methods to disrupt religious services (Manfred Rommel, "Then My Father Called for Me and Told Me He Had Ten Minutes to Say Goodbye," in Steinhoff, *Voices from the Third Reich*, p. 364).

51. The Book of Mormon, from which the name Mormon is derived, is viewed as scripture by members of the LDS Church, transcribed from ancient metal plates delivered to Joseph Smith. The book contains verses referring to the fate of those nations which fight against Zion, commonly held to be in America.

52. The Battle of Stalingrad is generally considered the turning point in World War II. Lasting from November 1942 until February 1943, the battle cost Germany more than a quarter of a million casualties.

53. The LDS Church practices baptism by immersion for persons eight years of age and older.

54. The Polish campaign ended on 6 October 1939. The Polish forces suffered casualties of approximately 203,000 and 700,000 prisoners. The German losses were 10,572 dead, 3,409 missing, and 30,322 wounded (Zentner and Bedürftig, *Encyclopedia of the Third Reich*, 1:715).

55. The French campaign lasted from 10 May to 22 June, 1940. In addition to Belgian, Dutch, and British losses, the French casualties were approximately 92,000 dead and 200,000 wounded. The German Wehrmacht suffered 27,074 dead, 18,383 missing, and 111,034 wounded (Zentner and Bedürftig, *Encyclopedia of the Third Reich*, 1:298).

56. When the Ministry of Propaganda was created in March 1933, it informed journalists in great detail what matters they could report and how their reports were to be written. Readers were to be spared any information about failures, retreats, and discontent. Emphasis was to be placed on positive matters such as sporting events and industrial and economic progress. Reports concerning England, France, and the United States were to stress racial conflict, social discontent, and economic problems such as strikes (Schorer, *Als Hamburg unter den Nazis lebte*, pp. 21–22).

57. Hans Kunkel maintains that Helmuth had access to extraordinary books in the archives and libraries, and read widely on politics, history, and economics (see Document 74).

58. Hübener "borrowed" some of the forbidden books and took them home to read, and showed them to some of his friends (Wobbe and Borrowman, *Before the Blood Tribunal*, p. 35).

59. Such sentiments were widespread after the beginning of the campaign against the USSR. Reports of the new front were "a real shock" to persons favorable to the regime, "while among those critical of the regime a thinly concealed malicious glee was observed" (Report of the Regierungspräsident for Central Franconia, 11 June 1941: BHStA, Abt. II, MA 106,681, cited in Steinert, *Hitler's War*, p. 99). To many Nazis the extension of the war was a "blow to the very foundations of National Socialism and the Party" (Report of the Regierungspräsident for Swabia and Neuburg, 10 June 1941: BHStA, Abt. II, MA 106,684, cited in Steinert, *Hitler's War*, p. 99). Many persons considered Operation Barbarossa to be a "lost battle" (OLG-president Frankfurt, 26 June 1941: BA, R22/3364, and Security Service of the RFSS, SD

section Leipzig, Außenstelle Leipzig, 17 May 1941: *Aus deutschen Urkunden*, p. 245, cited in Steinert, *Hitler's War*, p. 99). Reports from Nazi party and government sources reflected widespread astonishment and dismay (Steinert, *Hitler's War*, p. 118).

60. Johannes Sudrow was born on 7 February 1865. He became the second husband of Wilhelmina Gudat when they were married in 1923. Helmuth's maternal grandmother was born on 19 March 1877.

61. The National Labor Service (Reichsarbeitsdienst) required labor of all able-bodied male citizens. According to a law of 26 June 1935, all citizens between eighteen and twenty-five were obligated to work in labor camps under military discipline. Agricultural service was stressed. The average term of involvement was twenty weeks, which was increased later to six months. In 1939 labor service became mandatory for females (Snyder, *Encyclopedia of the Third Reich*, p. 284; Zentner and Bedürftig, *Encyclopedia of the Third Reich*, 1:775).

62. Because foreign broadcasts were vital sources of information about developments and reactions outside of Germany, as well as about anti-Jewish measures, military campaigns, and arrests of anti-Nazis, opponents of the regime and those concerned with knowing the truth violated regularly the law prohibiting the listening to foreign radio stations (Deutschkron, *Outcast*, p. 63).

63. In 1939 when Goebbels proposed a law against "black listening," Franz Gürtner, the non-Nazi Minister of Justice, opposed such an ordinance because it would destroy the trust between the populace and its government and cause the German people to lose faith in German newscasts. Most of the members of the cabinet shared Gürtner's viewpoint, so were astounded the following morning to read in the newspaper that the cabinet had approved the ordinance for "Extraordinary Radio Measures." Thereafter sentences of up to three years were imposed, even when there was no evidence that the news heard had been passed on to others (C. F. Latour, "Goebbels' 'Außerordentliche Rundfunkmaßnahmen' 1939–1942," *Vierteljahresheft für Zeitgeschichte* 11, no. 4 [1963]: 418–19; Balfour, *Withstanding Hitler*, pp. 62–63).

64. In August 1941 Hübener first invited his friends from the LDS branch to listen to the BBC broadcasts with him (Sander, "Helmuth-Hübener Gruppe," in Hochmuth and Meyer, *Streiflichter*, p. 330; Wobbe and Borrowman, *Before the Blood Tribunal*, p. 13).

65. Wobbe claims that Helmuth toyed with a radio on New Year's Eve 1940, attempting to "tune in a station other than those authorized by the German Reich" (Wobbe and Borrowman, *Before the Blood Tribunal*, p. 20). Hans Kunkel maintains that Helmuth began his resistance activity early in 1941, which is when their brother Gerhard returned from France with a shortwave radio (see Document 74).

66. During the Polish campaign, Germans who listened to the BBC were convinced that the British newscasts were more propaganda than truth, because the reports minimized German successes and emphasized minor Polish successes. Such British attempts "proved rather ridiculous and boomeranged right into their own faces" (Pabel, *Enemies Are Human*, p. 39).

67. On 6 August 1941, after a lengthy period of no news, the Oberkommando der Wehrmacht issued a report about major advances and the capture of large numbers of prisoners in the Russian campaign, claiming that "Russia has now only men but no weapons, especially tanks and aircraft. It is lost." Within a month, however, the SD reported that "there is now more talk of having underestimated the enemy. Citizens no longer seem nearly as self-confident as during the first weeks of the war. . . . The individual reports about battles and successes in sectors of the entire front were received without enthusiasm. People generally conclude that the tempo of the advance has slowed." By early September, internal reports noted that letters from soldiers at the Russian front "contributed to an impairment of public morale. . . . Reports of this kind are spreading like the wind and add significantly to an increase of uncertainty among the population over the course of the eastern campaign" (Heinz Boberach, *Meldungen aus dem Reich. Auswahl aus den geheimen Lageberichten des Sicherheitsdienstes der SS 1939–1944* [Berlin: Luchterhand, 1965], 4 Aug., 4 and 8 Sept. 1941, pp. 167, 172–73).

68. In the *Report of the Armed Forces* the nature of military situations was concealed. German losses were not admitted, and the names of rivers crossed and cities occupied were only given when the Germans were crossing them going east or conquering them. A new terminology was developed to avoid the impression of defeats or reverses. Instead of a unit being described as encircled by the enemy, it was said to have established a "hedgehog defense" (*sich einigeln*). A retreat was described as a "shortening of the front line" (*Frontverkürzung*) (Schumann, *Being Present*, pp. 89–90).

69. Schnibbe is probably referring to the *Ark Royal*, an aircraft carrier sunk on 14 November 1941, after being torpedoed the previous day by U-Boot U81. The *Royal Oak* was sunk on 14 October 1939, prior to when Hübener, Schnibbe, and Wobbe listened to the BBC broadcasts. The commander of U-Boot 47, Günther Prien, was responsible for sinking the *Royal Oak* and became an early Nazi hero for his exploits (Helmut Pemsel, *Atlas of Naval Warfare* [London: Army and Armour Press, 1977], p. 123; see also Zentner and Bedürftig, *Encyclopedia of the Third Reich*, 2:726–27).

70. From Steinert's study of German popular opinion it emerges that the Russian campaign "represented the turning point in his [Hitler's] relationship with the German people." He retained the "trust of large segments of the population . . . but his goals no longer meshed with the desires of the broad masses" (*Hitler's War*, pp. 129–30).

71. In early October the military reported that stunning blows had been inflicted upon the Soviet armed forces, which allegedly had lost seventy-three infantry and seven tank divisions and three million prisoners. On 9 October, Otto Dietrich, the Reich press chief, stated that the USSR was "militarily finished" (Willi A. Boelcke, ed., *"Wollt ihr den totalen Krieg?" Die geheimen Goebbels-Konferenzen 1939–1943* [Stuttgart: Deutsche Verlags-Anstalt, 1957], pp. 188–89, cited in Steinert, *Hitler's War*, pp. 130–31).

72. The Nazi propaganda ministry recognized that the barrage of propagandistic reports only increased indifference. People were tired of hearing "the same reports with almost identical commentary in various broad-

casts" (*Meldungen aus dem Reich*, 5 Aug. 1940: BA, R 58/153, cited in Stein-ert, *Hitler's War*, p. 75).

73. In a letter in March 1943 to Lionel Curtis, Helmuth von Moltke stat-ed that "there is only one way of communicating news and that is the Lon-don wireless, as that is listened to by many people who belong to the oppo-sition proper and by many disaffected Party Members" (Balfour, *Withstanding Hitler*, p. 77).

74. Schnibbe's comment was expressed earlier by high government offi-cials. The Reich Minister of Finance, Schwerin von Krosigk, worried about the possibility of peace and the effects upon the German population if Ger-many entered a two-front war by attacking the USSR: "Don't you believe that we are expecting too much from this willing, loyal and trusting Volk if this treaty with Russia, once celebrated . . . as *the* greatest guarantee of vic-tory, as *the* greatest political achievement, as *the* security against English blockade plans is perverted? I fear that most people will not be equal to so severe a test." His fears were substantiated by SD reports that many Ger-man citizens believed Germany would collapse eventually under the weight of its victories (*Meldungen aus dem Reich*, BA, R2/24243; BA, R58/160, cited in Steinert, *Hitler's War*, pp. 97–98). Inge Deutschkron overheard her neigh-bors bemoaning that "we're going to die of our victories" (Deutschkron, *Outcast*, p. 137).

75. It was common at the time to underestimate the military potential of the USSR. "There is talk within military circles of an invasion within, at the latest, eight weeks and that the war—if it can be called that—will be con-ducted with little bloodshed. . . . The German army is more likely awaited as a liberator than as an enemy" (Security Service of RFSS, SD section Leipzig, 3 May 1941, cited in Steinert, *Hitler's War*, p. 98).

76. Reinhold Pabel, who participated in the early advance of the Ger-man army into the Soviet Union, recounted seeing huge posters in Kiev which proclaimed: "HITLER THE LIBERATOR!" It was obvious to him that "the Ukrainians sincerely believed that the German Army would clear away the Bolshevist rubble and allow them to build up their nation under a free and independent self-rule." Peasants presented the victorious German troops with buckets of milk and baskets of cream-filled pies, or threw cans of cold water into the "heat-tortured" faces of the soldiers and sang folk songs to them as the German forces marched through the villages (Pabel, *Enemies Are Hu-man*, pp. 63–64, 83). Hitler launched a reign of terror, first by eliminating the Jews and Muslims, who were mistaken for Jews, because they were cir-cumcised. The indigenous population was driven back into the arms of Sta-lin and became active partisans against the Germans. In areas under mili-tary administration, efforts were made to avoid the problems that occurred in areas conquered earlier, so peasants were treated more leniently and there was no collectivization. As a result there were no partisans (Hans Herwarth von Bittenfeld, "The Party Succeeded in Driving People Back into the Arms of Stalin," in Steinhoff, *Voices from the Third Reich*, p. 130).

77. The German commissioners, referred to by the soldiers as "Golden Pheasants" because of their party badge, disgusted members of the Wehr-

macht by their cruel and inhuman behavior toward the Ukrainians and other peoples who surrendered. Besides being deprived of their land and animals, natives were shipped back to Germany to work in labor camps where many starved (Wolfgang Schöler, "The Soldiers Showed the Villagers Their Photos," in Steinhoff, *Voices from the Third Reich*, p. 137).

78. One of the most important economic goals of Nazi Germany was to derive enormous amounts of provisions from the "inferior" Slavic peoples of eastern Europe and Russia. It was well known in German military circles that the measures taken to obtain foodstuffs in the east would lead to catastrophic hunger for the peoples living there (Albrecht Lehmann, *Gefangenschaft und Heimkehr. Deutsche Kriegsgefangene in der Sowjetunion* [Munich: Verlag C. H. Beck, 1986], pp. 58–59). Of the 3,350,000 Russian prisoners taken by the Germans in 1941, 60 percent of them died before the end of the year. Of the 5.7 million Russian prisoners captured by the Germans during the war, 3.3 million died while in custody (Ulrich Herbert, *A History of Foreign Labor in Germany, 1880–1980* [Ann Arbor: University of Michigan, 1990], pp. 143–44).

79. The Iron Cross, a medal first awarded in 1813 for bravery in battle, was reissued in the wars beginning in 1870, 1914, and 1939. The former highest decoration of World War I, the *Pour le Mérite* was not reissued due to its French name. Instead, the *Ritterkreuz* (Knight's Cross) was awarded. At the beginning of the war such decorations were awarded infrequently, but it was not long before there was such a flood of medals that people spoke of a medal inflation. It was rumored humorously that Hitler had designed many of the decorations personally "as an outlet for his frustrated artistic talent" (Schumann, *Being Present*, pp. 55–56). By 1944 over 500,000 Iron Crosses (First Class) and more than three million Iron Crosses (Second Class) had been awarded. One-third of the members of the Wehrmacht had been decorated for bravery (Grunberger, *Social History of the Third Reich*, p. 141). Teenage members of the naval and air force assistance units felt some of their decorations were "laughable" (Granzow, *Tagebuch eines Hitlerjungen*, p. 126). See also Willi Nolden, "I'll Give You a Thousand Marks for Your Hand," in Steinhoff, *Voices from the Third Reich*, p. 144; *Reichsgesetzblatt* 1, no. 159 (2 Sept. 1939): 1573ff.; *Frankfurter Zeitung*, 7 June 1937, cited in Grunberger, *Social History of the Third Reich*, pp. 77–78.

80. Schnibbe could have gotten into difficulty easily. On 9 March 1940, the government promulgated the "Law for the Protection of Youth," which banned persons under the age of eighteen from the streets after dark, as well as from visiting restaurants, movie theaters, or other places of entertainment after 9:00 P.M., if unaccompanied by an adult ("Polizeiverordnung zum Schutze der Jugend," *Reichsgesetzblatt* 1, no. 47, pp. 126–27; Behrend-Rosenfeld, *Ich stand nicht allein*, p. 121).

81. The leaflets were printed on bright red paper, because it drew attention to the message. In the corner Hübener placed a swastika "to throw the Nazis off the track" and to lead others to believe that it came from the Nazi party (Wobbe and Borrowman, *Before the Blood Tribunal*, p. 37).

82. There is no extant copy of the flyer entitled "Hitler the Murderer of

General von Schröder, Commander of Serbia." In it Hübener discussed the rumored murder of General Ludwig von Schröder, the former general of the anti-aircraft artillery for Germany who was assigned as the Commanding General of Serbia (Wobbe and Borrowman, *Before the Blood Tribunal*, p. 37). It was reported that von Schröder had been "slightly injured" in a plane crash when the aircraft was attempting to land at Belgrade during a storm and hit a high tension line (Richard Brett-Smith, *Hitler's Generals* [San Rafael, Calif.: Presidio Press, 1977], p. 61; *New York Times*, 19 and 30 July 1941).

83. Wobbe claims that Hübener typed the messages twelve times, using carbon paper in order to produce five copies, thus making sixty copies of each flyer. The sixty copies came from fifteen sheets of paper divided into quarters (Wobbe and Borrowman, *Before the Blood Tribunal*, p. 37).

84. Wobbe was proud that none of the leaflets turned over to the police were in the area of Hamburg where he distributed them, which was a strong workers' area (Wobbe and Borrowman, *Before the Blood Tribunal*, p. 39).

85. In addition to the fact that remaining outdoors during an air raid was dangerous, it was illegal according to the *Luftschutzgesetz* of 26 June 1935. Violation of the law could result in a fine of 150 marks or imprisonment or both. Air-raid wardens patrolled the streets to assure that unauthorized persons were in shelters (*Reichsgesetzblatt* [1938], 1:827–28).

86. Rothenburgsort was one of several areas of Hamburg outside the inner core of the city where the working class had a strong tradition of cooperation and loyalty to the ideals of socialism. Drawn largely from the 25–to–30–year-old age group, workers were often third-generation socialists who had grown up in the movement and comprised the most active and largest resistance groups in Hamburg (Ditt, *Sozialdemokraten im Widerstand*, pp. 76–77).

87. "Hamburger bleibt in den Betten, wir fliegen nach Berlin zu den Fetten."

88. A line from a song of the era by Zarah Leander, "Es wird einmal ein Wunder gescheh'n, und dann werden tausend Märchen wahr."

89. A member of the SS, Kurt Gerstein listened regularly to the BBC broadcasts in the presence of his closest associates, who were well aware that they were risking their lives (Joffroy, *Spy for God*, p. 115). Peter Neumann, also a member of the SS, was stunned to discover that his father listened regularly to the British newscasts in German, because he was not "satisfied with all the nonsense we get from your Himmler and that little Goebbels man," but did not report his father to the authorities (*The Black March: The Personal Story of an SS Man* [New York: William Sloane Associates, 1959], pp. 238–39). To decrease the likelihood of being reported for listening to foreign broadcasts, many Germans used earphones, which were sold at a premium price. Persons purchasing earphones exercised extreme caution and rarely purchased such items in a store where they were not well known to the proprietors. After airing a newscast, the BBC reminded listeners to change the dial setting to avoid incriminating themselves (Deutschkron, *Outcast*, p. 64).

90. The distribution of flyers was a popular form of resistance, but, in the opinion of Wilhelm Leuschner, the former Minister of the Interior in

Hesse, such an activity did more harm than good because it left a trail the police could follow and provided evidence for trials. The Communists believed the distribution of flyers was good because, besides providing information, it indicated that there were those among the public who were struggling against National Socialism (Gerhard Beier, *Die Illegale Reichsleitung der Gewerkschaften* [Cologne: Bund-Verlag, 1989], p. 33; Balfour, *Withstanding Hitler,* p. 64).

91. Helmuth's plan was remarkably similar to that of the Directorate of the Social Democratic Party (SOPADE), which was in exile in Prague after 1933. Its work of "enlightenment" had three aims: (1) to inform the public about the violation of human rights; (2) to point out that the Nazi policies were not designed to promote domestic peace; (3) to show that the Nazi regime was aiming toward war. The early publications of the organization were later mirrored by the leaflets and flyers which Hübener produced, including the statement that the reader should consider the flyer a chain letter and pass it on. The SOPADE also deposited their publications in mailboxes (Ditt, *Sozialdemokraten im Widerstand*, pp. 79–85).

92. In 1934 the Communists distributed 12,000 copies of a newspaper entitled *Die Rote Fahne* every fortnight in the Rhine and Ruhr areas. Nearly a million Communist leaflets were distributed in Germany in 1937. The attack on Russia witnessed a great increase in the number of leaflets distributed, of which 24,500 were seized during the second half of the year. Hübener's association with Communist youths probably contributed to his method of informing the public about the falsity of the German newscasts and the deception of the Nazi regime (Balfour, *Withstanding Hitler,* pp. 64–65).

93. Hans and Sophie Scholl were university students in Munich who were involved in a later resistance group known as the White Rose. They distributed leaflets denouncing the Nazi regime and calling for the overthrow of the government. They were observed at such activities, sentenced to death by the People's Court, and decapitated on 22 February 1943.

94. By 1943 the Security Service reported that posters and flyers were appearing regularly in Berlin and other large cities, and that the populace, instead of removing the inflammatory statements and surrendering them to the police, were reading them and passing them to other persons. After the debacle at Stalingrad, the police noted that it was rare to notice someone rejecting such inflammatory writings (Security Service Report No. 367, 15 Mar. 1943, in Boberach, *Meldungen aus dem Reich*, p. 372).

95. The term includes the word *Brand* ('fire') and may be derived from the Brandenburg Division, which was a commando unit used to capture objectives behind enemy lines and prevent bridge and tunnel demolitions by the enemy during his retreat (Eduard Steinberger, "We Were Totally Convinced We Were Doing the Right Thing," in Steinhoff, *Voices from the Third Reich*, p. 112).

96. Because of the shortage of materials resulting from the war, German industry was obligated to develop substitutes (often artificial) for those items that were extremely costly or unavailable. Hence, the Germans used *ersatz* (substitute) coffee, rubber, silk, and other items.

97. In addition to the regular weekly service required of Hitler Youth members, male or female, service on the land was obligatory. Most of those engaged in such service were involved with harvesting crops. Others, such as Schnibbe's friend, served for a year in a variety of occupations, often domestic in nature. For many young men, service on the land meant the end of their schooling, because as soon as their year of land service ended, they were taken into the military. In 1938, because so many females were seeking better-paying jobs in commercial areas and in towns, the government required a "duty year" of all unmarried girls or women under the age of twenty-five entering the labor force as office workers or employees in the clothing, textile, and tobacco industries (H. W. Koch, *Hitler Youth*, pp. 231–32; Grunberger, *Social History of the Third Reich*, p. 255).

98. Although the Gestapo probably never comprised more than approximately forty thousand persons, it succeeded in creating the impression that the organization had penetrated all aspects of public and private life and that the secret police were "omnipresent and ubiquitous" (Crankshaw, *Gestapo*, pp. 16, 89).

99. "Golden pheasant" was a term of ridicule applied to Nazi party functionaries who paraded in fancy uniforms and decorations. The term stemmed from the golden German eagle displayed so prominently on their uniforms. Common soldiers regarded the wearers, many of whom were corrupt administrators, as ostentatious and self-important (Snyder, *Encyclopedia of the Third Reich*, p. 124; Zentner and Bedürftig, *Encyclopedia of the Third Reich*, 1:352).

100. An estimated 600,000 Germans were killed in air-raid shelters during the war. In Berlin 47 percent of all dwellings were rendered inhabitable, while the average in Germany was 32 percent (*Bericht des Statistischen Bundesamtes*, 4 Apr. 1962, cited in Grunberger, *Social History of the Third Reich*, p. 42).

101. The shortage of rural labor contributed to short supplies of food in the cities. As early as 1938 many fields were lying fallow, because of the need for 600,000 farm workers. By the summer of 1939, the production of milk and butter had declined to the extent that the Reich was living off the cooking-fat reserves stored in September 1938, in the event of war. By the winter of 1939–40 there were severe coal shortages, resulting in outbreaks requiring the intervention of the police. Even beer, the most German of drinks, declined so much in quality that the percentage of wort in the brew was increased "to create a better disposition among . . . German beer drinkers" (Steinert, *Hitler's War*, p. 72). By 1939 nearly everyone except the nobility, the wealthy, and high party officials were complaining of low wages in comparison to the high cost of living and the shoddy quality of goods. In Hamburg in October 1940 the rations for a single person consisted of "60 grams of semolina [coarse wheat breakfast cereal] and oats [per day], and 125 grams [of] butter per week, 1 lb. meat and sausage per month" (Wolff-Mönckeberg, *On the Other Side*, pp. 28–29). By the end of 1940 the sausage was often unpalatable and the increasing list of complaints mentioned "difficulties with cooking fat and meat allotments, a reduction of bread rations, inade-

quate market deliveries of fruits and vegetables, as well as the complete elimination of game, poultry, and fish deliveries." Textiles and footwear were often unobtainable (Steinert, *Hitler's War,* p. 85).

102. The Jews were considered the lowest form of creature resembling
humanity, while the Slavs, especially the Poles and Russians, were regarded
as subhumans who were greatly inferior to Germans. Even the prominent
scholar Max Weber declared that "it is only thanks to us that the Poles are
human beings!" The French were hereditary enemies considered to be
"breeders of decadence and revolution" and viewed with loathing, because
of the Treaty of Versailles. See Hans Kohn, *The Mind of Germany* (London:
Macmillan, 1961), p. 269, cited by Grunberger, *Social History of the Third
Reich,* pp. 32–33.

103. Wobbe recounted hearing similar comments from Hübener on an
earlier occasion and believes it was then that Helmuth decided a course of
action against the Nazis needed to be taken. While the boys were walking
home and singing popular American songs after church services they were
confronted by a Hitler Youth patrol which demanded to see their identification and inquired why they were singing "English songs." Hübener berated
the patrol members so vehemently that they withdrew. He then commented
to Wobbe that "our country is being run through threats, intimidations and
even brutal force. And something has to be done about this!" (Wobbe and
Borrowman, *Before the Blood Tribunal,* pp. 21–22).

104. On one occasion an elderly female member of the LDS branch picked
up a leaflet dropped by the British and brought it to church with her. She
casually showed it to other members until the branch president, Arthur Zander,
noticed what she was doing. He ripped the flyer out of her hand and told her
that "if you ever bring enemy propaganda literature into this branch house
again, I will see to it that you are brought into a concentration camp." When
Wobbe reported the incident to Hübener, Helmuth responded by saying that
"the evil influence of Nazism, with its disregard of human rights and feelings,
is making inroads even into the Church by changing people's priorities and
loyalties" (Wobbe and Borrowman, *Before the Blood Tribunal,* p. 31).

105. On a previous occasion, 1 January 1941, Worbs, while praying in
the presence of Wobbe, Hübener, and Arthur Sommerfeldt, had made anti-
Nazi statements. The boys warned Worbs to be careful of what he said in
public. He responded that "I tell the truth and nothing but the truth, and I
cannot tell a lie" (Wobbe and Borrowman, *Before the Blood Tribunal,* p. 20).

106. Denunciation was an integral and essential part of the Gestapo system of terror and was "one of the mechanisms that caused the Gestapo to
move into action on any particular case." Slightly more than one-quarter of
Gestapo cases began with an identifiable denunciation which "constituted
the single most important cause for the initiation of proceedings of all kinds."
There was no specific law that required citizens to inform on one another,
but §139 of the criminal code made it a crime if a person failed to communicate knowledge of possible treasonous activities, which included malicious
gossip, defeatist statements, or merely innocuous criticism of a party leader
(Gellately, *Gestapo and German Society,* pp. 132–39).

107. Those fortunate enough to be released from a concentration camp were forbidden to inform anyone of their experiences upon the threat of being arrested and incarcerated again. The silence maintained by those who returned, coupled with the obvious evidence of their experiences, fostered a greater fear of the camps. Anyone who learned from a former prisoner of the terrors of a concentration camp faced the challenge of remaining silent about the murders and tortures in order to avoid being imprisoned. Like others released from concentration camps, Worbs was obligated to sign a statement that he had been incarcerated for "educational purposes" and had been treated well (Hoffmann, *History of the German Resistance*, p. 16; Wobbe and Borrowman, *Before the Blood Tribunal*, p. 26; see also Klaus Drobisch and Günther Wieland, *System der NS-Konzentrationslager 1933–1939* [Berlin: Akademie Verlag, 1993], p. 138).

108. Worbs had been sent to the Neuengamme concentration camp near Hamburg, where he was detained for six months. Upon his return to Hamburg, he was scarcely recognizable and "was a broken man, a shadow of his former self" (Wobbe and Borrowman, *Before the Blood Tribunal*, p. 26).

109. According to the LDS branch records in Hamburg, Worbs did not die until 8 October 1945, when he succumbed to pneumonia. This record might be in error, because Schnibbe, Wobbe, and Otto Berndt state that Worbs died shortly after being released in 1941.

110. Not everyone in the church congregation felt the same toward Worbs as Schnibbe's father and Helmuth Hübener. Some members of the congregation gave Worbs the "cold shoulder" and refused to speak to him, accusing him of "kicking against the pricks." It is likely that his religious compatriots feared that by associating with Worbs they could be suspected of wrongdoing and be arrested by the Gestapo. Inflicting terror upon one person, whether in a family or some other form of community, served effectively to guarantee the cooperation or compliance of others (Wobbe and Borrowman, *Before the Blood Tribunal*, p. 26).

Chapter 3: Guests of the Gestapo

1. Workers were conscripted from the countries conquered by the German army. After the German victory over France, Germany retained approximately two million French prisoners as hostages and for conscripted labor (Klaus-Jörg Siegfried, *Das Leben der Zwangsarbeiter im Volkswagenwerk 1939–1945* [New York: Campus Verlag, 1988], pp. 124–25). Hübener apparently wanted to start a circle of acquaintances by distributing flyers in the French language in the Altona district of Hamburg (Sander, "Helmuth-Hübener Gruppe," in Hochmuth and Meyer, *Streiflichter*, p. 335). See also Heck, *Burden of Hitler's Legacy*, p. 74.

2. Mohns was a *Betriebsobmann*, a shop steward, appointed to a company of four or more employees. Selected from the ranks of the employees by the German Labor Front, he was in charge of ideologically "aligning" the other employees in the National Socialist sense and had political and social control (Zentner and Bedürftig, *Encyclopedia of the Third Reich*, 2:1064).

3. In Wobbe's account Mohns first talked with Kranz and Düwer together. Düwer, "not having any experience in these matters and having no support group . . . as frightened as a teen-age boy would be," agreed to get some materials later from Hübener (Wobbe and Borrowman, *Before the Blood Tribunal*, p. 40).

4. Before Helmuth returned to the apartment of his grandparents with the Gestapo agents to search the premises, he was interrogated by the Gestapo and "made soft." When his grandmother Sudrow saw him, she was distressed at his obviously severe mistreatment. She asked him why he had been arrested and what had happened, but the Gestapo agents would not permit Helmuth to answer and dragged him away (see Document 72).

5. As early as Christmas 1941 Hans Kunkel, the half-brother of Helmuth, had warned of the dangers in continuing his resistance activity (see Document 74).

6. Nazi block leaders ranked lowest in the Nazi party hierarchy and were part of the surveillance system to observe the German people. By January 1939 there were 463,048 block leaders who reported to the next higher echelon, the cell leaders. The large majority of block leaders performed such functions as compiling a "household card index" of everyone who lived in their area, collecting for Nazi charities and fund drives, and distributing ration books on an unpaid basis on their own time. The block leaders were also responsible for the party bulletin boards. Although they were told not to spy on those under their care, such behavior was difficult to avoid, because they were expected to be able to report on the political background and reliability of their neighbors. Block leaders also sought out Jews hiding in the premises over which they had responsibility. The block leaders compiled the reports on the reputations and generosity of investigated persons. It was their duty to discover persons circulating pernicious rumors and to report them to the *Ortsgruppe*, so the information could be relayed to the Gestapo. Block leaders also enforced blackout regulations and kept close tabs on room occupancy. Because of their pervasiveness, block leaders were usually treated with a respectful caution and with the motto "The enemy is listening" in mind. At the Nuremberg trials following the war, the American judge advocate, General Thomas Dodd, stated that "in no Nazi cell or block could a secret remain unknown to them. The switching on of a radio, the disapproval of a frown, the inviolate secrets between priest and penitent, and the ancient confidence between father and son, even the sacred confidences of marriage, were their stock in trade. Their business was to know" (Jacques Delarues, *The Gestapo: A History of Horror* [New York: Paragon House, 1987], p. 80; see also Gellately, *Gestapo and German Society*, pp. 73–74; Grunberger, *Social History of the Third Reich*, p. 67; Behrend-Rosenfeld, *Ich stand nicht allein*, p. 64; Mackinnon, *Naked Years*, p. 196; and Documents 17–20).

7. When the organizers of the fiftieth anniversary commemoration of Hübener's execution solicited information from individuals who had known Helmuth, some of the original flyers were acquired. These flyers, the possession of which was a serious criminal offense in Nazi Germany, had been hidden for more than a half-century. Ulrich Sander claims that Hübener

produced editions of sixty copies of some flyers, nine of which came to the attention of the Gestapo. It appears unlikely that Hübener produced any more flyers than were presented as evidence at his trial ("Helmuth-Hübener Gruppe," in Hochmuth and Meyer, *Streiflichter*, p. 330).

8. In 1948 Gerhard Düwer made a statement indicating that Hübener had organized several groups and was pursuing a more active resistance than Schnibbe suspected: "My friend Hübener gathered several friends in a resistance group. That was the beginning of our actual work. We met together often to listen to foreign radio stations. That which was heard was taken down in stenography and then reproduced, which at that time was done completely with a typewriter, an enormous chore. The resulting flyers were frequently distributed in the form of chain letters and at first, of course, in a narrow and outer circle of acquaintances. When we had become more accustomed to it, we began to distribute the flyers in greater numbers. We posted them on poster columns, tacked them on the bulletin boards of the Nazi Party, tossed them in mailboxes, or stuck them in the coat pockets of guests at shows, festivities, and dances. For the most part we singled out the city districts of Hamm, Hammerbrook, and Rothenburgsort. The circle got bigger and bigger and we found more and more people to work with us. In order to provide for a larger operation, we found a press in Kiel that wanted to produce the flyers in greater numbers; of course a secret job at night by two employees. . . . And then we started sending the flyers in letters to the front" (Sander, "Helmuth-Hübener Gruppe," in Hochmuth and Meyer, *Streiflichter*, pp. 334–35). Hübener likely received some of his ideas, such as producing the flyers and attempting to instigate a chain-letter effect, from the Communists, who used the same tactics and produced much of their literature in Kiel. See also Wobbe and Borrowman, *Before the Blood Tribunal*, p. 40; and Klaus Mammach, *Widerstand 1939–1945. Geschichte der deutschen antifaschistschen Widerstandsbewegung im Inland und in der Emigration* (Berlin: Paul Rugenstein, 1987), pp. 68, 146.

9. According to Jupp and Ida Wieczorek, Hübener met and associated with the Hamburg-Altona Communist youth resistance group in 1940 and 1941, before starting to listen to foreign radio broadcasts in the apartment of his grandparents. The group included, at least, the leader, Josef Wieczorek, Hans Beier, Paul Liedel, and Hübener. Josef was a member of the Communist youth organization, Red Pioneers, before 1933 and forced to drop out of the secondary school because he lost his scholarship and his unemployed family could not provide the necessary funds. In early 1941, Josef informed his father, who was imprisoned for illegal political activities, about the activities of the Communist youth group in Altona, which Hübener had joined. The youths met at the apartment of the Wieczorek parents and the garden house of a Dr. Horn in Hamburg-Bahrenfeld to discuss politics and listen to foreign broadcasts, which had a profound impression on Helmuth. It was at such discussions that he learned the fate of the great number of democrats thrown into prisons and concentration camps. In February 1941 Josef Wieczorek was inducted into the German army and he was sent eastward in May. After Josef Wieczorek entered the military, Hübener started listening

to the radio his brother brought from France (Franz Ahrens, "Er war nicht allein!" in *Blinkfeuer* [Hamburg], 27 Oct. 1966, cited in Sander, "Helmuth-Hübener Gruppe," in Hochmuth and Meyer, *Streiflichter,* pp. 328–29). Wobbe claimed that he learned later that Hübener had "cultivated ties with communistic youth organizations, like the Wieczorek group" (Wobbe and Borrowman, *Before the Blood Tribunal,* p. 39).

10. Wobbe believed that Arthur Sommerfeld "was also involved and knew of his [i.e., Hübener's] involvement to some extent," but that only Schnibbe, Wobbe, and Hübener were involved in the distribution of the leaflets (Wobbe and Borrowman, *Before the Blood Tribunal,* p. 39).

11. This saying was derived from the Nazi slogan: "Wheels must roll for victory!" which, among other places, was painted on the sides of the rail cars carrying German troops to the Polish front and was plastered in the German railroad stations and inside passenger cars until the end of the war. See Mackinnon, *Naked Years,* p. 62; Joffroy, *Spy for God,* p. 126; Graf von Christian Krockow, *Hour of the Women* (New York: Harper-Collins, 1991), p. 16.

12. In October 1939 Roland Freisler, a state secretary in the Ministry of Justice, introduced a new legal "system of values" to be applied during the war. Included in the "new state of affairs" were deeds which, under normal conditions, did not qualify as punishable transgressions. In one case, an elderly woman was sentenced to death as a "parasite of the people," because she knitted a pair of mittens for her grandchild from the wool gathered for the Winter Relief program (Meyer, *Nacht über Hamburg,* p. 61). Refusing to give the "German greeting" (i.e., "Heil Hitler") could be construed as resistance to the Nazi state and result in a sentence of death, as could refusing to make a small contribution to a Nazi fund drive, or commenting that the war was not going well (Hoffmann, *German Resistance,* p. 55). A single word could bring a person to the scaffold. Referring to Hitler as a *Teppichbeißer* (lit.: "rug-biter," i.e., lunatic) resulted in the execution of a highly gifted and famous piano virtuoso (Leo Schwering, *In den Klauen der Gestapo. Tagebuchaufzeichnungen der Jahre 1944–1945* [Cologne: Verlag J. P. Bachem, 1988], p. 84).

13. After the defeat of the German army at Stalingrad at the beginning of 1943 and the reverses in the North African theater, the terror inflicted by the special courts increased, particularly in relation to petty offenses such as robbing postal packages. Suspects were often tried and executed publicly on the scene to serve as a deterrent (Meyer, *Nacht über Hamburg,* p. 63). During a spot check at the post office at the Südbahnhof in Vienna, it was discovered that seventeen employees had stolen bars of chocolate and soap from gift parcels sent to the military. They were summarily marched to a nearby square and executed (interview with Rosa Chlupaty in Vienna, Apr. 1965, cited in Grunberger, *Social History of the Third Reich,* p. 38).

14. Looting after an air raid carried such severe penalties that pedestrians were known to make wide detours around areas that had been bombed (Grunberger, *Social History of the Third Reich,* pp. 37–38).

15. Offenses committed during a blackout were against the Public Inquiry Order and were particularly heavily punished, sometimes by death. The

Swedish newspaper *Stockholms Tidningen* reported eleven executions on 19 February 1942 (Martin Broszat, "Resistenz und Widerstand," in M. Broszat et al., eds., *Bayern in der NS-Zeit* [Munich: Oldenbourg, 1981], 4:697–99; see also *Reichsgesetzblatt* (5 Sept. 1939), 1:1679, §2, and Grunberger, *Social History of the Third Reich*, p. 124n).

16. For an enlightening assessment of the changes in German law instituted by the Nazis and the pervasiveness of harsh prison terms and death sentences, the reader is encouraged to consult Ingo Müller, *Hitler's Justice*, pp. 74, 90–91, 111–15, 130–34.

17. In July 1939 a conference was held in Berlin to outline a program for the elimination of the mentally ill in Germany. A note was presented to Hitler by proponents of euthanasia asking him to allow them to proceed with their program. In a document dated 1 September 1939, Hitler signed the letter. Even though the letter did not have the force of law, it was adequate for the implementation of the program (Steinert, *Hitler's War*, p. 79). Six hospitals were designated for the elimination of adults and four for children. The definition of the undesirables was changed to include the mentally retarded, the chronically and incurably ill, the unproductive elderly, and anyone else considered superfluous (Ernst Klee, *Euthanasie im NS-Staat* [Frankfurt am Main: Fischer Verlag, 1983], pp. 86–103). By the time the program ended officially in August 1942, more than 70,000 persons had been killed, while another 100,000 were murdered thereafter as a result of unofficial euthanasia. Some estimates ran as high as a total of 200,000 euthanasia deaths (Joffroy, *Spy for God*, p. 122). See also William Brennan, *Medical Holocausts I: Exterminative Medicine in Nazi Germany and Contemporary America* (New York: Nordland, 1980), pp. 52, 56, 104–5, 156–57; and Ingo Müller, *Hitler's Justice*, p. 128.

18. Because Lüdelsen was a small farm town, it was easier to secure provisions there than in Hamburg.

19. Hübener was excommunicated from the LDS Church on 15 February 1942, possibly in a move to protect the branch from recriminations by the Nazi regime. The record was annotated on 11 November 1946 to read: "Excommunication done by mistake" (LDS Records of Members, Hamburg, Germany [1922–48]).

20. The same questions ran through the mind of Rudi Wobbe, who considered fleeing Germany and going to Switzerland, England, or Sweden. He knew a journeyman at his place of employment who had an uncle living in Sweden, so Rudi engaged the acquaintance in a conversation about that country. Just as he was set to ask the journeyman if he could help Rudi escape to Sweden, "the shop Nazi stepped up and asked why I was asking so many questions." The chance passed and Wobbe never had another opportunity to ask the journeyman for help in escaping the country. He inquired later of a tenant in his house, who was from Holland, about the possibility of a person getting in touch with the Dutch underground and being smuggled into England. The tenant advised him against such an action (Wobbe and Borrowman, *Before the Blood Tribunal*, pp. 45–48).

21. Wobbe was arrested on Wednesday, 18 February, while he was in class

at vocational school (Wobbe and Borrowman, *Before the Blood Tribunal*, p. 49).

22. When Rudi arrived at church the following Sunday, Karl-Heinz's sister, Karla, after checking to see that no one was listening, informed him that "Karl-Heinz got arrested by the Gestapo last Tuesday [and]—they are going to get you next!" Others in the LDS branch suspected Rudi's involvement (Wobbe and Borrowman, *Before the Blood Tribunal*, pp. 46–47).

23. Wobbe was less cautious and had hidden some of the larger leaflets in his "secret hiding place," which was where the wallpaper had come loose behind a wall hanging, creating a small pocket which the Gestapo agents did not find (Wobbe and Borrowman, *Before the Blood Tribunal*, p. 50).

24. Wobbe estimated that Paul, who towered over the other guards in height and brutality, was at least six feet eight inches in height. His rubber truncheon was "never idle" (Wobbe and Borrowman, *Before the Blood Tribunal*, p. 53).

25. Late in the war Paul was still plying his trade as torturer. When Aenne Bohne-Lucko was imprisoned in Kolafu in March 1945, she met Paul, whom she described as "the most feared brawler and murderer" (". . . entkommen," in Gerda Zorn and Gertrud Meyer, eds., *Frauen gegen Hitler. Berichte aus dem Widerstand, 1933–45* [Frankfurt: Röderberg Verlag, 1974], p. 94). Wobbe heard later that Paul was identified one day on the streets of Hamburg by some of the former inmates of Kolafu, who beat him to death before the police could arrive (Wobbe and Borrowman, *Before the Blood Tribunal*, p. 137).

26. While imprisoned in Kolafu in 1945, Gertrud Meyer asked one of the female prison guards who appeared less crude than the others why she chose to serve in such a capacity. The answer, which stunned Meyer, was that the work was the "most convenient employment available" and that the "SS uniform appealed" to her. Meyer then asked how someone so apparently well educated could engage in such work. The response was that "at first it was a bit different from what I anticipated, but one can become accustomed to anything. When my shift ends here and I close the door, I simply turn it off" (Gertrud Meyer, "Begegnung mit der Schauspielerin Hanne Mertens," in Zorn and Meyer, *Frauen gegen Hitler*, pp. 78–79).

27. Physical assault usually accompanied one's arrest by the Gestapo and continued intermittently until formal methods of torture, if deemed necessary, were inflicted. The purpose of beating the prisoners was to break their will and shatter their nerves, thus stunning and humiliating them so they would confess more readily. By knocking their victims off balance and beating and kicking them, the Gestapo officials kept them off guard and made them more "cooperative." Only the bravest individuals were able to endure such treatment (Crankshaw, *Gestapo*, p. 127).

28. By 1938 the rearmament program had changed the mass unemployment of the early 1930s into a labor shortage. In order to continue the war program and the four-year plan, and cover the demand for agricultural labor, the German government imported 120,000 foreign workers in 1938. The government developed measures to procure and assure an adequate number of workers. Anyone considered a vagrant, that is, anyone without a perma-

nent abode, was persecuted as an "anti-social parasite on the people." All itinerants were to be rounded up and forced to work. Fearing it would lose potentially valuable workers, in 1939 the Hamburg city government ordered a comprehensive registration of all "vagrants, vagabonds and anti-social elements." When the various flophouses, homeless shelters, and the like were raided, it was discovered that the residents were not, as suspected, old and decrepit human wrecks, but mostly (75 percent) persons of middle age who were capable of working (Ayass, "Vagrants and Beggars," in Evans, *German Underworld*, pp. 228–32). Declaring that there must be "no more tramps in Germany," the local authorities placed those who refused to work in a labor welfare camp, a home for the destitute, or a concentration camp. Of an estimated 10,000 tramps imprisoned during the Third Reich, few survived (Noakes, "Social Outcasts," in Bessel, *Life in the Third Reich*, pp. 93–94).

29. Before 1914 protective custody was designed to protect someone from danger, such as being killed by a mob. During the Weimar era the meaning was expanded, but the person was to be released or brought to trial within twenty-four hours. As interpreted under the Nazis, protective custody made it possible for the police to arrest and detain anyone suspected of being an enemy of the state, which was an efficient means of eliminating opposition. The practice dealt with indictable offenses and was used to prevent "threats from subversive elements" (Gellately, *Gestapo and German Society*, p. 28). In a short time the prisons of Hamburg were so full of alleged opponents that a special prison (Wittmoor) was created for political prisoners. This prison was soon filled to capacity, so the former prison for women, Fuhlsbüttel, which was standing empty, was used. By the end of 1933, 682 citizens of Hamburg had been incarcerated on political grounds (Schorer, *Als Hamburg unter den Nazis lebte*, pp. 17–18). Protective custody was not limited in time and was not subject to any legal jurisdiction. During the war it was exceptionally rare for anyone in protective custody to be released, particularly those considered "asocial elements" or "enemies of the state having previous convictions" (Meyer, *Nacht über Hamburg*, p. 58).

30. The arrest and detention of "anti-social elements" was facilitated by the "Fundamental Decree on Crime Prevention by the Police" issued on 14 December 1937. In 1938 Heydrich informed the criminal police that "at least 200 male persons capable of work are to be placed under preventive police custody in your police division during the week from 13 to 18 June 1938 by applying the decree of 14 December 1937 in the harshest way possible." In the Hamburg police division there were 700 arrests, 300 of which were within the city boundaries. Those arrested were taken to the Fuhlsbüttel prison, the number of whose inmates increased from 72 to 1,006 during June 1938. A month later the number had dropped to fewer than 100, because the "work shy" prisoners had been deported to the Sachsenhausen concentration camp (Ayass, "Vagrants and Beggars," in Evans, *German Underworld*, pp. 229–30). "A Gestapo report of April 1939 showed 162,734 persons held in 'protective custody' for political reasons, 27,369 were awaiting trial for political misdemeanors, and 112,432 had been sentenced for politi-

cal misdemeanors." These figures do not include those political persons who died from mistreatment, were murdered, or were shot "while trying to escape" (Günther Weisenborn, *Der Lautlose Aufstand: Bericht über die Widerstandsbewegung des deutschen Volkes 1933–1945* [Hamburg: Rowohlt Verlag, 1953], p. 30, cited in Hoffmann, *History of German Resistance*, p. 16).

31. Wobbe was first imprisoned with a member of the SS who had been deceived by a supervisor, resulting in his arrest for theft and malfeasance. It was he who taught Rudi how to survive in prison (Wobbe and Borrowman, *Before the Blood Tribunal*, p. 54).

32. When asked why he was sent to Kolafu, Rudi answered "Tall Paul" that he did not know, whereupon Paul assailed him with the omnipresent rubber truncheon (Wobbe and Borrowman, *Before the Blood Tribunal*, p. 58).

33. Persons detained under protective custody were often not informed of the charges against them, but were left in ignorance so that they would be "prepared" better and succumb more easily to the brutal methods which always followed arrests (Schwering, *In den Klauen der Gestapo*, pp. 84–85).

34. Unyielding prisoners were sometimes retained in Fuhlsbüttel for weeks or months and kept bound hand and foot with metal bands. In the evenings their hands and feet were tied to the sides and feet of their beds (Ditt, *Sozialdemokraten im Widerstand*, p. 93).

35. In addition to political opponents, the persons most often denounced as asocial elements were drunkards, prostitutes, beggars, shirkers, and the like. They were often joined by others, such as gypsies, whom the Gestapo imprisoned because it did not know what else to do with them (Meyer, *Nacht über Hamburg*, p. 59).

36. Walter Schmedemann relates numerous instances of suicides by prisoners who could no longer face the torture or who did not want to risk endangering the lives of others ("Bericht von Walter Schmedemann über die Methoden der Nationalsozialisten gegen ihre politischen Gegner vom Januar 1934," in Ditt, *Sozialdemokraten im Widerstand*, p. 144). One prisoner perceived that "degradation was exactly what the Nazis wanted. The hunger, humiliation and constant beatings made us begin to believe that we actually were sub-human. . . . With the loss of dignity came the loss of a will to live" (Sala Pawlowicz, *I Will Survive* [New York: Norton, 1962], p. 146).

37. Once the beds were made and the room cleaned, a guard came with white gloves to try to discover evidence of filth of any kind. Prisoners whose cells were not clean enough were punished (Wobbe and Borrowman, *Before the Blood Tribunal*, pp. 54–55).

38. Wobbe recounts that the prisoners were herded outside and required to walk in single file in a line around the courtyard for twenty minutes without speaking to one another before returning to their cells. In the meantime, the guards turned their cells inside out, looking for illegal items (Wobbe and Borrowman, *Before the Blood Tribunal*, p. 62).

39. *Muckefuck* and *Mucke* were the slang expressions for *ersatz* (artificial or substitute) coffee.

40. "There was a broad cross section of society in prison. One of the most persecuted groups . . . were the Swing-Boys, who were . . . the 'preppies' of their

day. It was a kind of club in Hamburg. They listened to jazz recordings from England and America, wore their hair a bit too long for conventional Nazi taste, and danced in a style that Nazis considered decadent. The Gestapo came down on them with a vengeance. They were young men of my age. I felt sorry for the fellows. Without exception they all went to the concentration camp only because they had listened to certain English-language phonograph records. The Gestapo did not want to kill them, but reeducate them. They beat them up terribly" (Rainer Pohl, "Das gesunde Volksempfinden ist gegen Dad und Jo," in *Verachtet-verfolgt-vernichtet-zu den "vergessenen" Opfern des NS-Regimes*, ed. Klaus Frahm et al., Projektgruppe für die vergessenen Opfer des NS-Regimes in Hamburg e.V., 2d ed., [Hamburg: VSA-Verlag, 1988], pp. 14–45). The Nazi government saw the adoption of foreign culture as a trend toward deserting traditional German values and pursuing potentially treasonous activities. As a result, public and private dance parties were suspect.

41. Those forced to stand facing the wall were subject to punishment if they made any movement. The most frequent punishment was having one's face shoved into the wall until blood flowed, usually from the nose. Prisoners were not permitted to raise their hands or arms to stop the bleeding (Meyer, *Nacht über Hamburg*, pp. 20–21; Gerda Zorn, "Aus dem Leben der Charlotte Gross," in Zorn and Meyer, *Frauen gegen Hitler*, pp. 13–14; Lucie Suhling, "Aufmachen—Polizei!" in ibid., p. 37).

42. After he was returned to the hall of mirrors following his first interrogation, Wobbe was fortunate to stand next to an older man who whispered to him how he needed to behave in order not to be caught in a verbal trap or to give in to the harsh methods (Wobbe and Borrowman, *Before the Blood Tribunal*, p. 61).

43. "Wir tragen unser Schicksal mit Geduld, denn an der großen Scheiße sind wir selber schuld."

44. The hall of mirrors customarily held approximately twenty prisoners awaiting interrogation (Zorn, "Aus dem Leben Charlotte Gross," in Zorn and Meyer, *Frauen gegen Hitler*, p. 13).

45. When Lucie Suhling met her husband under identical circumstances after a week's absence from him, she was stunned at his appearance. He appeared to have aged several years and his face was so changed from the torture and sleeplessness that she was unable to refrain from crying over his condition (Suhling, "Aufmachen—Polizei!" p. 37).

46. It was assumed by the Gestapo that anyone arrested was, at the least, knowledgeable about subversive activities. Victims were often questioned on topics about which they knew nothing, on the chance that they might reveal something. If the earlier torture did not result in a confession, the pressure was increased until the victim was dead or nearly so before the Gestapo concluded that nothing was to be gained. The torture of innocent persons might last for days until the victim was so injured that he was then shot "as good for nothing" (Crankshaw, *Gestapo*, pp. 130–31).

47. Any denial was usually rewarded with a blow to the face (Zorn, "Aus dem Leben der Charlotte Gross," in Zorn and Meyer, *Frauen gegen Hitler*, pp. 13–14).

48. The two Gestapo agents played the roles of "bad cop" and "good cop," with Wangemann being "tough and brutal" and Müssener being "subdued and supportive." Wobbe gives details of the interrogations (Wobbe and Borrowman, *Before the Blood Tribunal,* pp. 56–57).

49. Many of the administrative and clerical personnel had no police training but were merely civil servants. The clerks and typists were frequently the wives or relatives of the Gestapo officials (Crankshaw, *Gestapo,* p. 95).

50. In the French Resistance it was expected that nobody could withstand for longer than twenty-four hours the methods used by the Gestapo for extracting confessions (Rothfels, *German Opposition to Hitler,* p. 11).

51. The resistance rings broken in Hamburg between 1933 and 1935 usually had contacts outside Germany and numbers of members far exceeding that of the Hübener group. There were occasional members in their teens, but most of the conspirators were adults, which is why the Gestapo could not believe that Hübener and others of his age conducted their own resistance movement (Ditt, *Sozialdemokraten im Widerstand,* pp. 88, 96–97). It was incomprehensible to the secret police that a boy of seventeen could lead a ring and produce such high-quality flyers, so they tortured him to learn the names of the adults (*Hintermänner*) behind the operation. Criminal Secretary Müssener stated that "only after lengthy remonstrances and emphatic admonishments was Hübener moved to make a confession about the extent of his destructive activity" (Sander, "Helmuth-Hübener Gruppe," in Hochmuth and Meyer, *Streiflichter,* p. 336; see also Wobbe and Borrowman, *Before the Blood Tribunal,* pp. 58–59).

52. Irmgard Becker, a member of the Mormon branch in Hamburg in 1942, relates that the parents of Karl-Heinz Schnibbe were "downright sick after the arrest" ("regelrecht krank nach der Verhaftung") (see Document 67).

53. The Holstenglacis prison was for persons confined temporarily on some charge. The prison had a capacity of 1,200. In 1935, 1,089 of these were men and 111 were women (Germany, Reichsjustizministerium, *The Prison System in Germany* [Berlin, 1935], p. 36).

54. Untersuchungsgefängnis.

55. It was not until 10 February 1936 that the Gestapo was finally given a legal basis and simultaneously raised above the law. There was no appeal from the decisions of the Gestapo and normal judicial bodies were forbidden to question the Gestapo's activities. A person arrested by the Gestapo had no legal basis for appeal. If a person was acquitted by a court of law or released from prison after serving a sentence, he could be rearrested immediately by the Gestapo and put under protective custody, which usually meant being sent to a concentration camp. The spirit of the Gestapo's extralegal power was explained by Hitler in 1938 when he declared that "every means adopted for the carrying out of the will of the Führer is considered legal, even though it may conflict with existing statutes and precedents" (Crankshaw, *Gestapo,* p. 89). A judge who considered a suspect innocent was disinclined to pronounce such a judgment, because he then might be arrested by the Gestapo (Schwering, *In den Klauen der Gestapo,* p. 131; see also Gisevius, *To the Bitter End,* p. 50).

56. According to an official report filed by the investigatory prison in Hamburg, 510 executions were carried out in Hamburg during the Hitler era. Many of the executions occurred after the start of the war in 1939, because of more stringent martial and special laws. During the Weimar period there were only three offenses for which a person could be executed. During the Nazi time, there were forty-six such crimes. The number of executions, of course, does not include those who died from other means. Not all those condemned to death in Hamburg were executed there (Meyer, *Nacht über Hamburg*, pp. 226–28).

57. Under the Nazi system of "justice," committing a political crime was the worst thing a person could do, whereas a person who committed a non-political crime would be tried and given the legal punishment, and "did not particularly need to be fearful" (Schwering, *In den Klauen der Gestapo*, p. 82).

58. Wobbe chose to remain in the cell with Bernhard Rubinke rather than move to a private cell, which turned out to be a mistake, because he was persuaded to divulge part of the contents of the secret document to his cellmate (Wobbe and Borrowman, *Before the Blood Tribunal*, pp. 63–64).

59. German law drew a distinction between high treason (*Hochverrat*) and treason to the country (*Landesverrat*). The latter was considered by many to be more serious (Balfour, *Withstanding Hitler*, p. 70).

60. On 24 April 1934 the People's Court (Volksgerichthof) was created, and replaced the Supreme Court (Reichsgericht) as the court of first instance. It was, in effect, a revolutionary tribunal for the Nazi party. Between 1937 and 1944, the People's Court tried 14,319 defendants, of whom 5,191 (36.3 percent) were sentenced to death, while 7,594 (53.0 percent) were incarcerated. Only 1,073 (7.5 percent) were acquitted (Ingo Müller, *Hitler's Justice*, pp. 140–52).

Chapter 4: Judgment and Destruction

1. Moabit was classified as a cellular prison for the imprisonment of convicts and the detention of others "for the protection of public safety and for the betterment of the detained person." The prison had a capacity of 620 and held only men. In 1935 it was filled to capacity and likely never had vacancies during the Nazi era (Reichsjustizministerium, *Prison System*, p. 33).

2. Wobbe's weight had dropped from 160 to 102 pounds during the six months of imprisonment. He was so weak he could scarcely climb the three flights of stairs to return to his cell in Moabit (Wobbe and Borrowman, *Before the Blood Tribunal*, p. 68).

3. "Each day we received three full meals. In the morning we were given 100 grams of bread with some unidentifiable beverage called malt coffee. At noon we were treated to some kind of watery soup. If a cabbage leaf happened to swim in it, it was cabbage soup; if there were a few kernels of barley and a few strands of beef, it was beef barley soup. The main ingredient was always water. The Berlin specialty was beef soup with herring—an awful combination. At night we were given another piece of bread (sometimes with a dab of margarine as a special treat) and some more malt coffee

to wash down our feast. Whenever the flap in the door was opened by the guard, he called out, 'Here you swine. Eat your swill'" (Wobbe and Borrowman, *Before the Blood Tribunal*, p. 68).

4. Wobbe's attorney, Karl Krause, a member of the National Socialistic Justice Association, treated him in like fashion. Rudi felt his counselor was distant and aloof and had no interest in his case. The interview was conducted much like an SS interrogation. The entire session was merely a superficial pretrial interview and the only contact between the two prior to the trial (Wobbe and Borrowman, *Before the Blood Tribunal*, p. 68).

5. Almost no attorneys in Germany were willing to represent diligently any person indicted by the Gestapo, even if the accused was totally innocent and a person of noble character, because any defense was a great hazard for the lawyer. An attorney was, in any "legal" dealings with the Gestapo, a "foreign body" and only those attorneys with "connections" with the secret police were allowed to plead for the accused. Of course, if the Gestapo chose, the attorney would be "shown the door" (Schwering, *In den Klauen der Gestapo*, pp. 148–49).

6. Bernhard Rubinke gained the confidence of Wobbe by going out of his way to befriend his inexperienced cellmate. He taught Rudi how to avoid problems with the guards. By standing in front of the peephole into the cell, Rubinke enabled Rudi to look out the window. "Before long he had me talking about my case and my feelings in general" (Wobbe and Borrowman, *Before the Blood Tribunal*, p. 63).

7. The use of fellow prisoners to ferret information was a common practice of the Gestapo (Ditt, *Sozialdemokraten im Widerstand*, pp. 97–98).

8. Upon entering the prison, Wobbe discovered that Rubinke had been shipped to Berlin at the same time, when he accidentally heard a guard in another room call out Rubinke's name and heard his former cellmate answer. The officer of the watch instructed the guard to keep Rubinke on a different floor of the prison until called to testify in court, but later it was decided not to call him as a witness (Wobbe and Borrowman, *Before the Blood Tribunal*, pp. 67, 71).

9. The complete statment to which Schnibbe refers is: "What the Hübener group of the religious community of the Church of Jesus Christ of Latter-day Saints did in the year 1941, as the Hitlerian war wagon appeared to be ascending to the sun, is simply inconceivable. Only someone who himself was active in the resistance movement can grasp what it means to compose, to reproduce, and to distribute more than thirty-five informational letters (*Aufklärungsschriften*) within a few months" (Franz Ahrens, *Helmuth Hübener*, Komitee ehemaliger politischer Gefangener [Hamburg: Hermes Verlag, 1948]; see also *Das Gewissen steht auf. 64 Lebensbilder aus dem deutschen Widerstand 1933–1945*, collected by Annedore Leber [Berlin: Mosaik Verlag, 1954]).

10. Pleitegeier.

11. Attendance at the trial was not open, which is why Johann Schnibbe requested permission to attend. Except for members of the press, who were present in a large number, there were few spectators (Wobbe and Borrowman, *Before the Blood Tribunal*, p. 69).

12. The questions were standard party questions, such as the birthdate of Hitler and points of the party program, in which the boys had been drilled in the Nazi youth organizations (Wobbe and Borrowman, *Before the Blood Tribunal*, p. 71).

13. "After passing this political IQ test, we were asked what we had against the Führer—a man who had freed Germany from foreign oppression, made her great among the nations of the world, and who had brought back a sense of national pride to all her citizens. Indeed, he asked, what could we hold against the man who was at this very moment leading the armed forces into a glorious victory against the Allies? This political tirade went on for several minutes. As the justice warmed to the subject he became angry and started shouting at us, 'You snot-nosed kids, what do you know of what is going on in the world today?' He caught himself, and tried to become objective again. (He didn't become more objective, just quieter.) He told us to sit down and then continued his questioning.

"At one point a judge asked us why we made special efforts to distribute the handbills in the workers' section of Hamburg. Helmuth answered the question, 'Hamburg will always be reactionary [*sic*] and opposed to the Nazis.'

"'Not true, you impertinent boy,' screamed the Chief Justice" (Wobbe and Borrowman, *Before the Blood Tribunal*, pp. 71–72).

14. Wobbe alleges that Düwer showed the leaflets to the Zumsande brothers in an attempt to persuade them to translate the writings into French, which they refused. Düwer then urged his acquaintances to read the leaflets for their political contents (Wobbe and Borrowman, *Before the Blood Tribunal*, p. 40).

15. On 12 May 1950, Heinrich Mohns was sentenced to a prison term of two years for "crimes against humanity." The *Hamburger Abendblatt* reported: "The Court of Assizes particularly took amiss that the defendant still does not see the injustice of his deed at that time." However, he never served his term. On 25 June 1953, the Fifth Criminal Panel of the Federal Court for Justice decreed (in legal jargon and logic reminiscent of the Nazi courts): "Upon the appeal of the plaintiff, the judgment of the Jury Court of Hamburg rendered on the 12th of May 1950 is nullified. The matter reverts to the Jury Court for new deliberation and judgment. . . . The Jury Court must therefore judge the deed of the plaintiff according to German Criminal Law. The central question to be investigated is whether the plaintiff is guilty of being an accessory to [Hübener's] killing or to the illegal deprivation of [Hübener's] freedom. The Jury Court must also determine whether the plaintiff's behavior was illegal, given the circumstances, if he was in fact obligated by law to denounce youthful offenders. If it should be found to be the case that the plaintiff is excused by virtue of the existence of emergency laws, then it should be investigated further whether the plaintiff was guilty of creating the state of emergency by his investigations. . . . The decision satisfies the petition of the Attorney General of the Federal Supreme Court" ("Wie bewältigen wir das schwerste Kapitel deutscher Geschichte?" *Beiheft*, p. 50).

16. Wobbe also received the impression "that Helmuth was purposely drawing attention to himself. Not to be in the limelight, but to focus the

court's attention on him and away from us. I think that he sensed that this would be his last battle, and he was willing to sacrifice himself to protect us. . . . If ever a man had a finest hour, this was Helmuth's" (Wobbe and Borrowman, *Before the Blood Tribunal*, p. 72).

17. In the German legal system the professional judges, not a jury, determined the guilt or innocence of the defendant. In Nazi Germany it was common for judges to confer with the prosecutors before a trial to determine the outcome. For some judges this was welcomed, because it absolved them of sole responsibility for the decisions. Because of the case loads, such conferences sometimes did not occur until the trial was underway, during a break in the proceedings (Werner Johe, *Die gleichgeschaltete Justiz* [Stuttgart: Europäische Verlagsanstalt, 1967], p. 187, cited in Grunberger, *Social History of the Third Reich*, p. 126). In the case of Hübener, Wobbe, Schnibbe, and Düwer, the judges did not leave the room to confer, but put their heads together at the bench for a few minutes and then announced they were ready to render a decision (Wobbe and Borrowman, *Before the Blood Tribunal*, p. 74).

18. Between 1937 and 1944 the People's Court went from sentencing 32 persons to death per year to 2,097 persons. In the year Hübener was sentenced to death, 1,191 others met the same fate, while only 107 defendants were acquitted, with 1,038 persons receiving prison sentences (Ingo Müller, *Hitler's Justice*, p. 143). Imposing the death sentence on youthful offenders was made easier by the decree of 4 October 1939, which transfered youths sixteen and older from juvenile courts to the more severe jurisdiction of the adult penal code if "their mental or moral development put them on a par with adults" ("Verordnung zum Schutz gegen jugendliche Schwerverbrecher," *Reichsgesetzblatt* [4 Oct. 1939], I, Pt. 1, p. 2000). One of the bases for considering Hübener qualified to be tried as an adult was his dissertation written at the *Oberbau*. Entitled "The Plutocrats," the work was so outstanding that it received a grade of A+ and moved Fikeis to comment that if the piece had been written at a law school it would have received honors (Wobbe and Borrowman, *Before the Blood Tribunal*, p. 71).

19. According to the account of the trial by the father of Karl-Heinz Schnibbe, Helmuth Hübener, who was bound in chains, collapsed when he heard the verdict. His friends were prevented from coming to his aid (see Document 72).

20. Even hardened Nazis were astonished at the verdict. Hübener was the first juvenile to be given the death penalty for violating the radio law (Erster Deutscher Rundfunk, 27 Oct. 1992, "Jugendfunk: Aktuelle Erinnerung an jugendliche Hitlergegner").

21. Wobbe was fortunate that the court sentenced him to ten years. On 21 March 1943, Roland Freisler, the president of the People's Court, informed lower jurisdictions in a threatening manner that "too mild sentences" were a stumbling block for the Gestapo. He instructed the presidents of the higher regional courts to cease giving sentences exceeding ten years imprisonment. For cases in which more than ten years was justified, the death penalty was to be applied instead of imprisonment (Meyer, *Nacht über Hamburg*, p. 63).

22. The crowd was astonished, because earlier resisters from Hamburg had received far less severe sentences for similar offenses. A group of approximately 150 persons sentenced before the *Oberlandesgericht* in Hamburg in 1935 for offenses strikingly similar to that of the Hübener group each received from one to two and one-half years imprisonment. The following year another group of Social Democrats was convicted and received higher sentences ranging from two to four years. Hübener, though, was accused and convicted under the radio ordinance of 1 September 1939. Hence, his sentence could be and was much harsher (*Stadtblatt der Frankfurter Zeitung*, 20 Jan. 1935, cited in Hellfeld and Klönne, *Die betrogene Generation*, p. 273).

23. None of the members of the People's Court were ever brought to trial or punished for their activities.

24. Wobbe recalled that those along the sides of the hall also bowed their heads and one of them whispered, "Have courage" (Wobbe and Borrowman, *Before the Blood Tribunal*, p. 76).

25. Wobbe's account differs in that he claims he was put accidentally into a cell with Hübener and a Swiss prisoner who were going to be taken to Plötzensee for execution. When the mistake was discovered, Rudi was removed from the cell and placed with the others of his party, thus making him the only one of the group to say farewell to Helmuth (Wobbe and Borrowman, *Before the Blood Tribunal*, pp. 76–77).

26. Wobbe maintains that it was the Swiss prisoner who spoke thus to Hübener (Wobbe and Borrowman, *Before the Blood Tribunal*, p. 76).

27. Plötzensee was a penal institution in northwest Berlin. Between 1933 and 1945 an estimated 2,400 persons were executed there. Many of those involved in the 20 July 1944 conspiracy were executed in Plötzensee. It is now the site of a memorial to the victims of Nazism (Zentner and Bedürftig, *Encyclopedia of the Third Reich*, 2:710).

28. Several appeals were made to the German Chancellery to grant clemency to Hübener and commute his sentence to life imprisonment. Among those appealing for clemency was the Gestapo (see Document 57).

29. According to Sommerfeld, the original letter, which was much longer than that reproduced here, was lost. She was able to recall only that which is contained in Documents 61 and 72.

30. Although he never belonged to one of the Communist or Social Democratic youth groups, Hübener associated with the Communists and can be counted among the youthful working-class opponents of the Nazi regime who were the predominant group of youth executed between 1939 and 1945. In the Brandenburg prison, 1,807 persons were executed for political reasons. Of this group, 75 were under twenty years of age, the youngest being sixteen (H. W. Koch, *Hitler Youth*, p. 223).

31. The boys had been in Berlin for twenty days (Wobbe and Borrowman, *Before the Blood Tribunal*, p. 81).

32. Walter Schmedemann, who was incarcerated in January 1934 and underwent the same experiences with the Gestapo and in the prisons in Hamburg, claims that the organ in Fuhlsbüttel was used to drown the screams of those being tortured. Lucie Suhling maintains that it was well

known in resistance circles that prisoners in Kolafu were tortured in the prison church so their screams could be drowned by the organ music ("Bericht von Walter Schmedemann," in Ditt, *Sozialdemokraten im Widerstand*, p. 145; Lucie Suhling, "Aufmachen—Polizei!" in Zorn and Meyer, *Frauen gegen Hitler*, p. 35; see also Meyer, *Nacht über Hamburg*, p. 22).

33. Glasmoor, which was regarded as a prison, had a capacity of 310 inmates, all of which were men in 1935 (Reichsjustizministerium, *Prison System*, p. 36).

34. According to information provided in 1935 by the Reich Ministry of Justice, "all prisoners legally obliged to work" were given work which made "the fullest possible use of their strength." Viewed as particularly important was "work in the open air," which included "the cultivation of waste and moor land." The type of sentence determined the daily hours of work, "usually ten hours for those sentenced to penal servitude and nine hours for those sentenced to imprisonment." The peat dug at Glasmoor was cut into squares and then stacked in the sun to dry. Later it was used as fuel in the prison furnace (Reichsjustizministerium, *Prison System*, pp. 13–15; Wobbe and Borrowman, *Before the Blood Tribunal*, pp. 81–82).

35. Glasmoor is situated thirty kilometers from the center of Hamburg.

36. Wobbe recalls the event differently: For a week prior to going to Glasmoor, he and Düwer were held in the UG (investigatory prison) in Hamburg, where they spent most of their time "chasing and exterminating bedbugs" before joining Schnibbe (Wobbe and Borrowman, *Before the Blood Tribunal*, p. 81).

37. Their primary task was to repair or make new uniforms for the other prisoners. They were infrequently given the special task of fashioning an unusual piece of clothing for some official (Wobbe and Borrowman, *Before the Blood Tribunal*, pp. 91–93).

38. Wobbe claims that it was the master tailor in the shop, Franken, who took a liking to the boys, chose Schnibbe as his personal orderly, and showed them the newspaper article announcing the execution of Helmuth Hübener on 27 October 1942 (Wobbe and Borrowman, *Before the Blood Tribunal*, pp. 82–83, 88).

39. Even though they were living on a farm, the daily fare of the inmates was not significantly better than it was in the other prisons, although they were able to "organize" (steal) food relatively easily. A major currency for food bartering was chewing tobacco, which was produced in a cord twenty-five inches long and one-quarter of an inch thick. Wobbe was successful in having his mother smuggle tobacco to him when she came for a visit. A centimeter of tobacco could be exchanged for 200 grams of bread, the equal of a morning's ration. Most of the prisoners, including Wobbe, smoked tobacco to deaden their hunger pangs (Wobbe and Borrowman, *Before the Blood Tribunal*, pp. 82, 93–94).

40. Wobbe makes no mention of the group of "Berliners" digging peat, although Schnibbe could have been involved in such an activity prior to the arrival of Wobbe and Düwer at Glasmoor.

41. Gerhard Düwer was moved at the same time to the prison office (Wobbe and Borrowman, *Before the Blood Tribunal*, p. 88).

42. In comparison with their habitations since their arrests, Glasmoor was relatively luxurious. "We also had the benefit of being under the supervision of our master craftsmen who were usually better to us than the hardened guards of the adult prisons. There the guards were long-term professionals who had spent a lifetime dealing with hardened criminals. Their methods were brutal and unfeeling. Our guards and supervisors were men who had made some kind of mistake while in the military, which landed them the assignment of prison duty. Having been civilians before the war, they still saw us a young people who would one day be set free. . . . In a sense our prison was a small community made up of people who provided support to each other." The prisoners usually worked approximately twelve hours per day, six days per week (Wobbe and Borrowman, *Before the Blood Tribunal*, pp. 88, 90).

43. *Sippenhaft* was the joint liability of a family for the crimes of one member. This practice was related to an ancient Germanic custom. In speaking to the Gauleiter on 3 August 1944, Himmler stated that "when they [the people's Germanic forebears] put a family under the ban and declared it outlawed or when there was a vendetta in the family, they were totally consistent about it. If a family was outlawed or banned, they said, 'This man has committed treason; there is traitor blood there; it will be exterminated.' And in a vendetta they exterminated the entire clan down to its last member" (cited in Hoffmann, *History of the German Resistance*, pp. 529–30).

44. Because Hamburg was the second largest city in Germany, it was believed that "the total destruction of this city would achieve immeasurable results in reducing the industrial capacity of the enemy's war machine" and "would play a very important part in shortening and in winning the war." On the first attack on the city the aircraft were to drop incendiary bombs in order to overwhelm the fire-fighting forces. Heavy attacks were launched against the city from 24 to 28 July. On the night of 24 July, 787 aircraft were involved in the bombing. Over 1,200 persons were killed and fire storms swept through several parts of the city (Gordon Musgrove, *Operation Gomorrah: The Hamburg Firestorm Raids* [New York: Jane's, 1981], pp. vii-viii, 65–102). On 27–28 July the night raid destroyed much of the city in the areas where Wobbe, Schnibbe, and Hübener had lived (Rodnick, *Portrait of Two German Cities*, pp. 234–37). The "atmospheric firestorm" unleashed on the city resulted in unimaginable damage to the buildings and to sheer terror for the citizenry. The heat and flames were so intense that some persons committed suicide rather than continue to face them. The parents of Schnibbe were extremely fortunate to escape relatively unharmed. Many of those who sought refuge in the water were burned or crushed by falling timber and masonry. In some instances the temperatures exceeded 1,400°F (Musgrove, *Operation Gomorrah*, p. 131). During the four major attacks on the city, 3,095 aircraft were used. Nine thousand tons of bombs, half of which were incendiary, were dropped. It is estimated that 55,000 persons were killed and 40,000 injured during the raids and that two-thirds of the housing was destroyed or badly damaged. Nearly one million persons fled the city (Noble Frankland, *Bomber Offensive: The Devastation of Europe* [New York: Ran-

dom House, 1970], p. 69). The American report of the bombing of Hamburg estimated that "the raids on Hamburg in July-August 1943 were among the most devastating of the war" (Martin K. Sorge, *The Other Price of Hitler's War: German Military and Civilian Losses Resulting from World War II* [New York: Greenwood Press, 1986], p. 102). Willy Schumann, who was living sixty miles away from Hamburg, recorded that he could see a large, dark cloud of smoke which hovered over the city for several days (Schumann, *Being Present*, p. 117). During the raid of 27–28 July, after thirty minutes of bombardment a single fire covered an area of twenty-two square kilometers. A vast suction developed which caused the air to storm "through the streets with immense force, bearing upon it sparks, timber and roof beams, and thus spreading the fire still further and further until it became a typhoon." The winds exceeded 150 mph, flinging human bodies into the air and sucking young children out of the arms of their mothers (Musgrove, *Operation Gomorrah*, p. 132). Wobbe claimed the prisoners in Glasmoor could smell the burning buildings and human flesh in Hamburg (Wobbe and Borrowman, *Before the Blood Tribunal*, p. 101). See also Erich Andres, "The Night of the Firestorm," in Steinhoff, *Voices from the Third Reich*, p. 203.

45. The citizens of greater Hamburg referred to the bombings of July and August 1943 as "The Catastrophe" and viewed it "as the end of the world for the inner city" (Irmgard Burmeister, "Although We Were Living in a Suburb, We Were Still Scared to Death," in Steinhoff, *Voices from the Third Reich*, p. 208). The detachments which cleared the rubble and gathered the dead bodies stacked the corpses as high as thirty-five layers deep on the streets. The smoke and dust remained so thick that for several days the work crews were obligated to go about with cellophane over their eyes. The intense heat often mummified the bodies and reduced them in size, so that entire families melted together could be put into a bathtub (Uwe Köster, "The Corpses Were beyond Identification," in ibid., p. 212).

46. Emma Hübener, Helmuth's mother, and his grandparents, the Sudrows, were killed during the bombing of Hamburg on 28 July 1943 (LDS Records of Members, Hamburg, Germany [1922–48]).

47. Robert Ley served the Nazi regime as the leader of the DAF (German Labor Front) and was, as a result, one of the most powerful Nazi leaders, although less well known than some of his contemporaries. He sought to have a modest home provided for each German family, a goal which was not realized. Because of Allied bombing and the enormous need for simple, inexpensive, and rapid housing, the scale of the projected houses was reduced until they became garden huts (Ronald Smelser, *Robert Ley: Hitler's Labor Front Leader* [New York: Berg, 1988], pp. 281–83). Even with the reduced size of lodgings, the number of new dwellings declined precipitously from 115,000 in 1940 to 28,000 in 1944, by which time the estimated shortage had reached eleven million (Jürgen Kuczinsky, *Die Geschichte der Arbeiter in Deutschland, 1933–46* [East Berlin, 1947], p. 211). See also Max Seydewitz, *Civil Life in Wartime Germany* (New York: Viking, 1945), p. 120.

48. By 1944 approximately four million apartments in Germany had been

destroyed by Allied bombing (Seydewitz, *Civil Life in Wartime Germany*, p. 308).

49. Wobbe claims that they were shipped to Graudenz during the last week of April 1944 (Wobbe and Borrowman, *Before the Blood Tribunal*, p. 101).

50. Graudenz is ninety-five kilometers south of Danzig.

Chapter 5: Poland and the Long Road Home

1. Graudenz served as a camp for prisoners of the German army during World War I also. It was virtually impossible to escape from the camp, because of the barbed wire and heavy posting of sentries. The rations of bread became increasingly smaller and the soup "steadily thinner." The prisoners became so weak that climbing the stairs of the barracks made them nearly collapse from exhaustion. The British were fortunate that they received regular shipments of packaged food from England, while the French were less well off (Robert Jackson, *The Prisoners, 1914–1918* [New York: Routledge, 1989], pp. 64–66, 111–13).

2. A geographical region of east central Europe in the upper Oder basin of approximately 17,500 square miles. Originally a Slavonic area of Poland, it was mostly incorporated into Prussia. In 1918 the Austrian portion of Silesia was divided between Czechoslovakia and Poland (Dudley Stamp, ed., *Dictionary of Geography* [New York: John Wiles and Sons, 1966], p. 384).

3. One of the drillmaster's particular sadistic pleasures was to require his charges to do a duckwalk, which damaged their knees (Wobbe and Borrowman, *Before the Blood Tribunal*, p. 82). A British captive reported that "we lost all POW rights and were subject to German military law and spent most of the day being drilled by a screeching German 'drill pig' who never let up" (David Rolf, *Prisoners of the Third Reich: Germany's Captives, 1939–1945* [London: Leo Cooper, 1988], p. 72).

4. Schnibbe and Wobbe rarely saw each other during their time at Graudenz. Rudi commented that Karl-Heinz got along well with those around him, because he learned to blend well into the prison life routine (Wobbe and Borrowman, *Before the Blood Tribunal*, p. 105).

5. When the Hübener group first arrived at Graudenz, the assembly plant was in the open, but because of enemy bombing raids it was moved to Corbiere fortress on the outskirts of Graudenz (Wobbe and Borrowman, *Before the Blood Tribunal*, p. 103).

6. Wobbe's job in reconstructing the airplanes consisted of repairing the fuselages by riveting patches over bullet holes, repairing the gas tanks, and checking the accelerator linkage and the connections to the engine (Wobbe and Borrowman, *Before the Blood Tribunal*, p. 102).

7. After Wobbe contracted cancer, from which he died in 1992, he quite naturally wondered if exposure to these chemicals had caused his illness.

8. Wobbe became well acquainted with a test pilot, who offered to give him a ride in one of the reconditioned planes. A guard heard of the proposal and put a stop to it, then reported the matter to the camp commander. The intervention of Dr. Krüger quashed the charges, so the guard called in

the Gestapo, which wanted to send the Hübener group to an extermination camp. Krüger refused to turn the young men over to the Gestapo, thus probably saving their lives (Wobbe and Borrowman, *Before the Blood Tribunal*, p. 103).

9. Tobacco was widely regarded as the most valuable commodity, because it "increased one's strength and lengthened one's life" (Tadeusz Wittlin, *A Reluctant Traveller in Russia* [New York: Rinehart, 1952], p. 7). Many prisoners considered tobacco more valuable than food. All prisoners smoked, even those who had never done so before their capture. For many the addiction to tobacco was so strong that they readily traded their food or clothes for a few cigarettes (Eberhard Pautsch, *Und dennoch Überlebt. Als sechzehnjähriger auf dem "Archipel Gulag"* [Dülmen: Laumann Verlag, 1984], p. 94).

10. One German prisoner in the USSR noticed that the most brutal camp guards he encountered were German deserters from a pioneer battalion formed of men who had been sentenced for crimes against army discipline. They called themselves the "Fighters against Fascism" and, "curiously enough, nearly all of them came from Saxony" (Godfrey Lias, *I Survived* [New York: John Day, 1954], p. 31).

11. In the last quarter of the eighteenth century Poland was divided among Russia, Prussia, and Austria and disappeared as a country. At the Congress of Vienna (1814–15) it was agreed that a small kingdom of Poland should be created. The area, the southeastern quadrant of modern-day Poland, was referred to as Congress Poland to distinguish it from other areas of the former Polish kingdom (Harold D. Nelson, ed., *Poland: A Country Study*, Area Handbook Series [Washington, D.C.: U.S. Government Printing Office, 1983], pp. 35–37).

12. Wobbe received an offer from his friend, Thaddius Dombrowsky, a member of the Polish underground, to help him escape from the camp and hide in Poland. Rudi's political "crimes" had already thwarted the military career of his uncle and he was quite unwilling to risk the arrest and possible deaths of his family members by escaping (Wobbe and Borrowman, *Before the Blood Tribunal*, p. 104).

13. Schnibbe's reference is to the fact that it was Düwer who succumbed to the pressure from Mohns and provided the flyers which led to the arrest of Hübener.

14. Besides executing the conspirators in the 20 July 1944 assassination attempt, Hitler used the occasion to settle the score with other political opponents. Estimates range as high as nearly 5,000 persons perishing in the subsequent reprisals. In addition, friends and family members of the accused were arrested and imprisoned (Hoffmann, *History of the German Resistance*, pp. 529–30, 720 n. 38).

15. The extermination camp Neuengamme was named after a city eighteen kilometers southeast from the middle of Hamburg. The camp was started in June 1940 and reached a capacity of 10,000 inmates. It was intended originally as a holding camp for political prisoners from conquered countries. In 1941 Heinrich Himmler designated the camp as Grade II, which was for "protective custody prisoners with less good records but who are

likely to benefit from education and reform." Relatively little is known about the camp's operations, but it was a center for "medical" research, particularly on tuberculosis. Approximately 90,000 prisoners passed through Neuengamme, of which 40,000 died (Konnilyn G. Feig, *Hitler's Death Camps: The Sanity of Madness* [New York: Holmes and Keier, 1981], pp. 209–14). At the end of 1940 the camp contained 3,500 inmates. By the beginning of 1945 the number had risen to 52,000. Between 26 December 1944 and 25 March 1945 there were 3,040 deaths in the camp. On 20 April 1945, seventy-one members of the resistance (fifty-eight men and thirteen women) were executed at Neuengamme (Ulrich Bauche et al., eds., *Arbeit und Vernichtung. Das Konzentrationslager Neuengamme 1938–1945* [Hamburg: VSA Verlag, 1986], pp. 118–19, 129, 167).

16. The demand for combat troops was so great in October 1943 that Hitler ordered sixty thousand workers from the aviation industry be drafted into the armed forces, which the Luftwaffe was unsuccessful in preventing. The resulting shortage of aircraft workers increased greatly the value of political prisoners working at Graudenz (Matthew Cooper, *The German Air Force 1933–1945: An Anatomy of a Failure* [New York: Jane's, 1989], p. 303).

17. The Germans usually identified their prisoners with a system of cloth triangles, which were sewn with the apex down on the right trouser leg and the left breast of the coat, the latter triangle being larger. A red triangle was usually given to political prisoners, a category including a wide variety of other offenses for which specific colors had not been established. The political criminals comprised a large and diverse group, ranging from those, such as Communists, who had opposed the regime to those who had merely told jokes about Hitler (Anton Gill, *The Journey Back from Hell: An Oral History: Conversations with Concentration Camp Survivors* [New York: Wm. Morrow, 1988], pp. 29, 31).

18. The standard uniform for prisoners was the familiar striped apparel and consisted of a cap, shirt, jacket, and trousers for men, while the women received dresses. For shoes the inmates were given clogs. No consideration was given for sizes, so prisoners either exchanged clothes or tried to survive with what they received. Prisoners were expected to care for their attire, which they tried to do because no more would be issued them and it was extremely difficult to locate more, which contributed to theft. Dead bodies were usually stripped for uniform parts. The uniform was most often given directly to some prisoner without being cleaned. In some camps the clothes were never washed. Prisoners performing heavy labor often discovered that their clothes had become rags within a short time. Because of the flimsy nature of the clothes, prisoners were often naked or nearly so, even in the coldest weather. Foot problems were common due to poor shoes (Gill, *Journey Back from Hell*, p. 36).

19. A. E. Bell, a British prisoner, recalled: "There was only one meal a day, a litre of soup, the morning and evening being quite ridiculous and consisting of one slice of bread cut so thin that the bloke who cut it damned near missed it" (Rolf, *Prisoners of the Third Reich*, p. 72).

20. The Battle of Stalingrad, at which the German Sixth Army, commanded by Field Marshal von Paulus, was surrounded and captured, resulted in
the loss of approximately 250,000 soldiers, including twenty-four generals
and von Paulus. Stalingrad is almost universally viewed as the most serious
loss suffered by the German army and the turning point of World War II.
Throughout Germany memorial services were held and a national period
of mourning was declared. See Ronald Seth, *Stalingrad: Point of Return. The
Story of the Battle, August 1942–February 1943* (New York: Coward-McCann,
1959), pp. 244–52; and Mackinnon, *Naked Years*, p. 114.

21. The Russians had been preparing the assault upon East Prussia and
the adjacent areas for three months, so when the attack was launched, it broke
through the front in several areas (Lehndorff, *East Prussian Diary*, p. 2).

22. The military, which always had the right of way, had blocked the
bridge, so the refugees were obligated to vacate the roads or weave their
way around stalled military vehicles (Wobbe and Borrowman, *Before the Blood
Tribunal*, p. 107). For a detailed account of the exodus from Graudenz, see
Document 63.

23. Wobbe claims that the prison was located in Prussian Stargard, which
they reached on the fourth day of their trek and where they remained an
extra day due to a blizzard. The prison was extremely crowded, because prisoners from a large area of eastern Europe were being shipped westward.
"They were . . . twelve in cells that were meant to hold only three. At least
it was warm and dry and most of us managed to sleep even though we
couldn't lie down" (Wobbe and Borrowman, *Before the Blood Tribunal*, pp.
109–10; see also Document 63).

24. When roll call was taken the following morning, it was discovered
that several of the prisoners who were from West Prussia had escaped during the night. The guards were not concerned, because it lessened their work
(Wobbe and Borrowman, *Before the Blood Tribunal*, pp. 107–8).

25. Schnibbe's skill at obtaining whatever was necessary for the group to
continue going was demonstrated by the procurement of the horse to pull
the sled when the prisoners were too tired to continue pulling (Wobbe and
Borrowman, *Before the Blood Tribunal*, p. 114).

26. Wobbe was amazed at the skill of Schnibbe and some others in "liberating" the pigs and obtaining carrots and potatoes to prepare a stew, which
comprised "one of the finest stews I've ever eaten." The kitchen crew,
Schnibbe, Düwer, and five others, was almost constantly on the lookout for
food, which consisted sometimes of flesh cut from the carcasses of frozen
animals (Wobbe and Borrowman, *Before the Blood Tribunal*, pp. 110–11).

27. The greatest fear of the refugees was the military police and the SS
patrols, which sometimes drafted men into the army on the spot. The patrols were also on the lookout for deserters, who were usually shot immediately. Because of their civilian clothing, the prisoners feared they would be
mistaken for deserters, so they gave the search patrols a wide berth (Wobbe
and Borrowman, *Before the Blood Tribunal*, p. 113).

28. General Lothar Rendulic established "flying courts-martial" to search
the rear areas in East Prussia. Every soldier who was not wounded and was

picked up outside his unit area was to be tried and shot immediately (Earl
F. Ziemke, *Stalingrad to Berlin: The German Defeat in the East*, Army Historical Series [Washington, D.C.: Center of Military History, 1968], p. 433).

29. On the third night of the exodus, the group slept in a barn. When
he awoke the following morning, Wobbe noticed that the prisoner next to
him had frozen to death during the night (Wobbe and Borrowman, *Before
the Blood Tribunal*, p. 109).

30. In the area of eastern Prussia adjacent to Graudenz the temperatures
were frequently between -20° and -30°C and were accompanied by severe
winds (Lehndorff, *East Prussian Diary*, pp. 177, 185, 198).

31. Erich Koch was regarded in Nazi circles as an exceedingly brutal and
uncontrolled person. He became the Gauleiter and the governor of East
Prussia. During the Russian campaign he conducted such a reign of terror
in the Ukraine that even members of the SS opposed him (Zentner and
Bedürftig, *Encyclopedia of the Third Reich*, 1:506–7). Following Hitler's orders,
he prevented the evacuation of East Prussia (Albert Seaton, *The Fall of Fortress Europe, 1943–1945* [London: B. T. Batsford, 1981], p. 187). He disappeared at the end of the war, but was captured by British military police in
1950. In 1959 he was sentenced to death for his role in the deaths of at least
400,000 Poles. His crimes in the Ukraine were not considered. Because of
his mental incompetence, he was not executed (Zentner and Bedürftig, *Encyclopedia of the Third Reich*, 1:506–7).

32. Retreating German troops engaged in enormous amounts of gratu-
itous looting and vandalism, including taking the property of their countrymen, whether in Germany or further east, in order to send supplies to their
own starving and deprived families. Field Marshal Erich von Manstein instructed his troops that "in enemy towns a large part of the population will
have to starve. Despite this, misconceived notions of humanity must not lead
to the distribution of goods among prisoners and the local population, those
are goods the home front goes without for our sake" (Ernst Niekisch, *Das
Reich der niedern Dämone* [Hamburg: Rowohlt, 1953], p. 304; in Grunberger, *Social History of the Third Reich*, p. 148). Such directives resulted in the
razing of entire villages and the massacre of their inhabitants. Of the Russian prisoners of war transported to Germany, the survival rate was between
10 and 20 percent (interview with Herr Lindlar, Düsseldorf, Apr. 1966; in
Grunberger, *Social History of the Third Reich*, p. 148).

33. For two nights during the eleven-day trek, the group spent the night
in barns, where they survived by burying themselves under the hay (Wobbe
and Borrowman, *Before the Blood Tribunal*, p. 108).

34. Wobbe confirms that Schnibbe saved Düwer's life that night (Wobbe
and Borrowman, *Before the Blood Tribunal*, p. 109).

35. The support of his friends probably saved Düwer's life, or at least
improved greatly his situation, because after the eighth day of the trek, it
was decided to leave twenty-five of the least ambulatory prisoners behind
in Neukrug, where they were captured by the Russians. Although weak and
feverish and still suffering from an infected carbuncle on his neck, Wobbe
was able to continue going. Düwer succeeded in hiding his frozen feet and

was assisted by the others in his group (Wobbe and Borrowman, *Before the Blood Tribunal*, p. 111).

36. The previous day Dr. Krüger gave orders for twenty more prisoners to be released. Only the worst offenders, which included the Hübener group, remained under arrest. By the end of the tenth day, they nearly gave up hope of reaching their final destination, the railhead at Bütow, but when they saw a sign indicating the town was only seventeen kilometers distant, their courage revived and they reached their goal. The original group of more than 250 was reduced to fewer than 100. They had traveled at least 157 kilometers since leaving Graudenz, not counting detours (Wobbe and Borrowman, *Before the Blood Tribunal*, pp. 111–12).

37. Schnibbe and a small group of others pushed ahead and arrived in Bütow early, thus enabling Karl-Heinz to reserve a compartment for his close friends (Wobbe and Borrowman, *Before the Blood Tribunal*, p. 113).

38. At nearly every railroad station along the way the Red Cross had established aid stations to provide food and drink to the refugees. Schnibbe always told the relief workers that he represented a group of refugees, so he returned loaded with food for his friends. The relief workers never asked questions, except "how many?" (Wobbe and Borrowman, *Before the Blood Tribunal*, p. 113).

39. Wobbe claims that the delay lasted for two days without provisions until Schnibbe dug into his bag and produced some stale, but nourishing, sandwiches. "He always seemed to obtain the things that were most needed at a particular moment" (Wobbe and Borrowman, *Before the Blood Tribunal*, p. 114).

40. Peter Neumann noted that Hamburg had been "terribly bombed" and that "most of the factories had been destroyed." Throughout the city he saw "interminable lines of refugees" standing for hours outside the soup kitchens, which appeared to be open day and night (Neumann, *Black March*, p. 238).

Chapter 6: From Political Prisoner to POW

1. Shortly thereafter Düwer was taken into the Wehrmacht and was stationed in northern Germany, where he was subsequently captured by British forces (Sander, "Helmuth-Hübener Gruppe," in Hochmuth and Meyer, *Streiflichter*, p. 340).

2. Oldenburg is 120 kilometers southwest of Hamburg and 35 kilometers west-northwest of Bremen.

3. Lüneburg, a city of 31,171 in 1933, was situated forty kilometers southeast of Hamburg (Frederich Müller, *Müllers Grosses Deutsches Ortsbuch*, p. 635).

4. An anonymous member of the German military units retreating toward Berlin near the end of the war commented that "many times I saw bodies of German soldiers hanging from trees, men who had been hanged for desertion" (Comrade X, *My Three Years inside Russia* [Grand Rapids, Mich.: Zondervan Publishing House, 1958], p. 20). In Berlin in April 1945 patrols

of gendarmes and "powerful soldiers with brass plates on their chests" were searching for fugitives and deserters, who were condemned immediately. The so-called express summary courts were operating in all districts of the city. The shortage of soldiers was so great that an order was issued in the cities informing all males that they were to enlist at the proper Nazi party or military headquarters to receive arms. Anyone who hid in an air-raid shelter was to be brought before a military court and sentenced to death (Borkowski, *Wer weiß, ob wir uns wiedersehen*, pp. 122, 124).

5. The Germans had two air-raid warnings. The first warning was sounded when the enemy was fifteen minutes away and consisted of three 15–second wails. Most persons took little notice of the early warning. The second warning occurred when an air-raid was imminent. On the night of 24 July part of the alarm system was rendered inoperable (Musgrove, *Operation Gomorrah*, p. 69).

6. The military received better provisions than the civilian population. The inhabitants of Hamburg in April 1945 were preoccupied with the military situation, bombings, and food. A large percentage of the population was completely without bread and some other foodstuffs. "It is no longer a rarity for soldiers to be approached on streets and in restaurants for bread and fat ration cards" (Stellv. Generalkommando X. A.K. II a/W Pro. No. 49/45 GKdos, concerning action "MPA," activity report No. 4, Apr. 5, 1945: MGFA, WO1–6/368, cited in Steinert, *Hitler's War*, p. 308).

7. The population of Oldenburg in 1933 was 66,951 (Frederich Müller, *Müllers Grosses Deutsches Ortsbuch*, p. 792).

8. Ferdinand Schörner was the last field marshal appointed by Hitler. As one of Hitler's most trusted officers, he rose rapidly through the ranks. In January 1945 he became the supreme commander of the German Central Zone, which included Berlin. During the war he took harsh measures to maintain morale (Snyder, *Encyclopedia of the Third Reich*, p. 313). After the war he was captured by American forces and turned over to the Russians, who put him in prison for ten years. Upon his arrival at the prison camp at Krasnogorsk, where some of the soldiers formerly under his command were also imprisoned, about two hundred of the German prisoners were waiting alongside the road with a rope to hang Schörner (Job von Witzleben, "One General in Particular Immediately Disguised Himself as a Supercommunist," in Steinhoff, *Voices from the Third Reich*, p. 515). When he returned to Germany in 1955, he was sentenced on charges of manslaughter (Snyder, *Encyclopedia of the Third Reich*, p. 313). For a short biography of Schörner, see F. W. von Mellenthin, *German Generals of World War II as I Saw Them* (Norman: University of Oklahoma Press, 1977), pp. 175–86.

9. As the end of the war approached, recriminations against the regime and the Nazis increased. Germans noted with intense feelings the words of Hitler: "Give me ten years and you will have airy and sunny homes, you will not recognize your cities, no one will starve or freeze" (Stellv. Generalkommando X A.K. II a/W Pr O No. 44/45 GKdos. Activity report No. 2 of 22 Mar. 1945: MFGA WO1–6/368, cited in Steinert, *Hitler's War*, p. 308).

10. It was customary for a rider to sit on a front fender and serve as a

lookout. The slang word *Lucki-Lucki* was coined from the English word "to look" to describe the function. When the lookout heard or spotted an attacking plane, he pounded on the fender, the truck stopped as quickly as possible, and the passengers sought shelter. Having seen one vehicle that was strafed before the passengers could escape, Willy Schumann was more desirous of traveling afoot and relying upon his own senses than a warning from someone else (Schumann, *Being Present*, p. 159).

11. Bremen, which had a population of 323,331 in 1933, lies thirty-five kilometers east southeast of Oldenburg and eighty-five kilometers southwest of Hamburg (Frederich Müller, *Müllers Grosses Deutsches Ortsbuch*, p. 122).

12. In 1943 the tonnage of bombs dropped on Germany was 200,000, five times the amount dropped in 1942. Among the cities listed as "virtually destroyed" was Hamburg. Bremen was listed as having been "seriously damaged" (Max Hastings, *Bomber Command* [London: Michael Joseph, 1979], p. 226).

13. Königgrätz (modern-day Hradec Králové), located ninety kilometers east northeast of Prague, was the site of the decisive battle in the Austro-Prussian War of 1866 which eliminated Austria's dominance in the German Federation.

14. As early as January 1944 the zones to be occupied in Europe by the Allied powers had been outlined. However, General Eisenhower was making a military decision to halt his forces at the agreed-upon boundary (Forrest C. Pogue, *Command Decisions: The Decision to Halt at the Elbe* [Washington, D.C.: Center of Military History, 1990], pp. 479–82; see also John O. Crane and Sylvia Crane, *Czechoslovakia: Anvil of the Cold War* [New York: Praeger, 1991], pp. 239–40; and Josef Korbel, *Twentieth-Century Czechoslovakia* [New York: Columbia University Press, 1977], pp. 175–76, 214–15).

15. Because of the treatment of Russian prisoners by the Germans, German soldiers feared that being captured by the Russians was a death sentence because "many of us believed the Russians didn't take prisoners." When they were loaded into trucks, the captured German soldiers "expected to be taken into the nearest ditch and shot" (Kurt Meer-Grell, "We Marched into Russian Imprisonment Singing," in Steinhoff, *Voices from the Third Reich*, p. 511).

16. Those prisoners who returned from the Soviet Union always remember the formula: *skoro domoj*, "going home soon," which was told them frequently by the officers, guards, and their fellow workers (Lehmann, *Gefangenschaft und Heimkehr*, p. 41).

17. Reinhard Heydrich formed the Sicherheitsdienst (Security Service) in the SS under orders from Heinrich Himmler and became the deputy and heir apparent of his superior. Heydrich, perhaps more than any other person, transformed the program for the Final Solution of the Jews and other "subhumans" into reality. Beginning in September 1941 he served as the Deputy Reich Protector for Bohemia and Moravia. On 4 June 1942, a group of Czech partisans assassinated Heydrich in Prague. In retaliation for the assassination, the SS obliterated the village of Lidice on 9 June. All of the men (198) in the community were killed and the women were sent to Ravens-

brück concentration camp. Ninety of the children of the village were taken to a camp elsewhere (Zentner and Bedürftig, *Encyclopedia of the Third Reich*, 1:543–44). Using the assassination of Heydrich as a pretext, the Gestapo conducted mass raids and arrested hundreds of German citizens in their homes (Deutschkron, *Outcast*, p. 118).

18. Tabor is sixty-five kilometers south of Prague.

19. After being assembled near Tabor, the German prisoners were visited by Russian soldiers who bore the marks of having been in a concentration camp. The recently released Russians walked along the rows of German soldiers, looking for their former torturers who might be concealed among the captives. The soldiers were apprehensive that the Russians might mistake some of them for former concentration camp personnel (Helmut Gollwitzer, *Unwilling Journey: A Diary from Russia* [Philadelphia: Muhlenberg Press, 1953], p. 35).

20. Because of their fanaticism and the atrocities they committed in Russia, members of the SS were convinced they had no chance of survival if they were captured by the Russians. Anyone wearing an SS uniform, regardless of past behavior, was subject to being shot without a trial. If they were taken prisoner, the SS believed, their fate would be worse than death (Neumann, *Black March*, pp. 268, 293, 305). The SS was considered the most aggressive and bloodthirsty German force and had the highest casualty rates of the German military forces, nearly one-third of their troops being lost in combat (Rudolf Würster, "I Was in Awe of My Comrades' Show of Fearlessness," in Steinhoff, *Voices from the Third Reich*, p. 260). When Klaus Granzow and some of his unit hitched a ride on a wagon driven by a Czech peasant, they were informed by gestures from the driver that his countrymen were checking under the arms of soldiers for the blood-type tatoos which every member of the SS bore. If any were found, the bearers had their throats cut. Anyone taken for an SS person would likely be liquidated on the spot (Granzow, *Tagebuch eines Hitlerjungen*, p. 180). See also Theo G. Klein, *Saftra Budjet. In russischer Kriegsgefangenschaft 1945–1949* (Grenchen, Switzerland: Spaten Verlag, 1951), p. 36.

21. Schnibbe was unusually fortunate. Helmut Gollwitzer, also a German prisoner at Tabor, estimated there were more than 40,000 prisoners and noted "at first there was nothing else to eat but what each one had brought with him, and that did not last most of them very long," so "friendly generosity could not be stretched beyond one's own little group." Because the Russians appeared to have made no provisions for feeding the prisoners, the conviction grew that they were going to be allowed to starve to death (Gollwitzer, *Unwilling Journey*, p. 32).

22. The number of prisoners became so large that most could not be accommodated in the barracks and were detained on the adjacent fields. It was several days before the camp was surrounded by barbed wire. To protect themselves from the sun during the day and the cold at night, prisoners dug holes or improvised "huts made of planks, old targets or bits of derelict cars." On Whit Saturday, 19 May 1945, the prisoners were besieged by a storm which dropped hailstones "as big as pigeon's eggs." When the storm sub-

sided, the prisoners were required to display all of their personal belongings. Anything valuable or not considered necessary for prisoners to possess was confiscated (Gollwitzer, *Unwilling Journey*, pp. 32, 35–36).

23. Tabor, whose population of 14,251 in 1945 was less than the number of prisoners, yielded all of its bakers to produce food for the prisoners and the Russian military. The potato stocks of the immediate area were confiscated and the citizens were obligated to purchase flour from their former bakers (G. Donald Hudson, ed., *World Atlas* [Chicago: Encyclopedia Britannica, 1945], p. 134; Gollwitzer, *Unwilling Journey*, p. 38).

24. Hermann Melcher, who was captured in Czechoslovakia by the Russians and interned there prior to being sent to the Soviet Union, recalled that fifty men were expected to share a loaf of bread weighing six pounds (Hermann Melcher, *Die Gezeichneten* [Leoni: Druffel Verlag, 1985], p. 50).

25. The entire prisoner-of-war camp was organized into companies, battalions, and regiments, with each battalion possessing a cooking stove constructed of "used petrol tins" (Gollwitzer, *Unwilling Journey*, p. 38).

26. To reduce the number of lice and to brand the prisoners, the Russians shaved off all body hair, including the armpits and pubes, on a regular basis. Sometimes the shaving was done so crudely and with such blunt instruments that prisoners fainted. In nearly all cases, it was a teeth-gritting experience (Pautsch, *Und dennoch Überlebt*, pp. 71, 147).

27. The average European freight car is only one-half to two-thirds the size of an American car and had only enough space to contain thirty persons without crowding. However, the cars nearly always held a greater number of prisoners, sometimes exceeding ninety. The crowding was often so severe that it was almost impossible to move, and lying down was unthinkable (Comrade X, *My Three Years inside Russia*, pp. 40–41). Some cars had three tiers of crude bunks along the sides. The only provisions for relieving oneself were usually either a metal funnel or a hole in the floor. Some cars did not possess even those amenities. Privacy was out of the question and the stench from the body waste, when combined with the dust and heat, was often overpowering. Because the cars were locked, the inmates often traveled in the dark and rarely saw much of the surrounding countryside (Yeshoshua Gilboa, *Confess! Confess! Eight Years in Soviet Prisons* [Boston: Little, Brown and Co., 1968], pp. 29–30). Sometimes prisoners determined their direction of travel by glimpses of the position of the sun (Otto Lasch, *Zuckerbrot und Peitsche. Ein Bericht aus russischer Kriegsgefangenschaft-20 Jahre Danach* [Pfaffenhofen: Ilmgau Verlag, 1965], p. 55). Those who traveled in cattle cars had more light and scenery, but suffered more from the cold. Water was a rare luxury and was always inadequate. In some cases, prisoners were deprived of water and food for three days or more and were kept in the car for a week before being allowed to exercise. Death was a daily occurrence and the bodies were usually removed once a day. The trip to their destination required several weeks.

28. In 1956 the Federal Republic of Germany estimated that the German prisoners captured on the eastern front exceeded 1.8 million (Sorge, *Other Price of Hitler's War*, pp. 73, 76). The total number of German troops

captured by the Soviets by the end of the war was over 3 million. When the displaced civilians who became prisoners are included, the total exceeds 4 million (Karl-Heinz Frieser, *Krieg hinter Stacheldraht. Die Deutschen Kriegsgefangenen in der Sowjetunion und das Nationalkomitee "Freies Deutschland"* [Mainz: v. Hase u. Koehler Verlag, 1981], p. 35).

29. Not all of the German prisoners from the Tabor camp were transported in train cars or sent to the same destination. Some went in trucks through Austria and Hungary to Rimnicu Sarat in east central Rumania, where the enlisted men were separated from the officers, loaded into railroad cars, and taken to the Ukraine (Gollwitzer, *Unwilling Journey*, p. 45).

30. The most common diet of prisoners transported in cattle and freight cars was rusks, a light, hard bread, much like that used aboard ships, dried or salted fish, and, sometimes, a little sugar. Warm food and water were a rarity. Prisoners were usually not permitted to obtain hot water, which was provided for Russian travelers at nearly all railroad stations, but the guards would distribute water to the inmates, although not every time the train stopped. The salted fish gave rise to the saying that "a fish loves to swim," which meant that eating fish increased a person's need to drink water (Gilboa, *Confess!* p. 30). The allowances of food and drink were highly irregular. Black, sour bread was distributed usually at intervals of two or three days. On very rare occasions a few buckets of fish soup with the heads, bones, eyes and entrails included were distributed. Some convoys never received hot food ([Zoë Zajdlerowa], *The Dark Side of the Moon* [New York: Charles Scribner's Sons, 1947], p. 71).

31. In most railroad cars the "convenience" was nearly constantly occupied, because so many of the prisoners had diarrhea. For those obligated to sleep adjacent to the toilet facilities, nighttime was dreaded (see Klein, *Saftra Budjet*, p. 77).

32. It was not unusual for prisoners to go twenty-four to thirty-six hours without water. When water was distributed, it was only one or two bucketsful, never more. Cries and entreaties were answered with curses, threats, or blows. On one train the prisoners in a car managed to make a small hole in the roof. A rag was stuck into the hole and the prisoners would suck what moisture fell onto the rag from the outside. If the perpetrators had been discovered, they probably would have been shot ([Zajdlerowa], *Dark Side*, p. 72).

33. Experienced prisoners were deprived of food so often that "it passed at times unnoticed" (Comrade X, *My Three Years inside Russia*, p. 63). After being imprisoned in jails or camps, the inmates became hardened to the disappointments, recognizing they could only wait patiently, because there was virtually nothing they could do to improve their situation (Lasch, *Zuckerbrot und Peitsche*, p. 158).

34. It was not uncommon for trains carrying prisoners to be stalled on a siding for several days to permit trains carrying troops, military supplies, or other higher-priority items to pass.

35. Prisoners who were undernourished and had a limited diet often overconsumed food or liquids when such rare opportunites occurred and became

ill or were unable to retain what they had devoured. In extreme cases prisoners died from overindulgence.

36. Camp Region Volga contained 18 main camps, 135 secondary camps, and 109 stations. In one of the larger camps a total of several hundred to several thousand prisoners lived. Although the camps were not in Siberia, they were commonly believed by the prisoners to be located in Siberia, which was a metaphor stemming from the extreme expanse and strangeness of the landscape (Lehmann, *Gefangenschaft und Heimkehr*, p. 39). In spite of occasional accidents, such as a crushed foot or broken collarbone, caused by the heavy labor of building a camp, the work raised the prisoners' spirits, because they knew they were improving their own condition (Bronislaw Mlynarski, *The 79th Survivor* [London: Bachman and Turner, 1976], p. 123). Prisoners who refused to assist in building the camps were put into the "cooler." After two weeks there, the recalcitrant would either be dead or have pneumonia (Wolfgang Kasak, "I Copied the Dictionary onto Five 'Volumes' of Cigarette Paper," in Steinhoff, *Voices from the Third Reich*, p. 520).

37. Swabian is a High German dialect of Swabia, a duchy in medieval Germany which was one of the ten circles into which Germany was divided prior to 1806. Swabia is in southwest Germany on the upper Danube.

38. German immigrants first moved to Russia in great numbers in 1763. Most estimates indicate a total German population of approximately 27,000 within three years. Most of the immigrants settled south, southeast, and northeast of Saratov, founding 104 colonies, which expanded to 192 towns and villages in the provinces of Saratov and Samara (Hattie P. Williams, *The Czar's Germans with Particular Reference to the Volga Germans* [Lincoln, Nebr.: American Historical Society of Germans from Russia, 1975], pp. 98–99). By 1914 the total German population in Russia was an estimated 1.5 million. By 1941 this number had been reduced, largely as a result of collectivization, to 788,000, of which 330,000 were Volga Germans (Fred C. Koch, *The Volga Germans in Russia and the Americas from 1763 to the Present* [University Park: Pennsylvania State University, 1977], pp. xv-xvi, 22–23, 282, 284). In 1926 there were 463,469 Volga Germans. See also Ingeborg Fleischhauer and Benjamin Pinkus, *The Soviet Germans Past and Present* (London: C. Hurst and Co., 1986), p. 70.

39. The lists of the Volga German communities are incomplete. The editors have been unable to locate Bochvisnievo, which was probably located northeast of Saratov.

40. A good description of the subterranean structures is contained in Fred C. Koch, *Volga Germans*, p. 25.

41. Toilet paper was an unknown commodity. When Godfrey Lias asked a nurse in a hospital for some paper, she inquired why he could possibly want some; after all, he was permitted to take a bath every ten days. When grass was available, prisoners used it; in the winter, snow "came in useful" (Lias, *I Survived*, p. 39).

42. In the winter the frozen pillars of excrement were cleared away with pick axes wielded by latrine wardens. In the summer the open pits "stank infernally" (Sorge, *Other Price of Hitler's War*, p. 78).

43. Prisoners learned that the Soviets had a different conception of truth. Rather than give a categorical refusal, "it seems to him unjust to disappoint a suffering person and he will consider any lie justified to avoid doing so. When it is not a case of pity then it is at least a convenient way of preventing further importunate requests." The lies of the Soviet camp guards and commanders, from their perspective, also served a useful purpose, because "a lie serves the truth and thus forms part of the truth." The hopes raised by lies often were a benefit to the prisoners, because to think something was "less painful than experiencing it." Prisoners recognized later that "for many years we allowed ourselves to be led on a piece of string" and "could not force themselves to suspend belief in a Russian assurance or promise until it had come true" (Gollwitzer, *Unwilling Journey*, pp. 82–83). Nearly all promises made to the prisoners went unfulfilled. The most common response to requests, however simple, was "budjet" 'it will be' (Lasch, *Zuckerbrot und Peitsche*, pp. 15, 18).

44. The roll call, with the prisoners arranged in ranks of five men, occurred each morning before they left for work and each evening upon their return to camp. The roll count was written with a pencil on a board similar to a breadboard with a handle. The numbers were recorded by using four vertical marks with the fifth mark crossing them. The writing was erased later by scraping the board with a piece of glass. In due time the board would be worn away and replaced (Pautsch, *Und dennoch Überlebt*, pp. 159–62, 322). Because of the enormous difficulty the Russian guards in some camps had in making an accurate count of the prisoners, the roll calls lasted sometimes for hours. In one instance, a prisoner remembered a roll call continuing for eight hours (Lasch, *Zuckerbrot und Peitsche*, p. 42).

45. Some prison camps were referred to by Russian authorities as "sanitoriums." German prisoners were astounded to discover that, although such "sanitoriums" were better than the average prison camp, they were far below the standards of what was anticipated. In comparison to how the average Russian lived, German prisoners in the better camps believed their lot was no worse than that of the indigenous populace (Lasch, *Zuckerbrot und Peitsche*, p. 48).

46. Godfrey Lias, who was in the area of Kuybyshev in early 1945, reported that the daily rations were supposed to consist of "400 grams of bread, 200 grams of porridge made from unhusked oats, 20 grams of sugar, and half a liter of cabbage soup." The prisoners did not always receive so much, and were sometimes given a salted fish in addition. About once a month a small piece of horse meat was provided (Lias, *I Survived*, p. 31).

47. Theo Klein recounts how lucky he was once to find a single pea on the ground. He swallowed it immediately, because "peas are said to be nourishing" (*Saftra Budjet*, p. 56).

48. The bread universally in the prison camps contained so little grain that it was referred to as "granary dust" (Klein, *Saftra Budjet*, p. 56).

49. German: Brei; English: mush, porridge.

50. Sunflower oil had long been the staple fat in Russian cooking. Starved prisoners who were inclined to consume an excessive amount of the rare oil

in its raw form were usually stricken with violent diarrhea (Mlynarski, *79th Survivor*, pp. 172–73).

51. The amount of nourishment provided prisoners varied over time and according to their productivity. In 1941–42 the amount Schnibbe received was that given to prisoners who failed to achieve the norm or who were invalids. The average prisoners received from 400 to 700 grams (14–25 ounces) of bread per day and a liter of thin soup with occasional vegetables, fish, or pieces of fat (Jerzy Gliksman, *Tell the West* [New York: Gresham Press, 1948], pp. 52–53; and American Federation of Labor, *Sklavenarbeit in Russland* [n.p., 1948], p. 89). The various camps had five to ten different allotments according to the status and achievements of the prisoners and camp personnel (David J. Dallin, *Forced Labor in Soviet Russia* [New Haven: Yale University, 1955], pp. 10–11).

52. The heads and entrails of herring were common components of the soup prisoners received. Theo Klein claimed that when a prisoner looked into his bowl at the brew, the fish eyes "looked at you suspiciously." The only thing that could be done was to close one's own eyes and pour the mixture down one's throat (*Saftra Budjet*, p. 327).

53. The diet of the German prisoners was noteworthy for two reasons: its meagerness and lack of diversity. Only those who were privileged to work in the food preparation areas or were able to "organize" something for themselves were able, in a relative sense, to escape a starvation diet. Food was often distributed according to the type and amount of work a prisoner did. Prisoners were divided into categories according to their health and ability to work. Those in the upper categories were obligated to work longer hours and received more food than prisoners who were less able. Those rare individuals or groups who succeeded in reaching their quota were rewarded with better or more provisions (Comrade X, *My Three Years inside Russia*, pp. 52–53). Prisoners raised on farms commented that on their farms the pigs ate better than they did. Some prisoners said they now gladly eat what they had once given to their dogs. The most common topic of conversation among the prisoners was food. Other pleasures of the flesh were seldom, if ever, mentioned. Because of their starved condition, tempers flared easily and "men, like hungry wolves would throw themselves on one another in impotent fury. . . . The fights were always of short duration. The opponents, weak with hunger, had not strength for protracted combats." The soups and fish and barley grains provided so few vitamins that vitamin-deficiency diseases, especially scurvy, were common. Gums and lips bled at every bite, and the generous ration of salt consumed by prisoners often caused running sores to break out on their legs (Wittlin, *Reluctant Traveller*, pp. 66–69).

54. Hunger edema, as it was called, was dystrophy and was the most common cause of death among the prisoners. The disease was also rampant in Germany following the war (Lehmann, *Gefangenschaft und Heimkehr*, pp. 60–61; Victor Gollancz, *In Darkest Germany* [Hinsdale, Ill.: Henry Regnery Co., 1947], p. 51).

55. Assignment to work details and the general ability to work was determined by the firmness of the buttocks, which was the last area of the body

to decrease (Sorge, *Other Price of Hitler's War*, p. 76). In the prison camp in Bistriz, inmates were ranked in three categories. Category 1 was those considered good. Category 2 were those who were "usable." Category 3 were the poor or useless. "When the buttocks do not droop and there are no wrinkles, you are still usable" (Melcher, *Gezeichneten*, p. 68).

56. Approximately 108 pounds.

57. Approximately 6'2".

58. This most likely occurred near Kuybyshev or between Kuybyshev and Ufa.

59. The "performance bread" (*Leistungsbrot*) was reserved for those who filled or overfilled their quota. The book listing the quotas described how much of each type of work a worker needed to accomplish to fill the quota, but "nothing was said about what he should eat in order to fulfill the quota" (Klein, *Saftra Budjet*, p. 140).

60. The food allowance was based on an imaginary norm, and each worker was expected to meet the norm as his *minimum*. It was rare for prisoners to meet their obligations. The brigade leader determined how close each worker came to the norm, which also determined how much food he received. If a prisoner was considered capable of work and did not work, he was given no food ([Zajdlerowa], *Dark Side*, pp. 115–16; see also Melcher, *Gezeichneten*, p. 333).

61. The various quotas were often established with little regard for the conditions under which the workers were required to work. As a result, during harsh conditions when more food for strength was required, workers often received the least (Klein, *Saftra Budjet*, p. 140).

62. Trenches for pipelines or building foundations were dug even if the temperature reached -40°C and the ground was frozen to a depth of three feet or more. In those instances, holes that would have been dug in one day during a warm period required up to several weeks. The lack of food and the cold weather rendered the prisoners able to work only at a snail's pace. Regardless of the threats of the brigade leader, the prisoners were absolutely incapable of "conjuring up any superhuman efforts" (Pautsch, *Und dennoch Überlebt*, p. 299).

63. The average work brigade of German prisoners numbered from twenty to forty persons and was usually commanded by a German prisoner. Some groups numbered as high as 150. The workday outside of the prison compound, which is where most of the prisoners worked, was eight hours, in addition to the normal march of several kilometers in both directions. Prisoners were also expected to complete projects such as maintaining or improving the camp (Lehmann, *Gefangenschaft und Heimkehr*, p. 93).

64. In 1941 the ratio of peasant females to peasant males who were involved in agricultural employment was 1.1:1. By 1945 the ratio was 3.1:1. Over 60 percent of the armed forces were rural residents (Alec Nove, "Soviet Peasantry in World War II," in Susan J. Linz, ed., *The Impact of World War II on the Soviet Union* [Totowa, N.J.: Rowman and Allanheld, 1985], pp. 78–79).

65. Estimates of the total casualties of the Soviet Union during World

War II run as high as thirty million (James R. Millar, *The ABCs of Soviet Socialism* [Urbana: University of Illinois Press, 1981], p. 42).

66. Some German prisoners had the misfortune of being put into camps which contained common criminals from the USSR. In those instances, the Germans, who were often few in number or isolated, received the worst treatment in the barracks, where the most aggressive criminals established a pecking order. The Germans found themselves being robbed almost as soon as they arrived and were given the most miserable place in the prison cell or barracks room to sleep, in addition to having their food stolen (Pautsch, *Und dennoch Überlebt*, p. 76).

67. During the course of World War II, five million Soviet soldiers were captured by the Germans. Only one million of these were alive in prison camps by the end of the war (Alexander Dallin, *German Rule in Russia, 1941–1945* [London: Macmillan, 1957], p. 427). In addition, several million Soviet citizens had been sent to Germany to provide forced labor. The Soviet authorities were suspicious of their loyalty, because nearly one million soldiers from the USSR had served in the German *Ostruppen* or had been members of General Vlasov's army of Russian turncoats (Sheila Fitzpatrick, "Postwar Soviet Society," in Linz, *Impact of World War II*, pp. 130, 134–35). (For more information about Vlasov, see chapter 7, n. 19.) According to the tradition of the Red Army, anyone who surrendered or permitted himself to be captured was a traitor. A soldier was to fight to the finish, killing as many of the enemy as possible, and commit suicide, if necessary, rather than let himself be captured (David Dallin, *Forced Labor in Soviet Russia*, p. 282). The Russian prisoners who returned to the USSR were mostly not permitted to return to their families, but were sentenced from ten to twenty-five years at hard labor, which meant the death sentence for a great number of them (Pautsch, *Und dennoch Überlebt*, p. 83).

68. It was dire necessity, not moral laxness on the part of the Russians and the prisoners, that moved them to steal. It was difficult for the Russians to survive during normal times, so the exigencies of the war and postwar periods increased by several orders of magnitude the need to "organize" enough food to survive (Gollwitzer, *Unwilling Journey*, pp. 253–54). The shortages of nearly all basic commodities had taught every Russian child "that it will have to search always for food, for clothing, for the thousand and one notions of which there is an endless shortage and what it is so hard to get by ordinary legal means" (Mlynarski, *79th Survivor*, p. 164). Any item which could prove useful or be sold was subject to theft. Prison camps sent inmates to steal from nearby factories or railroad yards (Gollwitzer, *Unwilling Journey*, pp. 253–54). German prisoners considered it a point of honor to steal from their Russian guards, but it was the opposite to steal from a fellow prisoner. Germans skilled at "organizing" soon learned that the Russians "were more active and skilful thieves than we were and . . . had no qualms whatever about stealing from one another as well as from the state." Because so much that is private property elsewhere belongs to the state in the Soviet Union, the Russians felt justified in taking it. After all, they reasoned with a new interpretation, "l'état c'est moi" (Lias, *I Survived*, pp. 77–78).

69. German prisoners of war in Russia commented frequently in their memoirs on the degree and prevalence of dishonesty in the Soviet Union. One prisoner attributed to Maxim Gorki the statement that "a Russian who neither lies nor steals is not a Russian" (Gollwitzer, *Unwilling Journey*, p. 84; see also Lasch, *Zuckerbrot und Peitsche*, pp. 15–16, 24, 36–37).

70. The material, economic, and population losses to the USSR in World War II were equivalent to the total earnings of the population for a period of eighteen to twenty-five years (Susan J. Linz, "World War II and Soviet Economic Growth," in Linz, *Impact of World War II*, pp. 24–25).

71. The Axis forces occupied a large portion of European Russia, an area with 85 million inhabitants, which was 45 percent of the prewar population. The Soviets claim that the Germans destroyed 1,710 towns and 70,000 villages, 32,000 industrial enterprises, and 65,000 kilometers of railroad. Vast numbers of livestock were killed or confiscated (Fitzpatrick, "Postwar Soviet Society," in Linz, *Impact of World War II*, p. 130).

72. Prisoners often received used Soviet army uniforms, which served them much better than the clothing provided by the German army. Prisoners also received regulation army shirts. No one was much concerned about the "corroded layers of filth" because they were pleased to have warm clothing (Pautsch, *Und dennoch Überlebt*, p. 151).

73. Although such a practice probably increased the danger of frostbite, accounts written by German prisoners usually mention this method of dealing with the cold.

74. Prisoners were seldom beaten severely without good reason, because they were valuable commodities due to their ability to work and rebuild the shattered Soviet economy. If a prisoner was beaten or killed without good cause, his assailant could be charged with sabotage (Klein, *Saftra Budjet*, p. 67).

75. Prisoners were often required to assemble at 5:00 A.M. or earlier. Reveille was sounded over the loudspeaker system or by striking a hammer on an iron bar. The word heard most often by the prisoners from their guards was "hurry" (Gilboa, *Confess!* p. 42).

76. Theo Klein described the urinary traffic at night as a "bustling traffic of passersby" who were in a hurry. After having drunk one or two liters of watery brew each day almost without any fat, "the strongest bladder could not withstand it." Most of his fellow prisoners were required to urinate ten times during a single night. Although they were berated the following day for urinating in front of the barracks, which was virtually impossible to avoid, the next night the process was repeated (*Saftra Budjet*, pp. 130–31).

77. The Russian prison-camp personnel found particular pleasure in requiring high-ranking German officers to clean the toilet facilities in the Russian housing area. One German general attributed the amount of excrement he found in the rooms and entries of the Russian apartments to the low cultural life of those in the Russian military who were posted to prison camps. At temperatures as low as -50°C, guards and prisoners relieved themselves as quickly and easily as possible (Lasch, *Zuckerbrot und Peitsche*, pp. 107–8). Libussa Fritz-Krockow recalled that the Russian occupation forces

in Pomerania were also not fastidious about the disposal of human waste and were known to let it accumulate in the rooms they occupied (Krockow, *Hour of the Women*, p. 73).

78. "Water . . . made life a misery. It possessed unimaginably strong diuretic properties which would result in endless nocturnal pilgrimages. At every hour of the night some unfortunate victim, enduring the painful pressure no longer, would leap from his bunk and, in a state of semi-consciousness, would stagger barefoot into the cold of the night. As the latrine was some hundred metres away it was impossible to reach without disaster striking first. And so . . . yellow icebergs would form around our huts and although regularly destroyed, new ones would spring up in their places" (Mlynarski, *79th Survivor*, p. 138).

79. During his captivity in the Soviet Union, Jozef Czapski learned that even the Russians living in rural areas lived on almost a starvation diet as early as 1939. The most common grievances of the Russian peasants were the lack of food and their obligation to give what they produced to the state. He was told that the Russian population received a ration of only 300 grams per day, and there was no guarantee of that amount. Neither meat nor sugar had been available for a long time and there was no assurance that other food would become available. Prisoners often noted that they were deprived deliberately of adequate food, but had a diet similar to the lower classes in Russia (Joseph Czapski, *The Inhuman Land* [London: Polish Cultural Foundation, 1987], p. 15). Josef Lücking observed that "the Russians were suffering terribly from hunger themselves" and that he had seen Russians on the streets of Moscow in 1945 who had died from malnourishment ("The Escapees Had to Be Brought Back Dead or Alive," in Steinhoff, *Voices from the Third Reich*, pp. 512–13). See also Comrade X, *My Three Years inside Russia*, p. 104.

80. In spite of the enormous difficulties in feeding its own population, largely due to the destruction of Russian agriculture by the Germans, the Soviet government tried to protect the German prisoners from starvation. They wanted to provide the prisoners with food of the same quality and containing the same nourishment as the native Russians received (Lehmann, *Gefangenschaft und Heimkehr*, pp. 58–59).

81. Although Sundays were usually free from work, it was certainly not unknown for prisoners to work seven days a week in order to meet a quota or if a project needed to be completed more quickly. The average workday was also supposed to be eight hours, but this was often lengthened by the great distances prisoners were marched from their camps to the work sites. In such cases, a normal day was often twelve hours. If the work time was increased, a prisoner could spend sixteen hours working and traveling. In 1948 most prisoners sentenced previously, as most prisoners of war had been, under the infamous §58, experienced an increase of working hours to twelve hours per day and an elevated quota. The crimes under §58 (a catchall law), for which the prisoners could have been executed though usually their sentences at forced labor had been reduced by ten to twenty-five years, covered a wide range of charges. Most common were "anti-Soviet political agi-

tation, counter-revolutionary activity, sabotage and espionage against the USSR" (see Pautsch, *Und dennoch Überlebt*, pp. 61–64, 282).

82. Visits to bathhouses were compulsory and were always made outside of working hours. Each prisoner was shorn and shaved and had his outer garments removed to be disinfected. If he wore state clothing he was given a clean set of underclothing. Private clothing was not washed. Each prisoner, if he had no clothing of his own, had the right to "two shirts, two pairs of pants, one vest, puttees, one pair of trousers (linen in summer, wadded in winter), a cap with ear flaps, a wadded short jacket, one pair of boots and, in winter, one other warm jacket and felted leg coverings." Few prisoners were fortunate to possess so much clothing. Some exchanged clothing for food or tobacco, while others had their clothing stolen or witnessed the disintegration of clothing due to harsh conditions. Most prisoners, rather than having boots, were forced to get along with cloth or felt for shoes, which, in some cases, were temporarily patched with pieces of wood or rubber from discarded tires. Prisoners were frequently known to wrap their legs and feet with straw or rags, cover the wrapping with mud, and then plunge their legs into cold water. When the limb was withdrawn, a coating of ice would form immediately on the outside, which helped protect from frostbite. Some prisoners of war survived better because of the high quality of the clothing they were wearing when captured ([Zajdlerowa], *Dark Side*, pp. 118, 125–26).

83. Some prisoners who lost faith that they would return home or decided to collaborate with the Russian authorities in order to improve their situations chose to remain in the Soviet Union rather than return and face a trial in Germany for their misdeeds (Gollwitzer, *Unwilling Journey*, p. 90).

84. In nearly all Russian prison camps bathing was a quick and incomplete procedure. Soap and warm water were at a premium and prisoners were not allowed to enjoy much time cleaning themselves, because the next group of prisoners was clamoring to enter. The clothing, which was laundered during the shower period, was rarely, if ever, clean and was thrown in a heap. The prisoners usually spent most of their bath time waiting huddled together in the nude for their clothing, which it took "a lot of time" to boil (Melcher, *Gezeichneten*, p. 189).

85. The most common "bathhouse" for prisoners consisted of a row of wooden basins. A large copper vat full of boiling water was available, from which each prisoner received a jugful, which he then took to a basin and mixed with cold water to his liking (Lias, *I Survived*, p. 33). On occasion, prisoners were given a small piece of "fish" soap and a washcloth (Pautsch, *Und dennoch Überlebt*, p. 297).

86. German prisoners noticed that there was no prison camp in the Soviet Union that was not besieged with bed bugs and other insects. Otto Lasch once killed one hundred insects during a ten-minute period. He gave up the effort, however, because the mass of crawling creatures was too overwhelming. As a result of the hordes of bugs, the sleep of the prisoners was often painful and they were covered with sores, boils, and bumps when they arose in the mornings. Some camps were disinfected approximately every two or three weeks on a regular basis, while other camps went several months with-

out any action taken to reduce the numbers of insects (Lasch, *Zuckerbrot und Peitsche*, pp. 93–94). The only insects which caused apparent concern to the Russian authorities were lice, because of the danger of a typhus epidemic, the traditional bane of military operations in eastern Europe and Russia. Between the start of the German invasion of Russia in June 1941 and the end of the year, over 10,000 cases of typhus were reported in the German army (Joffroy, *Spy for God*, p. 105).

87. Even "clean" laundry contained lice, which survived the boiling of the clothing which had also hung for several days in subfreezing temperatures (Melcher, *Gezeichneten*, p. 189).

88. German soldiers and prisoners in the Soviet Union soon learned to cope with lice, which often covered their bodies and "had almost become domestic animals." Spare time was often devoted to hunting lice. It was a great relief to be able to rid oneself of some of the creatures. No one got excited about the lice, because the lice-killing time was "just like brushing your teeth or cleaning your rifle" (Pabel, *Enemies Are Human*, p. 103).

89. The lack of medical supplies was universal in the prison camps, which frustrated the physicians to the degree that some asked to be sent to labor with the prisoners, rather than merely be "viewers of dead bodies" (*Leichenbeschauer*) (Klein, *Saftra Budjet*, p. 334). In the camps where he lived, Eberhard Pautsch noticed that the medical supplies were usually limited to "universal powder, a universal tincture, and a fever thermometer" (Pautsch, *Und dennoch Überlebt*, p. 242).

90. Officers received better provisions than enlisted men. Generals in some camps enjoyed white bread, butter, and twenty cigarettes per person per day. In remote camps the officers shared the mess of the other prisoners (Lasch, *Zuckerbrot und Peitsche*, p. 42).

91. Chess and checkers were the most popular games played by prisoners. One prisoner became unbeatable at checkers after he memorized all of the possible moves. Chess men were frequently fashioned from bread and regarded as works of art. Playing cards were fashioned from whatever substance was at hand, often cigarette papers. Upon leaving a camp, however, a prisoner was usually relieved of his diversionary equipment by the guards (Lasch, *Zuckerbrot und Peitsche*, p. 42).

92. The center of the code of ethics for university students in fraternities was one's honor. The caste spirit of the student *Corps* dictated that he never do anything to debase its honor. To defend or "satisfy" one's honor, it was necessary to duel. The retention of the duel was an identification with the social superiority of the officer class and aristocracy. There were, in reality, few duels and the threat of a duel usually sufficed. A court of honor decided the means by which one's honor was to be defended. For those who engaged in duels, the visible scar, preferably on the face, was considered an emblem of masculinity and courage (Steinberg, *Sabers and Brown Shirts*, pp. 37–38).

93. The lack of adequate vitamins resulted in prisoners developing scurvy, wounds that would not heal, "suppurating boils, bleeding gums, loss of teeth and, in the advanced stages, lameness, loss of control over arms and

legs, stiffening of the joints, and night blindness" (Wittlin, *Reluctant Traveller*, pp. 166–67).

94. Schnibbe probably had an outbreak of carbuncles, which was caused by dirt, lack of soap, and malnutrition. This affliction was common in postwar Germany (Gollancz, *In Darkest Germany*, p. 44).

95. It is no wonder that Tanya was skeptical of Schnibbe's claim. The Germans who opposed Hitler were incensed at those countrymen who joined the Nazi party or supported the Nazi activities and claimed afterward that "they had only joined the party in order to keep worse things from happening." All of the Nazis seemed to disappear overnight and "suddenly everyone had been in the resistance!" (Peter Petersen in the epilogue to Steinhoff, *Voices from the Third Reich*, p. 527).

96. For many prisoners, particularly Russian criminals, obscene language "belonged to the ritual that made them strong and superior to the other prisoners. Like mangy dogs they growled and yapped their curses with every utterance, whether kindnesses or offenses were connected" (Pautsch, *Und dennoch Überlebt*, pp. 141–42). Pautsch believed that more than half of the vocabularies of the criminals consisted of obscenities. In consideration of the amount of profanity heard by foreigners and the conditions under which they lived, it was hardly any wonder that the Russian vocabularies of German prisoners included substantial amounts of profanity of the most obscene nature (Pautsch, *Und dennoch Überlebt*, p. 321). Despite the use of obscene language as expletives, "dirty talk was not heard in the camps, and fantasies centered on food, a much more important deprivation" (Gill, *Journey Back from Hell*, p. 105).

97. Camps nearer Moscow and other large cities were more likely to have a greater supply of medical supplies, especially after the end of the war, when captured German supplies were distributed. Camps located far from major population centers rarely had the most basic medical supplies (Lasch, *Zuckerbrot und Peitsche*, pp. 96–97).

98. Medical supplies such as aspirin were often unavailable. In spite of the extremely primitive conditions, some German physicians succeeded in making "astonishing medical accomplishments during captivity" (Lasch, *Zuckerbrot und Peitsche*, p. 98). Many of the medical officers were sorely lacking in medical training and were often medical orderlies (*Felczer*), a combination of horse doctor and barber capable of letting blood and lancing boils ([Zajdlerowa], *Dark Side*, p. 129).

99. One of the numerous plagues of the prisoners of war was being tormented by enormous swarms of mosquitoes during the summer (Sorge, *Other Price of Hitler's War*, p. 78).

100. Seriously ill patients often showed remarkable progress toward recovery when permitted to rest, eat well, and sit in the sun, but they soon lost their healthy coloring upon returning to the "malarial ditch," the senseless battle with the bedbugs, and the bran soup (Klein, *Saftra Budjet*, pp. 336–37).

101. In some camps the promotion of culture was part of the Soviet attempt to wean German soldiers away from Nazi political indoctrination by

pointing out the barrenness of recent German politics when compared to the richness of pre-Nazi German culture (Gollwitzer, *Unwilling Journey*, pp. 39–40).

102. A common expression among the prisoners was "You'll get used to it." Those who survived often thought they would succumb to their situation and that some days would be their last, but they managed to adapt themselves and "feel at home," because "now and then some secret mechanism deep in the soul would produce a kind of self-encouragement." Rumors of improvements, such as increased food or easier conditions, and amnesties, usually the result of wishful thinking, often provided the encouragement prisoners required to continue their struggle to survive (Gilboa, *Confess!* pp. 64–67). Gollwitzer noticed that "the Russians themselves were frequently the instigators of these rumours." The prisoners finally recognized that such rumors were deliberately circulated when good weather arrived, because "it was the easiest means of avoiding attempts at escape in the summer." The "camp proletarians" were hard pressed to keep from sinking further into a subhuman state, whereas those who belonged to a "cultural group . . . who catered for the musical and theatrical entertainment of the camp, stood on an island of humanity" (Gollwitzer, *Unwilling Journey*, pp. 81–82, 85–86). Hermann Melcher discovered that the camp musical groups gave the prisoners a "renewed courage to live" (*Gezeichneten*, p. 276).

103. Marching to and from work was not always an easy task, particularly after working a ten- or twelve-hour day at hard labor. The prisoners were expected to march in ranks of five and maintain a rapid pace, which was not always possible. Those who lagged behind were often "encouraged" to move ahead by the butt of a rifle. As a result, the return in the evening often resembled a foot race to escape the wrath of the guards. For the prisoners, who often felt they were "dead from the hips down," it was agony to move their leaden feet and rubbery knees and lift their wooden-soled shoes, which "were as heavy as lead" (Klein, *Saftra Budjet*, pp. 115–16).

104. Prisoners who survived their experiences noted that they experienced "joylessness . . . to an extent almost unknown in civilian life" (Gollwitzer, *Unwilling Journey*, pp. 87–88). Because the present had lost all, or nearly all, value for the prisoners, the only thing that kept many of them struggling forward was the eschatalogical purpose toward which life moved. As each day ended, the prisoners sighed with relief that they were now one day closer to being released. Prisoners who emerged from the camps attributed their survival to having never given up hope that they would survive (Gill, *Journey Back from Hell*, p. 150).

105. Even though prisoners became better able to distinguish truth from falsehood, such was not always the case. One prisoner maintained that believing the Russians was a defense mechanism in order to "maintain our morale under the burden of our worries" (Mlynarski, *79th Survivor*, p. 110).

106. A few months after the German defeat at Stalingrad, Soviet officials encouraged former German soldiers to participate in active resistance against Nazism by joining the military unit commanded by former Field Marshal von Paulus. Passive resistance, which involved mostly spreading

anti-Hitler and pro-Communist progaganda among the German prisoners of war, was also possible. In some camps the passive movement was
"extremely popular." The prisoners were probably less than sincere in their
enthusiasm, but did it to have something new to do or to ingratiate themselves with the Russians and receive extra food. Some prisoners, including
an astonishing number of high-ranking officers, the foremost being General Walther von Seydlitz-Kurzbach, chose to join the Soviet-sponsored
National Committee for a Free Germany (Lasch, *Zuckerbrot und Peitsche*,
p. 35). The members of the committee were to be installed as the nucleus
of the new Communist government in Germany following the destruction
of the Third Reich (Sorge, *Other Price of Hitler's War*, p. 80). Not all members of the national committee, however, chose to become Communists
and some were given lengthy prison sentences in the USSR. The creation
of the anti-Nazi national committee (commonly called Free Germany) led
to outbreaks between the committee members and other Germans who
refused to participate in it. One prisoner observed that if the Soviets had
provided the two sides with guns and alcohol, the two German factions
would have exterminated one another (Lasch, *Zuckerbrot und Peitsche*, p. 29).
The League of German Officers was another Communist-front organization to obtain the cooperation of the former enemy in undermining the
German war effort and providing leadership in the German state of the
future (Jesco von Puttkamer in Steinhoff, *Voices from the Third Reich*, p. 171;
Lias, *I Survived*, p. 47). After the end of the war, some prominent members of the Free Germany movement, rather than returning to their homeland, were sentenced to twenty-five years in Soviet labor camps (Lasch,
Zuckerbrot und Peitsche, p. 160). See also Count Friedrich Ernst von Solms
in Steinhoff, *Voices from the Third Reich*, p. 173.

Chapter 7: Horror and Humanity along the Volga

1. For the German prisoners "home became the equivalent of paradise"
and was remembered only in its best light. Problems were smaller or had
not existed at home. Bad news from Germany did not worry the prisoners,
because "people at home are better off than the Russians are here." Life was
meant to be lived free, not with the meaninglessness that existed in a prison
camp, so the prisoners declared that "a bread soup at home in freedom is
better than a roast joint here" (Gollwitzer, *Unwilling Journey*, p. 88).

2. "Whosoever did not, in the course of the years, specialize in some
manner [i.e., have a special occupational skill], trotted through the countryside either behind or in front of a *nossilka*" (Pautsch, *Und dennoch Überlebt*, pp. 324–26).

3. Prisoners who could not endure the march and fell behind or who tried
to flee were shot, but the treatment of those who continued marching and
working in the camps and caused no problems was astonishingly free of beatings. Helmut Gollwitzer overheard a Soviet captain inform a guard that he
would be responsible if the prisoners were not delivered to their destination unharmed. On two occasions, after Gollwitzer had been struck in the

head by a rifle butt, his guard was "promptly relieved of his post" (Gollwitzer, *Unwilling Journey*, pp. 101–2).

4. Schnibbe was fortunate to have made the acquaintance of the physician, because patients were often extremely ill before they were admitted to the infirmary, because there was not always room. The rule of thumb was that a prisoner needed a temperature of 39°C (approximately 102°F) before it was possible to be admitted (Klein, *Saftra Budjet*, p. 328).

5. Because of the chronic shortage of beds inmates were released from prison hospitals not when they recovered but when there were more prisoners in worse condition than they (Melcher, *Gezeichneten*, p. 233).

6. The death of a fellow prisoner was so common that "the most alarming thing . . . was the indifference of others. It seemed as if they not only had to ration their physical strength with the utmost economy but also their feelings. They got as far as a brief regret . . . and after two days the dead man was forgotten." All corpses were buried naked so that other prisoners could use the clothing. It was considered criminal to steal from a living fellow prisoner, but few inmates had qualms about stripping the body of a dead comrade (Gollwitzer, *Unwilling Journey*, p. 60).

7. Not all deceased prisoners were granted such modest recognition at their burial. When Otto Lasch help bury one of his dead comrades, the grave was dug several kilometers away from the camp and was covered in such a way as to give no hint that someone was buried there. Erecting even a simple wooden cross was forbidden (Lasch, *Zuckerbrot und Peitsche*, pp. 151–52).

8. Of the German soldiers captured during 1945, 20–25 percent died while in captivity, a remarkable contrast to the 90–95 percent of the 1941–42 captives who died (Heinz Nawratil, *Die deutschen Nachkriegsverluste unter Vertriebenen, Gefangenen und Verschleppten* [Munich: Herbig Verlagsbuchhandlung, 1986], p. 41). Of the estimated three and one-half million German prisoners of war captured by the Russians, approximately two million survived (Ronald H. Bailey, *Prisoners of War* [Chicago: Time-Life Books, 1981], p. 119).

9. Prior to 1947 the prisoners who died were nameless and not registered. Beginning in 1947 it was mandatory for an account to be made of every prisoner who died. Prior to the arrival of the investigating commission, the prisoners saw a sudden improvement in the quality of their food, which declined again after the departure of the commission. Prisoners suspected that some of their provisions were siphoned off to be sold on the blackmarket (Melcher, *Gezeichneten*, p. 349).

10. A babuschka is a triangle, or triangularly folded, kerchief worn over the head by women and tied under the chin. Because nearly all elderly women wear the babuschka, the term became synonymous with an older woman or grandmother.

11. There is a Mongol and a Turkic theory for the origins of the Tatars, with the former view more widely accepted. The Tatars, an Asiatic people, were conquered by Genghis Khan and accompanied his son, Batu, in the conquest of the steppes of Russia. The main body of the Tatars settled along the central Volga area and adopted Islam as their religion (Azade-Ayse Ror-

lich, *The Volga Tatars: A Profile in National Resilience* [Stanford: Stanford University Press, 1986], pp. 4–7).

12. To most citizens of the Soviet Union a toothbrush was an unknown and useless commodity. Prisoners who were robbed by transport or prison guards often saw their toothbrushes thrown aside, because they were deemed worthless (Klein, *Saftra Budjet*, p. 70).

13. Makhorka was cut from the stalks of the tobacco plant and was a cheap, inferior type (Klein, *Saftra Budjet*, p. 427).

14. Besides their food rations, prisoners received "dry rations" of sugar, tea, a tiny scrap of soap, safety matches, cigarette papers, and makhorka tobacco, which were supposed to be delivered every ten days but in fact came irregularly (Mlynarski, *79th Survivor*, p. 173). The cheap tobacco was most often smoked in newspapers rather than ordinary cigarette papers, which were valuable for writing (Gollwitzer, *Unwilling Journey*, p. 72; and Czapski, *Inhuman Land*, p. 144). The ink in the newspaper added extra flavor to the tobacco (Mlynarski, *79th Survivor*, p. 117; see also Klein, *Saftra Budjet*, p. 72). A triangular strip of newsprint was rolled with a small bowl at one end and a narrow mouthpiece at the other. The mouthpiece was twisted upward so that the bowl became like a pipe. One or two packets of makhorka was supposed to last ten days, but the average smoker finished his tobacco in two days or less (Lias, *I Survived*, p. 26). It required considerable dexterity to roll a cigarette containing makhorka, because the tobacco was as "dry and loose as sand" (Mlynarski, *79th Survivor*, p. 205). The first attempts to smoke the tobacco often induced some form of sickness, but once a prisoner had adapted, he was known to swap his ration of sugar for more tobacco. The cigarette papers served to assemble collections of notes, stories, poetry, anecdotes, and the like (Gollwitzer, *Unwilling Journey*, p. 72).

15. German prisoners commented frequently that they were treated kindly by the peoples of the Soviet Union. One German nobleman attributed the retention of his health to the generosity of the Russians, who "were unbelievably kind and always brought us fruit or bread" (Count Friedrich Ernst von Solms, "To Me It Was Mostly a Matter of Betraying Our Country," in Steinhoff, *Voices from the Third Reich*, p. 174).

16. Flush toilets were unknown to many citizens of the Soviet Union. Accounts tell of Russian soldiers using the toilets in Germany to wash vegetables. In many public buildings, the toilet consisted of two footprints astraddle a hole in the floor (Lias, *I Survived*, p. 30).

17. To counter the negative accounts which prisoners often related, Gollwitzer posed three questions. First he asked a prisoner "whether during his captivity he has not seen some good in the Russians, or only evil—if not, then he is just being ingracious." Second, "whether he can contradict the fact that the orders of the directors of the Soviet POW administration were good but badly carried out by the lower-ranking officials." (The thick soup which prisoners received a few days prior to the arrival of inspection teams indicated that the local camp officials had been perverting the wishes of higher authorities.) Third, whether a German prisoner did not recognize "that we should have expected something quite different considering the treat-

ment of Russian POWs in Nazi Germany" (Gollwitzer, *Unwilling Journey*, pp. 99–100).

18. Many German prisoners received instruction from their fellow prisoners who were teachers before the war, particularly *Gymnasium* teachers. Many prisoners were interested in learning English, but relatively few wanted to learn Russian. It was unusual for a prisoner to return home with any significant amount of knowledge of the Russian language. One reason for the lack of skill and interest in learning Russian was the fear that fluency in Russian would make one suspected of being a spy (Lehmann, *Gefangenschaft und Heimkehr*, p. 108).

19. Andrei Vlasov was a lieutenant general in the Russian army. His forces fought against the Germans at Kiev and Moscow. In March 1942 he was moved to the Volkhov front where he was captured by German forces in July 1942. He agreed to cooperate with the German army and began urging Russian soldiers to desert and fight with the Germans to free Russia from the Bolsheviks. The Germans never trusted Vlasov enough to permit him to command forces until near the end of the war, when the situation was hopeless. He was captured by American forces in 1945 and was handed over to the Soviets, who executed him in 1946 (Zentner and Bedürftig, *Encyclopedia of the Third Reich*, 2:997).

20. Soap and water were such rare commodities in many areas that the Russians washed themselves by spitting into their hands and spreading the saliva over their faces. Bowel movements were often performed in public barely outside the doorsteps of the peasant huts (Pabel, *Enemies Are Human*, p. 91).

21. Because of the frequent unavailability of water under such circumstances, German prisoners adopted the Russian method, which was to take "a mighty gulp of water and let it run in a fine measure over the hands. The last fourth was captured in one's cupped hands and was used to wash the face" (Pautsch, *Und dennoch Überlebt*, p. 163).

22. Sugar, bread, and a weak tea were the most common provisions given to the German prisoners in transit, and had been traditional food in Russia for generations (Lasch, *Zuckerbrot und Peitsche*, p. 36; Maxim Gorky, *My Universities* [Moscow: Progress Publishers, 1970], p. 352).

23. According to the agreements signed at Yalta on 11 February 1945, the Allies determined "that Germany be obligated to make compensation for this damage in kind to the greatest extent possible." For details, see C. L. Sulzberger, *Such a Peace: The Roots and Ashes of Yalta* (New York: Continuum, 1945), pp. 152, 160.

24. Medical officers in Russian labor camps could free a limited number of prisoners from labor until their health improved, but the total number thus stipulated was small, regardless of the health of the other prisoners or the feelings of the officer ([Zajdlerowa], *Dark Side*, pp. 129–30).

25. Prisoners who were starved and then permitted to work in the kitchen often devoured enormous amounts of food at the first opportunity. One was reported to have eaten six liters of soup and one liter of porridge, or 2.5 kilograms of potatoes. One prisoner claimed to have eaten about 100 tomatoes in one day (Lehmann, *Gefangenschaft und Heimkehr*, pp. 66–67).

26. To work in a camp bakery was likely the most desired position. Those who did were obviously well nourished, because they were able to "organize" all they wanted to eat. Prisoners acquainted with bakery workers envied greatly their good fortune and dreamed of being in a similar situation. When the prisoners showered, it was immediately obvious who the well-nourished kitchen bulls (*Küchenbullen*) were. "Then you could see that we were all walking skeletons. Only the kitchen helpers and the hospital orderlies looked like men and were the only ones who needed to be ashamed of their looks in that situation" (Hedwig Fleischhacker, *Die deutschen Kriegsgefangenen in sowjetischer Hand. Der Faktor Hunger. Zur Geschichte der deutschen Kriegsgefangenen des Zweiten Weltkrieges* [Munich, 1965], vol. 3, cited in Lehmann, *Gefangenschaft und Heimkehr*, p. 45; see also Klein, *Saftra Budjet*, p. 95).

27. A common activity of the Germans privileged to be employed in prison-camp kitchens was the brewing of illegal beverages, either beer or *samogon*, a popular homemade whiskey.

28. The Waffen-SS was the collective term after 1939 for the armed units of the SS and police. This elite guard was changed gradually into a major force in the German military establishment, in spite of the opposition of the regular army. Near the end of the war, the Waffen-SS consisted of more than 600,000 troops. The ideological indoctrination and elitism of the SS made it a ruthless force against foreign enemies and civilian populations (Zentner and Bedürftig, *Encyclopedia of the Third Reich*, 2:1011–12).

29. The Leibstandarte-SS "Adolf Hitler" originated with a group of 120 men from Hitler's bodyguard in Munich. Although it grew greatly in size, it remained one of the elite units of the Waffen-SS. The unit was in charge of security measures and served as the ceremonial guard of the Third Reich. Because of its personal oath to the Führer, the LAH, as it was known, became the private army of the Reich Chancellor. It became a brigade in 1940 and a division in 1941. Much of its reputation was gained through brutal combat in nearly every theater of war (Zentner and Bedürftig, *Encyclopedia of the Third Reich*, 1:536–37).

30. Prisoners who worked in the bakery or kitchen were allowed to eat as much as they wanted, but were not permitted to take any provisions from the work premises. Of course, many of the prisoners used their opportunity to help their comrades (Lasch, *Zuckerbrot und Peitsche*, pp. 142–43).

31. Schnibbe was fortunate to escape with such a mild punishment. Theo Klein learned of prisoners who stole two kilograms and were sentenced to ten years of hard labor in Siberia (Klein, *Saftra Budjet*, pp. 112–13).

32. Prisoners were known to have assaulted a fellow prisoner who received a larger ration of bread for unknown reasons (Wittlin, *Reluctant Traveller*, p. 61).

33. General Lasch noted that at the end of the war, upon being taken prisoner, the German soldiers "very nearly lost all of their moral principles." Because the "honorably preserved discipline of the German soldier was as if blown away at the end of the war," they had no further respect for "previous authorities or age" and were concerned only with grabbing for them-

selves what they could (Lasch, *Zuckerbrot und Peitsche*, p. 36). The constant hunger and frequent cold weather contributed mightily to the observed loss of comradeship and resulted in conflict, beatings, and theft. "Every emotion, every manner of thought, every gathering, every loose tooth became repulsive. The week-long connection lead eventually to the dreaded prison rage, which resulted in a very regrettable result for us" (Pautsch, *Und dennoch Überlebt*, pp. 199–200).

34. A survivor of the death and prisoner-of-war camps was frequently a person who had a belief in his innate ability to survive and tried to live one day at a time and not brood over his situation. Those who survived the initial shock of their captivity and maintained an inner, covert, and relatively positive outlook were more likely to survive, despite the efforts of the prison guards to convince them they were animals and had no justification for being alive (Gill, *Journey Back from Hell*, p. 190).

35. Night blindness (nyctalopia) is caused by a deficiency of Vitamin A and was a common malady, even during the summer in Siberia when there is no night. The symptoms developed at dusk and disappeared at the break of day. A few spoonfuls of cod liver oil cured the disease, but "that excellent medicine was in short supply" (Wittlin, *Reluctant Traveller*, pp. 166–67). After night blindness, scurvy, and other vitamin-starvation diseases, kidney and skin troubles of an advanced nature were experienced by most prisoners, while diarrhea, typhus, and lung disease (frequently tuberculosis) were also common. Because of their starved conditions, the prisoners' wounds rarely healed. Sores usually remained open and no new flesh formed; scabs broke open repeatedly and released a new discharge. Because the flesh below scabs was usually soft and shifting, "the agony of walking and working in the open is very great; it is in fact agonizingly painful to use the limbs at all" ([Zajdlerowa], *Dark Side*, pp. 130–31).

36. The labor camp system in the Soviet Union was riddled with corruption. Those on higher levels did not distribute everything they should have to their underlings, while those at the bottom, or nearly so, forwarded false reports in order to obtain the most basic necessities of life ([Zajdlerowa], *Dark Side*, p. 124).

37. To increase the vitamin content of the camp food, invalids or others incapable of normal work were sent on foraging expeditions to gather stinging nettle, dandelions, orache, yarrow, sorrel, and other plants. Of course, those who went on such excursions ate raw what they could of the plants gathered (Melcher, *Gezeichneten*, p. 357).

38. Regular inspections, usually monthly, were carried out by the camp physician or a visiting commission of medical personnel. The prisoners were examined and graded in one of four divisions. Categories 1 and 2 were considered fully fit and able to continue normal work. Category 3 were those who were "fairly fit." The final designation was category *OK*, which was given to prisoners unfit for work. Prisoners were aware that there was a chance they would not be worked to death and if their condition deteriorated to a certain point they would be released. This limit and the hope of being released in the future enabled some prisoners to gather enough courage to

survive. The terrible conditions during combat, especially at Stalingrad, and the long marches to transportation centers contributed far more to the high death rate than did the Russian guards and the medical personnel (Gollwitzer, *Unwilling Journey*, p. 102).

39. The German prisoners in Russia had been told so often they were going home that they rarely believed it and were known to react violently toward their fellow prisoners who made the same claim. Nearly all of those who were released remembered that day as one of the most significant of their lives and rarely forgot when it was (Lehmann, *Gefangenschaft und Heimkehr*, p. 128). One prisoner estimated that of those who were in Category 3, i.e., those with no buttocks, only 5 percent had a chance of remaining alive long enough to return home (Klein, *Saftra Budjet*, p. 60).

40. The SS tattooed the blood type of its members under the left armpit. To be found with such a tattoo in Russia was tantamount to a death sentence (Heck, *Burden of Hitler's Legacy*, p. 5).

41. Until the end of their journeys, most prisoners were fearful they would be sent back to the work camps. Even upon crossing the German-Polish border, some were taken from the train and returned to the Soviet Union (Lehmann, *Gefangenschaft und Heimkehr*, p. 130).

42. Those who were released were in such a miserable physical condition that it could not be said they were psychologically healthy. There was "no jubilation, no exuberance, we had waited too long for this moment and could not and wanted not to believe it." The prisoners being released were usually given a small package of clothing, consisting of underclothes, a shirt, a work suit, a coat, slippers, and a pair of work shoes. During the return trip, prisoners often showed little emotion, because they could not conceive that they were traveling to freedom (Melcher, *Gezeichneten*, pp. 483, 488).

43. The German prisoners of war incarcerated in the Soviet Union were held in approximately 3,000 camps. More than 890,000 prisoners still remained in Soviet hands by March 1947. By 1957 only 1,950,000 had returned from captivity (Sorge, *Other Price of Hitler's War*, pp. 76, 80).

Chapter 8: Home and Healing

1. Brest-Litovsk was the major historical city on the Russo-Polish border where the treaty between Germany and the new Bolshevik regime in Russia was signed in 1918 ending World War I between the two states.

2. During his return from captivity in November 1949, one prisoner observed with astonishment that the few Germans still remaining in former German-populated cities in Poland came to the train stations to beg for bread. The returnees were shocked and gave what they had to their compatriots, who related their own terrible war experiences and begged to be taken to Germany (H. R. R. Furmanski, *Life Can Be Cruel* [New York: Vantage Press, 1960], p. 57).

3. Most prisoners believed they were returning to a "dreamed-of paradise" and were stunned to discover the reality of conditions in Germany (Lehmann, *Gefangenschaft und Heimkehr*, p. 134). The father of Karla Poewe

returned in 1947 and was "disoriented" because he had imagined Germany had recovered from the war and was "blooming again" (Karla Poewe, *Childhood in Germany during World War II: The Story of a Little Girl*, Studies in German Thought and History, vol. 4 [Lewiston, N.Y.: Edwin Meller Press, 1988], p. 86). General Otto Lasch described his return to Berlin in 1950 as a "depressing reunion with my homeland" and noted that the populace "created a tattered and timorous impression" (*Zuckerbrot und Peitsche*, p. 168). See also Klein, *Saftra Budjet*, pp. 423–24.

4. Because of overpowering hunger and the will to survive, some Germans were driven to serving as informers, oppressing their comrades, and agitating for Soviet politics. Extra food was used by the guards to enlist informers and to prevent prisoners from forming close associations (Pautsch, *Und dennoch Überlebt*, p. 336). There was a high level of fear that prisoners would revolt or try to escape, so they were moved frequently into different barracks and forbidden to gather in groups. The various levels of food served "to evoke a perpetual spirit of distrust inimical to the growth of friendship" (Wittlin, *Reluctant Traveller*, pp. 174–75).

5. During the period of incarceration in the Russian forced labor camps some informers and collaborators were drowned in the large barrels of excrement (Sorge, *Other Price of Hitler's War*, p. 78). In other cases collaborators were assaulted and thrown from transport trains (Lehmann, *Gefangenschaft und Heimkehr*, p. 130).

6. Tuberculosis was rampant among the prisoners of war and the residents of Germany in general. It was estimated that in Hamburg in 1946 active lung tuberculosis was five to ten times as common as it was prior to the war. Because most citizens were never examined, the official figures represent only those admitted to hospitals. In 1947 the situation worsened. The main causes of tuberculosis were malnutrition and overcrowding (Gollancz, *In Darkest Germany*, pp. 26–27, 40–44).

7. The "eating orgies" frequently had serious or fatal results. A large quantity of bread would swell in the stomach, while several kilograms of potatoes would either cause the stomach to rupture or necessitate pumping the stomach (Lehmann, *Gefangenschaft und Heimkehr*, pp. 67–68).

8. The wooden shoes of most Russian prisoners consisted of a slab of wood to which some fabric or rope was bound. When wire, a relatively rare commodity, was available, it was used to create a form of slipper with either wood or some other item, such as a piece of truck tire, as a sole (Melcher, *Gezeichneten*, p. 206).

9. Because of the lack of information concerning their husbands, some wives had their husbands declared dead. Upon returning home, the legally dead husbands discovered their wives had married a second time. For some prisoners the separation and lack of contact with their families were the heaviest psychological burdens they carried during imprisonment. Otto Lasch was convinced that the NKVD, the Soviet secret police, used the restriction of information to "wear down" the prisoners (Lasch, *Zuckerbrot und Peitsche*, p. 137).

10. In 1948 the official German estimate was that there were three mil-

lion late returnees in the three western zones who had no homes to which to return (Manfred Malzahn, *Germany 1945–1949: A Sourcebook* [New York: Routledge, 1991], p. 129).

11. The enormous losses of the war created a staggering imbalance in the sex ratio. By 1945 the number of men had been reduced by half. Overall in Germany there were almost three women to every man. The 1946 census indicated a ratio of 126 females for each 100 males in the population (Sorge, *Other Price of Hitler's War*, p. 66). The official German losses, which included those missing persons and prisoners of war assumed dead but were limited to ethnic Germans, not including those from Austria, was announced in 1958 as 5.3 million (Douglas Botting, *From the Ruins of the Reich: Germany, 1945–1949* [New York: Crown, 1985], p. 253).

12. When Wilhelm Hansen returned from captivity in 1955, he, as a man in his mid-thirties, was a highly desirable marriage partner. Women were not reluctant to approach him. Many threw slips of paper with their addresses in the window of the bus in which he was riding. He could have gotten married as soon as he entered Germany (Lehmann, *Gefangenschaft und Heimkehr*, pp. 151–53).

13. Many of those who survived the labor camps did so as a result of "luck, the ability not to draw attention to oneself and a talent for organization." As a result, they often continued their behavior for months or years following their return. For many who returned, their survival had been, in part, a result of their blunting of their feelings, a trait which continued upon their return home (Gill, *Journey Back from Hell*, pp. 59, 103).

14. Reinhold Pabel watched soldiers buy food in the presence of starving people in the Ukraine. A prisoner or soldier was soon "to acquire habits he would be ashamed of in normal times. He gets tough because he has to survive. And his toughness tends to cling to him. Tender feelings and sensations are readily sacrificed on the altar of the belly" (Pabel, *Enemies Are Human*, p. 105).

15. Because of the brutal treatment they experienced as prisoners of war, survivors often had an inability to concentrate, a fear of committing oneself to love, and the inability to obtain satisfaction from anything (Shamai Davidson, "Transgenerational Transmission in the Families of Holocaust Survivors," *International Journal of Family Psychiatry* 1, no. 1 [1980]: 95–111, cited in Gill, *Journey Back from Hell*, p. 62).

16. Captivity for German prisoners in Russia was more difficult than in other countries due to longer incarceration and more harsh conditions. In 1947 it was discovered that 90 percent of those who had been imprisoned in Russia were unfit to work. Many of them suffered from dystrophy and the "homecomer disease" (*Heimkehrerkrankheit*), a traumatic change of personality caused by long-term malnutrition and high emotional stress. Those who found it difficult to settle into a normal pattern of life were said to be suffering from "straitjacket syndrome" (*Zwangsjackensyndrom*). Many returnees were unable to talk about their experiences or repressed most of their memories (Malzahn, *Germany 1945–1949*, pp. 140–41).

17. The ailments Schnibbe experienced were widespread among return-

ees. Psychiatrists concluded that "the consistency and regularity of the constellations of the symptoms justify the name of syndrome." This KZ syndrome was characterized by failing memory and difficulty in concentration, nervousness, irritability and restlessness, fatigue, sleep disturbances, headaches, emotional instability, dysphoric moodiness, vertigo, loss of initiative, vegetative lability, and feelings of insufficiency. The KZ syndrome manifested itself "as a state of chronic, and often disabling, bodily and mental weakness which is manifest in the same way in those who have never completely recovered from their time in the KZ." See H. Hoffmeyer and M. Hertel Wulff, "Psychiatric Symptoms on Repatriation," *Acta Medica Scandinavica* 105 (1952): 365; and Paul Thygesen et al., "Concentration Camp Survivors in Denmark. Compensation—A 23–Year Follow-Up—A Survey of the Long-Term Effects," *Danish Medical Bulletin* 17 (1970): 81; both cited in Gill, *Journey Back from Hell,* p. 92.

18. Stimuli encountered during the day, could "precipitate a re-experiencing of the horrors of the traumitization resulting in considerable distress" (Shamai Davidson, "Long-Term Psychosocial Sequelae in Holocaust Survivors and their Families," in the proceedings of the Israel-Netherlands Symposium on the Impact of Persecution, Jerusalem, 1977, cited in Gill, *Journey Back from Hell,* p. 63).

19. There were wide-ranging differences in the abilities of former prisoners to adjust to their changed situation. "In general, people who were independent of family ties just before the war seem to have survived best in the camps and to have adapted most successfully after liberation. To be independent in this way meant that you were in your mid-teens to early twenties, no longer dependent upon your parents, and having not yet formed secondary dependencies" (Gill, *Journey Back from Hell,* p. 117).

20. Schnibbe's condition was not uncommon for those of his age. Upon his return from prison camp in 1947, after ten years of military service and captivity, Hans Scheuerl recounted that "it is difficult to say when my 'youth' ended and 'adulthood' began: there were duties and responsibilities that required maturity from persons. At the same time there were developmental retardations, which forced a 28–year-old, upon his release, to recognize that he was nothing except an older school graduate" (Klafki, *Verführung, Distanzierung, Ernüchterung,* p. 76).

21. Many of the former prisoners were unable to distinguish between reality and their thoughts. It often required many months to overcome the idea and the fear that they were only dreaming and would awaken and find themselves in prison once more. Some returnees still lived in the "hunger culture" and stole food, even though there was no reason for them to do so (Lehmann, *Gefangenschaft und Heimkehr,* p. 161).

22. Hamburg, which was founded in the early ninth century, was begun on the site of St. Peter's church (Rodnick, *Portrait of Two German Cities,* p. 193).

23. Prisoners who survived often delayed their grief at the death of friends or family members. Because grieving requires a significant amount of time and energy, the survivors could not mourn because they were caught up in

the need to assure their own survival. Only later, when they were in a psychological position to be able to grieve, did they give free rein to their emotions. This delayed grief sometimes resulted in feelings of guilt (the author's conversation with Colin M. Parkes, cited in Gill, *Journey Back from Hell*, p. 69).

24. Better-educated persons had an advantage in coming to terms socially with their changed lives. However, such persons did not adjust any better to family and private life (Thygesen, "Concentration Camp Survivors in Denmark," p. 68, cited in Gill, *Journey Back from Hell*, p. 117).

25. Returnees often experienced "bridge symptoms," which occur at the time of a traumatic event but do not surface until later. In the case of concentration and prison camp survivors, their postliberation euphoria was often so great that they did not recognize they were not completely well. "People wanted to be themselves again, that was the most important thing." As a result, the symptoms sometimes did not emerge for several years (Gill, *Journey Back from Hell*, p. 101).

26. The symptoms of the KZ syndrome could be manifested immediately or could remain submerged for several years before exhibiting themselves. In some cases the symptoms dissipated gradually, while other victims experienced prolonged bouts with the symptoms. Related to the nature, degree, and persistence of the symptoms was the weight loss experienced in the camps. For some the joy of life was gone and they functioned only because it was expected of them. They did not enjoy life and did not feel they were the same as they were prior to the war (see Gill, *Journey Back from Hell*, pp. 96–98).

27. A common behavior of those who had survived the various death camps was to pursue constant activity, thus trying to remain free from unpleasant memories (Gill, *Journey Back from Hell*, p. 59).

28. Dr. Jorgen Kieler, a survivor of the camps, noted that "the one thing they (members of the resistance) had in common was that they were active people, people who would take the initiative. . . . And they were their own men. . . . In one way the experience . . . made the strong stronger, if they survived with their minds whole" (conversation of Kieler with Gill, cited in Gill, *Journey Back from Hell*, p. 124).

29. "For many survivors this [adjustment to normal life] was the beginning of another struggle. The world was unable to comprehend at first that for these people liberation did not mean immediate recovery from what had happened to them, and the initial euphoria which stemmed from being free and the excitement of a new environment caused the mainly young survivors to give the impression of being healed. The desire to make up for lost time, to get on with the interrupted business of education or career, was strong" (Gill, *Journey Back from Hell*, p. 45).

30. After a long recuperation, Gerhard Düwer applied for employment in the social service administration, the same position he had held at the Biberhaus prior to his arrest. He was reinstated to his former position (Wobbe and Borrowman, *Before the Blood Tribunal*, p. 140).

31. The claims of those persecuted were divided into three classes which

were to be paid "according to the funds available for reimbursement." Class 1 included the costs for medical treatments and pensions for injured persons and surviving dependents, provision of benefits for officials, and indemnification to part of those who had been under detention. The remainder of those previously under detention fell into Class 2, as well as some of those who had suffered property damage or loss. All other payments were in Class 3. Those in Class 1 who had been imprisoned were to receive up to 3,000 marks (Constantin Goschler, *Wiedergutmachung. Westdeutschland und die Verfolgten des Nationalsozialismus (1945–1954)* [Munich: Oldenbourg Verlag, 1992], pp. 143, 152).

32. The Vereinigung der Verfolgten des Naziregimes was created under the auspices of the Soviet government as an ostensibly nonpolitical organization operated largely by undeclared Communists. Its primary function was the political surveillance of the population (Anthony Mann, *Comeback: Germany 1945–1952* [New York: Macmillan, 1980], p. 95). The VVN was involved in seeking and bringing to justice active Nazis and war criminals. Numerous former prisoners worked in the organization to help their fellow persecuted (Karl-Heinz Schöneburg, ed., *Errichtung des Arbeiter-und Bauernstaates der DDR* [Berlin: Staatsverlag der DDR, 1983], pp. 100, 266). Wobbe received 200 marks and coupons for new clothing from the organization, which included among its tasks informing the general populace of the resistance movement and the atrocities of the Nazi regime (Wobbe and Borrowman, *Before the Blood Tribunal*, p. 134).

33. The prisoners at Glasmoor expected the British to liberate them soon after Hamburg was captured, but such was not the case. After waiting for a couple of weeks for the anticipated liberation, some French prisoners escaped to Lübeck, where they contacted the British army and a contingent of French troops, which were sent to the prison camp. When all of the former guards had been rounded up and incarcerated, Wobbe was given a rifle and stood guard over the new prisoners (Wobbe and Borrowman, *Before the Blood Tribunal*, p. 125).

34. Schnibbe's experience was mirrored by most survivors of the camps. While the survivors wanted to explain their feelings and "externalize" them, those who had not experienced the camps were disinclined to listen to the survivors. "In general, survivors' war accounts were too horrifying for most people to listen to or to believe. Even people who were consciously and compassionately interested played down their interest, partly rationalizing their avoidance with the belief that their questions would inflict further hurt." The impression on the survivor was often one of callousness, causing them to withdraw into their own families and other survivors (Yael Danieli, "Families of Survivors of the Nazi Holocaust," *Stress and Anxiety* 8 [1982]: 407).

35. Following the trial, while conversing with Krüger, Wobbe learned that the former camp director had saved his life on three occasions: "I want to tell you now that there were three times, not one, when the Gestapo wanted you transferred to one of the local concentration camps, especially after the incident with the pilot who wanted to take you flying. The Nazi guard who intervened at the time went right over my head and reported the inci-

dent directly to the Gestapo, who wasted no time asking for an immediate transfer. If it wasn't for your performance record at the airplane factory and the additional testimony of the director of the plant, I'm afraid my statement wouldn't have been enough to save you. To be honest, I still don't know how you escaped their grasp. Perhaps it was the God you told me you believed in during our interview. You said that he would protect you and it looks like he did" (Wobbe and Borrowman, *Before the Blood Tribunal*, p. 139).

36. Divorce in Germany became relatively rampant when compared to the previous decade. In 1939 there were 30,266 divorces. In 1948 there were 88,374, an increase of 192 percent (Lehmann, *Gefangenschaft und Heimkehr*, pp. 146–49).

37. Those persons married prior to captivity experienced serious marital problems also, because "they could not settle down to domesticity; they had changed, and if their spouses had no inkling of what they had been through, they were unable to relate to the changed personality of their partner." Those who married after their captivity and prior to becoming adjusted had similar problems (Kieler conversation with Gill, cited in Gill, *Journey Back from Hell*, p. 135).

38. One way survivors coped with their years of misery was to get married, often after an extremely short acquaintance. "These marriages of despair disregarded differences in prewar socioeconomic and educational status, lifestyle, age, or other ordinary criteria for marriage. Recreating a family was a concrete act to compensate for their losses, to counter the massive disruption in the order and continuity of life, and to undo the dehumanization and loneliness they had experienced" (Danieli, "Families of Survivors," p. 406).

Documents

1. Heinz Bergschicker, *Deutsche Chronik 1933–1945. Alltag im Faschismus* (Berlin: Elefanten-Press-Verlag, 1983), p. 310.

2. Included among the "parasites of the people" were "a married couple which advised their only son to cultivate his bladder complaint to secure exemption from front-line service; two teenage lads who broke into the home of a soldier; an unskilled woman worker who pilfered five towels, one sheet and one pillow from an air-raid storage depot; a man who filed a bogus claim for war-damage compensation; and a pensioner who took a pair of trousers lying outside a bombed house during an air raid" (Grunberger, *Social History of the Third Reich*, pp. 124, 485 nn. 49–53).

3. Most likely Gestapo euphemisms for torture.

4. The Nazis took a dim view of teenagers (referred to as the "swing youth") who listened to foreign music and danced modern and "degenerate" dances such as the jitterbug and boogie-woogie, because it was felt that such persons were rejecting the traditional virtues of the German race and becoming morally warped and, possibly, disloyal to the Nazi state. As a result, private parties at which teenagers listened to records with such "negro" music and danced to them were grounds for interrogation by the Ge-

stapo and possible imprisonment. Hitler maintained that "when a people dances negro dances and listens only to jazz music, then we need not be surprised if it should perish and seek out parliamentary monstrosities" (*Völkischer Beobachter*, 20 Jan. 1928, cited in Prange, *Hitler's Words*, p. 7). In February 1940 a swing festival in Hamburg elicited the following response from the police observer: "The dance music was all English and American. Only swing dancing and jitterbugging took place. At the entrance to the hall stood a notice on which the words 'Swing prohibited' had been altered to 'Swing requested.' Without exception the participants accompanied the dances and songs with the English lyrics. Indeed, throughout the evening they attempted to speak only English; and some tables even French. The dancers made an appalling sight. None of the couples danced normally; there was only swing of the worst sort. Sometimes two boys danced with one girl; sometimes several couples formed a circle, linking arms and jumping, slapping hands, even rubbing the backs of their heads together; and then, bent double, with the top half of the body hanging loosely down, long hair flopping into the face, they dragged themselves round practically on their knees. When the band played a rumba, the dancers went into wild ecstacy. They all leaped around and mumbled the chorus in English. The band played wilder and wilder numbers; none of the players was sitting any longer, they all 'jitterbugged' on the stage like wild animals" (Bessel, *Life in the Third Reich*, p. 37). During 1940 and 1941 "Swingers" in Hamburg continued to bedevil local authorities. The records of forbidden music, usually English, continued to circulate and amateur swing bands were formed throughout the city. Goebbels, Borman, Himmler, and Heydrich believed the Swingers were "reactionary," "disputive," and "treasonable." Himmler ordered Heydrich to "eradicate the entire evil" in a "brutal" and "thorough" way. In light of the regimentation and leveling of life in Nazi Germany, it is easy to understand that many youths found music the means of "defying the regime and protesting an unbearably restrictive life within the Hitler Youth" (Rempel, *Hitler's Children*, pp. 93–94). See also Mackinnon, *Naked Years*, p. 102; and Detlev J. K. Peukert, *Inside Nazi Germany: Conformity, Opposition and Racism in Everyday Life* (New Haven: Yale University Press, 1987), pp. 166–69.

5. Rudi Wobbe recalled that his mother was obligated to arise at 3:00 A.M. to leave to clean offices. She applied later for a war veteran's pension, which was granted, but it was inadequate for her to survive, so she continued working (Wobbe and Borrowman, *Before the Blood Tribunal*, p. 6).

6. During the second year of the war, the *Eintopf* replaced the traditional family Sunday lunch, and the money assumed to have been saved by cooking a single pot of meat and vegetables (the nominal amount was fifty cents) was to be donated by each household to the Winter Relief program. The program was abandoned later in the war when the slogan "Guns before Butter" attempted to justify the meager diet of potatoes, cabbage, and turnips eaten by most Germans (Mackinnon, *Naked Years*, p. 63; Grunberger, *Social History of the Third Reich*, p. 79).

7. A euphemism for "Heil Hitler."

8. *Verführer* (seducer), a pun on the word Führer (leader).

9. The inept handling of the Hess affair by the German propagandists contributed to a satirical verse concerning Hess: "There is a song all o'er the land; we're setting out t'ward Angelland. But if one should arrive by plane, he'd surely be declared insane" (Steinert, *Hitler's War*, p. 99). The Berliners had a similar satirical verse: "For years they've trumpeted through the land; 'Just watch us descend on Engeland!' But when a fellow goes and lands his plane, they promptly declare that he's insane" (Krockow, *Hour of the Women*, p. 157).

10. Royal Air Force.

11. Adolf Hitler, *Mein Kampf*, trans. Ralph Manheim (Boston: Houghton Mifflin Co., 1942), p. 181.

12. Royal Air Force.

13. "As late as 18 November 1941 Goebbels had told the press to inform the public that the necessary winter clothing for the troops had already been procured during the summer and lay ready at railway terminal points. Distribution was already proceeding; only the transportation situation was still causing some delays." As a result of such deceit, the German people were astonished, shocked and enraged when the government called for a collection drive on 21 December for the needed supplies for soldiers on the Russian front, labeling the effort as a "Christmas present from the German people to the Eastern front" (Steinert, *Hitler's War*, p. 148; see n. 188, p. 177).

14. A large number of jokes in Germany stemmed from Göring's statement that the citizenry could call him Meier if enemy aircraft should enter German airspace. Air raid sirens became known as Meier's Buglehorns (Grunberger, *Social History of the Third Reich*, p. 334).

15. Göring was probably the most blatantly and possibly the most corrupt member of the Nazi party, "who carved out fiefs and sinecures for himself on a scale commensurate with his own Gargantuan bulk." Besides being the prime minister of Prussia and the economic overlord of the Reich, he was the commissar of the Four-Year Plan, the Minister of the Air, Speaker of the Reichstag, Marshal of the Air Force, and National Hunt Master (Grunberger, *Social History of the Third Reich*, p. 91).

16. In September 1940 the "youth service arrest" was introduced to discipline recalcitrant Hitler Youth members. Because the organization was disinclined to expel members, detention was deemed the best means of discipline. Less harsh than police incarceration, the "service arrest" permitted Hitler Youth leaders to incarcerate boys between fourteen and eighteen for up to ten days. The punishment was to be inflicted after a rapid hearing and within twenty days of the punishable incident. Those sentenced for a weekend subsisted on bread and water, while longer detainees received complete meals (Rempel, *Hitler's Children*, p. 71).

17. This flyer remained uncompleted, because the Gestapo found it in the typewriter when they searched Hübener's apartment following his arrest.

18. Because of poor planning and overconfidence, the German troops sent into the Soviet Union were unprepared for the harsh winter conditions. To remedy the situation, the German government appealed to its citizens to donate furs and woolen clothing to be sent to the armed forces. When such

items finally arrived at the front, they were often unusable, because they were the sweaters and fur coats of women. Worse than the light summer uniforms were the standard German army boots, which were inadequate for the weather, resulting in the loss to frostbite of the toes and feet of large numbers of soldiers (Hugo Volkheimer, "The Red Army Fought like Men Possessed," in Steinhoff, *Voices from the Third Reich*, p. 146).

19. As memorialized in Friedrich Schiller's drama *Wilhelm Tell*, this is a reference to the oath sworn at Rütli by representatives of the Swiss cantons as they created the Swiss confederation to overthrow the tyranny of Austrian rule.

20. Lines 1447–52 (act 2, scene 2) of Friedrich Schiller's *Wilhelm Tell*.

21. Reproduced here with similar spelling and grammatical errors.

22. Jan Gorter had been "drafted" to work in Germany and was a tenant in the Wobbe household at the time Rudi was arrested (Wobbe and Borrowman, *Before the Blood Tribunal*, p. 47).

23. Much of what Rubinke stated was corroborated later by Wobbe in his autobiography (Wobbe and Borrowman, *Before the Blood Tribunal*, pp. 64–65).

24. When the criminal court which first questioned Wobbe about the food stamps learned that he was imprisoned on political charges, he was dismissed and the charges were forwarded to the Gestapo (Wobbe and Borrowman, *Before the Blood Tribunal*, p. 63).

25. "During the war it was felt that pedantic distinctions between juvenile and adult criminality affronted 'the sound feelings of the people.' Youngsters from sixteen upwards could now be sentenced to death 'if their mental and moral development corresponds to that of adult criminals.'" In 1944 this ruling was extended to include persons as young as fourteen years (Andreas Frittner, *Deutsches Geistesleben und Nationalsozialismus* [Tübingen: Rainer Wunderlich, 1965], p. 166, cited in Grunberger, *Social History of the Third Reich*, p. 123).

26. Some women whose husbands were alive were jokingly referred to as widows because of the extreme involvement of their husbands in party affairs, such that the men seldom used their homes for anything more than room and board. The resulting clash between domesticity and political loyalty was so common that it constituted a new category of divorce. Women were informed that "it is a husband's duty to participate in National Socialist activities and a wife who makes trouble on this score gives grounds for divorce. She must not complain if her husband devotes two evenings per week to political activity, nor do Sunday mornings always belong exclusively to the family." To make the point more impressive, a court ruled that "the accused cannot excuse her refusal to participate in political activity on the grounds that she has been unable to lead the sort of family life she had anticipated when marrying, because the plaintiff had been kept away from home almost every night by Party work. At times of political high tension, German women must make the same sacrifices as the wives of soldiers in the present world war" (Grunberger, *Social History of the Third Reich*, pp. 240–41).

27. At the time of his incarceration in the concentration camp, Worbs, who was born 21 November 1875, was approximately sixty-six years of age.

28. The Nazi government first used the guillotine in the Stadelheim prison in Munich, which had been erected as a model penal institution. The guillotine chamber was constructed so that "heads could be cut off more efficiently and in greater numbers" (George N. Shuster, "Foreword," in Gollwitzer, *Dying We Live*, p. xvii). The guillotine was used until the end of March 1933, and then was replaced with the axe and the gallows for executing those sentenced to death, because the guillotine was considered a non-German invention. For the succeeding two years executioners used the axe, until witnesses to the executions complained that the instrument was too messy. As a result, the axe was replaced by the "falling-sword machine" (*Fallbeil*), a German euphemism for guillotine (Golo Mann, *Reminiscences and Reflections: A Youth in Germany* [New York: Norton, 1990], p. 292).

29. In 1948, when Hübener's case was reexamined by LDS Church authorities in Salt Lake City, a handwritten line was added to his membership record reading: "Excommunication done by mistake."

30. See Document 65, n. 28.

31. It was well known in Germany that open opponents of the regime soon disappeared, so the only alternative was to adopt underground methods. Some of the opponents, to cover their activities, "affected to be ardent supporters of the extremist Hitlerist ideas" (Rauschning, *Hitler Speaks*, p. 278). Wobbe believed that Hübener "was not an ardent follower of Nazi ideology but was putting up a clever smoke screen so others could not see his real convictions and suspect his intentions," which increased Wobbe's respect for his friend (Wobbe and Borrowman, *Before the Blood Tribunal*, p. 15).

32. Hugo Hübener held the office of *Rottenführer* (lance corporal) in the SD (Sicherheitsdienst) (Wobbe and Borrowman, *Before the Blood Tribunal*, p. 14).

33. France was the favorite area of occupation for German soldiers and officials. Although looting was relatively restrained below the officer and official level, an artificial exchange rate enabled German soldiers "to go through French shops like an army of locusts." Officers and officials had greater opportunities to enrich themselves by confiscating booty. Extensive amounts of furniture, art works, and other high-class items, as well as perfume, liquor, food, and lingerie were sent back to the fatherland. The cost of the occupation to France was estimated to be four hundred million Francs per day, a "colossal" amount of money (Alfred Cobban, *A History of Modern France*, vol. 3 [New York: George Braziller, 1965], p. 179; see also Hanns Peter Herz in Steinhoff, *Voices from the Third Reich*, pp. 305–6; and Shirer's account for 26 June 1940, in *Berlin Diary*, p. 433).

34. Wobbe, born on 11 February 1926, was younger than Hübener, born 8 January 1925. Schnibbe, born on 5 January 1924, was the eldest of the group.

35. After the trial of his half-brother before the *Volksgerichtshof* in Berlin, Gerhard Kunkel was brought to account for having supplied him with a radio and for having said nothing about receiving flyers from Helmuth. As

a consequence, Gerhard was expelled from the officers' training school he was attending (Sander, "Helmuth-Hübener Gruppe," in Hochmuth and Meyer, *Streiflichter*, p. 340).

Index

Anti-Nazi(sm) (*continued*)
372*n*95; Hübener moved toward being, 21; Hübener produced virulent
literature, xxvi; none of Schnibbe's
school teachers were, 6; POW participation in, 373–74*n*106; Russian encouragement of, 373–74*n*106; sentiment in Rothenburgsort, 36; slogans
on walls, xxv. *See also* League of German Officers; National Committee
for a Free Germany
Appearances, supernatural: common oc-
currences of, 294*n*5
Apprentice(ship): description of, 24;
treatment of, 320*n*21; Wobbe's, 25
Arendt, Hannah: banality of Nazi evil,
xvii-xviii
Aristocrats: did not oppose Hitler, xiii;
made peace with National Socialism,
xii; resistance of to Hitler, xxi; 20 July
1944 conspirators dismissed by East
Germany as, xix
Ark Royal: allegedly sunk twice, 192,
213, 223; sinking of, 31, 327*n*69
Arschbackenbrühe. See Coffee. *See also*
Ersatz products
Article of Faith, Twelfth: admonishes
obedience to regime, xiv. *See also*
Mormon doctrine
Aryan ancestry: Berndt questioned
about, 257; Hübener family of, 177;
Nazi genealogy determined, xv;
Wobbe family of, 176
Aryanization: extent of, 319*n*19; forced
registration of Jewish property, 23,
319*n*17
Asia: war in, 211
Asmus: Hitler Youth director, 235
"As now will be known": leaflet, 224
Asocials: groups that are considered as,
297*n*22; numbers of arrested, 340–
41*n*30; persons arrested as, 341*n*35
Atlantic, battle of, 208, 212
Attin, Rolf: report of Hübener's school-
mate, 267–69
Attorneys: Drullmann, 67; Grotefend,
W., 231, 232–33; Knie, Hans Georg,
69–70, 234–35; Krause, Karl, 345*n*4;
Kunz, Wilhelm, 65; obtained visita-
tion permission, 70; Ranke, First
State Attorney, 239, 241–42; roles of,

345*n*5; verdict of, 219–31
Auchinlek, General: retreat of, 199
Augerstraße: Wobbe's school in, 183
Augsburg: Hess departs from, 200
Auschwitz: fear of, 75; known to Poles,
82; Salomon Schwarz imprisoned in
and died at, 27, 324*n*47; unknown to
most Germans, 309*n*88
Ausschläger Weg: school in, 267
Australia: to be conquered, 205
Austrian soldiers die, 195
Authority: youthful aversion to,
312*n*106, 314*nn*114–16. *See also* Hit-
ler Youth

Babushka: definition of, 375*n*10; medi-
cal skills of, 119–20
"Badenweiler March": Hitler's favorite,
6; legal limitations on performance
of, 302*n*42; played to German
POWs, 302*n*42
Bad Kleinen: trek via, 255
Bähre: Schnibbe's painting instructor,
24
Bahrenfeld: Düwer resided in, 149, 151,
176; Dr. Horn's property in, 266;
Horst Zumsande resided in, 193, 266;
illegal Communist activities in, 336–
37*n*9
Bahrenfelder Kirchenweg: Düwer resid-
ed in, 149, 173, 176, 180, 185
Bakery: Schnibbe fired from, 126–27
Balalaika: music of, 125
Balkans: campaign in, 201
Baptism: LDS practice of, 325*n*53
Barbarossa: code name for Russian cam-
paign, 30–31
Bardia: fell to British forces, 205–6
Barmbek: Communists lived in, 3, 266;
Dr. Horn's property in, 266; suburb,
3
Barmbek LDS branch, 272; ban on Jews
in, 324*n*46; Sudrows attend, 265; wel-
comed Salomon Schwarz, 27
Barth, First Sergeant: on trek, 247, 255
Barts, Police Sergeant: in Glasmoor and
Graudenz, 76
Basedow, Hugo: owner of ferry boats, 15
Bathe, Rolf: army propagandist, 210
Bath facilities: construction of, 109–10,
377*nn*20–21; in Russia, 108

Bochvisnievo: oil production in, 105; village near Volga prison camp, 102

Bock, General Field Marshal Fedor von: removed from command, 211

Bodinus, Senior District Leader: at trial, 67; verdict of, 219–31

Bökmannstraße: Schnibbe worked in, 161

Bolshevik(s): casualties of, 197; forces of, 199; judges call defendants, 69

Bolshevism: deliverance from, 210

Bombers, American: controlled air, 95; strafed travelers, 95

Bonhoeffer, Dietrich: did not seek martyrdom, xv; religious convictions of, xiii; resistance to Nazis, xiii. *See also* Resistance to Nazi regime

Book of Mormon: records fate of those who oppose Zion, 325*n51*

Border crossing: attacks on collaborators at, 131; behavior toward Russians during, 130–31

Bornstraße: Mohns resided in, 163, 193

Brackdamm school: Hübener attended, 155, 166, 178, 267, 277

Brandenburgers: explosions, 40, 331*n95*

Brandenburg Gate: victory parade through, 28

Brandt, Nazi District Leader: letter from, 148

Brandt, Willy: resistance fighter, 293*n9*

Braunau: birthplace of Hitler, 311–12*n102*

Brazil: German colony Blumenau in, 6, 301*n40*

Bremen: bombing of, 359*n12*; destroyed, 96; location and population of, 359*n11*; Schnibbe departed for Czechoslovakia from, 95

Bremerhaven: Johann Schnibbe joined merchant marines in, 1

Brest-Litovsk: significance of, 380*n1*; travel through, 129

Brey family: ship owners, 13

British: Admiralty, 197; advanced in Africa, 205; air force, 191; army approached Germany, 263–64; atrocity stories about, 69; headquarters in Cairo, 205; military neared Hanöfersand, 92; not enemies of Germans, 42; radio stations, 156; tank units,

214; took Lüneburg, 93; troops of British Empire, 199; war news, 259. *See also* BBC; RAF

Broadcasts, foreign: few persons allowed to listen to, 305*n59*; nature of British news during Polish campaign, 326*n66*; only means of obtaining news, 328*n73*; source of information for many, 326*n62*; tactics to avoid suspicion of listening to, 330*n89*; widespread listening to, 330*n89*. *See also* BBC; Radio

Broszat, Martin: study of resistance in Bavaria, xv

Brown Shirts, 14; meaning of, 298*n26*. *See also* SA

Buchenwald: known to Poles, 82

Bühlaustraße: singing school in, 8

Bund deutscher Mädel: Hitler Youth female division, 311*nn99–101*. *See also* Hitler Youth

Burial of prisoners: no recognition for, 375*n7*; in Yablonka, 118–19

Buske, Heinz: did not see flyers, 41–42; school friend of Schnibbe, 24; took college preparatory courses, 5

Bütow: prisoners' arrival at, 357*nn36–37*; trains operating from, 89; trek via, 242–43, 250, 252

Buttocks: relation to prisoner survival of, 365–66*n55*, 380*n39*

Bützow: Bützow-Dreibergen prison, 263; overnight camp in, 90; trek via, 243, 255

Cairo: British headquarters in, 205

Campaign, Russian: German unpreparedness for, 388–89*n18*

Canalstraße: flyers in, 165

Capone, Al: boys compared with, 72

Capucco, Fort: German loss of strategic site, 205

Car: Gestapo Mercedes, 50

Caro, Dr.: delivered Schnibbe, 22; disappeared, 22; Jewish, 22; office in Ifflandstraße, 22

Catholic: cultural resistance to Nazis, xv; dominance of culture in Bavaria, xii

Chancellery, German: clemency appeals to, 348*n28*

Chemnitz: a center of German Mormonism, xiv
Chiang Kai-shek: opposes Tokyo, 205
Children: average number per family in Germany, 298n27
China: at war with Japan, 211; to be freed, 205
Choir practice: at St. Georg LDS branch, 13
Cholm: in Russian hands, 199
Christmas: Hübener warned during, 278; message of Hess, 200, 223, 256; parties at St. Georg LDS branch, 13
Churchill, Winston: Hübener made caricatures of, 24; predicted raids, 202
Church of Jesus Christ of Latter-day Saints, the: American church, 257; Hübener involved those outside of church in conspiracy, xxvii; not political, 271; suspected as influence in Hübener's crimes, 238; West German mission of, 184. See also Latter-day Saints; LDS Church; Mormon(s); St. Georg LDS branch
City Hall: Gestapo headquarters in, 51, 55
City Hall Square: changed to Adolf Hitler Square, 8
Civil service: dismissals from, 303n48; loyalty oaths required for, xxiii; reorganization law for, 303n48
Clark, J. Reuben, Jr. (Mormon church leader): attitude toward Nazi regime, 292n28; favorable impression of Germany of, 289n8; miscalculations by, xx
Clothing: effects of prison garb in Germany, 133; new clothes in Germany, 135; in prison, 106–7
Coffee: ersatz, 54. See also Ersatz products
Collaborators, German: causes for and treatment of, 381n4; fates of, 381n5; remained in USSR, 370n83
Collective guilt: differentiated from collective responsibility, xxii; emphasis on by Allies, xx; Germans seen as bearing, xxii
Cologne: Edelweiß Pirates in, xiii, xvii; murder of Gestapo chief in, xiii, xvii; resistance in, xiii
Communism: Mormons believed Nazis

fighting against, 27; Schnibbe and friends discussed, 26. See also Bolshevism; Communist(s); Communist Party; Marxism
Communist(s): arrested and incarcerated, 14; assassinated by SS, 14; at Bismarckbad, 48; Hübener drew ideas from, xxvii; judges refer to defendants as, 69; many employed at the harbor, 14; many in Barmbek, Altona, and Rothenburgsort, 3; many in Hamburg, 26; marched, 3; met with Hübener, 266; natives in Ukraine not, 32; neighborhood in Rothenburgsort, 36; Peters a, 270; resistance groups of, xiii; Schnibbes not, 3; shawm orchestras of, 3; thrashed people, 4; underground opposition of destroyed, xxiv; youth groups of, xxvi. See also Bolshevik(s); Communism; Communist Party; Rote Kapelle; Rotfront
Communist Party: Hübener's association with, 336–37n9, 348n30; influence on Hübener, 336n8; members arrested in Hamburg, 309n85; Nazi perception of and effect on, 308n83; opponent of National Socialism, 296n16. See also Communist(s)
Community Alien Law: purpose of, 298n22
"Comrades in the North, South, East, West": text of leaflet, 209–12
"Comrades in the South, North, East or West": leaflet, 192, 223, 226; text of, 205
Concentration camps: Communists and Social Democrats in, 308n83; German awareness of, 309n88; role of SS in, 307n76; treatment of prisoners in, 334n107. See also SS, Deathhead
Congress Poland: origin of, 353n11
Conscience: absence of, xiii; dictates of, xii; workings of, xiii
Conspiracy to commit high treason. See Indictment
Crimea: war in, 198
Crimes: number of, 344n56; punishments for, 337n13, 337–38n15; worst, 344n57
Criminals, adult: definition of, 389n25

Crohne, Dr.: letter of, 239
Crystal Night. *See* Kristallnacht
Curriculum, school: Nazi changes in, 300*nn*32–33; religious training in, 300*n*33; youth group activities replaced by, 300*n*33
Cyrenica: English drive into, 192, 223
Czech: farewells written in, 69
Czechoslovakia, 96, 98; German motor pool in, 99
Czechs: abused by Russians, 100; beaten by German prisoners, 100; celebrated German defeat, 97; mistreated German captives, 98; rebelled against Germans, 96; taken as hostages by Germans, 96

Dachau: fear of, 75
DAF. *See* German Labor Front
Dahl, Hans: chauffeur of Jean Wunderlich, 135
Dakar: Düwer mention of, 164
Daniel, Book of the Prophet, 209
Danzig: location of, 75
Darlan, Admiral: friend of Hitler, 201
Death sentences: after "Bloody Sunday," 296*n*17; estimates of numbers of, 293*n*19; laws regarding, 347*n*18
Decorations, military: overabundance of, 33, 329*n*79
Decree about Extraordinary Radio Measures of 1 September 1939: cited in indictment, 186, 226–27; text of, 145–46, 174; violated by Hübener, xviii
Demei: agents of, 205
Demonstrations, political: violent nature of in Hamburg, 295–96*n*14, 296*n*17
Denmark: murder in, 217, 218
Deserters: sought in Hamburg, 93; treatment of, 355*n*27, 357–58*n*4
"Deutsche Bergwald steht in grün, Der": sung, 8; text of song, 283
"Deutschland, Deutschland über alles" (*Deutschlandlied*): anthem on radio, 6; text of, 281–82
Diarrhea. *See* Diseases
Dietrich, Otto: Nazi press chief, 196
Dillinger, John: boys compared with, 72
Discipline: traditional nature of, 299*n*29

Diseases: blood poisoning, 130; conditions contributing to, 372*n*100; descriptions of, 379*n*35; diarrhea, 119; dysentery, 119; malaria, 113; most numerous, 379*n*35; in prison camps, 104; Schnibbe's afflictions, 111; valine fever, 113. *See also* Dystrophy; Night blindness; Remedies, folk; Tuberculosis; Vitamins
Doctor Clubfoot. *See* Goebbels, Joseph
Dokumentationsarchiv des österreichischen Widerstandes. *See* Widerstandsarchiv, Vienna
Dombrowsky, Thaddius: offered escape to Wobbe, 353*n*12
Domin: fanatical Nazi, 4
Donets Front: Russian military active on, 199
"Down with Hitler": leaflet, 33, 222; quoted, 181, 191; text of, 194
Drullmann, Dr.: First State Attorney at trial, 67; verdict of, 219–31
Drunkenness: prevalence of, 124; reaction of Schnibbe's mother to, 139; role in cure of malaria, 139; of Sascha, 123
Dunckersweg: Schnibbes' garden in, 10
Dutch Indies: in war with Japan, 211
Dutchman: beaten in prison, 52; helped Schnibbe, 53, 54
Düwer, Adolf Hinrich: father of Gerhard, 176; Nazi report on, 175–76
Düwer, Gerhard Heinrich Jacob Jonni, 163, 173, 174, 182, 186, 188, 190, 191, 193, 260, 261; alienated by Hitler Youth coercion, 317*n*1; approached Werner Kranz, 47; arrested, 47, 149, 150; co-conspirator with Hübener, xxvii; diary of trek from Graudenz of, xxvii–xxviii, 242–56; early resistance activity with Hübener, 336*n*8; friend of Schnibbe, 79; induction into army of, 357*n*1; interrogated, 158; in kitchen at Hanöfersand, 92; leaflet distribution of, 346*n*14; life saved, 356–57*n*35; mentioned by Hübener, 156–57; not yet fully recounted experiences, xxvii; postwar employment of, 384*n*30; protected by Jäger, 88; remained with Schnibbe, 76–77; report on, 151–53;

responsibility for group's arrest, 353*n13;* Schnibbe ignorant of, 48; with Schnibbe in Hamburg, 138–39; sentenced, 69, 220; sent to Berlin, 62–63; sent to Graudenz, 75; suffered frozen feet, 89; testimony for Krüger, 140; at trial, 68–70; verdict regarding, 219–31; worked in camp office, 73
Dysentery. *See* Diseases
Dystrophy: frequency of, 365*n54*. *See also* Diseases

East Germany, 125, 130. *See also* German Democratic Republic
East Prussia: cold wind in, 84; Koch Gauleiter of, 88; flight of citizens from, 88, 246
Eberswalde: trek via, 254
Edelweiß Pirates: activities of, 322*n33;* executed in Cologne, xiii; manner of execution, xvii; murder of Gestapo chief by, xiii, xvii; opposition to Hitler Youth of, 314–15*n117;* resistance of, xiii, xxvi. *See also* Hitler Youth
Education, university: limited to wealthy, 299*n30*
Eggers, Staff Sergeant, 243–56 *passim;* directed tailor shop, 73; in Graudenz, 76; from Hohenfelde, 74; saved Schnibbe from SS, 86
Egypt: British cross border of, 205, 214
Ehlers, Johannes: deceased, 138; master painter, 23; questioned about Schnibbe, 57
Eichwald, First Lieutenant: on trek, 243
Eiffestraße: leaflets distributed in, 159
Eintopf. See One-pot meal
Elbe river: hostels on, 15
Elisenstraße: destroyed in bombings, 74
Emigration
—Jewish: international attitude toward, 319*n15;* routes of, 319*n15*
—LDS: interwar era, 290*n12;* pre- and postwar, 306*n67*
Empire, German: persecution of Mormons under, xv; time of stability, 3
Engel: on trek with Düwer, 251, 252
"Engeland Lied, Das": sung, 15; text of, 286–87
Engels, Kurt: sang at prison camp, 113–14

Engert, Karl: verdict of, 219–31; vice president of the People's Court at trial, 67
England: declared war on Germany, 28; heard on shortwave, 30; to lose Australia, 205; Schnibbe thought to be spy for, 62; started war against Reich, 187
English: air raids by, 32; broadcasts, 37, 48, 152, 155, 159, 162, 170, 185, 187, 190, 191, 205, 213, 218, 220, 226; Hübener good at language, 178, 276; landing forces, 164; POWs, 246; POWs in Graudenz, 82–83; transmitter, 153. *See also* BBC; London
Entertainment: in prison camp, 114. *See also* Music; Singing
Erfurt: entertainment in, 130; Schnibbe's health status in, 130. *See also* Diseases
Ersatz products: necessity for, 331*n96*
"Es zittern die morschen Knochen": sung, 18; text of, 283
Euthanasia: number killed by, 338*n17;* origins of, 338*n17*. *See also* Mercy killing

"Fahne hoch, Die." *See* "Horst Wessel Song"
Fasting: LDS definition of, 306*n71*
Fatherland: deaths for, 28, 33. *See also* Germany
Federal Republic of Germany: considered antiprogressive by East Germany, xix; resistance gave legitimacy to, xix. *See also* West Germany
Feldherrnhalle: construction of, 313*n111;* Nazi march on, 18, 313*n111*
Fenner, I.: on trek, 243
Ferry boats: *Fortuna, Fortuna I, Fortuna II, Hugo Basedow,* 15
Fikeis, Higher Regional Court Counsellor: berated defendants, 69; estimation of Hübener by, 347*n18;* at trial, 67; verdict of, 219–31
Films, Nazi: nature and purpose of, 310*n95*. *See also Jud Süß*
Flex, Walter: song composed by, 309*n89*. *See also* "Wildgänse rauschen durch die Nacht"

Flögel, Bertha: turned in flyer, 147
Flottbeker Chaussee: Nazi locale, 175
Food: availability on ration cards, 136;
effects of, 107, 127; effects of overeating, 132; in Germany, 131–32;
good supply for German military, 94;
in Hamburg, 358n6; nature of in Tabor, 100; prison camp norms, 366n60;
prisoner procurement of, 355n26;
Russian, 107, 121, 125; in Russian
prison camp, 103–4; Russians provide, 99; shortage and rations of during war, 332–33n101; supplied to military, 358n6. See also Prison camps,
Russian
Forced labor: construction projects,
108; nature of in Russia, 105, 107
Foreign Legion: criminal joined, 73
France: bloodletting in, 201; declared
war on Germany, 28; German looting
of, 390n33; heard on shortwave, 30;
Hugo Hübener in, 271; invasion of,
28, 29; Kunkel brings radio from, 30,
155, 162, 171, 273; smashed in four
weeks, 32
Frank, Erwin: LDS church friend of
Schnibbe, 24
Frank, Frau Dr.: disappeared, 23; Jewish, 22
Franken, master tailor: in Glasmoor,
262
Frankenstraße: leaflet written in, 160
Frank family: shown flyer, 265
Frankfurt an der Oder: arrival and food
in, 130
Frederick II: battles of, 17; books about,
310n96; idol of Nazis, 17; influence
on Hitler of, 310n96; as role model,
310n94; success of, 310n92; students
learn about, 311n97. See also Hitler,
Adolf
Frehse: turned over flyer, 147
Freisler, Roland, 146; death of seen as
divine retribution, 291n21; instructions regarding sentencing, 347n21;
introduced new system of legal values, 337n12
French: farewells written in, 70; German perception of, 333n102; Hübener wanted leaflets translated into,
47, 150, 151, 153, 163, 188, 225, 226;

not enemies of Germans, 42; POWs,
246; POWs in Hamburg, 47; prison-
ers escaped, 264; results of campaign,
325n55
Fricke, Gerhardt: LDS church friend of
Schnibbe, 24
Fricke, Harald: LDS church friend of
Schnibbe, 24
Fricke, Karla: LDS church friend of
Schnibbe, 24
Friedrichstraße: Dr. Knie's office in,
234
Fritsch, General von: suffered accident,
211
Fritsche, Hans: Nazi propagandist, 196,
197, 199, 205, 207, 210, 212
Froehlich, Elke: study of resistance in
Bavaria by, xv
Frostbite: treatment of, 368n73
Fuhlsbüttel: concentration camp at, 15;
Düwer complained about, 217; Düwer incarcerated in, 242; Hübener in-
carcerated in, 278; Krüger director of
prison after war, 91; on route home,
255, 256, 260; Schnibbe taken to, 51,
163. See also Kolafu (Konzentrationslager Fuhlsbüttel)
Führer: blamed, 26; broadcasts by, 6;
deaths for, 28, 33; denied clemency,
237, 240; Hübener loyal to, 178–79;
Hübener's criticisms of, 159, 169,
171–72, 191, 192, 195, 197, 199, 206,
207, 208, 218, 224, 228, 259; infalli-
bility of, 43; loyalty oaths to, xxiii;
pun on, 387n8. See also Hitler, Adolf
"Führer's speech": leaflet, 68, 193, 224;
text of, 212

Gambut: German loss of, 205
Games, children's: military nature of,
309n90
Gauleiter (regional Nazi party leader):
education level of, 323n40; Kauf-
mann, 26; Koch of East Prussia, 88;
typical Nazi thugs, 26; Wächtler, xvii
Gebhardt, Master of the Protective Po-
lice, 147
Geesthacht: near Krümmel forest, 1
Genealogy: Berndt's, 257; determined
Aryan ancestry, xv
Georgenthal: Jungvolk camp in, 18

Girabub: British military advance from, 205

Gisevius, Hans: reported death of Horst Wessel, 297*n22*

Glasmoor, 242, 262, 264; capacity of, 349*n33*; conditions at, 73–75, 350*n42*; duties at, 349*nn37–40*; Düwer's position at, 349*n41*; food and tobacco at, 349*n39*; freeing of prisoners at, 385*n33*; labor camp, 72; location of, 349*n35*; prisoners at learned of Hübener's execution, 349*n38*; prisoners learned *verpflegungstechnisch* tricks in, 82; regimen in, 349*n34*; on route home, 91, 92, 255, 256; warm clothes left in, 81

Godesberg Declaration: churches' stance regarding Jews, 324*n45*

Goebbels, Joseph: instigated Kristallnacht, 317*n3*; mocked by Hübener, 197, 206, 210, 213; promulgated Extraordinary Radio Measures, 326*n63*; propaganda machine of, 196, 198, 200, 204; on radio, 8, 29, 195; radio program described as fairy-tale hour of the billy goat from Babbelsberg or Doctor Clubfoot, 29, 43. *See also* Propaganda Ministry

Goethe, Johann Wolfgang von: dramas of, 267

Gollnow: trek via, 243, 253

Gondar: captured by British troops, 206

Göring, Hermann: called Meier, 202; corruption of, 388*n15*; issued directive merging police with paramilitary groups, 298*n25*; made Reichsmarshall, 202; maligned in leaflet, 68, 223, 259

Gorter, Jan: boarder at Wobbe home, 389*n22*

Gospel of Jesus Christ: opposite of Nazism, 19

Götterdämmerung: Year Null, xix

Göttingen: behavior of former prisoners and women in, 135–36; entertainment in, 135; length of stay in, 133; Mormon children in, 132; Schnibbe in hospital in, 131

Graf, Director of cashier's office: superior of Mohns, 163

Grant, Heber J. (LDS Church president): assured German LDS members during Nazi era, 292*n28*; discouraged German emigration, 290*n12*; miscalculations by, xx

Graudenz (Grudziadz): aircraft assembly plant in, 352*n5*; conditions in, 263, 352*n1*; departure from, 84, 86; digging tank traps in, 84; Düwer's account of trek from, xxvii–xxviii, 242–56; food in, 81, 354*n19*; Hübener group association in, 352*n4*; location of, 352*n50*; parents unaware of flight from, 93; prisoner transfer to, 352*n49*; Schnibbe, Wobbe, Düwer sent to, 75, 262; treatment of prisoners in, 352*n3*; trek from, 86, 91, 263; weather in, 356*n30*

Great Depression: American missionaries poor during, 11; during Weimar Republic, 3

Greater German Reich: rise of, 6. *See also* Third Reich

Green Minna (paddy wagon), 51, 54, 62, 63, 64, 72, 75

Greifenberg: trek via, 243, 253

Grevenweg: leaflets distributed in, 159

Grindel: ghetto area, 27

Grindelallee: Pipo lived in, 164; Schnibbe witnessed arrest of Jews in, 22

Große Allee: site of LDS branch and union house, 3

Großen Bleichen: many elegant Jewish businesses in, 22

Großes Wollenthal: trek via, 242, 246

Grotefend, Dr. W.: attorney for Hübener, 231, 232–33

Grotefend, Werner: notary, 232

Grynszpan, Herschel: assassination of German diplomat launched Kristallnacht, 317*n3*

GSA: English shortwave station, 200. *See also* Radio; Shortwave radio

Guards, German: nature of, 353*n10*

Gudat, Emma. *See* Hübener, Emma

Gudat, Helmuth. *See* Hübener, Helmuth. *See also* Vater, Karl Oswald

Guddat, Emma. *See* Hübener, Emma

Guddat, Helmuth. *See* Hübener, Helmuth

Guderian, Heinz: portrayed as youth hero, 311*n97*

223
Ireland: Allied forces in, 208
Iron Cross: abundance of, 329n79; on obituaries, 28
Iron Savings: Nazi program, 192, 213, 223
Isesstraße: many Jews lived in, 22
Italian: armed forces, 199; broadcasts in, 205; colonial policy, 192, 224; strength of people, 192; tank units, 214
Ivan: slang for Russian, 85
"I've Calculated for Everything": leaflet, 192, 223; text of, 206–8

Jacobi, Franz: Nazi Mormon, 26; not evil, 27
Jäger, Staff Sergeant: in Glasmoor and Graudenz, 76; protected Schnibbe, Wobbe, Düwer, 88; took over kitchen at Hanöfersand, 92, 243–56 passim
Japan: attacked Pearl Harbor, 204, 211; attacked Russia, 198; entry into war of, 192, 223; nervous about Manchukuo, 200; victory of, 193, 224
Jehovah's Witnesses: many killed in Nazi camps, xiv; opposition to Nazis of, xiv; prepared for martyrdom, xv; refused to accept legitimacy of secular state, xiv
Jesus Christ. See Gospel of Jesus Christ
Jew(s): arrested, 22; Aryanization (registration) of property of, 318n7, 319n17; Dr. Caro, 22; "cause of our misfortune," 23; deportations of, 318n7; disappearance of, xxiii; driven from apartments, 23; effects of Kristallnacht on, 21, 317n3; exception to Nazi cooperation with churches, xiv; fate of intellectuals, 319n14; following Kristallnacht, 318n13; forbidden to attend LDS meetings, 44, 324n45; Frau Dr. Frank, 22; German attitude toward, 318n9, 333n102; lost medical licenses, 318n10; mass exterminations of, xxiii; Mormons helped, 271; not enemies of the state, 42; persecution of, 317n4; persecution of in Poland, 82; population in Hamburg of, 317–18n6; seldom seen physical characteristics of, 318n13; transients arrested

early, 318n8; treatment of in Hamburg, 317n5; wore yellow star with word Jude, 27. See also Godesberg Declaration; Physicians, Jewish
Jud Süß: Hübener's reaction to, 320n24; nature and effects of, 320n24. See also Films, Nazi
"Junges Volk steht auf, Ein": sung, 15; text of, 285
Jungfernstieg: many elegant Jewish businesses in, 22
Jungmädelbund. See Bund deutscher Mädel
Jungvolk: activities of, 17–18; camp in Georgenthal, Thuringia, near Wartburg, 18; children pressured to join, 303n49; division of Hitler Youth, 311n99; Hansen ordered to attend demonstration as member of, xvii; Hübener in, 178, 220, 268, 269, 277; mandatory membership in, 311n100; oath of, 313n109; Pimpfe members of, 17; purpose of, 314n113; Schnibbe joined, 17; Schnibbe's enthusiasm for, 313n110; test for membership in, 312n103, 313–14n113; Wobbe member of, 311n99. See also Bund deutscher Mädel; Hitler Youth

Kalinin: recaptured by Russians, 199
Kaluga: recaptured by Russians, 199, 210
Karstens: Pipo lived with, 164
Kaufmann, Karl: common misperceptions about, 323n40; not Nazi thug, 26; opposed Kristallnacht in Hamburg, 317n3; refused to defend Hamburg, 323n39; roles and positions in Nazi party, 323n39; treatment of prisoners by, 323n40
Keitel, Field Marshal Wilhelm: relationship to Hitler of, 305n61; ridicule of, 305n61
Kiel: bombing by RAF, xi; Hansen born in, xi; Hitler at launching of heavy cruiser in, xi; Johann Schnibbe worked at, 93; Kurt Zumsande born in, 164; Mormon community in, xi; press wanted to produce leaflets in, 336n8
Kiev: allegedly open to German forces, 194

Kuybyshev: food in, 364*n46;* medical supply caravan to, 111–12, 122
KZ (Konzentrationslager): Johann Schnibbe learned of, 15

Landwirt train station: flyer read in, 41
Langenhorn: school hostel in, 268
Lasch, General Otto: reported effects of imprisonment upon Germans, 378–79*n33*
Latter-day Saint(s): friends of Schnibbe in branch, 24; Schnibbe only one in school, 7. *See also* Church of Jesus Christ of Latter-day Saints; Mormon(s)
Lay ministry, LDS: duty of, 306*n72;* nature of, 306*n69*
LDS Church: branch, definition of, 324*n44;* damage to buildings in Hamburg of, 305–6*n63;* Hamburg membership, size of, 294*n6;* intellectual origin of Hübener's ideas in, 290*n11;* lay ministry of, 306*nn69, 72;* missionary service of, 305*n65,* 306*n66;* Schnibbe's attendance at, 140; Schnibbe's reception by, 140; supplies provided to Germans by, 135–36. *See also* Terminology, LDS
LDS Church Historical Department, xxix
LDS District Leader: definition of, 324*n43*
LDS missionary service: Germans perform, 306*n66;* length of, 306*n65*
Leaflets, illegal: alleged number of, 335–36*n7;* Communist distribution of, 331*n92;* description of, 329*n81;* form of resistance, 330–31*n90;* Hübener's resembled Communist leaflets, 331*n91;* later appearance of, 335–36*n7;* limited value of, 331*n90;* numbers of, 330*n83;* reaction of Zander to, 333*n104;* SD reports concerning, 331*n94*
League of German Girls. *See* Bund deutscher Mädel. *See also* Hitler Youth
League of German Officers: Russian establishment of, 373–74*n106. See also* Anti-Nazi(sm); National Committee for a Free Germany

League of Young Girls. *See* Bund deutscher Mädel. *See also* Hitler Youth
Legal system, Nazi: determination of guilt under, 347*n17*
Leningrad, 194; battles for, 214; defenders of, 198
Leuthen, battle of: idol of Nazis, 17; results of, 310*n93*
Ley, Robert: denied private life of Germans, 293*n17;* housing goals of, 351*n47*
Ley houses: named for Robert Ley, 103; prison barracks resemble, 103; Schnibbe family builds, 75
Libya: British cross border of, 205, 214
Lice: efforts against, 371*n88;* prevalence of, 255, 361*n26. See also* Insects
Lidice: destruction of, 98. *See also* Heydrich, Reinhard
Liedel, Paul: illegal association with Hübener, 336–37*n9;* met with Hübener, 266
Lightning war. *See* Blitzkrieg
Lindleystraße: flyers in, 165
Loherstraße: Kranz lived in, 151, 153, 193
London: arrests for listening to, 212; broadcasts from, 37; prison in, 195; radio station, 159, 165–66, 172, 180, 181, 183–84, 189, 191, 197, 221, 222, 224, 228, 237. *See also* English
Looting: absence of, 337*n14*
Lord Haw-Haw: disseminator of enemy propaganda, xviii
Lore: Schnibbe met on trek, 254
Louisenweg: Hübener lived in, 25, 150, 155, 171, 235; Kunkels lived in, 277; leaflet distribution route, 38; leaflet found in, 147, 148; radio listened to in, 149, 184; school attended in, 178, 184, 235, 267
Louse control: in Czechoslovakia, 101; in Poland, 129; SS discovered during, 128. *See also* Insects; Lice
Loyalty: of Germans to laws, xxiii
Lübeck: trek via, 243, 255
Lübeckerstraße: leaflet distribution route, 34; Police Precinct 24 in, 57; SA killed man in, 17
Lüdelsen: food acquisition in, 338*n18;* location and size of, 294*n4;* near

Lüdelsen (*continued*)
Salzwedel in Altmark, 2; vacation in, 49
Ludendorff, General Erich von: called Anti-Christ, 209
Luftwaffe: in Africa, 205; raids over Warsaw and Rotterdam, 196; weak, 202
Lüneburg: size and location of, 357*n3*
Lütkemüller, Berthold: Berthold Schnibbe named after, 4; killed in World War I, 2
Lütkemüller, Caroline Marie Elisabeth: died of broken heart, 2; mother of Pauline Schnibbe, 2
Lütkemüller, Friedrich Gustav (Fritz): drank, 12; father of Pauline Schnibbe, 2; joined in saying grace, 12; lived with Schnibbe family, 136; smuggled across border, 136; supporter of the Republic, 3

Machinery: deterioration of, 125–26; Russian import of, 125
Machines, sewing: confiscation by Russians of, 100
Maginot Line: impregnable, 201
Mahorka: source of, 376*n13;* use of, 121. *See also* Tobacco
Malaria: attacks in Göttingen, 135; cure for, 139; in Germany, 132; Schnibbe acquired, 113; in Yablonka, 118. *See also* Diseases
Malo Jaroslavecz: German losses in, 199, 210
Manchukuo: Japan nervous about, 200
Manstein, Field Marshal Erich von: orders during retreat, 356*n32*
Markmannstraße: flyers in, 165
Marmarika: events in, 205
Marxism: not eradicated in Hamburg, 230. *See also* Communism
Matthiessen, municipal bailiff, 148; sends Düwer for leaflet, 149, 154
Mecklenburg: route via, 90, 254
Medical conditions: in Göttingen, 131–32; in Russia, 110
Medical Corps: Hansen Sr. assigned to, xvi
Meetings, political: forbidden by Nazis, 295*n10*
Meier, Diedrich: custodian, 184

Meier: euphemism for Göring, 202
Mein Kampf. See "On page 199 in Hitler's *Mein Kampf* it states"
Meins, August: Hübener's teacher, 267; recollections of, 269–70
Merchant marines: Johann Schnibbe joined, 1
Mercy killing, 49
Messerschmitt ME-109 fighter plane: Hess departed in, 200; repaired in Graudenz, 77, 79
Meyer: Wobbe's teacher, 183
Military: Army Day, Navy Day, Air Force Day, 26; behavior of during retreat, 356*n32;* commission recruits at Hanöfersand, 92; High Command lying, 191, 193, 196, 197, 205, 210, 212, 222; Hitler Youth uniforms resemble those of, 26; loyalty oaths of, xxiii; rapid buildup of, 14; reports by, 31, 32; resistance efforts of, xxi; suffered serious reverses, xxiii; supported Hitler, xiii
Millenarianism: Mormon belief in, xv
Minister of Justice of the Reich, 145, 146
Ministry of Defense of the Reich: Council of, 145, 146
Missing persons: inquiries about, 131, 133
Missionaries: American, expelled, 271; broken German of, 11; invited for dinner, 11; Mormon, apparent wealth of, 11; poor, 11. *See also* LDS missionary service
Moabit: classification and description of, 344*n1;* Düwer reported on, 242; length of stay in, 348*n31;* Wobbe reported on, 261, 262. *See also* Alt-Moabit
Modshaisk: German losses in, 199
Mohns, Kurt Heinrich Martin: conviction as war criminal of, 68, 346*n15;* interrogation of Kranz and Düwer by, 335*n3;* observed Hübener and Kranz, 47; report of, 150, 152, 154, 163, 190, 193, 220, 226, 228, 229, 260; role as *Betriebsobmann* of, 334*n2;* sentenced, 279; summoned Gestapo, 47; at trial, 68
Mölders, Colonel: death of, 192, 223
Molotov, Foreign Minister: assurances from, 200

Moltke, Helmut James von: resistance leader, xiii. *See also* Kreisau circle; Resistance to Nazi regime
Mommsen, Hans: paraphrase of, xii
"Monthly Military Review December-January": leaflet, 191, 223; text of, 198
Moorwerder: hostel on Elbe river, 15; typical day in, 16
Morentz, Sergeant: on trek with Düwer, 251
Mormon(s): aided by modern infrastructure in Germany, xv; branch president Arthur Zander a Nazi, 13, 26; decline of religious persecution of, xiv-xv; desire for order and stability caused acquiescence of, xiv; from disadvantaged social strata, xiv; emigrated, after war, 265; evade Nazi past like East Germans, xix; faced disapproval of established churches, xiv; few joined Nazi party, xiv; genealogical research encouraged by Nazis, xv; helped Jews, 271; Hitler would persecute after war, xvii; Hübener as, 268; Hübener group evoked ambiguous response among, xvi; immigration to Utah discouraged by LDS Church and state, xiv; Jacobi a Nazi, 26; in Kiel, xi; made peace with National Socialism, xi; not prepared for resistance, xv; passive acceptance of Nazis by, xv; perceived early Nazi years as golden age, xiv; positive attitude toward New Germany, xiv; predicted defeat of Germany, 27; saw Nazis as fighting against Communism, 27; sought new beginning after war, xix; support for Hitler by, xiv; supposed similarities with National Socialism of, xiv; sweep Hübener affair under rug, xx; Wobbe family strong, 25. *See also* Latter-day Saint(s); Missionaries; Mormon doctrine; Mormonism
Mormon doctrine: advocated support for regime, xiv; of fasting, 12; of life before birth, after death, 2; millenarian beliefs of, xv; of Word of Wisdom, 12. *See also* Article of Faith, Twelfth; Mormon(s); Mormonism
Mormonism: drew Schnibbe family

away from drinking, 2; incompatible with Nazism, xvi, 19. *See also* Gospel of Jesus Christ; Latter-day Saint(s); Mormon(s); Mormon doctrine
Morse code: in BBC broadcast, 30
Moscow: express train from, 105; good military strategists in, 198; military road to, 194
Mosquito swarms, 372*n99. See also* Insects
Motor pool, German: in Czechoslovakia, 99
Mouzhaisk: German defeat at, 210
Muckefuck. *See* Coffee. *See also* Ersatz products
Mühlenweg: flyers in, 165
Müller, Heinrich, chief of SD: punishment directive of, 291*n22*
Munich: radio broadcasts from, 29; resistance in, xiii, xxvi
Munitions: gathered and destroyed after war, 100
Museumstraße: site of vocational school, 24
Music: balalaika, 125; effects upon Schnibbe, 115, 137; impact of, 304*n53. See also* Entertainment; St. Peter's Church; Singing
Müssener: arrested Wobbe, 260; Gestapo agent, 50, 51; interrogation method of, 57, 343*n48*; report of, 148–49, 153, 154, 158, 161, 164, 165, 166, 168, 170, 171, 173, 193, 220, 230; at trial, 68
Mutual Improvement Association: at St. Georg LDS branch, 13

Nagelsweg: decorating guild house in, 24
Napoleon: influence on Hitler of, 310–11*n96*
National Archives of the United States, xxix
National Committee for a Free Germany: fate of some members of, 373–74*n106*; purpose of, 373–74*n106*; Russian establishment of, 373–74*n106. See also* Anti-Nazi(sm); League of German Officers
National Labor Service, 157; description of obligations in, 332*n97*;

National Labor Service (*continued*)
Kunkel served in, 30, 155, 157; military training in, 214; obligations of German youth to, 326*n61*; Arthur Sommerfeld served in, 274, 276; van Treck served in, 156, 159, 169–70, 172, 181, 182
National Socialism: aristocrats made peace with, xii; competing religious system, 19, 222; considered to be overcoming modern problems, xxiii; drummed into children, 268, 273; end of terror of, xxvii; generation of Germans raised in spirit of, xxi; Hübener enthused about, 277, 278; incompatible with Mormonism, xvi; Mormons made peace with, xii; opponents in Germany faced different problems, xxvi; seen as worthy of toleration, xxiii; successes of, xxiii; supposed similarities with Mormonism, xiv; worked out modus vivendi with religions, xiv. *See also* National Socialist German Workers' Party; Nazi(s); New Germany; Third Reich
National Socialist German Workers' Party, 14, 40, 148, 175–77; denied clemency to Hübener, 237, 259, 260; Hugo Hübener member of, 177; Wobbes not members of, 177. *See also* Nazi(s); NSDAP
National Socialist Justice Association: Wobbe's attorney member of, 345*n4*
National Socialist Volk Welfare: Adolf Hinrich Düwer member of, 176; Emma Hübener member of, 177; Marie Wobbe not member of, 177
National Socialist War Martyrs' Welfare: Marie Wobbe member of, 177
Naugard: trek via, 243, 253, 254
Nazi(s): and Arendt's remark about banality of evil, xvii-xviii; Aryanized Jewish property, 23; battle of Leuthen idol of, 17; bestiality of revealed, xxii; blamed inflation on Weimar Republic, 3; block leaders' role, 335*n6*; drove Jews from homes, 23; efforts to weaken, xxiii; encouraged genealogy, xv; extent of crimes of, xxiii; fewer conflicts with Social Democrats, 4; fought with Communists, 3–4; Germans blind to crimi-

nality of regime, xxiii; helped mostly other party members, 14; heroism not lacking in era, xxv; Hübener opposed to, 272; improved economy, 14; incarceration by, xxix; indoctrinated schools, 5; informants of, xxiv; judges escaped judgment, xviii; law favored, 15; life cheap in state run by, 48; life in Germany, 59; many in Graudenz, 80; marched, 3; Old Fritz idol of, 17; orators on radio, 8; overthrow of regime, 42–43; party badges indicated teachers as, 5, 268; party discussed, 26; Plötzensee infamous center of death, xxviii; positive works of, 15, 278; power legally acquired, xxiii, 7–8; practiced *Sippenhaft*, 74; promoted radio drama, 9; propaganda, 201; rapid military buildup of, 14; refusals to salute flag, xxv; resistance to considered treason, xxvi; resisters joined army to be safe from, xxv; Rolf a fanatic, 5; Schnibbe's attorney a, 65; Schnibbe with, 18–19; Sommerfelds opposed, 273; state and party symbols, xi; takeover destroyed Communists, xxiv; teachers became, 7; took children to hostel sites, 15. *See also* National Socialism; National Socialist German Workers' Party; New Germany; Third Reich
"Nazi Reichsmarshall": leaflet, 192, 233, 259; text of, 202
Neo-Nazi movement: modern rise of, xxiii
Neuenburg: trek via, 242, 244, 245
Neuengamme: description and activities of, 353–54*n15*; extermination camp, 79, 263; location of, 334*n108*
Neuen Wall: many elegant Jewish businesses in, 22
Neukrug: trek via, 242, 249, 250
Neumann, Peter: report on Hamburg bombing of, 357*n40*
Neuss: apprentice with Düwer, 156
New Germany: Mormon attitude positive toward, xiv. *See also* National Socialism; Nazi(s); Third Reich
New Year's: parties at St. Georg LDS branch, 13
Night blindness: cause and treatment of, 379*n35*

Ranke, First State Attorney: attended execution, 241–42; visited Hübener in prison, 239

Ratcatcher of Braunau: plans of, 17. *See also* Hitler, Adolf

Ratzkowsky, Joseph: fellow painter of Schnibbe, 77–78; procured girl for Schnibbe, 79–80; took Schnibbe into city, 80

Rauschning, Hermann: political plan of SS and SA alleged by, 297*n*20

Realgymnasium: college preparatory courses in, 5; curriculum of, 300*n*31

Red Cross: health care in Göttingen, 132; provisions for refugees by, 357*n*38; services of, 131; stations of, 253

Red Relief. *See* Rote Hilfe

Rees, Alfred C.: article by designed to gain Nazi favor, 292*n*27

Refugees: precautions of, 358–59*n*10

Reichenau, Field Marshal von: death of, 192, 211, 223

Reichskristallnacht. *See* Kristallnacht

Reichstag: Nazi majority in, 209

Reich Teachers' League: Adolf Hinrich Düwer member of, 176

Reineke, Adolf: employment under, 138

Reismühle: destroyed in bombings, 74; friend of Schnibbe lived in, 35; Hitler Youth meetings in, 19, 35, 74

Relief Society: at St. Georg LDS branch, 13

Remedies, folk: cures by, 120. *See also* Diseases

Rendulic, General Lothar: established courts-martial for deserters, 355–56*n*28. *See also* Deserters

Renk, Secretary of Justice: attended Hübener's execution, 241; visited Hübener in prison, 239

Reparations: paid to Schnibbe, 139; paid to those persecuted by Nazis, 384–85*n*31

Reports, military: euphemisms for reverses in, 327*n*68; successes of Russian campaign discussed in, 327*n*71

Resistance to Nazi regime: in Bavaria, xv; began before Hitler seized power, xxii; considered illegal and treasonous, xxvi; 800,000 Germans imprisoned for, xxii; inadequate source material about, xxvii; involvement of Edelweiß Pirates and Packs in, 294*n*21; lacked political ambitions, xxiv; lack of records about, 293*n*16; largely neglected, xxii; memory of repressed, xix; more widespread, xxii; other groups involved in, xxvii; played role in legitimation of West Germany, xix; role of Hübener group in, 345*n*9; secret, xxv; size and nature of, 343*n*51; of soldiers and bureaucrats, xxiv; stemmed from war, xxiv; suffered from being scattered, xxiii; unsuccessful efforts at, xxiii; voluminous literature about, xiii; why it existed, xxiv. *See also* Bonhoeffer, Dietrich; 20 July 1944; Kreisau circle; Solf circle; Stauffenberg, Claus Schenk von

Rhineland: resistance in, xiii. *See also* Cologne

"Riddle of Hess": leaflet, 192, 223

RLB. *See* Reich Teachers' League

Roehm, Ernst: alarmed at SA violence, 311*n*98; homosexual associates of, 297*n*22

Rohde, Senior Administrative Inspector: attended execution, 241; visited Hübener in prison, 239

Röhrendamm: flyers in, 165

Rolf: English and German teacher, 6; Nazi, 5; officer in war, 6

Rome: minimized Allied war effort, 208; Palazzo Venetia in, 211

Rommel, Field Marshal Erwin: defeat of, 205, 210, 212, 225; errors of, 199; mentioned by Düwer, 164; portrayed as hero, 311*n*97; victories by, 31

Roosevelt, Franklin Delano: blamed for starting war, 204, 208

Roß, Hans-Theo: memory of Hübener, 267–69

Rossausweg: bombed out, 10; encounter with police in, 34–35; in Hohenfelde suburb, 3; site of Schnibbe apartment, 3, 172, 174, 180, 185, 214

Rostov: German loss of, 206, 210; Russian capture of, 214

Rote Grütze: composition of, 306*n*64

Rote Hilfe (Red Relief): relation to

Communists, 308–9n84; role of, 309n84; for Social Democrats arrested by Nazis, 14

Rote Kapelle: members of executed, xiii; resistance group, xiii. *See also* Communist(s)

Rotfront: in song text, 282. *See also* Communist(s)

Rothenbaumchaussee: many Jews lived in, 22

Rothenburgsort: anti-Nazi sentiment in, 36; Communists lived in, 3; Hanseatic athletic fields in, 271, 278; leaflet distribution route, 38, 159, 171, 180, 189, 222, 267; strength of Social Democrats in, 330n86; students in Brackdamm school from, 267; Wobbe lived in, 25

Rothfels, Hans: commemorative lecture by, xxi

Rotterdam: raids on, 196, 202, 221

Röttger: beheaded Hübener, 241; executioner, 71, 239

Royal Navy: German reports about, 196; against Rommel, 205

Royal Oak. See Ark Royal

Rubinke, Bernhard: in cell with Wobbe, 65–66, 344n58; gained Wobbe's confidence, 345n6; statement of, 217; statements corroborated by Wobbe, 389n23; transferred to Berlin to attend trial, 345n8; Wobbe's reply to, 218–19, 225

Rumania: German prisoners pass through, 101

Russia: campaign in, 30–31; German losses in, 83, 207, 214, 217, 222; Germans fared poorly in, 83; Hitler successful in, 32; Hitler won himself to death in, 33; labor camp in, xxviii; leaflet reported deaths in, 191, 195; weather in, 104, 129, 169; winter in, 197, 198. *See also* Soviet Union; Steppe, Russian

Russian(s): advancing, 218, 245–56 passim; broke through front in Czechoslovakia, 96; drew closer to Graudenz, 83–85; nature of, 121, 125; not enemies to Germans, 42; posing as Germans, 109, 263; in POW camp in Graudenz, 81–83;

POWs gave food to, 90; prisoners learned language, 377n18. *See also* Ivan

Russian campaign: behavior of German commissars during, 328–29n77; behavior of German forces during, 328n76; German aims during, 329n78; German attitudes toward, 325–26n59; German fears of defeat in, 328n74; reception of German troops during, 328n76; reports about, 327n71; turning point in German opinion, 327n70; underestimation of Russian military potential during, 328n75

Rütli-oath, 208; source of, 389n19

SA (Sturm Abteilung): arrested Jews, 22; brawls of, 3; created concentration camps, 15; fatherless joined, 297n20; Haase joined, 13; Hugo Hübener in, 177; involvement in Kristallnacht by, 317n3; Johann Schnibbe had no sympathy for, 14; killed man in Lübeckerstraße, 17; nature of members of, 297n20; perceived enemies of, 311n98; picketed Jewish shops, 21; police power in Hamburg of, 298n24; prowled haunts of unemployed, 4; role of, 295n13; Schulz in, 41; in song text, 282; transients and unemployed joined, 296nn18–19; violent nature of, 311n98; Wessel member of, 4. *See also* Brown Shirts

Sachsenstraße: Hübener arrested in, 149, 150; Hübener lived in, 171, 173, 177, 179, 180, 185

Sacrament: LDS definition of, 306n70

Sacrament meeting: at St. Georg LDS branch, 13

St. Georg: suburb of Hamburg, 3

St. Georg LDS branch: arrest of Hübener announced in, 49; choir practice in, 13; Haase wore uniform to, 13; Hitler Youth attempted to disrupt, 27; home teaching in, 13; Hübener clerk of, 259; Mutual Improvement Association of, 13; Peters attended, 271; priesthood meeting in, 13; Relief Society of, 13; Schnibbe

tenced, 69, 220, 256, 257; sent to
Berlin, 62–63; sent to Graudenz, 75;
story of important and overdue, xx;
story of in genre of resistance literature, xiii; at trial, 68–70; verdict regarding, 219–31; visited in prison by
mother, 60–61, 260. *See also* Kuddl

Schnibbe, Martin: brother of Johann, 1

Schnibbe, Pauline Louise (Paula): at
dentist during search of apartment,
50; homemaking of, 4, 16; joined
LDS Church, 294*n3;* modest background, 2; mother of Karl-Heinz, 2;
sent food, 78; talked about execution
of Hübener, 265; vision of brother, 2;
visited by son, 93; visited son in prison, 60–61, 260; warned husband, 46;
warned son, 35–36; witnessed murder, 17; worried about son, 53

Schnibbe family: Knapps, Bergmanns,
Berndts, friends of, 12

Scholl, Hans and Sophie: distributed
leaflets, 39; resistance activity and execution of, xiii, 331*n93. See also*
White Rose

Schools: eradication of denominational,
300*n33;* law against overcrowding of,
299*n30*

Schörner, General Ferdinand: commander of Fifth Army in Czechoslovakia, 95; military positions and fate
of, 358*n8*

Schreber, Daniel Gottlob: gardens
named after, 9, 305*n62*

Schrebergarten, 9–10

Schröder, General von: death of, 191,
221, 259

Schulauweder: Schnibbe traveled to, 93

Schulz, Otto: debated with Johann
Schnibbe, 20; harmless brawler, 20;
Nazi, 14; neighbor of Schnibbes, 14;
punishment of, 140; in SA, 41; saw
handbill, 40–41, 43; Schnibbe visited
after imprisonment, 140

Schutzhaft. *See* Protective custody

Schwarz, Annemarie: half Jewish, 274

Schwarz, Salomon: biological conception of, 324*n44;* Jewish Mormon, 26–
27; receives visits from LDS Church
leaders, 271; sent to Auschwitz,
324*n47*

Schwedlick: turns over flyer, 147

SD. *See* Sicherheitsdienst

Secret State Police. *See* Gestapo

Security Service. *See* Sicherheitsdienst

Serbia: Schröder commander in, 191,
221, 259

Seydlitz-Kurzbach, General Walther
von: anti-Nazi activity of, 373–
74*n106*

Shawm: in Communist bands, 3; description and use of, 296*n15*

Shortwave radio, Rola: 30, 193, 220

Shortwave station: English GSA, 200

Siberia: East Siberia to be taken, 205;
reserves from, 198

Sicherheitsdienst (Security Service): enrolled Hitler Youth patrols for surveillance of churches, 324*n49;* Hugo
Hübener member of, 233, 237; internal security reports of, xxvi; many informants from, xxiv; reported discontent of Germans during Russian
campaign, 327*n67;* ubiquitous in
Graudenz, 82

Sidi Omar: Rommel's position near, 205

Sieg Heil, 28; crowds roared, 6; Heil-
aluja, 43; meaning of, 302*n41*

Silesia: location of, 352*n2*

Singing: in prison camp, 114–15; Russian, 114. *See also* Entertainment;
Music

Sippenhaft: arrest of Stauffenberg family,
xvii; fear of, 79; Himmler's description of, 290–91*n17;* historic role of,
350*n43;* Nazi practice of, 74

Slammer-ology. *See Knastologie*

Slavs: German perception of, 333*n102*

Social administration office: access to
books in, 29; Düwer apprentice at,
151–52, 219, 260; Hübener apprentice at, 25, 151–52, 181, 219, 223,
259. *See also* Biberhaus

Social Democratic Party: Nazi impact
on, 308*n83;* numbers of members arrested in Hamburg, 309*n85;* rare opponent of National Socialism,
296*n16;* resistance activities of,
331*n91;* strength in Hamburg,
295*n11*

Social Democrats: fewer conflicts with
Nazis of, 4; flag black, red, gold, 3,

Street fights: police noninvolvement in, 298nn23, 25
Streifendienst: Hitler Youth activity in, 321–22n32; results of capture by, 322n34. *See also* Hitler Youth
Stresowstraße: Wobbe attended school in, 165
Struve, Sergeant: on trek with Düwer, 251
Student Prince, The: Schnibbe named after character in, 4
Sturm Abteilung. *See* SA
Stuttgart: a center of German Mormonism, xiv
Suderov. *See* Sudrow
Süderstraße: flyer found in, 147, 148
Sudroff. *See* Sudrow
Sudrow, Johannes and Wilhelmina: attended Barmbek LDS branch, 265; attended church after Hübener's death, 258; death of, 351n46; described Hübener after arrest, 335n4; grandparents of Hübener, 25; greeted Schnibbe, 36; Hübener lived with, 149, 155, 159, 166, 169, 171–72, 178, 184, 221, 233, 235, 272, 273; killed in bombing, 275, 276, 279; last letter of Hübener to, 71; marriage of, 264, 326n60; radio in apartment of, 181, 187; related Hübener's arrest, 274; retired early, 30, 35; took Hübener to church, 276
Sudrow: various spellings of, 320n25
Suhling, Lucie: procedures in Fuhlsbüttel, 348–49n32
Suhse, F. Georg: former employer of Schnibbe, 138, 161; painting contractor, 23
Sukov, General. *See* Zhukov, General
Sunday school: at St. Georg LDS branch, 13
Swabians: location and dialect of, 363n37; in Russia, 102. *See also* Volga Germans
Swastika: displayed by Hugo Hübener, 177; displayed by Otto Schulz, 14; on handbills, 40; on judges' robes, 67; LDS church flew, 271; in shadow of, 1. *See also* Vulture of rack and ruin
Swing Youth: activities and persecution of, 341–42n40; Nazi attitudes toward,

386–87n4; north German presence of, xiii; proclivity for Anglo-American music, xiii; threatened with concentration camp, xiii
Swiss: spy in cell, 261
Switzerland: armed, 212; sale of German gold in, 212
Symbols, political: coerced obeisance to, 322nn35–36; Nazi forbidding of, 295n10; Nazi wearing of, 301nn36–37

Tabor: bakers in, 361n23; description of prison camp in, 360–61nn21–22; German forces fled toward, 96, 360n19; Germans imprisoned at, 98, 99; location of, 360n18; population of, 361n23; prisoner transportation from, 362n29
Tall Paul: assault on Wobbe by, 341n32; brutal guard, 51; death of, 339n25; Wobbe's description of, 339n24
Tamara: innocence of, 124; interpreter, 122–23; saved Schnibbe, 124; trips with, 122
Tanya: embarrassed Schnibbe, 114; enlisted Schnibbe, 111–12; farewell from, 128; nursed Schnibbe, 113; Russian physician, 110
Tatar(s): folk healers, 120; theories of origin of, 375–76n11
Teachers: denunciations of, 302n45; dismissals of, 303n49; lowered requirements for, 303n50; methods of Nazi party members, 301n38; and political education, 302–3n46; political views of, 301n34; preferential treatment of, 303n50; pressured to leave Social Democratic party, 303n47; salary reduction of, 303n47
Terminology, LDS, 309n86
Thaliatheater, 8; role of, 304n55
"They are not telling you everything": leaflet, 191, 222
Third Reich: abomination of, 34; collective guilt in rise of, xxii; conscience of Germans during, xii; daily life in, 13; expansion of, 76; feared Hübener, 61; leaders viewed nation as congruent with, xxvi; resistance to broadly interpreted, xxv; rise of, 6. *See also* Greater

Upper Silesia: prison guards from, 76.
See also Beutedeutsche
USA: entered war after Pearl Harbor,
27, 208; German-language repertory
company in, 8; German Mormons'
dreams of immigration to, xvi, xx;
headquarters of Mormon church in,
xx; Hübener read books about, 278;
Schnibbe immigrated to, 8. *See also*
America
USSR. *See* Russia; Soviet Union
Utah: Mormon emigration to discouraged, xiv

Valine fever. *See* Diseases, malaria
Vater, Karl Oswald: Hübener's biological father, 235, 321*n*27
"Verdun": drama from World War I, 9
Verhaaren, Theodor: converted Johann
Schnibbe to Mormonism, 2
Verpflegungstechnisch (grocery technology): called liberating, 85–86; learned
in Glasmoor, 82; stealing food, 81–82
V for Victory, 30, 222. *See also*
Beethoven, Ludwig van
"Victorious advance into the shining
battles of annihilation": leaflet, 193,
224
"Victory over England": song, 213
Vienna: German prisoners pass
through, 101; Widerstandsarchiv in,
xxix
Violence: dominant trait of Nazis,
311*n*98; victims of police in 1933,
298*n*25
Vistula: frozen, 84, 244; Graudenz on,
75
Vitamins: acquisition of, 379*n*37; effects
of lack of, 371–72*n*93
Vlasov, General Andrei: activities and
fate of, 377*n*19; Schnibbe accused of
being supporter of, 124
Vodka: prevalence of, 123. *See also*
Drunkenness
"Voice of Conscience,": leaflet, 49, 192,
223; text of, 200
"Voice of the Homeland": leaflet, 193,
223; text of, 209
Volga: boatmen, 116–17; camp construction near, 363*n*36; frozen highway, 129; German prison camps near,

363*n*36; German prisoners arrived at,
102; German settlements near,
363*n*39; hygienic conditions near,
363*n*42. *See also* Immigrants, German
Volga Germans: prisoners of war work
with, 106; in Russia, 102
Völkerball: game played, 16. *See also*
Schlagball
Volksempfänger: nature and role of, 304–
5*n*57; official radio, 9. *See also* Broadcasts, foreign; Radio
Vorbeck, Willi: alleged theft by, 58;
Schnibbe worked with, 58
Voscherau, Karl: actor at Thaliatheater, 8
Vulture of rack and ruin: on robes of
judges, 67. *See also* Swastika
VVN (Vereinigung der Verfolgten des
Naziregimes, Union of Those Persecuted by the Nazi Regime): attempted to help Schnibbe, 139–40; purpose
of, 385*n*32

Wächtler, Fritz: organized demonstration against Stauffenberg family, xvii
Waffen-SS: prisoner in Yablonka, 126;
role and status of, 378*nn*28–29; Russian view of, 126. *See also* SS
Wallstraße: Schnibbe attended school
in, 179; site of elementary school, 5
Wangemann: Gestapo agent, 50, 51,
173; interrogation method of,
343*n*48; interrogator, 57; not at trial,
68; report of, 149
"War of the Plutocrats": school essay by
Hübener, 189, 193, 229
Warsaw: raids on, 196, 221
Wartburg: Jungvolk camp near, 18; significance of, 313*n*112
"Wave of oil": leaflet, 193, 224
Wedding: trek via, 254
"Weekend Incarceration": leaflet, 192,
223; text of, 203–4
Wegener, Adolf: position in sauna, 108–
9; problems of, 109
Wehrmacht: rapid career advancement
in, 301*n*39
Weimar Republic: hard days during, 3;
Nazis blame inflation on, 3; persecution of Mormons during, xiv-xv
Weltien, Carl Friedrich: turned in flyer,
147, 148

Wendenstraße: Frank family lived in, 265; Peters lived in, 271
Werner: on trek with Düwer, 249, 251
Wesermünde: near Hetthorn, 1, 175
Wessel, Horst: asocial element, 4; death of, 297nn21–22; importance of knowledge of song by, 312n103, 302n43; song by, 297n21
Western Europe: visitors from see Hitler working wonders, xxiii
West Germany. See Federal Republic of Germany
West Prussia: prisoners from ran away, 90, 244, 246
"Where Is Rudolf Hess": leaflet, 191; text of, 195, 222
White Rose: resistance of, xiii, xxvi. See also Scholl, Hans and Sophie
"Who is inciting whom?": leaflet in typewriter, 47, 149, 188, 224; text of, 192, 204–5, 223
"Who Is Lying?": leaflet, 191, 222; text of, 194
WHW. See Winter Relief Agency
Widerstandsarchiv, Vienna, xxix
Wieczorek, Ida: association with Hübener of, 336–37n9; report of, 266
Wieczorek, Josef (Jobi): illegal activities and association with Hübener of, 336–37n9; military service of, 336–37n9
Wieczorek, Jupp: association with Hübener of, 266, 336–37n9; report of, 266
"Wildgänse rauschen durch die Nacht": sung, 15; text of, 284. See also Flex, Walter; Songs
"Wild Geese Whir through the Night." See "Wildgänse rauschen durch die Nacht"
Wilhelmsplatz: propaganda office in, 196, 201, 211
Wilhelmstraße: propaganda in, 208
Wilhelm Tell. See Schiller, Friedrich von
Wilhelm II, Kaiser: Bertold Lütkemüller died for, 2; pompous ass, 3
Wille, Georg: farewell from, 128; German physician in Russia, 110; helped Schnibbe get job in bakery, 126; received medical supplies, 112; saved Schnibbe's life, 118; Schnibbe's asso-

ciation with, 110–11, 375n4; in Yablonka, 117–18
Winter, General: euphemism for Russian cold, 197
Winter Relief Agency: Hugo Hübener contributed to, 177; Marie Wobbe contributed to, 177
Wittenberg: trek via, 243, 255
Wobbe, Marie: letter from, 215–16, 260, 264; mother of Rudi, 176; occupation of, 387n5
Wobbe, Rudolf: alienation from Hitler Youth by, 321n30; altercation with Hitler Youth by, 316n125; arrest of, 338–39n21; boarder with, 389n22; caught smuggling, 80; co-conspirator with Hübener, xxvii, 30; considered flight, 338n20; death of, 141; discussed war, 29; distributed leaflets, 33–40; effects of prison on, 344n2; father's death, 321n29; freeing of, 140; friend of Hübener and Schnibbe, 13, 24, 140, 273, 348n25; goals of, 278; at Graudenz, 75, 352nn6–7, 352–53n8; health affected in Graudenz, 352n7; helped Jews, 271; Hübener questioned about, 57; immigration to USA of, 141; incautious hiding of leaflets by, 339n23; interrogation of, 165–66, 181, 182, 185, 188, 189, 190, 193, 260; investigative report, 180–82; LDS Church member, 140, 173, 180, 189, 221, 264, 307n73; learned of Hübener's arrest, 49; learned of Schnibbe's arrest, 337n22; learned prison survival skills, 341n31, 342n42; lived in Rothenburgsort, 25; mechanic at Hanöfersand, 92; memoirs published, xxvii; mentioned by Schnibbe, 162; mother a war widow, 25; not excommunicated from LDS Church, 258; offered escape from Graudenz, 353n12; posttrial association with Hübener of, 348n25; protected by Jäger, 88; questioning by criminal court of, 389n24; Rubinke relationship with, 218–19; Schnibbe questioned about, 50; sentenced, 69, 220; sent to Berlin, 62–63; slept with dead prisoner, 356n29; statement of, 259–64; testimony for Krüger by, 140; on